TWO NAVIES DIVIDED

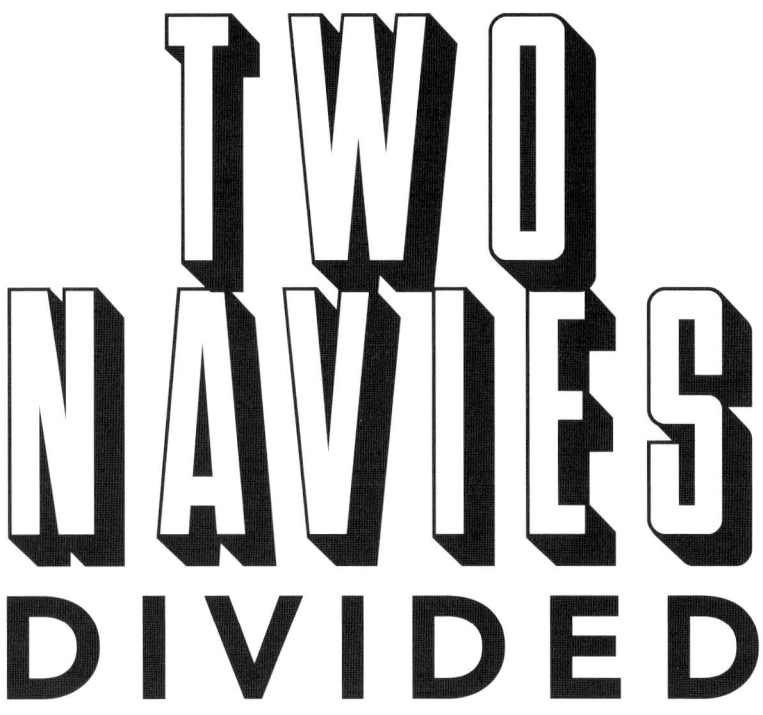

THE BRITISH AND UNITED STATES NAVIES IN THE SECOND WORLD WAR

BRIAN LAVERY

Foreword by Admiral the Rt Hon the
Lord West of Spithead GCB DSC PC

Naval Institute Press
ANNAPLOIS, MARYLAND

Copyright © Brian Lavery 2023

First published in Great Britain in 2023 by
Seaforth Publishing,
A division of Pen & Sword Books Ltd,
George House, Beevor Street, Barnsley S71 1HN
www.seaforthpublishing.com

Published and distributed in the
United States of America and Canada by the
Naval Institute Press,
291 Wood Road, Annapolis,
Maryland 21402-5034

www.usni.org/press/books

Library of Congress Control Number 2023946167

ISBN 978 1 68247 472 3

This edition authorized for sale only in the United States of America, its territories
and possessions, and Canada.

All rights reserved. No part of this publication may be reproduced or transmitted in any form or
by any means, electronic or mechanical, including photocopying, recording, or any information
storage and retrieval system, without prior permission in writing of both the copyright owner and
the above publisher.

The right of Brian Lavery to be identified as the author of this work has been asserted by him in
accordance with the Copyright, Designs and Patents Act 1988.

Printed and bound in the United Kingdom

Contents

Foreword		vi
Preface		ix
1	The Structure of Naval Power	1
2	Naval Society and Culture	34
3	Officers	61
4	Ratings and Enlisted men	96
5	Non-combatants	125
6	Marines	158
7	Bases and Logistics	182
8	The Ships	208
9	Weapons	227
10	Intelligence and Electronics	254
11	The Battle Fleet	278
12	Naval Aviation	303
13	Submarines	347
14	Anti-Submarine Warfare	376
15	Coastal Navies	415
16	Amphibious Warfare	453
17	Enemies	489
18	Allies	526
19	Conclusions	556
Notes		563
Bibliography		585
Picture Credits		596
General Index		597
Ship Index		610

Foreword

IN 1939 the Royal Navy was, as it had been for more than a century, the largest and most powerful maritime force in the world, but by 1945 the US Navy had overtaken it and was by a significant margin pre-eminent. And it was the overwhelming strength of the USN and RN that enabled survival and ultimately total defeat of Germany, Japan and Italy in the Second World War. Brian Lavery, with his recognised background in naval history, has produced an absorbing analysis of the two navies at this crucial juncture, showing the relative and absolute efficiency of each service. It is a tour de force and no aspect of the organisation of these vast services is overlooked. A must for naval historians and laymen alike, it is packed with fascinating facts and insights.

The strength of the Royal Navy had ensured victory and the defeat of Germany in the First World War. Churchill said in November 1918, 'nothing, nothing in the world, nothing that you may think or dream or anyone else may tell you, no argument, however seductive, must lead you to abandon that naval supremacy on which the life of our country depends', and this was just at the end of a war where the focus was on the army and the Western Front. Lavery shows how this strength was squandered over the next twenty years to the extent that, although still the largest navy, the RN had surrendered the lead in a number of key areas by 1939.

One of the most crucial of these areas, and echoes of which still reverberate today, was the control and development of naval aviation. There is no doubt that the fact the RAF owned and ran policy on naval aircraft was wrong, and certainly resulted in the loss of many maritime lives in Second World war. The RAF were obsessed with the strategic bombing of cities. One example Lavery highlights is that, at a conference in 1931, the RAF discounted the dive-bomber, claiming that it would need a specialised aircraft which no air force would be prepared to invest in. Instead, the RAF favoured the high-level bombing of ships. As a result of discounting dive-bombers, the 40-degree elevation of destroyer guns was considered more than sufficient and that the ships needed only light anti-aircraft armament, such as pompoms, to protect themselves. This was a terrible mistake that was only rectified later in the war.

The US Navy, with no interest in strategic bombing, made huge progress with dive-bombing and produced the aircraft designs to make such options possible.

Both the US and Japan forged ahead in carrier aviation capability and it was the dead hand of the RAF that lead to the RN being left behind. The struggles over CVA01, and more recently numbers and ownership of Harriers and now F35s, echoes this longstanding problem. Another area of weakness was the RN's failure to develop refuelling at sea. The Americans had planned for a trans-ocean war and were able to teach the RN a great deal.

Lavery asks the ultimate question, 'Was the American navy better than the British during the Second World War?' but as he admits the answer is not clear, despite the fact the USN had far greater numbers in the end, and better techniques, especially in aviation and engineering. Lavery also reminds us that America had many overall advantages in the war, size being fundamental. She is forty times as large as Great Britain, with three times the population. Remoteness was another factor, and the USA was never under serious threat of bombing or invasion. Britain had already been fighting for two years before America entered the war and, even then, America did not have to begin its major offensives for another two years after that. The scale of US defence production was staggering, helped by the fact she had been the allied arsenal in the First World War. Between 1940 and 1945 America would launch 141 aircraft carriers, eight battleships, 807 cruisers and destroyers, 203 submarines, 82,000 landing craft and more than 50 million tons of merchant shipping. The USN had more than 100,000 ships and vessels by the end of the war.

Defence against invasion and maintaining the nation's lifelines were the highest priorities for the RN and it is not surprising we were pre-eminent in anti-submarine warfare. Where I unusually disagree with the author is that defence against invasion was largely secured by the RAF victory in the Battle of Britain in 1940. It is quite clear from German documents that it was the certainty of destruction of any invasion force by the Royal Navy that led to the abandonment of invasion plans.

The author raises an interesting point in that, although the RN had maintained high levels of morale as it fought through six years of war, the maintaining of service morale should the Pacific war have continued might have proved problematic.

In summary, Lavery shows how the navies could learn from one another, but mostly the Royal Navy from the USN. Americans were best in carrier aviation, submarines and in building a modern battlefleet. The British were best in anti-submarine warfare. Both had strengths and weaknesses in amphibious warfare. The navies, despite some flaws and mistakes, adapted well to unforeseen circumstances and can be immensely proud of their superb heritage.

The author should be proud of an amazingly researched, detailed yet readable book, which gives context to any number of issues relating to the two largest navies the world has ever seen.

Admiral the Rt Hon the Lord West of Spithead GCB DSC PC
August 2023

Preface

THE TITLE of this book is derived from a common misquotation of George Bernard Shaw's supposed comment that 'England and America are two countries divided by a common language.' It is not meant to imply that the British and American navies were seriously at odds with one another (though occasionally that might have seemed to be the case), but to suggest, as in the case of language, that common roots and usages might vary significantly and sometimes seriously in detail.

My interest in the US Navy was inspired by two books, both by coincidence bought in the Scottish town of Helensburgh. One was E B Potter's *The Great Sea War* of 1960, which I bought as a schoolboy many years ago. It introduced me to the name of Chester Nimitz, one of the greatest commanders of the war. Unlike Eisenhower, MacArthur and Patton, his name was almost unknown in Britain outside the circle of naval historians, and so was the course of the Pacific War and the scale of American effort – Potter enlightened me on both. The second book was *Naval Orientation* of 1945, a guide to the American navy which is far more comprehensive than anything the Royal Navy produced at the time, and reflected the pattern for other American manuals of various types. It has its faults, including an undue emphasis on saluting, but it inspired me to write *Nelson's Navy* a third of a century ago. I started off imagining what a manual for Royal Naval officers on that level might be like around 1800. I hope to have the same comprehensive approach in the present work, though naturally there is far less detail. I have to cover two navies instead of one, and both are far more complex than Nelson's force, with specialised ships and sailors to interact with the air and land and to operate under the sea.

I have placed some emphasis on the social history of both navies, at many different levels. Millions of men and hundreds of thousands of women served in these navies during the Second World War. Only a tiny proportion of them left memoirs, whether published, manuscript or oral, but collectively they give a very detailed picture of life in the many different branches of the navies. These are combined with the official regulations and manuals explaining or decreeing how things ought to be done. This work is not technical in any full sense but to get a complete picture it is impossible to ignore the design of ships, which is fully covered in great detail on both sides of the Atlantic by D K Brown and Norman Friedman, and to some extent the shipbuilding chapters are a summary of their efforts. Weapons and sensors – especially sonar (Asdic) and radar – are covered in other works listed in the bibliography. These subjects are included to complete the picture of the life of those who sailed in the ships and operated the equipment.

The two navies had common origins and a history of both rivalry and co-operation over more than a century and a half. They faced different challenges during the war and dealt with them successfully, if sometimes belatedly. Both navies ended up on the winning side after making essential contributions to victory. The relative and absolute efficiency of each is the subject of this book.

1

The Structure of Naval Power

THE SECOND World War is a particularly appropriate moment for comparing the British and American navies. They fought on the same side, and sometimes side by side, for nearly four years, significantly longer than during the First World War. They exchanged information, technology and material in an unprecedented fashion, and it was not just one way; and for a brief period they were roughly equal in size. Equality had been formally recognised by the Washington Treaty of 1922, but the United States did not attempt to build up to the limits until after the Vinson–Trammel Act of 1934. Allowing for losses on both sides, true equality was reached around the end of 1942; that date marked the start of a massive American building programme, and the US Navy was soon the largest in the world by a long way, a status it has retained ever since. It marked the coming of age of American sea power, and the end of independent British naval power, except for occasional events such as the Falklands War of 1982.

Despite their differences, the Royal and United States Navies had a common origin and many elements of a common culture. Even when relations between the countries were at their worst in the War of 1812, Captain Thomas Truxtun wrote:

> notwithstanding the prejudice that exists in our nation against the British government, … yet I think none can be so much so, as not to acknowledge them, … the first maritime power on the globe, with respect to naval tactics, discipline, and the general management of ships of war; they are therefore a proper example for us to imitate in our infancy, in all those points of duty and regulation, in which precedents are wanting: and by a steady attention to their general naval system, we shall very early have our ships of war and marine affairs in good order, and our internal government on board the different ships, in the navy …[1]

In 1945 *Naval Orientation* told American midshipmen: 'The United States Navy has always, to a large extent, adopted the practices of the Royal Navy.'[2]

American interest in the Royal Navy was accelerated in 1889 when Captain Alfred Thayer Mahan USN published *The Influence of Sea Power upon History*. Using mainly British examples, he argued that the United States could only progress by developing a world-class navy of her own. The book was highly influential, being read by the German Kaiser and the officers of the new Japanese navy, as well as Theodore Roosevelt in the United States. The lessons were that the most important function of the fleet was to defeat the enemy fleet and anything else was a diversion, and consequently commerce raiding would never win a war. However, Mahan was mostly writing before the invention of the submarine and the aircraft, and he did not take account of the effect of the railway on transport, or the growing dependence of nations like Britain and Japan on imported food and oil. To follow his doctrines too closely, as the Japanese navy did, could be dangerously misleading.

Mahan's lessons seemed to be confirmed historically by Britain's defeat of the French, who invariably put 'the mission' before the battle. The writings of Sir Julian Corbett were far less popular, but he expressed another view, that 'the paramount function of a covering force in an amphibious operation is to prevent interference with the … landing, support and supply of the army.' It was a constant paradox in all naval operations and was highlighted at the battle of Leyte Gulf, when Admiral Halsey went in pursuit of a Japanese carrier force (a decoy with hardly any planes onboard) and neglected to prevent a counter-attack through the San Bernardino Straits. Fortunately, the Japanese failed to press home their advantage, and American destroyers showed exceptional bravery.

A special relationship?

Long before the term 'special relationship' was coined, the British tended to assume that Americans, who were largely of British descent and spoke the same language, would be naturally sympathetic. In peace, Franklin D Roosevelt was optimistic in a toast to King George VI: 'the greatest single contribution our two countries have been enabled to make to civilisation, and to the welfare of peoples throughout the world, is the example we have jointly set by our manner of conducting relations between our two nations.'[3] This reckoned without the Irish-Americans whose attitudes were frozen at the potato famine of 1846. When a royal visit to Chicago was in prospect, the populist Mayor 'Big Bill' Thompson promised to 'crack King George one in the snoot' if he ever came to the city. It also reckoned without a strong German element in the population, with disillusionment after the last world war, with the American desire to assert their role and culture against European domination, and the wish to keep the continent separate from world problems. In 1931 the United States adopted 'The Star-Spangled Banner' as its national anthem. It referred to an incident in the War of 1812 with Britain. Some of the lines in the rarely sung third verse were clearly anti-British, and possibly pro-slavery: 'No refuge could save the hireling and slave / From the terror of flight, or the gloom of the grave.'

The British upper classes could afford to travel across the Atlantic, and it became quite common for aristocrats to marry American heiresses – Winston Churchill's mother was one. But the British generally had seen little of Americans. During the First World War, soldiers usually landed in France and went straight to the front; sailors were mostly in isolated areas such as Scapa Flow, the Moray Firth, or Queenstown in Ireland. Emigration to the United States was restricted by the Quota Acts of 1921 and by the Great Depression, so fewer families had relatives who might write home.

The American tourist was now a recognised figure, but was far from common. Margaret Halsey's bestseller, *With Malice Towards Some*, of 1938 described a cold, wet land with poor food, narrow streets and tiny houses, mitigated by the beauty of landscape and townscape, and friendly service. She was particularly infuriated by the attitudes of the upper middle class: 'the people we met had been trained from childhood

The Sixth Battle Squadron of the US Navy sailing from the Firth of Forth in 1918, with the Forth Bridge seen dimly in the background. It shows a kite balloon for anti-aircraft protection and the characteristic masts of US battleships of the time. These were no longer in use by the Second World War.

to patronise Americans as Americans are trained from childhood to clean their teeth.'[4]

British impressions of America were largely derived from the most important medium of the age, the cinema. Hollywood dominance was so great that in 1927 Parliament passed the Cinematograph Act, which decreed that 5 per cent of films shown should be British, rising by stages to 20 per cent. The greatest star of the silent screen, Charlie Chaplin, was, in fact, British, but never spoke until 1940 so it was not obvious. The beginning of sound films or 'talkies' in 1927 made the American accent familiar. Stoker Albert H Jones later wrote: 'America to us ratings who had come from the working class was the land where glamorous film stars and amiable gangsters like Cagney and Bogart lived. ... These favourite stars had, if nothing else helped to brighten up many people's lives by taking their minds away for a couple of hours from the misery of the dole and the Means Test'.[5] Westerns were mostly low budget B-features until John Ford's seminal *Stagecoach* of 1939. They showed the individualism of the American character and the wide open spaces. Gangster films had a lull between *Scarface* of 1932 and *The Roaring Twenties* of 1939, but after that they flourished. The American RNVR officer A H Cherry was approached by his commander in 1941:

> 'Come, Yank, I'll take you to the cinema. You can explain some of the Americanisms to me.'

They saw an Edward G Robinson gangster movie.

> 'Look here. Old chap, do they really go about shooting each other up that way over there?'
> 'Hardly!'[6]

The British would see nothing of America's race problem on the screen – African-Americans were shown as faithful servants, or even as contented slaves in *Gone with the Wind*. But Hollywood's picture of the country was not all rosy – it included Chaplin's critique of mass production in *Modern Times*, the harrowing *I am a Fugitive from a Chain Gang* and John Steinbeck's *The Grapes of Wrath* on the desperation of displaced agricultural workers. But far more popular were the musicals, products of the sound age, such as Fred Astaire's *Top Hat* of 1935.

As American servicemen began to arrive in Britain in 1942, they were warned that the people were 'reserved, not unfriendly', they disliked bragging, and they did not care about being the 'biggest' of anything. Their sports were very different from American versions. The pub was 'the poor man's club', the local gathering place where much beer or ale was drunk, but whisky was rarely available. And they deserved respect for what they had been through so far in this war.

Naval co-operation between the two sides was equally ambivalent. In 1917/18 an American squadron joined the British battlefleet in the North Sea, though it saw no action. In 1918 D W Knox of Admiral Sims's staff wrote: 'It is very evident that extremely cordial relations exist between our officers and the British in the Fleet, and there is a very highly developed spirit of co-operation between them.'[7] Not everyone agreed: Ernest King was staff officer to Admiral Mayo and railed at the subservience shown to the British, their lack of aggression, and inadequate staff work.

One result of the contact was that in 1919 the US navy replaced the single-breasted, stiff-necked, blue jacket and adopted the British-style officer's double-breasted jacket with lapels, collar and tie. Instead of the eight buttons on a Royal Navy uniform they had six, as worn by the unconventional Admiral Sir David Beatty.

After the war and the elimination of the German fleet, the Americans became worried, as a member of the naval advisory staff wrote in April 1919:

> In the past our naval position has derived great strength from the potential hostility of the British and German fleets … The German fleet has ceased to exist, with the result … Under present conditions the British Navy, with its world wide supporting organisation, is strong enough to dominate the seas in whatever quarter of the globe that domination may be required.[8]

War between Britain and the United States was unlikely, but the Americans saw the possibility of disputes over the status of Canada, or a trade war. Britain was likely to avoid such a war at all costs, but saw the possibility of a new and extremely expensive arms race, as the Americans planned to build ships against the threat from Japan, reducing the United Kingdom to the second or even third naval power in the world. To prevent this, and to restrict Japan, British and American politicians negotiated the Treaty of Washington, and naval officers were obliged to go along with it. Britain and the USA were to be equal in 525,000 tonnage of capital ships, with Japan allowed three-fifths of that, and France and Italy having 175,000 tons each, while both the major powers were to have 135,000 tons of aircraft carriers with the others in proportion. The United States was content to be recognised as first equal among naval powers but Congress did not vote the money to support it until the Vinson–Trammel Act of 1934. Japan was only prepared to accept second-class status in return for an agreement not to fortify US bases in the Pacific.

If the Washington Treaty was largely based on mistrust between Britain and the United States, the conference in London in 1930 was inspired by co-operation between President Hoover and Prime Minister Ramsay Macdonald, who were equally determined to cut naval expenditure in the face of the Great Depression. Macdonald wrote that 'the two delegations worked in complete harmony'. This was largely due to the presence of an Anglophile American, Admiral W V Pratt, who was so unpopular on his return home that he considered resignation. The main effect was to limit the building of cruisers, but the Admiralty was very unhappy at being restricted to fifty.[9]

Relations continued to be ambivalent. A British authority reported in 1930: 'Among American Naval Officers there seems to be two currents of opinion; those who know and like the British Navy and British Naval Personnel, and those who do not know us and regard us with suspicion and even hostility.'[10] It is perhaps just a coincidence that three of the pre-war aircraft carriers – *Lexington*, *Saratoga* and *Yorktown* – were named after victories over the British. Admiral Harold G Bowen complained about 'our unbelievably long dependence on British technology', as represented by the textbooks at Annapolis early in the century.[11]

The end of isolation

While the US Navy was largely focused on events in the Pacific, politicians were more concerned with the other ocean. President Roosevelt was increasingly worried about the rise of the Nazis and Fascists in Europe, but that was not shared by the American public. In 1935 Congress passed the Neutrality Act, forbidding any support to nations at war. It was strengthened two years later, but with the important concession that belligerents could buy material in the United States, provided they paid immediately and carried them in their own ships – 'cash and carry'. This greatly favoured Britain, as German ships were likely to be stopped by blockade. Roosevelt reacted swiftly to the start of war in Europe in 1939, setting up the Neutrality Patrol to keep warships, especially U-boats, from activity within three hundred miles of the coast.

In July 1940, soon after the fall of France, Congress passed the Two Ocean Navy Act, allowing a 70 per cent increase in naval tonnage at presidential discretion. There was authorisation to 'acquire lands as the Secretary of the Navy with the approval of the President may deem best suited for the purpose, erect buildings and acquire the necessary machinery and equipment.'[12] Even that was not enough: fifty-six more acts would have to be passed during the war to facilitate naval operations. It was soon followed by the Selective Service Act, which instituted peacetime conscription for the first time, though the navy still relied on volunteers for now.

Roosevelt ignored the advice of Ambassador Joseph P Kennedy that Britain was finished, and in September 1940 he concluded the 'Destroyers for Bases' deal, by which fifty old destroyers would be given to Britain in exchange for long leases on bases in the Bahamas and Caribbean. In March 1941 Congress was persuaded to pass the Lend-Lease Act which allowed help to Britain on more generous terms, offering 'all aid short of war', and beginning the full mobilisation of American industry. A meeting between Roosevelt and Churchill in August off Newfoundland produced more promises of American support, but no declaration of war.

Meanwhile, in the Atlantic, American ships escorting convoys were confronted by U-boats. The US destroyer *Kearny* was hit by a torpedo in October 1941, but survived. *Reuben James* was not so lucky and sank with the loss of more than a hundred lives. Any doubt about American involvement in the war was removed with the Japanese attack on Pearl Harbor on 7 December, and Churchill 'slept the sleep of the saved and thankful.' Hitler, believing that America was a mongrel nation run by Jews and there would never be a better opportunity to defeat her, declared war on 11 December. But the road to victory would be far harder than Churchill imagined.

It was agreed that the main Allied effort should be against Germany and Italy rather than Japan, which was unpopular with some sections of American opinion, including Admiral Ernest King, who was particularly suspicious of the British. When Admiral Sir Andrew Cunningham asked for additional divisions of escort vessels to assist in the North Atlantic convoys, King interpreted this request as a 'needle' directed at him, and was very abrupt with Cunningham. He felt obliged to point out that 'although the British had been managing world affairs for some three hundred years, the United States Navy now had something to say about the war at sea, and that fact should be faced, whether palatable or not.'[13]

Command structures

From 1942 the Allied war effort was directed by the Combined Chiefs of Staff – not to be confused with the *Joint* Chiefs, who all came from the same country. The Combined Chiefs included Admiral Leahy, Admiral King, General Marshall and General Arnold for the US side, and the First Sea Lord, Chief of the Imperial General Staff and Chief of Air Staff from the United Kingdom. They first met in January 1942 during Churchill's visit to the USA after Pearl Harbor, and defined their tasks, including 'The strategic conduct of the war … the broad program

A meeting of the Combined Chiefs of Staff in Washington in October 1943 with the British on the left, including Rear Admiral W R Patterson, Field Marshal Sir John Dill, Brigadier Vivian Dykes, Lieutenant General G N Macready and Air Marshal D C S Evill. The American officers on the right include Ernest J King, William Leahy, Brigadier General J R Deane, General George C Marshall, and Lieutenant General J T McNarney.

of war requirements ... The allocation of munitions resources' and 'The requirements of overseas transportation.'[14]

The organisation had its headquarters in Washington. According to Churchill, eighty-nine out of about 220 formal meetings were held during the major international conferences, such as Casablanca, Quebec and Yalta.[15] Sir Alan Brooke, the Chief of Imperial General Staff, described the meeting on 14 August 1943 during the Quebec conference: 'Not a difficult one. Our first task being to settle the agenda for the conference, and secondly to run through a general outline of the war as we saw it. Before lunch we finished the European Theatre in compete accord. After lunch we went on with the Pacific Theatre till 4 pm.' But the meeting on the next day was far less successful. 'I entirely failed to get Marshall to realize the relation between cross Channel and Italian operations ... It is quite impossible to argue with him as he does not even begin to understand a strategic problem!'[16]

Just after the war Admiral Cunningham discussed the merits of two different command systems, which he called 'the triumvirate' and 'a supreme commander'. The first, with navy, army and air force commanders of equal status, was 'in accordance with the British spirit of compromise.' He drew on his own experience in the Mediterranean in the first years of the war, and admitted that the services did not understand each other's needs, but concluded that it worked well enough. The only British commander-in-chief of naval origin was Mountbatten, who 'did not know much of the higher side of naval warfare and nothing of soldiery or of the air, *and he had no judgement*.' Eisenhower had little effect on Operation Torch, which was really executed by the commanders of the individual landings. By the invasion of Sicily he was 'getting better, he was integrating his staff, and was showing signs of the very great man that he became.'

Cunningham claimed that 'The Supreme Commander was invented by the Americans because the Army and Navy could not agree, and when they reached a point in the Pacific, they still could not agree, and still did not have a Supreme Commander' – a little unfair, as both Nimitz and MacArthur were, in effect, supreme commanders in different areas of a vast ocean. But as Cunningham agreed, a supreme commander was essential when the force of two or more nations operated together, as in the Normandy invasion.

The British political system

The British sovereign had no political power, but a certain amount of influence. King George V, who died in 1936, and his son George VI had both been naval officers. George VI, who succeeded with the traumatic abdication of his brother Edward VIII, was shy and famously had a great deal of trouble to control a crippling stammer, but his frailty endeared him to his people. Both kings took a strong interest in the navy and there is evidence that George VI was far more relaxed in a naval environment. Admiral Cunningham had an audience with him and noted, 'We laughed a good deal as usual.'[17]

Under the British parliamentary system, the legislature and the executive were closely linked. Government ministers were members of the House of Lords or Commons. The prime minister was, by definition, someone who could command a majority in the House of Commons, which usually meant the leader of the party with the largest number of MPs. The Conservatives were dominant before the war, as Labour and the Liberals split over support for a so-called National Government in 1931. The numbers would remain roughly constant throughout the war, for unlike Congress, Parliament was able to prolong its own life and delay the next election until the war in Europe was over. But in 1940 Churchill came to power supported by a coalition which included the Labour and Liberal parties, with only a tiny number of members in opposition.

Except in extreme circumstances, a government with a majority could rely on the support of the House of Commons as long as it did not stray too far from the ethos of its party or coalition. The power of the House of the Lords was restricted, and it was not likely to challenge a Conservative government, or a coalition which clearly represented the vast majority of the country. Backbench MPs were subject to tight party discipline and rarely voted against the party line.

Winston Churchill seemed an unlikely focus for national unity until he took office as prime minister on 10 May 1940. Many people remembered the disastrous failure of his Dardanelles expedition of a quarter of a century ago. The grandson of a duke, he lived an opulent lifestyle and had never been on a bus. He had made many enemies. A fervent anti-Communist, he had motivated the British expedition against the Bolshevik government in Russia in 1919. He joined the Conservatives in 1924 as the Liberal Party declined. During the 1926 General Strike, he led the government against the trade unionists but spent most of the next decade opposing Conservative policies on India and Nazi Germany. No one could doubt his opposition to Fascism, but many suspected his judgement, and his associates knew that his wilder schemes had to be kept in check. But Churchill had seen war at many levels in India, the Caribbean, North and South Africa and France, with a perfectly balanced knowledge of all three services. He had been a reforming First Lord of the Admiralty before and during the last war, and later served as Secretary of State for War and Air. He offered strength and experience as a military leader.

Churchill immediately formed a coalition government which included the Labour and Liberal parties, and he took care to get the support of the powerful trade unions. The young journalist J P W Mallalieu was sceptical about the aims of the Chamberlain government when the war began, but in 1940, 'when Churchill formed the National Government with the full support of the Labour Party and when Germany smashed through Belgium, Holland and France and what remained of the British army escaped through Dunkirk; my own previous attitude to the war seemed irrelevant and possibly wrong-headed.'[18] The coalition had almost universal support but Churchill was not immune from criticism. He won a vote of confidence by 477 to one in the dark days of February 1942, and a vote of censure by 477 to twenty-five in July.

As well as prime minister, Churchill took on the title of Minster of Defence, which had no constitutional meaning, but gave him moral authority over the armed services, and he did not hesitate to interfere in

Winston Churchill remains seated with his elbows on his knees amid congratulations after his speech in the House of Commons on 4 June 1940, justifying the attack on the French fleet at Oran and emphasising Britain's determination to fight on. Clement Atlee of the Labour Party stand to the left and Neville Chamberlain to the right, while David Lloyd George, the prime minister in the last war, is in the right foreground.

the detail of the war effort. The service ministers – the First Lord of the Admiralty, the Secretary of State of War and the Secretary of State for Air – were relatively minor political figures outside the War Cabinet and mainly confined to administrative duties. Churchill dealt directly with the chiefs of staff on strategy. That was always an uneasy relationship, Admiral Cunningham reported in August 1944 that Churchill was 'in no state to discuss anything. Very tired and too much alcohol', but concluded 'in spite of his sometimes bad remarks, I had always known that he was basically sound.'[19]

The United States political system

In the American system, the head of state and head of government were combined in a single person. The common view that right-wing governments were pro-miliary and left-wing ones were against it was reversed in this case. The Republican Herbert Hoover had been regarded as anti-navy during his presidency in 1929–33 and was accused of 'abysmal ignorance' of naval affairs.[20] His successor, Franklin D Roosevelt (FDR), in contrast had served as a very active Assistant Secretary of the Navy in 1913–20. He loved the sea and maintained close contact with it, despite being crippled by polio. As president, he enjoyed annual trips in the yacht *Potomac* or naval cruisers. He was a highly skilled political operator who had 'the yachtsman's sensitivity to the way the wind was blowing'.[21] And expenditure on the navy was one way of reducing unemployment.

As the war in Europe intensified, Roosevelt tried to integrate members of the Republican party in his administration, though it was never quite a coalition in the sense of Churchill's administration. Among these

Eleanor Roosevelt, Queen Elizabeth, King George VI and Franklin D Roosevelt stand on the deck of the presidential yacht *Potomac* during the royal visit to America in 1939.

appointments was Frank Knox, a Republican who had stood as vice president against FDR in 1936. He became Secretary of the Navy alongside another Republican, Henry L Stimson, as Secretary of the Army.

According to the constitution, the president was commander-in-chief of the armed forces, but Roosevelt was the first since Lincoln to function in the role. Sir Alan Brooke, the head of the British army, wrote of his relations with the chief of staff of the army, 'The President had no military knowledge and was fully aware of this fact and consequently relied on Marshall and listened to Marshall's advice.'[22] The president did not go as deeply into the affairs of the military as Churchill did. With vast resources, their allocation was never quite as critical as it was in Britain, and the war fronts were some distance away. On the other hand, he had to take the lead in allocating resources over two different wars over different oceans and deploying a wide variety of materials and personnel. Roosevelt usually allowed the chiefs of staff to take the initiative, and only overruled them if it did not suit his purposes. He did so in approving Operation Torch, the invasion of North Africa, and later at Casablanca, when he was convinced by Churchill's plans for a Mediterranean offensive, and he announced the policy of 'unconditional surrender' off his own bat.[23]

In May 1942 Roosevelt appointed Admiral William Leahy as his chief of staff, as well as chairman of the newly formed Joint Chiefs of Staff, which also included George C Marshall as head of the army, Ernest King for the navy and 'Hap' Arnold of the army air force. Leahy had got to know Roosevelt while he was aide to the Secretary of the Navy from 1915. He was a confirmed battleship man, a member of the 'gun club'. Under Roosevelt he became Chief of Naval Operations in 1937. Retired in 1939, he became governor of Puerto Rico, then ambassador to Vichy France, being recalled after it seemed to be too close to the Nazi occupiers. As chairman of the joint chiefs, he was seen as an honest broker, who could gain the trust of the other members. Wearing his other hat, he was a key adviser to the president.

No president could go far without the support of Congress. Roosevelt had large majorities in both houses at first, but his Democratic Party included conservative southerners as well as the liberals who favoured more welfare and state intervention. And he lost some of his supporters in the mid-term elections of 1938.

In contrast to the British Parliament, the United States Congress exercised a detailed, and not always positive, control over government, including the navy. In 1937 one naval officer wrote of 'us who are so accustomed to the legislators having a legal or practical finger in all phases of military life'. It had powerful standing committees which had no equivalent in the British system at that time. Any policy had to go through the 'double jeopardy' of the Appropriations Committee and the Naval Affairs Committee in each house. The navy was greatly helped by Carl Vinson, the chairman of the House Naval Affairs Committee from 1931 until 1947. His interest went far beyond congressional matters. 'Mr Vinson came to [Admiral] King's office many times during the war to ask him if there was anything that he needed, and to urge King to be prompt to communicate his needs to Congress.'[24] Even Ernest King had to defer to him in appointing Bull Halsey to five-star rank, rather than Spruance, whom King and many others thought more worthy.

Congress was naturally far more supportive in war than in peace:

> No armed service could expect better support than the United States Navy received from Congress during World War II. It might be said that in peacetime the Navy proposes and Congress disposes; in wartime, on the other hand he legislators were far more ready to defer to professional judgement, and for the most part to give the Navy what it asks.[25]

It was necessary to hold a presidential election in 1944, and Roosevelt stood for the fourth time. Orvill Raines wrote to his wife from the Pacific:

> Yes, Honey, I was for Roosevelt too. He is the only guy for the office right now. Later after the war I hope for a change. My reasons are that his is too extravagant (but it is necessary to win the war now) and he is getting too much power. ... he is now in possession of emergency war powers that give him more authority than any president of the United States ever had. He very nearly approaches to a dictator ...[26]

Society and class in Britain

Margaret Halsey wrote in 1938, 'An American living in England is constantly fetching up with a whang against the caste system; ... and against that death-in-life which the Britons, with characteristic understatement like to call English reserve.'[27] But contrary to what many foreigners thought, the old aristocracy was no longer supremely powerful in Britain. Their decline had begun in the 1870s with the fall in land values, continued with the curbing of the powers of the House of Lords after 1911, and the loss of many heirs in the battlefields of Flanders. It retained influence, both with the royal family and as directors of numerous institutions which wanted the prestige of a title. The myth,

An image which came to symbolise class divisions in 1930s Britain. Public school boys maintain their stiff upper lips as they wait to enter Lord's cricket ground for the Eton versus Harrow match in 1937, while local boys look on in amusement.

however, was enough to make Hitler's deputy Rudolf Hess believe that contact with the Duke of Hamilton could help negotiate a peace in 1941. And in the same year, Commander Henry Eccles of the US Navy believed that 'the cold-blooded, stupid selfishness of the so-called aristocrats of England' was partly 'responsible for the present mess.'[28]

The influence of class was still strong in other ways, and it was maintained by the education system. Britain traditionally had an upper class, a middle class and a working class, and schools were divided into 'public', grammar or secondary, and elementary. 'A public school is one which has a real measure of independence, and can direct its own policy, which keeps its pupils to the full limit of age of eighteen and over, and which has a direct and regularly maintained connection with the Universities.' They were mostly boarding schools, where the boys lived in spartan conditions. Sport was emphasised, and boys were expected to learn leadership. They experienced military discipline in the officers' training corps, whose very name suggested where the army expected to find its leaders. School uniform, a private language and a rigid hierarchy were good preparation for life in the services, though in peacetime the navy did not use it, recruiting its potential officers at the age of thirteen.

Middle-class children mostly went to grammar schools if they could pass the entrance exams and their families could afford to keep them on beyond the age of fourteen in the harsh economic climate of the 1930s. Their main aim was to get its pupils to the level of the school certificate at around the age of sixteen. This was where the Admiralty would find its temporary wartime officers. Much of the middle class had arisen since the end of the last century and it thrived in London and other cities, despite the Great Depression. The 'breadwinner' was typically an office worker or businessman, and his wife ran the home with no live-in servants. The parents were proud of moving out of the overcrowded and unsanitary centre into the new suburban houses which were springing up around the cities; perhaps they were the first members of their family to have inside toilets, electric light and running water. Travelling by train though the new-built London suburbs in 1941, the aristocratic civil servant Sir Alexander Cadogan saw them as 'the encampment of the anti-Bolshevist horde.'

Life was very different from another Britain of extreme poverty, where unemployment was only interrupted by spells of grinding hard work, as seen by George Orwell in the north of England. Despite the building of council (social) housing, conditions were a striking contrast to the suburbs.

> 'Back to back' houses are two houses built in one, each side of a house being someone's front door, so that if you walk down a row of what is apparently twelve houses you are in reality seeing not twelve houses but twenty-four. The front houses give on the street and the back ones on the yard, and there is only one way out of each house. … The lavatories are in the yard at the back, so that if you live on the side facing the street, to get to the lavatory … you have to go out of the front door and walk round the end of the block – a distance that may be as much as two hundred yards …

Eight or more people might live in a three-roomed house. They tried to keep the living room respectable, so the overcrowding was at its worst in the bedrooms:

> In one family I visited there was a father and mother and a son and daughter aged round about seventeen, and only two beds for the lot of them. The father slept with the son and the mother with the daughter; it was the only arrangement that ruled out the danger of incest …

But not that of child abuse, which was not recognised as a problem at the time.

Britain was slightly less affected than the United States and Germany by the Great Depression after 1929, but George Orwell described the demoralisation caused by mass unemployment.

> I remember the shock and astonishment it gave me, when I first mingled with tramps and beggars, to find that a fair proportion, perhaps a quarter, of these beings whom I had been taught to regard as cynical parasites, were decent young miners and cotton-workers gazing at their destiny with the same sort of dumb amazement as an animal in a trap. … They had been brought up to work, and behold! it seemed as if they were never going to have the chance of working again.

Britain became the first industrial country by the early decades of the nineteenth century, with its iron works and cotton mills and a supply of coal to fuel them. Soon they developed the first railway network using more coal, and steamships to transport the coal, as well as goods and passengers. By the 1930s, however, industry was beginning to run out of steam in the figurative if not the literal sense. Oil rather than coal was the main fuel of the age, for warships, aircraft and vehicles. Transport was gradually moving onto the roads, but Britain was some way behind the United States and Germany in building them.

As well as providing employment for over a million workers and an export market, coal heated most homes, powered railway engines and merchant shipping, and fuelled gas and electricity production. But its older mines were less efficient compared with other countries, and the owners failed to modernise, preferring to keep wages down, with divisive effect. Textiles, at the centre of the first industrial revolution, employed around half a million women, mainly in the north of England, but had lost much of the overseas market during the war, and was finding it difficult to cope with competition from India and Japan. Steel was essential for ships, cars and armoured vehicles. It suffered from an excess of capacity and a lack of technological progress.

Of the newer industries, Imperial Chemical Industries was founded by merger in 1926. The American Ford Company had a large share of car production in Britain, while the Morris organisation adopted their mass production methods, and its owner, Lord Nuffield, had some of the autocratic style of Henry Ford. Electric generation increased, to supply numerous domestic appliances, as well as a few railways, and was helped by the setting up of the National Grid in the early 1930s.[29]

In wartime, the routine lives of the British people could not have been much more affected than they were, short of an actual invasion. Thousands were made homeless by bombing, others suffered nightly discomfort and anxiety sheltering from it, while children, and sometimes their mothers, were evacuated from the main cities. Street lights were extinguished and house lights were screened by thick curtains. Civilians routinely carried steel helmets and gas masks. Food and clothing were strictly rationed to minimal quantities. Life in the armed forces had many dangers and hardships, but at least the serviceman or woman did not have eke an existence out of meagre rations, or wait in a queue for basic foods. The naval man on leave might well be reminded of the importance of his mission to keep the sea lanes open.

Everyone who could make the slightest contribution to the war effort was obliged to do so, with unmarried women being conscripted from December 1941, to work in factories or join the women's services. For the biggest constraint on the national effort was the shortage of personnel. From the middle of the war the 'manpower' budget, rather than any financial restraint, was what decided everything from strategy to domestic life – 'the manpower budgets were the main force in determining every part of the war effort from the numbers of RAF bombers raiding Germany to the size of the clothing ration.' Britain from 1940 to 1945 was one of the most heavily regulated and mobilised societies in history. But as Americans were told by the British Information Services in 1943, 'the restrictions have not been imposed on them. The people have clamored for them at public meetings ... Working hours are long, leisure time is short, and wartime duties have been shouldered by every class.'[30]

Economy and industry in the land of opportunity

After the Civil War ended in 1865, the United States experienced unprecedented growth, led by Andrew Carnegie in steel, Henry Ford in automobiles and J P Morgan in banking. The Wall Street Crash of 1929 led to the Great Depression, ending the boom years of the 1920s and leading to a slow-burning series of bank failures and company closures, which the Hoover government did little to avert. The American economy, the first mass-consumer market, relied on prosperous farmers and businesses and well-paid workers being supplied by large-scale mass production. Europe was impoverished by war and depression and was no longer able to buy manufactures and food. In the Dustbowl Crisis, large numbers of farmers were ruined by the erosion of their land and moved west to California, where they were not welcome. The situation was desperate by the time Franklin D Roosevelt was sworn in as president

A sculpture showing unemployed men standing in line for bread during the Great Depression, in the Franklin Delano Roosevelt Memorial in Washington DC.

in 1933, with perhaps a third of the population of 126 million living in poverty – a reversal of the American dream. His New Deal offered large-scale public works, welfare benefits and banking reform, but it was only partially successful. From 1937 he was inhibited by the Supreme Court, by splits in his own party, and the loss of his congressional majority in the mid-term elections. When the war began in 1941, there were still millions unemployed and in poverty, with a great deal of slack to be taken up by a nation which was now united.

American war production was the industrial miracle of the century, and one of the main reasons why the Allies won the war. It actually began in 1940, with the supply of 'cash and carry' and lend-lease materials to Britain – by the end of that year, a quarter of a million tons of merchant shipping, nearly 12,700 aircraft, and thousands of tanks and field guns were on order for delivery in the next two years.[31]

The United States was the only major combatant that was never bombed or under realistic threat of invasion. It had time and Churchill said, in a slightly different context, 'In the military as in the commercial or production spheres the American mind naturally runs to broad sweeping, logical conclusions on the largest scale.' The British on the other hand, 'assign a larger importance to opportunism and improvisation'.[32] Up to 50 per cent of American industrial capacity was unused due to the Great Depression. It had space where new factories such as Henry Ford's

Willow Run could be erected, with a mile-long assembly line for B-24 bombers; and Henry Kaiser could build new shipyards among fields of mud. It was only in 1943 that the huge quantities of ships and aircraft were ready for the advance across the Pacific and for the invasion of Europe. Mass production was the great American innovation, started early in the century when Henry Ford stopped treating cars as individual, hand-crafted items and put them on production lines. William Knudsen, a Danish immigrant, left Ford after a heated disagreement and worked with General Motors, where he developed a much more flexible system of mass production, which could later be adapted to defence needs. In 1940 Roosevelt appointed him to the powerless and unpaid, but influential, post of chairman of the Office of Production Management, where he was able to improve the techniques of various companies and suggest ways to transfer production to defence needs.

Roosevelt had to modify some of the anti-business elements of his New Deal. A punitive tax regime for arms producers, derived from the myth of the 'merchants of death' of the last war, was mitigated. Government grants financed the building of new factories. Companies were alerted to possibilities to transfer their various efforts to war production, but with little or no compulsion, being motivated by patriotism or profit. General Motors, which was responsible for about 10 per cent of war production, made aeroplanes for Grumman and tanks for the army. Andrew Higgins developed the principal landing craft, and Donald Roebling the LVT, or 'amtrac', which became the main amphibious vehicle for the marines. Organised labour was brought on board, but that did not prevent a certain amount of industrial unrest, even after the invasion of the Soviet Union stimulated the Communist element. Women were recruited, though proportionately less than Britain or the Soviet Union. Many African-Americans escaped from the extreme poverty and vicious segregation of the south to work in munitions factories, though life there was far from free of racism.

During the war, besides hundreds of ships launched, American industry would produce more than eighty-eight thousand tanks, a quarter of a million artillery pieces, 2.4 million trucks, 2.6 million machine guns and forty-one billion rounds of ammunition. Even Stalin toasted, 'To American production, without which this war would have been lost.'[33]

The Lords of the Admiralty and naval administration
The Admiralty, based in its offices in Whitehall, was all powerful over the Royal Navy. Nominally it was headed by the First Lord, a civilian politician, whose real power might vary. When Churchill held the

The Board of Admiralty in 1943, showing the mix of naval and civilian members. The secretary sits at the nearest end of the table, with a recess to allow him to spread his papers. A V Alexander, the First Lord, sits on the grand chair at the other end, with the First Sea Lord, Sir Dudley Pound, two places to his left. The famous decorations, including a wind gauge surrounded by Grinling Gibbons carvings and a portrait of William IV, the 'Sailor King', have been removed for the duration.

office in 1911–16 and 1939–40, there was no doubt about who was in charge. In the coalition government of 1940–45, the position was held by A V Alexander of the Labour Party, who was an effective politician and administrator, but was left out of the main decision-making processes on war strategy. The First Sea Lord was the military head of the navy. Admiral Sir Dudley Pound took up the post in June 1939, after the death of several other leading candidates. He was in poor health and narcoleptic. He made at least one great mistake in dispersing the Arctic convoy PQ17 in 1942, but he oversaw a great naval expansion, the introduction of new technology, and fighting on many seas. Unlike Alexander, he was privy to strategic decisions as a member of the chiefs of staff committee, though he was said to wake up only when the navy was mentioned. Despite his tendency to fire unsuccessful generals, Churchill kept him on until he died in 1943.

His successor was Sir Andrew Cunningham, a much more forceful character – Churchill was reluctant to appoint him until other admirals declined the post if Cunningham was passed over. He had been a very effective commander-in-chief of the Mediterranean Fleet, then served as British naval representative in Washington, and led the naval side of the North African landings. The course of the navy had already been set by the time he took office in October 1943, but the work of the Normandy landings and the British Pacific Fleet still had to be done.

The other sea lords were responsible for different departments and activities – the Second Sea Lord for personnel, the Third Sea Lord was controller responsible for shipbuilding and materiel, the Fourth Sea Lord for supplies and transport, and the Fifth Sea Lord for naval air. Together with other politicians and officials, they constituted the Board of Admiralty, which had compete authority over the navy. Tactical power, however, was delegated to regional fleet commanders, with exceptions.

The naval staff was a relatively small but important part of the organisation, responsible under the First Sea Lord for intelligence and planning operations. Naval officers only served short terms of about two years at the Admiralty, for part of their function was to bring recent sea experience to bear. The bulk of Admiralty personnel were members of the Civil Service, a well-established and powerful institution, whose higher ranks were recruited by competitive examination among graduates of the older universities. They did nearly all the detailed administrative work and provided continuity, but it was often suggested that the set-up made any progress difficult. Files or dockets passed from office to office attracting many comments and delaying a decision, unless the matter was taken in hand by someone senior enough to give it priority.

By long-standing tradition, the Royal Navy avoided the attention of Parliament as much as possible. The Naval Estimates were presented by the First Lord in the spring of each year, after much discussion within the Admiralty. On one level they were very detailed. The salaries of civilian officials, such as £520 for a foreman of electric supply at Portsmouth, were listed. They detailed the amount spent on ships building or under repair – in 1937 it was noted that the battleship *Nelson* had cost £56 million to build and would need an estimated £331,000 to repair at Portsmouth. But statistical information was lacking on the active service navy. Parliament and public were only informed that during the year there would be 4970 flag and commissioned officers, 705 subordinate officers, 78,073 petty officers and seamen and 3489 boys in service, plus 466 cadets under training as officers, 4380 boys in shore bases and 874 artificer apprentices. All these figures except the first were up on last year, reflecting the slowly expanding navy.

The First Lord's printed statement was a good summary of naval activity during the year and was debated in the Commons. In 1937

Churchill, then out of office, lamented that the house, which had been full in his days as First Lord before the Great War, was now almost empty. He deplored the decision to fit the five battleships under construction with 14in guns as a backward step and wanted to know if there was any way to modify the design. Other members made valid points, but they had no real effect on the outcome. Eventually the division bell rang, and the members flooded in to vote on party lines.

Even this level of parliamentary control was suspended in wartime, as Churchill announced in 1940, 'it is not expedient to lay precise facts and figures of the proposed strength and cost of the Navy in the coming year before the House'. Instead, it voted for sums for 'such numbers of Officers, Seamen, Boys and Royal Marines and of Royal Marine Police, as His Majesty may deem necessary to be borne on the books of His Majesty's Ships and the Royal Marine Divisions.' Treasury control of expenditure, the bugbear of naval officers in peacetime, was also suspended. 'It will not be necessary to consult the treasury merely because a proposed service may involve an excess on the Vote or Subhead concerned.' It was protested that this was 'a complete abandonment of any system of financial control', but it was policy for the rest of the war.[34]

A chequered history: the status of the US Navy

The US Navy had had a far more chequered history in recent decades. It was neglected after the Civil War ended in 1865 and the army, with its campaigns against the Native Americans, was the premier service. Naval interest revived with the Spanish-American War of 1898, caused by the mistaken belief that the battleship *Maine* had been sabotaged by the Spanish off Cuba. In Manila Bay, George Dewey destroyed a Spanish fleet; Commodore Schley did the same job off Santiago in Cuba. It was the American navy's first real appearance on the world stage, and that was reinforced by the acquisition of Guam, Puerto Rico and the Philippines, following Rudyard Kipling's racially charged injunction to 'Take up the White man's burden.' This imperialist tendency was greatly reinforced when Theodore Roosevelt became president in 1901. He promoted the building of the Panama Canal, which would be of great strategic value to America, and he sent the 'Great White Fleet' on a world tour.

The US Navy had no opportunity to distinguish itself after America entered the Great War in 1917. A squadron of battleships was sent over to form a division of the British Grand Fleet, but the Germans did not venture out to meet it. American forces served in the anti-submarine war and laid a huge mine barrage. The navy languished in the 1920s and early 1930s, but began to revive as the Roosevelt administration tried to create work by shipbuilding, coinciding with the growing threats from Germany and Japan.

The United States Navy was run from Washington. The Navy Department on Constitution Avenue was an immense building, in which unadorned offices of standard size stretched interminably along dreary corridors. When built as a temporary structure in 1918, it had seemed a model of efficient use of space, but the additions and alterations of a quarter of a century – coupled with wartime crowding – had turned it into a curiously chaotic rabbit warren.[35]

The Secretary of the Navy was the civilian head of the department, and the post was held by significant figures during all the war years. Charles Edison was the son of the inventor of electric light, and supported the building of the *Iowa*-class battleships and the controversial introduction of high-pressure steam before stepping aside to become governor of New Jersey in 1940. Frank Knox, a newspaper publisher and one of Theodore Roosevelt's 'Rough Riders' in the war with Spain in 1898, was nominated to the post on the same day that France surrendered. He had to deal with the aftermath of Pearl Harbor and appointed Chester Nimitz to

The view from the top of the Washington Monument in Washington DC in 1944, looking towards the Lincoln Memorial. The area is dominated by temporary wartime buildings for the use of the Navy Department. They were eventually demolished after their function was taken over by the Pentagon, which was then under construction.

the Pacific command before supervising the greatest expansion in the history of this or any other navy. He made a habit of visiting bases, and Ted Mason was impressed: 'on 17 September 1940 ... his appearance in our mess hall, where he was escorted with the utmost solicitude and deference by two rear admirals, two captains, and a gaggle of civilians, seemed to confirm his importance.'[36] His deputy James Forrestal took over in May 1944 after Knox's death. He had already begun to reform the labyrinthine bureau system, and Forrestal would become the first Secretary of Defense in a unified structure after the war.

Under the secretary in 1944 were three other politicians, the undersecretary and two assistant secretaries (one of air). Of the twenty-seven branches, boards and offices directly under the secretary, nearly all were headed by naval officers, even the Director of Shore Establishments and Civilian Personnel, and the Chief of the Industrial Incentive Branch. Only the heads of the Transportation Branch and of Training, Liaison and Coordination and the General Counsel who dealt with commercial legal services were civilians. There were only three civil servants at the next level down, as assistant directors. Because of the dominance of naval officers, civilian clerks and messengers had few promotion prospects compared with other government departments. There were 2409 of them in 1938, rising to nearly twenty thousand during the war.[37]

The quasi-independent bureaus also had their headquarters in Washington – their status as almost watertight divisions was a serious weakness in the system. There was near-disaster in 1938, when the Bureau of Ordnance produced a design for a 16in turret which did not match the Bureau of Construction and Repair's plans for the new *Iowa*-class battleships.[38] They were reorganised in 1940, so that the Bureau of Navigation became the Bureau of Personnel or BuPers, which reflected its function much better; the Bureau of Construction and Repair and the Bureau of Engineering were merged into the Bureau of Ships, largely as a result of conflict arising from Admiral Bowen's fervent advocacy of high-pressure steam, and were all headed by service officers – line officers in the case of Personnel, Aeronautics and Ordnance, naval architects for the Bureau of Ships, Civil Engineering Corps for Yards and Docks, a supply officer for Supplies and Accounts, a doctor for Medicine and Surgery, a general for the marines, and one of their own officers for the Coast Guard.

The office of Chief of Naval Operations was created by Congress in 1916 against the opposition of the then Secretary of the Navy, and at first it had restricted power and status. During the Second World War, the post was held by Ernest J King, one of the most forceful and controversial characters of the war. He was the principal naval adviser to the president, as well as to the Secretary of the Navy, and he and Roosevelt were said to 'talk the same language'.[39] In March 1942, in a key step which gave him great power, he also took on the post of Commander-in-Chief of the United States Fleet – title which was abbreviated to Cominch rather than the all-too-apt CinCUS. As such, he was able to mitigate the negative effects of the bureau system. He had no patience with the British desire to build up forces in the European region without launching an invasion of northern Europe, and wanted to prioritise the Pacific instead. He must bear some responsibility for the losses to U-boats off the American coast in the first half of 1942, but overall he made a great contribution to the success of his navy. Roosevelt, Leahy, Knox, Forrestal and King all added their strong talents to the mix, largely overcoming the essential faults in the system, such as the independence of the bureaus.

In the British system, orders to individual ships and squadrons filtered down from the War Cabinet and Admiralty by means of fleet commanders. The Admiralty rarely interfered in the commands, and in October 1939 the First Sea Lord wrote, 'Why have Commanders-in-Chief and do their work for them? If they are not capable of doing it they must make room for someone who can.'[40] The Admiralty did interfere with good effect in co-ordinating the chase of *Bismarck* in

Chester Nimitz, to the left, and Ernest King in a Marine Corps vehicle while planning the unexecuted invasion of Formosa in August 1944.

1941, and disastrously in dispersing convoy PQ17 the following year. The Home Fleet was the primary naval striking force, a traditional fleet of battleships protected by cruisers and destroyers. Throughout the war, its main base was at Scapa Flow to the far north, to be clear of enemy bombing and protect the possible exits to the Atlantic. It had eight capital ships in 1939, two aircraft carriers (one for training), fifteen cruisers and seventeen destroyers, plus submarines, depot ships and minesweepers.[41] After 1941 its main task was in protecting the Russian convoys.

Apart from that, the British coast was divided into six commands. Portsmouth took up the central part of the English Channel and was headed by Admiral Sir William James at the start of the war, with destroyers and light forces for local defence. Dover, a new command, was under Sir Bertram Ramsey, who would conduct the evacuation from Dunkirk, and organise the main defence against invasion. The Nore Command was named after an historic anchorage at the mouth of the Thames, and was based at Chatham. It stretched north as far as East Anglia, where it met the Rosyth Command based in that port, and reaching up to the northeastern corner of Scotland. Between them, these commands protected the east coast, and the convoys which brought coal to the towns of southeast England. Orkney and Shetland was another new command, under the C-in-C of the Home Fleet and protecting the base at Scapa Flow. The whole of the west coast was under Western Approaches, centred in Plymouth until it moved to Liverpool in February 1941. It would conduct most of the Battle of the Atlantic from then on.

Overseas commands were usually geographically based. The Mediterranean Fleet was a desirable posting in peacetime for all ranks – 'Hands, knees and boomps-a-daisy' was lower deck slang for highly popular runs ashore in Cannes, Nice and Monaco. It was a major force, consisting of three capital ships, one carrier, seven cruisers and twenty-nine destroyers in 1939. It fought some of the major battles in the first half of the war, particularly under Andrew Cunningham. The North Atlantic Command had two cruisers and a destroyer flotilla in 1939. The America and West Indies Station, based at Bermuda, had a cruiser squadron and two escort vessels in 1939. These forces would be subsumed in the Battle of the Atlantic. The South Atlantic Command, based at Freetown in Sierra Leone, saw one of the first victories of the war when the German raider *Graf Spee* was cornered and forced to scuttle herself.

Force H was formed at Gibraltar in June 1940 to fill the gap in the western Mediterranean left by the fall of France. It was an elite force, including the famous battlecruiser *Hood* and aircraft carrier *Ark Royal*, with two more battleships, a light cruiser and four destroyers. In a sense, it was more like a task force in American style, but that created anomalies. It was not under the command of Sir Dudley North, the C-in-C at Gibraltar, and because of this he did not assume responsibility when six ships under the new Vichy government passed through the Straits and threated a British operation against Dakar. He was dismissed, which he contested bitterly for many years.

The China Station, based at Singapore, had four cruisers, one carrier, nine destroyers, five escort vessels and a miscellany, including submarines, river gunboats and motor torpedo boats. It was quickly liquidated by the Japanese advance of 1941/2. The Eastern Fleet, based at Trincomalee, had the task of stemming the Japanese advance into the Indian Ocean and included several old battleships. On taking command in 1942, Admiral Somerville signalled, 'Well never mind, there's many a good tune played on an old fiddle.' After heavy defeats, the British began to return to the Pacific as German and Italian naval power crumbled. The British Pacific Fleet was formed under Sir Bruce Fraser in December 1944, and included two battleships and five fleet carriers. The very need to include 'British' in the title acknowledged that the Royal Navy was no longer supreme in the area, and to the Americans it became Task Force 57.

In the 1930s the US Navy had a single main force, titled the United States Fleet, based in the Pacific partly to deter Japanese aggression, and partly to keep it together for training. It was divided into the Battle Force, composed of battleships with supporting cruisers, destroyers, submarines and aircraft, the Scouting Force for reconnaissance in force, and ancillary forces. It moved to Hawaii in 1940. The only other organisation with the title was the small Asiatic Fleet based in the Philippines and operating in Chinese waters. As war threatened in Europe, an Atlantic Squadron was set up to run the Neutrality Patrol, including seventy-seven destroyers and light minelayers rescued from the reserve fleet.

In February 1941 the system was reorganised, with a Pacific, Atlantic and Asiatic Fleet, each under a commander-in-chief who was subject to the orders of the Commander-in-Chief, United States Fleet, or CinCUS – renamed Cominch and combined with the Chief of Naval Operations in the person of Admiral King in 1942. Second-line units, such as coastal frontier forces, district craft and the Naval Transportation Service, were under the Vice Chief of Naval Operations from June 1942. Each fleet had type commanders for battleships, carriers, etc, but purely for administrative purposes.

The Asiatic Fleet was soon defunct owing to Japanese advances, and the Pacific forces were allocated odd numbers, the Atlantic, even.

Nimitz was in overall command as CinCPac and Commander-in-Chief, Pacific Ocean Areas, with his base on shore at Pearl Harbor, and later Guam. The First and Ninth Fleets were purely administrative concepts. The Third Fleet and the Fifth Fleet were the same ships, but alternated when commanded by either Bull Halsey or Raymond Spruance. The Seventh Fleet in the Southwest Pacific was a joint organisation including Australian forces, and it was under General Douglas MacArthur as supreme commander.

The task force was the characteristic organisation of the US Navy, and in a sense it was more dynamic that the essentially static and conservative 'fleet'. In 1921 a force was defined as 'a command composed of a number of vessels or larger units, organised for a specific task'. In peacetime that was largely for training, but in war, 'forces will be organized to perform tasks assigned by their immediate superior.' In June 1941 there were three task forces in the Pacific Fleet: the Covering Force, the Reconnoitring and Raiding Force, and the Amphibious Force. Task Force no. 4 was added during the year, 'of a type which became not uncommon during the war – a task force composed not of ships but of activities.' A task force was a collection of ships of various kinds assembled for a specific operation, which could be maintained or disbanded afterwards, that offered great flexibility. Its commander was free from administrative responsibility and able to concentrate on the strategic and tactical picture. One early task force consisted of a carrier, two cruisers and eight destroyers. Task Force 58, which conducted the battle of the Philippine Sea, consisted of most of the Fifth Fleet under Raymond Spruance. The Fast Carrier Group under Marc Mitscher was made up of Task Groups 58.1 to 58.4, each with three or four carriers, escorted by three to five cruisers and twelve to fourteen destroyers. The Battle Line, TF 58.7, comprised seven battleships, four cruisers and fourteen destroyers.

Once-mighty British sea power was brought to a new reality in 1944, when the British Pacific Fleet, the main force in the region, was designated T57 as part of the American Fifth Fleet.

Strategy, war and Empire

Britain and France both had inflated ideas of their importance in the 1920s and early 1930s. Both had fought throughout the greatest war in history with heavy losses, but were undefeated. Germany was laid low until 1933, the rising power of Japan was consistently underestimated, and the United States and Soviet Union were out of world affairs for different reasons. Meanwhile, Britain and France still ruled much of the world through their colonial empires.

Britain was a small country with a vast empire. The homeland was about a fortieth of the land area of the United States, while the Empire was on every continent and many islands. It was said to have been established 'in a fit of absence of mind', but before the Second World War it was much in the public consciousness. Classrooms were decorated with maps showing red covering a quarter of the world's land. The Empire Exhibition of 1924 attracted seventeen million visitors. The newspaper barons Beaverbrook and Northcliffe raised its profile with their unsuccessful campaign for 'Empire Free Trade'. The Empire came closer together. Princes Edward and Albert (later Duke of Windsor and George VI) visited it many times and radio allowed the King to broadcast to it. British civil aviation was largely aimed at fostering physical links. It was reported in 1938: 'The sea route from England to Bombay by the fastest and most luxurious liners takes about twenty days; … *Imperial Airways* will fly us to Karachi in India in two days eight hours'.[42]

None of this could eliminate the rising tensions. The 'White Dominions' of Canada, Australia, South Africa and New Zealand had been self-governing for many years and after an Imperial Conference in 1923 and the Statute of Westminster of 1931, they had almost total freedom of action, including foreign policy. The Crown was recognised as the 'symbol of the free association of the members of the British Commonwealth of Nations.' Less happily, the greater part of Ireland was quasi-independent after bloody uprising and civil war and was not likely to follow the British lead. In India, traditionally the 'jewel in the crown' of the Empire, there were growing nationalist movements and rising tension between Hindu and Muslim. The Government of India Act of 1935 did not go far enough for the nationalists, but it went too far for Winston Churchill. In Africa, the British believed they ruled the colonies in trust for the 'natives', except in Kenya, where white settlers predominated. The Caribbean islands had long lost their value as sugar producers. Despite the new-found enthusiasm, the Empire was a liability rather than an asset to the British.

Another deciding factor in British strategy was its closeness to Europe, which means that it can decide how much involvement it has in continental affairs – a question which dominates British politics to the present day. Throughout the centuries, the main strategy has been to maintain the balance of power by forming part of an alliance against the strongest land power – Spain in the sixteenth century, France from 1689 to 1815, Germany in the early twentieth century, and the Soviet Union in the second half. Until the twentieth century, Britain contributed sea power, finance, and a small but effective army. After that, British armies proved capable of expanding hugely in wartime, while finance and, later, sea power came increasingly from the United States.

During the early stages of the Second World War, the 'Phoney War' of 1939/40, the three services had their own ideas on how to win. The army would be built up to strength and eventually perhaps in 1942, launch an attack with their French allies. The RAF, if let off the leash, would bomb the German cities and force a surrender. And the navy would blockade Germany and eventually starve it out, as they had done in the last war. All this changed with the fall of Norway and France and the evacuation, largely conducted by the navy, of the army from Dunkirk.

Defence against invasion was, of course, the most immediate priority, but it was largely secured by the RAF victory in the Battle of Britain in 1940, with naval forces mainly held in reserve. And Churchill was never likely to be satisfied with a purely defensive posture. He instituted commando raids and special forces, which would 'set Europe ablaze' in co-operation with resistance movements. He backed army and naval campaigns in North Africa and the Mediterranean, mainly in an attempt to open the inland sea for convoys. He supported a growing and expensive bomber campaign, the ultimate success of which was doubtful. And he planned to get the United States involved though his diplomacy with Roosevelt, and the attacks by U-boats in the Atlantic. That ocean was where the main threat to Britain came from 1941, as Churchill later admitted.

Churchill always recognised that British and Allied forces would have to return to Europe to win the war, but this was matched by his fear of a long campaign of attrition, such as he had witnessed on the Western Front in the last war. He resisted strong pressure from both the United States and the Soviet Union to open a 'second front' in northern Europe until the forces were ready. He devoted a great deal of resources to the Mediterranean, where land forces were successful against the Italians but not the Germans, until they had overwhelming superiority in numbers and (largely American) materiel by late 1942. After that, he persuaded Roosevelt to support invasions of Sicily and Italy, instead of going on to invade France immediately.

The United States had long enforced the Monroe Doctrine, that the European powers should not interfere in the Western Hemisphere, and consequently their own interest in Europe was limited. They were drawn into the Great War of 1914–18 by attacks on American ships, the most common *casus belli* for the country over the centuries, but many of them came to regret taking part in a war which did not create a better world.

The United States Navy was always aware of the possible need to fight on two oceans, and the completion of the Panama Canal in 1914 greatly facilitated that. It had long planned for a war against Japan, as the two nations faced each other across the vastness of the Pacific Ocean. From 1907, not long after the Japanese defeated the Russians at Tsushima, the US Navy was working on plans for a Pacific war, based on the premise that Japan would try to capture the Philippines to clear the way to resources in New Guinea and Indonesia. War Plan Orange was based on the 'Through ticket to Manila', by which the US fleet would get to the area as quick as possible to fight a great fleet battle. But in 1933 war games in the War College showed that the American fleet, even if victorious, would have to withdraw to Pearl Harbor for repairs, leaving the Japanese in possession of the field. Improvised naval bases would have to be set up on the way, mainly by capturing islands and atolls. Marine training in amphibious warfare intensified, and orders were placed for floating docks for ship repair.

The dramatic sinking of the battlefleet at Pearl Harbor did not change this fundamentally as far as the navy was concerned, except that the loss of the Philippines and numerous Pacific islands would make the advance much harder, and that aircraft carriers would replace battleships as the deciding weapon. This was confirmed with the great carrier battles of Coral Sea and Midway. The alliance with Australia was a complicating factor, which led indirectly to the bitter battle for Guadalcanal in 1942/3. Another factor was the huge ego of General Douglas MacArthur who promised the people of the Philippines, 'I shall return.' This caused an army-led advance along the larger islands to the south, which required substantial naval support. Meanwhile, the navy, once it had acquired amphibious warfare vessels and aircraft carriers and trained thousands of pilots, began the Central Pacific Drive towards Japan. This was 'island hopping' in the sense that many of the strongest enemy bases were bypassed and neutralised, against the expectations of the Japanese. The Japanese naval air force was largely destroyed in the 'Marianas Turkey Shoot' during the invasion of Saipan, but then forces were diverted to the Philippines to fulfil MacArthur's promise. The Battle of Leyte Gulf which followed was the most extensive naval battle in history. It was followed by the costly invasion of Okinawa and Iwo Jima, to provide air bases within close range of Japan.

Rather like Britain at the beginning of the war, the three services now had visions of how to end the conflict. The army would invade Japan and eventually defeat it, despite fierce resistance and huge casualties; the air force would bomb the cities, kill perhaps millions of people and paralyse activity; and the navy would continue the blockade and starve the country of food, fuel and raw materials. All this ended with the dropping of the two atom bombs in August 1945.

* * *

Both countries were liberal democracies, each with a head of state and two houses of legislature. In practice, they operated in rather different ways, but with similar final results – strong wartime armed forces supported by popular will. Both navies, like all others, were ruled by bodies in their capital city, but operated in quite different ways. Both navies had exceptional global reach, but the British reach tended to decline, the Americans to expand greatly.

2
Naval Society and Culture

NAVIES ARE naturally more isolated from normal society than other armed forces. Soldiers might spend much of their time in horrific conditions in a battle zone, but they were in their natural element. Aircrews spent relatively short periods flying and lived comparatively comfortably at airfields. Sailors, however, had to bear all sorts of weather afloat, and live for weeks or months in closed societies. They often had skills which were very different from landsmen, and they had a specialised vocabulary filled with ancient and largely obsolete terms. One manual, written by two British ratings, commented:

> The Royal Navy has a language of its own. Coining phrases is one of the sailor's many specialities, and no author could be more descriptive or apt. Sea speech is essentially free speech, bright, breezy, exclusively nautical and sometimes naughty. The English language would indeed be enriched if many of the sailor's make-shift words and phrases could be put to more universal use.[1]

It was no different in the United States Navy:

> The chief started trying to teach us a bed was a bunk; upstairs was topside; the rifle was what you shot the enemy with; a gun was what you shot girls with. Anyone behind you was astern; to the right was starboard; to the left was port. The bath was the head; you drank water from a scuttlebutt. The window was a porthole. To work was called turning to; the kitchen was a galley; a light on a ship was a running light.[2]

The Royal Navy took this a stage further. Not only did one 'go ashore' on leaving a base, but it was actually considered a ship. It was not just 'cutely named' as Paul Fussell suggested,[3] it was a matter of law. Naval discipline only applied to those who were attached to His Majesty's ships and vessels, which was realistic in the mid-nineteenth century when sailors between ships or on training courses lived in old hulks in the dockyard ports. Rather than have the act amended to cover the modern 'stone frigates', the Admiralty maintained the fiction that they were still ships. The older ones retained the names of the ships they had once been, so the naming was largely random, and a small vessel was attached to maintain the pretence. Thus the training school HMS *Ganges* with thousands of men had a steam launch, and HMS *Heron,* the Fleet Air Arm base at Yeovilton and many miles inland, had a harbour launch.[4]

A sailor's basic loyalty was to his ship, though he was not likely to serve in the same one for more than two or three years, unlike a British infantryman who might spend a whole career in the same regiment. There were three stages in the birth of a ship – laying the keel, launch and commissioning – but the bulk of the crew was only likely to be involved in the last. A due amount of ceremony was held, even in wartime:

> On the *Abercrombie*'s broad fantail, officers and crew stood at attention in silent, white-clad ranks. On the dock ... sat the invited guests, mostly the wives, sweethearts and families of the crew ... In the center were Mr and Mrs C W Abercrombie of Kansas City.
>
> ... the supervisor of shipbuilding at Orange, representing the Commandant, Eighth Naval district, read the orders empowering

The commissioning of the battleship USS *Missouri* at New York Navy Yard in June 1944, showing the crew assembled under three of her 16in guns.

him to do so and then formally accepted the ship for the Navy. At the conclusion of his remarks, he ordered, 'Hoist the colours!' Forward, a sailor broke out the Union Jack ... at the jack staff. Aft, another sailor ran the national ensign up the short, aft-slanting flag staff. And amidships, a third sailor sent a fluttering sliver of red, white and blue soaring to the truck – the commission pennant. *Abercrombie* became in that instant the United States Ship *Abercrombie,* a commissioned warship.[5]

Leonard Charles Williams wrote:

> This was one of the good things about shipboard life as opposed to barracks. In a ship you were immediately accepted as one of the ship's company. Your shipmates slowly dissect you, find out what makes you tick, and then pass judgement. You are either a 'stinker' and no bloody good, or else you are OK and accepted as 'one of us'.[6]

Seasickness was a universal factor for civilians and naval men, especially those who were on their first ship and had never even seen the sea before, and the fear of it probably deterred many young men from choosing the navy. Frank Muir opted for the RAF because 'my father, who was a professional sailor, was seasick every time he went to sea, and no doubt he had passed to me some of the relevant chromosomes.'[7] And once at sea it could be chronic and widespread. 'Numbers of young seamen began heading for the side. They were joined by firemen and motor machinist's mates lurching up with ashen hue from the engineering spaces. Some took to their bunks and others lined up at the sick bay for relief.'[8] Even experienced sailors could suffer, for many of them were used to larger ships in smoother waters. The chief engineer of one of the fifty ex-American destroyers envied the small-boat sailors. 'What lucky devils these RNVR yachtsmen were, with their insides toughened by their crazy little sailing boats.'[9]

Research suggests that vertical movement, especially pronounced towards the bow and stern of a ship, is the main cause of seasickness, but it is exacerbated by such factors as tiredness, food and smell, for example of fuel oil. Pitching and especially rolling increase tiredness and tend to make it more difficult to work, for example in reloading depth charges in an escort vessel – and it was particularly prevalent in small escort vessels such as corvettes and trawlers which were pressed into service for the Atlantic War.

Officers and men in both navies worked to a common timetable, though as usual they interpreted it differently. British and American sailors used the watch system, in which nearly a half or a third of the crew (also known as a watch) were on duty for four hours, alternated with either four or eight hours off duty, according to whether they were divided into two or three watches. Large ships in peacetime usually had two watches, each divided into two in turn; at sea a whole watch would be on duty, in harbour perhaps half a watch. In the Royal Navy, the period between four and eight in the afternoon was divided into two, the first and second dog watches, to ensure that officers and men had a different routine every night and could have longer rest periods during darkness. In the US Navy, the term dog watch was mainly of historical interest, being 'A corruption of dock watch, that is, a watch which has been docked or shortened.' Thus officers and men might serve the same hours night by night, for example in the submarine USS *Jack*:

> 'You get the twelve to fours. Miles as senior watch officer gets the eight to twelve, and Goodman takes the four to eights.'
> I had expected to get the midwatches, the traditional lot of the junior watch officer. It's the toughest watch. Not only is your sleep broken up every night in the middle, but the times you are off watch are not the best to get to sleep.[10]

And there were variations within the individual ships:

> While the other divisions in the *California* stood the traditional four-hour watches, C-D Division was divided into four watch periods: morning (breakfast to dinner); afternoon (dinner to supper); evening (supper to 0100 the following morning); and 'mid' (0100 to breakfast). Thus, the day was split unequally among relatively short watches, and punishing ones …[11]

According to the official *Bluejacket's Manual*, 'During the night watches there is, as a rule, very little to do; consequently men not at work and not on lookout are usually permitted to lie down on the deck in a group, where they can easily be found.'[12] That might work in a battleship on two watches in peacetime, but it was unlikely in a wartime destroyer.

Crews were also split into divisions for welfare and disciplinary purposes, usually with men of the same occupational group, with larger groups split into several sections, with the senior officer in each responsible for 'the training, organisation, welfare, cleanliness and smartness of his men'.[13] A large American ship might have gunnery, navigation, engineer, construction and repair, supply and medical divisions.[14] When possible, divisions were paraded each morning so that officers could get a sight of their men. They were powerful institutions in the US Navy according to

Ted Mason. 'As I roamed the ship, I began to learn about her hierarchies and her twenty-three petty fiefdoms, or divisions. Each fiefdom was run by a chief or first-class petty officer from his command post near the ubiquitous coffee pot.'[15]

Larger British vessels were also divided into 'parts of ship' with the traditional titles of forecastlemen, topmen and quarterdeckmen. As far as possible, each would man the armament in the appropriate area, with the Royal Marines traditionally manning 'X' turret, the second from aft.

For action against the enemy, the Royal Navy had the Quarter Bill, the US Navy had the Battle Bill or General Quarters. It was not possible to maintain complete readiness during the long hours in which an air or submarine attack might be expected, so reduced forms were used. By 1945, the Royal Navy had four states of readiness, each of which could be applied to surface and/or air action. The first degree was used 'If enemy movements show probability of the enemy being encountered at any moment'; all the relevant weapons were manned. The second degree was used when 'there is a possibility of the enemy being encountered at any moment', and a limited number of men could be fallen out from full action stations. In the third degree, readiness was based on a two-watch organisation if contact was 'possible but not imminent'. And in the fourth degree, a four-watch organisation was used, when 'the disposition of our forces affords the necessary security from any surprise encounter.'[16] In the US Navy, at Condition I or General Quarters, every man was at his assigned battle station. Condition II and III were 'war cruising'. Steering, lookouts and sensors were fully manned, but only half the armament. In addition, there were duties allocated for tasks such as raising anchor, collision, fire, abandon ship and many others.

Nearly every armed force in the world, including revolutionary ones, maintains the distinction between officers and men. In operational terms it is perhaps more pronounced in navies, where the two groups have different roles – one to command, direct and navigate, the other to carry out the tasks. In an army, in contrast, NCOs and officers have essentially the same tasks, to command men in battle, while in air forces the main distinction is between flying and non-flying personnel. Armed service officers are generally distinguished by family connections in more traditional forces, and by education, by training and by technical skill. A British report of 1935 explained the difference between officers and petty officers:

> ... the officer holds his position by his personality and character, by his birth, by his superior general education, by his living apart

and on a different scale from the men and by his knowledge of such subjects as the navigation and handling of ships, which are a closed book to others.[17]

Even at that late date, distinguished officers considered 'birth' a significant factor.

Social distinction between officers and men did not keep up with changing mores. After the Invergordon Mutiny of 1931, Admiral Sir John Kelly noted a dangerous gap between officers and ratings. He listed intoxication among the officers, 'failure to attend to the wants and grievances of the men', and 'Rowdy parties in Officers' Messes which, if imitated on the lower deck, would not fail to be immediately suppressed, and would probably result in disciplinary action.' Able Seaman Len Wincott witnessed to this kind of 'high jinks':

> One night we had a remarkable spectacle of two officers, each wearing nothing more than a tie, swimming to the ship, whilst on the forecastle of the accompanying motorboat two women and some other officers screamed with hysterical laughter and shouted lurid observations to be heard all over Hong Kong harbour. Their innocent evening frolics ended up with one of the women quite drunk, literally riding totally naked up and down the officers' passage way on a bicycle, met at either end with officers with fire hoses. Of course all the mess had to be cleaned up by the seamen.[18]

Officers who behaved like this would never earn the praise, 'He's a proper gent, he is,' from the lower deck.[19]

From the US Marines, William Rogal discovered the officers' privileges onboard a troopship:

> Our chow line snaked past the windows, or portholes, of the officers' dining room. Such splendor, rows of white tableclothed tables attended by stewards in white jackets … Standing there with the sleet going down my neck, I truly felt like a homeless vagrant peering at the rich entering a fancy restaurant. It struck me then. The difference between the men dining in luxury and comfort and me was a college education![20]

According to Alvin Kernan: 'The gap between enlisted men and officers in the American navy during World War II was medieval … The enlisted men accepted the division as a necessary part of military life'.[21] Probably it was no more than in the Royal Navy or any other navy, but it was more noticeable in a nation which took pride in equality.

Saluting was something of an obsession with regular naval officers, and some reservists, but like many other British traditions it was not so old – it dated from 1890 when Queen Victoria saw something of German drill practices. Sailors were instructed:

> The naval salute is made by bringing up the right hand to the cap or hat, naturally and smartly, but not hurriedly, with the thumb and fingers straight and close together, elbow in line with the shoulder, hand and forearm in line, the thumb being in line with the outer edge of the right elbow, with the palm of the hand turned to the left, the opposite being the case when using the left hand.[22]

One medical officer went too far. When he and his captain were walking the quarterdeck in opposite directions he insisted in saluting very time they met, leading the captain to send a message via the first lieutenant – 'For God's sake stop saluting the Captain'.[23]

Saluting was also important in the US Navy and the midshipman's manual *Naval Orientation* of 1945 devoted its first eleven pages to the subject, including two pages of cartoons with twenty occasions 'When

A rare view of British and American sailors together, taken in the joint base at Londonderry early in 1942. Both sides are informally dressed, especially the Americans to the right, who show no sign of naval uniform.

to Salute', and ten on 'When not to Salute'.[24] However, it did not go so far as the US Army, where salutes were exchanged with the head uncovered.

When men of the two navies served together, the first thing that was noticed was the food. In the approach to the North African landings:

> Soldiers acquired sea legs slowly and did not 'beef' at British rations for some days. Gradually, as stomachs recovered and appetites were whetted by the sea air, that aspect of the voyage became all-important; the 'limey' cook on board *Keren* was deprived of his coffeepots in favour of more competent hands. … As the days passed … then gripes about the inevitably recurring herring, tripe and mutton [increased].[25]

According to Raymond Calhoun:

> Without question, the British tars found much about our ships for which to be thankful. The food was perhaps the most welcome of these advantages. Thumbing through Quartermaster Cleere's diary recently, I came across this passage. 'The ten English sailors aboard are really enjoying the quantity, quality and variety of food they are eating. I guess it is no joke that food is not too plentiful in England. One limey said they were eating like the lords and ladies of London, and it's probably true.'[26]

Then there was the perpetual debate about the value of ice cream compared with alcohol and the lure of the latter from dry American ships. Alongside HMS *Tyne* Calhoun discovered:

> We spent the first week alongside her, and every afternoon her officers came aboard the *Sterett*, rounded up all the officers who were not on duty, and took them aboard the *Tyne* for drinks. Despite the fact that their drinks were served without ice, the Scotch whiskey was excellent, and our little afternoon gatherings were tremendous fun … Commodore Moon … Told us that he did not want to see any more going aboard her with 'a thirsty look on our face.' We all complied with his directive: we continued to go aboard, but we made sure we did not look thirsty.[27]

Even the highest ranks were not immune. Admiral Nimitz visited *Duke of York*, the flagship of Sir Bruce Fraser of the BPF, mostly to get a Scotch and soda before dinner 'because our ships are dry.'[28]

Even on the humblest tasks there were small differences, according to Chief Petty Officer Miller USN: 'The British Navy does not use swabs but wet rags to mop up any excess water, not only requiring considerable [*sic*] more man hours but also not accomplishing an efficient job as a swab.'[29]

Houston Jones had started the war believing that the Pearl Harbor attack was not inevitable: 'we should have looked after our own business rather than England's [*sic*] and France's', an attitude he came to regret. In the Mediterranean he 'felt more kindly towards the "Limey Navy" after his ship was refuelled from a British LST; and he admired the spirit of British sailors when a boatload of survivors from HMS *Janus* 'burst into the saloon song, "Roll out the barrel".'[30]

Bell bottoms and blue jackets

Naval uniform was a relatively modern phenomenon. The Royal Navy only introduced it for officers in 1748, and for ratings in 1857. It was far less necessary than army uniform for identifying men in battle, but it did much to establish the seaman's self-identity and his pride in his service and unit. In many ways it had a common origin in the two navies, but the details were differently interpreted. Twentieth-century armies tended to reduce the visible distinctions between officers and men to protect the officers from sniper fire. But in practically all the world's navies, officers wore uniforms which had absolutely nothing in common with those of the junior personnel, except for its white or dark-blue colour. In working dress, the US Navy maintained even more visible distinctions – officers and chief petty officers wore khaki and later grey, enlisted men wore light blue shirts and dark blue trousers.

British seamen wore the 'square rig' uniform with bell-bottom trousers, a square collar and an uncomfortable round cap. It was very popular with the public. John Godley, who would later inherit the title of Lord Kilbracken, also noted the public respect:

> We could always hitch anywhere in bellbottoms. Almost everyone, not only nice girls, really did seem to like a sailor, especially if he were far inland and standing by a roadside. Elsewhere we were bought drinks, people called us Jack and dear old ladies came smiling up to us: touch a sailor's collar.[31]

Many sailors were proud of it but others found it very inconvenient: 'One has only to watch an A.B. dress to have pity on him, with a uniform consisting of tapes and ribbons and bits and pieces, and a blue jean collar which another person has to hold in place while the poor chap puts his overcoat on.'[32]

Uniquely among armed services, Royal Navy seamen had to pay for their uniforms, and most of them were skilled with needle and thread, so they had a strong tendency to adapt them. A 'tiddly sailor' might wear:

A well-dressed or 'tiddly' seaman, presumably ready for a run ashore, with a deep 'V' in his jumper and exaggerated bell bottoms, contrasted with the typical wartime working dress.

The 'little round hat' as far from the central position as authority will permit, with the bow of its ribbon teased into a flat, symmetrical rosette. The spotless 'blue jean' collar, with its white borders gleaming. The black silk ironed to impeccable smoothness. The ribbons attaching it to the jumper are as long as possible, with swallow tail ends: ... the longer the more dashing. ... The 'bell-bottoms' as wide as canny selection from 'Pusser's stores' or instructions to the ship's tailor can achieve ...[33]

The first issue of unform was a key moment in any new seaman's career, as recorded by Ted Mason of the US Navy:

> As we passed down an assembly line of storekeepers behind a wide counter, we pushed along an ever-growing pile of clothing: dress blues; dress whites (soon to be eliminated from the prescribed outfit): undress blues and whites; white and flat hats; double-breasted peacoat; blue denim work pants and lighter-blue short-sleeved shirts; T-shirts and drawers; a black silk neckerchief. After the clothing had been issued – by seaman's eye with no regard to the wearer's opinions – we picked up a mattress, a pillow, two white cotton mattress covers, a pair of white wool blankets, and a stiff canvas seabag.[34]

Only the first issue was free, replacements would have to be paid for.

The round white cap was the most distinctive feature of the enlisted man's uniform:

> Everyone hated or loved the white hats issued to us for dress and work uniforms. The hat was supposed to be worn rounded off two inches above the eyes, very tilted fore and aft, so that even a light stern breeze would dislodge it. … Each sailor had his own way of trying to look good in one of these hats so they would end up being worn as many different ways as there are sailors. I had a love-hate feeling for mine and still do.[35]

For Ted Mason:

> A good dress-blue uniform in hard-finished gaberdine with red flaring bell bottoms, lots of fancy stitching and a silk inner lining would cost from fifty to seventy-five dollars – a month's pay and more for a typical seaman first or petty officer. Nevertheless many sailors wanted them, precisely because the cloth and cut were not regulation. Such a uniform immediately identified its wearer as a man who knew his way around the navy.[36]

He described preparations for liberty, with the need to pass a gangway inspection as well as to cut a dash ashore:

> Making sure that my neckerchief was tied with ends even, that its square knot was aligned like a gunsight with the V of the jumper, and that my white hat was perfectly round and square over the eyebrows … At a safe distance, Johnson and I shifted the knots of our neckerchiefs towards our throats and crushed and bent our white hats before placing them on the back of our heads for a proper salty appearance.[37]

But James Fahey was relieved to get back to less formal dress: 'It felt good to put on dungarees again after having worn whites. Those white uniforms would make a good target'.[38] Houston Jones wrote: 'Our dress code at sea was very relaxed – blue cotton shirts, denim trousers, and white Dixie Cup sailor's hats – but we did receive instructions to dye our shipboard hats blue. From the air, a white hat could easily be sighted'.[39]

Rank distinctions were largely erased in working dress. According to Mason: 'In some of the divisions, chevrons were stenciled on the T-shirts to indicate petty-officer ratings, but [Chief Radioman] Reeves did not approve of the practice. In the radio gang, only one man had any real authority'.[40] In general, most enlisted men below chief, from petty officer first class to seaman second class, had no visible distinctions of rank while on duty. It was assumed that they would know the status of each of their colleagues.

Flags

Soldiers no longer carried flags into action, and aircraft had national symbols painted on the sides and wings, but warships still flew their ensigns with pride, in and out of battle. All true naval men were deeply concerned with flags, especially in the Royal Navy, which had a more complicated system than any other. To a sailor the Union flag was the national symbol and it should only be called the Union Jack when it was hoisted on the jackstaff in the bows of a man of war at anchor. It was and is a complex flag, incorporating the crosses of St George of England, St Andrew of Scotland and St Patrick of Ireland (though most of that island had left the union in 1922). The arms of St Patrick's cross were displaced slightly, which made it possible for the unwary to fly the flag upside down, a terrible solecism. But mostly on ships it was incorporated in one corner of either the red, white or blue ensign; red for the merchant navy, white (with an additional St George's cross in the main part) for the Royal Navy and blue mostly for non-naval ships under government control. The white ensign was flown from the stern of a warship during daylight, and at least two more were hoisted in various places during a battle, in case the loss of one might be taken for surrender. An Admiral of the Fleet would fly the Union flag from the mainmast; other admirals had the St George's cross with the addition of one ball for a vice admiral and two for a rear admiral. Other flags included the Royal Standard when the sovereign was onboard, and the Admiralty flag.

The US Navy, in contrast, used only two flags. The Stars and Stripes was universal, with its forty-eight stars representing the states as they were at the time. Confusingly to the British, they also used the term

46 TWO NAVIES DIVIDED

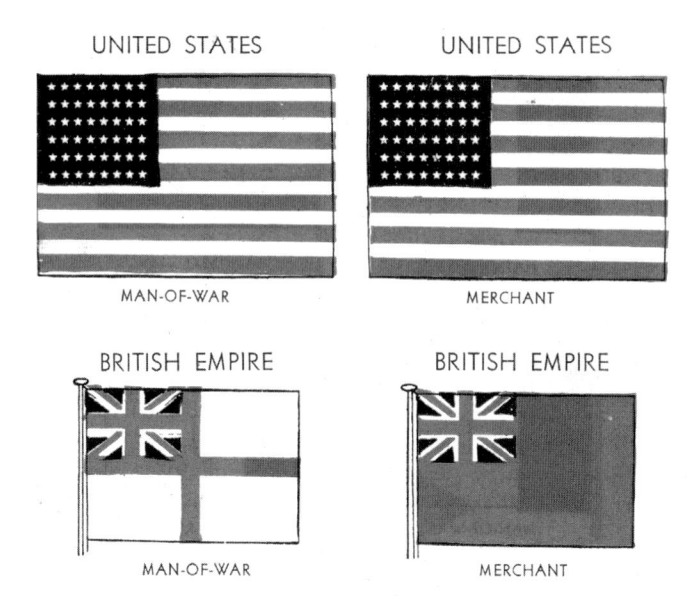

The American view of the the US and British ensigns. The latter flags are not drawn accurately, the red St George's cross on the 'man of war' ensign should have the white space above the red on the left-hand side, nearest the fly, and in the merchant ensign it is shown in the centre – a mistake which would be spotted by any member of the Royal Navy.

'union jack' for a flag consisting of stars only on a blue background, flown from the jackstaff in the bows of a ship at anchor. Whereas the Royal Navy's *Manual of Seamanship* devoted four pages of text and seven plates to various varieties of the national flag, the US *Bluejacket's Manual* of 1940 had less than a page on 'Our National Flag'. A commodore flew a blue flag with one white star and a fleet admiral had five stars, with the other ranks in between.

The King's navy

The Royal Navy was deeply, perhaps excessively, aware of its history, and the victories of Nelson were only the tip of the iceberg. Trafalgar Day, 21 October, was celebrated emotionally in every wardroom and officers' mess. Terms at Osborne and Dartmouth were named after great admirals of the past. Shore messes, such as the wardroom at Portsmouth, were decorated with paintings of great battles, whose names were proclaimed on the staircases.

The years before the war saw the publication of the first three of C S Forester's highly successful Hornblower novels. Set in the Napoleonic

Wars, they depicted a time when a captain might be months away from higher authority and had to make decisions of peace and war, life and death, by himself – the direct opposite of the highly centralised navy of the 1930s. Even in the German navy, one officer commented, 'Were there any among us who had not read Forester's Hornblower?'[41] There is no sign that they had any direct influence on the wartime navy, and in 1944 prospective captains were warned: 'the silent Skipper of last-century fiction, who in some way gained the devotion of his men by never uttering a word, will not be a success today.'[42] But they created an awareness of naval tradition which penetrated deep into the public mind.

The Royal Navy had won a higher proportion of its historic battles than most armed services in the world and had acquired 'the habit of victory'. The British army was a collection of regiments and corps, each with its own traditions, while the RAF was too new to have acquired many. Geoffrey Willans found that the navy, on the other hand, gave a sense of belonging:

> It is possible,' said one of our lecturers, 'that some of you may find yourselves in command of a dirty little ship dropping anchor for the night in a lonely little bay. I would suggest to you that it is worthwhile postponing your bath and your shave and seeing personally that colours are saluted at the proper time. … Meridians are passed, weeks and years go by, but this custom has survived. You, too, would do well to insist on this discipline of the colours, even if your White Ensign is only the size of a pocket-handkerchief.'
>
> You felt then that you were in contact with something that had roots. It gave you a sense of responsibility.

This was also true of the lower deck, and one medical officer wrote that the seaman's attitude was 'I am a British sailor. The British sailor has always been the best seaman, the finest fighter, the hero of the people. Therefore, I am a hero.'[43]

Before the First World War, there was no doubt that the Royal Navy was the senior service, the largest in the world and with a long history of decisive victory. This was shaken during the conflict, when it failed to win a decisive tactical victory at Jutland and had to be cajoled into the tactics which defeated the U-boat. The army had borne the great bulk of the fighting in Flanders and elsewhere, with casualties to match. Almost every town and village had a memorial with the names of the dead, and often a statue of a soldier. Furthermore, the rise of air power seemed to suggest that the navy was no longer the only, and perhaps not even the primary, means of defending the country. The Royal Air Force had a modern technological and demotic image, and entranced the public with its annual air displays at Hendon. In response, the senior service began its Navy Days in 1928, and they certainly worked for Bob Tilburn. 'I was born in Leeds and when I was ten we went on holiday to Portsmouth to visit relations. It was Navy Week and we went round all the ships. From then onwards, it was my one ambition to join the Royal Navy.'[44]

'I have not yet begun to fight'

The history of the United States Navy was, of course, much shorter than that of its wartime ally, and more erratic. It had done little in the First World War. The Spanish-American War produced a few heroes and there were plenty of glorious exploits in the Civil War, but they were performed by one side or the other and were obviously divisive. The navy tended to look back to the War of Independence or the War of 1812 with Britain. Traditions were impressed on midshipmen at Annapolis and during wartime training. It was largely centred on certain key figures, often with a signature quote: John Paul Jones the founder of the navy ('I have not yet begun to fight'); Edward Preble, the hero of *Constitution* in the War of 1812; James Lawrence ('Fight her till she sinks and don't give up the ship'); David Glasgow Farragut on the Union side in the Civil War ('Damn the torpedoes! Full speed ahead!'); his opponent Frank Buchanan ('If I fall, lay me on one side and go on with the fight') and George Dewey in the Spanish-American war ('You may fire when ready, Gridley').[45]

British officers tended to be sceptical about the extent of American naval tradition and Commander Parry commented in February 1941:

> the principle of naming destroyers after persons who had done well in the navy is causing some difficulty on account of the large numbers of destroyers now being built. In fact the names of individuals like doctors, paymasters and even marine officers are now being perpetuated. As an American officer told me the other day, 'all that is required is that you should be dead.' But the war that was about to come would add many more names to the list.

The old-timers derided the effete practices of the new navy. 'Goddam gedunk sailors!' they sneered, turning to their joe pots. But the gedunk stand, to us younger ones, brought back memories of the neighbourhood soda fountains that were teenage social centres in our home towns, and there were always fifteen or twenty of us in the service line.[46]

Sexuality

Perhaps the most obvious contrast from naval seafaring with normal life was the lack of contact with the female sex. Naval ports like Plymouth and Portsmouth had plenty of dance halls which allowed contact with women, but there were limits. The music hall song 'All the Nice Girls Love a Sailor' was not literally true, and perhaps the lines, 'Falls in love with Kate and Jane, Then he's off to sea again' contained a hidden warning. For 'nice girls' would not go too far in an age when contraception was primitive, abortion was illegal and an unwanted pregnancy could ruin a woman's reputation and life. Sailors far away from home had no time for wooing, except at dances and social events organised by the local authorities in friendly ports with mainly European populations, in places like Australia and New Zealand, at which the ladies were expected to be chaste. A few sailors did establish regular relationships while based in such ports, including Jim Calvert, despite being recently married.

Many sailors remained faithful to wives and girlfriends ashore or stayed celibate, but apart from that there were three outlets for sexual needs. One was masturbation, which was tacitly recognised in the Royal Navy's traditional wake-up call, 'Hands off cocks and on socks'. It could be difficult in the confines of a ship, though George Melly, one of the very few to write frankly about the subject, claimed that he had learned 'How to wank in a hammock without waking up the entire mess.'[47] And in a shore base, one of his colleagues insisted on masturbating at precisely 11am and 3pm each day, asking to go to the heads during a class.

Another outlet was to use prostitutes when ashore, and there was an element in lower deck culture which regarded that as acceptable, and even essential, for a good 'run ashore', or liberty. It was common in the main naval ports, though impossible in isolated bases such as Ulithi. Britain and the United States were both essentially puritan nations and neither would sanction prostitution officially or set up state-run brothels. Honolulu had around twenty brothels in 1941, each with three to eighteen 'girls', with the most famous on River Street. They were carefully regulated for health, but the chief of police had a corrupt hold over them. Some were 'exotic', that is, 'mostly Oriental, with a few Hawaiians, Portuguese and Negroes'. Others were staffed by American women, including Jean O'Hara, who came from a strict Catholic family in Chicago, but was lured by the instant riches. She came to regret her choice. It was:

> A slavery worse than the negroes of the South ever experienced. A life so filled with insults, sordid surroundings, disgusting diseases

and loathsome visitors that no attempt at portrayal can succeed in placing before you all the horrible experiences of this worst of all money rackets.[48]

Ted Mason describes the procedure in a brothel:

> A serviceman had scarcely to sit on a sofa or easy chair before the girls were paraded. Most wore only a flimsy, revealing peignoir held in place by a single snap or button … Once the selection was made, a girl led her customer down the hall to a tiny room that contained a bed, a nightstand, a lamp, and a stark white washbasin affixed to one wall … Before that, of course, one more part of the ancient protocol had to be observed: the exchange of money. The two dollars (three dollars if extra services were rendered) would be handed over, and the girls would usually put the bills casually on the night stand.[49]

After having his first sexual encounter with an inexperienced sex worker on a Greek island in 1937, Plumber William Batters of HMS *Resource* was greeted by his shipmates 'like a young lion.' 'Good old Kock! Have a drink – you need it.' Despite his ambivalence, 'After my experience with the Greek girl I had tried to come to terms with this sex skylark and decided that, having had one woman, I might as well try a few more.' In the French port of Oran, he went to a 'bagshanty' with some of his shipmates and found 'Sonia was a pro [who] took me to the sublime. She was a craftsman and I almost adored her before I left.'[50]

The third outlet was homosexuality, which was illegal under both national and naval law in both countries, and legislation was particularly harsh in England – it had notoriously been used to prosecute Oscar Wilde at the end of the last century. In the Royal Navy, homosexual acts were punished severely. AB Frank Escritt was convicted of 'Sodomy' and 'Committing an act of gross indecency with another male person', and sentenced to two years' hard labour. Marines Frederick Walker and Louis Tindall were found 'in the same bed together after lights out, both being in an undressed state'. Walker was given eighteen months' hard labour, Tindall nine months. Walker was convicted again a few days later alongside a marine corporal and given the unusually long sentence of five years, which the merciful Lords of the Admiralty reduced to three years, concurrent with his previous sentence.

George Melly was public-school educated: 'I left Stowe a convinced homosexual, believing and accepting that I would always remain one. I felt no shame, I considered myself part of an elite'. He found that his fellow ratings were tolerant and even co-operative. 'My relationship with the Petty Officers and Chief Petty Officers was, as usual, cordial, if flirtatious.' He was shocked when one partner told him that he picked up 'old queens' in London and if they did not pay generously, he 'knocked them about a bit and then walked off with whatever he fancied.' 'The expression "Winger" means, at its most innocent, a young seaman who is taken under the wing of a rating or Petty Officer older and more experienced than himself to be shown the ropes. It can also, although far from inevitably, imply a homosexual relationship'. In general, he found the sailors were tolerant, apart from his particular bugbear, warrant officers. True to form, a 'fiercely heterosexual' warrant officer found him asleep in a bunk with another rating, but the commander dismissed the charge as they were 'Far too drunk to have done anything about it even if they had wanted to.'[51]

Ted Mason suggests that the US Navy was less accommodating: 'Another group of men accosted service personnel in their own fashion: the homosexuals. Occasionally the tables were turned and the servicemen preyed on them. There was no such thing as "gay rights" in 1941. Homosexuality was considered a loathsome disease, a failure of masculinity and morality.'[52] In fact the official attitude to homosexuality had much improved since the aftermath of the First World War, when a combination of naval authorities had persecuted and entrapped sailors based at Newport, Rhode Island. During the Second World War, it was necessary to accommodate the preferences of huge numbers of men of all types and the Surgeon-General issued a circular recommending that homosexual relations be tolerated 'as long as they were private, consensual, and didn't disrupt the unit.'[53] Bob Ruffing found it remarkably easy to get past a screening test at the start of his naval service:

> I walked into this office, and here was this man who was a screaming belle – lots of gold braid but he was a queen if ever I saw one. And he asked me the standard questions ending up with 'Did you ever have any homosexual experiences?' Well, I looked at him right in the eye and said 'No.' And he looked back and said, 'That's good.' Both of us lying through our teeth.[54]

But toleration was not universal. After enlisting in 1943, Burt Gerrits was posted to a psychiatric unit in Treasure Island Naval Hospital, where he found some 'very pleasant patients' whose 'illness' was homosexuality and they were awaiting discharge.[55] In fact, very few men suffered this fate, but in 1943 David Barret did, his officer telling him, 'The only people who will hire you now are the Marine Cooks and Stewards Union,' so he signed up for service in the Merchant Marine.[56]

Naval law

Navies need special laws, because of the need for discipline, because ships operate a long way from the home environment, the possibility of a ship being isolated for a long period of time, even within a fleet, and the special facts pertaining to sea life. Navies and armies had very different legal codes at this time, with different origins, though often coming to the same draconian conclusions. It was only after the war that the British and American governments imposed similar rules on all three services.

British naval law was based on the Naval Discipline Act, which was passed in 1866 and amended in 1922. It was developed from the Articles of War first adopted in 1661, which in turn used features of the medieval Laws of Oléron. It dropped many of the most savage features of these acts, but not all. Many of the offences decreed that that a man found guilty 'shall suffer death', though it usually had the proviso, 'or such other punishment'. These included imprisonment, dismissal from the service, or lesser punishments such as reprimand, loss of pay, and others 'according to the Custom of the Navy'. Flogging of adults was no longer used after 1871. There were provisions against desertion, cowardice in battle, communicating with the enemy and disobedience. More general offences were punishable by ordinary law: fraud, theft, assault and murder were also included. After the Naval Discipline Act in authority was the *King's Regulations and Admiralty Instructions,* two thick volumes constantly updated by Admiralty Fleet Orders. Inexperienced officers were referred to specific clauses, for example on disciplinary procedures, complaints, good conduct badges and the duties of a divisional officer. They were advised, 'Punishments under the King's Regulations and Admiralty Instructions (KR and AI) and the Naval Discipline Act (NDA) should be used as a last resort. Bear this in mind and do your best to prevent serious cases arising.'[57]

The Judge Advocate of the Fleet was the head of naval justice. He was a barrister and usually of the highest rank, a King's Counsel. His main duty was to advise the Admiralty on court martial proceedings. He or one of his deputies attended each court in an advisory capacity. From 1933–43 the post was held by J G Trapnell, a King's Counsel who had served in the Royal Naval Air Service in the last war.

Onboard ship, discipline was maintained by the master at-arms, the 'Jaunty', and his assistants, the regulating petty officers or 'Crushers', though some complained that it relieved the ordinary petty officers of responsibility. The captain had wide disciplinary powers of imprisonment and other penalties, which were usually meted out at 'Requestmen and

Defaulters'. John Fernald lightly fictionalised his account in a destroyer, but it conveys much of the atmosphere:

> First the offenders and suppliants were paraded by the coxswain ... Then Lieutenants Waverley and Harker arrived and took up their positions on one side of the table, to be followed after an interval by the First Lieutenant, who stood by the other. Finally, the Captain, the star turn, emerged from his cabin and walked gravely to his place.

A diminutive seaman appears before his officers, both regular and reserve, and the coxswain during 'Captain's requestmen and defaulters' on a destroyer, c1942.

Ordinary Seaman Brennan was called, but his request for a transfer to be nearer his family was refused. Others asked about pay, allowances and promotion 'to which the Captain was always able to bring a penetrating insight and a ready judgement.' Then the only defaulter was brought in, an ordinary seaman accused of being absent over leave by nearly three hours. After some questioning the captain delivered judgement. He was 'a nuisance and a disgrace' and was sentenced to lose one day's pay, seven days' leave and the same amount of 'number eleven', or extra work.[58]

Unfairly accused of disrespect to an officer, John Whelan and a colleague feared that they would lose their petty officer rates. Their captain allowed them twenty-four hours to decide whether to accept his punishment or go up for a court martial. They pleaded mistaken identity and were kept in 'nail-biting suspense' for half an hour before returning to be told, 'I will not have my instructors being rude to my officers', and were deprived of one good-conduct badge with twenty-eight days' stoppage of leave, to their great relief.[59]

A rating coming before a court martial knew that he was only there because his captain's disciplinary powers were exhausted, and he could expect a severe sentence, usually custodial.

The court martial was the highest application of naval justice, though officers were inclined to avoid it as far as reasonable. It consisted of five to nine officers from at least three different ships, which would have to be in harbour for the duration of the trial, so it was a clumsy procedure. As a result, captains at sea were allowed powers of punishment which would not normally be accepted in a democratic society. The public had the opportunity to read about a naval court martial in 1928, when one resulting from a dispute among the officers of *Royal Oak* was held onboard the carrier *Eagle* at Gibraltar. It ruined several careers and showed the navy in a very bad light. But such publicity was not allowed in wartime.

During the second quarter of 1944, when the navy was close to its peak strength, there were 104 courts martial of officers and 164 of ratings. The disproportion is explained by the fact that a captain had few disciplinary powers over his officers, so he often had to refer the case to higher authority. And punishments awarded to officers were usually rather mild – a reprimand in most cases, perhaps accompanied by dismissal from the ship and/or loss of seniority, with dismissal from the service in more serious cases. It was assumed that these career-damaging penalties would be enough to deter a regular officer, though perhaps they were less effective against temporaries. However, Sub Lieutenant George Templeton of HMS *Trumpeter* was sentenced to six months' imprisonment for desertion, with dismissal; Lieutenant Harry Weston suffered the same fate for security breaches, including 'writing a letter referring to plans of future operations'; and Warrant Writer Clifford Williamson had the same punishment plus forfeiture of his Long Service and Good Conduct Medal for fraudulent conversion, negligence and attempted suicide.

Most offending officers were in the junior ranks of lieutenant and sub lieutenant, with only a few lieutenant commanders and two commanders. Sixteen RNR skippers were tried; as ex-fishermen, they did not take well to naval discipline. Common offences included smuggling, drunkenness and fraud. Fleet Air Arm pilots were often convicted of low-flying against orders, and invariably punished by loss of seniority. Relations with ratings were a sore point, at one extreme or the other. Lieutenant Frank Walker behaved 'with undue familiarity' towards Royal Marine ranks. Lieutenant Sutcliffe-Hatfield was convicted of indecent assault and 'lying on a bed with a rating in a locked cabin.' Lieutenant Reginald Lee, on the other hand, was found guilty of striking and fighting with a rating. Lieutenant John Lidstone seemed to cover both ends of the spectrum, using insulting language to a rating as well as 'giving intoxicating liquor to ratings.'

Two men were convicted of manslaughter in separate cases, and both were given the relatively lenient sentence of nine months' detention. There were several cases of fraud, mostly among the administrative branches. Petty Officer Writer James Dole was sentenced to a year for making a false entry with intent to defraud; Supply Petty Officer Kenneth Berridge, two years for fraudulent conversion. The most common charges, however, were desertion or absence without leave, which might lead to sentences of nine months to three years. There were cases of striking a superior officer, and theft. The most spectacular was that of Seaman Sidney Hiscutt of the Patrol Service, who deserted his post, stole a vehicle, drove 'to the danger of the public', and acted 'to the prejudice of good order and naval discipline in contravening Trinidad Government traffic regulations by driving a motor vehicle in the wrong way on a one way street.' He was sentenced to nine months' hard labour and to forfeit one day's pay.

By ancient custom, the officers and crew of a lost ship might be tried under Article 92 of the King's Regulations. At the beginning of the war, the Admiralty announced that it did not intend to apply this in normal circumstances, since in general there was no way of attaching blame for the loss of a ship by air or submarine attack. It was used occasionally, as with the loss of *Ark Royal*, when all were acquitted, but the lines between a court of enquiry and criminal trial were blurred. When Captain Harold Drew was reprimanded for scuttling *Manchester* in 1942, the Judge Advocate pointed out that he had entered the case without being told of any charges against him and with no chance to prepare a defence. 'In all other respects the system of naval justice as administered by Courts Martial is of such a high standard that the continued use of this procedure appears regrettable', and it was later dropped. Peter Bull 'found it difficult to contain myself when serving on a Court of Enquiry as to why one LCT had given a slight biff to another. After three hours of ridiculous questioning, I gave a graphic description to the offending officer as to what constituted a real biff in the Good Old Days.'[60]

American naval law shared a common origin with British. The original *Rules for the Regulation of the Navy of the United Colonies* was drawn up by John Adams in 1775 and based on the British system. The 1920 edition of *Navy Regulations*, reprinted in 1942, was approved by Congress and ran to nine hundred pages. It too could be quite savage, with the death penalty applicable for twenty-two offences, including sleeping on watch, leaving station before being regularly relieved, and 'Wilfully stranding or injury to vessels' – though it was rarely, if ever, applied in such cases.[61]

Naval law was supervised by the department of the Judge Advocate General in Washington, a combination of civilian lawyers and naval officers who had been sent to law school. However, courts martial and other fleet matters only formed a small part of their duties; mostly they were concerned with contracts and procurement, jobs which were done by the civil service in Britain. Here too the court martial was at the pinnacle of the legal system. According to Ted Mason:

> The justice system in the navy didn't operate like the one practiced in civilian courts. … the assumption was that you were guilty as charged. Except in rare cases, no allowance was made for mitigating circumstances. You were guilty of being thirty-one minutes AOL, as logged by the JOOW, or you were not. You were guilty of telling your leading petty officer that he was a hostile, surly prick, or you were not. You were guilty of landing a haymaker on the jaw of another member of the naval service, or you were not. The provocation was irrelevant.[62]

Captain's mast could award sentences of confinement of up to ten days, or seven in solitary or five on bread on water, or reduction in rating, or loss of liberty. A more serious offence might lead to a deck court convened by the captain and consisting of some of the ship's officers; it could award up to twenty days' confinement and other punishments.

An enlisted man could take it to the next level, at the risk of more severe punishment. That was a summary court martial. Edward Stafford found himself defending a petty officer accused of assault:

> ... the wardroom became a courtroom ... the three members of the court, in unaccustomed neckties and looking appropriately solemn, sat along the forward side of the green-baize-covered mess table, each with a lined pad and a sharpened pencil. Keith [the Recorder and prosecutor] sat at the narrow port end, with his dark red volume of *Naval Courts and Boards* open before him. Miles [the defendant] and I sat across from the court. ...

With the expression, 'Let's bring the guilty bastard in, give him a fair trial and then hang him,' in mind, Stafford successfully challenged the composition of the court and got the relatively mild sentence of a fine, not a reduction in rate as feared.[63]

Awaiting sentence, 'Johnson was, in fact, a prisoner at large. "Sweating out" a summary court-martial, he was forced to muster several times a day at the master-at-arms shack next the ship's service store.' Though he had joined another ship and been absent from his own for two weeks he was only sentenced to ten days in the brig and a twenty-dollar fine, 'a mere slap on the wrist.' In contrast, a fireman got twenty days' solitary confinement on bread and water and a thirty-dollar loss of pay for

A very rare view of a court martial, on fifty Black sailors (in the background) charged with mutiny after the explosion at Port Chicago, Yerba Buena Island, in 1944. Sentences of fifteen years' imprisonment were widely regarded as a miscarriage of justice and were reduced. The vast majority of courts martial were far fairer.

shirking duty and insolence to a petty officer.[64] The most severe cases would go before general courts martial, usually convened by a fleet or squadron commander and consisting of five to thirteen officers and a judge advocate. It could award any sentence up to death.[65]

Among the sentences to be awarded were various types of discharge. An honourable discharge or a discharge under honourable conditions brought no reflection on the character of the recipient; an undesirable discharge was the result of unfitness, fraudulent enlistment, desertion or conviction by a civil court. A bad conduct discharge came as a result of a summary or general court martial, but the most serious was a dishonourable discharge by a general court martial, which could take away some of the recipient's civil rights and might follow him for the rest of his life.[66]

Imprisonment might be in the ship's own brig or prison:

> ... the proper adjective for the marine guards was sadistic. They woke up the prisoners several times a night for the sole purpose of turning their mattresses over. They forced them to run in place or do push-ups to the point of collapse. They harassed them in a dozen other ways designed to abase, from using abusive language to withholding of reading and writing materials – and even meals from those not on bread and water. If a prisoner was provoked into retaliating, the best he could expect was a working over by the marines with fists and clubs. He might then find himself on report for 'insolence to a brig sentry.'[67]

Detention barracks ashore were no better:

> This was the famous detention barracks, where regular navy enlistees underwent twenty-one days of purgatory without hope of salvation by priest, mother, or congressman. The satanic overseers of this place of penance for civil sins were hard-bitten chiefs and petty officers from the fleet, men with impeccable records who, after six years at sea, knew good shore duty when they saw it and knew exactly what they were expected to do with these scrawny, undisciplined civilians.[68]

On shore, the naval police were obtrusive and disliked by the seamen according to Ted Mason: 'Despite the boatswain's mate ratings on their right arms, these SPs wore their uniform like boots and did not walk with the typical rolling gait of the sailor. They looked, in fact, like ex-cops masquerading as sailors – and that in fact is what most of them were.'[69]

Ships were also expected to patrol their own men while ashore. In January 1943 *Sterett* was ordered to provide a lieutenant, a chief and ten petty officers for a shore patrol in Vallejo. Calhoun went with CPO Hodge and ten petty officers picked 'for their leadership abilities and physical toughness'. As always, there was rivalry between ships, for 'Our sailors and those of the cruiser *San Francisco* frequently got into altercations into which ship had single-handedly won the war.' Indeed, there was trouble during which Hodge was injured, but Calhoun had a perverse but not untypical pride in his men when they came before captains' masts. 'I was secretly pleased that only three were *Sterett*'s men. Against eight from the *San Francisco* and other ships.'[70]

The public on both sides of the Atlantic was well aware of the concept of naval mutiny, if only through an inaccurate but highly popular 1935 film. George Melly wrote, 'my notions of the Senior Service were still coloured by the Charles Laughton version of *Mutiny on the Bounty*.'[71] In fact, that kind of mutiny, with the captain being overthrown, was very rare, and it was far more common for the crew to have a kind of strike against their conditions. That was the situation with the Invergordon affair of 1931, though it was never officially classed as a mutiny. There were many small-scale mutinies during the Second World War, though most of them were barely reported.

As the war approached its end, the authorities were seriously worried about large-scale mutiny. For one thing, naval mutinies had mainly been responsible for the overthrow of the Kaiser and the Tsar at the end of the last war and one British admiral noted, 'We have seldom got through a major war without some breakdown of morale'. Moreover, when the war with Germany ended, many ships would be sent to the Far East, deploying seamen who had perhaps volunteered to save their country from invasion in 1940, but were now being ordered to revive the British Empire. A document, *Notes on Dealing with Mutiny or Massed Disobedience*, of August 1944 contained frightening passages such as 'shooting to kill should only be resorted to as a last emergency.' Several senior officers objected to the tone and it was never issued. The sudden ending of the war with the atom bomb, and perhaps the election of a reforming Labour government, ended the threat, if it ever existed.

There was far less of an history of mutiny in the US Navy, possibly because officers were reluctant to show their problems by reporting it as such. Even the fictitious *Caine* mutiny was actually classed as 'Conduct to the Prejudice of Good Order and Discipline' when the matter came to court.[72] According to the regulations:

> Mutiny consists in an unlawful opposition or resistance to or defiance of superior military authority, with a deliberate purpose to usurp, subvert, or override the same. Simple violence without proof of purpose to usurp, subvert, or override authority is not mutiny. Specific intent is an essential element.[73]

But the crew of the destroyer *Dale* reported two incidents in 1945 in which they used the term. In one, an unpopular officer was thrown over the side of a landing craft by drunken crewmen. The captain took it lightly: the only result was that one petty officer was reduced to seaman and a duty section was restricted to the ship for a short time. In the other, the crew, supported by a brave ensign, objected when the captain wanted to issue ice cream to the officers only, and the men had their way.[74] The same term was used unofficially aboard the destroyer *Saufley*, when some of the more experienced members of the crew were refused liberty.[75] It is quite possible that 'mutiny' in a more general sense of the terms was as common in the American as the British navy.

3
Officers

IN A war emergency, a navy can build thousands of ships, train tens of thousands of new officers and men, develop and exploit radically new technology, and learn to fight and maintain itself in undreamt of ways. What it cannot do is improvise a corps of senior officers who can cope with all these changes. That depends on recruitment and training of young men around thirty years earlier. Character was an essential factor:

> Funny thing about this war business is that you can send people to the Naval Academy and teach them to fight, but you can't make them fight when the time comes. … There is no substitute for leadership in combat. You can never be certain you are doing the right thing, but you have to make a decision and fight![1]

There was a difference between success in peace and success in war. Some of the greatest British leaders – Ramsay, Somerville, and especially Horton and Walker in Western Approaches – were in retirement or in dead-end jobs when the war started.

Superficially at least, the officer corps of the British and United States navies had much in common. During the nineteenth century, the US Navy developed a rank structure which was similar to the British, with captains, commanders and lieutenants, rather than continental European titles which might translate as battleship-captain, frigate- or corvette-captain and battleship-lieutenant or captain-lieutenant. Important ships were mostly battleships or cruisers, each of which merited an officer with the rank of captain, or post-captain as the older British called him, in command. But with the rising importance of smaller ships such as destroyers and submarines, more junior officers might find themselves in charge.

The United States Navy instituted the rank of lieutenant commander in 1862. Since 1877, Royal Navy lieutenants of more than eight years' seniority had worn a thin gold stripe between the two thicker ones on their sleeves. In 1914 Churchill changed the title of such officers to 'lieutenant commander', making it a substantive rank. Though its

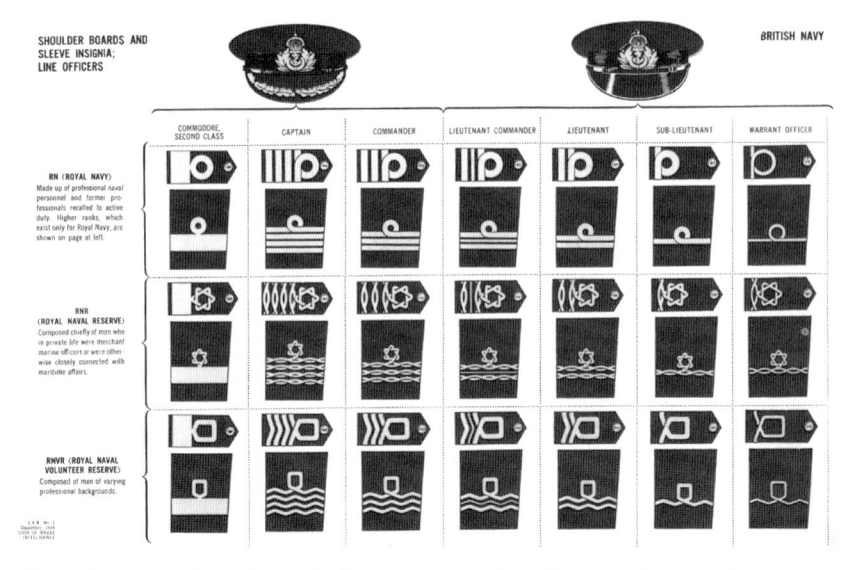

The rank stripes of British naval officers, showing the differences between the regular navy, the merchant seamen of the Royal Naval Reserve, and the 'Wavy Navy', the non-seamen of the Royal Naval Volunteer Reserve, who made up the bulk of the wartime officer corps.

effect was moral rather than material, the rank proved very useful in two world wars. The great majority of British destroyers, submarines and escort vessels were headed by lieutenant commanders, who also led the squadrons of the Fleet Air Arm. It is no exaggeration to say that the lieutenant commander played a greater role in winning the naval war than any other rank.

The commissioned ranks differed most at the lowest level, below lieutenant. The Royal Navy only had one rank, sub lieutenant, which was usually held for a comparatively short period until becoming a fully fledged officer as a lieutenant. The United States Navy had two, the ensign who was equivalent to a second lieutenant in the army and the lieutenant (junior grade) or JG to a first lieutenant. It is difficult to find an exact equivalence between the two navies, but the JG tended to have more responsibility than a senior sub lieutenant

At the upper end of the scale, the ranks were seemingly identical, but the United States was traditionally much more reluctant to hand out the very highest ones. When the Joint Chiefs of Staff met during the war, the British members – mostly Admirals of the Fleet, field marshals and marshals of the Royal Air Force – were always one rank higher than their American counterparts. And when the British fleet arrived in the

OFFICERS 63

The National Geographic Magazine

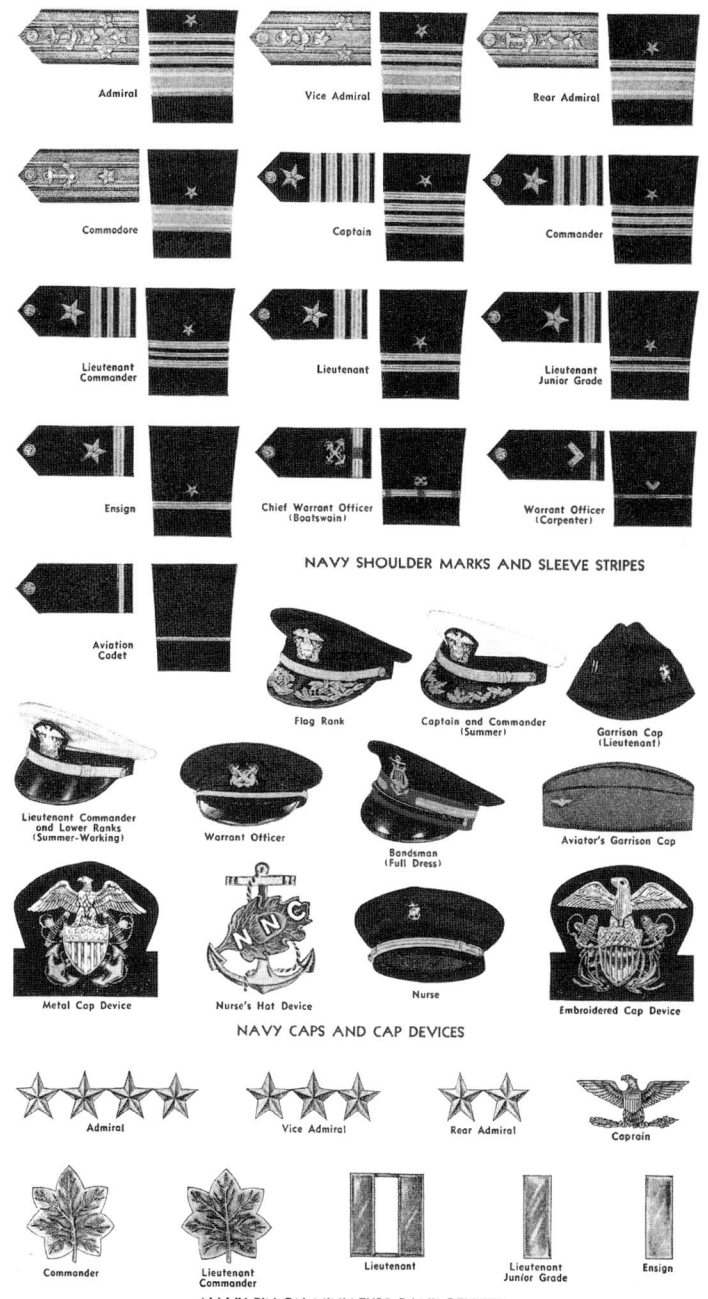

NAVY SHOULDER MARKS AND SLEEVE STRIPES

NAVY CAPS AND CAP DEVICES

NAVY PIN-ON MINIATURE RANK DEVICES

USN officers' rank stripes, similar to their RN counterparts except for the star instead of the 'curl' for line officers, and the 'pin-on' badges adapted from army practice, which were far more common in operational areas in the Pacific war.

Pacific late in the war, comparatively small forces were commanded by full admirals, such as Sir Bruce Fraser. There were a dozen Admirals of the Fleet on the Royal Navy List in 1945, but the equivalent American five-star rank, Fleet Admiral, was only created by Congress in 1944 and was only ever held by four men – Leahy, King, Nimitz and Halsey.

The gold stripes worn on lower sleeves or shoulder boards by regular officers were similar in the two services, except that in the Royal Navy they were surmounted by a 'curl', in the US Navy by a star for line officers, which seemed to point downward. In the US Navy all officers had the same straight stripes, with no equivalent of the braided or wavy stripes of the British reservists. The Royal Navy had no equivalent of the 'pin-on' badges worn by American officers in informal dress – a system of bars, laurel leaves, an eagle, and stars for flag officers, which was adopted from army practice and was far more common in the Pacific theatre than the gold stripes. The system of stars did attain some universality, the concept of a 'four-star admiral' for example, became well known, and senior officers in many services had plaques or flags with the stars on their cars.

The early selection of officers did much to set the character of an armed force. In peacetime, all officers of the United States Navy, and most of those of the Royal Navy, had trained at their respective naval academy or college. Both had restrictive entry systems, partly based on political influence or family wealth, which meant that they did not necessarily enrol the most suitable candidates. In wartime, training as an officer depended largely on pre-entry education.

Ship-handling was an essential skill of a seaman officer in any navy:

> Shiphandling is the most public demonstration possible of a naval officer's professional competence ... There is no hiding poor Shiphandling, especially in harbor ... The Captain is high up on the bridge, as prominent as a bronze statue in a park ... His every order as he handles the ship is relayed and repeated. The entire operation is performed in full view of – as a minimum – the whole deck force of his own ship ...[2]

The heirs of Nelson

By 1939 regular Royal Navy officers (apart from the small numbers who entered via the Merchant Navy or were promoted from the lower deck) had been trained under four different schemes. The oldest had learned the trade in HMS *Britannia*, an old wooden warship permanently moored in the River Dart. One of these was William 'Bubbles' James, who entered in 1895 and served as Commander-in-Chief at Portsmouth for the first half of the Second World War. 'The officers responsible for seamanship instruction had been brought up under sail, and they firmly believed that good seamen and good seamanship were only to be found in a sailing ship, and they turned a blind eye to the impending disappearance of sail-power in men-of-war.'[3] Yet the system produced great commanders in Andrew Cunningham of the Mediterranean Fleet, Bertram Ramsay of Dunkirk and the Normandy invasion, Max Horton of Western Approaches, and Bruce Fraser of the British Pacific Fleet.

Navigation was the defining skill of a Royal Navy seaman (or executive) officer, separating him from the engineers, accountants and others who were not eligible to command ships and fleets. It also separated him from the ratings of the lower deck, more so than in other navies. A German U-boat was navigated by the *Obersteuermann*, between a warrant officer and a chief petty officer. In the USN the quartermaster took over many navigational duties and might be the principal navigator of a PT boat. The Royal Navy rating of navigator's yeoman was not created until 1944 and had a far smaller range of duties. Navigation was the most important single subject for trainee temporary officers at HMS *King Alfred*, taking up fifty-two hours of instruction out of 235 and 130 marks out of 1000.[4]

The Royal Navy first came ashore in the 1890s and 1900s with the building of barracks and bases to replace the hulks where officers and men had lived when not at sea. This coincided with the reforms of Admiral 'Jacky' Fisher, including the attempt to integrate the seamen, marine and engineer officers. The new college at Dartmouth was not ready when the innovative and controversial Selborne Scheme started in 1903, and it was not likely to be big enough for four years of cadets. Queen Victoria's palace at Osborne House on the Isle of Wight was hated by her son, now King Edward VII, and he gave it to the navy for initial training of boys. Up till then entry had been at various ages during the teens, but Fisher regularised it at between thirteen years five months and thirteen years nine months.

It was expensive for parents, unless the cadets had bursaries, or were sons of serving officers. In 1914 it cost a total of £460. Additional costs such as uniform and spending money might bring that up to about £700 – a good suburban house could be bought for that. It could cost parents £40 per term completed if a boy left before reaching the rank of sub lieutenant. Bob Whinney was disillusioned with naval life: 'I tried to get my father to have me removed but that ... would have meant paying an indemnity.'[5]

It was different at the beginning of a career. Stephen King-Hall reported, 'the great day dawned in January 1906 when, together with eighty other creatures, I was herded on to a tug at Portsmouth … transported to Cowes and marched, if a struggle can so be called, up the hill to Osborne College'.[6] The cadets were divided into terms named after famous admirals, such as Drake, Blake, St Vincent and Hawke. One cadet recalled:

> The rules were very stringent. You had to get up as soon as reveille blew … then you stripped off your pyjamas, rushed down the dormitory stark naked into the cold plunge at the end where you were watched by your cadet captain who jolly well made sure that you totally immersed yourself and you rushed back, dripping wet, to your sea-chest, dried yourself as quickly as you could, threw on your clothes and reported ready for a day's work.[7]

Another commented: 'I think we were all much too young in the first place, and I think too much time was devoted to general education which you could have got anywhere rather than to grounding in naval things.'[8] Boat instruction was rather grudging. Caspar John noted that 'We are allowed to go for rows this term but there is no bathing which is horrid.'[9] Stress was placed on naval history, particularly the 'lives and exploits of the most famous seamen and the most striking episodes in naval wars'.[10] The cadets had a general education with a strong technical bias, but without the Latin which was a staple of the public schools of the time, and a large amount of naval tradition and discipline.

Homosexual affairs were taboo but not uncommon. According to King-Hall, 'Two cadets had been discovered experimenting with what are called the facts of life. One was expelled; the other received twelve cuts of the cane'.[11] Prejudice took other forms. Stephen Roskill's tutor was overheard to remark: 'I don't like him. He is a Jew boy'.[12] After confessing to supporting the Liberal Party, Stephen King-Hall was labelled a 'Filthy little Rad [radical] stinker'.[13]

Those ex-Osborne cadets who survived the First World War and were successful in the promotion ladder were in or around the rank of captain during the Second World War. Brian Schofield wrote:

> Out of the seventy-two of us of the Hawke term who joined Osborne in September 1908, only twenty-two were still on the active list when the Second World War began (not counting five who had transferred to the Royal Air Force). Of these, seven had reached the rank of captain and five subsequently attained flag rank.[14]

Notable alumni included Philip Vian, who commanded a famous destroyer flotilla and later supported the landings at Salerno and

Normandy, Lord Louis Mountbatten, and the promising cruiser captain Rory O'Connor, who was lost with *Neptune* in 1941.

Osborne House gained a bad reputation because of illnesses among the cadets: it was rumoured that the site of Victoria's stables was responsible, and the hastily built dormitories were certainly cold in the winter. The navy was reduced at the end of the First World War, and from 1920 all new cadets went straight to Dartmouth.

After two years the Osborne cadets went on leave, then travelled 150 miles further west to join the college at Dartmouth for another two years. Schofield was enthusiastic. 'The spirit of Drake is firmly implanted in the people of Devon and it was a happy circumstance that led to the establishment of the principal naval college in the rich loam of that county.'[15] It was designed by Aston Webb, who had produced the facade of Buckingham Palace. To some it looked like a prison, a lunatic asylum or 'the house of a profiteer'.[16] To Bob Whinney it was 'a vast, shiny, spotless place with highly polished floors throughout'.[17] Life was no less harsh:

> The first ring of the fire bell at six am sent us down the dormitory through an icy, over-chlorinated plunge bath and out again before the ringing stopped. Betowelled but still wet we stood at attention in front of our basins awaiting the order to *wash necks*, followed by *wash teeth*. As 0610 approached, the order came to *get dressed* followed five minutes later by *say prayers*. After early morning studies life was conducted at the double. We double to breakfast and rushed it so that we could get a chance to secure a cubicle containing rough square pieces of paper known as 'Admiralty brown'. Then to the parade ground for divisions, from where we doubled to our classroom or down several hundred steps to the river for sailing or engineering instruction.[18]

Like Osborne, Dartmouth had naval officers under a captain, and teachers under a headmaster. In 1937 the captain was Frederick Dalrymple-Hamilton, who was well-connected with the royal family and proud to be considered part of the Scottish aristocracy. Under him were six officers of the executive branch, three engineers, a marine captain, a chaplain, six instructor officers, three paymasters, a shipwright lieutenant, two gunners and a boatswain. The civilian staff was led by a headmaster, with departments of mathematics, science and modern languages, and a total of thirty-four teachers.[19]

The naval officer's education was excellent in places, according to Charles Owen:

Cadets at Dartmouth, already wearing officer-style uniform and cap badge march past Edward, Prince of Wales (later King Edward VIII, then the Duke of Windsor after his abdication) in 1922.

For the most part what emerged was a definite breed of fit, tough, highly trained but sketchily educated professionals, ready for instant duty, for parades or tea parties, for catastrophes, for peace or war; confident leaders, alert seamen, fair administrators, poor delegators; officers of wide interests and narrow vision, strong on tactics, weak on strategy; an able, active, cheerful, monosyllabic elite.

The Special Entry Scheme, by which potential officers entered at the age of about eighteen, was founded by Churchill as First Lord of the Admiralty in 1913. He was sceptical about current training, remarking that Osborne had 'a certain air of kindergarten', while the Dartmouth course was 'so ambitious for boys of that age as to provoke doubts that it is thorough.' There was a more immediate reason. It took more than seven years to train a fully-fledged naval lieutenant, but war was clearly not far away, new dreadnoughts were coming off the stocks, and they had to be manned.

Selection was mainly by interview. C A Jenkins feared it would be 'a fearful ordeal', but was questioned about cricket by a group of senior officers. Despite the doubts of the housemaster of his school, he passed fifth in the exam and was accepted for the Special Entry in 1919.[20] In 1934 prospective cadets and their parents were told, 'This examination is in no sense competitive, its object being to ensure that the cadets shall conform to the ordinary standard of a boy of 13–14 at a preparatory school. …Very few boys fail to pass the qualifying examination.'[21]

By 1937, about 35 per cent of new officers were Special Entry. In March 1939 the forty-fifth Special Entry term had six first-class passes, the Dartmouth entry only had one; seventeen out of eighteen prizes were won by the Special Entry. It was noted that 'the Darts show less enthusiasm for their work than do the Special Entry.' When the Special Entries took all the prizes at the next passing out, the Admiralty proposed separate prizes for the Darts.[22]

Because of the relatively late start of the scheme, no Special Entry officers reached the flag list until 1945, when Geoffrey Oliver was promoted. He had first been commissioned in 1917 and took charge of Force J for Juno Beach in the Normandy invasion, with the acting rank of commodore. Guy Grantham, who entered in 1918, commanded the carrier *Indomitable* during the invasion of Sicily; and Robert 'RED' Ryder who entered in 1926, gained the Victoria Cross for the raid on St-Nazaire in 1942.

The Dartmouth and Special Entry boys came together for the training cruise, using a succession of slightly eccentric monitors and cruisers – the 7.5in-gunned *Frobisher* and *Vindictive* for most of the 1930s. The cadets lived the life of the lower deck in broadside messes. Typically they would travel round the UK and over to Scandinavia, the West Indies or the Mediterranean. Occasionally their schedule was interrupted by ominous world events: the Abyssinia Crisis of 1935, and Munich three years later. Staff were well chosen and seamanship training was good, but the course had its limitations. According to Roderick Macdonald of the Special Entry, 'Public school boys were for some reason assumed to have absorbed leadership at school since it was not taught or alluded to in the training cruiser.'[23]

Engineer officers were an inferior and largely despised class within the Royal Navy until the Selborne Scheme was set up by Admiral Fisher in 1903. In future, all officers at Osborne and Dartmouth would be trained in engineering, and after commissioning they would be able to specialise in it in the same way as navigation or gunnery. Unlike their American contemporaries, they would not switch from job to job aboard ship, but would remain in the engine room or in staff jobs at least until they reached flag rank. An officer so qualified would wear the same stripes as a seaman officer, and would be distinguished by the letter E after his rank, eg Lieutenant (E). It was controversial from the start, and some upper-class families believed that boys might be forced to become engineers against their will, while Reginald Plunkett wrote, 'The requirements for the two branches are so widely different that all attempts at amalgamation can only be harmful.'[24] The system was abolished in 1920, in what engineer officers regarded as 'the great betrayal'. They lost their executive status and had no direct power of command over officers and seamen. Due to health problems, Louis Le Bailly had to transfer to the engineering branch in 1933. 'Eventually I had to discard my dirk and telescope, sew purple stripes on my sleeves and officially become a "civilian" in the Royal Navy.'[25]

In 1920 a scheme began for young ratings to be selected at the age of twenty to train as 'mate' and potentially reach the rank of lieutenant at around twenty-three, at the same time as Dartmouth cadets, but only a hundred mates were allowed on the establishment. In 1930 a committee proposed to seek out suitable boys at an early age in the training schools. Only single men could apply, for 'if he is made to wait till much later in his career when he has had the social opportunities which his officer's position will have given him he is likely to marry someone who will help him in his social life, and he will for ever bless those who deterred him from an improvident marriage.'[26] In the lower deck view, the authorities put obstacles in the way of candidates for officer rank, and when finally promoted they were in an unhappy position, often lonely in the wardroom, unable to afford the drinks bought by their colleagues and socially awkward.

It was not much better in wartime. The 'CW' Scheme of 1940 was intended for young men of good education who had entered the navy for 'hostilities only' as volunteers or conscripts, not for the regulars of the lower deck. The question was discussed in Parliament in 1942:

> ... no one who has not at least had a secondary school education is even considered ... The official excuse for this is that without a secondary school education men cannot master the officers' training course. This ... is not true. Any intelligent man can easily master the course ... the system as at present worked definitely prevents the average rating from ever being considered for a commission.[27]

Ambitious officers tended to specialise after commissioning. Gunnery offered the best career prospects, though Kenneth Dewar was sceptical about the value of the long course at HMS *Excellent* in Portsmouth Harbour. 'If Whale Island's methods were followed in other walks of life, applicants for driving licences would be examined in thermodynamics, and the manufacture of motor car steel, while medical students would undergo a course of cutlery before being allowed to handle surgical instruments.'[28] Peter Dickens was taught by his admiral father 'to mistrust all "super-plumbers" as narrow minded bigots; "nuts and bolts" were no foundation for sound judgement in command.'[29] But the result could be impressive, according to one American officer.:

> ... a British 'subleftenant' (an ensign) had briefed us on gunnery matters in a way that clearly indicated a knowledge far beyond that of the most knowledgeable among us ... someone ... made everyone feel better with the simple explanation that in accordance with long tradition, British officers specialize in a particular aspect of their profession – gunnery, navigation, aviation, submarines, engineering and so forth – to a much greater extent than we do. In all probability, it was agreed, the young gunnery officer knew very little outside of his speciality ...[30]

To be fair, the 'subleftenant' probably had a good grounding in seamanship before specialising in gunnery.

Torpedo officers trained at HMS *Vernon* in Portsmouth Harbour. For historic reasons 'Torpedo' was largely about electricity, and the First Sea Lord wrote, 'The torpedo officer appears to be growing less suitable relative to other branches for promotion to the higher ranks ... This is undoubtedly due to the growth of electrical machinery in ships and the ever-increasing need for the Torpedo Officer to spend time between decks rather than on deck.'[31] But he was not a professional electrical engineer, and the Electrical Department at the Admiralty was dominated by civilians who knew little about conditions at sea. The navy would struggle to maintain increasingly complex equipment.

John Iago was a qualified electrical engineer who was taken on in 1939, but the navy found it very difficult to place him: 'I volunteered as an Engineer (who wears a purple stripe) but was put into torpedo as an executive with no coloured stripe at all. Then in March they decided we were Special branch and had to wear an emerald green stripe'. This led to reduced pay so 'we are to become Electrical officers with an olive green stripe instead!'[32]

Navigation, despite its paramount importance in training, did not develop leadership faculties. According to C A Jenkins, the four-and-a-half-month navigation course was 'far too theoretical and "x-chasing," and I have found use for little or none of it since.'[33] It was carried out in HMS *Dryad* in Portsmouth Dockyard, which was bombed in 1941 and moved to Southwick House, later the headquarters for the Normandy invasion. During the war it had to cope with many new techniques, including radar and fighter direction. Anti-submarine was the least fashionable before the war.

Other officers were 'salt horse' non-specialists, but that did not necessarily debar them from promotion. Andrew Cunningham spent the greater part of his earlier career in destroyers, which he regarded as the best training for command, and rose to the very top.

According to Admiral of the Fleet Lord Chatfield, out of fifty cadets passing from Dartmouth:

> … allowing for resignations from health, accident and other causes, some 40 per cent reach commander's rank. Fifty per cent of these Commanders become Captains, and 50 per cent of these captains become Rear-Admirals, say five out of the original fifty! The exceptional men who have the ability and stamina, who have not had some professional misfortune (always possible even to the most able), and who have stood the strain of naval life and command, are few. To them the Navy looks for its leaders, to administer and command its fleet.[34]

He was confident about the fairness of the procedure:

> Promotion in the Navy is carried out absolutely fairly within the limits of human fallibility. It is, however, an agonising task that falls finally on the First, Second, Third and Fourth Sea Lords. For the higher ranks, all six Sea Lords take part. For non-executive officers, there is a committee of each branch – Engineering, Medical. Accountant – to make recommendations in the first instance to the Sea Lords. The Board gives its final approval.[35]

Promotion to lieutenant commander was virtually automatic but involved a change in responsibility:

> It is at this moment in their career when these officers are first entrusted with the command of destroyers, submarines and other smaller units, or when they are about to become gunnery, torpedo and navigation officers of the larger units, or when the signal specialists are about to assume control of the communications in the larger commands, or when they are about to undertake staff work.[36]

A lieutenant commander fell into the 'promotion zone' after three years in the rank, and left it after seven years. C A Jenkins was one of the disappointed:

> … the half-yearly promotion lists came out as usual and showed that I was now finally 'passed over' for promotion. … having achieved eight years seniority as a Lieutenant-Commander without catching the selector's eyes, I would not in future even be considered as a candidate for promotion. … Being passed over means being retired at forty-five with a pension which … is practically worthless.

Another officer who fell foul of this system was C R Thompson, who had earned a black mark by putting his submarine aground in 1931. In 1939 he was about to be retired at the age of forty-five, but instead became Winston Churchill's aide.

Angus Cunninghame Graham, on the other hand, had no difficulty in reaching commander in 1928, with the recommendations of two of his captains, but he was unhappy about the next stage.

> I … preferred the old way when their lordships chose their promotions from all the commanders serving, and the promotion zone [four to eight years in this case] was more loosely designed. By the batch system the sea lords were still choosing their promotions from all the Navy's commanders, but each batch only had a fixed quota of promotions … So I was put into competition with my zone-mates whom I knew, some being personal friends. This inevitably caused tension … some batches had a large proportion of the best officers, while others were chiefly composed of those who could be styled average. Thus, … the Navy lost good ones who were being crowded out …[37]

But again he made the promotion with the support of two admirals.

The commander's duties might include staff appointments with the fleet or at the Admiralty, command of certain warships, or instructional duties. But the most important was as the executive officer of a large ship, and his performance there would be a key factor in his subsequent promotion to captain.

The wardroom

The writer H V Morton was a guest in the wardroom of *Prince of Wales* during Churchill's voyage to meet Roosevelt in 1941. It was:

> … a large room some sixty feet in length … It was divided into two parts: on the port side was the ante-room, furnished with easy chairs, a club lounge, a bookcase containing *Chambers Encyclopaedia* and a number of novels and other works … and on the starboard side was the dining room. In the dining-room were two long tables and a hatch where Royal Marines in white mess jackets served the food. Above the mantelpiece hung an irreverent Gillray caricature of the Prince Regent … At the end of the ante-room was a small bar, which was opened before lunch and dinner, where gin was sold at 3d and whiskey at 5d a glass.

Ted Mason of the US Navy was impressed on visiting HMS *Warspite*:

The wardroom of *Indomitable* in November 1943, showing places at dinner for the large number of officers borne in an aircraft carrier. The deckhead seems to be unusually high.

> ... we passed through officers' country, something we could never have done in my ship. Rich walnut paneling had been polished over three decades in a deep, mellow luster and staterooms were filled with comfortable chairs and books and the kind of casual disorder that reminded me vaguely of what I had read about Oxford and Cambridge. I felt sure it would not be out of order to quote Shakespeare or Chaucer, Wordsworth or Houseman in these staterooms, as it would have been in the *California*.

The wardroom was far more compact on destroyers and smaller vessels. Wartime captains were told that: 'He should normally have lunch and dinner in the wardroom, as this will help him to know his Officers, but his continued presence is bound to have a somewhat restricting influence, ... A captain should therefore not outstay his welcome.'[38]

Warrant officers

Warrant officers, wearing thin gold stripes on their sleeves, had usually risen from the lower deck and were treated as specialised junior officers rather than senior NCOs, unlike the army and the RAF, or the modern Royal Naval warrant officer. The schoolmaster, however, was recruited directly from graduates of teacher training colleges. He was mainly responsible for the literacy of the boy seamen and was junior to the instructor officer, a science graduate who taught the midshipmen. In the age of sail the warrant officer had been a substantial figure, but the boatswain, responsible for rigging, was no longer the man who kept the ship mobile; the carpenter no longer kept it afloat, while the gunner was sandwiched between the highly trained gunnery officer and the chief gunner's mate. New categories were introduced for the modern age, including warrant electricians, engineers, mechanicians, cooks, photographers, shipwrights, stewards and telegraphists. Despite the high degree of specialisation, they wore no badges to distinguish their roles. They were mostly found in larger ships and shore bases, though warrant engineers and mechanicians might serve as chief engineers of frigates and similar ships.

The warrant officer was in a limbo, according to John Whelan, 'those forlorn and most pathetic of creatures'. To George Melly, they were 'martinets, sticklers for the letter of the law, hard resentful men who realised they had risen from the ranks on merit but been blocked for a commission on class grounds.'[39] But it was possible for a warrant officer to rise slowly; after ten years he would become a commissioned warrant officer with the thicker stripe of a sub lieutenant, and eventually he could qualify for lieutenant, though further promotion was unlikely in view of his age.

Annapolis

In contrast to Dartmouth, the United States Naval Academy at Annapolis offered a largely free education which was of great value to some families. A midshipman was given tuition to the level of Bachelor of Science, four years' board, books and clothing, full medical treatment and two cruises to Europe of 'great educational value.'[40] James Calvert was a pre-medical student in Ohio when the family money began to run out, so he went to Annapolis in 1939.[41]

If Dartmouth was modelled on the practices of a sailing ship of the line, Annapolis was based on an American college education. Entry to the Academy was later than Dartmouth, between the ages of seventeen and twenty-one. It normally required the nomination of a US congressman, some of whom used the system as a means of rewarding political favours, while others conducted competitive examinations. Marc Mitscher was appointed in 1904 through his father's 'long-term crony'.[42] Raymond Spruance passed the examination with flying colours in New Jersey where he was living, while his mother successfully lobbied her congressman in his home state of Indiana; due to family pressure he accepted the latter appointment.[43] It was not always the young man's first choice – both William Leahy and Chester Nimitz wanted to go to the army college at West Point, but the nominations were filled.[44]

The United States Naval Academy was founded in 1845 on the River Severn, where it flows into Chesapeake Bay. It was rebuilt from 1899 to designs by Ernest Flagg, an imposing Beaux Arts complex and largely coinciding with the navalism and imperialism of Theodore Roosevelt's presidency. One of the most dramatic buildings was the domed chapel which was influenced by the Dôme des Invalides in Paris. Sunday attendance was expected and almost compulsory – one daring cadet who described himself as an atheist in Ernest King's time was ordered to read books on atheism every Sunday.[45] Bancroft Hall was for accommodation and was designed to be expanded, as indeed it was – by 1941 it covered 40 acres with three miles of corridors and the midshipmen living mainly in double rooms. The ordnance laboratory in Dahlgren Hall was named after the pioneer of rifled guns, the library was in Mahan Hall and was decorated with numerous trophies, mostly from the war of 1812 with Britain. Maury Hall dealt with navigation, and Sampson Hall with science and electricity

On arrival the young man was examined mentally and physically before he was accepted and if successful he became a midshipman. He began his naval career as a 'plebe' in June, when more senior midshipmen were on leave or on summer cruises. Uniform consisted of 'Blue service' – a double-breasted coat with a gold anchor on each lapel; and 'white works' – a white jumper and trousers not unlike a seaman's summer uniform, distinguished by a blue band round a seaman's cap. To 'Bob' of the class of 1931, 'When I first put them on they felt so much like pajamas that I hardly dared leave my room.'[46] The senior years returned in August and soon began to 'haze' the plebes, who were expected to do menial work for them. The Youngster Year began in August the following year, with the first summer cruise. 'Bob' had to get used to a hammock in the battleship *Utah*, he scrubbed the decks and watched movies on a canvas screen from a perch in the maintop. He noted of the Midshipmen's Practice Squadron, 'It's surprising how many maneuvers three battleships can think up to do.' Back in college in September he noted, 'It's great to be a youngster … to stroll down the alley, … and in general to act like a freeborn American citizen instead of like a novice in some medieval and very ascetic monastery.'[47]

Having completed another year of studies, the midshipmen began another cruise. In 1930 they visited Cherbourg, then they saw 'more of Paris in three days than most tourists see in three months.' On to Kiel, 'a handsome little place', and a trip to Berlin with its famous *Kaberets* and a

Name and Laundry Number

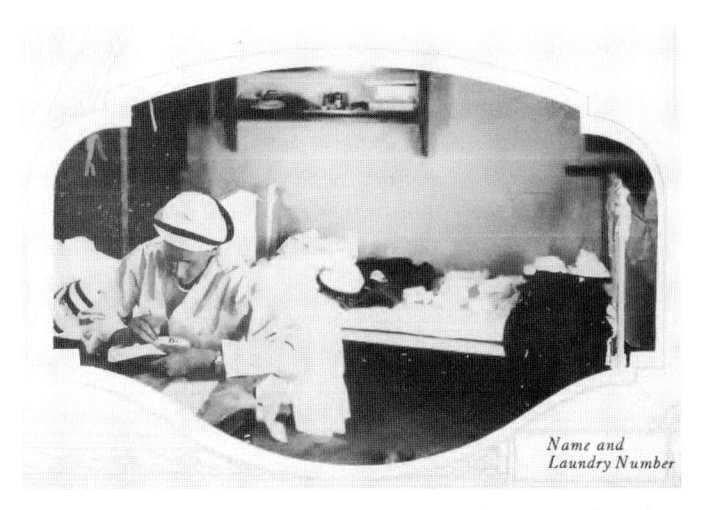

A midshipman in his spartan quarters at Annapolis, wearing his 'white works' uniform with a seaman's cap distinguished by a blue band, and writing a letter home.

magnificent airport. Norway seemed to be 'more like the United States', Scotland was 'quite a nice little country' to 'Bob', and Edinburgh was 'the most beautiful city I've ever seen.' A four-day excursion to London involved visits to 'the usual points of interest.'[48]

The midshipmen were put into battalions officered by senior year midshipmen. Ernest King was advised to acquire a lot of gold braid, a hint that he would be appointed to the highest grade, cadet lieutenant commander or four-striper.[49] 'Bob' of the class of '31 was content to be a company chief petty officer, 'not a striper, but in the higher ranks of the POs.' He soon found that 'the first class are kings around here' and looked forward to 'a great eight months' until graduation.[50]

Harold G Bowen wrote:

> Education at the Naval Academy consisted of trying to read the lessons assigned earlier in the day, but so many pages were assigned that it was usually impossible to finish. It was certainly impossible to find time to ponder anything that seemed particularly interesting. In the classroom the instructors handed out questions and we wrote the answers on the blackboard. A mark was assigned for the work and that was all there was to it. There was no actual instruction.[51]

Discipline was strict, with demerits to control behaviour. Failure rates varied from 27 per cent for the class of 1925, to a savage 42.8 per cent for 1929. The class of 1935 was more successful with only 24 per cent withdrawal, including forty-nine for academic failure and thirteen for medical reasons. Marc Mitscher was near the bottom of his class and was bilged. He was reappointed due to the influence of his congressman, but had to repeat the first two years. In 1910 he graduated near the bottom of his class, and it was only in 1915 that he found his true metier as a pilot.

Like any American college, Annapolis had its rituals and attachments. June Week was a round of parades, family visits and social events, culminating in the graduation of the upper class. Graduates were issued with rings to wear at the ball which followed. At the end of their year, the barefoot plebes were expected to form pyramids and replace a hat on top of the lard-covered 21ft Herndon Monument. The Army–Navy football game in November was supported enthusiastically, though the navy rarely won. The anthem 'Anchors Away' was originally written for it in 1906, with the lines, 'Sail Navy down the field and sink the Army, / Sink the Army grey!'

The annual magazine, *Lucky Bag*, contained a photograph and description of each midshipman, and much more besides, a striking contrast to the typical British production, as described by Schofield. 'After the accounts of cricket, rugger, soccer and hockey matches, of assaults at arms, sports, sailing and pulling regattas, meets of the Beagles, there follows on the last page the term order giving the numerical position of each cadet'.[52] Every Annapolis graduate would be forever one of the 'Class of '35', or whatever year he graduated.

Admiral Leahy told a graduating class: 'You will all have to a greater or lesser degree something else that is intangible … a combination of loyalty to ideals, tradition, courage, devotion, clean living and clear thinking. It is more than "esprit de corps" because it reaches far beyond the corps and comradeship.'[53] From 1933, each was entitled to the degree of Bachelor of Science. The 'hat toss' began at Annapolis when the midshipmen's caps were thrown in the air to be replaced by new officers' headgear, and it was copied throughout the country. Until 1912 graduates had to serve two years at sea as 'passed midshipmen'. After that they were commissioned straight away as ensigns. In the class of 1937, 219 members became ensigns in the navy alongside twenty-five second lieutenants in the marines.

The Annapolis system had its limitations, but it produced a surprising variety of alumni. Of the four five-star admirals appointed later, Vice Admiral Roland Smoot remarked:

> You have a man like King – a terrifically 'hew to the line' hard martinet, stone steely gentleman; the grandfather and really

The graduation of the class of 1940, the culmination of 'June Week'.

loveable old man Nimitz – the most beloved man I've ever known; the complete and utter clown Halsey – a clown but if he said, 'Let's go to hell together', you'd go to hell with him; and then the diplomat Leahy – the open-handed, effluent diplomat Leahy. Four more different men never lived …[54]

In peacetime, the officer corps was tightly controlled by Congress, with numbers in a fixed proportion of enlisted strength, a relatively high figure of 5½ per cent in 1938. Regulations for promotion were prescribed by law, and the numbers of the higher grades were limited. In addition, they had to cope with particular problems – a 'hump' of officers promoted as a result of the First World War, the increase in junior officers to man destroyers, submarines and anti-aircraft armament, and the integration of naval aviators.

The system of promotion was supposed to be fair to individual officers, to increase the efficiency of the navy, and to be economical. As in the Royal Navy, interwar promotion depended on keeping out of trouble rather than brilliance. It was reported in 1940, 'those who have had general courts [martial], boards of investigations, debt letters, one or more average fitness reports, domestic troubles, severe sickness [or] lack of some type of duty' were likely to be eliminated at an early stage.[55]

After graduation, ensigns were normally assigned to battleships, cruisers and carriers to learn the duties such as commanding a division of guns, as signal officer, and deck or engine room watchkeeper. As the rules stood, they were promoted to lieutenant (junior grade) after three years' service, and were eligible for promotion to lieutenant after a further three. It was not automatic, but more than 95 per cent were considered 'best fitted'; the others were discharged with one year's pay. This happened at the age of about twenty-eight, so an American lieutenant was usually more experienced than his nominal British equivalent. After a further seven years, including at least four at sea, an officer might be considered for lieutenant commander by a board of admirals. The class of 1924 was so assessed in 1938 and 70 per cent of 267 officers were deemed to be 'best fitted' to be promoted immediately, 23.6 per cent were 'fitted' and the rest were to be retired. Promotion to commander was after seven more years, including three at sea, and around 95 per cent were selected by 1938, an increase on earlier years. They were far more likely to command destroyers and submarines than British commanders. Promotion demanded flexibility: Admiral Kelly Turner commented, 'For each grade to which I have been promoted, I have found that it was necessary to make good all over again, and to spend a great deal of time in careful thought and study.[56]

Traditionally Congress was reluctant to give up its powers and promote too many officers to the higher ranks. In the summer of 1941, however, with a state of national emergency caused by the war in Europe and the growing threat from Japan, it relinquished much of its control of the officer corps. Under a bill sponsored by Chester Nimitz, then head of the Bureau of Navigation, temporary officers could now be appointed from the retired list, from warrant officers and enlisted men, and from the reserves. Temporary promotion was also allowed, and the number of vice admirals was increased because of:

> the desirability of being able to detail officers of specified rank to represent this country from the standpoint of relative rank with officers of other navies, and also the desirability of giving increased

rank to an officer commanding a special unit afloat if the importance of the command should warrant it.[57]

Unlike in the Royal Navy, commissioned officers were expected to take on any task onboard ship without specialised training. Raymond Calhoun joined the destroyer *Sterett* in the autumn of 1939 and was appointed assistant engineer officer, with the usual duties for the most junior officer onboard, of mess treasurer, welfare officer and leader of the landing party. He became communications officer, then gunnery officer in several heated Pacific battles, before becoming executive officer.[58] Navigation was normally done by the executive officer. Appointed to the role in *Sterett* after some 'musical chairs', Calhoun was worried: 'I had some concerns about my ability to locate the stars well enough to carry out my new responsibilities as navigator. But after a few days of practice I was able to take my sights and work them out with no difficulty.' One of his successors wrote: 'Navigation with its precision had always interested me, and although I had worked out navigation problems alongside the exec and chief quartermaster, I now got the job for real'.[59]

The policy of non-specialisation included engineering, which surprised Commander Parry of the Royal Navy in February 1941:

> … the engineer officer, who is a lieutenant junior grade, is expected to keep Officer of the Watch on the bridge when numbers get short in the watchkeeping list, or when required. Nothing unusual is seen in this sudden transference for one end of the engine room telegraphs (annunciators) to the other. In fact, in the former ship [*Coyningham*] the engineer officer was considered to be about the best station keeper.[60]

The Engineer Corps of the US Navy was abolished in 1899 and merged with the line, because 'it had no vision and didn't reach out for postgraduate education.' All midshipmen at the Academy were now trained in engineering and the slogan was 'every naval officer his own engineer.'

The main exception to the rule was the officers appointed for Engineering Duties Only or EDO. According to a scheme established in 1937, they already had at least fifteen years' service and had presumably carried out a range of duties in that time. They were shore-based and unlikely to be put in charge of a ship's engine room, but would aid the development of engines and take charge of maintenance facilities in bases. The most famous of them were two exceptionally feisty officers. Harold G Bowen wrote: 'I had decided that I preferred engineering duty.

Deck duty, watch standing, and gun drills bored me … Fortunately, in 1912, I was able to join the first class of the new postgraduate school with one year at Annapolis and one year at Columbia University.'[61] He would convert the navy to high-pressure steam just before the Second World War. Hyman Rickover, later 'the father of the nuclear submarine', worked in the electrical section of the Bureau of Ships from 1939–44, then took charge of the repair facility at Okinawa, but was only there a month before the atom bombs made it unnecessary.

Mustang officers, those who had come up the ranks, were quite rare and had a definite character:

> Nearly all the young officers in our outfit were college graduates. The few officers who had come up through the enlisted ranks of the regular Navy were almost always a few years older. These old-timers invariably had their ships in better physical and mechanical condition than the Reserve officers and almost without exception had a physical trait of their own that was noticeable – they were, to a man, more serious minded and unsmiling. The young Reserve officers were more eager and venturesome, and as they formed the overwhelming majority of the force, planning was patterned to their capability.[62]

The American wardroom

As in the Royal Navy, commissioned officers ate and socialised in the wardroom. As described in 1935: 'The wardroom … is a combination library, clubroom, and dining room. … in the wardrooms of the 10,000 ton cruisers there is a great difference of ages of the members due to the fact that there is no junior officers' mess.'[63] As fitted out by the shipyard, it was likely to be spartan. Appointed to the cruiser *Tuscaloosa* during her building, D A McElduff was told by a yard official, 'that a man-of-war should not in any sense be considered the home of seagoing officers.' Another issue was the quality of the food, for there were no specialised officers' cooks as in the Royal Navy, and older hands recruited specifically for the role were dying out.

It could become overwhelming in a large carrier and Dusty Kleiss wrote: 'the *Enterprise*'s mammoth wardroom … always appeared full, and despite its impressive size, *Enterprise*'s officer corps overflowed the room if all the officers sat together.'[64] Nevertheless it was impressive to an enlisted man like Ted Mason:

> In the *California,* which had been designed as a force flagship, the wardroom was large and luxurious. It ran clean athwartships on

the second deck … The atmosphere, I judged from my readings in Somerset Maugham, was that of an exclusive gentlemen's club.

On the starboard side were sofas and easy chairs in soft, rich leather. The ports were draped with heavy dark-green curtains. On the other side were refectory tables covered with green baize and decorated with siler bowls piled high with fruit. Filipino and negro stewards in starched white uniforms stood by in respectful attitudes.[65]

The same was true of the surrounding areas:

The decks in officers' country were covered with thick, highly polished battleship linoleum in familiar rust-red. Bulkheads and overheads were painted a contrasting pale green. The metal doors to the staterooms were kept discreetly closed … trading these passages as an enlisted man, one felt small and insignificant …[66]

USN warrant officers

As in the Royal Navy, an American warrant officer was treated as a junior officer rather than a senior NCO. He was entitled to a salute and might mess with the commissioned officers if the unit was too small for a separate mess. Typically, in 1941 the cruiser *St Louis* had nine warrant officers compared with forty-nine wardroom officers – a boatswain, gunner, chief electrician, chief radio electrician, chief machinist, machinist, carpenter, chief pay clerk and acting pay clerk. His real status was higher than his British counterpart, for American officers did not specialise to anything like the extent of the British, and the warrant officer's experience was valuable, while he was likely to remain at the same level rather than be promoted to higher things. According to Admiral Bowen, 'Engineering afloat or operating engineering became more and more in the hands of the Warrant Machinists, very able and practical men as a rule, but usually with no theoretical engineering education.'[67] When the carrier *Wasp* was damaged off Guadalcanal, 'On watch in the engine room at the time of the hit was Chief Machinist Chester M Stearns, who immediately took steps to correct the heavy list.'[68]

The warrant officer's position could still be uncomfortable, according to one chief radio electrician. On promotion, 'he would move into that curious limbo of the broken stripe: neither officer nor enlisted man, neither gentleman nor gob.'[69] William F Namemy had been closer to the enlisted men than the officers: 'While I was a warrant I used to regularly have young trainees come to me with their problems, and they felt perfectly comfortable discussing all sorts of family, marital and other problems with me. … However, after I received my commission all that ceased'.[70]

The Wavy Navy

Most British naval officers had left the conventional education system at the age of thirteen, and very few of them had any experience at all of state schools. Perhaps this is why they paid little attention to it. In peacetime, there was practically no naval presence in schools and universities, though the army had the Officers' Training Corps and the RAF trained pilots in the University Air Squadrons. In wartime, the first batch of trainees at *King Alfred* included a few university entrants alongside the yachtsmen and they were considered to be of high quality, but there was no plan to increase the supply until the University Naval Divisions were set up in 1943. Officers at *King Alfred* considered the scheme to be 'a complete flop' for 'Candidates … were never quite sure whether they were to become sailors or Masters of Art, and it takes a clever man to learn even the elementary rules of the navy in 1½ days instruction per week'.[71]

A petty officer interviewer often had little knowledge of the national education system, as John Davies found out:

> 'Education?' The rough, deep voice startled me.
> 'Oh! I took an honours degree in English at the University of London.' …
> The arbiter of my destiny gestured briefly with impatience.
> 'Never mind about that. Have you got the School Leaving Certificate?'
> 'Er – yes, of course.'[72]

The Royal Fleet Reserve consisted of men who had served their time in the navy and it had nineteen thousand members in 1939, supplemented by twenty-nine thousand rating pensioners and twelve thousand retired officers. They could be recalled and they were steeped in naval tradition (if sometimes reluctant to leave their firesides), but they knew little or nothing about modern fields such as aviation or radar. Royal Naval Reserve officers were merchant seamen who had trained with the Royal Navy in peacetime and were called up in war; though as it transpired, merchant seamen would be needed urgently in their own service. They would often be put in command of smaller escort vessels such as corvettes. They included Monsarrat's hero, Lieutenant Commander Cuthbertson of the corvette *Zinnia*, 'a tall, friendly, capable man', the model for Captain

Ericson in *The Cruel Sea*. He contrasted with Monsarrat's own captain, 36-year-old Richard Case, who had been educated in the training ship *Worcester* and with the Pacific Steam Navigation Company. Something of a bully, his rare official reports were terse, his private diary banal; though Monsarrat conceded that he was 'a superb professional.'[73] Another group consisted of the convoy commodores, who had often served in very high rank before retirement and had to drop several grades to take up the post. RNR officers wore intertwined lace on their sleeves.

Permanent Royal Naval Volunteer Reserve or RNVR officers were from many different professions and trained part-time in their local divisions in peace. They wore wavy stripes. At the beginning of the war D A Rayner had been told, 'the Navy won't give RNVRs command of a ship, no matter how long the war lasts.'[74] But this did not allow for the huge number of escort ships needed in wartime, and in 1940 he was given command of the old destroyer *Verbena* in the Western Approaches. They gradually overcame the prejudice of the Royal Navy proper.

The temporary members of the RNVR fell into two groups. A minority, including Monsarrat, were former yachtsmen who were hastily trained in naval ways early in the war. They were given a smattering of naval discipline at HMS *King Alfred,* a converted leisure centre on the seafront in Hove. According to one of its officers:

> Our job was to rig a fair sized Officers' Training Establishment, as it were, on the beach. There was a syllabus of training to be chopped into periods of instruction, into time-tables and into Routine. … There were lectures to be written, class rooms to find and furnish, billets to arrange and the Paymaster Captain alone knows what problems of administration to be solved by *leger-de-main* in the small hours of the morning …[75]

One of his staff wrote: 'The standard to be reached by a Sub-Lieutenant R.N.V.R. in September 1939 was the possession of a full uniform. An additional pair of trousers would almost certainly have led to accelerated promotion.'[76]

Monsarrat dismissed the training as 'learning how to salute and how to respond in a seamanlike manner to the Loyal Toast (don't stand up), and studying an ambiguous manual called *Street Fighting for Junior Officers*.'[77] Ludovic Kennedy and his comrades 'did extensive drills, learnt the rule of the road and the meanings of flags, practised boat handling in nearby Shoreham Harbour – and one dreadful day were taken to a nearby football field to be instructed in the one form of warfare I had joined the Navy to avoid: bayonet attack.'[78]

Cadet ratings wearing the uniform of the lower deck and relaxing with sandwiches.

The second group of temporary RNVRs comprised men who had joined the navy as ratings in wartime, either as conscripts or volunteers, and spent at least three months on the lower deck before being selected for training in *King Alfred*. Captain Pelly outlined the aims of the course:

> 'King Alfred' must, within ten weeks, instil in every man the alertness, enthusiasm, sense of responsibility, conscience and good humour (as well as a basic knowledge of technical subjects) which centuries of Service experience have shown to be necessary if a Naval Officer is to carry out his normal duties.[79]

One candidate was surprised on his first arrival at Lancing College, a former public school. It was:

> … one of the greatest surprises of our lives. … I stood dwarfed in the great doorway and looked down the long dining hall. I saw the stained glass windows, the oak panelling, the officers' tables and the bright red rope. I saw long tables stretched from one end of the room to the other; there were tablecloths! glasses! real knives and forks! Waitresses hurried to and fro with entrée dishes: cadet ratings in green gaiters and clean collars took their seats at the tables. Somehow I felt proud that I had been honoured to sit with them.[80]

Cadet ratings at HMS *King Alfred* practising navigation with sextants – a defining skill of an officer, but rarely used in practice except by specialist navigators.

Each cadet was interviewed by Captain Pelly who told him: 'We are all on the steps of a ladder, the ladder of promotion. There are many rungs; I'm on one, you're just starting to climb. Rung by rung we can both climb the ladder of promotion together.'[81]

The more technical side of things – gunnery, signalling, mines and torpedoes was left to petty officers, who tended to do things by rote.[82]

> 'This 'ere's the trigger. You put your finger on the trigger and you squeeze 'er. Finger thinks "Oi've been squeezed, Oi ave," and 'e presses the little old trigger. Little old trigger thinks, "Oi've been pulled by little old finger, Oi'd better move." So 'e moves and 'e 'its little old spring.'
>
> 'Chief, I didn't quite get what the little old detonator said to the little old cartridge. Could you repeat it?'[83]

The transfer to Hove after six weeks brought a completely new atmosphere and a change of pace. Lancing was academic, Hove was like 'bees in a beehive', according to F S Holt. Cadet-ratings took their tea in the ante-room, but had their other meals in a special part of the officers' mess, partitioned off by red ropes.[84]

A good officer, according to the *Aide Memoire*, had to steer between the limits of becoming 'popularity Jack' and neglecting his men. He was urged to get to know their names and interests, to remember that loyalty 'can only start at the top and grow downwards', to encourage the best men without showing undue favouritism, and to set a good example of smartness and confidence:

> Your demeanour should be cheerful and enthusiastic – it is your business to inspire enthusiasm and pride of ship and Service. Never appear bored or fed up, however irksome the work may be. The British have a capacity for cheerfulness in adversity. Give it a chance; it is infectious.[85]

Exercises were imaginative:

> ... we concluded that part of the course with a navigation exercise conducted in a large field ... dotted with scaled-down buoys, a miniature lighthouse, a church steeple, and a small rock or two. ... Working in pairs, we were provided with a chart of this 'ocean' and an ice cream vendor's tricycle, the top of the freezer box being fitted out as a chart table with a bearing compass, dividers, parallel rule, and binoculars. ... Not much was learned from this otherwise totally enjoyable and ludicrous exercise, given ... that the all-steel frame of the tricycles rendered the compasses nearly totally ineffective ...[86]

'Lower deck attitudes', the opposite of OLQs (officer-like qualities), were fatal to the prospects of a commission. It was widely believed that staff snooped around trying to find examples of inappropriate behaviour: 'legends were handed down from division to division of conditions and eccentricities. Certain officers, for instance, were reported to hide between pillars and take down particulars in note-books of every small breach of behaviour.'[87]

The method of announcing the results was quite cruel. The men were paraded and the names of those who had passed were read out: '[August] 21st and the announcement of our examination results. We were lined up and the results read out, starting at the back end. I stood and waited, the swine got to 18 before he called out my name. Phew! If name not called out, back to sea.'[88] The rejects went off to become the 'most abject of creatures, a failed CW candidate.' Unlike failures in other walks of life they did not go home to consider a different profession, but faced the rest of the war on the lower deck.

The new officers discarded their square rig uniforms and emerged, butterfly-like, from the tailors:

> The rest of us, dressed as ratings, crossed the road and changed into our best doeskin uniforms. A uniform with a single gold stripe. I was now an Acting Temporary Probationary Sub-Lieutenant in the

R.N.V.R. ... At the door, the sentry clattered to attention and gave us a butt salute. It was ... quite terrifying.[89]

They wore the same stripes as permanent RNVR officers, which caused some resentment as they were neither volunteers nor reservists.

Admiral Stark of the US Navy called *King Alfred* training, 'Britain's greatest experiment in democracy'. One of the trainees, Ronald Gellatly, wrote that it was 'without doubt the most efficiently run establishment that I met during my Naval career.'[90] The novelist Evelyn Waugh, sailing in the landing ship *Glenroy*, was far less positive. 'The RNVR lieutenants and sub-lieutenants were a pathetic collection of youths straight from insurance offices ... Besides being dreary fellows to talk to, they were hopeless seamen.'[91]

Promotion to full lieutenant was almost automatic. An officer under twenty-five needed two and a half years' service and a watch-keeping certificate from his captain ('I took damn good care of that one,' wrote Monsarrat). Above that age he only needed one year's service, and over thirty he only needed three months, and could dispense with the certificate.[92] As a result, there were few mature sub lieutenants, though their numbers were always quite high owing to the numbers going through the system at any given moment.

Ninety-day wonders
In contrast to the Royal Navy, the USN built close links with the nation's universities and colleges. This was important, because a college education was far more common in the United States – in 1943 there were 1702 accredited institutions of higher education in the country, including 690 senior colleges or universities.

In 1925/6 the navy set up the Naval Reserve Officers' Training Corps, initially in six colleges and universities – Harvard, Yale, Northwestern, Washington, Georgia Institute of Technology and Berkeley. The last was commanded by Chester Nimitz, a pioneer in many things. By 1939 it had spread to twenty-seven colleges. Training, however, was left at the discretion of the officers appointed to the corps, except to recommend that the standard of Annapolis should be seen as a model.

C Snelling Robinson enrolled in the Harvard unit in September 1940, and a quarter of his courses were in what was known as 'naval science': 'In addition to the classroom requirements of the program and the practice drilling under the supervision of chief petty officers and marine drill sergeants, the NROTC cadets were obligated to go to sea for training each summer while in college.' He did that in June 1941 in *St Augustine,* a converted 300ft yacht, supervised by old-time reserve officers who gave a good indication of sea life. They were scheduled to graduate in 1944, but it was accelerated after Pearl Harbor, and they were commissioned as ensigns in May 1943.[93]

The V-7, or 'Reserve Midshipman Program', was announced by the president in June 1940 for 'Unmarried male citizens of the United States [though married men might also be accepted] between the ages of 19 and 28 years, who have been citizens of the United States for a period of at least 10 years preceding enlistment, and who are college graduates or seniors.'[94] It provided a ready means for expansion after Pearl Harbor. Herman Wouk was close to the upper age limit when he was interviewed in 1942: 'five blue and gold uniforms confronted me. Questions came at me from five faces more or less alike. Why was I applying for midshipman school at my age? What was my major in college? What was my favourite sport? My physical condition?' The board was impressed that he had worked as scriptwriter for the comedian Fred Allen and asked, 'Is he funny in real life?' It was less pleased that he had already registered for the draft with the army, and that had to be sorted out before he was accepted.[95]

The first stage of the programme was a month as an apprentice seaman, as described by Douglas Leach: 'So it was that on 24 January 1942, again at Headquarters, First Naval District, I raised my right hand and was sworn in as an apprentice seaman, class V-7.' At Notre Dame College in Illinois: 'We drew our bedding and uniforms. Once in the possession of the latter, again as instructed, we stripped off our college-boy clothing in which we had come, climbed into sailor whites, and packed our discarded garments for shipment home. That snapped the last tie with the civilian world.' As with all American officer training, there was the danger of bilging by earning too many demerits or being found unsuitable, for the course was designed to accomplish two things – 'weed out the incompetent and prepare the remainder for later rigorous training at Midshipmen's School'. As a result, 'We watched from a respectful distance as those unfortunates on the bilge list assembled outside Morrisey Hall with their luggage, a forlorn little band, awaiting transportation to the railway station.'[96]

Reserve midshipman training was carried out at six different sites by the later stages of the war – Columbia University in New York, Northwestern in Chicago, Cornell in New York State, Notre Dame in Indiana, Forth Schuyler in the Bronx, New York, and in the Academy at Annapolis. It took three months and the successful candidates were invariably known as '90-day wonders'.

There was an immediate change in status as marked by clothing:

Upon arrival we were issued with new uniforms consisting of visor cap with changeable covers, khaki shirt and trousers, black necktie (worn tucked into the shirt), and web belt with shiny brass buckle. Earlier, at Notre Dame, we had been measured for our dress blues, including the traditional midshipman's double-breasted jacket with brass buttons, uniforms that arrived a little later.[97]

Herman Wouk fictionalised the process as avoiding demerits and learning by rote from outdated textbooks:

One night Willie came upon the following statement in his tattered green-bound manual, *Submarine Doctrine, 1935*: 'Submarines, because of their small cruising range, are chiefly suitable for coastal defence' at that time the Nazis were torpedoing several American ships each week around Cape Hatteras, four thousand miles from Germany's coast.[98]

The principal subjects were navigation with Dutton's *Navigation and Nautical Astronomy* as the main textbook; seamanship from Knight's *Modern Seamanship*, which was cherished by many officers in the fleet; ordnance and gunnery; communications; and damage control and engineering. They also learned about chemical warfare, ship and aircraft recognition, and leadership. From June 1945 the midshipman had the thorough 480-page *Naval Orientation* to guide him. According to Leonard W Tate: 'I had thought my last year of college had been difficult, but that turned out to be just a warm-up for midshipmen's school. … we were to learn everything in four months that a person learned at Annapolis in four years.'[99] If successful, a young man was commissioned as an ensign. Houston Jones described the 'proverbial' 90-day wonder as 'formal, exacting, less at ease; even his log entries were fuller and more formal.'[100]

The aim of the V-12 programme was to bring the students up to the level of a college education before sending them on to naval training as midshipmen. It allowed those whose families could not afford college a way in, and was also an opportunity for enlisted men to rise. For example, Herbert L Fritz was a first-class petty officer when he was sent to the University of Washington in 1944, though like many V-12 candidates he did not have time to be commissioned before the end of the war.[101] Houston Jones was assessed by his officer: 'One of the best sound operators in the business – best I ever worked with. Young, clean, Southern, handsome, well-liked, not exceptionally industrious, but dependable and bright. He had one year of college, interrupted by war … Recommended for V-12'.[102] But for some reason that did not happen.

According to Eugene Sledge: 'Life at Georgia Tech was easy and comfortable. In short, we didn't know there was a war going on. Most of the college courses were dull and uninspiring. Many of the professors openly resented our presence. It was all but impossible to concentrate on academics.' As a result, half the class of 180 flunked in order to go straight in as enlisted men.[103] Sledge perhaps regretted it later:

> ... I passed a porthole that gave a view into the officers' mess. There I saw Navy and Marine officers clad neatly in starched khakis sitting at tables in a well-ventilated room. White-coated waiters served them pie and ice cream. As we inched along the hot companionway to our steaming joe and dehydrated fare, I wondered if my haste to leave the V-12 college life hadn't been a mistake.[104]

The uniformed V-12 men attended classes with other students. They did little military drill, but were woken by reveille at six in the morning – though 'Taps' was not sounded in the evening to signal lights out, to let the men study late. Each semester lasted sixteen weeks and there were often lectures on Saturdays because of the intensity of the course.

Members of the V-12 unit in Washburn University, Kansas, in 1944, on a break from their studies and training. Typically they are wearing enlisted men's uniform, but they seem to be enjoying a normal undergraduate social life.

Appointments direct from civil life were offered to qualified men in certain professions – civil engineers, medical and dental officers, chaplains and communicators, amateur or professional sailors, and intelligence, ordnance and legal officers. By 1944, they made up half the officers in service, and their numbers included future presidents Lyndon Johnson, Richard Nixon and Gerald Ford, who applied to become an intelligence officer but was offered a post as a physical training officer because of his college athletic prowess. He served as an instructor in a pre-flight school, then as assistant navigator, athletic officer and anti-aircraft officer in the light carrier *Monterey*.[105]

After commissioning as an ensign, further promotion was en bloc and almost entirely by seniority. If ten thousand more JGs were needed:

> … BuPers runs smack into one plain fact: 10,000 ensigns are a lot of ensigns. A war is going on and that war makes demands which outweigh the individual study of ensigns. Moreover, because their naval careers have been brief, these ensigns have necessarily skimpy performance records and so the study wouldn't prove too much anyway.
>
> So … the promotions section has to lean on another reasonable assumption – that the average ensign has turned into neither a disciplinary problem nor an incompetent. And, lacking the manpower and sufficiently detailed records to process the whole lot to j.g. as individuals, the entire field of 10,000 is promoted, except those whose promotions are withheld by their COs.[106]

There was no reference to age or experience in the system, so older men might spend some time in the rank of ensign, and they were occasionally to be found in posts that might have merited a higher rank. Houston Jones was surprised to find that all three officers of his subchaser, including the captain, were ensigns, though they were soon promoted to JG.[107] Despite his lack of any advanced base experience, Ensign Libby compiled the *Catalogue of Functional Components* which was the essential tool in planning Seabees work in Acorns and Cubs from 1943.[108]

Promotion to the senior rank of lieutenant commander needed different techniques. If the navy needed 4300 men, and 6500 were qualified:

> The Bureau now takes steps to get to know Joe better. So, for the first time in his Navy career, he is put closely under the lens. This scrutiny is done by a selection board appointed by the Secretary of the Navy. …The touchstone to promotion, all things considered, is his fitness report … did the man's CO recommend him for promotion? If he did, his chances are good.[109]

According to Admiral Kelly Turner: 'Reserve Officers who have been intelligent and determined enough to follow this strict course of procedure have gotten along as well as, and often better than, Naval Academy Officers.'[110] From the other end of the rank structure Ted Mason compared the different officers:

> More often in the late months of 1941 … the [junior officer of the watch] was not a sword-straight Annapolis graduate but a reserve officer … The USNR junior officers had just as much authority as the career navy types to put a man on report or turn him back from liberty for the slightest deviation from a shipshape appearance, and they were accordingly, just as feared. Perhaps more so, since their lack of familiarity with navy regulations and the unwritten customs of the navy made them somewhat unpredictable.[111]

Bad officers will inevitably slip through in any system. According to Olson:

> … aboard the *Dale*: everyone hated Axelrod! He was a sleazy lawyer who had pissed someone off at the JAG office in Washington DC, and got sent out to sea. He went by the book like he wrote it with God telling him what to say.
>
> Now, Axelrod had been telling everyone who would listen that he had been sent out to the *Dale* by mistake. 'I've got connections in Washington,' he would say, 'and they're going to get me released from this rust bucket any day now!' this, of course, did not endear him to the crew.[112]

* * *

Both navies had their share of failures in the early stages of the war, mostly caused by admirals who had failed to adapt to the conditions of modern warfare. This was more than balanced by a clutch of commanders who could stand alongside the greatest in the history of naval warfare – Cunningham, Horton, Ramsay, Fraser and Vian on the British side; King, Nimitz, Spruance and Mitscher on the American. At a lower level, there were captains who sacrificed their ships needlessly or failed to engage fully, but many more who exceeded expectations – the escort commanders who kept their ships efficient through months of gruelling conditions in the Atlantic, the American destroyer captains who sacrificed their lives but saved the day off Samar during the Battle of Leyte Gulf, and the many who had to learn a completely new trade of amphibious warfare. Neither Dartmouth nor Annapolis was perfect in its selection principles, but both produced the officers who would win a war over all the oceans of the world.

It is difficult to assess the British policy of specialisation against the American one, because it was not always applied effectively. Royal Navy engineers were segregated from executive officers and unnecessarily debarred from command. Gunnery training included far too much scientific material that only a very few would ever need. 'Torpedo' was more about electricity and inhibited the development of a fully electrical branch. On the American side, the lack of deep knowledge of any subject by commissioned officers led to reliance on warrant officers, who did not always have the vision needed.

A naval officer leaving Dartmouth could look forward to a career as a seaman officer in the Royal Navy, perhaps specialising even more in gunnery, signals, navigation, torpedo or anti-submarine, all skills which had little or no market value in the outside world. He was likely to be entirely focused on his career in the navy, one of Charles Owen's 'poor delegators' with 'narrow vision'. An Annapolis graduate, on the other hand, might have the option of flying or becoming a ship designer within the navy, or he might spend much more time on shore-based administration than his British counterpart; in a more senior rank he would have to understand the political ways of Congress; and he had a bachelor's degree which could get him a job in the outside world – for example, as a teacher. All this suggests that the American officer was likely to be more flexible in his approach to life, and that is perhaps borne out by wartime experience. Admirals like Leahy and King were far more politically aware than Pound, or even Cunningham, on the British side.

At the junior officer level, both navies had to mass-produce men to command smaller vessels or take charge of watches. Both used education as the initial principle of selection, though in different ways – the Royal Navy largely ignored the education system of the country, the Americans worked closely with it. Both navies had long believed, like all others, that it took years to train a fully fledged naval officer. Both had to evolve systems in which a man might find himself in charge of a ship as officer of the watch less than a year after entering the navy. Naturally there were incompetents who slipped through the net, but the great majority rose to the occasion, probably for the most intense, gruelling and dangerous period of their lives. Among their many duties was the effective leadership of their men.

4

Ratings and Enlisted Men

Personnel below commissioned or warrant rank were known as 'enlisted men' in the United States services, and as 'ratings' or the 'lower deck' in the Royal Navy, as 'other ranks' or 'rank and file' in the British army, and as 'airmen' in the Royal Air Force – paradoxically most of them never flew except as passengers.

The lower deck

In the Royal Navy, non-commissioned men were the 'lower deck', from the place where they had eaten and slept on sailing men-of-war. Regular seamen, known as 'active service' or 'continuous service' men, were usually recruited as boys and went through a rigorous training programme before joining the fleet. They signed on for twelve years from the age of eighteen, though as the war approached, others were taken on for seven years with the fleet, and five in the reserve. After leaving, they were kept on the lists of the Royal Fleet Reserve and recalled in wartime, so there were many in the fleet. Twelve years was acceptable in Victorian times when it was common to spend a lifetime devoted to a single employer, and guaranteed employment was highly desirable in the hungry thirties, but already the system was under question. A wartime petty officer wrote:

> Is our public aware that its young sailors are kidnapped into its senior service at the tender age of 15, and, to ensure that the sentence is binding, they have to sign or have signed for them a document stating that for 12 years, from the age of 18, their souls belong to the Admiralty. Imagine: 15 years signed away by children unaware of life's meaning.[1]

Boys' training establishments were attached to the main naval bases – HMS *Impregnable* at Plymouth, *St Vincent* near Portsmouth, *Caledonia* at Rosyth and *Ganges* near Harwich, attached to Chatham. Tristan Jones was on one of the last boys' courses there in 1940:

> Life for a boy trainee at HMS *Ganges* was one long harassment from dawn – when the bugler sounded 'Charlie' – until lights out at nine-

fifteen p.m. There was hardly a minute of the waking day when we boys were not on our feet and doubling, or sat at attention in a classroom, being yelled at. Even when the 'working' day was over, our time was taken up hand-sewing our names on to our uniforms (red chain-stitches, each not longer than the rest). Some of the class were still busily engaged in this pastime, even though they had been in *Ganges* for ten weeks.[2]

Discipline was enforced by the 'Stonicky' (variously spelt): 'A short stick or canvas-covered rope ... used for belting boys up the back-side to hurry them along ... very painful it was too.'[3]

Some of the boys were selected to become visual or radio signallers. The rest joined ships as boy seamen and were strictly segregated from adult ratings. At eighteen they qualified as ordinary seamen, then as able seamen. Boy training continued in wartime, but it was switched to HMS *St George* on the Isle of Man, while the older bases went over to training adults.

By June 1940 the navy had doubled in size, to 271,000 officers and men, and by the end of the year it had increased again, with 333,000 men. It did this mostly by taking on men, both volunteers and conscripts, for 'hostilities only', or HOs. The navy's prestige tended to attract the right kind of man. According to the Mass Observation report of 1941, the most common attitude to the navy was 'one of unqualified but unspecified respect.'[4] For most of the war, the navy had about three times as many applicants as it needed, so it could be selective. Only with the great

Seamen boys drilling in cold weather at HMS *St Vincent* near Portsmouth in 1935, wearing the gaiters that were a common dress of naval trainees, also worn for foot drill and shore operations.

expansion on the eve of D-day in 1943/4 did it take nearly everyone who came up to the minimum standard. Early in the war, it used recalled regular chief petty officers. In a few minutes, 'the Naval Recruiter concerned made his assessment of the man; obtained answers to standard questions about his willingness to be inoculated, vaccinated and so on; decided whether or not to accept him; and, if he accepted him, allocated him to a branch of the service.'[5] After 1942, Wren petty officers used more modern psychological techniques. The candidates were asked questions on 'such topics as sickness absence from civilian work, headaches, accidents, dieting, and reaction to air raids.' They would ask candidates 'to fill up a simple form, … which would yield facts about the school and work record and leisure activities … the group would go on to take a paper-and-pencil intelligence test … Then, as the men trickled back one by one from the medical board which saw them on completion of the form and the test, each would be given an interview lasting about 8 minutes.'

As well as the former boys' training establishments, new bases were set up, often in converted holiday camps round the coast. George Melly found that *Royal Arthur* at Skegness had 'a certain architectural frivolity completely inappropriate to a Royal Navy Shore Establishment. … The ceiling of the lobby was painted to represent a summer sky with fluffy white clouds passing over it.'[6] According to Alec Guinness, *Raleigh* near Plymouth was 'a vast parade ground, with concrete quarter-deck and rows of long wooden huts housing two-tier bunks, offices, gym, dining hall and bomb shelters.'[7]

There was no leave of any kind for two weeks and to one entrant, 'It was just like being in jail and the food was the worst I encountered during the whole time I was in the navy.' At *Ganges* the day began on the huge parade ground, with three thousand men arranged by divisions, classes of about seventy, and watches. After that, one watch in each class went off to train in gunnery, the other in seamanship, with the order reversed next day. Geoffrey Ball found that the titles were misleading. The first 'seamanship' period consisted of advice on how to live in the barracks, followed by training in the points of the compass. Gunnery was largely foot drill on the parade ground and around the site. They trained on guns, usually without firing them, including the standard destroyer weapon: 'Most of their instruction was on the 4.7 quick firer. They were drilled in the details of the job to be done by each member of a crew'. Foot drill, also known as 'square-bashing' or 'gravel grinding', was intended to weld the men into a unit and teach them to obey orders. According to the *Royal Naval Handbook of Field Training*: 'The chief prop of discipline is drill, for although of itself of little fighting value, its utility as a means of exercising officers and men in instant obedience cannot be overestimated.'[8]

In general the training was a compressed version of what the boys had learned, but without the brutality. An officer described what he hoped had been achieved as men prepared to leave.

> Each could look after himself and his kit; whatever his category, each could swim, and pull and sail a lifeboat; each knew enough about fighting a ship not to be a nuisance at sea. And, above all, they had a sense of belonging, a rock-bottom foundation for living together, in preparation for the time when they would be locked together for months on end in a steel box far from land.[9]

Boot camp

In peacetime the US Navy recruited young men from the age of seventeen. It was not particularly difficult during the years of the Great Depression and in early 1941:

> Everyone was young – for the most part, kids who couldn't get jobs. Here and there were men in their twenties, jobless workers at the end of third rope, or incorrigible 'fuck-ups' who had gotten into some kind of trouble at home and had been given the ancient choice by the judge of going to jail or joining one of the services. Most were from small towns, usually from broken families, notable for bad teeth and bad complexions, the marginal young produced by more than ten years of the hardest of time.[10]

Selective Service or conscription was applied, and later that year:

> As the summer wore on, it became apparent that the navy's previously high enlistment standards were being relaxed. There was a noticeable decline in the quality of the recruits reporting for shipboard training, a decline both physical and mental. The draft was now in full operation and many young men were choosing the navy as the lesser evil. A number of them had no business being in a battleship (or any other ship): they were a menace to themselves and to their shipmates.[11]

The situation regarding basic training, or 'boot camps', was assessed in 1930, at the height of the peace:

> The bases were spread evenly round the country, at Newport, Rhode Island, Hampton Roads, Virginia, San Diego, California

and inland at Great Lakes near Chicago. The course of nine weeks was intended to change recruits 'from purposeless, immature boys to self-reliant, disciplined patriotic men-of-war's men'. It included teaching them to row a whaleboat, swim 50yds, learn the *Manual of Arms*, take care of themselves, operate small arms and be classified for future training. Leave and liberty were forbidden during the first three weeks.

As in the Royal Navy, new arrivals were greeted with cries of 'suckers' and 'you'll be sorry'. They slept in hammocks and started with callisthenics and infantry drill. Selected men became recruit petty officers with the eagle or 'crow' on their arms, but little real authority.

Foot drill played a large part:

> At the bottom was the feared rectangle of asphalt … known to generations of boots as the Grinder. Several companies of about one hundred men each were already hard at work executing the hoarse commands of their petty officers. 'Right shoulder *harms!*' and 'Right, face, forward, *harch!*' And 'column, half left, *harch!*'[12]

Floyd Beaver wrote of the chief petty officers who dominated the camps, 'Their patience was limited … But I never saw any gross abuse or pointless cruelty.'[13] Unlike British recruits, they had plenty of ship visits if they wanted: 'That was my special pleasure. I visited, at one time or another, light cruisers, minesweepers, and auxiliaries. Once I even visited the aircraft carrier *Saratoga* at her anchorage off Coronado.'[14]

The course was shortened in wartime but the content did not vary much:

> We spent four weeks in training and lived in barracks. … A Chief Petty Officer was in charge of each company and our chief was liked by all. Some of the chiefs are hated because they go out of their way to make it as miserable as possible. …
>
> You learned that your days of privacy were over while you were in the Navy and they would not return until you were back in civilian life again. When you ate, slept, took a shower, etc, you were always part of the crowd, you were never alone.
>
> No one enjoyed sleeping in the hammocks because they were too tight. It was like sleeping on a tight clothesline.[15]

In 1930, the recruits took English, spelling and mathematics tests after six weeks Then they were examined by an officer, the CPO in charge of their company and a yeoman to take notes. Officers were warned to take notice of the chief in case he sent cryptic signals to his men. In 1930 about a third – 3971 out of about 13,000 in 1930 – were selected for further training in Class A Schools and the rest went on to the fleet as seamen second class.

Floyd Beaver was delighted to be selected in 1939. 'The Navy then had advanced and more specialized schools beyond boot camp for selected men. I applied for communication school and was accepted as one of fifteen men chosen from 550 applicants' – though that did not take account of the men who were selected for other schools.[16]

With the growth of aviation and the increased use of electricity and electronics, many more specialists were needed in wartime, both in absolute terms and in proportion to the size of the navy. By December 1943 there were more than 88,000 enlisted men in Class A schools compared with 124,000 men in boot camps at the time. Numbers in the schools peaked at more than 91,000 in June 1944. In late 1943 the most populated schools, by far, were for aviation machinists' mates (14,000), diesel engines (12,000), electrical (10,000), machinists' mates (10,000), and radio (14,000).[17] They were assessed by petty officers of the Specialist (C) – Classification Interviewer group. They relied on education and intelligence tests with pass marks set according to the needs of the navy, previous experience and personal qualities such as age and fitness, but interviewers were told that 'men who have had considerable experience in a field directly related to a rating should not be excluded solely on the basis of low test scores.' Furthermore, 'In some cases, more efficient classification may be effected by considering the recruit in terms of the billet in which he is likely to serve – ie whether he is more apt to be assigned to shore stations'.[18]

* * *

A modern navy is a collection of specialists – gunners, engineers, electronics operators, cooks, and many more – the seamen, the elite in a sailing ship, were reduced to rather menial roles. A few men, mainly in the engineering trades, might come into the navy fully skilled, but the great majority were trained within the service.

Royal Navy manning was under the control of the Second Sea Lord, but his authority was limited and the different branches in the Admiralty largely set their own policies, leading to a complex and arcane system of badges. A star above or below a man's branch badge might mean proficiency at the trade or just repeat his rank as leading seaman, etc, on the other arm. A crown above the badge was equally ambiguous unless one knew the system. But a badge was important to a new seaman: 'I was now an anti-aircraft gunner, an AA3 (LC), and as proud as the proverbial peacock. I could not sew my badges on quick enough.'[19]

Seamen made up about a third of the navy. They might specialise as torpedo or gunnery, which included the military side of naval life. As such they would hold 'non-substantive' ratings, which brought a badge on the right arm and extra pay, but were separate from the 'substantive' ratings as leading seamen, petty officers and so on. As an American official publication put it in 1943:

> In British naval practice, speciality and rating are generally unrelated. A man may have a high status in a speciality without advancing beyond a seaman's rating; or he may be a CPO but still not highly qualified in his particular speciality. In such cases, advancement in rating would depend on leadership, education, etc.

Nevertheless, gunnery ratings were told: 'Although the regulations permit advancement to Leading Seaman and Petty Officer without first qualifying for a "non-substantive" rating, such qualification is of great assistance and should in any case be undertaken as soon as possible after "substantive" advancement.'[20]

The gunnery branch was the largest within the seaman category. Its men were trained at Chatham, Plymouth and Portsmouth, where HMS *Excellent* was sited on an artificial island within the harbour. The course included a great deal of foot drill, and the branch saw itself as being 'responsible for the high standard of drill required to work the gunnery armament which is reflected in the general smartness and spontaneous reaction to words of command.'[21] Just before the war, the branch was divided into quarters ratings, who supervised the working of guns as turret or gun captains; layer ratings for laying, training and firing; control ratings, who operated rangefinders, while senior ones might form part of the control team; and anti-aircraft ratings, who operated the directors and guns for close range and distant weapons. Radar control ratings were added later.[22]

The torpedo branch mainly dealt with low-power electricity, as there was no actual electrical branch until after the war. Highly trained but rare artificers maintained high-power equipment, with 'dilutee' electrical mechanics, who had a much shorter training course. Wiremen were also members of the branch; they had served as civilian electricians. It was recognised that the situation was unsatisfactory, but it was decided not to change it during the war.[23]

The anti-submarine branch was separated from the torpedomen in 1925. They were mainly employed in destroyers and sloops, which was

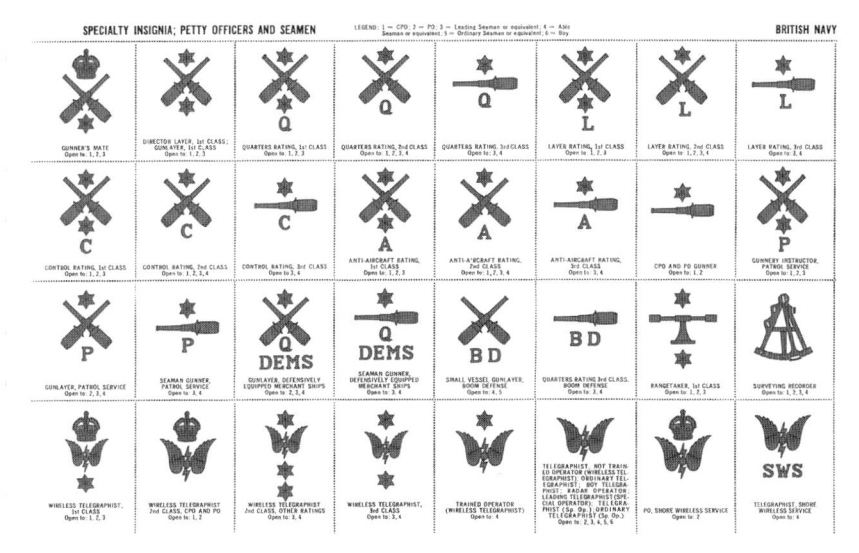

Some of the 'non-substantive' badges worn by Royal Navy ratings, with various types and grades of gunnery ratings towards the top, and 'wireless telegraphists', or radio operators, below. This by no means exhausted the range of possibilities, which filled several pages.

an advantage to John Whelan: 'if I became an Asdic operator, the odds were heavily in favour of my staying in small ships for the rest of my naval service. I promptly volunteered – and was accepted.'[24] The captain of HMS *Osprey*, the pre-war training base at Portland, drafted a notice to attract volunteers:

> We nearly lost the last war because we had no suitable device for detecting and attacking submarines.
>
> We now have such a device and special ratings known as S/D [Submarine Detector] Operators are trained to work it. …
>
> His job is a very responsible one as any submarine he fails to hear may slip through.[25]

During the war, men were trained in the Firth of Clyde at Dunoon and Campbeltown. From 1200 men at the beginning of the war, the number of submarine detectors rose to 7600 at the end.

The next largest group after the seamen was the stokers. Very few of them actually shovelled coal, since modern ships were oil-fired, so they became semi-skilled mechanics, supervised by the highly skilled engine room artificers, who had served apprenticeships inside or outside the navy and were equivalent to chief petty officers. Stokers had a different culture from seamen and were kept apart aboard ship. In peacetime they joined as adults, so had not endured the discipline of the boys' training establishments. Their work was much dirtier and carried out in the bowels of the ship, so they had different standards of cleanliness.

The third largest group was the marines, who had their own customs and rank structure. Other specialist branches included cooks, writers (clerks), stewards and stores assistants, who wore the 'fore and aft' uniform with collar and tie instead of the seaman's square collar. It was not popular: one wearer described it as 'a cross between that of a taxi driver and a workhouse inmate.'[26]

Rated men

The seaman branch of the US Navy included many non-rated men as well as the boatswains' mates who supervised them. It also included petty officer gunners' mates, torpedomen's mates, quartermasters and fire control men who would help aim the guns. The artificer branch included a variety of skilled trades such as radiomen, radar and sonar men, shipfitters, carpenters' mates and metalsmiths, as well as the most skilled of all, the radio technician. The artificer branch (engine room force) was made up of low-skilled firemen, plus machinists' and motor machinists' mates, electricians' mates and watertenders who looked after the ship's boilers. The special branch was mostly domestic and administrative, with yeomen or clerks, mailmen, buglers and many others. The commissary branch included stewards and cooks, mostly black or Filipino. The aviation branch had is own versions of some of the other rates, including aviation machinist's mate, aviator metalsmith and aviation boatswain's mate.

James Fahey had no qualifications and presumably did not do well in the tests at boot camp. He remained a seaman for the rest of the war, helping at one of the 40mm guns on the light cruiser *Montpelier* and subject to heavy duty with working parties, especially loading ammunition. He was also required to clean decks, whereas Floyd Beaver was quickly taken off the duty as a signalman. Fahey described his duties:

> … we break out the big fire hose and soak the deck with the ocean's water. Scrubbing comes next with big enormous brushes. We then use rubber squeegees and finish the process with swabs or mops. The men are shoeless and stockingless and pants rolled up to their knees as the work is being performed.[27]

Seamen could strike for higher ratings, usually in the deck force, but Fahey never achieved that. His engineering equivalent, the fireman, could strike for ratings in the engine room force.

Ratings and Enlisted Men   105

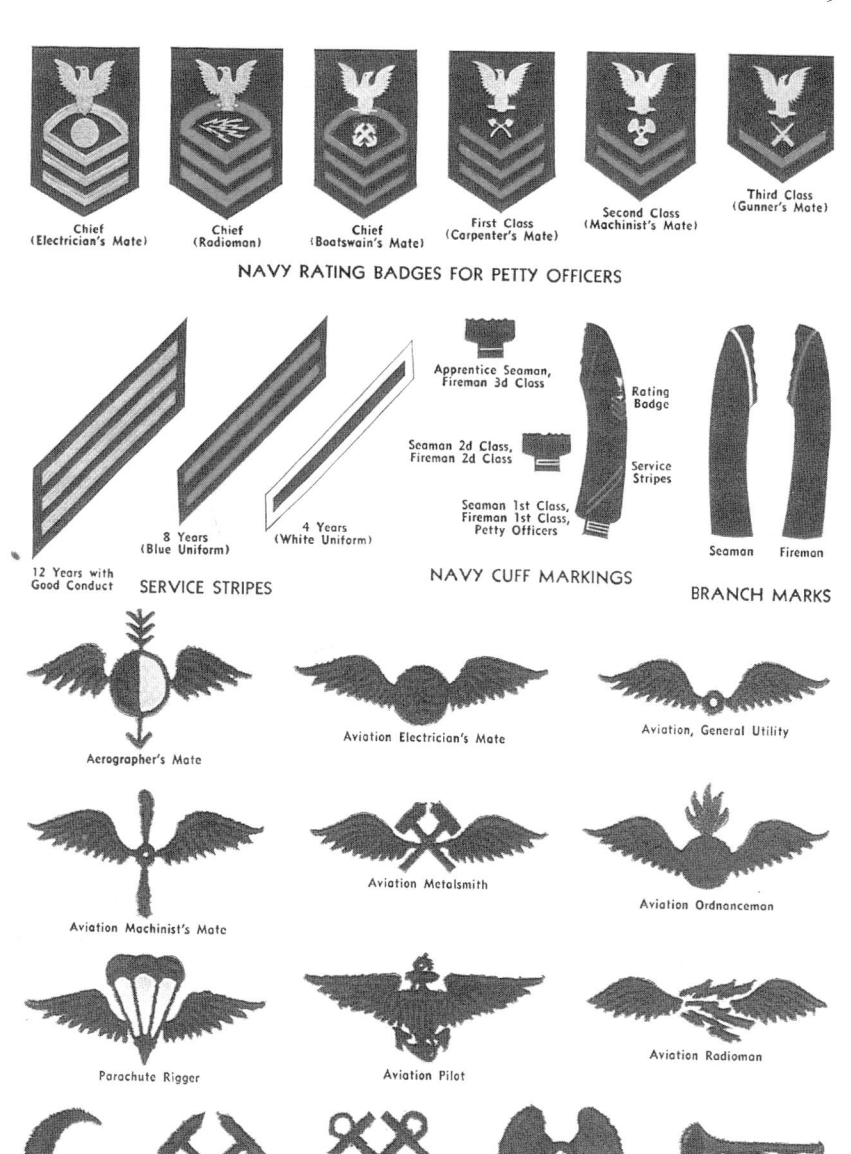

NAVY RATING BADGES FOR PETTY OFFICERS

Chief (Electrician's Mate) — Chief (Radioman) — Chief (Boatswain's Mate) — First Class (Carpenter's Mate) — Second Class (Machinist's Mate) — Third Class (Gunner's Mate)

SERVICE STRIPES
- 12 Years with Good Conduct
- 8 Years (Blue Uniform)
- 4 Years (White Uniform)

NAVY CUFF MARKINGS
- Apprentice Seaman, Fireman 3d Class
- Seaman 2d Class, Fireman 2d Class
- Seaman 1st Class, Fireman 1st Class, Petty Officers
- Rating Badge
- Service Stripes

BRANCH MARKS
Seaman — Fireman

Aerographer's Mate — Aviation Electrician's Mate — Aviation, General Utility

Aviation Machinist's Mate — Aviation Metalsmith — Aviation Ordnanceman

Parachute Rigger — Aviation Pilot — Aviation Radioman

Baker, Cook — Metalsmith, Molder, Shipfitter — Boatswain's Mate, Coxswain — Boilermaker, Engineman, Machinist's Mate, Water Tender — Bugler

NAVY SPECIALTY MARKS

Some of the specialist badges worn by US Navy enlisted men, combined with chevrons in the case of petty officers, and worn alone by 'strikers' – on the right arm for members of the seaman branch such as gunners, quartermasters and signalmen; on the left for administrative, domestic and technical branches.

Seamen were supervised by boatswains' mates, who wore the rating badges on their right arms, and it was stated that each 'must first of all be a leader, as more military demands are made of them than any other rating.'[28] Augustus P Johnson found this difficult:

> There was a great barrier. You slept two feet apart, yet you had to give them orders. You wanted to be friends with them, but you couldn't. I was more friendly than some guys. I could go ashore with them, but being a Bosun's mate, you aren't liked that much.[29]

Ted Mason describes one example:

> We found ourselves at a table … presided over by a deeply tanned sailor who looked just as rough as boatswain's mates were supposed to. I figured that was his rate because he was wearing a bosun's pipe on a cord round his neck. … he was regular navy through and through.[30]

There was no real equivalent of the three-badge AB in the American service, where people were generally more ambitious, but Edward Stafford encountered a multi-talented man who refused promotion: 'he had made an early decision to remain a seaman second for the duration. It made for a simple, relaxing life, he said, and with no responsibility there was nothing he could be blamed for and a minimum of trouble.'

US Navy Class A schools were 'those designed to assist the forces afloat by giving such elementary instruction to recruits as will make them more immediately useful and give them the groundwork necessary for the lowest petty officer ratings.'[31] The aim of the training was that each man should be able to perform the basic functions of his speciality, to understand his part in the task, and be capable of absorbing further training. Schools were not expected to teach too much theory. 'For example, the man trained in the class A school for electricians' mates will need to be an intelligent learner of his rating, but the few weeks he spends in the school should not be spent upon theory he will not need until he reaches his first-class rating'.

Floyd Beaver found a very different world:

> Our routine was completely different from that in boot camp. We no longer marched at all, not even in parades, and inspections were few. We ate in the same mess hall with the boots, but we no longer wore leggings and we had two thin white stripes on the cuffs and a white braid around our right sleeves at the shoulder. We were officially seamen second class …[32]

Alvin Kernan found the aviation ordnanceman course surprisingly easy:

> … a few simple facts about electricity and some rudimentary circuits, learning the difference between one type of bomb rack and another, some information about various explosives and the fuses used to ignite them, how to break down, clean, and adjust machine guns, pistols, rifles. …
>
> For someone with a good memory and a feel for simple systems, it was all ridiculously easy, but for others, I learned, it was a slow drudgery, involving sitting up in the heads all night to try to get the facts down for one of the dreaded weekly exams. Many flunked out, but most passed …[33]

Successful trainees left the school wearing the badge of the branch, but not the white eagle or 'crow' and red chevrons of the petty officer. They were 'strikers', or apprentices who would learn the trade on the job before further promotion. 'Ordnancemen worked in pairs: an experienced petty officer and a striker … learning the ropes,'[34] Ted Mason was told by his instructor:

> In case you haven't guessed, … a striker is the lowest form of life in a radio gang. Your duty is to make coffee. You wake up the watch standers. You run messages. And you do mess-cook duty. If you have any time left over, you might get a shot at the code machine.[35]

A quartermaster needed high scores in the tests, along with 20/20 vision, good memory and leadership. He was preferably a high-school graduate with a knowledge of mathematics, for he was expected to assist the navigation of a large or medium ship, and even carry out most of the navigation of a PT boat. Edward Stafford was surprised that the quartermaster of a destroyer escort did not know how to 'double the angle on the bow; … this elementary exercise in piloting.'[36] During the Pearl Harbor attack, Chief Quartermaster Robert Sedberry was on the bridge of *Nevada* with a junior officer and played a key part in getting the ship clear of the doomed *Arizona*: '[Lieutenant] Ruff gave the order "hard left rudder" when while backing should have been the opposite so as to swing the bow to port. Sedberry said "Did you say hard RIGHT rudder, Sir." Ruff responded by giving the correct order and then said "Thank you, Chief."'[37] Roger Bond became a quartermaster striker in *Saratoga* after an interview with the navigator, part of a team of eight which kept charts up to date in harbour. At sea, 'A quartermaster always steered when the ship was at general quarters, flight quarters, or special sea detail.' When he subtly questioned an order from the captain, he was congratulated: 'I really appreciate the fact that the quartermaster is thinking with me, and is thinking ahead'.[38]

A radarman was also a high-school graduate with above-average scores, at least twenty-two years old, with a clear speaking voice and the ability to remain alert during long periods of inactivity. The radio technician needed even higher scores, along with manual dexterity and interest in studying. He was aged from seventeen to forty and would undergo a total of forty weeks' training. Musical experience, for example in a band or glee club, or playing an instrument, was desirable in a sonarman, who would have to distinguish changing notes of echoes. Houston Jones had expected to be trained as a yeoman and was surprised when an officer in boot camp told him that tests showed he had a 'musical ear' and was to become a sonarman or 'ping jockey'.[39]

A watertender had a responsible job in ensuring that the ship's boilers were kept efficient and safe. His test marks were only average, but he should be at least twenty-five, capable of leadership and calmness under stress. The ordinary routine was 'very boring', according to Thomas Hair: 'Standing watch in the fire room for four hours, watching the burners and oilers. You were watching the gauges to be sure of maintaining steady steam pressure. Other than that, cleaning up and stuff like that.' But things could change in action: 'You are down there in the fire room and bells are ringing because you are always changing speeds. You are lighting off boilers and cutting them out, operating the safeties, etc., so you are pretty well occupied with what you are doing.'[40] The penalties for failure were severe: 'the ship suddenly lost all power. It was restored in time to avoid drifting onto the rocks, but we had, all hands agreed, a very close call. … Apparently, a Watertender had failed to keep the feedwater at the proper level in his glass.'[41] A 36-year-old resented Watertender Cromie for being 'young, lazy, and in charge', but came to respect him more when 'One night when everything seemed normal, Cromie suddenly leaped up and flew around like crazy, turning valves off and on, jumping over steam lines, and yelling to the other men. The pumps had lost suction, and no-one had noticed it quick enough to react.'[42]

A yeoman, known as a 'yogi' or 'feathers', after his badge, ought to have touch-typing skills, which was no problem for Orvill Raines as a former newspaper reporter. He needed a 'capacity for detailed work.' Shore patrol specialists did not need such high marks, but had to be at least twenty-five and of good personal appearance. They ought to be in excellent physical condition, above-average strength, medium to tall, and 'well proportioned'. A laundryman did not need high scores and he would supervise washing and pressing. The highest rate available to him was seaman first class, though he could strike for rates in other branches.

In peacetime, a Royal Navy seaman who passed his examinations for leading seaman might wait several years for a vacancy. It conferred little real authority, but the man was expected to keep order in his messdeck: 'the leading seamen have a difficult job. They find themselves in charge of men older than themselves, some of whom endeavour to trip them up.' Many men preferred to become 'three-badge' ABs, proud of the service stripes awarded after three, eight and thirteen years. They were described by Nicholas Monsarrat:

> ... either he hasn't the brain and energy to pass for Leading Seaman, or he doesn't welcome responsibility, or he 'likes it where he is', or for any other reason ... He may sound dull and stupid but he is rarely that; more often than not he knows it all ...[43]

Ambitious men rose from leading seaman to petty officer, with a greater pay differential and living in a separate mess. After a year, they would change to the 'fore and aft uniform' with peaked cap and collar and tie. Eventually they could advance to chief petty officer, the highest ratings on the lower deck. A report of 1935 explained the difference between officers and petty officers. The latter:

> has little superiority of education, he lives among and on the same scale as the men and comes from the same social class. Some Petty Officers are born leaders, but many may be said to maintain their position by the authority conferred on them by the Naval Discipline Act and by their superior knowledge of the equipment of the ship and of the work of the Seaman ...

They might take command of a gun or turret in peacetime, but 'the stress of action requires the reserve of leadership and the higher moral qualities of the officer immediately things go wrong.'[44]

Expansion created a much greater demand and promotion came much faster, which created other problems. Even in 1938, officers joining HMS *Hood* were warned: 'Do not expect too much of your Petty Officers. We cannot expect that their standard shall be a very level one; large numbers are being made up and many are of very limited experience.' Fast-tracking promising men was not popular: 'It is well known that ... Trade Unionism and an innate fidelity to their own kind limit their aim to one of general security, i.e. equal opportunity to rise steadily on a pay scale.'

George Melly liked his petty officers:

Long association with the sea and its ports had given them a certain tolerant sophistication, part cynical but certainly affectionately so. They had learnt to mistrust the moral imperatives of any one place because they had seen them replaced by others, often equally rigid and ridiculous, elsewhere. They made allowances too for us temporary sailors. We were there because we had to be. One day the war would be over and the Navy its old self; a machine for sailing in.[45]

Some of the engineering categories were exceptions to the rule that technical skill did not necessarily bring a high rating. The most prominent were the engine room artificers, who served apprenticeships in various trades, inside or outside the navy, and were awarded the rating of chief petty officer when fully qualified. They were supplemented by mechanicians, who were selected from promising stokers and trained to the same standard; and in wartime by engine room mechanics who had a shorter training and were expected to 'dilute' the ranks of the artificers.

Captain Oram of the cruiser *Hawkins* commented:

The Jolly Jack of peacetime was a rare bird indeed, so rare that one was tempted to pipe a tear of affection for the breed, now a practically extinct prototype. The wartime sailor, faithfully modelling himself upon his glamorous predecessor, was conscious of the ready-made aura which attached to his own interpretation of the part. ... The model set for them to follow was good and by his exacting standards we were able to run our complicated machines on a very weak mixture of RN spirit![46]

Petty officers

In no case were the two navies more divided by a common language than in the role of petty officers. It is often difficult to find an equivalence of non-commissioned rates and ranks between different countries, but one might note that an American petty officer first class corresponded to an army technical sergeant, the senior NCO of an infantry platoon and therefore equivalent to a British army sergeant, who was equal to a Royal Navy petty officer. The American petty officer first class did not have the privileges of a peaked cap and collar and tie or a separate mess, but in other respects he was roughly equal to the Royal Navy petty officer. Therefore a petty officer second class might be equated with a leading seaman, and a third class with an able seaman holding a non-substantive rate.

It was stated that a petty officer must be, first, a leader, and second, a specialist. Many petty officers in the US Navy were described in traditional fashion as 'mates' or assistants to certain warrant officers, who were not always present in the ship or station concerned. These included relatively modern rates, such as photographer's mate and aerographer's mate. The term 'rating' was also used differently. A man who succeeded in his examination would get the rating, for example, of gunner's mate third class and became a 'rated man'. But potential midshipmen were warned: 'Note the confusing terminology: a man holds a rating of seaman 2c, but when he holds that rating he is a "non-rated" man; petty officers are often referred to as "ratings".'[47]

Ted Mason was pleased to reach the first rung: 'Having worked very hard, we had passed the first and most critical test to receive the first reward: the silver eagle, stylised lightning bolts, and single red chevron of radiomen third class. That was an event worthy of celebration.'[48]

In 1945 a detailed programme for 'enlisted advancement' was prescribed, involving planning by the ship's training officer, practical and classroom training aboard ship and, finally, examination of a board of three officers.[49] In fact, 'Promotion was easy too in an expanding navy. Ratings were now given away with the stroke of a yeoman's typewriter, to the disgust of the old-timers who had often waited years for promotion.' Kernan's chief petty officer promised him promotion if he carried out an unpleasant task: 'I thought he was joking, but I did it anyway, and the next week the squadron orders listed my name and the new rating of ordnanceman second class.'[50] Presumably the chief had influence with the officers. Beaver recorded: 'I don't remember being especially elated at the news of my promotion. Promotions were so readily available during the war they had lost much of their meaning.'[51]

Ted Mason described the difficulties of those on the lowest level of authority in all armed forces. In *Pawnee*, the first class petty officers were allowed to mess with the chiefs, leaving the second class in charge of the messes:

> We bunked in the crew's compartments and had to share head and mess facilities with the seamen and firemen. The perceptive observation that 'familiarity breeds contempt' applied with special force in the confined quarters of a navy ship. Required to give orders to men who knew them too well, the seconds often had the hard choice of enforcing discipline through channels, with the report, or unofficially with their fists.[52]

Tribal divisions were to be found in all large ships:

The deck divisions considered the radio gang effete (they would have used a different word) and sneeringly referred to us as radio girls. Confident of our superior skills and education we in turn thought the members of the six line divisions gross and stupid, and called them deck apes.[53]

At the top of the enlisted scale was the chief petty officer. More perhaps than in the Royal Navy, he was 'a man apart', the only grade of enlisted man (apart from the lowly stewards) with a peaked cap and collar and tie, and separate quarters. They were quite clear about their status: '"Don't call me sir, Mason. I'm not an officer." His tone left no doubt that he was devoutly pleased about that.'[54]

Officers were always aware of the importance of chiefs: 'There is an oft-quoted saying that it is the chiefs who run the Navy, and it is true that they provide the day-to-day, man-to-man leadership, along the lines established by the Captain and implemented by his officers'.[55] The image of a grizzled veteran is not entirely untrue, but Alvin Kernan was promoted in 1945 after five years' service: 'Despite my young age, by seniority roles my appointment to chief petty officer was long overdue, and I decided, since I would be leaving the service shortly, to push for the appointment before discharge.'[56] Floyd Beaver was promoted for exceptional bravery (which he always denied) and became a 'slick arm chief' – 'one who has been promoted before he has been in the Navy long enough to have a hash mark on his sleeve.'[57]

Every new chief petty officer was given a clothing allowance of three hundred dollars to buy a uniform: 'My blues were resplendent with eight shiny brass buttons, silver embroidered crow, scarlet chevrons, and hash mark'.[58] But a chief was appointed temporarily for the first year and could still 'lose his buttons', and revert to the 'low necked gown' of the seaman.

In the attack transport *Florence Nightingale* Floyd Beaver found:

The chiefs' quarters, however, were comfortable. The mess itself was on the main deck at the forward end of the superstructure. It was large and well, if simply appointed, with a permanent table fitted with a soft rubber cloth and wooden fiddles to keep dishes from sliding off in rough weather. There were individual chairs for eating and leather benches along the bulkheads for lounging and off-watch socializing. Large opening ports in the forward bulkhead made it pleasantly light and airy in good weather …[59]

They had their own customs and practices:

Meanwhile, our chief petty officers were demonstrating their own brand of shipboard savoir-faire, one honed by long Navy service. The *Pawnee* was lacking a few articles they considered necessary for her efficient operation. They sortied for a 'midnight requisition' at the San Diego Destroyer Base. By some means they appropriated two ladders, miscellaneous tools and a bicycle …[60]

The doyen of the chiefs was the master-at-arms, the senior enlisted man in the ship and responsible for its discipline:

Murphy was so tough, according to legend, that he chewed up stanchions and spat out iron filings. He had been sent to the *California* as chief master-at-arms to clean up the ship's petty loansharking, gambling, and laundry and liquor rackets.

As number one enlisted man in the ship, Murphy lived in lordly splendour in his own stateroom, near the bow on the main deck.[61]

Messdecks

The messdeck, where Royal Navy ratings ate, slept and had their recreation was at the centre of the naval rating's life. On a typical destroyer:

At most, the mess deck was about 70 feet long – the length of the ship was only 300 feet. The widest place in the ship was only 27 feet. The mess deck was not at the widest place and One Mess was not at the widest part of the mess deck. It would be the only place where they could eat, sleep, read, and write, and stow their gear. It would not be comfortable.[62]

Hammock hooks or bars were fitted from the deck above, 21in apart and 10ft 6in long, to allow room for the ropes, or nettles, from which each hung. New seamen were instructed:

Sling the hammock between two hammock bars by passing the lanyard over the bar, back through its own ring and form a sheet bend over the nettles. Then distribute the bedding evenly over the length of the hammock and tauten up the slack nettles if necessary. To keep the head of the hammock apart a stretcher can be used, but this is optional. It consists of a length of wood two feet in length with a V cut at both ends.

In the daytime the hammocks were stowed in racks. With wartime overcrowding, it was not always possible for a man to find space for his hammock.

The messdeck of a British destroyer in 1940, showing the crew during their limited leisure time, and the typical overcrowding. A few hammocks are slung above, personal belongings are stored in cases to the left, and the men in the foreground are engaged in reading, 'uckers', or ludo, and card-playing.

British officers noted that American-style bunks led to increased weight, and made access more difficult for damage control purposes, but recognised their advantages. A hammock needed 10ft to sling it, a bunk needed only 6ft, and could be in three or four tiers instead of one.[63]

The long-established serving of the crew's rum was an essential feature of lower deck culture. It was issued to the leading hand of the mess and brought down below to accompany a meal. Each man was supposed to drink his own 'tot', but it was a kind of currency in the messdecks. A small favour would be rewarded by 'sippers', a larger one by 'gulpers', and an exceptional debt might be paid by 'downers' or 'grounders', in which a whole tot was given up. John Whelan's messmates were shocked when a group of CWs began to drink them one sip at a time. "'Knock them blasted tots back," growled guns, "The messdeck's taking on the atmosphere of a blasted cocktail party.'"[64] Sailors were allowed to decline the tot for a small payment.

Smaller ships used the antiquated standard ration and messing allowance system. Each mess provided two 'cooks' in rotation, who actually had to prepare food, rather than just fetch it. Most received no training for this, though at HMS *Ganges* they were given a booklet:

> The mess caterer will decide what the mess will have to eat. You, when cook of the mess, will prepare the food – on the mess table

– and take it to the galley to be cooked – after which you will hear what your messmates think about it as a MEAL.

They were recommended to learn how to make pastry and dumplings, and prepare different kinds of vegetables, using simple recipes such as cottage pie, apple dumplings and suet puddings.[65]

There was a strong hidden economy on the messdecks, as some men paid others for tailoring, barbering, laundry and so on. Cliff Smith asked his messman why he had never gone for promotion: 'He told me he could make more money with his dhobying [washing] firm and barbering, not forgetting his "Crown and Anchor" board circuit (strictly illegal) more than any chief petty officer's earning inboard.'[66]

Doctors complained that the overheated and under-ventilated atmosphere of the messdeck was unhealthy. According to the surgeon of a frigate the men had:

> ... unhealthy disrespect, that seems to be traditional among seamen, for fresh air on the mess decks. Punkah louvres were often closed, flaps closed down over exhaust trunks although the latter was justified to some extent as some cases are on record where considerable quantities of ocean found their way to the mess decks via these passages.[67]

But the seaman got plenty of fresh air on deck; coming down from a cold, wet watch he wanted to dry and warm himself as quickly as possible in his limited off-duty hours.

Swearing was extremely common on the lower deck and was noticed by CW candidates. John Wilson felt it was almost poetic in its strange way. It was easy to be caught up in this:

> Language deteriorated quickly. An anxiety to appear as street-wise as the next man frequently turned what should have been everyday conversation into obscene nonsense. Sanity slowly regained control over insecurity but the vocabulary of the vast majority underwent a profound change and the few who resisted the trend were regarded with suspicion.[68]

Messdeck culture tended to produce disregard for danger. No sailor would show fear in front of his messmates, which was a key factor in British naval success. A report of December 1942 summed up his attitude: 'I am a British Sailor. The British Sailor has always been the best seaman, the finest fighter, the hero of the people. Therefore, I am a hero.'[69]

Bunks and canteens

Living conditions were generally superior in the US Navy. As early as December 1918 it was noted:

> ... It is indisputable ... that the living conditions of the crews of the US ships are above comparison with those which obtain in the British Service ... It is considered that we have nothing to learn from anyone in the question of sanitation, cleanliness, ventilation, or in the installation of what are in most services conceived to be luxuries for the men. ... British ships are notoriously too cold for the comfort of men brought up in American homes. They are likewise poorly ventilated by comparison with our standards. They do not go in for laundries and other labor saving devices such as a motor driven dough mixer, potato peelers, etc ... Now, whereas the average British sailor is not used to these refinements at home and does not miss them, our men are so accustomed to them that their removal would work a serious hardship and militate against efficiency.[70]

Differences between the two navies increased during the 1930s as the US Navy began to replace the traditional hammock with bunks in three or four tiers:

> Our bunks were just large enough to lie on and were covered with a fitted sheet, a regular sheet and a wool blanket. The bunks were held by chains and separated by two steel posts to which they were

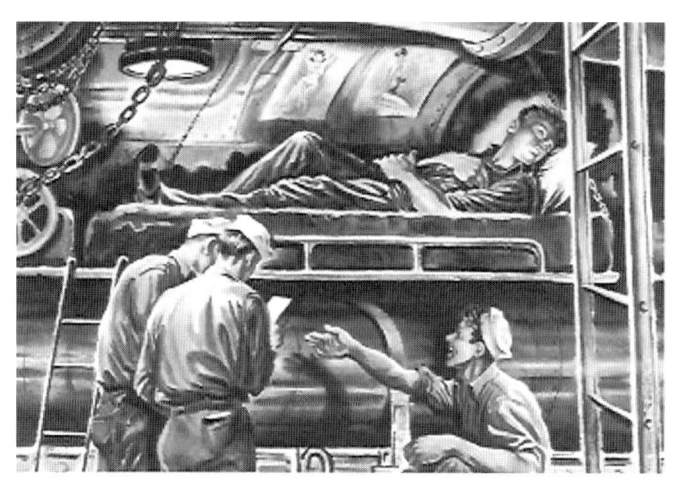

Crew accommodation in an American submarine showing a typical bunk above a torpedo, and pin-ups. The seamen in the foreground are reading a letter from home.

fastened. When you were out of the bunk, it was folded upward to the post and fastened to give you more room. When they were unfastened, you were only inches away from another sailor.[71]

The hammock did not disappear instantly, Commander Parry of the Royal Navy reported on the old *Colorado*-class battleships in 1941: 'The ship's company sling in hammocks, which by day are stowed in large linen bags thrown in nettings all along the messdeck ship's side bulkheads.' The *Bluejacket's Manual* devoted two pages to its care until 1946, but few of the wartime sailors slept in one. Alvin Kernan was an exception onboard *Enterprise*, when surplus crew had to sling theirs in the mess hall – very inconvenient as it was in use all day.[72]

US Navy policy was to disperse men on different trades round the ship, very different from Royal Navy practice.

> … the various gangs in the ship split apart so that no one speciality all slept in the same compartment. This was rationalized on the grounds that a single bomb or torpedo might destroy an entire speciality. Signalmen slept with machinists, deck apes, electricians, or whatever other odd life forms might surface at the moment. The effect of this policy was to destroy the old family identification of men who lived and worked and ate together.[73]

Instead men grouped together round the coffee pot:

> The forward engine room coffee pot was by the throttle board. It was handmade by George Abner Stoneham from Rose Bud, Texas. Instead of electricity, it used live steam and small coils for heat. … Everyone drank lots of coffee. Each man had a cup and as soon as he came on watch it was always kept full by the messenger of the watch, and a new pot was made for the men coming on watch.[74]

Coffee was as important to the American sailor as tea was to his British counterpart. 'If we had run out of coffee, the exec would have been visited by a delegation of angry petty officers, in defiance of regulations. Fortunately for moral and good order, we never did.'[75]

A constant complaint was that bunks became hot and stuffy: 'It is hard to breathe and you would wake up in a pool of sweat. Some of the men sweat so much in their bunks that they could not stand up, they were sick and dizzy from heat and sweating'.[76] But Orvill Raines had to admit that it was better than being a marine or soldier ashore:

> We have it so much better than the Army or Marines on those blasted islands. My bed is clean and most important of all, I *have* a bed instead of the ground. I can 'come in' out of the rain and a lot of other conveniences are to be had by us on ships.[77]

Toilet facilities were not luxurious, especially on destroyers. On *Dale* in 1942:

> Where the officers had individual stalls, enlisted men had a long wooden plank, with half a dozen round holes spaced a few inches apart from each other. Beneath that plank was a long meal trough with a continuous flow of seawater running through it. We lined up on that plank for our morning dump, which then flowed down the trough and out to sea.

Perhaps swearing was far less common on the decks of American ships – at least it is rarely recorded by the writers of letters and memoirs. But perhaps that is because the American ships did not have the CW candidates whose sensitive middle-class ears were impressed by it. From the Marines, William Rogal recorded, 'We all spoke the same language – foul. In fact if the "F word" hadn't been invented we would have been almost tongue-tied.'[78] Another source claimed:

> Submariners were profane. Swearing was a custom that had been honed to a fine art over their years of service by the chiefs, senior petty officers who could flavour the English language by inserting swear words to give it rhythm and spice. Young submariners stumbled through speaking with synthetic profanity as they tried to emulate the old salts.[79]

Floyd Beaver described the old-style messing which survived in some ships:

> The signalmen's mess in the *Indianapolis,* for example, was two tables set in a recess on the port side forward of number two mess hall. This allowed us to be set off from the main body of slurpers and grunters, and we had two nice big portholes that could be left open in good weather to let in pleasant light and air.[80]

Each division's mess was ruled by its senior petty officer. This man determined the character of the conversation and the general demeanour of the mess. Some of these were strict, some not. The tables were set up and the food bought from the galley by men known as mess cooks. They were not cooks at all, but did all the work of waiters and busboys in shoreside restaurants.

A Royal Navy surgeon-captain reported on the US Navy's modern feeding arrangement:

> Enlisted men in all US ships are fed on the cafeteria system. This entails a centrally placed galley to which is attached a large servery.

At meal-times men queue up to form a chow-line, and as they approach the serve each man picks up a metal tray, compartmented into six irregular divisions. He also gathers a knife, fork and spoon and a porcelain mug. At the servery six stewards serve the six main components of the meal directly onto the tray and the man's mug is filled with coffee. He then carries his rations to any mess table he chooses. In this way he may sit down at a different place each meal and seamen, firemen, radiomen and signalmen, etc, may all mess together.

Queuing [ie standing in line], it was claimed, led to some delays. 'After the meal each man scraped his leavings into a bucket and then it was rinsed and put into an "Instone automatic dishwasher", which was unknown to the British at the time.

Cafeteria-style dining was not always successful and Floyd Beaver complained:

> The *Chester* had already been converted to cafeteria-style feeding. Instead of clean tables, set and waiting for us when we came off watch, we had to stand in line for our meals and to eat them off cold aluminium trays with table mates we might or might not know. We even had to carry our own trays to the scullery, for Christ's sake. Cafeteria-style was undoubtedly more efficient in getting food into sailors' stomachs, but it was a damn poor way for a man to eat.[81]

Orvill Raines was not impressed with the quality of the food:

> Honey, the meals here are edible but that's about all. Occasionally we have chow that would make a real meal but it's never cooked satisfactorily. We have had steaks a few times but they are too rare and underseasoned. … Boy the Navy would be in a hell of a shape if it weren't for spuds. … The tables we eat from reach arm-pit level almost and consuming the food is purely a matter of 'scooping it in'.[82]

To Ted Mason:

> Our food was as predictably bad as the weather. Nearly everything came out of a can or carton: spam and chipped beef, anaemic small peas, clingstone peaches, sour grapefruit juice. The eggs, milk and potatoes all were powdered. The Rice Krispies in their individual-serving boxes were stale and tasteless. Occasionally we received a side of frozen 'ox-meat' from Australia or New Zealand. Once it may have been beef. By the time the cook had finished with it, the resemblance to roasted shoe leather was unmistakeable.[83]

In 1941 a *Brooklyn*-class cruiser had sixteen men devoted to 'ship's service' – three barbers in a well-equipped shop, four in the soda fountain, which was a combined canteen and bookstall and could take up to 80 gallons of ice cream, two tailors, a cobbler, and four or five in the laundry which was 'fully equipped for pressing and starching work.' Two men operated the cash register when men bought tickets for these services, and the accounts took up a good deal of a lieutenant's time. They had the advantage that standard of cleanliness of clothes was more certain, and that services such as haircuts did not have to wait until the barber came off watch.

There was less need for hidden economy. If a sailor wanted a better class of uniform he might buy one ashore, as Alvin Kernan did when in funds – 'a highly fitted gabardine dress blue uniform: bell bottoms, zipper up the side of the skin-tight blouse, a dragon sewn in gold and green thread in the satin lining inside the front flap of the pants secured with thirteen buttons.' Wearing this on home leave he found 'Girls who would never speak to me before were now willing to dally and to charm.'[84]

Gambling was a partial substitute for the hidden economy. It was 'a way of life in the navy, and everything we did was made more interesting by wagering on it.' Fahey describes the 'anchor pool' by which men bet on the exact time of the ship arriving: 'We dropped anchor at 2.01 PM. I should know the time because I won $250 in the anchor pool. The ship moved very slowly as it came alongside the pier but just slowly enough for me to win.'[85]

Cleanliness was easier in larger ships like the *Lexington*:

> … the washrooms themselves were a jolt. Carrier sailors apparently had never heard of water hours. We could take showers any time we liked. The wash-room decks were often ankle deep in soapy oil-and-dirt-streaked water that rushed from side to side with the rolling of the ship and sometimes slopped over into the passageway outside.[86]

The sailors had their code of honour as much as the officers:

> What the enlisted men in fact evolved (and many former navy officers may be wholly unaware of it) was a code of conduct, a rough-and-ready approximation of the honor code of the military academies. I will not lie, cheat or steal; and I will not tolerate anyone who does. … The code, however, only applied to navy personnel in general and one's shipmates in particular; it was not extended to civilians.[87]

Race

The basic premise of the British Empire was racial, in that it involved white people ruling over indigenous peoples, but there were comparatively few black and Asian residents in the United Kingdom at the time, so it was not a great issue in the navy. But Churchill, despite his later reputation as a racist, was surprisingly liberal in 1939 when he wrote, 'I cannot see any objection to Indians serving in HM ships where they are qualified and needed, or, if their virtues so deserve, rising to be Admirals of the Fleet. But not too many of them, please.'[88] But the country was not free of prejudice.

In the United States the problem was much more immediate, with African-Americans making up about 10 per cent of the population, with the legacy of slavery still predominant, and with strict and formal segregation in the southern states, and less formal prejudice in other parts of the country.

Black sailors had served well in quite small numbers in the old navy, but recruitment of them was stopped in 1919. It was reopened in 1932, but only for messmen, the traditional role of servant to the officers. Even then many officers preferred Filipinos, and certainly not northern blacks, who were 'apt to be independent, insolent and over-educated, according to one officer.'[89] Ted Mason thought it was reasonable:

> The negroes or 'coloreds' … were considered equally fortunate to be accepted in the navy, where they had status equivalent to Pullman porters or waiters in private clubs or the better restaurants … most of them were limited to being boot blacks, house servants or sharecroppers.
>
> Most of the crew (and I am sure, the officers too) accepted the proposition that negroes were inferior in certain ways.[90]

Thomas Allen was a messman in the carrier *Yorktown*: 'I served in the wardroom and cleaned the staterooms – but most of the time as the steward [a supervisor]. … I learned the art of how to talk and listen at the same time. The officers would talk amongst themselves … but we had big ears.'[91]

The Selective Service and Training Act of 1940 was ostensibly unprejudiced, decreeing that 'in a free society the obligations and privileges of military training and service should be shared generally', and that 'any person, regardless of race or color, … shall be afforded an opportunity to volunteer for induction into the land and naval forces of the United States'. But that would be difficult to apply in the circumstances of the time. Roosevelt would have liked to do something about segregation, and his wife certainly would, but he was dependent on southern votes in Congress. Moreover, it would be impossible to apply segregation in the grossly overcrowded conditions of a wartime ship, but integration would affect morale, to say the least:

> ... it was not possible to provide separate quarters for the officers' cooks and steward's mates in a ship as small and congested as the *Pawnee*. They were lodged in a cul-de-sac formed by the ladder up to the main deck, the forward transverse bulkhead, and the portside shell plating. A bank of lockers provided for the further isolation of these third-class Navy citizens, who were virtually ignored by the rest of the crew.[92]

And there would be a further problem when a black petty officer was placed over a white seaman.

Frederick Peterson thought he had enlisted for training at Great Lakes, which meant he would be one of the first African-Americans in general service. 'But six of us black recruits were put on the train to Norfolk. We were going to Unit X ... and we found that MA didn't mean "master-at-arms"; it meant mess attendant.' The navy tried to augment their status with the title of 'steward's mates', but that did not impress the recruits, who felt they had been deceived and made sure they were discharged from boot camp.[93]

Roosevelt decided not to try to remedy the situation 'at one fell swoop'. The General Board was asked to look at it, but concluded: 'It is but part and parcel of similar discrimination throughout the United States', and recommended recruitment only to the messman branch.

On the other side, the National Association for the Advancement of Colored People pressed for change. As a compromise, it was suggested that African-Americans might serve in construction battalions, either in all-black stevedore units or as unskilled labour under white craftsmen; in shore bases where there was room for separate accommodation; and if it was necessary to let them serve afloat, in yard craft and coastal vessels.

Joseph Small finished his training at Great Lakes in 1943 and was drafted to an ammunition depot at Port Chicago, California: 'Everybody above petty officer was white. All of the munition handlers were black. We off-loaded ammunition from boxcars and loaded it onto ships.' There was a huge explosion in which 320 sailors were killed, and Small was one of fifty men court-martialled for a mutinous gathering and sentenced to fifteen years' hard labour, which was later commuted after protests.[94]

The army solved the problem by having all-black units mostly under white officers, but a naval ship needed a whole array of specialists, and there was no pool of African-American petty officers and technicians to get them from; and recruits tended to score far lower than whites in tests due to poorer education, so far fewer of them were sent to Class A schools, which were in themselves segregated. Only two ships, the destroyer escort

Some of the crew of USS *Mason*, one of only two ships manned with a mainly African-American crew, but with mostly white officers, including Lieutenant Commander William M Blackford, the captain, shown in the centre. The ship is being commissioned at Boston in driving snow.

Mason and the subchaser *PC-1264*, were commissioned with largely African-American crews, still under white officers. By June 1945 the navy had 165,000 enlisted African-Americans, of whom about 45 per cent were stewards' mates (as the messmen were renamed in 1943).[95]

In 1945 BuPers issued the relatively liberal *Guide to the Command of Negro Personnel*. It stated: 'The Navy accepts no theories of racial differences in inborn ability, but expects that every man wearing its uniform be trained and used in accordance with his maximum individual capacity determined on the basis of individual performance.' It was aware of African-American sensitivities, using the vocabulary of the time:

> Negroes prefer to be referred to in their individual capacities as Americans without racial designation. The word 'nigger' is especially hated and it has no place in the Naval vocabulary. Negroes are suspicious that the pronunciation of the word Negro as though it were spelled 'Nigra' may be a sort of genteel compromise between the hated word 'nigger' and the preferred term 'Negro'. The terms 'boy', 'darkey', 'coon', 'jig', 'uncle', 'Negress' and 'your people' are also resented. If it is necessary to refer to racial origin, 'Negro' and 'colored' are the only proper words to use.[96]

* * *

There is no doubt about which navy was the most advanced in its treatment of non-commissioned personnel. The Second Sea Lord and his department which was responsible for personnel policy in the Royal Navy was less effective than its equivalent, the Bureau of Personnel, for its head was perhaps more involved in general Admiralty affairs than the detail of administration, and his staff had a far higher proportion of civil servants rather than naval officers. The individual branches, such as gunnery and torpedo, were responsible for the personnel in their own departments, hence the over-complicated system of ratings.

Any naval reform is difficult to force through against the innate conservatism of the profession, ratings as well as officers. This was equally true in the US Navy, where the old-timers sneered at the 'Goddam gedunk sailors' of the new navy. Buy BuPers was able to reform the practices in many ways.

For some time after the war, the Royal Navy authorities denied that bunks and cafeteria messing had any advantages – the bunks themselves were costly and added to the weight, they did not move with the ship, and the use of them in American fashion would destroy mess life, the key to naval morale. But eventually they were forced to concede and bunks were standard in all naval ships from the mid 1950s.[97]

Though the US Navy had occasional events classified as mutinies, it was nothing like the level of the Royal Navy, and it is difficult to believe that any American admiral would have written that 'shooting to kill should only be resorted to as a last emergency.' The level of discontent discovered in the Royal Navy by Hannen Swaffer in 1945, though perhaps exaggerated for journalistic effect, was far higher than anything to be found in the US Navy:

> ... if hundreds of witnesses are to be believed, the Royal Navy is ridden with a caste system that has been abolished in our civilian life; its lower deck is ruled with a discipline that is out of date; and its traditions belong to that age of Squiredom when villagers bowed and curtsied if the landlord passed on his way.[98]

The Royal Navy fought through six years of intensive war in all sorts of climates, partly drawing on its traditions and prestige in the past to maintain morale, but it is not certain that it would have been able to do so had the Pacific war lasted much longer. The US Navy showed far fewer signs of strain in 1945 after nearly four years, though its combat experience was just as challenging. The more advanced personnel policies probably had an effect on that.

5

Non-combatants

EVEN IF their jobs and stations kept them well away from the battle zones, members of the armed forces were expected to be ready to fight. The exceptions were medical personnel and chaplains, who are forbidden from active fighting by the Geneva Conventions; and women, who were forbidden by the customs of the time.

Medicine in the navy

Naval medical officers no longer had to deal with diseases such as scurvy, and epidemics were far rarer than in the past. Indeed, Sir Sheldon Dudley, the Medical Director General of the Royal Navy from 1941, claimed that sailors were healthy enough while aboard ship, with strict hygiene, good food and water and adequate exercise, and it was only when they came ashore, especially in foreign parts, that they were subject to disease; though that optimistic view did not take account of wartime stresses such as excessive overcrowding, sickness in ships that were not designed for ocean conditions, extreme temperatures, and the general mental strains of possible action and separation from families. And the horrors of battle were a different question altogether. The naval doctor or surgeon, however, did have an unusual role. Onboard ship he had a practice consisting entirely of fit young men and he did not normally have to deal with the problems of children and the old, pregnancy, or specifically feminine complaints.

A potential sailor was likely to encounter naval medicine from the moment he tried to enter the navy, in the form of a strict examination. No navy could afford to take on potential health risks, especially if they were to be sent to sea for months at a time in ships with limited medical facilities:

> Ratings are given a preliminary examination at the many Naval Recruiting centres throughout the country, and are thoroughly investigated on arrival at their Depots. They are first seen by the Psychiatrist, by whom they are thoroughly investigated. This officer determines the wishes of the recruit as to the branch of Service he

has in mind, and recommends that he should or should not be accepted ...

The physical standard of the recruit is assessed by the Medical Officers of the Depot to which he has been sent ...[1]

Royal Naval medical services were headed by the Medical Director General of the Navy. From 1937 the post was held by Surgeon Vice Admiral Sir Percival Nicholls, who carried out his duties in an 'unflurried' manner until his retirement in 1941. His successor, Sir Sheldon Dudley, was born appropriately enough in naval sick quarters in 1884, the son of a naval surgeon. After graduating from St Thomas's Medical School in 1906, he joined the navy against his father's advice and he would serve thirty-nine years, twelve of them at sea. He wrote later, 'I would join the navy again as a doctor if I had my time over again. I have had a splendid life, playing, working and lazing all over the world, meeting all sorts and conditions of men, and being a member of the finest herd in the world, the Royal Navy.' He researched in diphtheria and epidemiology and as director general he set up the Naval Personnel Research Committee, besides overseeing the huge expansion of medical facilities during the war.[2]

Naval doctors were known as surgeons for historical reasons. Starting as surgeon lieutenant, in peacetime an officer was promoted to surgeon lieutenant commander after six years and surgeon commander after another six, with 44 per cent going on to surgeon captain, and with prospects of promotion to surgeon rear admiral as director of one of the main hospitals, and surgeon vice admiral and head of the service.

In the 1930s the government was worried about the status of medical officers in the services. According to an 'extreme view', which was nevertheless shared in many medical schools, 'that the life the services offer is an idle one, that the amount of professional work available is slight, that is average quality is poor and its scope limited.' The navy tended not to take responsibility for families, so a medical officer was not likely to treat women and children. Retirement was at fifty, too old to enter general practice but too young to become completely inactive.[3] Enough doctors were lured by the prospect of foreign travel, but the Admiralty always worried about quality.

All this changed in wartime. According to Dr R Ransome Wallis:

> Doctors in general practice were selected by a local medical committee as being able to be spared to join the Forces. This was usually by virtue of having a partner who could carry on the practice. ... Having been notified that I was expendable, I lost no time in volunteering for the Royal Navy ...[4]

In peacetime, a naval medical officer would have a very through training in preventative medicine and the treatment of casualties. There was no time for that in war; a temporary surgeon lieutenant RNVR would be given a few weeks of lectures in one of the naval hospitals at Chatham, Portsmouth or Plymouth. From 1943 he was issued with a booklet, *Notes for Medical Officers*, which said as much about naval etiquette as medicine. It concluded optimistically:

> You are at the beginning of a fine adventure and new experiences. No-one is 'behind the lines' in a ship nowadays, and you will share the risks and dangers equally with your brother officers and men. It is a great privilege. Strive to be worthy of it.[5]

The surgeon lieutenant of the River-class frigate *Aire* described his routine in a quiet period.

> ... First aid lectures have been given to all members of the gun's crews, and I hope shortly to start a refresher course. Health lectures were given to small groups of the ship's company at the start of the commission, and I have been extremely fortunate in the small number of infectious diseases that have occurred. Only about six cases of Scabies, Tinea Cruris, and Pediculosis all together. I have had one case of Venereal Disease, and he contracted Syphilis a short time ago and is expected back on board in about a month. ...
>
> It was found difficult to treat the minor infections that seem to be prevalent in warmer climates such as the Mediterranean Station, and lately the Levant Station, so a small amount of Sulphathiazole Emulsion was obtained ... This was found to be so successful that some more was obtained from the manufacturers[6]

The British military had seen the birth of modern nursing, when in the 1850s Florence Nightingale elevated the profession from notoriously negligent, drunken and unskilled practitioners, to well-educated and dedicated upper- and middle-class women. Each of the British services had a corps of nurses nominally under royal sponsorship – the Naval Nursing Service was formed in 1884 and in 1902 it was taken under the wing of Edward VIII's consort to become Queen Alexandra's Royal Naval Nursing Service or QARNNS. Its members were all fully-trained nurses, known as sisters, equivalent to a naval lieutenant. They were regarded as superior to staff nurses in civilian hospitals: 'it by no means follows that the sister who has been successful in civil hospital work will be equally successful in taking charge of a number of sick berth ratings.'[7] Under the rank structure which came into effect in 1942 they could be promoted to senior nursing sister, superintending sister, matron, principal matron and matron-in-chief, equivalent to a naval commodore. At the start of the war they had nurses' uniform for ward wear, and a greatcoat and tricorn hat, and a coat and skirt were introduced in 1942 to bring them into line with other services. It was quite a small corps, with eighty-five members and fifty-five reservists in August 1939, reaching a total of 1129 in service in April 1945; 327 had married or retired. Only two were killed by enemy action, but some suffered imprisonment with the fall of Hong Kong.

Miss J Woodgate knew very little about the service in 1938, 'but on the staff of my hospital, there was someone who had a niece in QARNNS, so I wrote to her for advice on what to bring. A nice friendly letter came back and she said to bring some safety pins and some wide black elastic – a mystery.' She discovered that the safety pins were needed for the apron and the black elastic for a belt. Miss J E Tinne had a matron who 'pulled strings' to get her accepted and in May 1941 she travelled to Portsmouth by train, in first class for the first time in her life. Once there, 'I loved the naval atmosphere but I had a lot to learn …'[8]

They worked in the main naval hospitals, where they were expected to do theatre work and to help train the numerous sick berth attendants and VADs coming through in wartime. A hospital ship had four to eight of them, according to its size, and they were eligible to serve in bases abroad.

Voluntary aid detachments, or VADs, were civilian women recruited from the first-aiders of the Order of St John of Jerusalem and the British Red Cross Society. They could be trained as nurses, cooks, clerks and dispensers in naval hospitals, mainly to free up sick berth attendants for other work. They could rise to the grade of head nursing member, or head cook or head clerk, the equivalent of a chef petty officer. More than five thousand of them were employed. They could be sent overseas, but unlike the sick berth attendants they could not be drafted to sea, except in hospital ships, so they tended to be more settled in their jobs. Mona Stanton reported:

> My colleagues had come from all walks of life. There were office workers, typists, telephonists, housemaids, shop assistants, and dancers, and many of the British gentry also joined up as nurses. … I was lucky as I had learned first aid in the Girl Guides and had a fortnight pressure-cooker course given by the Red Cross in London. … even though we did not have the theory, we became very efficient practical nurses, and we did the work of nurses who had trained for many years to pass exams.[9]

Sick berth attendants were the principal ratings of the medical branch. They might fulfil a wide range of duties, from hospital orderly to what would now be called a paramedic. They were trained in the naval hospitals, where the nursing sisters often made an impression. Eric Alleson was one of twenty at Haslar taught by 'Rectum Rosie', so-called because of her constant reference to the alimentary canal. A J E McCreedy's sister tutor was 'the fastest bed-maker I have ever seen'.[10]

SBAs wore the 'fore and aft' uniform of the domestic and administrative branches, with peaked cap and collar and tie, and a red cross on a white background on the right arm. They could rise through the normal ratings of leading hand, petty officer and chief, and a warrant officer was known as a wardmaster.

Medical officers were told: 'The relationship between you and your Sick Berth staff is of course primarily that between any Officer and any rating, but there is also the normal relationship between a doctor and a nurse. In addition your Sick Berth rating is, in a sense, your confidential clerk or secretary'.[11] On hospital work, one petty officer reported: 'As duty PO in the hospital you have a lot of responsibility being in charge of about 4 leading hands and 12 SBAs.'[12] In the hospital ship *Maine*, R Sebbage commented: 'Below decks our work in the Wards was much the same as the daily routine in any Naval Shore Hospital, except for the steady rise and fall of the vessel as she ploughed towards Malta which made the use of surgical trolleys an acrobatic act.'[13]

Ships such as corvettes had no doctor and the SBA was an important figure:

> In small ships where no medical officer is borne, the Sick Berth Rating has a great responsibility and a high privilege … that of the care of the sick and wounded. He should conduct himself with dignity, having in mind that his general bearing and ability will decide the degree of confidence that both officers and ratings will repose in him.[14]

Naval hospitals and sick quarters

Each of the main home bases had its hospital. Stonehouse at Plymouth and Haslar at Portsmouth had been built in the 1750s, Chatham was more modern and dated from 1905. In peacetime, they serviced the naval population of the base and in 1940 they took in casualties from actions in the English Channel, including those from *Lancastria*, sunk off St-Nazaire in June, and they supplemented the local hospitals in dealing with air-raid victims. Haslar received casualties from the Dieppe raid in 1942, and from the Normandy invasion. According to one nurse, 'The patients were brought back from France in returning Tank Landing Craft so they arrived in large batches. Some of them still had sand in their clothes.'[15] However, in general they served as clearing stations for patients who transferred elsewhere for long-term treatment. All were heavily involved in training medical staff at different levels. Stonehouse treated more than sixty thousand patients during the war, Haslar more than eighty-three thousand and Chatham eighty-six thousand.

Chatham was regarded as particularly vulnerable to air raids in the early stages when the main threat was from the east, but in fact no bombs fell within its boundaries. Haslar was on a peninsula across the harbour from the town and dockyard, and suffered only minimal damage, though numerous alarms caused considerable disruption. Plymouth suffered much more, especially during April and May 1941, with some casualties and much damage to buildings. At its peak in 1944 Haslar had thirty-five medical officers, 110 nursing sisters, and 700 SBAs and VADs. There were smaller hospitals near bases, at Portland, and Port Edgar for Rosyth.

Auxiliary hospitals were set up, including Barrow Gurney near Bristol, which dealt largely with mental health cases. Kingseat was inland in Aberdeenshire and was chosen as the base hospital for Scapa Flow, due to likely immunity from air raids. Patients were transferred by ship and road. Sherborne in Dorset was mainly for orthopaedic purposes, with a rehabilitation centre at Bromley near London. Those at Londonderry, Seaforth, and Woolton near Liverpool served the crews in the Battle of the Atlantic. That at Southport was mainly for tuberculosis, which was quite common at the time. In addition, there were around a hundred sick quarters, of varying size but larger than the mere sick bays which were to be found in practically every naval facility.

As war approached, the navy reached agreement to share the army's medical facilities at Alexandria, which was regarded as 'a remarkable line of thought' at the time – though on a smaller scale the navy had long used the army facilities at Gibraltar. The naval hospital at Bighi on Malta was in a dramatic site overlooking Grand Harbour, but it was vulnerable to bombing and patients had to be evacuated to other sites. In the Atlantic, there were hospitals at Bermuda and Simonstown in South Africa, while the Indian Ocean was largely served by hospitals in Ceylon, as Sri Lanka was then known. The British Pacific Fleet used bases at Sydney and Brisbane in Australia, but had to rely mainly on hospital ships and American resources for long-distance operations.

Maine, 8599 tons, was the navy's only hospital ship at the beginning of the war. Plans to build a new one came to nothing, so a dozen merchant ships of varying sizes and capabilities were requisitioned. The Royal Navy, with its longstanding aversion to building shore bases, tended to favour hospital ships for mobile operations. Some, such as *Vita,* were coal-fired, and coaling ship was a problem: 'Coaling, especially at Aden, was a nightmare, coal carried aboard in baskets with coal dust trickling through the wickerwork.' As a result, 'The wards are covered in coal dust and the linen is grim.'[16]

A hospital ship could fulfil several functions. It differed from army ships in that it had to do more than transport patients from A to B: it was the equivalent of a field hospital which had to give full treatment as far as possible. It could follow the fleet as *Maine* did with the Mediterranean Fleet in peacetime, or it could become a more or less static ship in an improvised naval base, as *Oxfordshire* did for a time at Freetown. Often they combined several roles. *Isle of Jersey*, with her short range of only 700 miles, usually spent three or four weeks at Scapa Flow, then sailed to Aberdeen with patients.

Vasna was badly converted in Bombay in 1939, with very poor accommodation for the medical staff, especially the SBAs. In addition, it was reported, 'women patients had to be carried without warning and at times European patients had to share accommodation with Asiatics'. She served mainly in the Indian Ocean. *Amarapoora* was the largest of the ships, carrying up to 503 patients. After service at Scapa she supported the North African campaign and was narrowly missed by bombs during the Salerno landings. *Oxfordshire* was converted efficiently to carry 505 patients, ten medical officers, nine nursing sisters and sick berth staff. She spent much time in the improvised base at Freetown, but during 1943 she supported the campaigns in the Mediterranean, then joined the BPF fleet train. In July and August 1945 she was loaned to the Americans in Subic Bay, and after the war, like many of her sisters, she treated former prisoners of war. *Vita* was about half the size and another unsatisfactory conversion in Bombay. She was hit by bombs off Haifa in April 1941, abandoned, then salvaged. She rescued the survivors of *Hermes* and *Vampire* after an attack by Japanese aircraft in April 1942. *Tjitjalengka* had been built in 1939 for the Dutch and was requisitioned in July 1942. She took American and Canadian invalids to Halifax, Nova Scotia, before service in the Indian Ocean. She too was loaned to the Americans in the Philippines. *Ophir* was taken over in 1942 and retained her Dutch merchant crew. She was small and slow and mostly used for ferrying services in the Indian Ocean.

Faults were showing by 1944 when attention turned to the Pacific. It was found that accommodation for five hundred had to be reduced to three hundred for long voyages in tropical waters, and only two out of five promised extra ships were available, while the older ones were in bad condition. Only the surrender of the Japanese prevented a crisis.

The sick bay of the River-class frigate *Cam* was described by her medical officer:

> The sick bay is excellent in its size and appointments, there are 2 cots and hooks for 3 hammocks, an operating table and 2 instrument tables and a ring of 6 lights over the operating table. There is also an ablution room next to the sick bay containing a WC, 2 wash basins and a portable bath.[17]

In a small vessel such as a submarine, the coxswain was expected to take on medical duties and had some training for it. And other officers and men might be obliged to help, such as Nicholas Monsarrat in the corvette *Campanula*: 'Since my father was a surgeon … I was also appointed the ship's medical officer within a few hours of reporting on board. … At first it meant nothing much', but as the Battle of the Atlantic intensified:

> I would soon be stitching up a gashed throat without benefit of anaesthetics, or trying to coax a dangling eyeball back into its socket. If I had known that a man with a deep stomach would … could actually smell so awful … I might well have kept my yachting experience as secret as the grave, and settled for the Army Pay Corps, or for prison, or for shameful defeat itself.[18]

Eventually sick berth attendants were drafted to corvettes, and frigates had surgeons.

The supreme test of a ship's medical organisation was in battle. In 1942 medical officers were warned not to do what had happened to Nelson at the Battle of Trafalgar – to carry a seriously wounded man down through several decks, which must have 'grievously exaggerated the shock from his injuries!' Instead, men were to be treated as far as possible on the deck on which they were injured. In normal times, the sick bay was in the upper part of the ship, convenient to main living and working spaces, and sited where 'natural light and ventilation are available.' But in war this could become extremely vulnerable, so it was 'necessary to provide a more protected place to which existing sick can be quickly transferred and where casualties can be received.'[19]

Distributing stations were to be set up, 'under protection and so situated that there is easy access for stretchers and sufficient room for treatment.'[20] The cruiser *Norfolk* had two emergency distributing stations, forward in the sick bay and aft in the wardroom anteroom. Each was manned by fifteen or sixteen personnel, including administrative and catering staff as well as medics. If these became untenable, they would move to the torpedomen's messdeck or the gun room or warrant officers' mess. In addition, there were three first aid posts, in the meteorological office, the torpedo parting shop and the officers' galley, each manned by three or four men.

Shipwreck survivors

The Battle of the Atlantic and the Russian convoys produced more shipwrecks than any conflict before or since, and often left survivors clinging to floats or crammed into lifeboats, sometimes for weeks at a time – the record was two men who spent seventy days in a lifeboat after the wreck of *Anglo-Saxon* in 1940. The Shipwreck Research Committee dealt with this and in 1943 Surgeon Captain Macdonald Critchley produced a report. He had 279 modern examples to study, but he also relied heavily on history, starting in ancient times and passing through Bligh of the *Bounty*, the wreck of the *Hesperus* and the loss of the *Titanic*. Cold was an obvious problem, severe in the Arctic, but serious enough in the Atlantic: 'In most cases of exposure after shipwreck, the factors of low temperature, high wind, wetness and inadequate clothing exist in combination.'

Even if he was lucky enough to be in a lifeboat, rather than clinging to a float, a survivor might well have to endure water in its bilges. A new ailment, immersion foot, was identified as separate from frostbite and trench foot. Thirst was also common, as few lifeboats carried an adequate water supply. Critchley was doubtful if drinking urine, as occasionally practised, was advisable. Drinking seawater was certainly not:

> … The condition of the lips, mouth, and tongue worsens and a peculiarly offensive odour has been described on the breath. Within an hour or two delirium sets in … colour is lost … Death may take place quietly … more often it is a noisy termination, and not infrequently the victim goes over the side in his delirium.

Hunger was the next hazard. By law, lifeboats were provided with 'hard tack' plus what other items the shipowners might see fit, such as bully beef, nuts, dried fruits and chocolate. But 'food is of very secondary importance under such conditions and the adequate water is the dietic factor which will determine survival.' And as losses occurred all over the world, he considered survival in tropical waters, where the passengers in a boat might become euphoric at first, and where sharks were a danger.

A new pattern of 32-person lifeboat as demanded by the British Ministry of War Transport regulations of 1941. It carries a range of compact foods, but the main problem is shortage of water, so it is designed to carry three litres per person instead of one. Like most modern lifeboats it has an engine, with sails to be used to conserve fuel.

If the survivors were fortunate enough to reach a rescue ship or a shore base, they should be warmed up, though not in the lower limbs until immersion foot had been dealt with. Blood transfusions were not advisable in cases of shock, but glucose-saline transfusions should be given instead. Sedatives might encourage sound sleep at night, but drugs such as morphine should be used sparingly.[21]

Medicine in the US Navy

The US Navy had 841 medical corps officers in 1939, which more than doubled to 1957 in June 1941, and soared to more than fourteen thousand by 1945. Since the navy did not train doctors, all were graduates of Class A medical schools. In addition, by that year there were more than seven thousand dental corps officers, nearly eleven thousand women in the Nurse Corps and 3429 administrators in the Hospital Corps. Enlisted men of the Hospital Corps rose from 4267 to 132,500 and there were 1125 Waves on medical duty in 1945.

The V-12 programme was used to augment the supply of doctors and dentists by helping them through college, with 55 per cent of places allocated to the army, 25 per cent to the navy and 20 per cent to civilian needs. For dentists, 35 per cent went to the army, 20 per cent to the navy and 45 per cent for civilians. In 1944 the director of Selective Service began to draft some men into the forces, to the annoyance of the medical authorities. Nevertheless, four thousand medical and dental students completed their training under the programme and another five thousand medical and 1400 dental students received part of their education. By the end of the war 23 per cent of naval medical officers had been trained under V-12, and 20 per cent of dental.[22]

A ship's surgeon might be shared between several vessels in the case of destroyers. 'As the medical officer, I was responsible for the health of crews and staffs. When we were together, I would hold sick call once a week or whenever necessary.'[23] Boredom was a problem in normal times according to the medical officer of *Sterett*:

> As a fully qualified surgeon with a hell of a lot of expensive and hard-earned training behind me, I felt ashamed to take Uncle Sam's money … for I think the *Sterett* had the healthiest damn crew in the entire Navy. … a few residual cases of gentlemen's diseases left over from glamorous Norfolk an occasional runny nose, and a bit of seasickness were all that ever came my way. And even those poor patients I soon learned to leave to the tender ministrations of my worthy Chief O'Briant, who had twenty years more experience behind him, and knew more about medicine as it is uniquely practiced in the Service than I shall ever know …[24]

Captain Copeland of *Samuel B Roberts* reported:

> After about a week or ten days of sheer boredom, Doc came to my cabin one afternoon and wondered if there wasn't something he could do to relieve his own monotony and at the same time do the ship and the crew some good. … After discarding several other ideas I venally asked him how he would like to get out a ship's newspaper – something on the lighter side to stimulate the interest of the crew in their shipmates and shipboard happenings.

The result was *Gismo,* which had seven cyclostyled issues in 1944.

Of course, it was very different in action:

> Harry Nyce had performed his duties in superb fashion. His foresighted preparations were a blessing. He had distributed well-selected first-aid equipment to each of several subdressing posts and outfitted the wardroom as the main battle dressing station in a thorough manner. As the wounded began to arrive he received, evaluated, and administered emergency first aid treatment to them in the wardroom. Then, when it became apparent that he was going to be overwhelmed by the number of casualties, he transferred his base to the little sick bay.[25]

USS *Pecos* had transferred survivors from other ships when she herself came under attack, as her medical officer recorded:

> When I heard the machine and antiaircraft guns rattle, I knew that we had about 30 seconds before we would sustain another hit or near miss. We would treat a patient for a few moments and then drop down alongside him, the pharmacist's mate on one side and I on the other, and wait for the ship to jump. As soon as the ship stopped shuddering we would again attend the injured until the next bomb burst. Often the interval was less than a minute.[26]

The US Navy nurse corps, established in 1908, was open to unmarried registered nurses who were US citizens. Ann Bernatitus joined in 1936 after training. 'I always wanted to be a nurse. There was nothing else for girls to do in those days but be a school teacher or a nurse. My parents couldn't afford to send me to college.'[27] Nurses had no regular ranks at first: 'We were neither fish nor fowl. We were not officers and we were not enlisted.'[28] In July 1942 they were given relative ranks, with the superintendent becoming a lieutenant commander – at the end of the year that was raised to captain. A nurse remained the equivalent of an ensign, a chief nurse to lieutenant JG and an assistant superintendent or assistant director to lieutenant. Until then, 'When the war started we couldn't go to Honolulu without an uniform so we had to wear our white ward uniforms and carry gas masks at all times. We were really cute.'[29] Uniform could be uncomfortable in the heat of the South Pacific: 'We had to wear duty uniforms, which were cotton dresses with long sleeves and a big wide belt. The chief nurse came around to see if we were dressed properly, but when she wasn't there we hung our belts up near a fan to dry them out.'[30]

Treating burns was perhaps the most traumatic experience: 'I recall making rounds in the ward when the strong odor of burns and dressings was so pungent, and I had to get out because I was going to get sick. I pitied the corpsmen who worked there all the time.'[31] But patients were often desperate for feminine contact. One hospital ship nurse recounted:

> A soldier who wanted me to put powder on his pillowcase because he wanted to smell a woman's powder. One day in a triple-deck-bed ward, a soldier reached out and touched me on the shoulder, and I turned around thinking he wanted to tell me something. He said, 'Excuse me, lady, I just wanted to touch a woman again.'[32]

Flight nurses tended patients as they were evacuated by air:

> On March 1 [1945] we made our first evacuation flights in DC-3s to Iwo Jima. During the six-hour flight, the nurse and a corpsman set up about twenty litters for the return trip. We landed amid anti-aircraft firing, and the patients, mostly marines right from the battlefield, were often just lying on the ground, waiting for us. The flight doctor evaluated the wounded; there were always a lot of abdomen wounds from hand grenades and shrapnel. There were no pressurised cabins, so we couldn't bring back those with head injuries.[33]

Enlisted men and women of the medical service were mostly trained within the navy, though any previous experience could be useful. Hospital apprentices were defined as:

> … non-rated men in the Hospital Corps who are striking for the rating of Pharmacist's Mate. Perform elementary duties such as arranging dressing carriages with sterile instruments, dressings, bandages, and medicines; applying dressings; recording pulse, temperature and respiration; catherizing and giving evening and morning care to patients, and administering hypodermic injections to patients. Keep medical records and perform routine clerical duties.[34]

The duties of petty officer rate, pharmacist's mate, were also defined:

> Perform numerous types of medical and clerical duties in the Hospital Corps. In addition to the usual duties of applying first aid to men injured in combat, many Pharmacist's Mates are technicians in specialized fields such as X-ray, clinical laboratory, pharmacy, epidemiology and sanitation, fever therapy etc.[35]

At boot camp, Forrest Walker had a typical mixture of motives for choosing the hospital corps. 'Any training or education I received would come in handy in raising a family ... The other reason actually had to do with my basic faith beliefs. I would really rather help people than kill people.'[36] In December 1943 potential recruits were told that they could 'contribute directly to the job of keeping the guns firing', as well as learning skills that could be useful after the war. Candidates were expected to have some knowledge of biology, chemistry, commerce, first aid, general science, mathematics, physics, physiology or typing, and they were trained in several hospitals, including Farragut in Idaho and at Great Lakes. To Forrest Walker: 'Most of the six-week training program was in a classroom setting, and we studied from the Hospital Corps Handbook primarily. Topics covered included *materia medica*, nursing practices, tropical diseases, food sanitation and cross infection control in hospital settings.'[37] Those with a professional background could go straight into petty officer rates, the others started as apprentice seaman, then to hospital apprentice second and first class. Higher rates could be achieved in various ways, including in battle. Louis Ortega was told: 'For

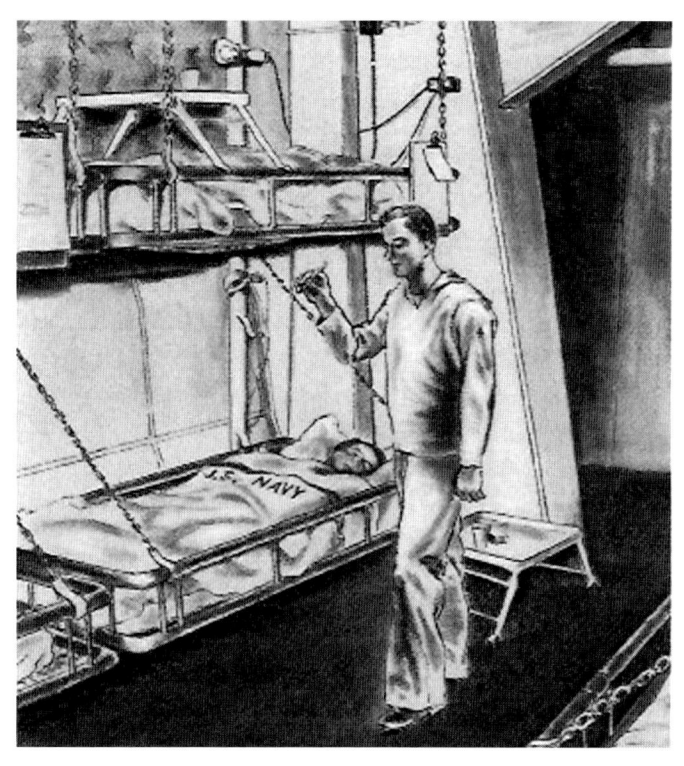

A hospital corpsman, or pharmacist's mate, takes the temperature of a patient in the sick bay of the carrier *Yorktown*. The bunks are in two tiers, allowing room for treatment.

the Battle of Matanikou, you and Smitty, and Kyle have been promoted to pharmacist's mate third, and for the Battle of Lunga, you, Kyle, Williams and Scotty have been promoted to pharmacist's mate second.'[38]

Many of them were on the staffs of hospitals, with roles ranging from orderlies to highly skilled technicians. Daniel Goolsbee was offered training in operating room technique in Treasure Island Hospital because of his grades in hospital corps school: 'I assisted in many different types of surgery, such as orthopedic, general, and brain surgery'.[39]

They might serve in ships, either under a medical officer or as the sole source of medical advice:

> ... the typical first- or second-class pharmacist's mate of 1941 had ten or fifteen years of navy service, which included independent duty on small ships that did not rate a doctor. As a result, he acquired a broad if nonacademic knowledge that enabled him to sort out complaints from symptoms and make intuitive diagnoses that were surprisingly accurate.[40]

Each of the destroyers had a chief or first-class pharmacist's mate, and they were 'as good as any doctors.'[41]

The most demanding assignment was in a submarine as the only medically qualified member of the crew. He was usually experienced and was highly trained at New London or Norfolk, and his duties were wide.

> ... the pharmacist's mate is responsible for the care of the sick and injured and the maintenance of the health of the crew. He is thus responsible for all of the routine medical duties laid down in the *Manual of the Medical Department*. However, in addition to this, war experience demonstrated the desirability of the pharmacist's mate performing general submarine operational duties and other special duties such as were assigned, such as sonar operator, radar operator, day or night lookout, librarian, compartment cleaner, oiler of the periscope etc.[42]

One of the thorniest problems was appendicitis, which could not be predicted before sailing and might prove fatal. At the beginning of the war, it seemed to reach epidemic proportions in submarines, but regulations explicitly forbade the pharmacist's mate from operating for it, because of the very real danger of misdiagnosis. Nevertheless, it was done three times during the war. The most famous case was *Seadragon* in September 1942, when a seaman fell unconscious. Pharmacist's Mate First Class Wheeler B Lines made the diagnosis and obtained the permission of the captain, who ordered the boat to be submerged in quiet water, while tools were made from spoons and a tea strainer. Three officers served as operating room assistants and the permission of the patient was sought: 'Like a veteran Lines made the incision, found the appendix, sewed up the incision with catgut.'[43] But overall, 127 cases of acute appendicitis were reported in submarines during the war, and not one death, so the recommended 'conservative' treatment seemed to work.[44]

It was reported just after the war:

> The accomplishments of submarine pharmacist's mates during the recent conflict have received high acclaim … This splendid record and the more-than-adequate service rendered by the Pharmacist's Mates during this war makes it appear that rigid selection and adequate training … is the answer, rather than assigning medical officers.[45]

Corpsmen could serve with the marines and endure all the dangers and hardships of battle, wearing combat uniform and carrying their full equipment like Louis Ortega on Guadalcanal: 'The Unit 3 was like a horse harness you put over your head and it had two bags full of first aid equipment.'[46] They were armed, because the Japanese did not treat them according to the Geneva Convention and, indeed, often picked them off to do the most damage to their enemy.

The most famous of them was Pharmacist's Mate Second Class John Bradley, who was one of the six men who raised the stars and stripes over Mount Surabachi on Iwo Jima. He was awarded the Navy Cross of 'extraordinary heroism' during this, his only operation, for bandaging a wounded marine under intense fire and pulling him 30yds to a position of safety. Unlike the marine flag-raisers, he was not killed or traumatised, and lived to the age of seventy.

Surgeon Captain Critchley of the Royal Navy was impressed with the sick bay of a new American battleship in July 1943. It had seventeen separate compartments, including a main ward with thirty-four cots and an isolation ward with six, operating theatre, offices, X-ray room, dispensary, laboratory, venereal treatment room and a dental surgery. The ship had a staff of four medical and two dental officers and twenty-three hospital corpsmen, headed by a warrant pharmacist and a CPO pharmacist.[47]

As an enlisted man, Ted Mason was also impressed:

> Sick bay occupied the entire athwartships section of the second deck … Except for the piping and conduits suspended from the overhead and the circular ports, it looked (and smelled) like a small hospital.

On the starboard side, it was equipped with dressing stations, a laboratory, and a dental office. To port were an examination room, a six-bunk isolation ward, and the compact operating room. …

Most of the forward transverse bulkhead was occupied by some two dozen luxurious berths, two-high and fat with Simmons interspring mattresses. We crewmen cast many a covetous glance at these accommodations, so luxurious by comparison with out pallets.[48]

It was very different in a destroyer in 1939: 'Our sick bay was nothing more than a small closet. If I wanted to examine a patient, I took him out of sick bay and laid him down in one of the crewman's bunks.'[49]

As always, sexually transmitted diseases were a major concern of the authorities and the doctors, while preventative measures, 'short arm inspection', could be humiliating for the crew:

As you came abreast of the medical officer, you had to drop your pants and underpants and raise your T-shirt so that you were exposed from navel to knees. The corpsman targeted his flashlight on that seemingly insignificant part of your anatomy. Selecting a tongue depressor, the doctor flipped your private parts back and forth, up and down, looking for an infestation by crab lice …[50]

Before the war, the US Navy had three overseas hospitals and eighteen in the homeland. These included Chelsea Naval Hospital in North Carolina, founded in 1836, which was expanded with six H-type wards, each including solarium; Newport, Rhode Island, which expanded from 245 beds to a capacity of 1419 patients; and San Diego, which 'grew astronomically' from fifty-six buildings with 1424 beds in 1941 to 241 buildings with 10,499 beds in 1945. By 1945 there were fifty-six stateside hospitals, sixteen base hospitals and sixteen convalescent hospitals, which included Naval Hospital Oakland, commissioned in June 1942 and intended to treat casualties from the Pacific in 135 buildings, including a chapel, Navy exchange and library and had three thousand staff catering for six thousand patients.[51] Naturally, most hospitals were clustered around the main naval bases, but a few were far inland: for example, at Glenwood Springs in Colorado and Norman in Oklahoma.

In 1939 the Bureau of Medicine and Surgery planned a prefabricated hospital that could be transported and set up without skilled labour; US Naval Mobile Hospital No. 1 was set up at Guantanamo Bay, Cuba, in November 1940, with five hundred beds. It was then shipped to Bermuda. Mobile Hospital No. 2 was disembarked at Pearl Harbor on

26 November 1941; eight five-hundred-bed mobile and base hospitals had been erected in battle zones by the end of 1942. Despite the name, they 'did not possess a high degree of mobility'. It was reported from the Seventh Fleet in 1944:

> They are bulky and require considerable shipping space to transport, time and effort to establish, and even more effort to dismantle, refit, and move forward. In a fast moving type of warfare over the vast distances typified in the operations in the Southwest Pacific, hospitals have not been capable of receiving casualties until the assault beaches moved far ahead.

Eventually, ten of them would be set up, all except the first in Australia, New Zealand or the Pacific.

The hospital at Netley on Southampton Water on the south coast of England had been built as a reaction to scandalous conditions in the Crimean War of 1852–54, though its design was criticised by the legendary Florence Nightingale. Its main building was a quarter of a mile long, the longest in Europe. In 1944 it was taken over by the US Navy to treat casualties of the Normandy invasion, and it was in poor condition:

> It was a very cold monstrosity. The wards were huge. … There was a fireplace at either end, which made the place terribly cold and damp and certainly not conducive to treating patients
>
> The Seabees came over and remodelled the whole thing to make it usable. They converted those wood-burning fireplaces … to gas and that kept us warmer.[52]

According to nurse Helen Ramsey:

> The first casualties came into my operating room. I remember how busy we were and how they kept coming and coming and we had no place to put them. We put them out in halls and everywhere. We were only there as a receiving hospital. We received the casualties, took care of them, removed the bullets and shrapnel, did the debridement, cleaned them up, poured penicillin and sulfa into the wounds, and wrapped them up. Then we sent them inland to the Army or to British hospitals inland, or by air to the United States …[53]

Because they relied more on building hospitals on shore, the US Navy had proportionately fewer hospital ships than the British, and they tended to be patient carriers rather than bases. At the beginning of the war they had two, *Relief*, which dated back to 1920, and *Solace*, which was commissioned in August 1941, the only one built as such from the keel up. The three ships of the *Comfort* class had naval crews, but the medical teams were provided by the army. *Bountiful*, *Samaritan* and *Refuge* were converted from transports built between 1916 and 1927. Later in the war, *Rescue* was converted from a passenger and cargo liner. The six ships of the *Comfort* class were fitted out in the hulls of C-4 transports, but did not enter service until 1945.

Refuge served initially in the Mediterranean theatre, taking wounded back to the United States, and ferrying German prisoners of war, which caused problems: 'Patients were always divided onboard according to injury, and this resulted in allied patients being mixed with Germans in the same ward. That proved to be a major mistake.'[54]

Though the Japanese did not respect the Geneva Convention, the American authorities insisted on obeying the rules, so hospital ships were painted white with red crosses and green stripes along their sides, and they kept their navigation lights on at night. Some officers would have preferred service in a combat ship, for the hospital ships were targets without any means to defend themselves.[55] *Solace* was indeed attacked in 1942, but it later emerged that it was a 'friendly fire' incident.

It took some time to evolve the best use of hospital ships in the Pacific, compounded by a shortage until the *Comfort* class became available near the end of the war. At Tarawa, they were kept about eighty miles away and did not anchor to take on casualties until the operation was completed. One hospital ship took approximately 265 casualties from the transports and the other did not receive a patient. At Saipan no hospital ship was available until the third day, and thereafter only at irregular intervals.[56]

In *Bountiful* during that operation, one nurse reported: 'As we dropped anchor, Higgins boats, motor launches, motor whale boats, amphibious ducks, and the like, were all heading in our direction. … We loaded over 500 patients in six hours, there were only 150 ambulatory patients admitted.'[57] At Leyte, five army-staffed ships were offshore with the naval *Solace*, *Relief* and *Bountiful* available at Ulithi. In the final operation at Okinawa, two hospital ships and two casualty carriers were present at all times.[58]

As well as exposing women nurses to danger, supporting a landing often brought them into contact with horrific injuries, as in *Bountiful* at Saipan:

> The patients were received were the severest kind of casualties one could ever imagine. Many were in shock and hemorrhaging. Some were shot through the head and probably would be blind the rest of their lives. … Some had badly mangled legs that had caught mortar fire, and it was a question whether the legs could be saved or not.[59]

Forrest Walker helped to unload the former luxury liner *Lurline*:

> I particularly remember carrying a stretcher case out of the emptied swimming pool where many of the patients had been stacked four tiers high. All this was not a problem for most of the patients as they were glad just to be back stateside. One could still see beautiful paintings, murals and chandeliers that were still hanging, along with other signs of former opulence.[60]

Many of the hospital ships arrived too late to see much action, but they spent the immediate post-war period treating and repatriating former prisoners of the Japanese.

Naval medics often had to deal with casualties during a landing, especially in the Central Pacific where the marines landed first. The use of LSTs was established early in the South Pacific and they were known as LST(H) for hospital. LST464 was fitted as a hospital ship for close support on the beach. At Saipan one amphibious tractor was stationed off each beach equipped with litters, blankets and splints, plus cases

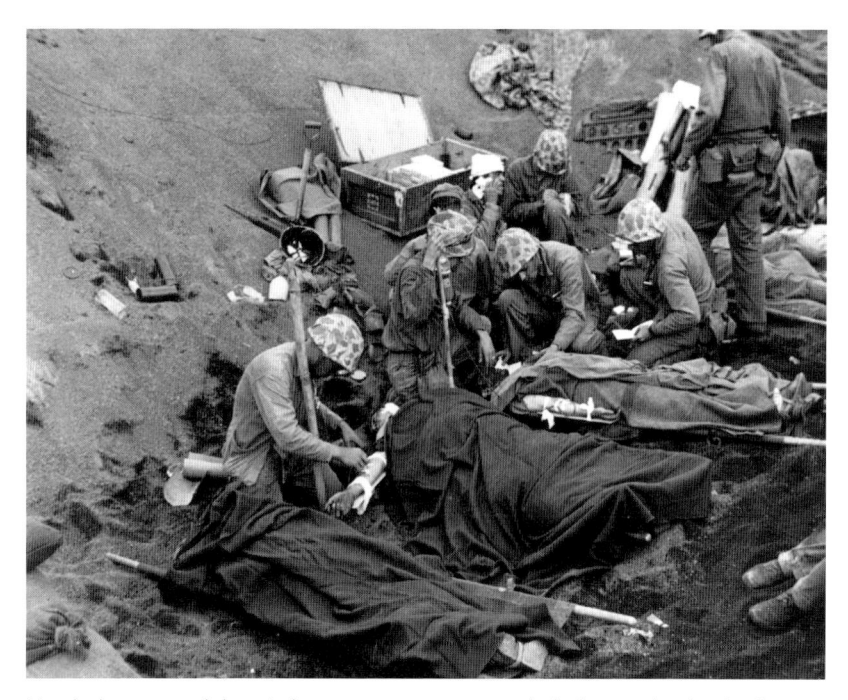

Naval doctors and hospital corpsmen treat wounded during the battle for Iwo Jima. Chaplain John H Galbreath is kneeling in the centre of the photo. They are indistinguishable from marines in their combat dress, because it was believed that the Japanese deliberately targeted medical personnel.

including plasma, dressings and morphia.[61] 'Medical section landed in the fourth and fifth waves on Red Beach at H-plus-21-minutes. The battalion surgeon was hit by a mortar shell in the first 10 minutes. The aid station was set upon the beach and wounded treated where they fell and evacuated in amphibian tractors.'[62] Out of 1750 casualties on the first day, 350 were killed outright, 700 needed immediate treatment and 700 were slightly wounded.[63]

In the Southwest Pacific landing at Arawe in December 1943:

> The conversions of LCTs for the care of casualties entailed the installation of a watertight hatch in the tank deck bulkhead, thus affording access to the forward troop compartment from either port or starboard. Spaces were converted into a receiving room, sterilizing and scrub-up room, and operating room, without interfering with the ship's capacity to carry troops and cargo. Thus, wounded could be brought in over the ramp, onto the tank deck and passed into the receiving room through the hatch. The ship's medical officer was responsible for triage, those requiring surgery were prepared for the surgical team, and those with minor injuries being treated on the spot.[64]

Casualties were lighter than expected on most of the Normandy beaches, as reported from LST 293:

> I went back to France for a total of five trips. On the third trip we had fewer than the 220 casualties of the second. And we got hardly any on the fourth. By the fifth trip we may not have had any. By that time C-47s were using the improvised runway they had built …[65]

The most important advance in medical science was penicillin, which was discovered by Alexander Fleming in London in 1929, but only developed for mass production after a visit to the United States by the Australian Dr Florey in 1941. By 1943 it was being manufactured by thirteen American and two Canadian companies, but supplies were still limited and rationing was needed – 85 per cent of production went to the armed services, with the rest for research and a small quantity for civilian needs: 'The remarkable results obtained with penicillin in the treatment of certain infections promise to establish new drug as the most outstanding medical discovery of the World War II era.'

* * *

Both naval medical services were proud of their efforts during the war – they dealt with a greater variety of injuries than ever before, from a greater variety of weapons, and a greater range of climates and battlefields, but the recovery rate from injuries was higher than ever.

The US Naval Medical Service was proud of its record during the Second World War:

> … in the First World War an average of 11.09 percent of those wounded in action subsequently died of their wounds, while in World War II the figure was 2.92 percent … the two main reasons for this great saving were the advances in medical science in the nearly 25 years between the two wars, and the medical administrative measures that permitted first aid to be brought directly to the wounded in the field, and then rapidly transporting them to medical installations where future definitive treatment was instituted.[66]

Apart from the usual work of naval medics, the two services had different problems. The British had to deal with numerous shipwreck casualties (not all naval) in the Battle of the Atlantic, and the extreme cold of the Arctic convoys. The Americans had to put large resources into casualties during landings in the Pacific, especially as the naval medical service also covered the marines. They also had to cope with burns and other injuries from kamikaze attack.

As with the training of officers, wartime experience tended to show that long professional medical training was not always necessary, at least for some of the more specialised tasks. It was recognised, even by doctors themselves, that the best pharmacist's mates, especially on submarines, were almost as good as the doctors themselves. And as to nurses, Mona Stanton's experience suggested that hastily trained VADs could carry out many tasks without the theoretical knowledge of nurses. This is perhaps reflected in the increasing use of paramedics after the war.

Religion at sea

The United States and the United Kingdom were both nominally Christian countries, and Jews were the only significant minority, for Muslims, Hindus, Sikhs and Buddhists had not yet begun their mass migration to Britain. The naval chaplain was at the centre of religious effort. An essential problem was that only the largest ships could carry them – the US Navy allocation was one per 1250 men – in an age when the small ship came to predominate. Moreover, he would not be able to represent all the different faiths likely to be onboard. Therefore, most chaplains were to be found in shore bases.

Beyond the obvious religious duties of conducting services and, in the case of Roman Catholics, hearing confessions, ship's chaplains usually had many other tasks. They were forbidden from direct participation in action, but they could act as cipher officer, help to censor letters and act as ship's librarian. General welfare was an important aspect. Rabbi Roland Gittelsohn dealt with numerous and varied cases and concluded:

> ... the chaplain's job is ... to be a wise and understanding counsellor, to 'square away' consciences that have some how become 'fouled up', to help remove those burdens of the heart and mind that become too oppressive and thereby destroy an asset more valuable than the finest of equipment: the spirit and morale of the men who will use the equipment – or misuse it.[67]

Another of their functions was to inspire the men in action, as in the British cruiser *Penelope*. As a large formation of bombers approached, it was suggested that church service be stopped:

> Then that was changed, so that guns' crews went to their posts ... but that others carried on. Thus we had the thrilling experience of singing 'Stand up for Jesus' at the top of our voices and even, on one memorable day, 'Grant us thy peace' while our own four-inch were hammering away noisily ...[68]

But the most famous quote from any naval chaplain came from Howard L Forgy of *New Orleans*. During the Pearl Harbor attack he passed along lines of men encouraging them and came up with the phrase, 'Praise the Lord and pass the ammunition.' It was turned into a patriotic song which reached number one in 1942.

On the face of it, the Royal Navy was committed to the episcopalian Church of England, though Scotland had an established presbyterian church and there were numerous other churches in England and Wales, known as Nonconformists, as well as Roman Catholics from Ireland and elsewhere. The first paragraph of *King's Regulations*, however, demanded that a service be held every Sunday according to Church of England rituals. In 1937 the Chaplaincy Service was headed by the Venerable Archdeacon Thomas Crick, with nearly a hundred Anglican clergymen under him, some with commissions dating back before the First World War. In addition, there were five 'Temporary Methodist Chaplains', and eleven 'Temporary Catholic Chaplains', along with one Congregationalist, two from the Church of Scotland and one other.[69]

Temporary chaplains RNVR were recruited as soon as the war started and came from a wide variety of experiences, from young curates to canons and university dons perhaps in their fifties. Until June 1940, they wore civilian clothes, but were allocated a special cap badge similar to an officer's, and a uniform. Some continued to wear their clerical dress, but in the atmosphere of wartime most preferred a uniform. It had no rank badges, which might have inhibited ratings. They were allocated to the main naval barracks to learn about naval ways, serving under the regular chaplain of the base, before being sent out to a ship or shore station. Stoker Fursland of *Belfast* found that off duty the chaplain was 'down to earth', indulging in swearing and smoking, and he once had to take him back to his cabin drunk.

Battleships, fleet carriers and cruisers were entitled to a chaplain each, usually of the Anglican faith, though in 1944 the battleship *Anson* and carrier *Victorious* of the British Pacific Fleet each had a Roman Catholic priest in addition. A destroyer flotilla had a single chaplain. In theory, he would lead a nomadic life, spending a few weeks in each ship, but in practice most flotillas were so dispersed that that proved impracticable.

Some served with the Royal Marines and went ashore during landings. In the Normandy invasion, Thomas Holland, a Roman Catholic chaplain, was on Sword Beach:

A service in the chapel in the carrier *Indomitable* attended by officers and men in working rig. Part of the ship's structure is exposed on the left. Only the largest ships had a dedicated chapel, others had to 'rig for church' in any available space.

> I remember saying Mass and telling the men that that one way or another the little saint of Lisieux (not so far away) would let one of her roses fall for them. In fact not another man was killed though the reason for this is not particularly creditable; the order came to evacuate ...[70]

Meanwhile offshore, there were chaplains in all but three of the nineteen Royal Navy ships bombarding the shore.

During Ewen Montagu's first formal parade at *King Alfred* in 1939, he stood fast when the order 'Fall out the Roman Catholics' was given – as a Jew, he waited for an order to cover the other religions. But he found himself in a Church of England service, including the naval prayer:

> O Eternal Lord God, who alone spreadest out the heavens and rulest the raging of the sea; who hast compassed the waters with bounds until day and night come to an end. Be pleased to receive into thy most Almighty and most gracious protection the persons of thy servants, and the fleet in which we serve.

He found it completely appropriate 'at that moment, with a group of us dedicating ourselves together to a common effort in anticipation of unknown dangers, saying *that* prayer together was exactly right and a most moving experience.'[71] As Montagu hints, the instruction could be used by others. Stoker Fursland of the *Belfast* resented the pressure to attend services and obeyed the order 'Fall out the Roman Catholics', though he was not of that faith, claiming he was not against religion, just compulsion. Then he hid until the service was over.

On the messdecks, religion was often the butt of humour, as Mallalieu recorded, with perhaps some exaggeration. A sceptical seamen was confronted by another reading the Lord's Prayer:

> 'The Lord is my shepherd.'
> 'That's right. We're just a flock of flicking sheep. Wouldn't 'ave joined if we weren't.'
> 'I shall not want.'
> 'Not want? Not want? I want to go home.'
> 'He maketh me lie down in green pastures.'
> 'Wet hammocks more like.'
> 'He leadeth me beside the still waters.'
> 'STILL waters? Oh, Flicking yeah!'[72]

There were 534 chaplains in the navy in 1945; sixteen had been lost, mostly when their ships went down. The 118 non-Anglican chaplains included sixty-eight from the Church of Scotland and Free churches (whose views were not always compatible). Roman Catholics sometimes had to improvise. Father Walter Meyjes had already served in *Renown* and was offered a transfer to *Rodney* on her way home, which he declined. Instead, he met with Father Pitt of *Oxfordshire*, and Father Devine, and they realised that they were the only Catholic naval chaplains on the North African and Italian coasts, so they divided the area between them.[73]

American sailors were not any more religious than their British counterparts. 'Religion was not a major factor in navy life,' according to Ted Mason.[74] In theory, there was no dominant religion in the United States, and indeed the Constitution prohibited the establishment of one, though the great majority of the population professed the Christian faith, with a significant Jewish minority. Early in 1941 the US Navy had seventy-seven Protestant chaplains from nine different sects, of which Methodist, Presbyterian and Baptist predominated, along with twenty Catholics. By the end of the war there were eighty-seven regular and 2624 reserve chaplains, and denominations included Unitarians, Russian and Greek Orthodox, and even pacifist Quakers.

Alvin Kernan reported, 'The old navy was, among other things, covertly anti-Semitic and openly racist. Few Jews were in the navy, and they were looked upon as extremely odd, as indeed they were to have enlisted in the navy.'[75] Ted Mason's officer was Lieutenant Bernstein, who 'did not look any more Jewish than Commander Carney looked Irish or Admiral Nimitz looked German', but he was a rare Jewish Annapolis graduate. The team also included two enlisted men, and Mason remarked:

> In early 1941 there were there were few Jews in the navy, and practically none in the battleship navy. Here were three of them in one radio gang, all with some college and engineering backgrounds and all well grounded in radio code and theory. Into the predominantly Anglo-Saxon C-D Division they brought the accents of Brooklyn and the Bronx …[76]

The war naturally brought in many more Jews, and their chaplains were given a badge showing tablets and the star of David.

Chaplains were sent to Williamsburg, Virginia, to learn about naval customs and language. Rabbi Roland Gittelsohn found it an enlightening experience:

> … the interplay of three major religions in a living democracy was not limited to our personal and informal relationships. It was a conscious and deliberate part of our schooling. Every class,

for example, hears lectures on both Catholicism and Judaism … Men belonging to each of the three groups were told, clearly and concisely, what they could do to comfort and sustain a dying sailor or marine of a faith other than their own.[77]

It was far less happy for James Russell Brown of the African Methodist Episcopal Church, the first African-American chaplain, who was very lonely in a heavily segregated town. He was followed by Thomas Parham of the United Presbyterian Church.

Chaplains were taught how to 'rig for church', though improvisation might be needed. In *California* in 1940/1, the Catholic chaplain conducted services under a canvas rigged on the forecastle at 0900 and the Protestant at 1000.[78] The ecumenical atmosphere of Williamsburg did not necessarily prevail onboard ship. In the cruiser *Montpelier* in 1944, Protestant services were held on the bow and Catholic on the stern.[79] Festivals were, of course, celebrated where possible and Ted Mason reported:

> The 800-foot-long hangar deck of the *Enterprise* had been strung with Christmas lights and converted for church services with many rows of mess benches. At the forward end stood a large, portable altar with its six candles, tabernacle, white altar cloths, and white antependium decorated with silver crosses. Over the altar, a large crucifix had been suspended from the overhead … The area nearest the altar had been roped off. The rows of wardroom chairs were occupied by officers and their ladies.
> I nudged Daley. 'Officers' country up forward. Do they think they're going to the head of the line at St Peter's Gate?'[80]

But a burial at sea was the most poignant of all:

> The burial ceremonies were held on the starboard side of the catapult on the stern. All hands assembled with life jackets on. The American flag was over the casket, prayers were said by the Chaplain, taps were sounded by the Marines and the Marines also fired a 21-gun salute. The casket slid down a chute and dropped into the deep Pacific.[81]

Women in the navies

Women had often been present unofficially in warships in the age of sail and one British ship at the Battle of the Nile in 1798 may have carried up to a hundred of them. This practice was stamped out by increasingly tight Victorian regulation, but by the First World War the idea of women in the armed services was beginning to revive, in a very different form. The shortage of manpower, and the assertive Suffragette movement, caused the British army to set up the Women's Army Auxiliary Corps in January 1917, and the navy followed with the Women's Royal Naval Service in November. It was a fine title, every word of it had strong associations, and it made the memorable acronym 'Wrens'. The WRNS attracted seven thousand women before it was disbanded at the end of the war.

During the peace which followed, the Suffragettes achieved their main aims when women over thirty were given the vote in 1918, and those over twenty-one in 1928. More women entered the professions and found employment outside their traditional roles in domestic service, factory work, childcare, office work and education. But they rarely reached the highest ranks, and most were still housewives, whose role was expanded by the decline in the employment of servants in middle-class homes. The idea of reviving the Wrens began in 1939, when the navy advertised for about fifteen hundred women 'to take the place of Naval and Marine ranks and Ratings in the Naval establishments upon secretarial, clerical, accounting, shorthand and typewriting duties; and domestic duties as cooks, stewardesses, waitresses and messengers' – for there was no question of them serving onboard ship, and certainly not in action. At the same time, the army formed the Auxiliary Territorial Service, a weak title for a force which was never as popular as the Wrens, and gained a bad reputation in some quarters, until Princess Elizabeth, the future queen, joined their ranks in 1944. The RAF formed the Women's Auxiliary Air Force which was rather more popular, with its association with glamorous fighter pilots. But the Wrens were always the most popular of the three and able to pick and choose its entrants.

The revived service was headed by Vera Laughton Matthews, daughter of a great naval historian and a veteran of the original force, nicknamed 'Tugboat Annie' for her progress during numerous visits to naval bases. The name 'Wren' was be adopted as a rating title, as in Leading Wren and Chief Wren. The women were never subject to military discipline, unlike members of the other women's services; the Admiralty believed that their standard was so high that such compulsion was unnecessary, and desertion was practically non-existent. They were divided into 'immobile' Wrens who would continue to live at home, and 'mobile' Wrens who lived in barracks and could be posted anywhere, including overseas later in the war. They were paid less than male sailors, which Laughton Matthews defended. Though many men in naval bases would never go to sea, they 'were recruited to a life of hardship and danger and sacrifice beyond all comparison of what was demanded of women.' The

Wrens were largely of middle- and upper-class background and regarded as 'officers' girls' by the lower deck.

Officers' ranks were closer to the merchant than the Royal Navy, which might show that the Admiralty was reluctant to give them too much status. A third officer had the single stripe of a sub lieutenant, a first officer the 'two and a half' of a lieutenant commander, a superintendent the four rings of a captain. The commandant sported the broad and medium stripes of a rear admiral. The rings were in blue rather than gold and surmounted by a diamond as in the merchant navy, rather than a naval officer's circle. Formally, they gave no command over male officers, but in practice they carried a good deal of authority. The original officers were largely wives and daughters of naval officers, but after that they were selected from the ranks, with a training course of two to three weeks in the grand surroundings of the Royal Naval College at Greenwich.

Wrens were recruited by posters with slogans like 'Free a Man for the Fleet' showing a demure young lady, which was perhaps designed to reassure parents. A recruiting film of 1942 was not a great success – audiences thought it was too good to be true – but there was no real problem with recruitment. Even after conscription for women was introduced in 1941, the service continued to rely on volunteers. Around eighty-six thousand women entered the Wrens during the war, with a peak strength of seventy-two thousand in 1945.

New Wrens were given a two-week training period on naval life in several sites close to the main naval bases. They wore 'bluettes', which 'would have looked more at home in a penal settlement', and was evidently designed to test their determination. After that they were issued with the proper uniform, a source of great pride. The 1917 Wrens had worn a uniform based on the 'square rig' of the naval rating but with voluminous skirts. That of the 1939 force was more like that of officers and petty officers and proved very popular. The officers' cap was very successful. 'It suited nearly everyone I ever saw in it', wrote Angela Mack. The ratings hat, based partly on a yachting cap of the period proved too floppy and was unpopular. From 1942 it was replaced with a version of the seaman's cap.

Originally Wrens were confined to clerical and domestic duties, but from 1941 they began to train as wireless operators and to spread into fields such as cinema operators and range correctors. Many were employed to operate equipment in training bases. As non-combatants they were excluded from the gunnery branch, but the torpedo branch was largely about electrical maintenance and they were used there. They were not intended for sea service, but from October 1941 they served as crews of harbour craft, including ferrying sailors to and from shore

A Wren officer (centre) and ratings in their uniform, which was based on the petty officer outfit rather than the 'square rig' of junior ratings. The hats were particularly popular.

liberty. 'None of them ever get fighting drunk. You have just got to treat them like a lot of small boys.' Officers might join the Naval Control of Shipping as boarding officers who would take instructions out to incoming merchant ships. Wrens played a large part as mechanics in naval air stations, and since they could not be sent to sea they could stay long enough to form a stable staff.

Wrens were allowed to serve overseas, though their first expedition ended in disaster in August 1941, when twenty-two were lost in a troopship on the way to Gibraltar. Numbers remained quite small at the end of that year, but by 1945 six thousand of them were overseas, all volunteers for the service.

Eighty-six thousand women would serve in the Wrens during the war. For some it was just an exchange of one drudgery for another, from the kitchen of a hotel or home to a naval base, for example. But for many more it was a new and revealing experience, opening up prospects they had never thought of. And for well-connected women, such as the daughters of Lord Mountbatten and Vera Laughton Matthews, it brought them into contact with ordinary women and the work they had to undertake. The WRNS retained its name after the war, unlike the other women's services, and kept it until it was merged with the Royal Navy in 1993.

In the US, in 1916 Josephus Daniels, the Secretary of the Navy, got round the need for congressional approval for a women's naval service by asking, 'Is there any law that says a yeoman must be a man?' So they were recruited and given the rating title 'Yeoman (F)', so that they would not be confused with male rating. But in 1925 Congress tightened the law to preclude the possibility of recruiting women.

As the next war approached, the Bureau of Aeronautics was by far the keenest on recruiting women, including its then director Ernest King, and Joy Bright Hancock, a former Yeoman (F), who was the widow of two naval officers and a civilian administrator in the bureau. In 1941 it asked the Bureau of Navigation, in charge of personnel, for help in setting up a programme, but it met with scepticism. The Bureau chief, Chester W Nimitz, later admitted to being 'one of the doubters in the early days'.[82] Meanwhile, the Women's Auxiliary Army Corps had been formed. After pressure by Navy's Women's Advisory Council and Eleanor Roosevelt, congressional approval was obtained on 21 July 1942 to recruit women for the duration of the war plus six months.

Elizabeth Barnard, an academic and special assistant to the new Chief of Naval Personnel, originated their name after newspapers mocked the women as 'sailorettes':

> I realized there were two letters that had to be in it: W for women and V for volunteer, because the Navy wants to make it clear that this is a voluntary service and not a drafted service. So, I played with those two letters and the idea of the sea and finally came up with Women Accepted for Volunteer Emergency Service – WAVES. I figured the word Emergency would comfort the older admirals because it implies that we're only a temporary crisis and won't be around for keeps.

The term 'naval' was not used, but the title 'Waves' was enough to indicate the maritime significance.

The Waves found their original officers from academe, including the first director, Mildred H McAfee of Wellesley College, and teachers remained a large part of the officer corps, as they often had a large role in training: for example, in air navigation. Wave officers had to have a college degree, or two years of college with at least two years of business or professional experience, and be of high moral and physical standards. Unlike Wren officers, they could be recruited direct, though promotion for the enlisted ranks was also allowed for those without college education. They were given two months' intensive training in the United States Naval Reserve Midshipmen's School in Smith College, Northampton, Massachusetts. Until the law was changed late in 1943, McAfee was the only lieutenant commander; there were thirty-five full lieutenants in the corps, the rest were JGs and ensigns. After that, McAfee was promoted to captain and other women followed her to commander and lieutenant commander.

After training in several centres, and then in Iowa State Teachers College, from the end of 1942, all Waves were trained at Hunter College in the Bronx, New York, which was commissioned as USS *Hunter*. Women were instructed in navy ranks and rates, ships and aircraft of the fleet, naval traditions and customs and naval history. More than eighty thousand Waves had completed the course by the end of the war, along with 1,844 SPARS, and 3,190 women marines, before the Coast Guard and Marine Corps set up their own courses in 1943. More than 80 per cent of Waves went on to more specialised training, the rest remained seamen second class for, unlike the Wrens, the Waves kept masculine titles for its members.

A recruiting pamphlet for the Waves.

Enlisted Waves were offered '$200 worth of clothes free!'; $180 went into the issued uniform, the remaining $20 was for underclothing and shoes, which the woman was expected to provide, with heels not over 1½in. If anything, it was even more attractive than the Wrens' uniform, being designed by the New York fashion house of Mainbocher at the instigation of Josephine Forrestal, the wife of the Assistant Secretary of the Navy.

Initially, Waves were restricted to the continental United States, which tended to restrict their usefulness, as much of the fleet was stationed in European and Mediterranean waters, or in the distant Pacific. It was only in 1944 that the first Waves arrived in Hawaii, as reported in the naval newspaper *All Hands*:

> While a Navy band played Aloha, 203 enlisted Waves and 11 Wave officers from 40 states filed down the gangplank of a transport at Pearl Harbor on the morning of 6 January 1944 – the first large contingent of naval women reservists to report for duty outside the continental United States. … They constitute the vanguard of a total of 5000 which have been requested by the 14th Naval District to fill vacancies in complement or release men for duty at sea or in forward areas of for return to the US under the rotation program.[83]

Women marines were recruited from February 1943, after some resistance from the commandant general, with about five hundred per month entering for a six-month boot camp period, first at Hunter College, New York, and at Camp Lejeune. They too did many duties, including domestic and administration, but about half of them were employed in aviation, as link training instructors, parachute packers and navigation instructors. The SPARS (*Semper Paratus* – Always ready) were the Coast Guard equivalent, and numbered about eleven thousand enlisted women. Harriet Writer was one of the first women to join the navy in Boston: 'I went to radio school and on the day of my graduation they said the Coast Guard would like ten per cent of the WAVES to become SPARS. I raised my hand because I didn't want to sit at a desk with headphones on sending and receiving Morse Code.'[84]

In some ways the US Navy treated the Waves better than the Royal Navy did the Wrens – it gave them the same pay and status as the men and the same officer ranks. On the other hand, they peaked at eighty-six thousand members, not much more than the WRNS's seventy-two thousand, though the US navy was three and a half times as large, which suggests that there was still a lack of enthusiasm at the top; and they were constrained by the lack of overseas service until near the end of the war. But in both navies the principle of women's service was established and they would gradually attain equal status and prospects with the men.

6
Marines

SEA SOLDIERS have a long history. They formed the main fighting power of Greek and Roman galleys, apart from the ram in the bow. In the age of sail, among other roles, they fired small arms onto the enemies' decks, and they often formed landing parties. Their role changed again in the second half of the nineteenth century when long-range artillery made their onboard role with small arms redundant, but marines are always flexible and they found new tasks, in colonial landings with many European navies, or in the national backyard of Latin America in the American case. During the First World War they served mainly onboard major warships, but some served alongside army units on the Western Front. The Second World War would bring much wider roles.

The Royal Marines trace their origin back to 1664, and they have a continuous history from 1755, when they were brought fully under Admiralty control. They were given the title 'Royal' in 1802, and two years later the Admiralty formed the Royal Marine Artillery to man the mortars on bomb vessels. These 'red' and 'blue' marines were merged in 1923 and adopted the blue tunic, but individual marines were still able to qualify for non-substantive gunnery rates in the same manner as seamen, and they usually manned one of the main turrets in a battleship or cruiser, and a proportion of the light and anti-aircraft armament. Like stokers, they were recruited as adults, but unlike them they dressed smartly and they were fiercely proud of their corps. Traditionally they were seen as a barrier against mutiny, though it is doubtful how effective they were; their role in landing parties was less unique than in the past, as all seamen were now trained in military drill and weapon handling. But marines were adaptable and would find new roles in the course of the war.

The Royal Marines remained quite a small corps, with 12,600 regulars in 1939 and a maximum strength of seventy eight thousand during the war. It was generally subordinate to the Royal Navy. Unlike their American counterparts, they shunned the limelight, according to Evelyn Waugh: 'The regular Marines are delightful people rather smugly obsessed by their obscurity. "How on earth did you hear of us?"'[1]

According to General Holland M Smith of the USMC, the typical Royal Marine was 'heel-clicking, loyal, immaculately turned out, wise in his way like a family retainer, carefully restricted in latitude of opinion and activity.'[2] There was some truth in this, and Royal Marines did do duty as servants, a job which was done by African-Americans or Filipinos in the US Navy. But they also had an aggressive role, and they formed the majority of commando units by the end of the war. The duality was experienced by John St John as early as 1939, when he answered an advertisement for officer training for a 'marine naval base ... which he thought had a tolerably safe ring.' Instead, he found himself interviewed by a colonel who was perplexed: 'Never heard of it. Must be some other show. The task allotted to your outfit will be to raid the enemy's coastline – go in under cover of darkness – establish a temporary beachhead ... that sort of thing.'[3]

The marines were headed by the Adjutant General, retitled the Commandant General in 1945. He was directly under the Admiralty Board and usually had the rank of lieutenant general. The corps was divided into three 'grand divisions', with headquarters at Chatham, Portsmouth and Plymouth, plus a depot at Deal, which was used for training recruits at the start of the war. In addition, by 1945 there were commando groups, beach groups, assault forces and Fleet Royal Marine Officers for each of the main fleets. The divisions matched those of the navy as a whole and their main job was to house and, to a certain extent, train men between drafts, and to appoint them to ships.

The officer structure of the Royal Marines was identical to that of the army. In peacetime, the training course lasted three years. A young man would enter as a probationary second lieutenant and study drill and military procedure, weapons and tactical training, naval gunnery and seamanship. On passing he would be promoted to probationary lieutenant for a period of sea service, 'for practical instruction in their detachment duties afloat and in the duties of an Officer of the Watch in harbour.' By the late 1930s he was also expected to 'undergo a fortnight's course in elementary naval aeronautics'. He might even train as an aviator, though very few did so – only thirty-one marine officers flew as Fleet Air Arm pilots during the Second World War, with two as observers, and nine NCOs transferred to the navy. Up to two men per year might be commissioned from the ranks. They had to be under twenty-three, unmarried and of high educational standard.

In October 1939 the Admiralty concluded 'that the Royal Marines will have to undertake certain new services and that a substantial expansion of the Corps will be necessary', requiring large numbers of extra officers.

The training period for regulars was to be reduced to eighteen months, twenty sergeants were to be commissioned, and fifty civilians were to be selected for temporary service. They were 'Not to be available for sea service, but to be trained for service in one or other special units.'[4] Training of officers began at Chatham and at Kingswood House near Deal, fictionalised as 'the Halberdiers' by Evelyn Waugh in *Men at Arms*, and described more authentically in his letters and diaries. It was dominated by Brigadier St Clair Morford, 'who looks like something escaped from Sing-Sing and talks like a boy in the Fourth Form at school … eyes alight like a child paying pirates, "We have to biff them, gentlemen."'[5] John St John was on the same course and described:

> …sand-table exercises and TEWTs – tactical exercises without troops – based on the lessons learned in 1914–18, on India's North-West frontier, at Omdurman or fighting the Matabele. … We practised receiving orders from a company commander, synchronising watches, going forward to make our own reconnaissance, 'appreciating the situation' from both our own and the enemy's point of view, and finally giving orders ourselves to imaginary platoon sergeants and corporals.[6]

Training of regular officers continued in the early stages of the war, with the course reduced to eighteen months and eventually to sixteen. John Day started at Plymouth as a probationary second lieutenant in January 1940, one of a batch of twenty-one split between the marine depots. They often drilled among the recruit squads, in the first part of the course, which was 'almost entirely physical', apart from a few lectures and essays. Then the whole batch was gathered at Eastney, near Portsmouth, for training in naval gunnery for, unlike Waugh's group, they were clearly intended for sea service. Seamanship 'consisted mainly of sailing and pulling a cutter in Plymouth Sound and learning how to handle a beautifully maintained ancient steam launch.' After a final course in infantry training they were promoted to lieutenant.[7]

It is not clear whether St Clair Morford ended Waugh's and St John's course, as Waugh's fictional Brigadier Ritchie-Hook, 'pronounced, "The rule of attack is 'Never reinforce a failure'. In plain English that means: if you see some silly asses getting into a mess, don't get mixed up with 'em. …This course has been a failure. I'm not going to reinforce it.'[8] In any case, later officers were selected from among recruits on the basis of academic qualifications. They had to be under twenty-three and unmarried, trained in an officer cadet training unit, or OCTU, at Thurlestone in Devon, in the style of the army. This was disliked by

A Royal Marine sergeant, wearing the blue dress uniform, drills trainee officers wearing utilitarian battledress early in the war. The trainees are holding the standard Lee-Enfield rifle.

Major Patrick Ennor, who later wrote that they were too much under the direction of NCO instructors, who would tend to produce 'merely a super sort of private soldier.' It was 'very different from the atmosphere which prevailed among us second lieutenants under instruction at Deal.'[9]

In peacetime, the corps was attractive to young men who wanted the variety of a sea life, but were too late to enter as boy seamen and did not want the claustrophobic life of a stoker. Like seamen, they normally enlisted for twelve years. In wartime, conscripts were advised, 'Men within the registration ages who wish to serve in the Royal Marines should express a Royal Marine "preference" when registering.' The smart blue uniform was still in occasional use. 'The picture in all our minds was the blue uniform shown in all the adverts, but in truth very few were seen at Pompey.'[10] Medical conditions were similar to the navy, though colour blindness was not a disadvantage.

As always, NCOs were far more important than officers during basic training:

When we were all sorted out he introduced himself as Sergeant Lyle and that he was to be our squad leader. He called in two corporals who would assist him to make us the best squad ever. To quote him though, we 'weren't exactly the best material he'd worked on'!

To achieve the desired morale there was a need to develop an 'esprit de corps' which had been the backbone of the Royal Marines over the centuries.

They were not issued with full uniform for the first three weeks, partly so that they could work off excess fat by drill and PT. The first part of the programme, according to Pollitt, was learning cleanliness and tidiness, how to live together, and the washing of clothes. Foot drill soon began to dominate. 'Drill in the first few days was elementary; sorting out our lefts from our rights; swinging our left arm forward as our right leg goes forward, and viccy vercy'. And the base at Deal on the east coast of Kent had its hazards:

One very windy day, the corporal had difficulty making himself heard; got us marching towards the cliff but couldn't shout loud enough to either halt or reverse our direction. On we went towards the cliff edge … until a bellow from the sergeant came above the wind 'say something' he shouted to the corporal 'even if its only goodbye'.

For the second part, recruits were introduced to weapons and tactics:

Probably the most important thing, and the reason we were issued with a rifle, was to know how to use it. … with one particular instructor, we were told that all bullets … followed a trajectory and to quote him, 'imagine a coat hanger fixed to the rifle and sticking out from the end of the muzzle – that's the trajectory the shot would take'.

Some were selected for commando training: 'It was here that we learnt the basic skills of survival, both in concealment, shooting and weapons in field conditions and living on rations and the countryside without showing our presence.' They also went on the naval gunnery course which 'included live firings from the old six-inch MK12 guns at Penlee Point which gave us the first taste of the noise and smoke one could expect from the explosions in the turrets of ships.' Finally, they spent:

a full month on the parade ground to ensure that the squad could be fully kitted out with tropical kit for overseas, could be fully inoculated whether or not the injections would be needed, and the arrangements made for the recruits to move to units and ships as applicable.[11]

When ashore, a sergeant was the second in command of a platoon under an officer; as in the army, a corporal was the leader of an infantry section of eight to ten men, though onboard ship the duties might be different. The senior NCO of a detachment was usually a colour sergeant. Sergeant majors were to be found in the battalions and depots; unlike their army equivalents they were senior NCOs rather than warrant officers. Rank was more permanent than in the navy; officers in courts martial were reminded, that 'whereas Naval Ratings can regain their rate after a few months, RM NCOs will take years to regain their rank if they regain it at all.'

In peace, an intelligent marine of good character might be promoted to corporal after about five and a half years, sergeant after eleven and colour segreant after sixteen. In wartime, potential NCOs were identified early in the training process. Normally, a marine was eligible for promotion eighteen months after his entry. If he attended a section commanders' course during basic training that was reduced by three months, and if he was the star recruit who won the King's Badge it was reduced by a further three months. J W Pollitt recorded:

> The corporal informed the squad that persons wishing to enter a Section Commander training class would have additional instruction three nights a week ... When the class first assembled there were about thirty members of the squad of fifty-six who wanted to take the first steps, but by the end of the first week the class had dwindled to about fifteen.[12]

On completing the course the marine was entitled to wear a diamond on his shoulder, 'the proud experience I have remembered all of my life' to J W Pollitt.[13]

When the time came, the NCO candidates were sent to the NCOs' School at Deal for a six-week course, 'the syllabus being much the same as in peace, stress being laid on "man management."' At the end, they were examined by a team consisting of 'the adjutant, and that most fearsome of characters the Regimental Sergeant Major.'[14] By the beginning of 1944, the school had trained 5358 junior NCO candidates.

Shipboard units were known as detachments and varied according to the size of the ship – a battleship of the *King George V* class had 350, a *Southampton*-class cruiser had eighty, and an *Indomitable*-class carrier 128.[15] They were not a growth area during the war; numbers of capital ships, cruisers and fleet carriers were mostly stable as wartime construction was matched by losses. The expansion of the corps would come in other areas.

Marines lived in messdecks and slept in hammocks like seamen. Their quarters were known as the 'barracks', the reverse of the naval habit of referring to a shore base as a ship. At sea, they took a full part in the routine of the ship, and trained at the guns. In HMS *Valiant* in port in 1942, the gangway sentry had a ceremonial role in daytime and marched 20yds on either side of the after brow [gangway] with his magazine uncharged. At night-time it was far more serious: his magazine was charged, he patrolled the length of the ship with orders to challenge anyone approaching – as a last resort he had orders to fire low at him, aiming not to kill. Training for shore service was carried on, including landing, boarding, field parties and battle drill, as well as seamanship. One manual even included instructions on how not to leave tracks across fields, which might be spotted by enemy air reconnaissance, suggesting some time ashore. In the *Valiant* wardroom attendants were mustered at 0600 and cleared up the officers' breakfast by 0900, so that the wardroom would be ready for inspection an hour later. Cabins were to be ready for inspection by the corporal in charge by 1040, and the routine continued throughout the day.

Since 1904 the Royal Marines had provided bands for the Royal Navy. Apart from those in headquarters and the grand divisions, each major warship had bandsmen in the detachment – a fleet flagship had twenty-four men under a bandmaster, a small cruiser had twelve. In action they would serve in the transmitting station well below decks, operating the 'gunnery nerve centre'.

Boys could join to train at the age of fourteen and a half, and only slight musical knowledge was required. Professional musicians were recruited during the war to be trained at Deal, and later in a hotel in Scarborough. They learned a full range of military music, as well as popular tunes for the entertainment of the crew and guests.

The marines largely followed the army in ranks, weapons, and procedures. Of fifteen books which were supposed to be in the possession of officers and NCOs, all but two were produced by the army. The most common marine weapon was the well-tried Short, Magazine, Lee-Enfield rifle, much improved since its introduction in 1903. The British did not develop a semi-automatic rifle as the Americans did, but placed more emphasis on accurate aim, and the possibility of running out of ammunition. 'It can not be over-emphasised that the survival of Royal Marine detachments ashore will depend on every one of the few bullets that can be carried hitting their mark. It is unlikely that the Royal Marine landing party will have any supply echelon to rely on.' Furthermore, the principal armament of a section was the Bren light machine gun, jointly developed at Brno in Czechoslovakia and Enfield. It had a curved thirty-round magazine on top and was usually fired from an integral bipod. The other members of the section carried spare magazines, and their ammunition pouches were designed round them. It could fire 120 rounds per minute, though it was far more common to use bursts of five rounds, up to five per minute.[16] The Thompson sub machine carbine, the famous 'Tommy gun' was used extensively by Royal Marine commandos. It was 'a short range weapon introduced for the purpose of engaging the enemy at ranges from 10 to 100 yards. … The weapon is especially useful when on patrol or for fighting in close country such as woods and villages.' It was also used by section leaders, as well as the native Sten.

In temperate climates, a marine wore the drab army 'battledress', with a blouse which stopped at the waist and all buttons concealed. They had the standard web equipment, including gaiters and heavy hob-nailed 'ammunition' boots, which American marines deplored. 'This boot of pain! It was working on the soles of my feet with the exquisite delicacy of a vise!'[17] For the rare occasions when he wore his blue uniform in a 'utility' version, the marine had a peaked cap with a blue or white top according to climate, and a red band. It bore the corps badge, a globe surrounded by a laurel wreath to signify distinction all over the world, and a crown and lion on top, symbolising a royal regiment. More commonly, he wore the khaki 'fore and aft' forage cap until it was replaced by a blue beret from 1943. In action he wore the round steel helmet, known as the Kelly helmet to Americans, that was issued to all servicemen, and to civilians for use in air raids.

The unit for which John St John thought he was volunteering in 1939 was presumably the Mobile Naval Base Defence Organisation (MNBDO), which had its origins in the X Organisation formed at Fort Cumberland near Portsmouth in 1923. It developed techniques for landing equipment and from 1935 it worked on the defence of Alexandria. Its main function was to man naval and anti-aircraft guns, but it also had a team of men experienced in construction of piers. MNBDO I was formed soon after the start of the war, mainly from HO recruits, with an initial strength of seventy-eight officers and 2150 other ranks, but very little of its authorised equipment of searchlights and vehicles. In 1941 the unit, now increased to 202 officers and 4089 other ranks, sailed for the Middle East. It deployed in Egypt and Palestine before elements were sent to Crete for a naval base in Suda Bay. It lost 1200 men, mostly prisoners, as a result of the German airborne landings. It was then sent east for the defence of Ceylon before being disbanded in September 1944. MNBDO II was formed at the beginning of 1941 at Hayling Island near Portsmouth and it arrived in the Middle East in succession to MNBDO I in 1943. It was deployed in the defence of Malta and in Sicily after the invasion.[18]

The other side of the marines' dual personality was to be found in the brigade formed in 1939 under the special eye of the then First Lord of the Admiralty Winston Churchill, who valued aggressive action and had always craved a military force under his direct command. He wanted them for Operation Catherine, an ambitious and almost certainly impracticable plan to raid the Baltic, which was to be overtaken by events – in May 1940 Churchill was elevated to prime minster, while the fall of France gave much greater urgency to events nearer home.

The Marine Brigade was almost almost fully formed by that time and it might have been ideal for the new commandos that Churchill proposed, but it was one of very few units in a condition to fight after the bulk of the army was evacuated from Dunkirk. It was divided into 101 and 102 brigades and the first of these was held in readiness for various expeditions but put on coast defence duties. At the time it had a strength of sixty-six officers and 1350 other ranks, about half that of an army brigade. In August it was sent on an abortive expedition to the French colony of Dakar. The Royal Marine Division was formed with the addition of the newly-formed 103 Brigade in September, but like the MNBDOs it never realised its full potential before being disbanded in September 1943, with its well-trained personnel moving on to commandos and landing craft crews.[19]

It was only in February 1942 that the Royal Marines found their true metier for the modern age, with the formation of the Royal Marine Commando at Deal, though marines had already served with army commandos. Appeals for 'volunteers required for special duties of a hazardous nature' had yielded good results among bored personnel. 'This was an opportunity not to be missed,' recorded Marine J Forbes. As planned in 1942, the Royal Marine Commando was headed by a lieutenant colonel. There were three companies headed by captains, each with a headquarters and three platoons of an officer and thirty-two men each. As well as a twenty-seven-man signals platoon and a close support platoon, a demolition platoon was necessary during raids, and a medical section of one doctor and three naval sick berth attendants. There was a grand total of 446 men, compared with more than seven hundred for a regular battalion. This unit would be retitled 40 Royal

Marine Commando as seven further commandos were formed during the war.

The main training establishment was at Achnacarry in the Highlands of Scotland, with its usual cold and rain. It was far more challenging than the regular marine training, with exercises such as the 'death ride', in which a man had to descend a rope across a fast-flowing river secured by a toggle, or the 'Tarzan' course, a series of ropes and nets on the topmost branches of trees. The course concluded with the night opposed landing exercise in which trainees landed to be met with live fire from the instructors. The Achnacarry course was copied by other units and nations.

Royal Marine Commandos would serve in the Mediterranean and Burma. On 6 June 1944, 46 and 48 Commandos landed in Normandy while 47 and 46 Commandos took part in other events surrounding the invasion, and in 1945, 45 Commando was in the crossing of the Rhine. After the war, all marines except bandsmen would be trained as commandos.

With the growing redundancy of the MNBDO and the Royal Marines Division, Lord Louis Mountbatten, now Chief of Combined Operations, was keen to have them as crews of landing craft and it was commented that 'there is no better disciplinary training, and that required by the Jack-of-all-trades, than that given by the Royals.' Initially it was intended to use them in minor landing craft such as LCAs, which were boats rather than ships, and in support craft such as Landing Craft Flak (Large) which would go close inshore to provide anti-aircraft support for a landing. The revolutionary suggestion was made that Royal Marine officers might take command of them. Though it was 'a marked departure from tradition', it was extended to the Landing Craft, Gun (Medium), which carried two 17pdrs which were expected to beach during a landing and engage in the land battle. Training took place on rivers in Wales, where fierce tides gave a strong awareness of the effects of currents. By February 1944 there were 9300 marines serving in landing craft.

The Second World War transformed the Royal Marines. They moved well beyond Holland M Smith's 'loyal, immaculately turned out … family retainer' to play a leading, though not dominant, role in amphibious operations, large and small. But they would never match the dynamic, strident and largely independent force that was developing across the Atlantic.

'What are the Marines?' asked Holland M Smith when he was proposed for a commission in the US corps in 1905.[20] Within forty years the world would know all about them, not least because of Smith's activities and

US Marines of the detachment aboard carrier *Wasp*, also wearing blue uniforms, are inspected by Captain Forrest P Sherman at San Diego in June 1942.

writings. In 1940 William Rogal had at least heard of them, but had no idea what they did. He was attracted by the fine uniform and accepted his friend's misleading information that 'They ride around on Navy ships. And boss the sailors around.'[21]

The Marine Corps was founded in 1775, even before the Declaration of Independence, and landed for the first time to capture a fort in 1776, though they served mainly on shipboard like their British opponents. The corps was revived in 1798 for a quasi-war with France, and in 1805 they landed in Libya, 'The Shores of Tripoli'. They fought the British again in the War of 1812 and then served in the Mexican War of 1846 – 'The Halls of Montezuma'. Marines were the first Americans to set foot on Japanese soil with Perry's expedition in 1854. The corps remained small during the Civil War, and in the late nineteenth century they served mainly as a seaborne police force, landing to protect American lives and property in Latin America, and against the Boxer Rebellion in China. They landed in Cuba during the Spanish-American War of 1898, and a brigade of more than nine thousand men fought in the trenches in the First World War, facing a well-equipped modern army for the first time.

According to Samuel Hynes, 'The Marines are administratively attached to the Navy, but no Marine likes to admit, and the Navy is generally regarded (by Marines that is) as a softer, more gentlemanly, less belligerent service.'[22] By 1939, it was established that the Marine Corps was 'not an integral part of the Navy, but a part of the Naval Establishment.' The headquarters was in the Navy Building in Washington, on a par with the various agencies. It was headed by Major General (later General) Thomas Holcomb from 1936–44, who had attended both the army and navy war colleges and oversaw the development of amphibious techniques in the late 1930s. He was succeeded by Alexander A Vandergrift, who had commanded at Guadalcanal.

Despite General Smith's contempt for the 'heel-clicking, loyal, immaculately turned out' Royal Marines, they did have their equivalent in the American service, in battleships, cruisers and large aircraft carriers; in 1941 the cruiser *St Louis* had forty-seven, out of a complement of 976. In *California*, Ted Mason found them oppressive: 'While they looked resplendent at inspections in their "seagoing bellhop" dress uniforms, they were still cops. When they weren't guarding the brig or doing rifle drill, they seemed to spend most of their time standing around practicing the marine look: erect, hard-eyed, thin lipped, hostile.'[23]

Very different from the shipboard detachments, the Fleet Marine Force was a largely self-contained organisation which was formed in 1933 with a Pacific war in view, but with the experience of many landings of various sizes over the years. It was defined as:

> ... a balanced force of land, air and service elements of the US Marine corps which is integral with the US Pacific and/or Atlantic Fleet. It has the status of a full Type command, and is organized, trained, and equipped for the seizure of advanced naval bases and for the conduct of limited amphibious or land operations essential to the prosecution of a naval campaign.

The first *Landing Operations Manual* was prepared in Marine Corps schools in 1934, and tested and developed during Fleet Problems and marine exercises. Originally the FMF had three thousand officers and men, rising to 264,564 in the Pacific alone. As early as August 1941, Commander Parry of the Royal Navy recognised that the Fleet Marine Force was 'Considerably better than a highly-trained British Royal Marine Force; has its own aviation units; and has specialised in surf landings.'

The Marine Corps had 19,432 men on active duty in July 1939, plus 16,025 reserves. It expanded by several stages, with a new programme often coming into operation before the last one was completed, to peak at a strength of 485,113 in August 1945. It had no difficulty in recruiting before the war: in 1939, 36,356 men applied and only 5861, less than a sixth, were accepted. With the attack on Pearl Harbor, there were long lines outside the recruiting offices, but with the great expansion it became necessary to reduce the standards, with officers given authority to waive slight defects. From December 1942, voluntary enlistment was ended and all men were drafted. Seventeen-year-olds, however, were allowed to volunteer from February 1943, and were placed in the reserve subject to recall.

The East Coast training base was at Parris Island in South Carolina, the West Coast one at San Diego. During the war, Camp Pendleton was activated near San Diego in April 1942. Camp Lejeune was hastily built in North Carolina, with a thousand tents before the building could be erected, and opened in July 1942. Another base was set up at Mountford Point, South Carolina, to train twenty thousand black marines. Basic training methods had not changed much since the First World War, except in the need to deal with far larger numbers. The normal basic training period was eight weeks, reduced to five weeks in 1941, and back to eight weeks by 1943.

Eugene Sledge described his introduction to the Corps:

> My name is Corporal Doherty. I'm your drill instructor. This is platoon 984. If any of you idiots think you don't need to follow my orders, just step right out here and I'll beat your ass right now. Your soul may belong to Jesus, but your ass belongs to the Marines. You people are *recruits*. You are *not* Marines. You may not have what it takes to be Marines.[24]

The issue of the uniform was a defining moment: 'A cascade of clothes falls upon you, washing you clean of personality. ... a rain of caps, gloves, socks, shoes, underwear, shirts, belts, pants, coats, falls upon your unfortunate head. When you have emerged from this, you are but a number: 351391 USMCR.'[25] The schedule was hectic.

> In the six weeks of training there seemed not to exist a single pattern – apart from meals. All seemed chaos: marching, drilling in the manual of arms: listening to lectures on military courtesy: 'In saluting, the right hand will strike the head at a forty-five degree angle midway of the right eye'; listening to lectures on marine jargon – 'From now on, everything, floor, street, ground, everything is "the deck"'; cleaning and polishing one's rifle until it shone like an ornament; shaving daily whether hairy or beardless. It was all a jumble.[26]

'Manila John' Basilone, the hero of Guadalcanal and Iwo Jima, had already done a hitch in the army when he enlisted but noted, 'If you thought Army training was tough it was soon put out of your mind. When you train to become a Marine, you either fall by the wayside or you emerge as the best damn fighting man in the services.'

Naturally shooting played an important part, in American tradition:

> Most of us knew how to shoot; even, surprisingly, the big-city boys ... All the southerners could shoot. Those from Georgia and the border state of Kentucky seemed the best. ... But when live ammunition was issued and the shooting butts were run up, they scorned such effete support, cuddled the rifle butts under their chins and blazed away. The drill instructors let them get away with it. After all, there is no arguing with a bulls-eye.[27]

Sledge found the training was a success:

> By the end of eight gruelling weeks, it had become apparent that Corporal Doherty and the other DIs had done their jobs well. We were hard physically, had developed endurance, and had learned our lessons. Perhaps more important, we were tough mentally. One of our assistant drill instructors even allowed himself to mumble that we might become marines after all.[28]

Peacetime marine officers came from three sources. Midshipmen at the Naval Academy might volunteer for the corps. Others came from civil life, usually having served in the army or navy ROTC at college. At college, students were enlisted as privates first class and attended two six-week training camps before being commissioned as second lieutenants in the Marine Corps Reserve. Holland M Smith joined after an unsuccessful career as a lawyer. He attended a 'crammer' run by Mr Swaverly with about forty candidates for commission in the services, followed by examinations in the Marine Barracks in Washington: 'I passed successfully. It was the proudest day of my life. ... I received a commission as a Second Lieutenant and was assigned to the school of Application ... at the Marine Barracks, Annapolis'. He joined a class of fifty for 'an intense, thrilling year'.[29] Finally, a small number of NCOs were commissioned.

As expansion got under way in September 1940, the corps tried to recruit eight hundred extra officers from college graduates. After a slow start, there was a surplus of suitable applicants. There was no problem obtaining volunteers after Pearl Harbor, and by January 1942 the officer candidate schools were taking in men at a rate of 225 per month. Civilian specialists were taken on in large numbers, while promotion from the ranks was extended to include NCOs who were high-school graduates, and privates who had two years of college. In 1942, 5618 officers entered, including 2723 from the officer candidate classes, 1236 field promotions, 1408 specialists, 222 from ROTCs and twenty-nine from the Naval Academy. From 1943 the corps participated in the V-12 programme alongside the navy.[30]

As in other services, the distinction between officers and men was noticed, and resented more by Americans. Leckie mistakenly tried to enter an officers' tent: 'I ... gazed into the unblinking formidable glass eye of Captain High-Hips. What disdain! It was as though the holder of a coach ticket had tried to enter a parlor car! His hostility was as curt as a slap in the face.'[31]

Lieutenant General Holland M ('Howlin' Mad') Smith (1882-1967), the most formidable and controversial officer in the Corps. He played a large part in the development of amphibious warfare and was a protagonist in 'The War Between the Smiths', after he dismissed his army namesake during the battle for Saipan.

The non-commissioned officer structure also mirrored that of the army, with some detailed differences. A corporal led a fire team, a sergeant a rifle squad. 'Manila John' Basilone trusted his first command of a fire team. 'These boys seemed to be part of me and looked up to me for leadership. I knew they would never fail me when the chips were down.'[32] A platoon sergeant , with a 'rocker' under his three chevrons, was the second in command of a platoon under an officer who was often very inexperienced. There were first sergeants as the senior NCOs of companies, and sergeant majors of battalions.

William Rogal made it to corporal quite quickly in 1941 and was put in charge of a BAR squad before they were merged into the platoon. He was recommended for sergeant, but his battalion demanded that he pass a quiz from a senior NCO in another company: 'The knucklehead who concocted this scheme to take promotion authority away from company officers who knew the man and give it to an enlisted man who did not know him should have been drawn and quartered.' He failed, because, he believed, 'my questioner looked at me as too young and unworthy of becoming a sergeant.'[33]

The gunnery sergeant was already beginning to attain his legendary status. According to the *Marine Manual*: 'Gunnery sergeants will be appointed habitually from platoon sergeants. Candidates for promotion to gunnery sergeant must be well qualified ordnance technicians.'[34] At company level one was in the 81mm mortar platoon like their doyen, the legendary 'Lou' Diamond, whose battery at Guadalcanal was heard 'making twice the noise a battery usually makes … the extra noise was shouting.'[35] Another role was weapons instructor, which he also filled in boot camp. 'The first time I sat on the firing line, with two five-round clips beside me, and the warning "Load and lock!" floating up from the gunnery sergeant, I felt as a small animal must feel upon the approach of an automobile.' In training camps they were noted for the 'jaunty angle of the campaign hats worn by the gunnery sergeants', and their tendency to reminisce.[36] They also served as platoon sergeants and might show great leadership in battle, like John Basilone at Iwo Jima:

> Among all the prone figures I noticed a lone Marine walking back and forth on the shore, kicking asses, shouting cuss words and demanding 'move out an get your butts off this beach!' He gave the Marine corps signal for 'follow me'. … The Colonel and the Gunney got the invasion under way … it was more by example than anything else that inspired the Marines to start the attack instead of digging in on the beach … I couldn't see the lieutenants from B Company or any other officers.[37]

The first sergeant was the senior NCO in a company, and he combined administrative duties with military skills:

> First sergeants will be selected habitually from the list of platoon sergeants or staff sergeants (clerical). Leadership should be the outstanding characteristic of a first sergeant. He should be in fact as well as in name a first sergeant, capable of maintaining discipline, conducting drills and instruction, and handling the organisation either in barracks or in the field. His clerical qualifications and duties should be given weight and importance, but placed secondary to the qualification of leadership.[38]

Robert Leckie acted in the role as company clerk when his first sergeant was ill, but found it was 'a boring job, hardly less tedious than the duties of company clerk'.[39] But his own experiences with first sergeants had not been happy, especially with 'Sergeant McCaustic', who 'had taken charge of H company as First Sergeant. He was a slender man hardly above the minimum height requirement, possessed of filthy tongue, twisted by an openly sadistic temperament but saved from being a monster by an excellent sense of humour and a quick brain.'[40]

At the head of the battalion NCO structure was the battalion sergeant major, as described by Leckie: 'Tall, sharp-featured, his sandy hair thinning and the hairs of his military mustache bristling like bayonets, he seemed more like a sergeant of Scots Guards than an American Marines.'[41]

There was a clear distinction between older NCOs who had spent years achieving their rank, and the newer, brasher ones:

> A few weeks earlier these corporals and Pfcs had been privates. Some predated us as marines by that margin only. But in such an urgent time, experience, however slight, is preferred to none at all. … But the First also received a vital leavening of veteran NCOs. They would teach us, they would train us, they would turn us into fighting troops. From them we would learn our weapons. From them we would take our character and temper. They were the Old Breed.[42]

The US marines relied on the navy for medical and chaplaincy services, but in other respects it tried to be a self-contained military force. All marines were trained as infantrymen and that remained their primary role, but most were trained in some other specialisation, in twenty-one different groups. There were nearly thirty thousand artillerymen in 1945, and more than twenty-two thousand engaged in motor transport as drivers or mechanics; 7545 were employed in tanks of amphibian tractors. During the war, men were selected at boot camp according to education, previous experience and aptitude. Among many examples, civilian experience was needed for photographers and band members, two years' high school for fire control and gunnery instructors, a high-school education for radar operators and parachute riggers, and including maths for advanced fire control. The marines preferred to train men within the organisation, though some communicators and radar operators were trained by the army, and fire control and bomb disposal men by the navy.

Signallers mainly comprised field telephone and radio operators. A six-week course for the former was found to be long enough, but a radio operator needed twelve weeks. Between them the communicators made up nearly 9 per cent of the force in 1945. Administrative and clerical staff made up more than 6 per cent. They were selected from among high-school graduates and trained in typing, shorthand and routine Marine Corps administration at the Marine Barracks in Philadelphia Navy Yard and at San Diego. One of Manila John's men was a trained

BAR

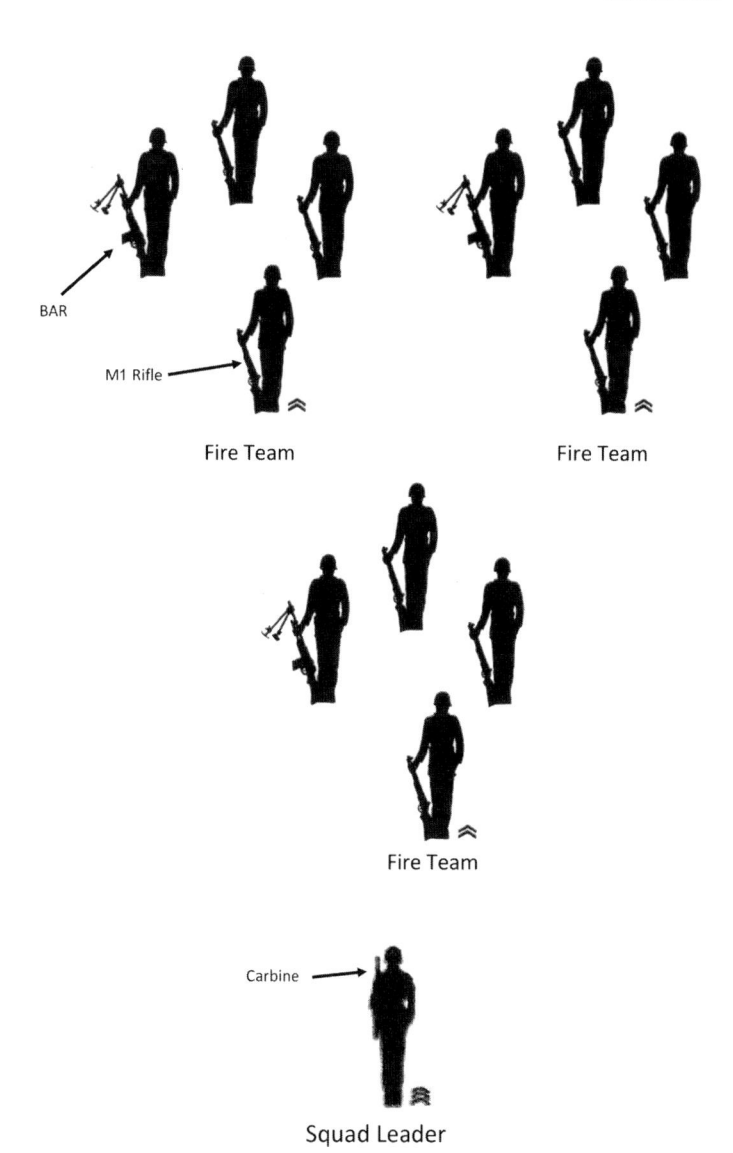

M1 Rifle

Fire Team

Fire Team

Fire Team

Carbine

Squad Leader

The composition of a US Marine rifle squad led by a sergeant, formed of three fire teams each under a corporal, and equipped with M1 rifles, carbines and Browning automatic rifles – the basic unit of the marine infantry.

typist, but he had 'joined the Corps to fight – not type.' Basilone used his influence to allow him to stay with his platoon.[43] The 'Food' group included more than fifteen thousand men in 1945 and was made up of cooks. There were more than twenty-three thousand engineers. Less common specialisations included dog training and post exchange bookkeeping. By 1945 only 57,052 men were pure infantry, less than 13 per cent of the force, and only sightly more than the 55,786 enlisted men in aviation.[44]

The basis of marine infantry organisation was the fire team, consisting of four men led by a corporal, with three M1 rifles and a Browning automatic rifle, or BAR. A rifle squad was made up of three fire teams led by a sergeant, who carried a carbine. Three squads formed rifle platoon led by a lieutenant, who had a platoon sergeant to assist him, with a guide, a demolition corporal and three messengers. Three platoons formed a company under a captain or major, which also had a light machine gun platoon of an officer and fifty-two men, with six Browning light machine guns; and a 60mm mortar section with an officer and nineteen men, and three mortars. The company had a total of seven officers and 247 men if up to full strength. Three of these formed an infantry battalion, which also included an 81mm mortar section and intelligence and communication sections. If up to strength it had a total firepower of twenty-seven flame throwers, nine bazookas, four heavy and eighteen light mortars, eighteen light machine guns, eighty-one BAARs, 421 M1 rifles and 449 carbines. It also had a medical team of two navy doctors and forty pharmacist's mates.

Marines called soldiers 'doggies' or 'dog-faces', and regarded them as greatly inferior in skills and morale, often conscripts who could not be fitted in anywhere better. But they were pleased to see them at Guadalcanal, according to Leckie:

> So we were glad to see the soldiers when they came trudging up to our pits. They came after another air raid; a very close one. But the Thing had not infected them yet. War was still a lark. Their faces were still heavy with flesh, their ribs padded, their eyes innocent. They were older than we, an average twenty-five to our average twenty; yet we treated them like children.[45]

At a much higher level, relations between the two services reached a very low point during the Saipan campaign. One army division, the 27th, part of the New York National Guard and under Ralph M Smith, was placed under the command of General Holland M Smith of the marines. It was ordered to advance up the centre of the island with a marine division on each side. Soon the advance developed in a U-shape, with the marines moving as fast as possible and the army much more slowly. According to one sergeant, 'when the Army came in, and hit a pillbox, they stopped the entire line of their troops until they knocked out that pillbox completely. ... That kind of left the Marines here and the Army there, you know?'[46] Holland M Smith fired his namesake, as he was entitled to do, but that incurred the wrath of Lieutenant General Robert C Richardson, commanding the army forces in the Central Pacific, who ran a heavy-handed campaign against the marine general, reaching Washington and the national press. To the army, the marines were mere 'beach runners', who had no capacity for a sustained campaign (despite the evidence of Guadalcanal), and the army should never be put under their command. Holland M Smith was backed up by his superiors, admirals Spruance and Nimitz.

The M1 Garand rifle was the standard weapon of army and marine infantry. It was 'a self-loading shoulder weapon … gas operated, clip fed and air cooled.' According to the army manual: 'The principal characteristic of the weapon is its mechanical operation which enables the individual rifleman or group of riflemen to deliver a large volume of accurate fire upon any designated point or area within range.'[47] Despite its name, the M1 carbine had very little in common with the Garand rifle. It was mostly used by men whose main job was elsewhere – platoon leaders and sergeants and members of specialist units operating light machine guns and mortars. It was also used by the Seabees. Its 300yd range was much less than the rifle, but it was lighter at 5lbs, and shorter, so that when slung over a marine's back it did not interfere with other duties.

The Browning automatic rifle was also a gas-operated, air-cooled, magazine-fed shoulder weapon, but it was equipped with a tripod because of its greater weight and higher rate of fire. This was 'the infantry's basic automatic rifle. It fired the same cartridges as our Springfield rifles from 20-round reliable clips. It was rather heavy, weighing about 21 pounds with a loaded clip.'[48] It was not intended for single-shot, semi-automatic fire, though it could be done by manipulation of the trigger. Instead, it could fire at the normal rate of 550 rounds per minute or slow rate of 350; but allowing for reloading, the sustained rate was 40 to 60 rounds per minute.[49]

The 60mm mortar was 'a smoothbore, muzzle loaded, high-angle-fire weapon', weighing 45lbs:

> Mortars have a high angle of fire and are particularly effective against enemy troops taking cover in defilades or behind ridges where they are protected from our artillery. The Japs have mortars and know how to use 'em, too. They will be particularly anxious to knock out our mortars and machine guns because of the damage these weapons can inflict on their troops.[50]

According to Sledge:

The job of flamethrower gunner was probably the least desirable of any open to a Marine infantryman. Carrying tanks with about seventy pounds of flammable jellied gasoline through enemy fire over rugged terrain in hot weather to squirt flames into the mouth of a cave or pillbox was an assignment that few survived but all carried out with magnificent courage.[51]

William Rogal describes the typical kit carried by the men for the landing at Guadalcanal:

Most men carried an entrenching tool, either a small shovel or a pick. I reasoned, correctly as it turned out, the shovel would be next to useless in hard compacted soil. ... a few, probably one in four, carried machetes which proved to be very useful in the jungle ... Infantrymen carried 100 rounds of 30-caliber ammunition for their Springfields and an extra 100 rounds in a bandolier. The BAR men and their assistants carried about 20 clips between them. ... Rounding out everyone's armament were two fragmentation grenades and, for riflemen, a bayonet.[52]

In the Pacific War, marines wore a reversible combat uniform with one side in speckled camouflage and the other in green; after the initial landings, the green was usually on the outside, though the helmet cover was still camouflaged. Marines went into action with few visible rank distinctions; as Holland M Smith remarked: 'you can't tell a Pfc from a General in this working outfit, and that's exactly why it was adopted. No amount of pressing will transform our utility clothing into any semblance of a well-tailored uniform.'[53]

The shoes [boots] were known as 'boondockers' and were much valued, according to Leckie. They were 'of buckskin and crêpe rubber, a wonderful soft and comfortable shoe designed to make no noise.'[54] The marine pack was carefully designed, which was necessary on active service conditions:

Each bag was carefully stencilled with our company markings. Then all were carried off on trucks. I never saw mine again until I returned to the states. From that day forward – save for brief intervals in Australia – we lived out of our packs, the single combat pack about the size of a portable typewriter case.[55]

Sailors usually fired their big guns at an impersonal ship or an inanimate land target. Airmen and anti-aircraft gunners fired at machines and glossed over the fact that they contained fellow human beings. Most

Marines in action at Okinawa in 1945, showing a carbine and an M1 rifle. Typically they are wearing helmets with camouflaged covers and green battle uniforms.

soldiers fought at long range and barely saw the enemy as human beings. But the marine battles in the Pacific were far more personal:

> ... we had another motivating factor, as well: a passionate hatred for the Japanese burned through all Marines I knew. ... This collective attitude, Marine and Japanese, resulted in savage, ferocious fighting with no holds barred. This was not the dispassionate killing seen on other fronts in other wars. This was a brutish, primitive hatred ...[56]

Morale was reinforced by strong unit tradition, which was rarer in the United States than the British service:

> It was 'my' company. I belonged and nowhere else. Most Marines I knew felt the same about 'their' companies in whatever battalion, regiment, or Marine division they happened to be. This was the result, or maybe a cause for, our strong esprit de corps. The Marine Corps wisely acknowledged this unit attachment. Men who recovered from wounds or returned to duty nearly always came home to their old company.[57]

Leckie was devastated when he was transferred out of his company. 'Goodbye Chuckler, so long Hoosier and Runner, farewell to H Company. My spirit sank within me. I wept as I walked'.[58]

Sledge noticed the difference when the first conscripts began to appear: 'That was my first encounter with men who had no esprit. We might grumble to each other about our officers or the chow or the Marine Corps in general, but it was rather like grumbling about one's own family – always with another member.'[59]

It was not just technical skill which allowed marine morale to survive the long and often isolated battle for Guadalcanal, the heavy casualties of Tarawa, the slaughter caused by new Japanese tactics at Peleliu, or their most famous battle, Iwo Jima. Watching the famous raising of the Stars and Stripes, the visiting Secretary of the Navy James Forrestal commented to Smith, 'Holland, the raising of that flag on Suribachi means a Marine Corps for the next five hundred years.' In fact, the situation was more complex than presented. The famous photograph actually showed the second raising of a flag, replacing a smaller one; and the identities of the six men involved were never established with certainty, as all but three of them were killed soon afterwards.

But the marines had already proved their endurance in the Guadalcanal campaign, when they lived for months in the most primitive of conditions:

> We still slept on the ground – a poncho under us if it was dry, over us if it was raining. But the mosquito nets were a boon. Now we could use our blankets to sleep on, rather than guard our head against mosquitos … but the nets really came too late. We were full of malaria.[60]

The marines watched as their much-vaunted navy was often defeated off the coast, leading to a shelling by the heavy guns of Japanese cruisers. They were under constant threat of attack by aircraft, and by suicidal Japanese soldiers. Battles were often chaotic. 'Everyone was firing, every weapon was sounding voice; but this was no orchestration, in terribly beautiful symphony of death … Here was cacophony; here was dissonance … for everyone fires what, when and at what he chooses; here was booming, sounding, shrieking, wailing, hissing, crashing, shaking, gibbering noise.'[61] Between battles, there was a 'period of tedium – with its time for speculative dread – [which] leaves his foundation worn lower, his roots less firm for the next trial.'[62] 'With the Japanese, the battle was all night long. Infiltratin' the lines, slippin' up and throwin' in grenades. Or runnin' in with a bayonet or saber.'[63] All this time they believed that the world had forgotten them. On being evacuated after four months, Leckie's colleague asked a soldier: 'had you ever heard of the place before you got here?' The answer startled him. 'Hell, yes, Guadalcanal! The First Marines – everybody's heard of it. You guys are famous.'[64]

The Marine Corps had pioneer aviators by the beginning of the First World War, and during the conflict a force of 282 officers and 2180 enlisted men was raised to support the troops on the Western Front and mount patrols off the Azores and Miami. After the war, it concentrated on support of the marines ashore, and in that sense they were ahead of the RAF and the US Army Air Corps, both of which were obsessed with strategic bombing. In 1927 they pioneered dive-bombing during operations in Nicaragua. From 1933, they were intended to support the Fleet Marine Force. According to the mission statement of 1939, 'Marine Aviation is to be equipped, organized and trained primarily for the support of the Fleet Marine Force in landing operations and in support of troop activities in the field; and secondarily as replacement for carrier based naval aircraft.'[65] But during the first two years of war they spent most of their time protecting the fleet and shore installations. After that they played vital roles in the landings in New Georgia, Bougainville and the Philippines, co-operating with other air forces and developing techniques for close support of infantry. In 1944 they began to operate from carriers on a regular basis.

Pilots were trained as flight cadets as part of the navy, and opted for the marines towards graduation at Pensacola or Corpus Christi. To Samuel Hynes, 'Marines were rough, romantic and elitist; virtually all marine officers got into combat, and though they were supposed to be officers and gentlemen, they were, in our minds, fighting men first.'[66] Potential mechanics were selected at boot camp and sent to a naval technical training centre for aviation machinist courses, with the chance to specialise in engines, propellers, hydraulics and many others.

A fighter squadron at full strength had eighteen aircraft with two spares, eighteen pilots and the same number of reserve pilots, to a total of forty-seven officers and 212 enlisted men. A scout bomber squadron needed more enlisted men as radiomen and gunners. A few larger aircraft were used, including the PB5A, PB4Y and R4D. By the end of the war, aviation was almost a third of the total Marine Corps with 116,628 personnel and 103 squadrons, though it had actually peaked in September 1944 with five wings, thirty-two groups and 145 squadrons.

The marines of both countries developed dramatically during the war. The Royals took on amphibious warfare and commando duties, but despite service in the Falklands War of 1982, even today the British public is only just aware of their existence. The US Marines developed into a much larger and better-known force, celebrated in film by John Wayne's *Sands of Iwo Jima*. Its establishment is larger than that of many world armed forces, and its reputation is universally known.

7
Bases and Logistics

WARSHIPS NEEDED bases for shelter from storms, to rest their crews, to replenish and to make repairs to hulls, especially underwater. British bases were usually built round a series of dry docks which could be emptied to reveal the hull of a ship, and the older ones were therefore known as dockyards. But that was only the core of a base: it would include armament, fuel and victualling facilities, as well as barracks for crews. British bases usually had a large anchorage outside, and Spithead and Plymouth Sound played large roles in naval history, though less in the twentieth century. Bases ranged in age from Portsmouth in England, which was more than four hundred years old, to Ulithi, which was occupied in 1944 and was briefly the largest naval facility in the world.

Dislike between the seagoing navy and dockyard workers was perennial. They were known disparagingly as yardbirds to the US Navy:

> Their hair was too long, their clothes were filthy, and most of them had misplaced their razors. And we were sure that, beyond this, they were devout cowards. They would seldom meet our provocative stares and ignored the insults we delivered when tripping over their power cables, which snaked everywhere, or shielding our eyes from the brilliant blue-white light of their welding arcs, or dodging showers of molten metal from their cutting torches.[1]

'Dockyard mateys' were no more popular with the Royal Navy. According to Nicholas Monsarrat:

> Each day the *Campanula* became a dirtier shambles ... All the decks which we had kept scoured and scrubbed since the day we commissioned became a barnyard of cigarette ends, cartons, crates, wood shavings, oily rags, strips of welding, bits of wire: slices of metal, bottles, cans, half-eaten sandwiches, and gobs of prime Liverpool sputum ... The sight of a filthy raincoat dangling from a gun-barrel had, on day one, seemed scandalous and insulting. Presently it became a natural part of the infected scene ...[2]

But it was different for James Calvert when the submarine *Jack* had its unreliable HOR MAN engines replaced:

> Within half an hour of our arrival workmen were using torches to burn off the superstructure over our engine rooms. They had clearly been coached ahead of time and knew exactly what they were doing on this particular submarine. … The time to complete the entire job was estimated at an unbelievable seven weeks.[3]

The dry dock as used for ship maintenance was at the centre of an established naval base. Entry to one was described by Ted Mason:

> After the tugs had butted the *California*'s bow into the open maw of the dock, they cast off and the dockmaster took over, assisted by muscular riggers and a ship's docking party. With much manhandling of eight-inch manilla hawsers, run from the bitts on the ship to dock bollards, in response to shouted orders and hand signals from the dockmaster, the *California* was hauled in and centered in her granite and concrete sheath. The hollow caisson was closed against the waters of Sinclair Inlet, the pumps were started up and, in a remarkably short time, the ship was resting securely (I hoped) on the keel blocks in the rapidly draining dock.[4]

Yeoman Orvill Raines described one to his wife in 1944:

> We are tied up to a pier. A great big hole is setting over there about a block away. They fill up the big hole with water after setting numerous props and stanchions in the right places. They open the 'gate' or 'lock' and in we go. They close the gate and pump the water out. The ship settles slowly onto the props and stanchions. With all the water gone we look upon the bottom of the ship, scrape its bottom (I said scrape, not scratch) and put on a new paint job.[5]

Shore bases usually provided recreation for sailors, but it was not always wholesome, in any ocean. After an encounter with 'a slender, dark-eyed woman, who looked a little like my seventh-grade teacher', Ted Mason wrote, 'I departed San Diego with my education as a sailor advanced on two fronts. To me, the bordello experience was no less a rite of passage to full manhood than the boot-camp had been':[6]

> I was seconds away from being engulfed by the tide of swinging, ducking, surging, retreating, falling sailors when Johnson grabbed me and pulled me down.

'Take cover, damn it!' he cried. Sure enough, we had no sooner settled under the solid oak table when a whiskey bottle bounced off the topside and shattered into a hundred flying fragments.

As fists flew in the center and glass from the periphery of the moving front, the doors burst open and the peacemakers stormed in, shouting, 'Shore patrol! Break it up, goddamit, break it up![7]

Imperial spread

Over the centuries the British had acquired bases through the world, and places were often captured or retained because of their naval value – Gibraltar in 1704, Malta in 1800, Alexandria from 1882. Others were built within the Dominions, including Simonstown in South Africa. The Singapore base was a major part of defence investment between the wars, but it became a political football, and was not opened until 1938 and completed in 1940. It had the largest dry dock in the world and one of the largest floating docks, as well as the usual range of storehouses and workshops. It was defended from the sea by 15in guns, but the Japanese attack would come from the land.

At home, the Royal Navy had long been centred on three southern English bases, Chatham, Portsmouth and Plymouth, which were well sited for a war with France, but less so for conflict with Germany. They

Rosyth Dockyard in October 1941, as drawn by Muirhead Bone. The new battleship *King George V* is in a dry dock at the centre. Rosyth was safe from bombing compared with the southern English bases, so it was used to fit out the main capital ships.

were more than naval bases: all sailors, except the Fleet Air Arm and various specialist groups, were attached to one or other of them and would return there between ships for training. The towns themselves had large populations of sailors and the means to entertain them and their families. The new base at Rosyth in Scotland, built early in the century with Germany in mind, never took root in that way, and it was in 'care and maintenance' for much of the interwar period, though it had excellent dock facilities.

The home bases saw very little development between the wars and essentially each relied on an infrastructure created in Victorian times, rather like British railways. Each of the main bases had a large wet dock to keep ships afloat and safe, with a number of dry docks leading off, or entered separately. Portsmouth Harbour, for example, was roughly triangular in shape, though the channels within it were more of a Y-shape. On entering, one passed antiquated fortifications to port and starboard, then the torpedo depot of HMS *Vernon*, followed by the great mass of the dockyard, with historic buildings to the south followed by more recent ones. Then came the artificial Whale Island, the navy's principal gunnery school, then the range at Tipner. The northern part of the triangle was dominated by the ancient Portchester Castle, and on the other side were several training bases, followed by the armaments depot at Priddy's Hard and the Royal Clarence Victualling Yard, the successor to the infamous Weevil Yard of Nelson's day, then the submarine base at Fort Blockhouse. Further inland were numerous training bases and residential camps, with the Royal Marine Barracks some way to the east at Eastney.

The British would find that their fixed bases were vulnerable in the age of the bomber and submarine. At home, Scapa Flow was penetrated by *U-47*, which sank the battleship *Royal Oak*. The three southern bases were all subject to heavy bombing, particularly Plymouth, which was the most heavily bombed town in Britain. Shipping in the Firth of Forth near Rosyth Dockyard was bombed in the early stages of the conflict, but the yard was safe once the radar chain was operational, and it was the main site for fitting out capital ships. The Battle of the Atlantic was conducted from the merchant ports of Liverpool, the Clyde and Londonderry, where civilian facilities were adapted for naval use, but Liverpool too was subject to heavy bombing during the winter of 1940/1.

The overseas bases were no safer. In the Mediterranean, Gibraltar was constantly under the eyes of German sympathisers across the bay and was attacked by Italian human torpedoes. Malta was largely neutralised by bombing and blockade and strategically, it has been argued, it might

The heavily bombed entrance to Portsmouth Harbour as painted by Richard Eurich. The battleship *Revenge* is sailing out, escorted by a destroyer. One of the walls of the bombed building is inscribed 'Good old Bubbles' – a reference to the commander-in-chief Sir William James, who was the model for a famous soap advert as a child. There is a refuelling rig in the centre of the picture, barrage balloons fly overhead, and the Isle of Wight is seen in the background. Old Portsmouth is to the left of the entrance with Fort Blockhouse, the submarine base, to the right.

have been better to abandon it. Alexandria was also penetrated by Italian human torpedoes with severe damage to two battleships, and it was under threat of capture every time Rommel's Afrika Korps advanced eastwards. And in the Far East, Singapore and Hong Kong were quickly captured by the Japanese.

Scapa Flow was a ten-mile-square anchorage among the Orkney Islands to the north of Scotland, remote from most facilities, but well situated for controlling Germany's exit into the Atlantic. It had formed the main base of the huge Grand Fleet during the last war, much to the frustration of the sailors, who expected more action and entertainment. It was neglected after the war and only revived in 1938 when it was designated a Category A defended port. But initially it was not well defended, and *U-47* found a way through the sunken blockships in Kirk Sound to torpedo *Royal Oak*. It would serve as the main base for the battlefleet for the rest of the war. It was a bleak area, and Ludovic Kennedy of the destroyer *Tartar* wrote early in the war:

> The islands were treeless, just heather and grass, seabirds and sheep, and across the bare face of the Flow tempests blew, often for days

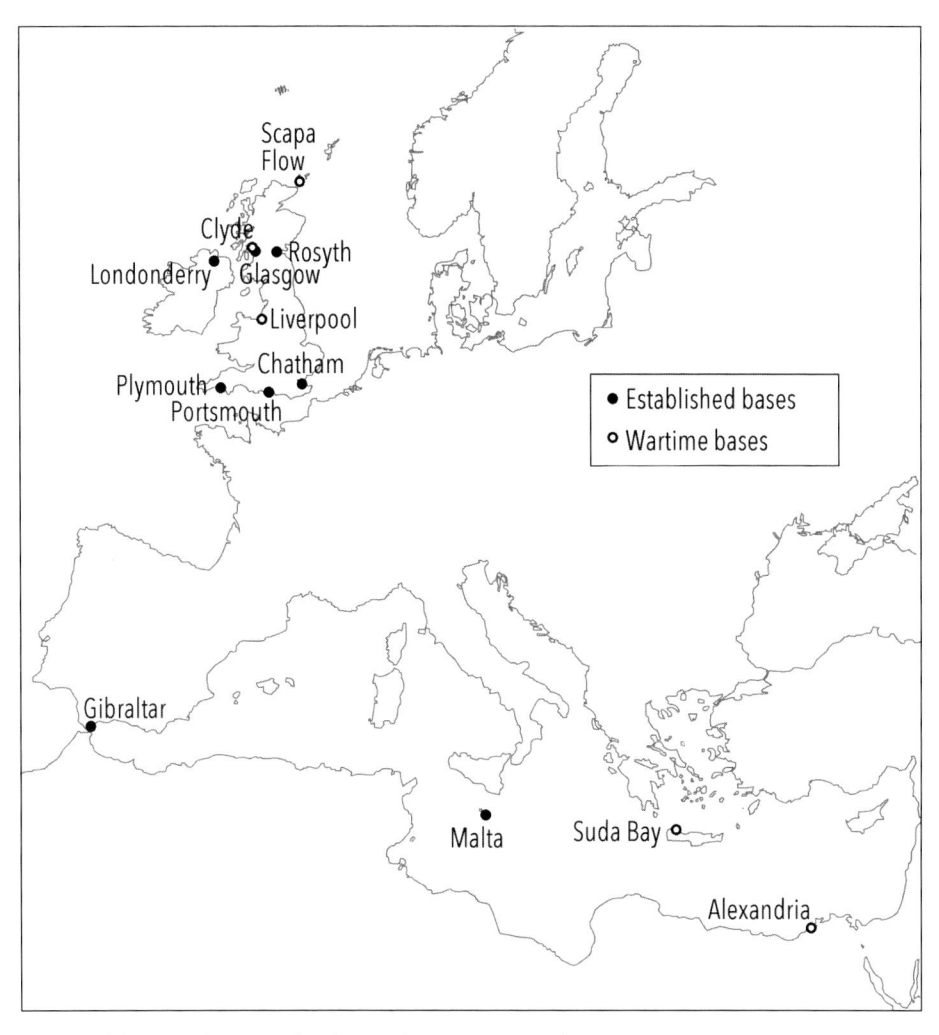

British bases at home and in the Mediterranean. (*Stephen Dent*)

on end. There were no women, shops, restaurants, just a couple of canteens that dispensed warm beer, a hall for film shows and the occasional concert party, and football fields that too often displayed the sign 'All grounds unfit for play.'

The passages to the east where *U-47* had entered to sink *Royal Oak* were blocked by the permanent Churchill Barriers, but friendly ships entered through mines and anti-submarine booms in Hoy Sound to the west and Hoxa Sound to the south. The birdlife and archaeology did not usually attract the young sailors, but the new naval base at Lyness on Hoy

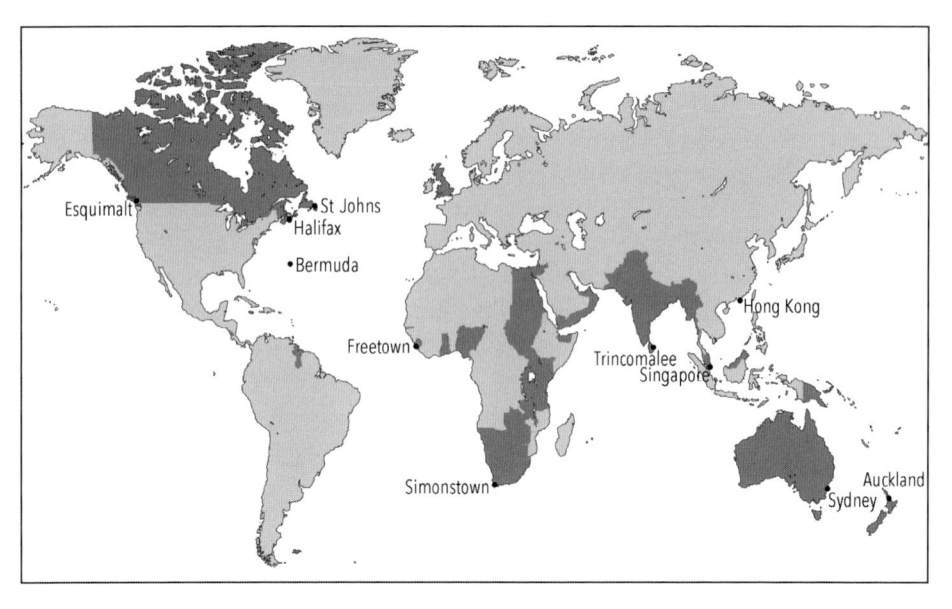

British bases throughout the world, with the Empire and Commonwealth shown in darker grey. (*Stephen Dent*)

had maintenance and leisure facilities which improved over the years, as D A Rayner of the destroyer *Shikari* observed when he returned in August 1943 after three years:

> Where there had been miles of muddy roads and open fields there were now hard roads and serried ranks of good huts. There were canteens for the men and there was also a giant mess for the officers. A busy town had spring up in the salty wilderness, and there were even Wrens about on roads where before only the male of the species had ever been seen.

But as one sailor recounted: 'Harbour routine at Scapa was the same day after day: clean guns; clean ship; watch-keeping; divisions; evening quarters; store parties and sometimes a day on the Island of Flotta doing military training and fraternizing with the local crofters and A.-A. gunsite crews based on the island.'

Obviously, good harbour facilities for sheltering large numbers of ships were a prime requirement in choosing a base. Some were natural harbours such as Spithead and the Clyde, others were largely artificial creations such as the great dock complexes of Liverpool, but it was essential that these facilities were already in existence during the war, as there was neither time nor labour for extensive civil engineering works in wartime.

Some were large harbours such as Halifax, others such as Londonderry were comparatively small and served a more specialised function. Most of the ports were used to assemble large numbers of merchant ships before the convoy sailed, though again Londonderry was an exception as a pure escort base. Some, such as the Clyde and Liverpool, also had loading and unloading facilities for merchant ships in a greater or lesser degree. As to the United Kingdom ports, safety from enemy attack by air and sea was a primary factor. The ports of London and Bristol were largely closed, as were most on the south coast of England. Atlantic convoys were routed round the north of Ireland to the great ports of Liverpool and the Clyde.

Across the oceans

If Britain had a tendency to lose some of its bases during the war, the United States added to them on a huge scale. Perhaps more than any other conflict in history, the Pacific War was about naval bases, beginning with the attack on Pearl Harbor and the loss of Singapore and Hong Kong, followed by the American loss of Guam and the Philippines.

One defining factor in American strategy in the Pacific was Article XIX of the Washington Treaty, yielded only to persuade Japan to accept the 5:5:3 ratio in battleship construction. It was agreed that 'no new fortifications or naval bases shall be established in the territories and possessions specified', which in the case of the United States meant that Guam and Philippines would remain unfortified and vulnerable to be captured – which they were. It caused the navy to make plans and build ships for long-range operations, and eventually to the drive across the Pacific.

The Americans, of course, suffered severely from the bombing of Pearl Harbor, but ironically the Japanese did not target the actual base facilities, the submarine depot and the oil tanks. The continental bases were too far from the enemy to be attacked, despite some panics in the early stages of the war. And the Pacific War was conducted from ports in Australia and New Zealand, and hastily built and temporary bases, mostly on small islands.

In contrast to Britain, the United States saw much investment in naval bases as soon as war threatened, and of course it had the advantage of creating work during the Great Depression. Alongside the Two Ocean Navy Act, the Naval Appropriation Act of 1938 allocated $20 million for public works at navy yards, followed by $116 million in the following years, to a total of $590 million to 1945.

Admiral Yates Stirling tried not to be disappointed when appointed to command the Third Naval District in New York, which included the

Brooklyn Navy Yard, but he knew it would be his last post in the navy. He found the duties were largely ceremonial, involving 'the acceptance of responsibility' and attending numerous official dinners.[8] The real work was done by the Captain of the Yard and the manager who was in charge of production. In 1938 Holden A Evans, a former naval constructor, complained about the policy of using and rotating naval officers in management positions:

> Let us assume you are general manager of a plant employing, say, five thousand people. There are numerous departments: manufacturing, sales, maintenance, personnel. Would you shuffle the heads of these departments every three or four years …? You would not, unless you were anxious to bankrupt the company and ruin yourself. … The British don't do things that way. They have learned their lesson. Their naval industrial activities are controlled by civilians. An admiral superintendent is in charge, but if he does not obtain results a civil servant from the Admiralty advises him …[9]

At lower levels, potential employees were examined by a board including several practical tradesmen and put on two weeks' trial, followed by six months' probation, which might lead to a permanent appointment.[10]

On the East Coast, Portsmouth, New Hampshire, was established in 1800 on five islands at the mouth of the Piscataqua River, near the town of Kittery. It was protected by the Isle of Shoals, but its entrance was well marked. It was mainly used for submarines, constructing approximately half those built during the Second World War, and employed 20,466 workers at it peak in December 1943. The Boston installation, sometimes confusingly known as the Charlestown Navy Yard, was on a site chosen by Josiah Humphreys, the great constructor of the early American navy, at the confluence of the Mystic and Charles rivers. It was situated in the great harbour, well protected from weather and close to the town of Boston. It was greatly extended during the war, while retaining most of its historic buildings. The yard built forty-six destroyer escorts during the war, more than any other yard, and employed about forty-seven thousand people, the great majority in industrial trades.[11]

New York was another great natural harbour, offering a four-mile-wide stretch of water in Upper Bay, and a large number of wharves on the east and west sides of Manhattan just to the north, serving the Atlantic liners and much other traffic. The navy yard was across the East River in Brooklyn. It was largely inactive in the 1920s, but revived with the Roosevelt administration, culminating in the battleship *North Carolina* ordered in 1937. Land area was expanded to 289 acres and two dry docks were enlarged to 1100ft. *Iowa* and *Missouri* were begun in 1940. During the war, repair was its most important task, with around five thousand ships being treated and others converted for war service. Philadelphia was nearly ninety miles up the Delaware River from the ocean and repaired 574 ships during the war and built fifty-three, including two battleships and three aircraft carriers. Its forty-five thousand workers included five hundred women welders. Washington Yard in the capital city was largely devoted to gun production by this time.

Norfolk was situated in the great natural harbour of Hampton Roads, which had seen the first battle between ironclads in 1862, but it was only the Jamestown Exposition of 1907 that brought the area to naval attention, and it was 1917 before land was purchased to set up a base. By the 1930s it was considered the largest operating base in the world. In wartime, it would be the main support for the Atlantic battlefleet, though it was never needed in that role. In 1937 it included a naval training centre, a receiving station, air station, marine barracks and an inactive submarine base sharing its 375 buildings. More land was acquired and a thousand new workers were recruited every month in 1940. It served as the base for the American component of the North African landings of late 1942. HMS *Illustrious* was repaired there in 1941.

Charleston, South Carolina, also had a natural harbour, but the navy was reluctant to set up a base there, and it remained under threat of closure in the 1920s and early 1930s. It revived with Works Progress Administration money, but was still small in 1938 with 1239 employees. It expanded rapidly to a peak of nearly twenty-six thousand workers in 1943, working nine-hour days in three shifts with the yard looking 'like a giant amusement park lighted by neon lights, welders' arcs, the glow of forges and the sparks of molten metal', not something that would have been possible in British yards. Though its main function was designated as repair, it produced many destroyers, destroyer escorts and tank landing ships.

In the Gulf of Mexico and Caribbean, the United States had the primary aim of protecting the Panama Canal, which was essential both in getting ships for the East Coast shipyards and navy yards to the war in the Pacific, and even more important in the supply of oil from the Texan fields to the battle zones. During the war it became the scene of much U-boat activity. The small yard at New Orleans had been closed several times during peace, and it served mainly for personnel administration. It had no dry dock at the beginning of the war, until a small floating dock arrived in May 1943; it would dock 235 vessels during the rest of the war. The yard serviced small minesweepers and escorts, and later landing craft. Cuelbra near Puerto Rica remained insignificant, but the base at St Thomas was developed further.

Guantanamo Bay was sovereign US territory and a base was built round the huge natural harbour, but it played a small role in the war, including the naval postal service. There was a naval air station, Coco Solo, at the entrance to the Panama Canal. The bases were acquired under the deal of 1940 and were all in the Caribbean area except one, on St Lucia, Antigua, Jamaica, British Guiana and the Bahamas. They saw some development by Seabees, mostly as air bases.

On the West Coast, the construction of Puget Sound Yard, fourteen miles west of Seattle in the state of Washington was started in 1891 and saw much investment just before the Second World War with the building of two new dry docks fit to take the *Iowa*-class battleships then under construction. It would repair five of the battleships damaged on 7 December 1942, as well as many aircraft carriers, including *Saratoga* after a torpedo hit in January 1942, and the same ship four more times. Arriving in *California* in 1940, Ted Mason observed:

Puget Sound Navy Yard at Bremerton in Washington State in July 1941. Ships shown include the seaplane tenders *Barnegat*, *Biscayne*, *Casco* and *Mackinac*, the battleships *Colorado* and *Utah*, the cargo ship *Aroostook*, and the repair ship *Prometheus*.

I could see many long red-brick shops, some with tall chimneys, four dry docks of various sizes, and an impressive two-story brick residence crowning a hill to my left – the quarters of the commandant I guessed. The city of Bremerton, cramped on its small peninsula, crowded up against the navy yard fences and gates. Just to my right, a single-ended wooden ferry was backing into a creaky slip. Sprouting from the pier and extending its hammerhead shape across the ship was the biggest crane I had ever seen.[12]

Bremerton had its limitations, but according to Olson, Seattle was the best liberty port of the war.[13]

San Francisco harbour was perhaps the finest of all, with the entrance under the new Golden Gate Bridge. Jim Calvert wrote: 'there is no way one can pass under that beautiful bridge without experiencing a surge of emotion. It is so graceful, so distinctively American, so much a symbol not only of a great city but also of a great nation'.[14] Under it was Treasure Island, almost square in shape and created for the international exposition of 1939. It contained an electronics training facility and a departure and receiving point for crews, as well as a naval air facility. The harbour itself was large enough to hold any fleet, while the main naval facility was at Mare Island thirty-five miles northeast of the city, with facilities for repairing and building ships without recourse to the East-Coast yards and employing more than forty-one thousand at its peak. The Hunters Point shipyard on the west side of San Francisco Bay was taken over by the navy in 1939.

In the Los Angeles region, more facilities were created at Long Beach during the war. Further south, San Diego had a range of facilities and was used to provide logistical support for operation in the ocean.

In the Pacific, Pearl Harbor can claim to be the most famous naval base in history, if only because of the world-changing attack on it in December 1941. The United States annexed Hawaii in 1898 and its two large harbours, Honolulu and Pearl Harbor, began to attract naval attention According to one description: 'Pearl Harbor resembles a great hand of water reaching into the sugar fields … The wrist of this great hand forms the harbor's channel … the palm and outstretched fingers the harbor … the fingers [known as lochs] are two, three and four miles long.' The channel needed much dredging over several decades. The mixed population of the islands, including many Japanese, provoked racial incidents and a fear of sabotage, which altered policy but proved largely unjustified.

The main naval facilities were in East Loch, which had the naval air station of Ford Island in the centre, with cruisers and carried moored to the northwest of it, and the famous battleship row to the southeast. South of that was the naval station with dry docks and a large tank farm; just east of that was the submarine base. South of the naval complex was Hickham Field of the Army Air Force, one of several airfields on the island. There was also a strong army presence on the island, centred on Schofield barracks.

In April the main battlefleet was based at Pearl for manoeuvres, and in an unsuccessful attempt to deter Japanese aggression, it was ordered to stay there instead of returning to San Diego. Admiral Husband E Kimmel concentrated on intensive and exhausting training rather than readiness, to his cost. In March 1941 Commander Parry of the Royal Navy observed, 'Personnel – officers and enlisted men – are being worn out with the present tempo of training'.[15] Crews were enjoying a seemingly well-earned rest when the Japanese struck in the morning of 7 December. The air force suffered heavy losses but the submarine base, dry docks and fuel tanks were largely intact. Salvage work began immediately on the sunken battleships and other vessels, and on the repair of others damaged in the attack. And the sight of the damaged ships, flashed round the world in newsreels, united American opinion in favour of the war effort. On arriving there in May 1943, Jim Calvert of the submarine *Jack* was moved: 'Looking at the actual scenes of this disaster, I felt as though something very sacred to my country had been raped and pillaged – not in the fair give and take of war, but without warning on a calm and peaceful Sunday morning, while men slept in their bunks.'[16]

Pearl Harbor became the centre of American effort in the Pacific, with 5554 ships entering the port for repair, including 1945 treated in the four dry docks. Airfields were built, fuel storage was expanded and barracks were built to receive men. Admiral Nimitz's headquarters was situated in the officers' bungalow compound at Makalapa on the crater of an extinct volcano overlooking the harbour. He lived in a large house with his chief of staff and the fleet medical officer.[17]

The western Pacific bases, Cavite and Olangapo in the Philippines and the island of Guam, were taken by the Japanese soon after their entry to the war. These losses, and the westward advance of American force from 1943, created a need for new bases in the Pacific involving the construction of airstrips, floating docks and harbours.

New bases had to be built in a hurry and in the face of enemy attack and counter-attack. The Japanese assaults on Wake, Guam and Cavite in the Philippines showed that civilian workers were a liability in defence. They were untrained in military discipline, and could be shot as

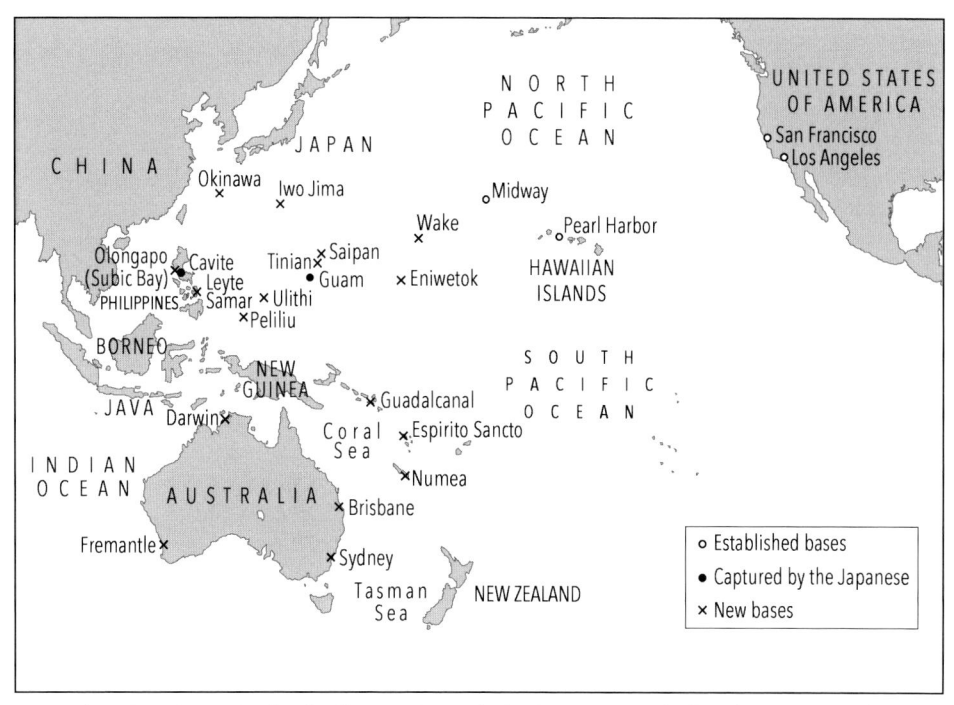

American bases in the Pacific mostly newly built or occupied after the war started. (*Stephen Dent*)

irregular combatants if captured. They could not be ordered to remain in a dangerous area, nor deployed with advancing troops. But the attack on Pearl Harbor caused many thousands of construction workers to want to play their part. Rear Admiral Ben Moreell of the Bureau of Yards and Docks already had plans for a force of base builders in naval uniform, and on 5 January 1942, less than a month after Pearl Harbor, such a force was established. It was soon known as the Seabees, from the initial letters of 'construction battalions'.

It was to be headed by the officers of the existing Civil Engineer Corps. They wore a device of laurel leaves above their stripes instead of the star, and like other non-line officers they had no executive authority. It would not have been practicable to divert line officers from their normal duties to take command of Seabee units, so in 1942 Congress gave them full authority. The Corps had 267 officers at the start of the war; civil engineering graduates were recruited to bring it up to a strength of more than ten thousand by the end.

The second deviation from naval practice was to recruit experienced construction workers directly into petty officer grades after their basic training, instead of sending them to Class A schools, then making them serve as strikers for an indefinite period. The construction worker was something of a blue-collar hero, featuring in the anthem of the Great Depression which was written in 1932: 'Once I built a railroad, now it's done. / Hey Brother, can you spare a dime?'

He had worked on such iconic structures as the Empire State Building, the Grand Coulee Dam and the Golden Gate Bridge. In naval service, he was freed from the main plagues of the construction industry – the constant battle between capital and labour was subsumed in patriotism and sense of purpose, and the worker's fear that he would be discharged as soon as the current job was finished was replaced by the knowledge that there was plenty more work to follow.

The average age of Seabees was about thirty-one, compared with twenty-two and a half for the navy, twenty and a half for marines and twenty-seven for the army. Coming ashore at Guadalcanal, they were greeted by the marines with cries of, 'What the hell, pop! Are we running out of men at home already?' But soon they gained their respect and the two forces worked closely together for the rest of the war.[18] *The Fighting Seabees* of 1944 is unique among John Wayne films in that his character comes to believe in the importance of paperwork: 'That's the Navy way, and that's the way you're gonna do it. And don't forget those daily reports.' In it, the Seabees fight a Japanese invasion on their own, without the support of marines, and using construction equipment as weapons in inventive ways. In real life, they mostly relied on marines and army. Voluntary enlistment ended in December 1942 under the Selective Service Act, but draftees could volunteer for the force until October 1943. By 1945 the Seabees had a total of just under a quarter of a million men, 83 per cent of them serving overseas.

The original complement of a construction battalion was thirty-two officers and 1073 men, divided into four companies plus a headquarters. Construction workers from about sixty different trades were given seemingly nautical titles. A carpenter's mate (CB) was usually a builder; a gunner's mate (CB) might be a demolition expert. 'Shipfitters (CB)' included blacksmiths, welders, plumbers, draughtsmen and steelworkers. At the heart of the corps were the machinist's mates (CB) (equipment operators) who were tasked to 'Operate and maintain trucks, tractors, bulldozers, power shovels, cranes, carryalls, pile drivers, ditchers, rock crushers, rollers and blade grinders in advanced base construction'. Their training was mainly military, as they were assumed to have mastered their trades. Camp Endicott, set up in Rhode Island in June 1942, was able to train ten battalions at a time and had a capacity of fifteen thousand men. Unusually, they were sent into action already formed in units.

The bulldozer was perhaps the most iconic piece of Seabee equipment. According to the *Advance Base Equipment Catalog* of 1944, the 'Tractor, Crawler Type, Class-3' had 50 to 60hp and was:

> diesel powered with electric starter and front and rear lights, mounted on crawler treads, equipped with radiator and crankcase guards, front-pull hooks and rear draw bar, muffler, heavy-duty track roller guards, from idlers and sprocket shields, and power take-off. When furnished as an allowance list item a bulldozer is mounted on each of this class tractor, with a single drum winch on 1 of every 5 and a double drum cable control on 4 of every 5.[19]

During an invasion a bulldozer was often landed first from an LST in order to clear the way, and during the invasion of the Treasury Islands, Machinist's Mate First Class Aurelio Tassone used his blade as a shield, then raised and dropped it on a pillbox, killing a dozen Japanese.[20] It was more mundanely used for clearing a site, often starting by removing trees, in which it was assisted by the 'Puller, Tree and stump, Tractor Operated'. The 'Scraper, Carryall' was 'for excavating, carrying, and spread dumping for the cut and fill operations necessary in the construction of roads, streets, and airfields.'

The iconic Seabee vehicle – a bulldozer in use at the training centre, Camp Endicott, Rhode Island, in 1943.

The Seabees had various models of mobile crane, which could be used in unloading cargo or as a power shovel, among other functions. Jack Cornwell landed at Iwo Jima from an LST:

> A Northwest 25 was a big, slow thing on treads with a rotating cab and a long boom; even with its big diesel engine it could only do about two miles an hour. … I needed to work on the airfield, so the mechanics changed my rig over from a bucket to a shovel. I put in nine or ten hours a day extending the original airstrip to make it big enough to accommodate B-29s. Marines were fighting for the very piece of ground where we were trying to enlarge the strip. We had to watch out for snipers and mortar fire and live ammunition and mines.[21]

They used the 'Spreader, Box to distribute materials for the construction, maintenance and repair of roads, streets and airfield runways.' The sheepsfoot roller was intended for 'deep tamping of fills to prevent settlement under road, street and airfield traffic'.

Seabees became expert at erecting Quonset huts, the American version of the ubiquitous British Nissen hut, which was actually invented by a Canadian colonel. The standard 20ft by 48ft model could accommodated twenty enlisted men in double-deck bunks, or ten officers in single bunks with a toilet in the corner – though the Seabees themselves mostly lived in pyramidical five-man tents while construction was in progress, then moved on to other jobs. Quonset huts could also be used for hospitals, headquarters, offices, stores, magazines and many other functions. One refinement was the Quonset redesigned, with 4ft vertical side walls to save space. Twenty-five thousand of these were erected out of a total of 153,000 huts built.[22]

Floating pontoons were another Seabee icon. Before the war, Captain John N Laycock experimented by joining cigar boxes and found the assembly had surprising strength. Steel boxes 5ft by 5ft by 7ft were to form the basic unit. These could be joined together to form part of a pier or landing stage. They first saw action in the invasion of Sicily, linking LSTs to the shore over beaches which would otherwise have been impossible for landing, and this was followed up at Kwajalein and the Marshalls. A string of pontoons 175ft long could be carried on each side of an LST and dropped into the water, to be towed into place by an amtrac. To form a longer causeway to the beach, strings of pontoons overlapped in 'slide-rule' fashion. They could be fitted with a curved bow with an outboard motor astern to make a barge. Others could be used in servicing PT boats.

Airstrips were perhaps the most important construction jobs, which might be made entirely of live coral in the Pacific:

> The strips were a beautiful hard white, made of living coral dredged up from the nearby bay and kept alive by being watered daily with seawater sprayed from a sprinkler truck. So long as it was watered it continued to live and every day the steamrollers crushed it smooth and hard again.[23]

Lieutenant-Commander Sam Mathis described the process in 1942:

> We arrived at Espirito Sancto on the afternoon of July 8. There wasn't a damn thing there but jungle. We began unloading and clearing. … We set up floodlights and worked around the clock. I had twelve Seabees who operated nine big pieces of equipment twenty-four hours a day for a month. … On a typical day – say July 21 – here is who we had working on the field: 295 army infantrymen, 90 marines, 32 Seabees and 50 natives. The Seabees were running the equipment; the rest were clearing by hand. We and six tractors, two scrapers, one grease truck, one gas wagon, three weapons carries and one 50-kw light generator.[24]

Others were covered with Marston mat, named after the village near where it was first tested. Later known as 'pierced steel planking', it

The 62nd Seabee Battalion uses a mechanical digger to remove steaming volcanic ash at Iwo Jima in 1945.

consisted of a number of 10ft by 15in steel plates each pierced with eighty-seven holes in three rows, to allow drainage. They could be stacked for stowage, and a 5000ft runway would take up about 20 per cent of the cargo of a Liberty ship. On site, the sections could be moved by hand, and they would interlock with L-shaped hooks and be secured by U-shaped spring clips.[25] It was easy to replace. At Guadalcanal, 'We found that 100 Seabees could repair the damage of a 500-pound bomb hit on an airstrip in 40 minutes, including the replacing of the Marston mat.'[26]

Fuel tanks are a defining feature of any twentieth-century naval base. Tanks of one thousand-barrel capacity were of 29ft diameter and were 16ft high, or 30ft by 8ft. They were used for storing high-octane aviation fuel and were made up of sections to be erected brickwork-style. The higher tank could be built in ten eight-hour man-days and the lower version in six. Tanks of ten thousand capacity were for oil or diesel for ships. Each took eighty man-days to erect.[27]

Regular troops disliked loading and unloading ships, known as stevedoring, while civilian workers would not be available in forward areas. Stevedore battalions were formed from the autumn of 1942, trained on a full-sized model of a Liberty ship at Camp Peary in Virginia. About forty of these 'special' battalions were formed, each including a construction platoon to set up dock facilities. Some of them, in accordance with the segregation policy, were manned by African-Americans.

Chaplain Clemen McHale watched the specials at work:

> Aboard ship the hatches are open, booms are rigged, winches are in neutral, the Seabee gangs are waiting. As the barge comes alongside, the cargo nets and slings move upward from the holds carrying tons of vital needs. Guns, grenades, serums, plasma, food, fuel, clothing tobacco, bulldozers and tanks – they all move upwards high in the air, then over the side and down to the pitching barge, where the Seabees jump in and lash them fast. ... Deep in the hold of the ship, too far down to feel even the whisper of a breeze, the Seabees are stripped to their waists. Sweat pours in torrents ... but they keep rushing. Always the next lift must be ready when the hook comes back from its journey over the side. Keep that hook moving![28]

Admiral Mitscher compared the Seabees favourably with army engineers, though perhaps not without bias: 'The sea and air battles off Okinawa could have been shortened considerably if the army had established airfields and put them into operation as rapidly as the Seabees had done in other places.'[29]

They also contributed to the war in the Atlantic, building a base at Argentia in Newfoundland, and impressing Commander Donald Macintyre of the Royal Navy:

> So out of nothing a base was to be created. The dock facilities, the repair shops, the supply organisation and the refuelling arrangements of old-established ports like Liverpool or Greenock, as well as a full-sized air station, had to be provided in a few months. It was a project to daunt the heart of anyone accustomed to the orderly and deliberate progress of peace-time civil engineering. But to the Americans with their tireless, New World enthusiasm and utter disregard of the cost, it was just another job.[30]

On the other side of the Atlantic they built facilities at Londonderry in Northern Ireland and Roseneath on the Firth of Clyde.

The servicing of ships' hulls was an essential base operation, normally done in large docks which formed the core of navy yards. At the beginning of the war, the USN only had three floating dry docks, which could be towed from place to place and sunk to allow the entrance of a ship, then raised again. It was sceptical of their value, but clearly they had a key role in the island-hopping of the Pacific war if ships were not to be sent thousands of miles back to Pearl Harbor or the mainland for routine repairs and battle damage. They built 150 during the war, fifty of timber, a dozen of concrete and eighty-eight of steel. The largest were the Advanced Base Sectional Docks, or ASBDs, usually made up to ten sections to a total length of 927ft, with a lifting power of 90,000 tons. Bow and stern were faired to aid towing, and the walls could be folded down to reduce wind resistance. The smallest ones, the twenty-nine ARDs, or Auxiliary Repair Docks, were made in a single piece and could service smaller vessels from destroyer escort downwards.

Fahey was impressed with the large floating dock at Havannah Harbour in the New Hebrides: 'The huge dock floats in the water with our ten thousand ton cruiser snug inside. It's quite an experience. The ship looks as if it were sitting in the centre of a huge ballfield.' He was less impressed to be chosen to scrape the bottom of the ship, after which, 'I looked like a coal miner. The stuff really sticks to you.'[31]

Perhaps the most spectacular achievement was the great base at Ulithi, which consisted of four large islands and many smaller ones and reefs, forming an atoll described as looking 'like a mushroom with a broken stem or a dishevelled necklace'. It was around twenty miles in each direction and enclosed an area of eighty-five square miles, mostly suitable for anchorage. The Japanese had discounted it, because they believed it would not be possible to build an airfield on any of the islands, so the American landing in September 1944 was unopposed. The survey ship *Sumner* began to sound and buoy the lagoon and it was considered capable of accommodating over seven hundred vessels. Seabees arrived to construct an airfield on Falalop where the Japanese had failed, and it accommodated a marine air wing for defence of the harbour and its ships. Asor was used as headquarters for Commodore Oliver Kessing, and Sorlen was the base for a fleet of four hundred small boats used to service the ships. Lieutenant J L Vollbrecht wrote the forty-seven-page *Ulithi Encyclopaedia*, which said much about the natural history of the island and its amenable people under King Ueg, who were evacuated to the island of Fassarai on the southern tip of the atoll.[32] But like their equivalents at Scapa Flow, the great majority of sailors took little interest in these matters and looked for recreation, which was available on the island of Mogmog. As an officer, Edward Stanford saw it positively:

> It was all sea and sky, you had to look for the land. The lagoon inside a thin ring of reefs and low islands was so large (twenty miles by about eight miles) that ships at one end of the anchorage were invisible from the other. Except for the lack of ground swell it was like anchoring in midocean. And add to sea and sky the trade wind. This was a continuous fact of life, like night and day, steady, always from due northeast … on the tiny islands … there was a short airstrip, a small hospital, a post office, and on flat, sandy little Mogmog at the northern end, a glorious recreation area. But the lagoon could comfortably hold seven hundred … so that Ulithi was in effect a secure base in midocean for warships needing those services, and a rest area for battle-weary seamen …[33]

Not everyone agreed that Mogmog was 'glorious', certainly not Alvin Kernan:

> Fights broke out now and again between the crews of different ships … Mostly, however, even hardened sailors, wild for liberty and drink, blanched at the sight of Mog Mog, and there was – an unheard of thing – a long line of men back at the landings waiting to return to their ships.[34]

The number of cans consumed of beer and soft drinks amounted to 7.6 million, showing how the area was used.

The anchorage at Ulithi, Caroline Islands, containing dozens of ships in November 1944. At the time, it was the largest naval base in the world.

Logistics

With the short range of British destroyers and corvettes, and the unexpected extension of the Atlantic War, some means of refuelling at sea had to be found. Captain Donald Macintyre summarised the development:

> ... the technique of refuelling at sea was perfected, at first by means of a floating hose towed astern of a tanker and picked up by the warship and connected to her fuelling system. This method, though at first sight simple and safe to employ in rough weather, suffered from unexpected difficulties ...[35]

Peter Gretton experienced it in 1943:

> There was an escort tanker to be visited, too. This ship, the *British Lady*, was fitted with a buoyant rubber hose which she streamed astern and which we picked up and secured at our forecastle. Oil could be pumped through the hose at a reasonable rate, and once secured the operation did not take very long, perhaps two hours for a normal refuel. But picking up the gear was not easy, especially in bad weather, and station-keeping astern of the tanker was a difficult task.[36]

Macintyre describe the alternative, the alongside method:

> As the destroyer draws nearer to the tanker, the speed has to be adjusted with extreme accuracy and down in the engine room, knowing the importance of this, the artificers on the manoeuvring valves stand with their eyes glued to the revolution counters ... At the right moment on the upper deck, the line throwing gun cracks and a line goes soaring over the tanker's decks to be quickly grabbed by her crew ... As the two ships get closer, their mastheads swinging in giddy arcs towards and away from one another, the seas heave and foam between them. ... Meanwhile, in the tanker a derrick swings out, carrying the oil hose in a large bight or loop. ... Oiling may take an hour or more ...[37]

But he had to admit that 'It was never a manoeuvre that I learnt to take light-heartedly in a seaway'.[38]

As a young lieutenant Chester Nimitz had participated in early experiments in refuelling ships at sea in 1916, and it proved its worth in getting destroyers across the Atlantic to join the European war in the following year. The idea gained further prominence in 1938 when Leahy, as CNO, became more aware of the problems of a Pacific war. Nimitz, now a rear admiral, recommended the 'broadside approach' based on past experience, and in subsequent exercises it was applied to the largest ships. In 1941 a Royal Navy observer onboard the battleship *North Carolina* was impressed and remarked that the procedure had been so perfected that 'no orders whatever were given when securing the destroyers alongside' while the ship's band played sprightly tunes and ice cream was passed across.[39]

Refuelling at sea was used in the early stages of the war, but an expedition to relieve Wake failed in December 1941, because of difficulties with the tanker *Neches*, which was sunk the next month on the way to attack the island with the carrier *Lexington*. In February and March tankers supported *Enterprise*, *Yorktown* and *Lexington* in several raids, and in April the tankers *Cimmaron* and *Sabine* refuelled *Hornet* and *Enterprise* in the famous Doolittle raid on Tokyo. Carriers were supported in the battles of Coral Sea and Midway, and by the time the United States began offensive operations the technique was well honed.[40] It was described by Edward Stafford:

> *Abercrombie* went alongside *Hase* for her first actual underway refuelling. *Hase* slowed to twelve knots and Katschinski eased the ship up parallel to the tanker's starboard side, fifty to seventy-five

feet away, until her bridge was opposite the 'Sugar' flag draped across a guntub on the larger ship, then slowed to maintain position. A line-throwing gun cracked from *Abercrombie*'s fo'c'sle and a long brass pin trailing a light line arched over and draped itself across the transport. It was quickly picked up and a heavier 'messenger' line was secured to it. On *Abercrombie*'s deck the shot line and messenger were hauled back in, bringing over an eight-inch manila towing hawser. With the hawser secured well forward on the *Hase* and tending aft at a sharp angle to the big towing bitts under *Abercrombie*'s bridge, other messenger lines went over fore and aft and were hauled back aboard, bringing with them two heavy, black, four-inch fuel hoses, which were thrust down the *Abercrombie*'s fuelling trunks and secured with light line to pad eyes so they could not pull out. A heaving line from the transport brought over a phone rigged bridge-to-bridge, and a distance line, marked off by red, yellow, blue, white and green flags every twenty feet, was secured on the transport and kept taut by the sailors. For a constant check on the width of the twelve-knot river of Pacific blue water rushing between the ships. Then after a go-ahead by phone, the *Hase* started pumping, and the black Navy Special fuel

The oil tanker USS *Manatee* refuelling the battleship *Massachusetts* at sea off Okinawa in 1945, showing the lines passed from ship to ship.

oil gushed into the *Abercrombie*'s tanks at a rate of fifteen thousand gallons an hour from each hose.[41]

The main tankers of the US Navy were the thirty ships of the *Cimarron* class, with the name ship being launched in 1939. During the Gilberts operation, each carried 80,000 barrels of fuel oil, 18,000 of aviation gasoline and 6782 of diesel. In addition, a dozen ships of the *Suamico* and fifteen of the *Escambia* classes were built during the war, carrying between 130,000 and 150,000 barrels of oil, besides other classes.

Any success that the Royal Navy had in the Atlantic was not reflected in the Pacific, where distances were much greater and fleets consumed huge quantities of aviation fuel and ammunition for shore bombardment. The idea of a fleet train was new to the Royal Navy, which had relied on its numerous worldwide bases since the advent of steam power. But at the Quebec conference of September 1944 Churchill promised that they could produce a force to operate for a long period independent of shore resources, to American scepticism. But already the task was becoming harder: by November it was clear that the fleet would have to operate 3500 miles from its bases in Australia and at Manus, rather than 200 miles. British shipping was in very short supply after the losses of the Atlantic, and merchant shipping had been left to the Americans during the war, so the fleet train that was assembled had many deficiencies. In September 1944 it had two armament supply issuing ships instead of the thirteen required, with eight coming forward; two naval stores issuing ships instead of twelve, with three being built in Canada; and there were similar deficiencies in other types. As it turned out, the US Navy was quite generous in its help, but there were limits. By the spring of 1945, during the Leyte operations, there were sixty-nine ships in the fleet train, including escort carriers and vessels, minesweepers, headquarters ships and a dozen tankers.

Perhaps the biggest problem was in tankers, and only a scratch force could be assembled, of many different types, slow and poorly equipped, and manned by inadequately trained merchant navy crews from many different nations. Some of them still tried to use the astern method, which failed in June when *King George V* suffered from parting of messengers and bursting of buoyant hoses and was forced to use the alongside method which she was not equipped for. But this set a precedent: all fuelling of battleships would now be alongside. It was not the final solution; in July refuelling was well behind when a typhoon delayed the operation, and allowed the British to save some face with the Americans. Admiral Fraser reported, 'With dogged persistence the British Pacific

Fleet is keeping up … but it is tied by a string to Australia, and much handicapped by its few small tankers.'[42]

At the end of the war the Royal Navy's fleet train in the Pacific consisted of 121 vessels under a rear admiral, including six escort carriers and thirty-seven other escort vessels; two floating docks, eighteen oil and four water tankers, thirteen armament-carrying and issuing ships, three hospital and four accommodation ships, as well as aircraft maintenance and repair ships and sundry others.[43]

As early as 1904 a floating naval base had been suggested for the US Navy, and some support facilities were provided for Theodore Roosevelt's Great White Fleet of 1907–09. And the experience helped in setting up bases at Queenstown and Brest during the First World War. The fleet train featured in the Fleet Problems between the wars, but that did not anticipate the scale of what was to follow.

The advanced bases built by the Seabees were essential, but were still not enough. In the Gilbert Islands operation of November 1943, the base at Espirito Sancto was more than a thousand miles away, which would have necessitated a round trip of five days for each ship refuelled. Essentially, a mobile naval base was needed, not just with fuel, but with all other facilities needed. The Mobile Service Squadron under Captain Schull in the Gilberts operation included a destroyer tender, oiler, repair ships, survey ship, a salvage vessel, fleet and rescue tugs, minesweepers, subchasers and transports. Groups like this operated with great efficiency during all the later operations. In the Leyte campaign, the Third Fleet was supported by the Sea Logistics Service Group under Captain Acuff and included thirty-four fleet oilers, eleven escort carriers, nineteen destroyers, seagoing tugs and various civilian ammunition ships. It delivered 8.5 million barrels of fuel oil and 14.5 million barrels of aviation gasoline.[44]

The practices of the two navies were almost the direct opposite during the Second World War. Apart from a few short-lived expedients such as Suda Bay on Crete, the British relied on long-established fixed bases, while the Americans built hundreds of new bases around the world. The British failed to develop effective refuelling at sea until late in the war, greatly reducing their tactical effectiveness. Essentially, this was because the Americans had planned for a long-range war, the British had not.

8
The Ships

MOST OF the ship types of the Second World War had an Anglo-American origin. Despite its deliberate isolation from world affairs for most of its history, the United States contributed more to the delineation of the basic types than any other nation apart from Britain. Britain had ruled the seas with the sailing ship of the line, which became the line of battle ship, or the battleship. The Admiralty was far less conservative about technology than its popular reputation suggests, and it had steam-powered ships of the line by 1845; the Crimean War of 1854–56 confirmed that the pure sailing ship had no place in warfare, but it was the American Civil War which brought about the next step. The Confederates deployed the first armoured ship in *Merrimack*, or *Virginia*. The Union quickly replied with *Monitor*, with its guns in turrets, and this changed the face of naval warfare. The British had already started an armoured ship in *Warrior*, but the attempt to use turrets and a sail and steam ship, *Captain*, resulted in her catastrophic loss. In 1871 they built *Devastation* with no sail power. The post-Civil War US Navy was severely starved of funds and it was the British, inspired by competition with France and then Germany, who reached the next stages – seagoing battleships with the *Royal Sovereign* class of 1891, and the famous all-big-gun, turbine-powered *Dreadnought* of 1906. Though the term 'dreadnought' was no longer used – all battleships of the Second World War era followed that concept, but with the addition of anti-aircraft armament on much bigger and faster ships carrying bigger guns.

The submarine was invented by the Irish-American John Holland, though he was not the first American to attempt such a vessel. As well as inventing the aeroplane, Americans were the first to launch one from a ship. The British, however, developed the first true aircraft carrier by the end of the First World War. They built the first destroyers as an answer to French torpedo boats, and necessity caused them to develop the first anti-submarine escort vessels. All these types, plus the cruiser, were in existence by 1922, when the game changed again with the Washington Treaty.

Naval architects on both sides of the Atlantic were familiar with the principles of ship design, which were taught at many universities. Hydrodynamics and hydrostatics were unchanging sciences, but mastery of them was only part of the naval architect's skill. He had to fit all the necessary armament, armour, accommodation, engines, fuel, sensors and other features into a given size of hull, while keeping cost down in peacetime and expediting construction in wartime. He had to concern himself with safety, reliability, seakeeping and maintenance. He was usually working to a specification provided by his superiors and the limitations of that, rather than any faults of the designer, were generally the cause of the weakness of a particular type: for example, the British *King George V*-class battleships.

Every ship design is a series of compromises. According to Mahan, 'You cannot have everything. If you attempt it, you will lose everything ... On a given tonnage ... there cannot be had the highest speed, *and* the heaviest battery, *and* the thickest armour, *and* the longest coal endurance, which the tonnage would allow to any one of these objects by itself.'[1] In later years, he might have mentioned the need for anti-aircraft and anti-submarine armament and for sensors such as radar and sonar and the means to assess the information provided by them.

A warship combines three main features. Most obviously, it needs armament – some combination of guns for use against ships, targets on shore and aircraft, torpedoes, depth charges and other anti-submarine weapons. In the case of an aircraft carrier, that might include the aircraft, and for a landing ship or craft it comprised the troops and equipment which would be put ashore. And these types usually had an anti-aircraft armament for their own protection.

Secondly, a warship needs mobility, which includes speed and range, as well as seakeeping and stability in all kinds of weather. It also includes habitability, that the crew can be fed and rested and can stand the conditions over a long voyage without loss of efficiency. Thirdly, it needs protection – armour in the case of battleships, cruisers and some aircraft carriers, anti-torpedo bulges in the largest ships, and subdivision so that a single hit does not do too much damage. It also includes the manoeuvrability which might protect against submarine or aerial attack, and systems of firefighting and damage control when an attack is partially successful. It is the resolution of these compromises, rather than any mystical skill in drawing the lines of a ship, that produces a successful design.

According to Hovgaard, who had trained at Greenwich and taught several generations of American warship designers at MIT:

Warships are built primarily for war service. The conditions likely to obtain in war should be determinative in all questions where the efficiency of the ship as a fighting machine is involved. …

Nautical and technical requirements, such as those concerning stability, buoyancy, strength, seagoing capability, and maneuvring, in so far as they affect the safety of the ship and military efficiency, should rank in importance with military requirements, and in fact be regarded as such.

Efforts should be made to save weight and space wherever possible, but must not be carried beyond the point where the reliability and efficiency of the materiel begin to suffer thereby … Likewise, where the living conditions and comfort of the personnel are below a certain standard, efficiency will fall off in the length of time.[2]

A fourth factor by the second quarter of the twentieth century was sensors, for the lookout's eye was no longer enough for a warship to function. Anti-submarine vessels used Asdic or sonar from the aftermath of the First World War. Radar was developed just before the war and fitted to all substantial vessels towards the end. Its interpretation needed areas like the combat information centre, which took up space onboard, and its high-level masts and aerials tended to create stability problems in ships which had not been designed with it in mind.

Stability was especially important in a warship, which often had to carry its armament well above the centre of gravity, and might have to operate in all kinds of weather (though the Royal Navy did not take account of Atlantic conditions before the war). High radar aerials, layers of paint and Arctic ice could add to the problem. Stability was 'a measure of the moment of force trying to bring the ship upright from a heeled position.' The centre of gravity was fixed at any given moment, the centre of flotation would move as the ships heeled, creating a righting movement until went beyond its 'range', when the ship would capsize. Detailed weight calculations were needed to establish these factors, and British naval architects tended to use previous experience as a standard. Destroyers were particularly vulnerable, with their long and narrow hulls and extensive additions of radar and anti-aircraft armament. The British were proud that none of theirs capsized due to stress of weather, whereas the Americans lost four, including three in the typhoon of December 1944. This led to new standards which were adopted by other nations, including Britain.[3]

The speed of a surface ship was limited by its bow wave – if that exceeded the length of the ship, then at high speed it was permanently climbing up it. Speeds of more than about 36 knots were only obtained at high cost. The fast cruiser-minelayers of the *Abdiel* class were roughly equivalent to the later Battle-class destroyers in size. They had a speed of 40 knots rather than 36, but that was only obtained by a 44 per cent increase in horsepower, from 50,000 to 72,000. One way round this was to design a 'planing' craft, with a hull shaped to lift most of it out of the water at high speed. This was the general principle of the motor torpedo boat.

The shape of the hull, the 'lines', was drawn out, often based on previous experience. A very accurate model was made and towed through the water in a test tank, the Admiralty one at Haslar near Portsmouth or the David W Taylor tank which was built in 1939 at Bethesda in Maryland to succeed one in Washington. Completed ships were subjected to inclining experiments in a dock to test their stability.

Britain took the Washington and London treaties very seriously. The legalistic minds of the British civil service were determined to stay within the limits to set an example to other powers. The Royal Navy was equally determined to get the maximum use out of every pound of displacement. The naval constructors had to resolve this conflict by building almost exactly to the limit. Each section of a shipbuilding contract carried the injunction in bold type, 'Economy of weight in this vessel is of utmost importance. The Contractors are required to keep this continually in view, and when detailed drawings are prepared for submission to the Admiralty all proposals are to be closely analysed with a view to economy of weight.' In the yard, an official known as the Recorder of Weights was 'responsible for obtaining the duly certified weight of each such article'. One solution was to use a special type of steel known as D-quality, which was lighter and stronger than normal steel, but it needed special equipment to work it. Ironically, it was very difficult to weld, which would have saved much more weight as compared with traditional riveting.

Though the US Navy was not able to build up to the overall treaty tonnage until the Vinson–Trammel Act of 1934, officials were just as strict in imposing the limits on individual ships, and an isolationist Congress was likely to object to any violation which might give an excuse to other naval powers.

Ship designers

British warships were usually designed by members of the Royal Corps of Naval Constructors under the Director of Naval Construction. Sir Stanley Goodall was born in 1883, the son of a London firefighter. He was a brilliant student at the Royal Naval College. He worked with American designers during the First World War, and then went through a frustrating period when many of his designs failed to reach fruition.[4] He was appointed to the post in 1936, in time to supervise most of the post-treaty construction, including the *King George V*-class battleships, the *Belfast*- and *Arethusa*-class cruisers, the wartime destroyers and the new corvettes and frigates. He retired in 1944 to be succeeded by Sir Charles Lillicrap.

Naval constructors were recruited from among dockyard shipwright apprentices, using a rather cruel and wasteful Victorian system by which about half of them were weeded out every year. According to one of them:

> In 1927 only 50 apprentices were accepted at Portsmouth. At the end of each (school) year an examination was held and apprentices who failed to qualify had to leave. So after four years only a dozen of the original fifty survived and these, together with the fourth year students of Plymouth, Chatham, Sheerness ... had to compete for one *only* constructor cadet post and one only electrical engineer cadetship.

Successful youths went to the Royal Naval College at Greenwich to study naval architecture to degree standard. A qualified man might be sent to the Admiralty Office in Whitehall. As an assistant constructor second class, he would join a team, perhaps designing a new class of ship:

> ... the Constructor had his desk in the middle of the room with his team around him (Constructors were then usually in their early-middle forties having had to pass through Second and First Class AC stages) ... Constructors were always addressed as 'Sir' by all members of the team ... Christian names were very seldom used except between equal grades or personal friends.

As well as the drawings, numerous and accurate calculations were needed. The constructor in charge of the Hunt class of destroyer escorts miscalculated the height of the centre of gravity and the short-staffed department had no one available to check it. It was not discovered until inclining tests in February 1940 and the constructor concerned was said to be 'very contrite'. Major modifications had to be made to the design.[5] As well as ship design, constructors supervised building in private yards, and played a leading role in the Royal Dockyards at home and overseas.

In 1937 the department of the Director of Naval Construction, besides clerical and administrative staff, had thirty-four senior draughtsmen, eighty first-class and 122 second-class draughtsmen, for they would

The inboard profile of the destroyer *Glowworm* as designed in 1935, showing the engines and many other features – perhaps the most sophisticated type of plan produced by the draughtsmen of the Royal Corps of Naval Constructors.

have to produce the plans of new ships in great detail. There figures were more than double those of the previous year, reflecting the end of the treaty system and the demands for new types of ship.[6] In 1939 it was decided to evacuate the department to Bath because of the threat of bombing, though Goodall objected that it would sever direct contact with ministers and Admiralty Board members. Long-term residents were displaced from hotels such as the Grand Pump Room and the Pulteney and bathrooms were fitted with drawing boards. About five hundred staff and families arrived by train and car and made the best of it until huts were built nearby. In 1942 Goodall and some of his key staff returned to London.

By the end of the war the Department of Naval Construction had expanded to include thirty-six senior staff, sixty-three chief and senior constructors, both permanent and temporary; thirty-six permanent and seventy-two temporary constructors; and forty-one permanent and forty-four temporary or acting assistant constructors.[7]

Ship design for the United States Navy was the responsibility of the Construction Corps, who were naval officers, unlike their British counterparts. In the early part of the century, the course was a desirable option which attracted the best midshipmen. It offered a far more settled life and a qualification which was marketable outside the navy, and interesting work without the long periods of boredom associated with sea service. Richmond Kelly Turner did well in his final examinations at Annapolis in 1908 and wrote to his mother, 'With that standing, I could probably get into the Construction Corps, but I prefer the Line.'[8] Eighteen of the twenty men who finished top at Annapolis opted for the Construction Corps in the first twenty years of the scheme. That began to decline in the 1920s and 1930s, and in 1940 the Construction Corps was abolished and the officers transferred to the line with the same status as Engineering Duty Only officers.

From 1897 potential members of the corps were sent on an intensive three-year course at the Massachusetts Institute of Technology leading to a Master of Science degree. Until 1933 it was taught by the Danish naval officer and naval architect William Hovgaard, who had initially trained at Greenwich in 1877, and was the author of several textbooks, including *General Design of Warships* and *Structural Design of Warships*. Since the students already had a general knowledge of ships and seamanship from their Annapolis education, they could perhaps appreciate the needs of seamen better than their British counterparts.

From 1862 naval shipbuilding was controlled by three of the semi-autonomous bureaus – Construction and Repair, Engineering and Ordnance. The controversy over high-pressure steam led to a merger of the first two of these, which was in effect by 1939 and was approved by Congress in June 1940. And many believed that Ordnance should have been included in the new bureau, especially after the affair with the guns of the *Iowa* class.

By that time the Bureau of Construction and Repair included forty-six officers, mostly of the Construction Corps, and 541 civilians. The Bureau of Engineering had seventy-one officers, mostly Engineering Duty Only, and 449 civilians. These numbers would expand tenfold during the war. The new Bureau of Ships was headed by a naval architect (Vice Admiral E L Cochrane from November 1942 until 1946), with an engineering officer as second in command. The feisty Harold G Bowen, whose term as head of the Bureau of Engineering had conveniently just expired, lamented that there was no longer an Engineer-in-Chief of the Navy. Other bureaus were involved in the design, especially of carriers. James S Russell, the carrier desk officer in the Bureau of Aeronautics, worked with Constructor Commander Kniskern of the Bureau of Ships on the design of the *Essex*-class carriers. 'We in Aeronautics fought to get that ship optimized for its primary mission, namely flying and service aeroplanes.'[9] The Bureau of Navigation (later Personnel) might comment on the habitability, and Supplies and Accounts on other facilities onboard.

Ship design usually originated with the General Board. Individual members might be associated with a particular design – Thomas C Hart with the *Atlanta*-class cruisers and *Marlin*-class submarines, Ernest King for the *Alaska*s, while Admiral William V Pratt sponsored the 6in cruiser.[10] Wargaming at the Naval War College also played a part, essential in view of the US Navy's lack of operational experience before 1941. And there might be conflict with the Chief of Naval Operations; for example, over the characteristics of the *North Carolina*-class battleships in 1936/7.

The design division of the shipbuilding branch of the Bureau of Ships included the preliminary design branch which would work with the Chief of Naval Operations and the General Board in producing studies for a proposed design – up to fifty of them for a radical idea, more typically six in the case of what became the *Brooklyn*-class cruisers or three for the *Iowa*-class battleships. These were known as the 'spring styles', after the practices of women's fashion, and each might be on a single sheet of paper. Once the departments had approved a general design, lines and general arrangement plans were drawn up, weight calculations were made and a model was towed in the David Taylor tank. That would usually result in some modification to the lines, but once the characteristics had been established with reasonable certainty, the project passed to the contract design branch, which had drafting rooms for hull, machinery and electrics. A specification was prepared in consultation with other bureaus such as Ordnance, and a set of fourteen

Draughtsmen in the Construction and Repair Division of the US Navy Department work on the plans for two new 35,000-ton battleships in 1937. They will become *North Carolina* and *Washington*, launched in 1940.

basic working plans was drawn up for the shipbuilder, whether a naval dockyard or a private contractor. In 1940 the New York Shipbuilding Corporation, lead contractor for the *Cleveland*-class cruisers, suggested changes in the hull lines which made the design practicable.[11] Until 1940 commercial contracts were awarded to the lowest bidder, after that it was by negotiation.

Thousands of working plans were needed beyond the basic ones, and these were the responsibility of the shipbuilder, subject to the approval of the Bureau. In 1933 the traditional builders were reluctant to take on the design of the new high-pressure steam plants for the *Mahan*-class destroyers and the navy turned to Gibbs and Cox, who had worked on fast liners for the Grace Line. From that point they became the main design agents for the US Navy.[12]

Much of the detail was still settled in situ; in the case of the *Cachalot*-class submarines, Stuart Murray reported:

> ... it wasn't scientific, to say the least. The draftsmen would come down from the planning section when we had the pipe installed and draw their plans from where the pipes went rather than where they were going. It was a very good method. There was no argument about where a pipe went, or anything like that, because it was a reality.[13]

Rear Admirals David Taylor and William Moffet join congressmen to examine a model with a lift-off top, showing the projected conversion of the battlecruiser *Lexington* to an aircraft carrier in 1922.The funnel of the carrier is even larger than what emerged in real life.

Engineering

Before the First World War the Royal Navy applied the steam turbine engine to the battleship *Dreadnought*, and subsequently to all new battleships, cruisers and destroyers. It became the standard power for all surface warships throughout the world, as well as fast passenger ships such as liners and ferries. Under the guidance of Fisher and Churchill, the navy converted to oil rather than coal. Not only was it more efficient, it eliminated the necessity for the gruelling labour of 'coaling ship' at the end of each voyage, which greatly improved the life of the sailor, and allowed a reduction in crews (though the semi-skilled men of the engineering team were still referred to as stokers). On the negative side, it made the country more dependent on imported oil rather than native coal. Initially, the turbines drove the propellers directly, though that was inefficient. From 1912 ships were fitted with fairly simple single reduction gears.

The Royal Navy had apparently lost its innovative spirit by 1918. With limited budgets for research, the steam turbine saw little improvement. Charles Parsons had been the pioneer of turbine engines early in the century, but he died in 1931 and his company became a dead hand, repressing future development with contractual rights over new shipbuilding. A separate division of the Parsons company developed more fuel-efficient turbines for the electrical industry, but the link was not made by the naval engineers, who were perhaps disillusioned and demoralised by their 'great betrayal' of 1920 and tended to prefer reliability to innovation. They failed to develop a chemical means of cleaning boilers, and had to rely on manual cleaning, an arduous and unpleasant process which necessitated putting the ship out of action for days. They continued to rely on high-grade Persian oil, which would cause difficulties when they had to switch to American and Caribbean products in wartime. And the navy did not develop any means of refuelling at sea, making it dependent on shore bases.[14] Though it had the mighty Atlantic Ocean on its doorstep, the Royal Navy had not anticipated having to operate in it over long ranges. The situation began to improve in 1943 when the Admiralty and the shipbuilding industry formed the Parsons and Marine Engineers Turbine Research and Development Association (PAMETRADA). It took over the Parsons patents and began to foster development, though too late to have much effect on the war.

The machinery of HMS *Belfast* represented the stage of development when the war began. It consisted of four boilers and four sets of turbines. Steam was provided by four Admiralty three-drum boilers in two separate boiler rooms, side by side in the forward space and one behind the other

The complex piping in the engine room of the cruiser *Mauritius* in 1945. The engineer officer stands in the middle of the picture with his pipe, with an engine room artificer and numerous dials to the right. The engine room log can be seen open in the centre foreground.

in the after one. In each boiler the lower drums were filled with water and linked to the upper one by tubes forming a tent-shaped structure. Oil fuel was burnt to boil the water, and the steam collected in the upper drum. A superheater consisting of more tubes was fitted between the other tubes; the superheated steam thus created was 'dry' with no moisture content. It was passed to the engines to provide the power.

Each engine consisted of three units. At high speed the steam entered the high-pressure turbine, then went to the low-pressure turbine to get full use of it. At normal cruising speed a cruising turbine was geared through the high-pressure unit and used to save fuel. With either system, gearing was used to reduce the revolutions to an efficient speed for the propellers. There was a condenser under each engine to return the steam to water to go back to the boilers to begin the process again. Each boiler could be linked to any of the engines so that various combinations were possible, catering for both peacetime economy and wartime damage.

Turbine blades required precision engineering, which was in great demand in wartime. The navy regressed, in that corvettes and frigates were powered by old-fashioned triple-expansion engines because they were easier to manufacture, though they were far less efficient. Some requisitioned trawlers even revived coal as a fuel.

Diesel engines were a German invention. The British had never excelled at them and they were not needed by the railways or merchant shipping, which were firmly wedded to steam. Their use was largely confined to submarines. Steam had been tried in the 'K' class of the last war, but it demanded too many holes in the hull, which probably contributed to the sinking of the unfortunate *K-13* in 1917. Diesels remained the standard power on the surface. They might also have been useful in coastal forces, as their fuel was not inflammable like petrol. They were produced in large numbers for the smaller landing craft.

Auxiliary power for electricity and habitability was normally provided by the main engines, which meant that knocking them out could have a fatal effect, particularly on pumping water out. Diesel generators were only in limited use, and when *Ark Royal* was torpedoed in 1941 she sank partly because of this. Diesel became more common later but often it was barely adequate. *Belfast* had four generators, and during the action with *Scharnhorst*, Stoker Fursland used his initiative and kept one in action using an improvised cooling system. He found a fire hose on the deck above and used it to circulate cooling water to keep the engine cool, for which he was decorated.

The US Navy was tentative in its adoption of turbines, because its need for longer range was undermined by the basic inefficiency of the direct-drive engine in which the high speed of the turbine was transmitted direct to the propeller. In 1916 it adopted it for a large battleship programme, using a turbo-electric system to reduce revolutions to a more acceptable level for propellers.

When warship construction resumed in the 1930s, they had moved on from electric drive and developed a double reduction gear which was far more efficient than the British system. The United States Navy had no more money that its British counterpart for the development of engines in the 1920s and 1930s, but it did link up with the major electrical companies – Allis Chambers, de Laval, and especially General Electric and Westinghouse – as they developed new technology for a rapidly expanding industry. The warship turbine manufactures operated under licence from Parsons until 1935, when the Espionage Act was invoked to prevent the transfer of technology. To Admiral Harold G Bowen, who would lead the Bureau of Engineering from that time, the process which followed was as much about American independence as naval development:

> The date of our political emancipation from England is well known and justly celebrated. On the other hand, we attained our engineering and industrial independence so slowly that the phenomenon scarcely attracted attention. By the time the rebuilding of the US Navy began in 1933 we had not only completed our industrial emancipation but had taken the lead in many engineering and industrial lines.[15]

High-pressure steam was the key to development and was introduced with the *Mahan*-class destroyers, with turbines designed by GEC.

220 TWO NAVIES DIVIDED

Bowen commented that it was 'the first time that high-speed turbines with double reduction gears and direct coupled cruising turbines had been installed in a Naval vessel.'[16] They had a steam temperature of 700 degrees compared with 650 of the *Farragut* class; a high-pressure speed of 5850rpm compared with 3460; and introduced economisers and deaerating of the feed water.[17] They were followed by the *Somers* class which introduced air-encased boilers and steam temperature increased to 850 degrees. The number of turbine blades was greatly reduced. The *Somers* class needed 14,730 compared with 98,750 in the *Porter* class.

The gearing was an essential element and Bowen commented, 'The double reduction gears have much higher factors of safety than have the single reduction gears used with the older design. In addition, they are much quieter.'[18] They required expert construction. Newport News Shipbuilding decided to cut its own for *Yorktown*, but failed to make them accurate enough and they had an unacceptable noise level of 120

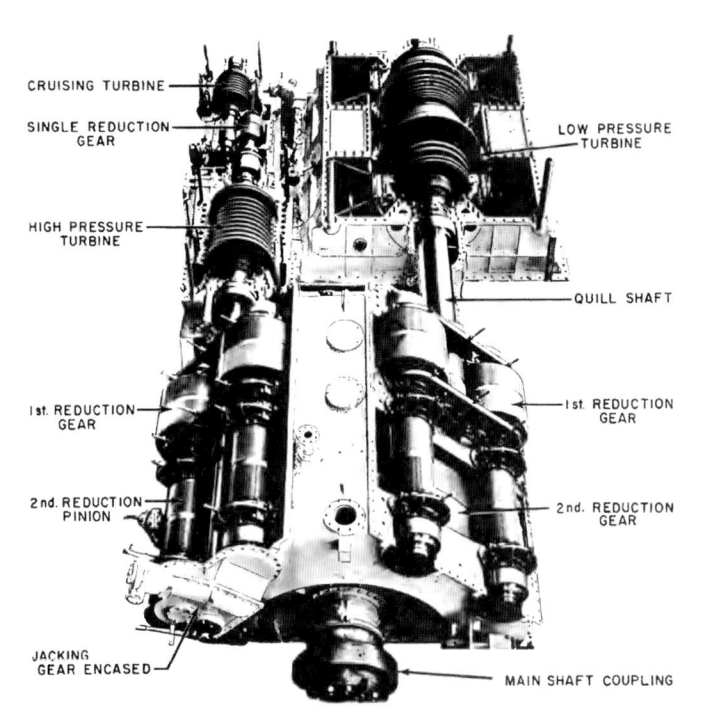

The engine of a wartime American destroyer with the covers omitted from the turbines to show the blades. Steam enters the high-pressure turbine first, then goes to the low-pressure turbine, and finally the condenser. The cruising turbine is used at moderate speeds. Revolutions are brought down to an acceptable level by the reduction gearing.

decibels. They had to be lifted out through a hole cut in the deck and replaced by gears made by a professional gear-cutting company.[19]

Until 1937 high-pressure steam had been confined to destroyers, but in that year Bowen ordered that the temperature in the engines of *North Carolina* and *Washington*, battleships under construction in the New York Navy Yard, be raised from 700 to 850 degrees, introducing the high-pressure concept to the battlefleet. Unfortunately, he failed to consult the General Board, which helped to stimulate a conflict. In 1938 Bowen admitted: 'there is a great schism in the engineering profession of the United States.'[20] On one side behind Bowen were Charles Edison, the Assistant Secretary of the Navy, the officers of the Bureau of Engineering below the rank of captain, some of the shipbuilders and the president of Gibbs and Cox. Against were the General Board, senior members of the Bureau of Construction and Repair, and the 'big three' shipbuilders. One senior officer reported: 'The Chief of the Bureau of Engineering has not sold the high-temperature design to operating naval personnel. They question the advisability of gambling with National defence by installing experimental and unproven engine designs which are not required to meet the military characteristics laid down by the General Board.'[21] But with the support of Charles Edison, the son of the great inventor and Assistant Secretary of the Navy from 1937–40, high-pressure steam was adopted for all new surface warships.

The proof came when the British Pacific Fleet arrived on station in 1944. The battleship *King George V* needed 39 per cent more fuel at low speeds than her contemporary *Washington*, and the American naval attaché in London claimed, 'On the whole we are many years ahead of [the British] technically. This is true in practically every phase of naval engineering.'[22]

In parallel with the liaison with the electricity suppliers, the US Navy was able to link up with the railways in the development of diesels for submarines, an option which was not available to the British, whose railways remained coal-fired. As a result, there was considerable development in the 1930s, though as usual Admiral Bowen did not avoid controversy, mainly over the role of diesel-electric drive.[23] Fairbanks Morse and Winton, a division of General Motors, both developed highly effective machines. But those produced by Hoovens-Owens-Rentschler (HOR) based on designs licensed from the German Maschinenfabrik-Augsburg-Nurnberg (MAN) were far less successful:

> To everyone's dismay, in the rush to build new submarines after Pearl Harbor, the Bureau of ships decided to install these same

HOR MAN engines in the first squadron of twelve submarines to be started at Electric Boat. Although we were at war with Germany and in spite of the HOR's poor performance in the early American fleet submarines, the plans went forward.

Jack made a traumatic voyage back to San Francisco, during which all but one of her engines failed, and they were replaced with Wintons.[24]

Shipbuilders

In 1939 British shipbuilders still regarded themselves as the best in the world by a long way. They had pioneered the use of steel and steam, they dominated the world supply of merchant ships and the export market for warships, but they had serious weaknesses. They had peaked before the First World War and had developed little since. They had suffered heavily in the Great Depression with an unemployment rate of 62 per cent, more than any other industry. They lost nearly all the export market to new builders in Denmark and other places. Yards had been closed with ruthless efficiency by the National Shipbuilders Security Ltd, most famously the one at Jarrow on the Tyne, which inspired a march to London, and there were few apprenticeships to train a new generation.

There were fifty-two main firms by 1939, forty of them capable of producing oceangoing ships. A few, like Harland and Wolff of Belfast, John Brown's on the Clyde and Cammell Laird on the Mersey, were 'great undertakings of international fame'; others such as Vickers-Armstrong were parts of larger organisations. The bulk of them were medium-sized family businesses, often still controlled by the descendants of their founders, who had perhaps lost the dynamism of earlier years. They tended to be complacent and conservative, objecting to the Admiralty plans to build ships with longitudinal framing. Denny of Dumbarton, once the pioneer of steel shipbuilding and turbine engines, was now seen as 'a little old-fashioned'.

This was matched by their workforce, dominated by craftsmen protective of their skills and resisting the use of welding to replace riveting. Their sites on rivers such as the Clyde, Mersey, Tyne and Tees had been more than adequate when they were set up, mostly in the second half of the nineteenth century, but they were limited as ships became bigger and bigger. The Clyde was only about 200yds wide off John Brown's yard at Clydebank and great ships like the liners *Queen Mary* and the battleships *Howe* and *Vanguard* had to be launched into the mouth of the River Cart opposite. Further upstream, Fairfield's had to launch diagonally into the river. On the land side, houses and amenities had been built

The River Clyde. Ships showing part of the Fairfield yard, which launched the battleship Howe in 1940 and the aircraft carrier *Implacable*. In the centre is the Barclay Curle yard, with Alexander Stephens across the river. All ships launch diagonally into the river, and the site is also restricted by blocks of working-class tenement housing in the bottom left.

for the workers, often financed by the yards themselves and it would cause great disruption to remove them to expand the yards. There was little space and no time to set up new yards, so the existing ones had to be used. Some ships, such as the Castle-class frigates, were deliberately kept short to fit existing yards. A particular wartime restriction was the blackout – in the winter, work had to stop at dusk as very few building slips were covered.

No new yards were set up in wartime and only a few of the old ones were reopened. A visitor of September 1942 found a variety of practices. John Brown was well equipped with cranes and was improving the plating shops. Yarrow in Glasgow had an efficient engine works but 'in the shipyard there was more congestion and less method.' Cammell Laird had a great variety of work and some plans for improvement with three new 15-ton cranes, berths were to be strengthened with steel posts and a new electric substation was to be set up to help with welding. Smith's Dock of Middlesbrough was producing corvettes at the rate of one every six weeks, whereas Robbs of Leith produced one every fourteen months. Fitting-out arrangements were the biggest problem; ships and workers had to be moved around various parts of Leith Docks.

Bombing caused less damage than might have been feared, partly because the main shipyards were away from the most vulnerable areas in the south. That did not stop occasional forays, including the mass raid on Clydeside on 13 March 1941. The Yarrow destroyer yard in Glasgow was one to suffer:

Two bombs and one land mine fell on the yard. The first bomb, which landed directly on an air raid shelter, killed forty-seven men, completely demolished the electrical department office, the tracing office, the galvanising shop, and damaged the boiler shop. The land mine demolished the cost office, damaged the east end of the engine shops severely, blew the roof off the main office block and killed one man. The second bomb fell on the stockyard and did only slight damage. …

The yard appeared to be utterly devastated, but a closer examination showed that despite the mess most of the vital services had survived. None of the four ships on the building berths had been disturbed. The damage to the machines in the engine shop was repairable …[25]

The British shipyard workforce numbered 182,700 in 1941 and peaked at 254,800 in December 1943, with 98,300 on naval construction and 45,600 on repair, a similar number on merchant shipbuilding and 65,300 on repair. 'Dilution' or the employment of less skilled labour was practised less than in other industries. The use of women varied, one major yard had none at all, and others were sceptical about how they could cope in the environment. More yards were using welding rather than riveting, despite concerns about its safety. Prefabrication was difficult because of restricted space in the yards, but a scheme was set up for the Loch-class frigates.

American shipbuilding

In peacetime, American naval shipbuilding was carried out in six navy yards at Portsmouth, Boston, Philadelphia, Norfolk, Puget Sound and Mare Island, and in six private yards. Bethlehem Shipbuilding, the largest of the 'big three', was founded when the Bethlehem Steel Company took over a San Francisco shipyard in 1906. By 1940, in addition to repair yards, it had four shipyards – Fore River at Quincy in Boston Bay for the largest vessels, including the battleship *Massachusetts* and the carrier *Wasp*; Sparrows Point in Maryland for tankers and cargo ships; San Francisco, which was not then building ships; and Staten Island, New York, for small vessels such as tugs. It soon began to expand under the Two Ocean Navy programme to take over 5 per cent of private construction. By the end of 1940 it was building seventy-three warships, before taking on the lead role in the Liberty Ship and destroyer escort programmes. New yards were added, including Bethlehem Fairfield in

Baltimore harbour, which employed forty-seven thousand workers at its peak, nearly all newly trained.[26]

Newport News Shipbuilding was close to the great Norfolk Navy Yard and built many of the ships in Theodore Roosevelt's Great White Fleet, and some of the first American dreadnoughts. In the 1930s it built the carrier *Ranger*, followed by *Yorktown* and *Enterprise*. In all, it built 243 ships in the Second World War, including 186 Libertys. The third member of the trio, the New York Shipbuilding Corporation, was funded by a bridge builder in 1899 and established a yard at Camden, New Jersey. It pioneered the use of covered building slips and prefabrication, and during the war it built all the *Independence*-class carriers and the battleship *South Dakota*. American yards also serviced British ships, including *Rodney* at Boston in 1940.

Of the three smaller yards, the Federal Shipbuilding and Drydock Company was founded in 1917 by the United States Steel Corporation to take part in the massive First World War building programme, but had hardly completed any ships before that war finished. In its yard at Kearny in the Port of New York, it survived the depression era by building merchant ships, including ocean liners, until orders for *Mahan*-, *Somers*- and *Benham*-class destroyers came along in the mid 1930s. In August 1941 there was a strike of sixteen thousand workers and the navy took it over under Harold G Bowen. It prided itself on fast construction, launching four destroyers in May 1942, with four more being laid down immediately; in the following year it built the destroyer *Thorn* in 137 days. The Bath Iron Works was based in Maine and by 1943/4 it was producing a destroyer every seventeen days. The Electric Boat Corporation took over the patents for Holland's original submarines. When submarine construction resumed in 1931, it settled in Groton, Connecticut, near the New London Navy Yard. During the war it built seventy-four submarines, and its subsidiary Elco built nearly four hundred PT boats.

As well as the enormous expansion of the established yards, new factors came into play. Henry J Kaiser, the son of German immigrants, took up photography and worked as a star hardware salesman before entering the construction business to take advantage of the road-building boom created by Henry Ford's cars. In 1931 he joined a consortium to build the Hoover Dam, followed by other New Deal projects. He foresaw American participation in the coming world war, and in 1940 he set up a huge shipyard at Richmond, California, to build thirty cargo ships for the British. He expanded to the Portland and Vancouver region and by 1944 he employed nearly a hundred thousand workers. Nicholas Monsarrat was impressed with his yard near Boston:

It was an enormous place, ... a swamp before the war until Henry Kaiser came along and turned it into one of the biggest shipbuilding concerns on the East Coast. Certainly, it was a monument to his fabled high-pressure drive. The acres of sheds, connected by wide roads and miniature railway lines, were in a spate of activity: the welding shops had enormous charts outside, recording the footage welded by each shift ... there were forests of cranes and derricks, there were whole chunks of ships waiting to be joined up, ... here was an administration centre like a wooden cathedral.[27]

Using mass-production methods, he built 1490 vessels during the war, including fifty escort carriers. Shipyard workers took unusual pride in their work, even with the mass-produced products of 1943: 'I watched with the others each time one of our ships was launched. And as each hull slid into the water I murmured with them "There goes my door", or "There goes my bulkheads", or "That's my deck plate."'[28]

In 1940–45 America would launch 141 aircraft carriers, eight battleships, 807 cruisers and destroyers, 203 submarines and more than 50 million tons of merchant shipping.[29] Including 82,000 landing craft, the navy had more than 100,000 ships and vessels by the end of the war.

The function of a warship was to carry weapons in one form or another, and most were designed round a particular weapons system.

A woman welder at work in a Kaiser shipyard in Richmond, California, in 1943. Though there was much publicity for 'Rosie the Riveter', welding was becoming increasingly common in American yards.

9
Weapons

OBVIOUSLY THE main function of a warship has always been to deploy its weapons, or to threaten to deploy them. That weapon might be the ship itself, as in the days of Greek and Roman galleys, and early twentieth-century battleships were fitted with ram bows. Though they often proved more dangerous to friend than enemy, in the Second World War they were still to be found on the British battleships of the *Queen Elizabeth* and *Royal Sovereign* classes. British escort vessels sometimes rammed surfaced U-boats, but they were not built for it and often had to spend weeks under repair – orders were issued banning the practice except when it was the only way to prevent an imminent attack. Some American destroyers had strengthened bows to cope with this.

Some of the newer ship types – aircraft carriers and landing ships – launched their main military force in the form of aircraft, troops and vehicles, though they were usually equipped with defensive gun armament as well. Escort vessels relied on specialist anti-submarine armament. Some, such as storeships and minecraft, carried only defensive armaments to allow them to execute their main functions. Apart from that, warships were mainly intended to carry and use guns and torpedoes. Guns predominated in the case of battleships and cruisers, they were roughly equal with torpedoes in destroyers, and torpedoes were the principal armament of submarines and motor torpedo boats (in theory at least).

The big gun
Battleships and cruisers were identified by the calibres and numbers of their guns. The dreadnought battleship was defined as an 'all-big-gun' ship with batteries from 12in upwards. By the Washington and London treaties, cruisers were rated as 'heavy' and 'light' according to whether they had 8in or 6in guns – their tonnage was restricted to 10,000 in both cases. Before the war, advocates of the big gun – alumni of HMS *Excellent* in the Royal Navy and the 'gun club' in the US Navy – regarded themselves as the elite of the navy and despised the upstart aviators.

The British 15in gun was ground-breaking when it was designed for the *Queen Elizabeth*-class battleships in 1911, outclassing the 12in and 13.5in which had dominated the dreadnoughts until then, and it benefited from the experience. According to an article of 1945:

> The difficulties in designing heavy LA mountings lie chiefly in the enormous weights which must be manipulated at high speeds, eg a 15in gun weighs 100 tons and the shell about a ton. Enormous recoil stresses must be smoothly absorbed and then transmitted from the trunnions through the clips and tollers to the supporting structure provided in the hull of the ship. By 1914 these difficulties had been overcome and the 15in gun mounting of those days does not differ in essentials from the heavy LA mounting of the present day.[1]

In 1945 it was still the most common gun on British capital ships and large monitors, equipping the *Queen Elizabeth* and 'R' classes and the three battlecruisers. It would continue in action until the invasion of Normandy in 1944, and surviving examples would be fitted to *Vanguard*, which was not launched until 1944. Its only rival in the fleet of 1939 was the 16in which equipped *Rodney* and *Nelson*. Up to that time such large guns had wire wound round an inner A-tube. This was heavy and did nothing to stop the barrel from drooping, so the new 14in guns, designed for the *King George V* class in the late 1930s, were made by heating and shrinking tapered tubes – the A-frame, jacket and breech ring, one onto another. As with all guns, the rifling was cut inside to spin the shell and make it much more accurate.

The British never liked the 8in gun prescribed for heavy cruisers by the Washington Treaty – it was overweight and had mechanical problems. They agonised about its value compared with the 6in. On the one hand, the 8in had greater power to penetrate armour and a longer range –28,000yds compared with 20,000 – which might be vital in the early stages of an action. But more 6in guns could be fitted in a given hull and they could fire much faster – six or eight rounds per minute, compared with two.

The mechanism of a big gun turret was extremely complex. At the lower levels deep inside the hull were the magazine handling room and the shell room, from where projectiles and charges were hoisted up by chains inside tubes – well armoured, as the charges were highly dangerous, in bags rather than brass. They passed through the spaces with machinery for training the guns directly below the gunhouse, which contained the guns and the mechanisms for elevating and loading them. Mountings were mostly designed by the private firm of Vickers-Armstrong, for in

WEAPONS 229

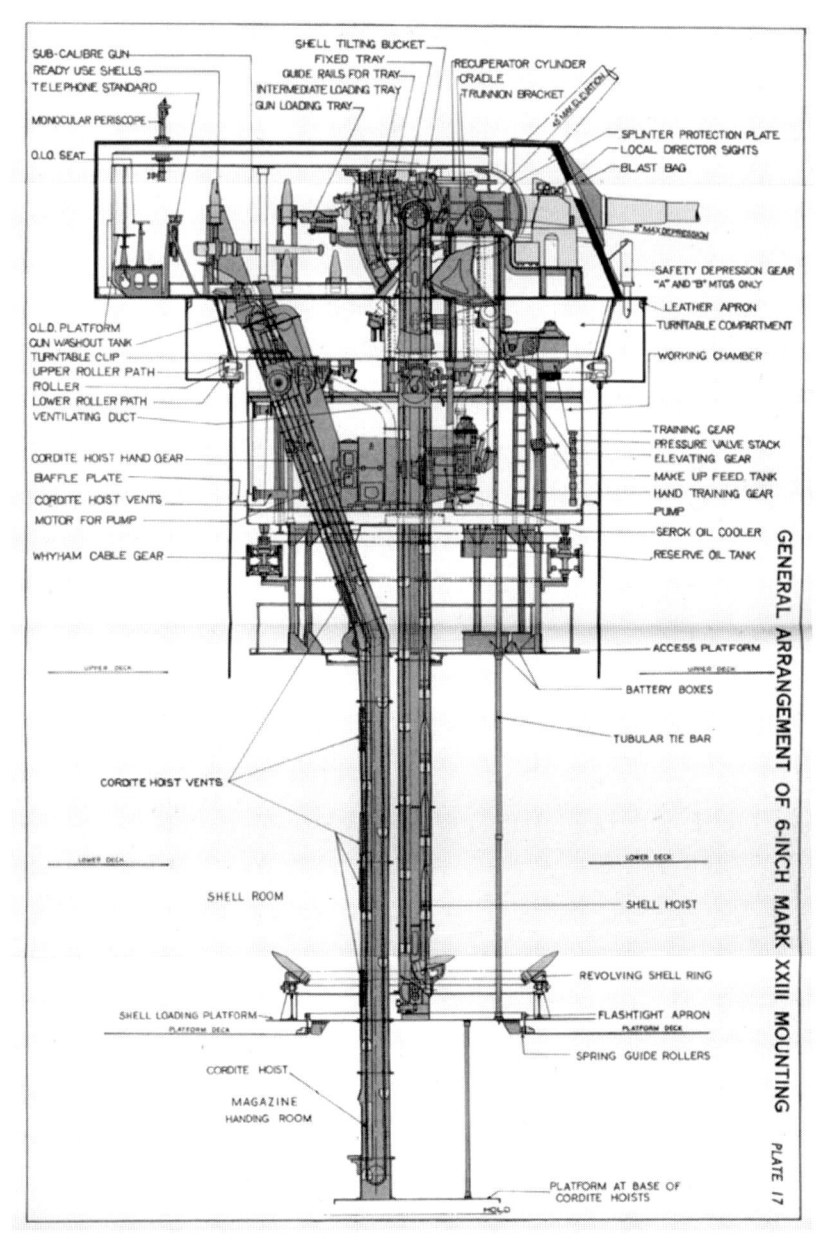

GENERAL ARRANGEMENT OF 6-INCH MARK XXIII MOUNTING
PLATE 17

Details of a British 6in turret. Cordite is passed up through a tube from the magazine handling room in the bowels of the ship, and shells by way of another tube in the shell room above. The mechanisms for rotating the turret and elevating the guns are shown. The sub-calibre gun is fitted for firing practice with smaller rounds.

lean times they could also work for foreign governments to maintain their design teams and plant. They had a tendency to accept over-ambitious specifications from the Admiralty, which could lead to failure. The 14in mountings of *Prince of Wales* failed against *Bismarck* in 1941, and in 1944 those of *Duke of York* underperformed against *Scharnhorst*.

Lieutenant Henry Leach describes the situation in a 14in turret of *Duke of York* in the *Scharnhorst* action:

> 'Follow director,' and the huge turrets swung round in line with the Director Control Tower.
>
> 'All guns with armour-piercing and full charge load, load, load.' The clatter of the hoists as they brought up the shells and cordite charges from the magazines. The rattle of the rammers as they drove them into the chambers of the guns. The slam of the breeches as they closed. These were music to all.
>
> Then a great stillness for seeming endless minutes, disturbed only by the hydraulics as Layers and Trainer followed their pointers in the receiver from the Director.
>
> 'Broadsides' and the interceptors completing the firing circuits right up to the Director layer's trigger were closed.
>
> A glance at the Range Receiver whose counters were steadily inexorably ticking down until … 12,000 yards … the fire gong rang 'ting ting' and … CRASH, all guns fired and the battle of North Cape had started.[2]

US Navy gun design and production was the responsibility of the Bureau of Ordnance in Washington, with the support of the Naval Research Laboratory, its own Naval Ordnance Laboratory, the Naval Proving Ground in Virginia, and many universities and institutions throughout the country. The big gun was at the centre of the old battleship navy, as Ted Mason wrote of his beloved *California*:

> All the machinery and equipment the men operated, the braid and chevrons and regimentation, were dedicated to one task: loading, elevating, and training the twelve gargantuan rifle barrels, so that they would speak with tongues of flame and shattering sound, hurling 15,000-pound projectiles across the horizon in lofty, decaying curves to descend upon, penetrate, and destroy the ships of the enemy.[3]

The standard big gun at the start of the war was the 14in, which equipped the battleships of the *Texas*, *Nevada*, *Pennsylvania*, *New Mexico*, *California* and *Maryland* classes, launched in 1912–21. It had originated in 1908 as the British began to design 13.5in models for their 'super-dreadnoughts' and the Germans seemed likely to move away from their 11in. It introduced the triple turret with the *Nevada* class launched in 1914. The *Pennsylvania* class of 1916 had four triples and that was followed by the others begun before the Washington Treaty. The guns were often sited too close together in the turrets, which caused problems with accuracy.

From early on, the navy was interested in larger guns. The 16in 45-calibre gun had its origin in a design of 1913. They were used in two-gun turrets in the battleships *Maryland*, *Colorado* and *West Virginia* completed after the First World War. A 50-calibre version was also adopted, intended for battleships and battlecruisers which were never completed due to the Washington Treaty, so many of them were fitted in shore batteries. With the resumption of battleship construction in 1936, there was fierce debate about whether to invoke the escalator clause of the new London Treaty and fit such big guns, in the face of pacifist sentiment with Congress and the public. After tests in the Naval

The battleship USS *Iowa* fires a salvo of two 16in rounds from her number 2 turret during the bombardment of Tinian in 1944. A full broadside of all nine guns would do considerable damage to the ship itself and was best avoided.

War College showed its superiority, the 16in 45-calibre gun, the latest development of the 1913 design, was adopted for the *North Carolina* and *South Dakota* classes. There was a major upset when BuOrd and BuShips were found to be using different turret designs.

Ironically, the 16in guns were never used as intended, against enemy battleships. The execution at Leyte Gulf was done by the 14in guns of the old *Mississippi*, *Maryland*, *West Virginia*, *Tennessee*, *California* and *Pennsylvania*. But in 1945 the Japanese surrender was signed alongside the great 16in turrets of USS *Missouri*.

The debate between supporters of the 8in and 6in gun for cruisers was just as intense as in the Royal Navy, though the 8in was favoured at first. Long ranges were expected in the Pacific and the American 8in could reach 30,000yds, more than any other cruiser gun.

American gun turrets were powered by electricity rather than hydraulics as in the British system. The Bureau of Ordnance was proud of the success of its large turret design:

> Guns larger than the 5in are installed in huge turrets of thick steel. Extending down into the very vitals of cruisers and battleships, the turret protects the gun and mount as well as the supply line from the ammunition rooms to the breech. A single turret of a modern battleship weighs as much as a destroyer, yet the tremendous structure rotates so smoothly and effortlessly that the guns may be brought to bear on a target in a matter of seconds. Each gun can be elevated separately as well as in unison with the others in the turret, and they can be fired singly or in salvos.[4]

Design of the turrets for the 16in guns of the *North Carolina*-class battleships began in 1937, and two years later for the *Iowa* class:

> Three 16-inch gun turrets, two forward and one aft, commanded the entire circle of sea around the ship. Maximum gun elevation of 45 degrees permitted the delivery of 2700 pound projectiles to targets well over 20 miles away. Behind one minute of fire, according to a statistician, lay 3600 man-hours of labor required for the production of the 100,000 pound of alloy steel … the 1300 pounds of carbon steel … and the more than two-thirds of a ton of copper and brass expended. … The ships of neither ally nor enemy mounted turrets of comparable efficiency.[5]

Fire control

Aiming techniques had come a long way since gunlayers had sighted them by eye, for increasingly long ranges were expected, and aircraft posed a new set of problems. The US Bureau of Ordnance claimed that every year it had to 'inform several prospective contractors that while fire control is properly its province, equipment for putting out fires is procured by other agencies.' Fire control meant solving the problems of naval gunnery, firing them over long ranges or against fast-moving targets, while taking into account the movements in all directions of one's own ship, and many other factors. Modern battleships and cruisers were designed to fire at ranges of up to twenty miles, and accurate and rapid calculations were needed.

The main and secondary guns of battlefleet ships – battleships, battlecruisers, cruisers and destroyers – were aimed by means of directors set high in the superstructure away from the effects of smoke and vibration. It had been a contentious issue with the Royal Navy since 1913, when the Admiralty rejected the Argo mechanical computer designed by the industrialist Arthur Pollen, partly on the grounds of cost. Instead they adopted a system designed by their own Captain Frederick Dreyer, who was accused of plagiarising Pollard's system. But the Admiralty fire control table, as fitted to *Nelson* and *Rodney* in the 1920s, used the best of both and was developed and fitted to the capital ships and cruisers of the Second World War.[6]

When an action began the captain chose the target, perhaps guided by fleet orders or tactical instructions. He aimed his sight at it and that was transmitted to the director tower.

The director was manned by the control officer, the leader of the gunnery team, who sat in the centre. He was assisted by the primary spotting officer, who would press buttons marked 'over', 'straddle' and 'short' to indicate the fall of shot, and the rate officer who would estimate the seed and inclination of the target. Also in the director were skilled ratings, a layer and a trainer who sat on either side of the gyro director sight. Each had a stabilised telescope which he would keep trained on the target. It was stated, 'On the Director Layer, more than any other individual in the ship, except perhaps the Control Officer, depends success of a gunnery action.'[7] The cross level operator was expected to compensate for the movement of the ship. This might involve 'hunting the roll', firing at the right moment for best effect.

British rangefinders each had a single eyepiece which relied on bringing together the upper and lower half of a view of the target or 'coincidence' of sights from mirrors as far apart as possible, often in ear-like projections from the sides of gun turrets. During the war they were superseded by radar, which at the time was more accurate in distance than direction.

In cruisers and capital ships the Admiralty fire control table was situated in the transmitting station deep on the ship. Destroyers used the slightly simpler Admiralty fire control clock, based on the same principles. The complexity of the task is indicated by the description of the Admiralty fire control clocks Marks 1 and 1*:

Calculates the Deflection due to own ship, enemy and wind, and provides a means of adding these and applying deflection spotting correction to give Gun Deflection.
    Transmits Gun Training to the guns ...
    Applies the rate of change to the range set.
    Calculates range corrections for enemy, wind and ballistics, and provides a means of adding these and applying range spotting corrections to give Gun Range.
    Calculates the tangent elevation, plus dip (from the director to the standard level) necessary for this range ...
    Transmits gun deflection and gun range to the guns for gunlayers and quarters firing ...
    Provides means for accurate calculation of PIL corrections to datum range and datum bearing
    Incorporates a Time-of-Flight unit automatically set for range ...

During the action against *Scharnhorst* in 1943, Reginald Mountfield spent long hours in the director tower, needing his 'quiet and able appreciation of the opportunities' and 'foresight to visualise beforehand' when they might next have a fleeting contact with the enemy. Deep in the ship, Gunner Frederick Northam in charge of the transmitting station had to keep up his men's attention during the lulls in the action. He was missing a team of the midshipmen who had gone off to do their exams, but was assisted by Royal Marine Bandmaster Douglas Colls, who supervised the inexperienced clock operator and spotting plot operator at the fire control table.

It was common to fire one gun in each turret from a button in the director, so that the fall of shot could be spotted. Firing more guns at once could cause damage to the ship, as with *Rodney* in action with *Bismarck* in 1941. 'Damage sustained by contusion of broadsides was very considerable, causing undue discomfort to the personnel and much work on tier part to make compartments arbitrable.' That included breaking tiles in washrooms, loss of urinals, broken beams, rupture of water mains and loss of electric lights.[8]

The US Navy's *Basic Fire Control Mechanisms* of 1944 explained the essence of the gunnery problem:

If the enemy were to announce six or eight hours beforehand just where the target would be at a particular instant and just how it would be moving, a lightning mathematician would be able to calculate where to point the guns to hit it at that one instant. But, the results would be good only for one instant.

Instead:

What is needed is an instrument which will predict quickly and accurately what will happen when the shell is in the air, compute the necessary corrections for the guns, and in addition continuously correct for the pitch and roll of own ship. As soon as a target is picked up the instrument must be able to solve the fire control problem in a few seconds and thereafter is must keep on solving the problem *continuously* and *accurately* as own ship and target move in relation to each other.[9]

In 1917 the US Navy acquired rights to the Pollen system and fitted it to at least one ship, and incorporated its best features in the existing Ford system. It continued to assess British methods, while developing in its own way. In the US Navy, the plotting room or 'central' was at the core of the action, rather than the director as with the Royal Navy. American directors were smaller and more numerous than British: 'The director was a metal shell, a cube of perhaps fifteen feet, that swivelled in a complete circle and housed the computers, radar, optical rangefinder, communication circuits, and controls that were the electro-mechanical brain directing the fire of the 5-inch battery.'[10] Bill Ryan recorded: 'As firecontrolman, I was stationed up in the gun director, which is above the bridge at the highest part of the ship. My job was to bring the gun director's diamond over the target and keep pulling the trigger.'[11]

The plotting room held the rangekeeper or analogue computer and it was from there that signals were sent to the gun crews. Originally, the US Navy used the coincidence rangefinder, as did the British, but during the 1930s they went over to the stereoscopic system with two eyepieces. The operator would bring the images from opposite ends of the rangefinder together in roughly the same way as human eyes compensate for parallax. The British tended to admit that this system, used by the Germans at Jutland, was more efficient, but that the highly skilled operators might be put off in action. Contrary to British practice, it was normal to fire each individual gun when loaded and on target, rather than in a co-ordinated salvo.

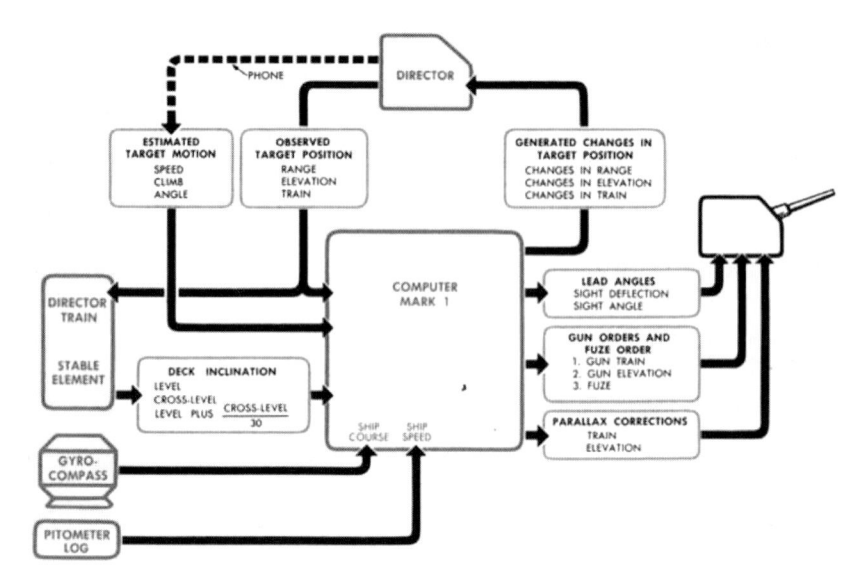

The input to the Computer Mark 1, which takes many factors into account to aim a 5in anti-aircraft gun. The process starts with the director, whose crew track the movement of the target, and ends with the gun itself.

In the destroyer *Sterett*, Calhoun was the gunnery officer; Ensign J D Jeffrey was his assistant: 'If anything happened to me, he was ready to step into my shoes.' Chief Fire Controlman Chapman was 'a gem' who could 'visualise the inner works of the gun director and pinpoint any malfunction within seconds.' The rangefinder was Jack Shelton, who had risen from seaman second class while in the ship, and 'was infallible in his capacity to identify ships and aircraft.' The director pointers and trainer 'both had steady nerves and excellent visual acuity and were … completely unflappable.'[12]

Medium-calibre guns

The design of British medium-sized guns was affected by many factors – economy, conservatism, the desire to use up old stocks of ammunition, misunderstandings about the effect of air power, piecemeal improvement before the war and too fast movement during it. And as was often the case with the Royal Navy, decisions were made at the wrong time when the full picture was not clear.

The ideal gun would be dual or double purpose, able to serve in the anti-aircraft role, but also to fight off light craft such as destroyers and torpedo boats. The British 4in gun, first introduced in 1913, had a niche as 'the largest [high angle] which can be loaded and rammed "uphill" without the aid of a loading tray and rammer'. Even so, it needed a strong man to handle its 63lb round. The advantages of a twin mounting were that one gun did not interfere with another, only one trainer and layer were needed, the same shield could protect the crews of both guns, and ammunition supply was simplified. Its effectiveness was doubtful, but it formed the secondary armament of the older battleships, many cruisers and the Tribal-class destroyers. A low-velocity version in single mounts was used in trawlers, corvettes and frigates, mainly against surfaced submarines.

Destroyers were fitted with 4.7in guns in various forms, of a type which had distinguished itself ashore at the Siege of Ladysmith in 1899 to 1900. The V-Ws left over from the last war used a a 50lb shell, a screw breech which restricted the rate of fire, and a bagged cartridge. The whole equipment weighed 7.9 tons. The interwar 'A' to 'I' classes used the same shell, but with brass cartridges which improved safety and increased the rate of fire, so the gun had to be redesigned to take account of that. They had shields rather than turrets, so the rear was exposed, and an elevation of only 40 degrees. The Tribal class of 1936 used them in twin mountings. A new 4.7in shell, weighing 62lbs, was designed for the 'L' and 'M' class ordered in 1936. The guns were designed for an elevation of 50 degrees, which necessitated power training (but elevation by hand), an enclosed mounting and ammunition hoists, without giving a full anti-aircraft capability. This led to a very high all-up weight of 34 tons and increased costs, so only a few were made.

The 4.7in guns of the British destroyer *Foxhound*. They had limited elevation and therefore poor anti-aircraft capability, though they were effective in other roles. The ship is off Freetown, Sierra Leone, in 1943, and the crew wear minimal clothing in the heat.

Meanwhile, plans were being made for the 'war emergency' destroyers, and economy was obviously necessary. The 50lb shell was revived but in the new single mountings, elevation was increased to 55 degrees. Power ramming gear developed by Vickers-Armstrong was fitted and the weight was kept to a manageable 13.3 tons.

During the Norwegian campaign and Dunkirk evacuation, it became clear that increased anti-aircraft armament was essential and the possibility of a more effective dual-purpose gun was raised – an elevation of at least 80 degrees was needed. One problem was that destroyer guns had a long recoil to prevent excessive strain on the ships' light structure. That would make it necessary to raise the trunnions of the gun, making it more difficult to load and, incidentally, tending to spoil the view from the bridge. A completely new 4.5in anti-aircraft gun was under development from 1935 for the new fleet aircraft carriers, with greatly improved shells of 55lbs and a recoil length of only 18in. It needed some modification for dual-purpose use, and a spare turret for *Illustrious* was used to develop it. But first there was a debate about whether to continue with the old 4.7, with enormous quantities of ammunition already available, or continue with a new project. Early in 1942 a decision was made in favour of the latter. Then there was a discussion about whether to use fixed ammunition of separate cartridge and shell; that was decided after experience in the cruisers *Scylla* and *Charybdis* showed that fixed ammunition was difficult to handle in bad weather, even in these relatively large ships. The 4.5in gun entered service with the last ships of the emergency programme near the end of the war, and with the larger ships of the Battle class but was rarely used in action. Even then, one member of the Naval Ordnance Department felt it necessary to explain that:

> ... the 4.5-in Mark IV mounting was a compromise designed to produce a quick and reasonably adequate solution to a very urgent problem ... and if its present performance is not as good as could be wished, it is very difficult to apportion much blame to those involved in the design and development.[13]

The 5.25in gun was developed to be fitted in twin mountings in the new *King George V*-class battleships, and as the main armament of most of the *Dido*-class cruisers. As a measure of the growing needs of dual-purpose armament, each 5.25in assembly weighed 90 tons, compared with 3 or 4 tons for a 4in twin of around 1930, and cost £50,000 compared with £2000.

The British had clearly developed too many types of guns in the 4–5½in range, and were behind in the development of dual-purpose guns. It was a strong contrast to the situation across the Atlantic.

The 5in 38-calibre gun was developed by the US Bureau of Ordnance in the early 1930s, using funds set aside for the relief of unemployment. Unlike British piecemeal and reactive development, it had the advantage of starting from a clean sheet, as no new destroyers had been built since the flush-deckers of 1918 vintage. A double-purpose weapon intended for anti-aircraft and surface use, it first entered service with the *Farragut*-class destroyers in 1934. Work began on a twin version in 1936, and an enclosed mount in the following year, so it was well developed by the time of Pearl Harbor. It had a range of ten miles and a ceiling of six with its maximum elevation of 85 degrees, and a powered rammer gave it a high rate of fire, for a gun of its size, of twelve to fifteen rounds per minute. In the twin version it became the standard secondary armament of battleships and cruisers and the main anti-aircraft armament of carriers. The single turreted gun became the main gun of destroyers and escorts, as well as serving in many merchant ships. Unlike British guns, it was well-timed and developed when the threat from aircraft could be assessed correctly, and Admiral Hussey wrote 'we had it years before … actual hostilities … when there was ample time to prove its potentialities, to eliminate any bugs that might show up, to incorporate new techniques of fire control, and to prepare tooling facilities for manufacture.'[14] More than eight thousand were made, with production peaking in the second half of 1943.[15]

As with all major guns, the crew operated at several levels to fire them, starting in the lowest part of the ship:

> Ammunition handling rooms, seated deep inside the ship, were crowded, hot, and noisy. We had five. When we were firing all out (22 rounds per minute), extended action would work you so hard that, when you had a chance to rest, you would just sink to the deck where you were.[16]

The main manual element was in loading shells into the tray inside the turret, which led to a contest onboard *Sterett*, with a $4000 betting pot:

> Big Willie attacked each shell as it came up shell hoist, handling them as if they weighed five pounds instead of fifty-five. His movements were fluid and graceful, the shells were put in the hoist, were put in the tray, and went into the breech. … Big Willie averaged about four seconds per load at first, and I waited for the pace to slow as he grew tired. But it did not slow. [His rival Jim Grann] was younger and an inch or two taller than Big Willie, but not quite as muscular. He started out like a sprinter … But after twenty minutes the pace slowed …[17]

In the destroyer *Dale*, 'Shorty' Smith reported:

> I was a powderman on gun one, which was the first gun on the bow of the ship. The gun had a protective metal shield, but the only thing it protected you from was the spray off the bow. My job was to take the twenty-four-pound cases off the hoist and hand them to the rammerman.[18]

And after firing, Richard Martinez recounted: 'My job in the gun crew was to catch the hot shells being ejected and throw them over the side. And though we were about as busy as you could possibly be, every once in a while I would look up'.[19]

A twin turret on a battleship, cruiser or carrier had a crew of twenty-six men, half in the turret or gun house, and half in the ammunition-handling room below. The mount captain was usually an officer. Each mount had a pointer and trainer, but the guns were normally using the primary method of fire control in which they were moved by the director, in which case the men were on standby in case the system failed. They might go on to 'follow the pointer' operation using signals from the director, or local control if the director communication failed or the director was knocked out. The sight setter and fuse setter were also on standby for most of the time, though they were expected to see that their equipment was functioning. There were men to handle the powder and shell for each gun and a rammer man to close the breech. In fact, the gun was semi-automatic; the only actions needed in normal times were to load the ammunition into the slide tray, and operate the manual control mechanism when required. The hot case men were responsible for the disposal of the spent cartridge cases, though only if the elevation was more than 40 degrees and the automatic system could not be operated. Down below, the crew of the ammunition-handling room was divided into projectile and powder men, who would receive the ammunition from the magazine below and put it into hoists as required.[20]

Anti-aircraft gunnery

The essential problem of anti-aircraft gunfire was explained in the US Navy's manual:

> To aim the guns correctly under these conditions about 25 things must be taken into account all at the same time. These include the target speed, climb and direction; target range, elevation and bearing; own ship speed and course; wind speed and direction; pitch and roll; and initial shell velocity.[21]

The British first thought about anti-aircraft gunnery about 1916, when the main target was the large and slow-moving airship, but that phase soon passed as faster, heavier-than-air craft came into service. In 1921 contracts were placed with Vickers for a 2pdr pom-pom, so called from its sound. It was far-sighted for its day, with power-operated elevating and training at speeds of up to 15 degrees per second. Ready by 1929, it was intended for eight-barrel mountings, or four in smaller ships, to provide a great volume of fire with 720 rounds per minute from each barrel. It could use up two million rounds of 2pdr ammunition left over from the last war but it soon proved to have a serious flaw – its muzzle velocity was only 1920ft per second, which meant a large deflection that made aiming even harder. That was increased to 2300ft per second by the start of the war, but that was not enough. The eight-barrel pom-pom would equip battleships, fleet carriers and large cruisers; the four-barrel version was to be found on smaller cruisers and carriers, and on destroyers and smaller ships.

Another early attempt was the four-barrelled Vickers half-inch machine gun, which was developed from 1918 using captured German ammunition and with a muzzle velocity of 2630ft per second and 700 rounds per minute per barrel, on a quadruple mounting from 1931. But a single non-explosive round was unlikely to do much damage to an aircraft unless it hit the pilot or a vital part of the engine. Nevertheless, it was fitted in ships of all sizes until replaced by the Oerlikon. The Royal Navy had to look elsewhere for its most effective close- and medium-range weapons.

Again, the Royal Navy suffered from making developments at the wrong time (usually too early) and from the independence and strong views of the RAF. In a conference in 1931, the airmen discounted the dive-bomber, claiming that it would need a specialised aircraft which no air force (presumably obsessed with the strategic bombing of cities) would be prepared to invest in. Instead, the RAF favoured high-level bombing of ships, which could be done with ordinary bombers. The navy accepted this, and that the main targets would be the battleships, the destroyers were simply their bodyguards, which might engage the bombers on their way, but at long range. If the attackers were flying at 5000ft they would be 18 degrees above the horizon, and the current 40-degree elevation of destroyer guns was more than sufficient. And destroyers only needed light anti-aircraft armament, such pom-poms, to protect themselves.

It was a deeply misguided view of air warfare. The US Navy, with no interest in strategic bombing, would soon make progress with dive-bombing, and the Luftwaffe would take it up within a few years, with devastating effect on land and sea warfare. And high-level attack was never viable, as a ship simply had to alter course, as Midshipmen Terrence Lewin and Roddy Macdonald found in 1940 in *Valiant* in 1940:

> … we were both posted at the back of the bridge with binoculars to alert the captain. 'Bomb doors open, sir.' Then 'Bombs away!' He then put the wheel hard over one way or the other. It always worked, as the explosions and columns of water erupted where we would otherwise have been.[22]

The mistaken belief that battleships should and could defend themselves led to a concentration on the high-angle control system, or HACS, which was already under development by the late 1920s and entered service in HMS *Valiant* in 1930. It used a standard layout of a director mounted high up with an unobstructed view, and a transmitting station deep in the ship, but it was originally intended for aircraft with speeds of up to 200 knots, later raised to 250 knots in 1940 and then 350 knots. It could only cope with planes in level flight and it relied far too much on estimation of target speed, wind effect and other factors. Several attempts at tachymetric systems, which would have measured the speed of a target far more accurately, failed to materialise, and there was little attempt to stabilise the system with gyroscopes. The manual calculations in the transmitting station were far too slow, and transmission of them to the guns added another delay. It was only suitable for battleships, which carried four directors, cruisers which usually had three, and fleet carriers. A smaller version was later fitted to destroyers.

Admiral Chatfield was complacent in May 1936 when he advised Winston Churchill that a single gun in a merchant ship would deter an aircraft from attacking. But soon naval officers had a chance to see the effect of Stukas in the Spanish Civil War, while a radio-controlled Queen Bee target was able to circle the Home Fleet for two and a half hours without damage. It was too late to alter the fundamentals of the HACS, but wartime improvements included adding Type 285 radar, analogue computers known as gyro rate units, and remote power control, or RPC, to speed the reaction time of the guns; it remained inferior to the American Mark 37, which was the cause of many ship losses during the war.[23]

For the US Navy, the Mark 37 gun fire control system (technically not a director as it incorporated elements remote from the director itself) was developed from 1936, only two years after its predecessor, the Mark 33, entered service. It corrected the worst faults of the HACS, with a full tachymetric system, it had an analogue computer, the stable element which corrected for the movement of the ship well below decks to aid stability, and it had the facility to set the time fuses in the shell hoists, eliminating the need for human intervention and making the process much more accurate. It allowed firing when each individual gun was ready, rather than having to wait for a salvo, providing for a faster rate of fire. Thus it could fire a 'rolling barrage', in which the pattern followed the movement of the attackers, instead of only threatening them at single moment, as with the barrage created by the HACS. It was first fitted to the destroyer *Sims* in early 1940 and was quickly adopted for new ships of destroyer size and above; in all 841 units were produced and there were ninety-two modifications to keep it up to date.[24]

The Royal Navy first encountered it in late 1941 when the cruiser *Delhi* was fitted with an example in New York Navy Yard. Its superiority was immediately recognised and eighty-two more were ordered, but that was overtaken by events and it only reached other British ships, like the battleship *Vanguard* and the carriers *Eagle* and *Ark Royal*, after the war.

The 40mm Bofors gun was a truly international development. The design was originated by Krupp in Germany, but disarmament after 1918 caused them to acquire the Swedish Bofors firm, until that was outlawed by Sweden. The gun was found useful in the Spanish Civil War of 1936–39 and it was noticed by an American engineer, Henry Howard, on a visit to Stockholm. He brought it to the attention of the Bureau of Ordnance, but attempts to import an example were jeopardised by the German invasion of Norway. Meanwhile, it was tested on a Dutch ship in the Caribbean, and Captain Blandy of the USN reported, 'American planes towed targets for a Dutch ship firing Swedish designed guns with a combined Dutch-German fire control system, the test taking place in the Caribbean Sea off a British port.' The Dutch ship *Van der Zaam* arrived in Britain after the fall of its homeland, and its pairs of 40mm Bofors in three-axis mountings created a sensation.

In America, it was assessed against the British 2pdr pom-pom of similar calibre, which had a much lower muzzle velocity and, fatally, used cordite, which was not manufactured in America. Negotiations with the Swedish government were protracted, but plans were eventually acquired. They were to Swedish standards and dimensions, which did not convert easily to American practices. The essential design of the gun was very sound, but it was designed for craftmanship rather than mass production. Now the thousand or so parts were made to exact dimensions rather than being filed down to fit the individual gun, and castings were reduced in size, then machined to shape. Initially, the York

Safe and Lock Company ran the project but it had its difficulties. The Chrysler Corporation of Detroit, part of General Motors, the apostles of mass production, took the lead and they reported:

> ... 65,589 man hours were saved by changing the material from which 9 parts were made from casting or bar stock to powdered metal. Another 43,266 man hours were saved in the Company's Kercheval Plant by improving manufacturing methods on rammer rods and spindles, by changing the design of the recoil cylinder, by changing the material from which the piston rods were made from bar stock to a forging, and by improving machining methods on the piston rod ...

These and many other improvements made it possible for twelve Chrysler plants, employing ten thousand workers and three thousand machines, to produce 28,892 Bofors guns for the army and navy by the end of 1943, with the help of two thousand subcontractors. The mount was made by Blaw Knox, best known for civil engineering equipment. In the naval version, the guns were usually joined in pairs, which could be used in a twin or quadruple mount. They were used in single mounts in submarines.

The 40mm Bofors was used at the Battle of Santa Cruz in *Enterprise* and *South Dakota*, and was found to be vastly superior to 1.1in.[25] Later

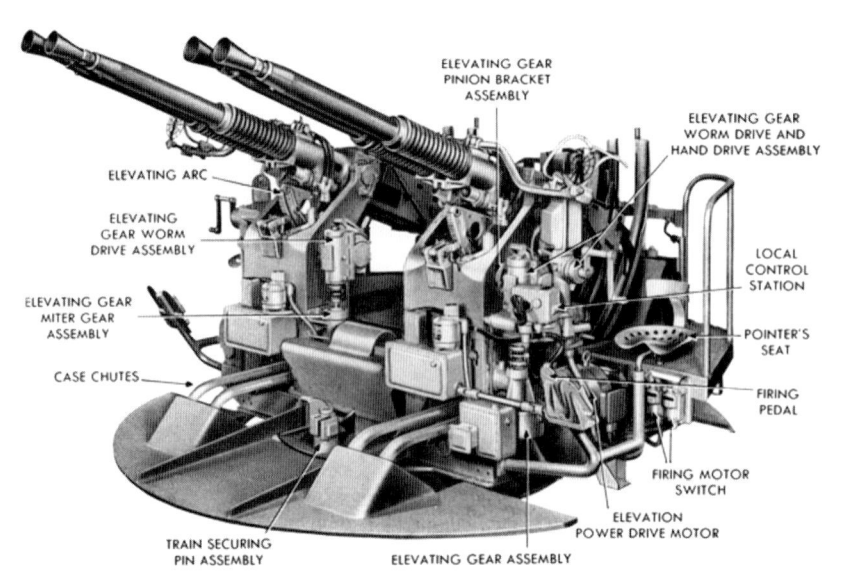

The classic quadruple 40mm Bofors gun, in many ways the best medium-range anti-aircraft weapon of the war.

the British came to appreciate the value of the Bofors in the Pacific. In August 1945 Admiral Edelstein was pleased that the fitting of them was going 'hot and strong' (though too late for the war).[26]

The 20mm Oerlikon gun was another international development. During the 1920s Werkzeugmaschinefabrik [Machine Tool Works] Oerlikon, based in the eponymous suburb of Zurich, developed a gun on the blow-back principle: 'The major difference between this gun and others is that the force of the explosion is absorbed in checking and reversing the forward motion of a relatively heavy bolt, or breechblock, that is never locked.'[27] It was sold to several governments, including China. It attracted British interest in 1935, when their overseas sales manager, Antoine Gazda, stopped there and showed a film of its operation to Captain Lord Louis Mountbatten, who became a great enthusiast and used his presentational skills to the full. In 1939 the Admiralty finally ordered five hundred guns. The fall of France cut off supplies, but the British were prepared to ignore restrictions on licensing by the neutral Swiss.

The US Navy had tested an example in 1935, but it was an earlier model which did not come up to standard. In 1940 the British looked to source supply from the United States, but first they had to establish that it was a standard weapon of the US armed forces to meet the export regulations. It was tested against its rival, the Hispano-Suiza, and recognised as an 'excellent weapon' by November 1940. Production was set up, initially for lend-lease, involving firms such as Pontiac Motors and the Hudson Motor Company, and numerous subcontractors, and it too was redesigned for mass production. It was soon taken up by the US Navy and production peaked at 4693 mounts and 5630 mechanisms in September 1943. Eventually nearly 147,000 mechanisms were produced.[28] The British had 55,000 of them, which would have taken up a seventh of the navy if all were fully manned with two men.

The 20mm Oerlikon was mostly used in a single mount aimed by the gunner moving his shoulders:

> The double shoulder piece, which is adjustable for width and is fitted at the rear end of the casing …, together with the harness fastened round the body, gives adequate control of the mounting enabling a rapidly moving target to be followed with precision. Accuracy of aiming is largely dependent on smooth footwork which requires constant practice.[29]

It was aimed using a foresight with concentric rings to match the supposed speed of the target.

Diagram 35.—20mm. OERLIKON GUN.

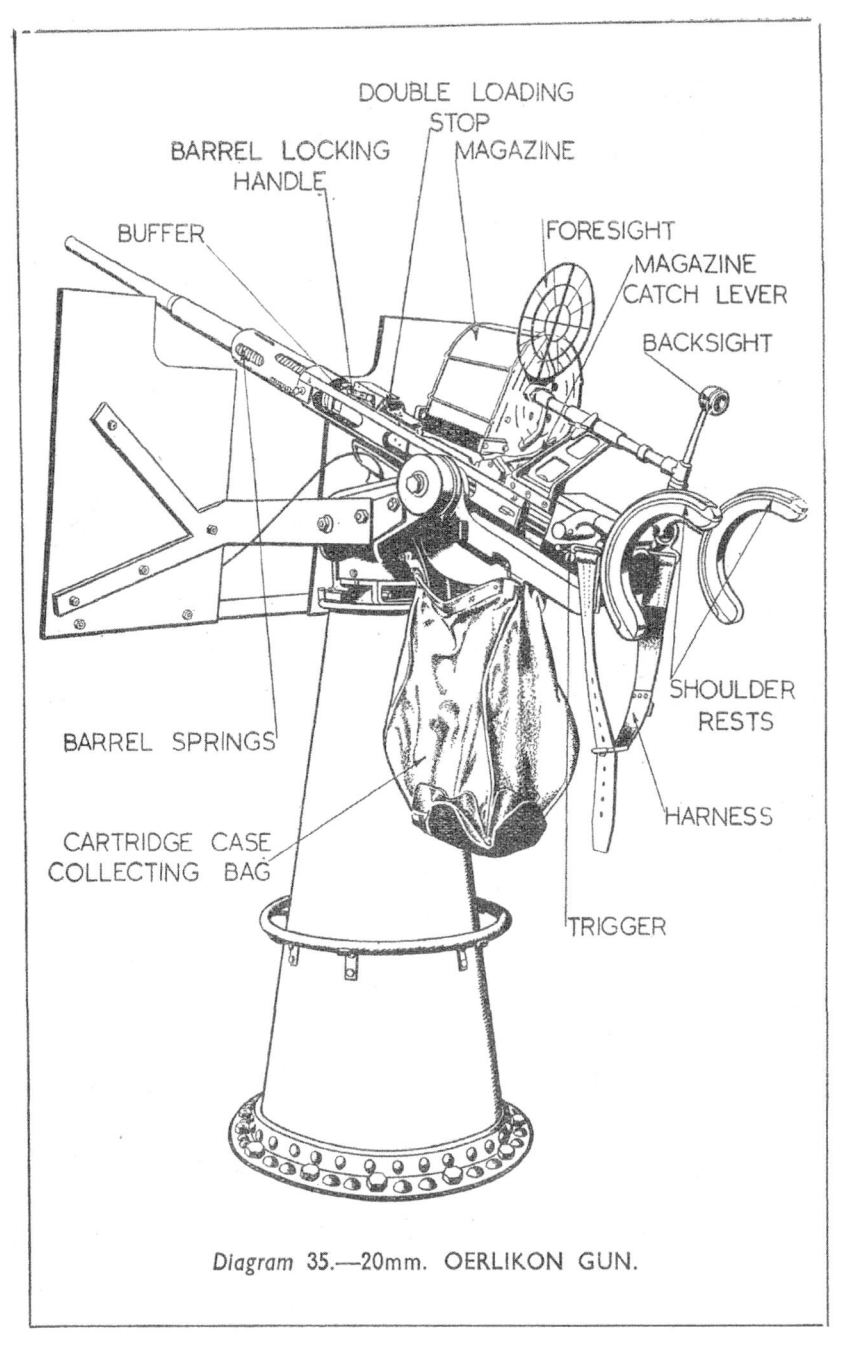

The 20mm Oerlikon gun, manned by a crew of two, showing the shoulder rests and straps by which the gunner aimed the weapon. It tended to be outclassed by the end of the war.

> You could tell a good gunner's tracers from a bad one. He would lead the plane well and his tracers would look like they would miss the plane by a mile. The tracers would start to form a line that arched out in front of the plane and started back bent in the shape of a strung longbow. ... the good gunner's tracers looked like a miss halfway to the target. Then they seemed to bend back to the plane and hit it.[30]

Its cylindrical magazine was 'easily and quickly changed' by the second member of the crew.[31] By the middle of the war it was to be found on the great majority of naval vessels, for example, one on each side of the bridge of a British frigate, to batteries of up to ten on American battleships, one of which might carry fifty or more in total. It was credited with 32 per cent of kills by American ships up to September 1944, which declined to 24 per cent when it was found to be ineffective against the kamikazes, which had to be destroyed to stop an attack. Compared with the Bofors, in August 1945 Admiral Edelstein thought that 'The Oerlikon was "abso-bloody-lutely hopeless" in the circumstances.'[32] But a successful Oerlikon gunner would be a hero to his shipmates:

> A/B Day in the twin Oerlikon turret had him exactly in his sights and gave him a long searing burst which ripped down his fuselage ... The attack was over and 658 had made her first kill. Young Day was surrounded by grinning matelots all promising their tots next day![33]

Another problem was to detonate the shell where it could do damage to the attacking aircraft. Contact fuses required a direct hit, which was rare except at short ranges. Fuses could be timed to explode near where the attacker was expected to be, but it took four or five seconds to set each by hand, which greatly reduced the chances of a hit. Automatic fuse setters only helped a little. One possibility was to use barrage fire, timing all the shells to explode at a fixed distance from the ship and create a wall of fire, but pilots soon learned how to pass through it undamaged.

As an alternative to the contact and timed fuses, the British began to develop a shell to detonate in close proximity to the target in 1939, and the Americans in 1940. The principle was simple enough, a small radio transmitter in the shell would be reflected from the target and it would explode, sending fragments towards it; but scientists at John Hopkins University had to deal with the shock of being fired from a gun, premature explosion damaging the crew, and safety in transit among many others. A hundred and ten factories were involved in production

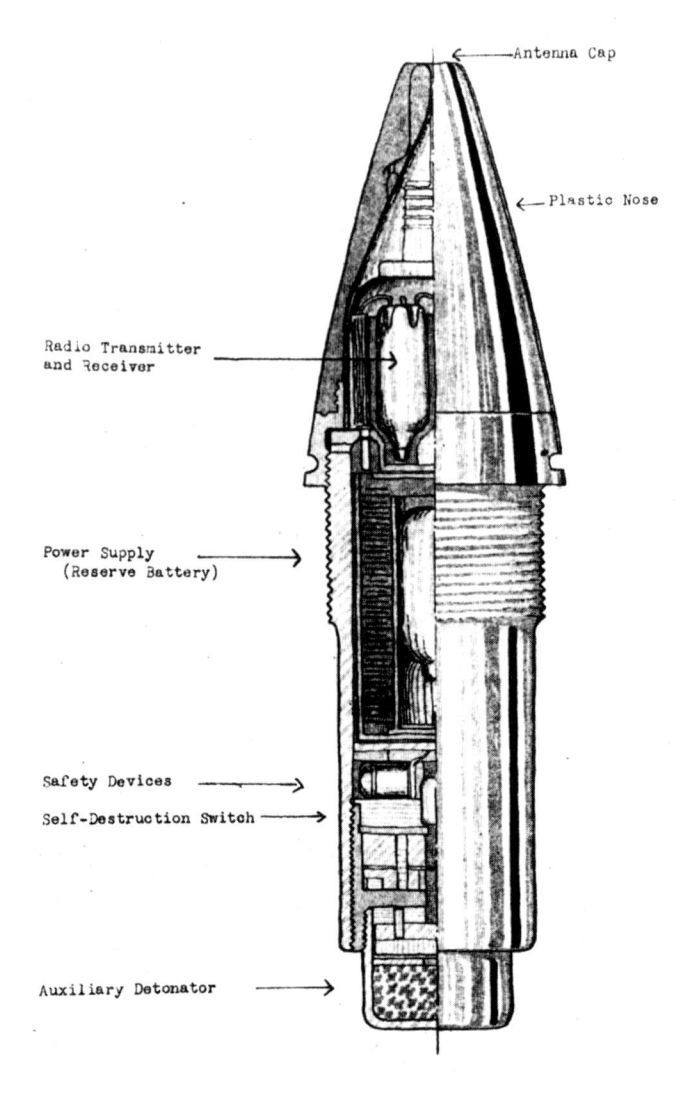

A VT-fused shell which would use radio signals and explode in proximity to the target rather than on contact. It transformed anti-aircraft gunnery towards the end of the war.

of the final version, the VT fuse, and five in assembly; more than 22 million were built during the war. It was first used by the cruiser *Helena* to shoot down a Japanese bomber in January 1943

The 5in/38 was the main gun to be fitted with the VT proximity fuse, as the Bofors was too small and the 6in was too slow. It came into its own against the kamikazes in 1944/5, as its shell was enough to destroy an aircraft totally before it could crash. Without the VT fuse it had a kill rate of 252 'rounds per bird' in 1942, rising to 1157 RPB in 1944 as more guns were fired at each target and high attacks increased, then falling to 627 in 1945. With the VT fuse, it achieved a RPB of 366 in 1945. In comparison, a 20mm Oerlikon might fire more than nine thousand rounds for a single kill.[34]

Torpedoes

The torpedo, in the modern sense, was invented by the British engineer Whitehead on behalf of the Austro-Hungarian navy. It was an obvious threat to a predominant navy like the British and could be launched by surface ships, submarines or aircraft. A torpedo is a sophisticated machine. Unlike a gun, most of the equipment is contained within the projectile itself and the launching mechanism is usually quite a simple tube. This meant that practice torpedoes were not expendable, which had a profound effect, particularly on American weapons.

The torpedo had played a decisive role in the First World War. The very threat of it had caused Admiral Jellicoe to turn away from a commanding position at the Battle of Jutland. It was the key weapon of the 'unrestricted submarine warfare' campaign which not only nearly brought Britain to its knees, but also caused the American entry to the war. Yet the Royal Navy itself had only expended 781 torpedoes in action during four years. This, and the general parsimony of the age, meant that reserve stocks were kept low during peacetime. Nevertheless there was some development based in the Royal Naval Torpedo Factory, with testing in the straight and deep waters of Loch Long across the Firth of Clyde. The 21in Mk VIII was developed from 1927 and powered by a burner-cycle engine, a kind of semi-diesel using kerosene. It was quite efficient, although it gave off a track – the Royal Navy did not do much to develop electric power which would have been trackless, though with a poorer performance. The Mk VIII*** version was in service in submarines in 1939 with a range of 5000yds at 45.5 knots and a warhead of 805lbs of Torpex. The Mk IX of 1930 had a longer range and hitting power and was issued to modern cruisers and destroyers. The 18in Mk XII was the standard airborne torpedo with a range of 1500yds at 40 knots and a charge of 388lbs of TNT. It was followed by the improved Mk XV, but in general the interwar torpedoes proved satisfactory, and effort was concentrated on increased production rather than further development.

The torpedo armament of cruisers was generally reduced to allow tonnage for aircraft and AA armament, usually leaving three tubes per side. Interwar destroyers of the 'A' to 'H' classes had two sets of four torpedo tubes mounted amidships and were able to fire on either side, though only with hand training. It was feared that any more might cause them to interfere with one another, though perversely with the 'I' class, a fifth tube was introduced to compensate for having one less ship in the flotilla. No reloads were carried. The Tribal class had only one set of quadruple tubes, with power training to switch quickly from one side to the other. Later destroyers mostly reverted to the two by four arrangement, though many had one set removed to make way for anti-aircraft armament.

Destroyer torpedo control officers used the torpedo deflection sight to aim them, probably passing the bearing of the target to a communications rating who fired when pointers came into line on a dial. Torpedoes in a salvo were spaced two degrees, or three for wide spreads. One problem was that the attacking destroyers had to turn just before launching their weapons, giving the enemy notice of their intentions, which was highlighted during the 'Channel Dash' of 1942. After that torpedoes could be gyro angled to fire 60 degrees ahead or astern of the beam.

A torpedo attack could be an exciting affair, as Tristan Jones observed during the final hours of *Scharnhorst*:

> Faster and faster, plunging and swaying, pulsing with strain until her whole hull screamed in protest, *Obstinate* headed for the flame and smoke to the south-east now, closer and closer. All we could see of the other nine destroyers was their pale wakes, until Captain (D) in *Onslow* opened up with his four-inchers. Crash after crash shook out hull, already battered by the flashing seas crashing alongside. *Obstinate* reared and pitched and rolled and wallowed, and how the Torps got the tinfish out away in any semblance of an aim I'll never know. Out slid the tinfish, long and sinister, and splashed into the darkness.[35]

Submarines were fitted with six ahead-firing torpedo tubes, though with the coastal 'U' class, firing all at once would cause the bow to rise out of the water. Astern-firing tubes were out of favour at the beginning of the war, but came back into use. The 'T' class also had four external tubes which could be fired in a massive salvo of ten against a very important target, though that was only used three times during the war. Salvoes of six were by far the most common. They could only be fired ahead or 90 degrees on either beam, which meant that the submarine had to be manoeuvred carefully and dangerously into position for an attack. The attack was controlled by the submarine torpedo director, or 'fruit machine'.

Edward Young describes the firing of an unsuccessful salvo in *Storm*:

I yelled the order down the voice pipe.

'FIRE ONE!'

The submarine gave a little arrested lurch as the first torpedo slipped away. Still crouched over the sight, I waited until the enemy's bow had crossed the line.

The black shape moved steadily on, unaware of the torpedoes racing towards him at forty knots.

'FIRE THREE!'

And when his stern had drawn just clear of the sight I sent off the last of the salvo.

'FIRE FOUR!' …

To my horror he crossed the line of fire unscathed, as he did so he saw the tracks of the torpedoes and began turning towards us.[36]

Out of 7770 torpedoes fired by the Royal Navy during the war, 5121 were by submarines. Capital ships only used them once, cruisers forty-three times and destroyers 606. MTBs, designed round the torpedo, used them 1328 times and aircraft launched 609, including the famous attacks at Taranto and on *Bismarck*. On average, they were successful 42.3 per cent of the time, with submarines having the highest rate at 46.4.[37]

Like practically all torpedoes, the Mk 14 used by American submarines was cylindrical for most of its length with a rounded head and a tapered tail. It came in four sections. The nose could contain either the warhead filled with TNT or Torpex, or the exercise head which was filled with liquid ballast which was expelled at the end of its run to allow it to be recovered. Aft of that was the air-flask section, the largest single compartment, filled with compressed air, with much smaller alcohol fuel and water compartments in the midship section behind. In combination, these would power the engine situated in the afterbody along with the depth and gyro mechanisms to control depth and direction. The tail was fitted with two propellers rotating in opposite directions, and depth and steering rudders. Destroyers used the Mk 15 with a heavier warhead.

Though the essential designs were sound, lack of practice and testing allowed serious problems to remain undiscovered. In the destroyer *Sterett*:

> … we rarely fired the 'fish' for fear that we might lose one: they occasionally sank instead of surfacing at the end of their run. The loss of a torpedo usually resulted in a letter of reprimand for the torpedo officer and unfavourable comments on the skipper's report of fitness. … Our highest priority on torpedo firing was not hitting the target but recovering the torpedo.[38]

During peacetime exercises, the depth was set for the torpedo to pass under the target to avoid any damage. There was no way of telling if it went well below that, unless it touched the bottom – which happened in 1938 when some surfaced with the heads covered in mud, but that was dismissed as poor maintenance. Once the problem had been identified in tests in 1942, it was relatively easy to reset the depths, but that exposed another problem. The torpedoes were fitted with magnetic exploders, which were supposed to detonate under the hull of the target, avoiding the armour and anti-torpedo bulges on a large warship. They were tested satisfactorily in 1926 on the hull of an old submarine, but there were no more trials during the peace. The device was very complex and unreliable, a 'Rube Goldberg [Heath Robinson]' device according to one American admiral. Excessive secrecy, and the stubbornness of the Bureau of Ordnance did not help. It might fail to detonate, which was more than frustrating for a submarine crew who had used their skill and risked their lives to get into firing position. Even worse it might detonate prematurely, giving away the presence of the submarine. The crew of *Jack* had that experience in June 1943 and even the puritanical commander was driven to moderate swearing:

> '*Damn* those exploders … damn them all to *hell*!' said Dykers as he looked through the scope. 'The first torpedo prematured … just before it got to the MOT … and I don't know whether the other two passed under without exploding, or missed. Son of a bitch from *Baghdad*!'

After surviving a counter-attack, Dykers decided to disobey orders. For the next attack he set the depth at less than the draught of the target, so that the firing pin rather than the exploder would take effect. It was successful: 'There was exultation all through the ship. Backs were slapped, and men were yelling in glee.'[39] This became general policy

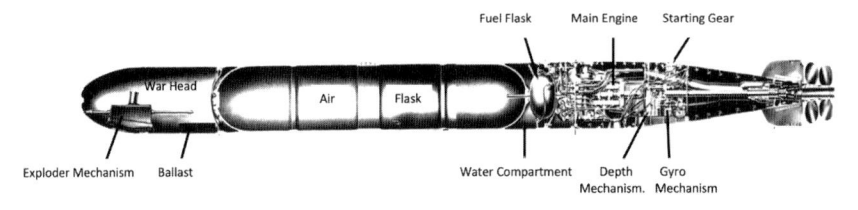

Details of the standard American ship-launched torpedo. The warhead and exploder mechanism are forward, the air flask in the middle, and the engine and depth mechanism towards the rear. After its design problems were solved, it became a very effective weapon.

from June 1943, when Admiral Nimitz ordered the deactivation of the magnetic device on all torpedoes.

This brought out another problem. On the very day when Nimitz issued his order, *Tinosa* fired fifteen torpedoes at a large tanker and only two exploded; *Haddock* had a similar problem a few days later. At Pearl Harbor the submariners fired directly at a cliff and found that the friction on the firing pin was too great, while on the East Coast the Bureau of Ordnance made the same discovery. The Pearl Harbor researchers tried dropping torpedoes on steel plates at different angles and concluded that a lighter pin and a stronger spring would solve the problem. At last by January 1944, the US Navy had a torpedo for its great offensive against Japanese shipping, and to defeat the Imperial Navy at Leyte Gulf.

* * *

The dominance of gunnery at the start of the war was never really tested to the full, in that there was no fleet battle on equal terms, but it was clear that aircraft were a far more effective weapon in most circumstances. British performance was adequate but unspectacular in heavy guns and torpedoes. American performance varied from the early faults of the torpedo to the triumph of design that was the 5in gun.

The Second World War saw the last gasp of the gun and uncontrolled torpedo – guided weapons were already under consideration with homing torpedoes, German glider bombers and, in a sense, the kamikaze. But all that would depend on the development of electronics, a process much boosted by the war.

10

Intelligence and Electronics

RADIO, OR wireless telegraphy as it was known at the time, was developed at the beginning of the twentieth century specifically for navies, at a time when all the important land sites were already linked by electric telegraph. The Royal Navy took the lead in co-operation with Guglielmo Marconi and with experiments in HMS *Vernon*, an old wooden warship moored in Portsmouth Harbour. The link between radio and intelligence was established during the First World War, when Room 40 at the Admiralty used German signals to track the movements of the High Seas Fleet. That set a pattern for the future – intelligence was rarely provided by secret agents, but by patient analysis of information that was publicly available, reports from neutrals, photo-reconnaissance and especially by listening to enemy radio signals.

Both navies began their active phase of the Second World War with a spectacular intelligence failure – the British in Norway, the Americans at Pearl Harbor. Warnings of a possible German invasion of Scandinavia came via the military attachés in Stockholm, reports on the movements of German forces in the Baltic and North Sea, and the first contact between the Operational Information Centre of the Admiralty and the Government Code and Cypher School on the eve of invasion, reporting a great increase of radio traffic in the area. But the reports were not co-ordinated and the different departments were still riddled with rivalry, even within the Admiralty and War Office. This was compounded by a belief that the Germans would not dare such an attack in the face of British sea power, and if they did, it would be easily defeated.[1] The invasion of Denmark and Norway, which ended the 'Phoney War' on 9 April 1940, caught the British and French forces wrong-footed.

In December 1941 American intelligence was well aware that the Japanese were moving south, and that the war would probably start on 7 December, but the great task force heading for Pearl Harbor kept radio silence, while radio messages intended to put the forces on alert failed to get through. Two army privates saw a number of aircraft approaching from the north on their radar, but their report was ignored, and an attack on a Japanese submarine attempting the harbour was discounted, so the main attack came as a complete and devastating surprise. Both nations had much to learn, and they did so.

Between the wars the Royal Navy did little to develop radio, only reluctantly increasing from low to medium and high frequencies, expecting it to be needed mainly for a Jutland-style battlefleet and operating mostly within close range of the shore. It was matched by a reluctance to replace wireless telegraphy, which relied on Morse code and a large number of trained telegraphists, with voice radio, known as radio telephony. The navy mistrusted voice communication, believing that it was much more difficult to control and record. Many of its sets were obsolete even in these terms, and due for replacement.

At the beginning of the war the Home Fleet read the routine area broadcast from nearby shore stations and the commander-in-chief would read the adjacent areas as well. The Fleet Wave was used for intercommunication on matters such as enemy movements and fleet manoeuvring, on very low power when cruising, and much higher power in action. Area low frequency was for reports from detached ships, area high frequency for senior officers' intercommunication. There was an RAF reconnaissance wave, and a striking force wave for use by aircraft carriers if necessary.[2]

The need to use very high frequency (VHF) to communicate with aircraft began to change this; and since VHF waves did not bounce off the Heaviside layer, they were generally secure when used between surface ships in a fleet or a convoy. The navy was not successful in its own VHF equipment, but relied on what was supplied by the RAF and the Americans.[3] For Donald Macintyre, who commanded various escort groups during the Battle of the Atlantic, an American system transformed the communications.

> It was not until the American VHF set known as TBS (Talk Between Ships) became available through lend-lease that our desires were met. The transformation TBS worked in the cohesion of the group dispersed around the sprawling convoy was wonderful. Instead of the tedious process of call-up by lamp and the laborious spelling out of an order, or the shorter but insecure communication by HF radio, each ship was in immediate touch with the others by simply speaking into a telephone, the message coming through on a loudspeaker on the bridge.[4]

By 1944 TBS circuits had been added to the Home Fleet's repertoire as the main circuit for fleet manoeuvring and surface radar reports, while detached units might use another TBS frequency. The Admiral's Wave was 'Kept by carrier-borne reconnaissance aircraft, by cruisers and above when these aircraft were operating, and by all ships in action.' A high frequency was reserved for communication with detached senior officers, there was an auxiliary wave, and an action information wave for urgent tactical information. The air plot control wave was used for 'Exchange of air information and radar reports of aircraft.'

This was not enough for the fast-moving warfare in the Pacific. Ships had to listen to five different broadcasts – two operational, one for intelligence, a senior officers' broadcast and the Admiralty administrative messages. The TBS circuit used by larger American ships for plans and reports of air strikes was kept by British task force and task group commanders. There was inter-group communication between all task force and group commanders, a local air warning circuit and a circuit for fighter direction officers. There was an inter-carrier co-ordination wave, another for briefing and intelligence and an inter-force fighter defence officer wave, kept by carriers in action.[5]

Commander Parry of the Royal Navy was impressed with American equipment early in 1941:

> All destroyers are fitted with radio telephony, known as TBS, which I gather is its type designation. A handset is available on the bridge for the use of the captain and the loud speaker receiver is nearby. The installation works well and was of the greatest value in directing ships when picking up torpedoes. It is also largely used in the destroyer night attack organisation, but its use has recently been restricted for other purposes owing to 'skip' distance trouble. It is said that messages have been picked up on the West Coast of the States, and as the wave length corresponded with that of police cars some confusion arose. The set is small, has a signal working range of from 20 to 25 miles, and a frequency of 7.82 megacycles. At present only one wave length can be used but this defect is being remedied in the near future.

According to American instructions of 1945, 'VHF radio channels are so essential for the efficient function of CIC that the benefits derived from their employment usually outweigh the loss of security. For this reason, radio silence on these frequencies is usually only ordered under extreme conditions.'[6]

Operation required considerable skill:

> No sooner had we worked up to copying eight or ten five-letter code groups per minute than a new challenge was presented: learning

to transmit with the telegraph key. This was more difficult than it seemed, since it required a 180-degree reorientation. In copying, what the ear received in aural symbols the brain must translate into letters (or numbers) that the hand, reinforced by the eye, can record on paper. But sending messages begins with the eye, not the ear. The message is converted by the brain in reverse, from sight to abstract Morse equivalent. It must then be forwarded by the hand and wrist, working in harmony with the eye and brain, the feedback sound in the earphones providing assurance that the retransmission is an accurate one.[7]

There were three ways of obtaining radio intelligence. First, by the volume of traffic, known as traffic analysis – one officer remarked, 'a great deal can be obtained from the study of enemy wireless traffic without having the faintest idea of the content of the message.'[8] Secondly, by finding the direction from which signals were coming and using that to fix the position of the sender, known as direction finding. And finally by actually decoding the signals.

As to direction finding, the Admiralty set up 'Y' stations at Flowerdown in Hampshire near the south coast of England, Scarborough and Cupar on the east coast of the United Kingdom, and at Chicksands in inland Bedfordshire. Overseas there were stations at Malta, Alexandria, Kilindini in Kenya, Gibraltar, Bermuda, Freetown in Sierra Leone, and later Polarnoe in northern Russia. They provided ocean-wide coverage, but over such distances they only gave approximate positions. Eventually, shipboard equipment would provide a more accurate picture in the Battle of the Atlantic.

The Royal Navy played a large part in cracking the German Enigma code, and it would be the greatest beneficiary of it. The first breakthrough came when two of the machines, rather like typewriters and capable of encoding messages that the Germans continued to believe were unbreakable, were supplied by a Polish officer just before his country was invaded. The Government Code and Cypher School (descended from Room 40 at the Admiralty) moved from London to Bletchley Park between Oxford and Cambridge, largely under naval auspices. It would use a combination of individual geniuses, such as Alan Turing and Gordon Welchman, and meticulous work by a staff of up to ten thousand, including many Wrens, and innovative machines such as the Bombe and the Colossus computer. Decrypts were known as Ultra and were one of the best-kept secrets of the war, and for nearly thirty years after.

The keyboard of a German Enigma machine, December 1943.

Naval activities during the war kept up the flow of information. In February 1940 *U33* was sunk during a minelaying operation in the Firth of Clyde, and one of the crew members was foolish enough to put some of the machine's rotors in his pocket before he was captured. The patrol boat *Krebs* was captured off the Lofoten Islands in March 1941, with some secret material, as was the weather ship *München* in May, and *Lauenburg* in June. In October 1942 *U559* was captured in the Mediterranean and yielded material which enabled Bletchley to end a long drought of information after the Germans introduced another wheel to the machine.

For the supply of information was not consistent over the war. It was February 1941 before information was available, but only spasmodically, and the speed of decoding it was equally important – during the chase of *Bismarck* in May 1941, decoding took forty-eight hours; the ship had already been sunk before the later ones were available. From June it was completely available with a delay of twenty-four to forty-eight hours. That ended when a fourth rotor was installed in February 1942, a dearth which lasted until December, when all traffic was read with delays of a few hours to a week. That continued for ocean operations until the end of the war, though extra German measures made it more difficult to decode messages from U-boats operating close inshore.[9] But there is no doubt that Ultra played a key part in winning the battle of the Atlantic.

American codebreakers never acquired the mystique of their British counterparts, perhaps because after the war the British wanted to believe that, despite their decline as a world power, they still retained a hidden potency. But the American codebreakers had at least as much impact on the course of the war, and in a much wider range of activity. They broke two main Japanese codes, the diplomatic one which transmitted signals to and from embassies, and the naval one. Like the Germans, the Japanese never realised that their codes had been broken. They upgraded them occasionally, which caused short-term difficulties, notably during the start of the Guadalcanal campaign, but never changed them radically.

The Japanese diplomatic code, known as Purple because of the year of its origin, had two main weaknesses. It only gradually replaced the older Red system, which had already been broken, so parallel messages were often sent; and in encrypting, vowels were only substituted for vowels, consonants for consonants. It was broken in September 1940 using the system known as Magic. Famously, on the eve of Pearl Harbor it revealed that an attack was imminent on 7 December, though not its location. Magic continued to provide insight into Japan and her allies; the Berlin embassy reported on German policy, for example alerting the Allies to Hitler's mistaken belief that they intended to invade Norway, and showing that the effect of air raids on German cities such as Hamburg was not devastating to industrial production.

There was already close co-operation with the British even before America entered the war, despite reluctance on both sides to reveal their techniques. In particular, two Bletchley Park representatives visited America in the spring of 1941, and around the same time an American mission visited Singapore to exchange information. This resulted in a Japanese-speaking British naval officer, trained in cryptanalysis, being sent to Corregidor in the Philippines.[10]

The naval code, JN25, was broken early in 1942 by a system also known as Ultra, operated by a team known as Op-20-G which, like its British counterpart, employed both ingenuity and large numbers of people. As one report put it, 'solutions which could once be achieved by relatively few experts and by simple means in a short period of time, now require complex machinery, large forces of personnel and extensive time-consuming research.'[11] Edward Van Der Rhoer, a Japanese linguist, reported of his work at Arlington Hall near Washington:

> It seemed to me as if, without knowing it, I had been preparing all my life for this work. I had always been fond of higher mathematics as well as all sorts of problem solving. I enjoyed the sophisticated

riddles, crossword puzzles, and acrostics. I also liked the intricate calculations that went into chess. And in foreign language I had sought, in reality, to break a kind of code, to get into an inner meaning represented by symbols that were unknown to me in the beginning. Now I realised that my mind and personality had a special affinity with codebreaking.[12]

It provided the intelligence which allowed the US Navy to draw with the Imperial Japanese Navy in the Battle of the Coral Sea, and to win at Midway two months later. It allowed American aircraft to shoot down Admiral Yamamoto in April 1943. The Japanese merchant shipping code had already been broken and that aided the devastating submarine offensive which threatened to starve Japan of strategic materials.

One particular difficulty for the Americans was that the flow of information by press and politicians was hard to control. As early as 1929, Herbert Yardley, a disgruntled former codebreaker, published a book revealing some of the secrets. In 1942, just after the Battle of Midway, the Chicago *Tribune*, owned by an isolationist, published an article misleadingly headlined 'Navy had Word of Jap Plan to Strike at Sea', giving away something of the secrets, but to prosecute the case before a grand jury would only reveal more detail. Later in the year, *Time* magazine referred to a station in South America from which 'coded and transposed messages were turned over to the US experts, who broke the code.' And in 1944, presidential candidate Thomas Dewey was only persuaded with difficulty not to make a speech revealing some details of US intelligence before Pearl Harbor.

Radar

Several nations, including Germany, Britain and the United States, were developing radar (then known as RDF to the British) before the war and had fitted it to a few ships. But for the British, the air had to take priority and stations were set up along the coasts. These soon proved their value in the Battle of Britain in 1940, but in the winter of that year there was a new threat as the Luftwaffe began to bomb cities by night. Ground radar was ineffective in countering night raiders, so a set had to be devised that could be fitted in an aircraft.

In September 1940, as the fate of Britain seemed to hang in the balance, a mission led by Sir Henry Tizard, the scientific adviser to the British government, arrived in Washington. They would discuss many things with their American counterparts, including Asdic, jet engines and atomic bombs, though the US Navy's Norden bombsight was off the

Intelligence and Electronics 261

table. But the key moment was when the British delegation produced what they called a cavity magnetron. It was:

> ... a simple-looking device whose operation is rather complicated. Holes, or cavities, are located in a ring that acts as the positively charged anode; a rod through the center of the anode acts as the negatively charged cathode. A magnet surrounds the anode so that as an electrical current is applied to the magnetron, the magnetic field causes the electrons to circulate. As they move in a circle the electrons pass over the cavities and create an electrical frequency

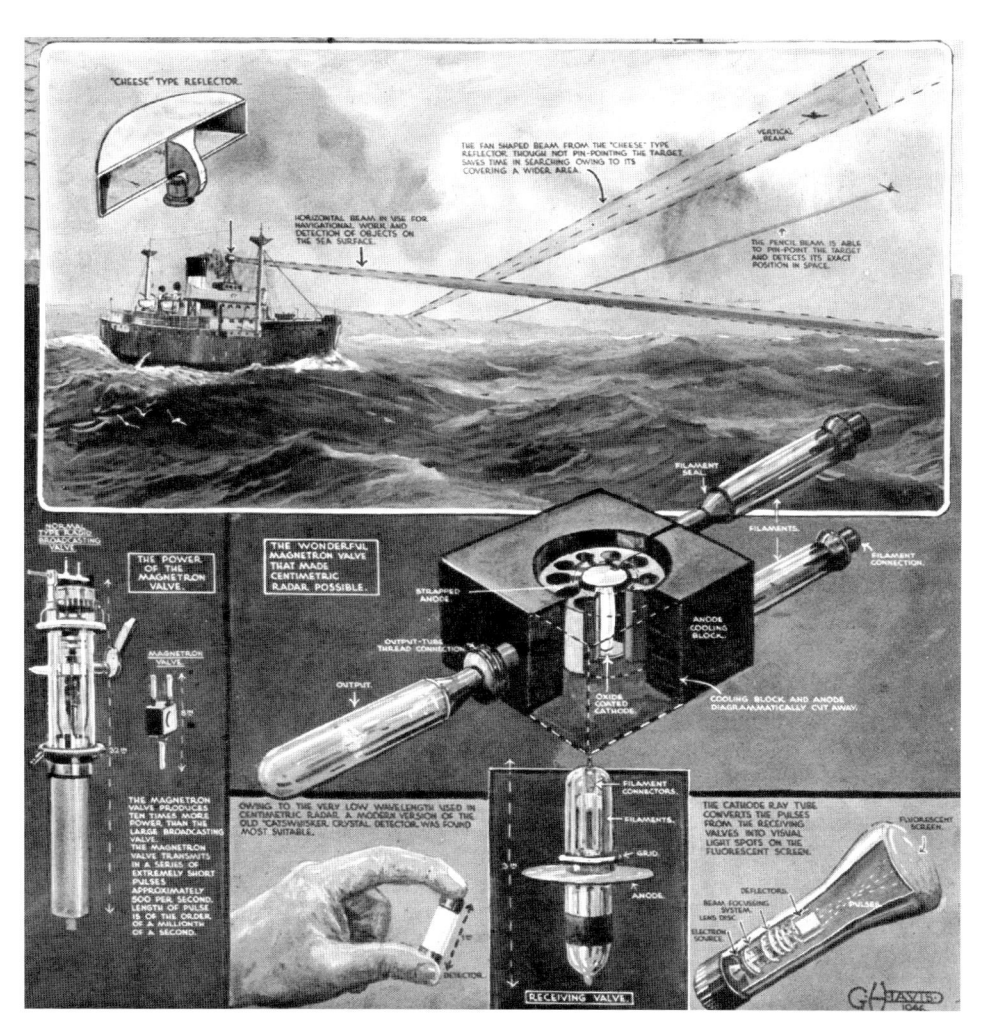

The cavity magnetron, as revealed after the war, one of Britain's most significant contributions to the Allied war effort.

based on the size of the holes. This frequency is conducted away from the magnetron in microwaves.[13]

It had been developed in Birmingham University by John Randall and Henry Boot without much official support, but it greatly increased the power of a radar set fitted into a ship or aircraft, making it possible to use a wavelength of 10cm, which would allow, among other things, the detection of surfaced submarines. Only a dozen models had been produced so far and it had never been tried in action, but when it was demonstrated before a group of American scientists, to radar expert Edward Bowen's immense relief it produced an inch-long 'glow discharge', power of more than 1.5 kilowatts as promised, and a wavelength of 9.8cm. Even the Anglophobic Admiral Harold G Bowen agreed that 'One of the inventions which the British disclosed to us was a great contribution to radar – an oscillator tube of unusual power output, known as the multi-cavity magnetron.'[14]

The U-boat's main tactic was to attack on the surface at night, undetected by Asdic, and a radar which could counter this was essential, replacing the primitive Type 286 with its fixed aerial and 1.5m wavelength. This demanded a much smaller wavelength of 10cm, known as centimetric or microwave. Type 271 radar was first tried on the corvette *Orchis* in the spring of 1941. Initially, its double semi-circular 'cheese' aerials were protected inside a hexagonal structure of ground Perspex with teak supports, but the wood caused back echoes so an all-Perspex structure replaced it. By April 1942 the whole assembly was prefabricated and fitted to ships as they came in for boiler cleaning. Type 271 and its successors were a decisive factor in winning the Battle of the Atlantic. Later models included the Type 273 with parabolic aerials which could be fitted at greater height, and was often used in larger ships, and the 277 with higher power and greater range.[15]

Another result of the Tizard mission was the proliferation of Identification Friend or Foe, or IFF systems. The first one was developed by Warson-Watt's team as early as 1938 and consisted of a transponder which would react to the Chain Home system. It was crude and was quickly followed by the Mk II which would respond to army and navy radars. Initially fitted to aircraft, it was used in ships by 1942. The Tizard mission had already shown it to the Americans, who were persuaded to adopt it for the army and navy, though they were developing a more sophisticated system of their own. But it could only respond on a limited number of wavebands and might be susceptible to German radar. The RAF scientist F C Williams developed Mk II, which would respond to signals from a separate transmitter. But off Salerno in 1943, four different systems were in use, causing confusion.[16]

The Royal Navy divided its radar sets into several types – WA for air warning, WS for surface warning, GS for gunnery against surface targets and GA for anti-aircraft gunnery.

Early radars used enormous 'bedstead' aerials and a great deal of power, so they could only be fitted in larger ships. The first one was Type 79 (numbered in a sequence intended for radio sets), which was fitted to the battleship *Rodney* and the cruiser *Sheffield* in 1938, and several other ships in 1939. It was mainly intended for anti-aircraft warning and could pick one out at a range of up ninety miles. Its definition was poor by later standards and its 5 to 10 degree beam and 7.5m wavelength made it inaccurate, but it proved to be reliable. When fitted with gunnery ranging it was known as Type 279, and it was succeeded by an improved version, Type 281, from 1940. This operated on 3.5m with a range of up to 110 miles and could pick out a battleship at eleven miles. It was later fitted with beam-switching which gave much greater directional accuracy. In different versions it remained in use for the rest of the war, for its successor type 960 was not ready until 1946. Other sets had different functions. Type 285 of 1940, with its pointed 'fishbone' aerials, was used to direct the long-range anti-aircraft armament of larger ships, and the high-angle and low-angle guns of destroyers. With beam-switching it was accurate to within a quarter of a degree in good conditions. Type 282 of 1941 also used a fishbone aerial and was for close-range anti-aircraft control in destroyers and above. Type 283 of 1943 was for controlling anti-aircraft barrage fire.

The cathode ray tube was one of the inventions that made radar possible, by providing a means to display the information. However, this was the linear A-scope, with a single line across the tube and blips displaying the distance of one or more objects on a scale which ranged from 15,000 to 150,000yds. In the case of a Type 271 in a corvette or frigate, the operator had an indicator to give a rough bearing as shown by the position of the aerial, but for more accuracy he had to look through a periscope to find its exact position. It was awkward for the operator in that he had to use two instruments at right angles to one another. Tactically, only one object might be in view at once and its relative position to others could not be found without plotting on paper – a U-boat approaching a convoy could be found, but not if it was among the ships.

From 1942 it was replaced by the plan position indicator, or PPI:

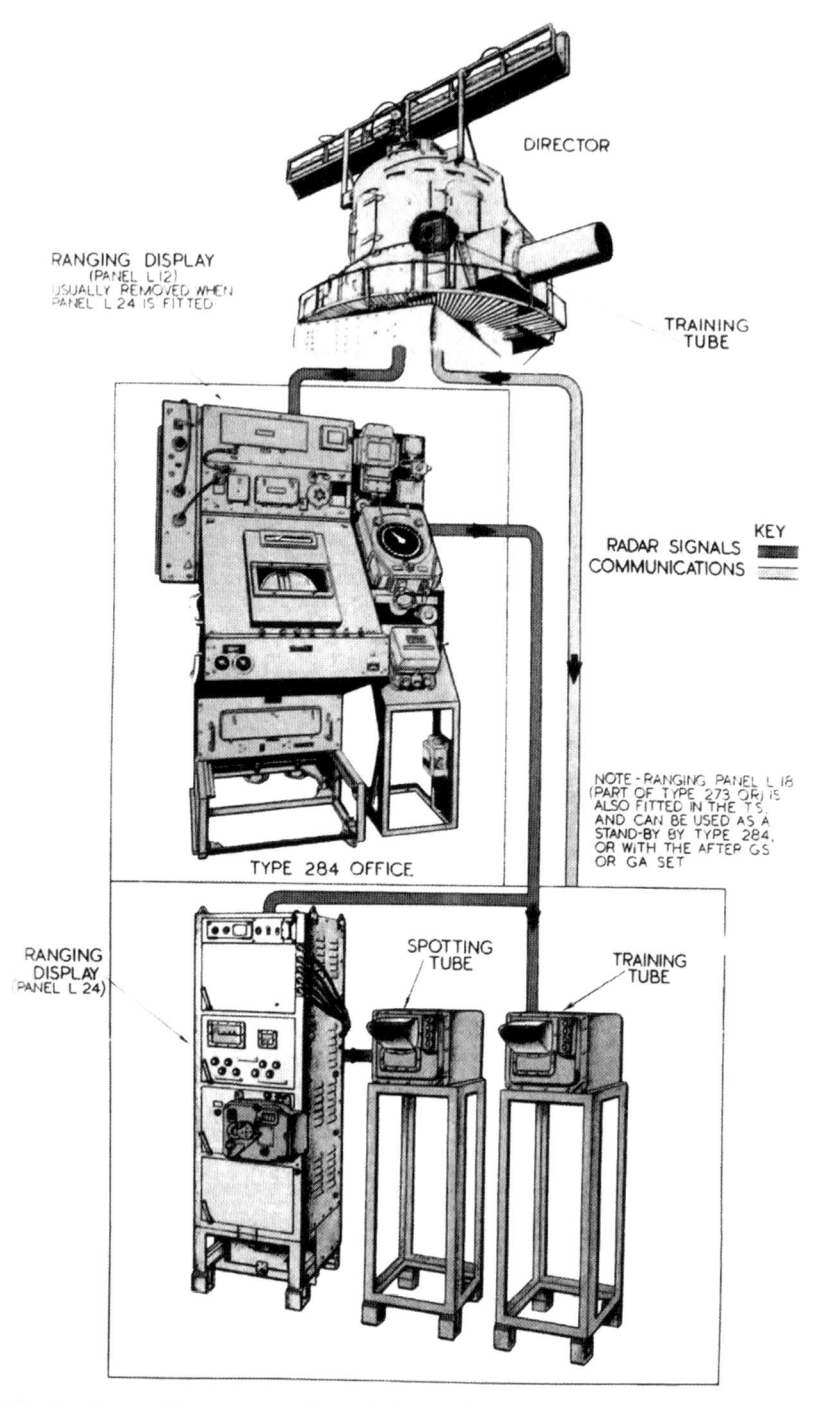

The British Type 284 gunnery radar, with the aerial mounted on top of the director and showing the various displays and the 'office'.

As the aerial sweeps round, echoes are traced out (or 'painted') not only at their correct range (from the centre of the tube) but also on their correct bearing, leaving a bright arc to mark their position. An after-glow tube is used, so that the echoes do not immediately die away, and provided the aerial is kept rotating at a reasonable speed the result is a complete picture or plan display of the relative position of all objects withing radar range.[17]

The PPI was not possible for older sets like the Type 271, which was turned by hand at an irregular rate, but for other sets it was a great advance, giving a map-like picture of ships, aircraft and land features.

There were two main types of American naval radar – search radar produced by the Bureau of Ships and fire control by the Bureau of Ordnance, each with its own designation system. The first American naval radar was the XAF, developed by the Naval Research Laboratory and fitted to USS *New York* in 1938. It became the CXAM1, which used a 17ft square rotating 'mattress' or 'bedspring' aerial and was fitted to about twenty capital ships, cruisers and the carrier *Yorktown* by 1942. In *California* in 1941, Ted Mason reported, 'no-one except Commander Bernstein, Ensign J N Renfro ... and the two enlisted operators had been allowed inside the locked compartment off the signal bridge. The only part of the radar I had seen was the "bedspring" antenna mounted atop the superstructure.'[18]

It was succeeded in production by the SC search radar, which was lighter and had a smaller aerial, but was turned manually and used the A-scope. The SC2 had a wider, narrower aerial with less altitude resolution, but it used the PPI and was fitted to destroyers. SG (Sugar George) of 1942 was a microwave set for destroyers and above, intended 'to search for enemy surface ships, to coordinate attack by surface vessels, and to assist in navigation.' It had a small parabolic aerial 4ft wide, which took up little space on a masthead. After teething troubles it proved reliable and effective. SK, introduced in 1943, was a long-wave search set for large ships which kept the big aerial of the CXAM and the more advanced technology of the SC2. Reflections off the sea tended to produce nulls, which were a significant problem during the kamikaze campaign. SF was used in frigates and corvettes for anti-U-boat work and used a 24in paraboloid reflector in a radome. Other search sets were designed for merchant ships, SJ for submarines, and SO for search and torpedo control on PT boats.

The SM radar was a microwave set of very advanced performance, originally developed by the Army Air Force as the SCR-584. It was able to detect a submarine periscope six miles away or a surfaced submarine as far as the horizon, with an accuracy of 200yds. But it was heavy, needing twenty-three different components, including a 131ft mount weighing 4600lbs to support the 6ft by 8ft antenna. The whole outfit weighed 9 tons, so its use was confined to large aircraft carriers, beginning with the new *Lexington* in the spring of 1943, followed by *Bunker Hill* and *Enterprise* that autumn – twenty-three examples of a lighter version were supplied to the Royal Navy. It was a 'Microwave set with three axis stabilised antenna, installed on aircraft carriers to search for enemy planes, particularly low-flying and shadow planes, and to supply height, speed and course data so that a Fighter Direction Officer can direct fighters to an interception.' Its narrow beam made it unsuitable for search, but it was effective in the fighter direction role.

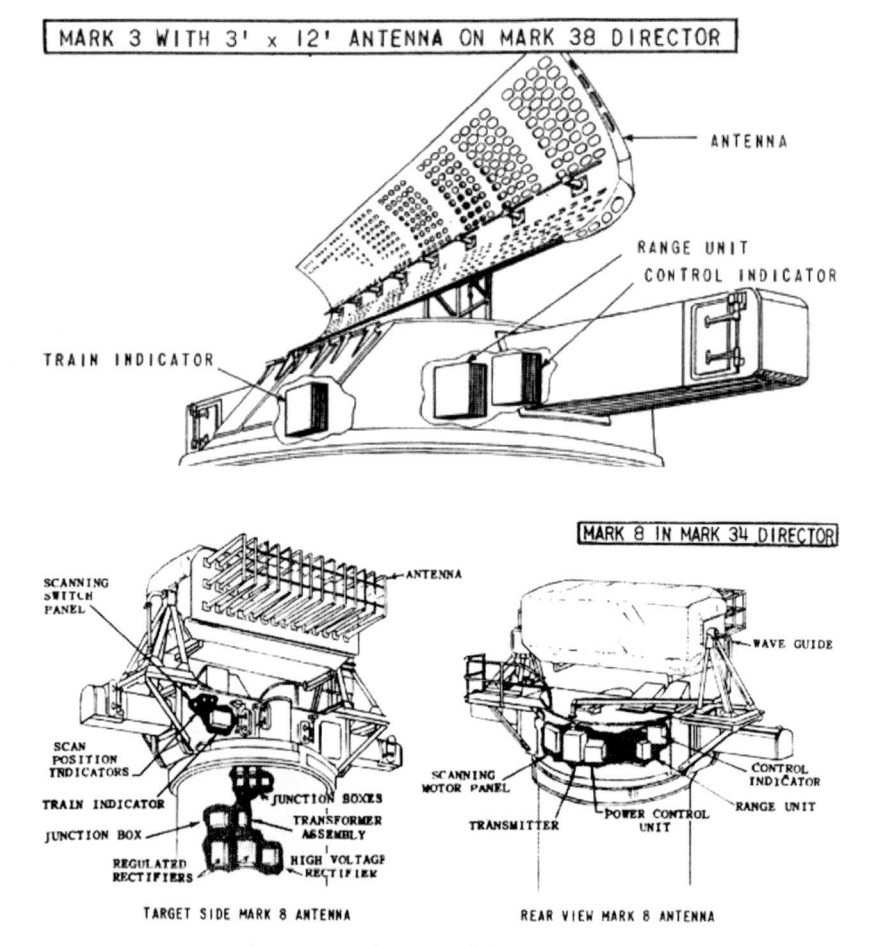

American gunnery radars, mounted on top of directors. The Mark 3 could pick up a battleship at a range of 28,000yds. The later microwave Mark 8 could pick one up at 40,000yds and also spot the fall of shot.

The first fire control radar (Mark 3 or FC in the Bureau of Ordnance system), had a semi-cylindrical antenna and was mounted on the Mark 34 or 39 main armament director of a battleship or cruiser. It was first used in the Guadalcanal campaign, in which it allowed *Washington* to sink the Japanese battleship *Hiei*. It had range gates which blocked returns except from a narrow window, so that the target would be isolated. It was obsolete by the time of the Battle of Surigao Strait in 1944, when ships equipped with it performed poorly. However, its successor, the Mark 8 or FH, played a decisive role in the same battle, directing the fire of *West Virginia, California* and *Tennessee* to devastate the Japanese force. It had a complex 'polyrod' antenna with numerous spikes, it had superb accuracy in range and bearing, and it could detect shell splashes. The Mark 4 or FD set had a double curved antenna and was fitted to directors for the 5in dual-purpose guns, making it a primary player in the defence of the task forces. The Mark 10 or FJ was mainly used to direct 40mm Bofors guns.

Off the Oregon coast in a fog, the captain of *California* did not use his new facilities for navigation, to the annoyance of one of the radiomen:

> 'God damn!' he said in disgust. 'Here we've got the new CXAM radar that can see right through fog and the *Tennessee* has got nothin' but a crappy old direction finder, and she's running away from us.'
>
> 'The old man doesn't trust any newfangled electronic gadgets. All he can think of is goin' aground and facin' a court of enquiry.'[19]

There were several early failures with radar, especially in the battles round Guadalcanal in 1942, in which the new SG system might have been used to offset the Japanese advantage in night warfare. Commanders did not always choose a fully radar-equipped ship as their flagship, as at Savo Island, and at Cape Esperance *Helena* had new SG radar, but it was not used promptly enough, though it was sometimes used effectively for aircraft warning, and for gunnery control.[20] Experiences like these would emphasise the need for what developed into the combat information centre.

Training and operation

Royal Navy signal officers were trained at Greenwich to have equivalent status to gunnery or navigation specialists. It was less fashionable than gunnery, but it did allow contact with an admiral as flag lieutenant. The most famous of them was Lord Louis Mountbatten, who served as assistant fleet wireless officer in the Mediterranean Fleet, then as a highly successful lecturer at Greenwich, then as fleet wireless officer in the Mediterranean from 1931. He used his private means to finance technical publications, and brought in several innovations.[21] It remained a small branch with 108 officers in 1939, plus twenty-eight that could be recalled from retirement. In wartime, expansion was mostly in specialist branches such as convoy signallers and H/F D/F specialists.[22]

Before the war, Royal Navy radio operators – known as wireless telegraphists – were trained to a high standard in the Signal School at Portsmouth. This had to change quickly in wartime – the course for second class W/Ts was reduced from thirteen weeks to ten, for third class from nine to seven. New branches were added with increased specialisation – coders, operators of automatic Morse machines and less well qualified personnel for the patrol service. The radar mechanic branch, with artisan status, was created in 1941 and its members were carefully selected and needed long training so that they could maintain radio and radar sets in detached ships.

The radar branch of the navy was the newest of all – aviation and anti-submarine, though subject to vast expansions, at least had some existence before the war. At first, ratings were members of the signal branch and only 150 men, nearly all 'hostilities only', were needed, but soon there was a huge expansion. By March 1941 men were being trained in old patrol boats and yachts in the Clyde and Irish Sea, but standards were low. 'The construction is designed to accustom ratings to take ranges and bearings, to make intelligible reports to the bridge, and to make good small defects at sea. After joining their ships they might learn to detect a submarine.' By 1942 all ships were being fitted with radar, up to fourteen sets on a battleship and one or two on a corvette. Intelligent men were now selected at the training bases, without completing the course in seamanship.

One man described his training in HMS *Valkyrie* at Douglas Head on the Isle of Man, which had accommodation for 1500 ratings:

> First impressions were that it appeared to be of bewildering complexity with a mass of coloured knobs, dials, meters, switches, co-axial cables, handles and cathode ray tubes. It was the size of a bulky wardrobe and the transmitter, buried in the basement, the size of a small room. The Instructor gave details of how the instrument was switched on and gave a practical demonstration with the CRT [cathode ray tube] lit up with a vivid emerald green tinge, on the left side a large blip caused by the ground returns and the top of the trace, an 'A' trace, looking like grass, which was the term for it, this was the equivalent of noise in a radio set plus odd returns from mountains and the like. Turning a large wheel in the front of the

set rotated the aerial so that it was pointing at the mountains of the Lake District some 60 miles away and on the CRT appeared a large blip on the 60 mile range; our first echoes.

In addition, captains were allowed to train men as acting operators. Trained men were highly valued, as John Davies recorded. The captain sent a car to recall a man named Barker. The boatswain's mate thought it was him, but the captain said, 'Oh I didn't want you. I meant Barker the radar man.' Partly for security reasons they did not wear badges until 1944 when a radar plotter branch was set up to operate search radars. The gunnery branch took on radar control ratings to operate their rangefinders. Radio mechanics were trained to repair radar and other radio equipment. They were carefully selected, sometimes from failed officer candidates, and trained in seventeen civilian colleges. They wore the fore and aft uniform of artificers with fast promotion to petty officer.

A typical set employed six men to cover three watches, with one on the set and one standing by, to change over after twenty or thirty minutes. The operation of a radar set began with the order to close up and the operator should switch it on – it might take five to twenty minutes to warm up. He was expected to deal with problems that might occur due to ground effect or atmospheric conditions. For an A-scope these might include beating echoes, inverted echoes, 'tram lines', or a criss-cross pattern; for a PPI, double echoes, 'telegraph poles', 'railings', a star, or a 'fingerprint'.

Normally he would begin an all-round sweep, though he might be ordered to concentrate on a specific sector. The rate would depend on the type of set, from half a revolution per minute for a Type 271 without a PPI, to 15rpm for a Type 276 or 293 being used for target indication. He would be given information on the situation, such as the positions and movements of ships in company. If he got an unidentified echo, speed was more important than accuracy and he might report, 'Echo bearing two seven oh, distance twenty'. He would provide more detail soon afterwards.

At this point the IFF (identification friend or foe) system, might come into play. It was first developed by the RAF as a means of separating returning aircraft from raiders and Mark I consisted of a small transmitter-receiver known as the transponder fitted in the friendly aircraft. Mark II was designed to work with the navy's Type 79 radar and other sets, while Mark III used a secondary radar set combined with the parent set. IFF could also be fitted to ships, and it might have to be switched off at times to prevent interference with an incoming echo.

When an identification was established, the control officer might then order 'watch' or 'disregard', while individual targets would be labelled A, B and so on. The operator might be ordered to 'hold' on a particular target and he would attempt to further classify the echoes, while they were plotted to establish course and speed.

In the US Navy the communications officer of a large ship had a radio officer, a signal officer (concerned with flags and semaphore) and the ship's secretary under him. On destroyers and smaller he combined the duties of these. He was also the divisional officer for the signallers.

Immediately after the Pearl Harbor attack, William C (Bill) Eddy, a former naval officer and director of an experimental radio station, offered his services in training men to operate the new and still largely secret radio equipment. The first problem was to find the right men. College graduates were likely to be in officer training programmes, so he devised the stringent Eddy Test to find intelligent, if sparsely educated, enlisted men. Once the veil of secrecy had begun to lift, it was advertised: 'No technical experience necessary – if you pass the Eddy Aptitude Test you will be made a Seaman First Class at once, followed by 10 months of specialised training ending with a Petty Officer rating.'

The issue was very urgent in view of the war situation and there were specific problems. The new equipment was far more complex than anything used before, it was changing rapidly and any training might soon be out of date, and operators might find themselves in ships without access to the company representatives that could be called in ashore, or spare parts. They would have to be self-reliant. The electronics training programme was carried out in six civilian schools throughout the country. Eventually around eighty-six thousand trainees entered it, though not all were successful.[23]

The duties of a radarman were defined in official publications:

> Stands radar watch and remains alert throughout long periods of inactivity. Uses and regulates radar equipment. Handles dials, reads indicators. Plots and reads polar coordinates and converts to rectangular coordinates. Coordinates numerous data. Solves maneuvering board problems.

The radio technician 'Maintains and repairs radios, radar and sonar equipment. Must understand circuit diagrams, principles of various types of vacuum tubes, direct and alternating current, wave theory, etc. (Considerable theoretical knowledge is required).'

Operation required motivation and concertation:

In the radar shack, ten minutes might seem like an hour, or an hour might seem like ten minutes, depending on what was going on at the time. Generally, you think you should be doing a lot all the time, but most of the time you only do a little. In fact 99 percent of the radar work was navigation and only 1 percent spotting enemy aircraft.[24]

The command system on a mid-war escort vessel, for example, a River-class frigate, was partly determined by the limitations of the Type 271 radar, in which the operator had to be close to the aerial. The captain stood in the centre of the bridge on a wooden platform to minimise deviation of the compass. There were numerous voice pipes on either side, with controls to release depth charges, and Oerlikon guns on wings. Behind the compass platform was the radar, with the 'parrot's cage' above and the operator in a small compartment below, where the officers could consult the screen if necessary. Forward of the compass platform was a compartment on a lower level and under a sloping roof, with a viewer through which the captain could consult the plotting table below. Beside that was the Asdic compartment, accessible via a door from the bridge. Underneath the whole was the steering compartment with the wheel and two telegraphs to send signals to the engine room. Aft of that was the chart room for the navigator, and a tiny sea cabin where the captain would get what rest he could while at sea. It was a system geared to the Battle of the Atlantic where threats, however lethal, would tend to develop slowly and air attack was rare.

The perpetual danger with all intelligence is to use it without revealing its extent. British Ultra was most useful in the Battle of the Atlantic and it was filtered through the submarine tracking room and Western Approaches Command in Liverpool, who were both aware of the issues. With the American forces there was always the fear that the data would be used with far less discrimination by the different commands – especially South-West Pacific Area under the maverick General MacArthur.

To make the best use of the intelligence, the Special Branch of the Military Intelligence Service was set up by the army, with officers and civilians in each of the main commands, but with a certain independence from their control so they could give the best advice.

Early in the war, Rear Admiral John Godfrey, the chief of naval intelligence from 1939 to 1942 (Commander Ian Fleming's superior officer and the model for 'M' in the James Bond novels), disputed with Churchill (then First Lord of the Admiralty) about the number of U-boats sunk, claiming nine rather than forty. He considered that intelligence was not a flexible commodity and that intelligence reports should not be wishful. He was dismissed in 1942, in a decision which is generally regarded as unwise.

His principles were followed in the submarine tracking room in Room 41 of the Citadel, a modern building attached to the Admiralty. Civil servants or 'civilians in uniform' of the RNVR Special Branch were preferred for work there, in contrast to regular naval officers, whose hierarchical attitudes often prevented them from expressing their real opinions. The room was headed by Rodger Winn, a barrister commissioned in the RNVR and rapidly promoted to commander and then captain. His legal training gave him exceptional skill at assessing evidence, which came from many sources – radio reports, air reconnaissance, D/F fixes and even enemy broadcasts, including 'even the most verbose and boastful'. However, it was agreed that special intelligence was by far the most important. 'Evidence was voluminous, and a large proportion of it was false. It had to be carefully scrutinised, and the facts sifted from the rubbish by comparing with other information.'[25] The reputation of the submarine tracking room was so high by 1942 that its advice was accepted by much more senior officers. Recommendations to re-route convoys to avoid concentrations of U-boats were passed to the Trade Division of the Admiralty, who might issue orders direct, or pass it on to Western Approaches Command.

The Royal Navy later developed the action information organisation, the equivalent of the American combat information centre, though it differed in many ways. According to an AFO of 1944, 'The primary object of an AIO is to serve the Command with a picture of the tactical and strategic situation, bit surface and air, which is up to date, comprehensive and readily intelligible … The secondary object of the AIO is to direct the weapons, including the air weapon, onto the targets.'

It was far more dispersed then the American system. In 1945 a *Colossus*-class light fleet carrier had a compass platform from which the ship was steered. The bridge plotting room received information constantly from the other elements. Below that, in the island, was the operations room: the nearest approach to the American CIC, it was 'responsible for over-all control of operations, and maintaining and evaluating the surface situation and reporting it to all interested parties.' It was dominated by a 6ft by 4ft general operations plot. The aircraft directions room was below decks and was charged with 'handling all defensive flights, for homing planes and, and for maintaining a complete air information picture'. It used a vertical display plot and a skiatron which projected the PPI picture. Also below decks was the target indication room where the gunnery officer was stationed, and the radar display room.[26]

Internally, the US Navy was well on the way to replacing the voice pipe by early 1941, and Commander Parry of the Royal Navy noted that on a cruiser:

> There are approximately 780 telephones in this ship and ease of communication thereby is remarkably efficient. The sound powered telephone, which requires no outside energy from batteries etc is now rapidly becoming the standard method of communication, and its effectiveness is of an exceptionally high standard. I have tested out the ordinary hand set in noisy compartments and have not had any difficulty in hearing perfectly.

The combat information centre, as developed in the mid 1940s, was the *pièce de résistance* of American electronic warfare. At the beginning of the war, radar was interpreted by a fighter direction officer and the operators. The campaign around Guadalcanal showed the need for the work to be done in a separate room, which became known as the 'radar plot' and was usually supervised by the executive officer:

> Gradually the radar plot absorbed other functions, becoming a terminal for radio, radar and lookout reports. Information received would be correlated and passed to the bridge, gunnery, flag and other stations depending on its character. Thus radar plot, as its scope and importance broadened, became the combat information centre, CIC. By the end of the war the CIC was big business conducted in well-protected compartments below, manned by as many as 50 men.[27]

Progress was fast, and by 1945 *Enterprise*'s equipment of 1943 was regarded as 'Ancient History.'[28]

The CIC was responsible for target indication, control of aircraft in the area both offensive and defensive, small craft in the area, and the location of the ship in proximity to the land during an amphibious operation. To these were added radar countermeasures and as siting in anti-submarine operations.[29] The captain still took his position on the bridge during general quarters and was fed the processed information from the CIC, though at Leyte Gulf, in the destroyer *Hutchins*, the first with CIC below decks, Captain McManes directed the ship from below, contrary to tradition.[30]

Information came into the CIC from many sources. Internally these included air and surface search radar, radio direction-finding, sonar, aerology [meteorology], lookouts aloft, weapons control, and the captain and admiral. The CIC collected and digested this and gave

The combat information centre of USS *Anzio* during the Okinawa operation in April 1945. A lieutenant sits to the left, with three enlisted men at the instruments behind, a small proportion of the crew of a typical CIC.

instructions and advice when required to surface ships of various sorts, aircraft in both attack and defence, and shore units in the case of an amphibious landing.

> In the Big E's Combat Information Center (CIC), the FDO sat at his scope with earphones on his head, a microphone in one hand and a grease pencil in the other, marking the positions of friendly and enemy aircraft each time the sweep of the antenna seemed to move and relight the little blobs which stood for aluminium and high explosive and high-octane fuel and flesh and blood rushing through the night sky twenty miles away at 200 miles an hour. The speakers overhead amplified his words to Phillips and O'Hare.[31]

By 1945 it was 'a weird and eerie jungle of electronic gear, illuminated tables, shining dials and gadgets which, at first, makes Flash Gordon look like a piker and Buck Rogers an anachronism.'[32]

The dead reckoning tracker, or DRT, had originally been designed for navigational purposes and was roughly equivalent to the ARL plotter. It was in a square cabinet with a recess which could be fitted with a chart and pencil carriage or 'bug' moving over it. There was a glass panel above that, so that movements of the ship and a possible target vessel could be marked on it for interpretation. It was most useful in tracking the movements of a submarine, and in shore bombardment.

CICs were now universally equipped with radar with plan position indicators to display the air or surface picture. In a relatively sophisticated outfit, a large carrier's CIC would be fed by SK radar for long-wave search. The most modern CICs had the VG1 or VG2, which projected the PPI picture onto a 24in diameter surface, so that it could be interpreted by more officers, though its resolution was less clear.

The compartment contained a number of status boards for displaying information that was non-plottable. Ideally, in 1945 they were edge-lighted lucite with chinagraph pencils for marking. In the Pacific the most urgent was usually the VF or fighter status board which included: 'Information pertinent to all VF in the task force, such as the tactical call of all available fighter planes, the divisions airborne, and their status, time of take-off, altitude information, station or mission, radio channel, IFF code, controlling base, present fuel and ammunition and last order.' The aircraft status board gave information on search and attack planes and the surface status board showed the course, speed and zigzag plan of accompanying ships. There might also be boards for the weather, recognition including IFF codes, and radio countermeasures.[33]

The CIC team was led by the evaluator, who was usually the executive officer in a battleship, carrier or cruiser, because the post needed an officer with tactical experience. As to the other officers, according to one report: 'Your average CIC officer may be (and this was the actual officer complement of the USS *Wasp* at one time) a college professor, a graduate student in forestry, a high school principal, a meat salesman, a lawyer, insurance salesman, and a recent college AB' – in other words, a cross-section of the more intelligent reserve officers.[34]

In action, the evaluator had no fixed station, but moved around the various positions according to the tactical situation; his job was to assess the value of the information and pass on advice to the captain on the bridge. His assistant was the CIC officer, the divisional officer for the CIC personnel and responsible for their training. He too had no fixed station, but was 'a first class trouble shooter who sees to it that the CIC is what its name implies, a centre for information of all kinds.' The fighter director used SP or SK air search radar on a plotting table and was ready, as the name implies, to direct fighters onto enemy raiders. The geographic plot officer stood by the DRT and was responsible for navigation and for shore bombardment. The gunnery liaison officer was beside a VF plot ready to assist with target identification, though the choice of target remained the prerogative of the captain. The surface plot officer was nearby and would provide data on other ships in the formation. The radar officer was responsible for checking the consoles and for maintenance while the communications officer was responsible for supervising the personnel, maintaining publications and coding. Most of these officers had enlisted assistants and, in addition, there were several radio operators, and talkers to maintain communications. To maintain understanding between the bridge and the CIC, personnel were to exchange duties occasionally.

In the destroyer *Dale*, as Lieutenant Hugh Melrose reported:

> We fed this information to the bridge over the sound-powered phones to a phone talker who was standing right next to the captain on the bridge. Since words transmitted over a sound-powered phone tend to lose their emotional impact, I editorialised a bit. 'Target is now within range of our 5-inch guns … Target is now within range of our forties … Target is now within range of our twenties.'[35]

The admiral in charge of a task force or group needed information that was even more carefully filtered and he usually had a flag plot in the island of a carrier to interpret it. In the Battle of Kolombanga in July 1943:

> In the flag plot under the chartroom, hot and crowded with 25 officers and men, the admiral gazes at the radar screen as reports flow in from bridge, combat information center and other points; everyone waits tense and sweating for his verdict … Some 'wise guy' insists that the radar targets are the *Nicholas* and *O'Bannon*. The admiral remarks quietly that it is strange that we, making only 18 knots should be overhauling them.[36]

> The heart of Admiral Mitscher's command was a compact room in the flagship's island called the Flag Plot. Packed with a staggering amount of tracking and communications equipment that hummed incessantly, Flag Plot had as its most prominent feature a huge chart table. Around the bulkheads were radar repeaters, showing the disposition of ships and aircraft, both friendly and enemy. There were huge translucent ship- and aircraft-status boards to indicate, for example, the availability of aircraft, the type of bomb loads carried by the various planes in the force, and the times of launching of planes then in the air. …
>
> Also important in Flag Plot life was a brown leather couch – the transom – a long, comfortable seat which Mitscher occupied most of the time he was in the room.
>
> From twelve to twenty people occupied the Flag Plot, depending on the situation.[37]

In the Pacific War there was another source of intelligence, which ultimately relied on electronics in the form of radio. The Coastwatching Service was set up by Eric Feldt, a lieutenant commander in the Royal Australian Navy who had retired after the First World War and became a colonial administrator. He gave it the code-name Ferdinand, after the bull who refused to fight in Munro Leaf's highly popular children's story of 1936 – the coast-watchers were expected to observe rather than fight, though they did have the capacity to defend themselves.

Australia had set up about a hundred coast-watching stations by 1941, stretching two thousand five hundred miles from the northern coast of New Guinea to the New Hebrides. They were manned by plantation managers, naval officers and others with local knowledge, with the support of the local population. Many of them, like Kenneth Dalrymple Hay, were 'immensely wise in the ways of the Islands.' Before the war, they had not expected to operate in enemy territory but the rapid Japanese advance of 1941/2 left many of them cut off. At great danger to their lives and with the likelihood of torture if captured, they sent messages on Japanese movements, especially in the Solomons Campaign. Martin Clemens in effect started the Guadalcanal campaign, when he observed the Japanese building an airfield, then worked with the US Marines after they landed.

The electronic element was the Teleradio, developed by Amalgamated Wireless, which was both an essential asset and a liability:

> They were grand instruments, standing up to heat, wet, and amateur handling, with a range up to 400 miles on voice and 600 miles if keys were used to transmit Morse. The model we used … consisted of a transmitter, receiver, and loud speaker, with four alternative transmission frequencies which could be tuned to complete accuracy. All parts were enclosed in three metal boxes, each about a foot deep, a foot wide and two feet long. Power was supplied by batteries like those a car uses, which were charged by a small gasoline engine weighing about 70 pounds, the heaviest part of the set.
>
> The instrument had one serious disadvantage. It was difficult to carry, requiring twelve to sixteen porters.[38]

11

The Battle Fleet

THE 1914–18 war did not produce the great naval battle that had been expected and the Royal Navy's disappointing performance at Jutland, through strategically decisive, divided the navy for the next two decades. During the 1920s it was extensively studied at the US Naval War College. The naval treaties of 1922 and 1930 affected battleship design more than anything else. The great naval arms race between Britain and Germany from 1906–14 was seen as one of the causes of the war which followed, and the number of battleships ordered each year was often a trigger for the other side to order even more. To prevent such a situation arising again, the main naval powers agreed to the Treaty of Washington and its successors.

In the 1930s all major navies saw the battleship, carrying the heaviest possible guns, with strong armour plate and a good speed, as the arbiter of naval warfare, with cruisers, destroyers, and even aircraft carriers, as its supporters. In Britain, Admiral Chatfield defended the capital ship against the advocates of air power:

> If we rebuild the battlefleet and spend many millions in doing so, and then war comes and the airmen are right, and all our battleships are rapidly destroyed by air attack, our money will largely have been thrown away. But if we do not rebuild it and war comes, and the airman is wrong and our airmen cannot destroy the enemy's capital ships, and they are left to range with impunity on the world's oceans and destroy our convoys, then we shall lose the British Empire.[1]

The General Board of the United States Navy proclaimed in 1934:

> The capital ship is the backbone of the modern navy. The command of the sea cannot be exerted only by surface vessels which can occupy the sea areas as the infantry occupies the land; air or submarine craft may threaten this occupancy by capital ships but cannot of themselves occupy and control such areas. The basic strength of the surface fleet is in its heaviest vessels, under the protection of which its lighter craft may operate.[2]

Both would have to change these views.

Heirs of *Dreadnought*

The British invented the modern battleship with the launch of *Dreadnought* in 1906. Development was rapid after that, main guns increased from 12in to 13.5in and then 15in, though the 'all-big-gun' concept was undermined by the increasing use of anti-destroyer guns and anti-aircraft armament. The huge First World War fleet was largely scrapped due to the Washington and London treaties, and its own obsolescence. Only a few of the older ships remained in 1939, some of them extensively modernised.

The oldest British capital ships in 1939 were the five vessels of the *Queen Elizabeth* class, launched in 1913–15, and four of them had been present at Jutland. Winston Churchill, never one to understate his role, claimed to be responsible for their inception as First Lord of the Admiralty. Certainly he had to take a huge gamble on the design of a new 15in gun – if it or its mounting had not worked, five very expensive ships would have been useless. He also steered through an equally important and far-reaching decision, to fuel them with oil rather than native coal. As well as the largest guns of the day, they had a high speed, for a battleship, of 25 knots. They survived the Washington and London treaties and were modernised in the 1930s, retaining the armament, but being almost gutted to be fitted with more efficient engines and anti-torpedo bulges. In 1940 *Warspite* justified her existence by leading a destroyer flotilla into Narvik Fjord to sink a large proportion of the German destroyer force, with profound strategic effects. They played a large part in the Mediterranean campaign, and *Barham* was torpedoed and sunk there in November 1941.

Queen Elizabeth's successors, the *Royal Sovereign*, or 'R', class, were a cheaper and slower version, but retaining the 15in guns. They too were fitted with bulges, but otherwise they were modernised far less than the *Queen Elizabeth*s, making them a kind of second-class battleship. *Royal Oak* was torpedoed in Scapa Flow in 1939, the first battleship loss of the war. The others served mostly in covering Atlantic convoys from surface raiders in 1940/1, before being sent to join the Eastern Fleet. They had all been reduced to non-combatant duties by the end of the war.

The battlecruiser was a faster version of the dreadnought battleship, but with less armour. The concept was called into question at Jutland when three of them blew up. *Repulse* and *Renown* were the first with 15in guns, but they only joined the fleet after Jutland had exposed their weaknesses so they were little regarded. *Repulse* was sunk by Japanese bomb and torpedo attack in December 1941. *Renown* was fitted with new engines in 1936 to become the fastest capital ship in the fleet and

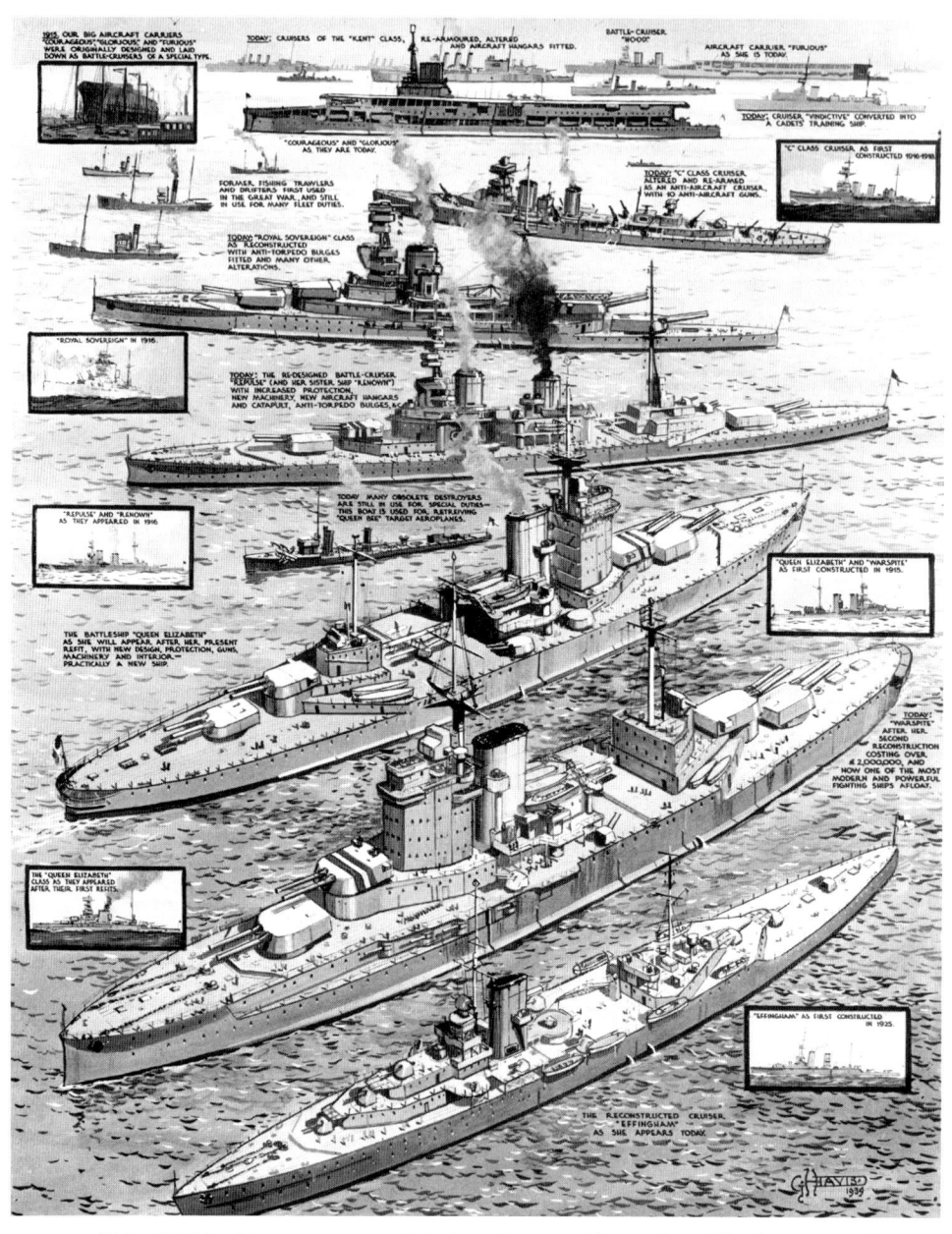

Older British ships reconstructed before the war. The cruiser *Effingham* is in the foreground, reduced to a single funnel like many other ships. Behind is the battleship *Warspite* and her sister *Queen Elizabeth*, followed by a destroyer, the battlecruiser *Repulse*, a *Royal Sovereign*-class ship fitted with anti-torpedo bulges, and an old 'C'-class cruiser and the carriers *Courageous* and *Glorious* converted from battlecruisers. A notable absentee is the battlecruiser *Hood* which was never reconstructed, with fatal effect.

she was often used by Churchill for his wartime voyages, which had the advantage of keeping her well away from enemy action. Two other ships, *Glorious* and *Courageous,* were converted to aircraft carriers in 1928–30.

The ship that became HMS *Hood* was designed just before Jutland and her deck armour was increased in the light of the battle, but not enough, as it turned out. A proposed reconstruction of 1939 was overtaken by the war. She was a good-looking ship, a favourite with crews and with the public on world tours and Navy Days. It was a huge shock when she blew up in action with *Bismarck* in May 1941; in all, five out of fifteen British battlecruisers were sunk by enemy action, and two more were lost after conversion to aircraft carriers, a loss rate of 47 per cent.

After the Great War, the Admiralty began work on remarkable 48,000-ton capital ships with nine 18in guns, but they were cancelled when the Washington Treaty limited ships to 35,000 tons and 16in guns. Britain was only allowed two more, which would emerge in 1927 as *Rodney* and *Nelson*, known as the 'Cherry Trees' because they were 'cut down by Washington'. They had three triple turrets, all forward of the conning tower, which was intended to reduce the need for armour protection, and very angular conning towers to prevent shot being trapped in it. To the lower deck they were 'the pair of boots' or 'the ugly sisters'. They had a speed of 23 knots, up to 15in armour plate, and were considered the most advanced battleships of the day. They were the only class which did not lose one of its number during the Second World War.

After that there was a 'battleship holiday' and by the Washington and London treaties no new ships were laid down. As these were about to expire in 1936 and be replaced by a new treaty, the Admiralty expected that guns would be limited to 14in, and they began the design of a ship to carry them. But Japan refused to renew the treaty and it was found impossible to change the new design. Four-gun turrets were designed to save weight of side armour, but the forward upper one had to be reduced to two guns, causing delays and leaving them with ten main guns. The five ships of the *King George V* class entered service from December 1940 to June 1942.

Churchill damned the ships with faint praise. They were 'of course most useful ships', but they could have been much better with 15in or 16in guns.[3] When he crossed the Atlantic in *Prince of Wales* in 1941, he had to move out of his cabin in the stern due to intolerable vibration because the circles of the propellers overlapped. Her gun turrets, designed to an ambitious specification, had already failed during the action with *Bismarck*, and in an exercise on the way back, 'Y' turret was hampered because of failure to follow procedure. He crossed again in *Duke of York*

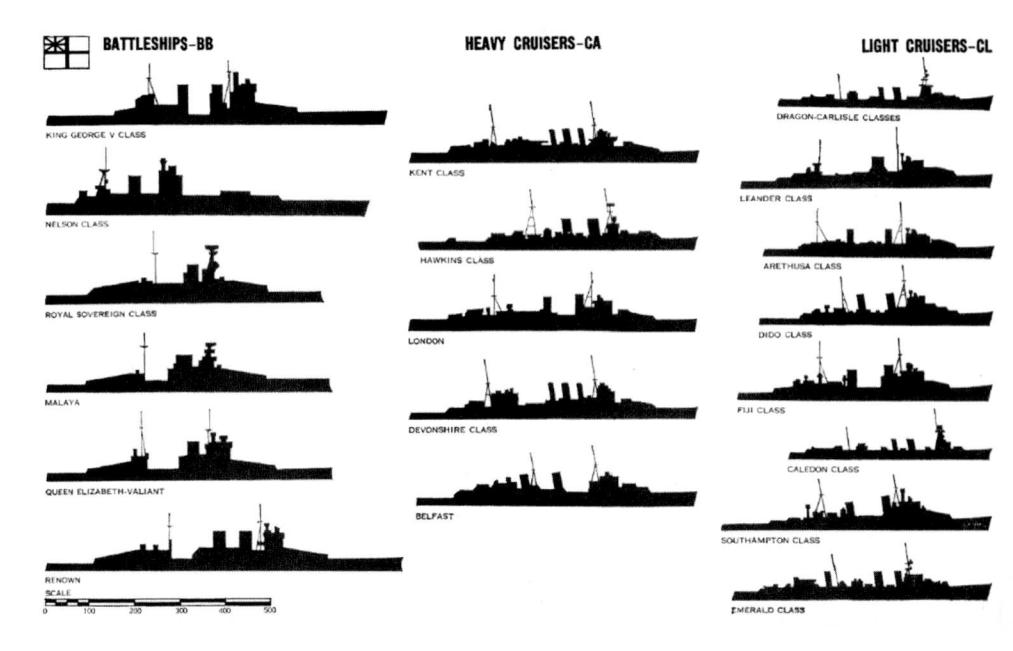

Silhouettes of the main British types of capital ship and cruiser, simplified and intended to aid American sailors with recognition. Apart from the battlecruiser *Renown* at the bottom of the first column, the battleships are arranged in ascending order of age. The heavy cruisers have the three-funnelled *Kent* class at the top, and *Belfast*, with her engines and funnels further aft than usual, at the bottom.

in December 1941 and witnessed another design fault. The Admiralty had insisted that the guns be able to fire directly forward so the bows were low. The party endured eight days of 'the dull pounding of the great seas on the ship's ribs', and Lord Beaverbrook refused to countenance a return voyage in 'that submarine the *Duke of York*.'[4]

When Lord Chatfield criticised the lack of new capital shipbuilding in February 1942, Churchill replied that the great new 45,000-ton battleships *Lion* and *Temeraire* were not being proceeded with 'as the construction effort has been concentrated on vessels likely to reach the line earlier' – and they were never finished, as priority had to be given to aircraft carriers, landing craft and escorts. The last British battleship, *Vanguard*, was not commissioned until the war. Admiral Cunningham attended her launch and thought she 'looked mighty impressive with her raked up bow.' At least one lesson had been learned from the KGVs.[5]

Like practically all classes of traditional warship, British capital ships did very little of the duty they were designed for. Since Germany only had individual capital ships, rather than a great fleet, they did not fight in line of battle. The nearest approximation was against the Italians at Matapan, when four British battleships, a carrier, four cruisers and thirteen destroyers took on a single Italian battleship, eight cruisers and fourteen destroyers. The Italian battleship escaped, despite damage by aerial torpedoes, and three cruisers were sunk. British ships did not do particularly well in individual combat with the sinking of *Hood*, and only the 14in guns of *Duke of York* allowed her to sink *Scharnhorst*, with 11in guns, in 1943. They suffered heavily, with *Royal Oak* and *Barham* lost to submarines, *Repulse* and *Prince of Wales* to air attack, and *Hood* to *Bismarck*'s gunfire. Apart from that, they mostly served as a deterrent, escorting convoys against surface attack in the early days, and then at sea or in readiness at Scapa Flow in case *Tirpitz* came out against the Russian convoys. And like their American counterparts, they found a new role in shore bombardment.

Surviving Pearl Harbor

The US navy had a longer battleship holiday than the Royal Navy, for there was no equivalent of *Rodney* and *Nelson* to fill the gap. Instead, three ships of the *Wyoming* and *Texas* classes survived in the mid 1930s, with 12in guns, and a dozen ships of the *Nevada*, *Pennsylvania*, *New Mexico*, *California* and *Maryland* classes with 14in guns, except for *West Virginia* which had 16in. All had been laid down just before or during the First World War and some were completed just after it. They were slow by modern standards; none could exceed 22 knots. These were the ships that would suffer in the Pearl Harbor attack: *Arizona* and *Oklahoma* were sunk and *Nevada*, *California* and *West Virginia* were only restored after long and extensive repair. Four others were still available for action, but America was catapulted into war without a battlefleet, which traditional admirals would have considered unthinkable.

Meanwhile, new and very different ships were under construction. In 1935, with the end of the treaty system in sight, the General Board inquired about the possibility of a fast battleship to accompany the aircraft carriers, breaking with the American tradition of slow but well-armoured ships. A ship with 14in guns in quadruple turrets was planned to fit with the current treaties, but unlike the British, there was provision to upgrade them if the escalator clause in the London Treaty was invoked. It was, and the two ships of the *North Carolina* class had nine 16in guns and a speed of 28 knots. They were begun in 1937/8 and commissioned in 1941. There were doubts about the effectiveness of their armour protection, so the *South Dakota* class tried to improve on that with the same displacement (38,000 tons), armament and speed,

A dramatic view of the mighty battleship *Missouri* on her shakedown cruise in August 1944, showing the Oerlikon guns in the bows, a small part of her anti-aircraft armament. Two of the powerful 16in guns can just be seen.

which resulted in very cramped ships. The four ships were laid down in 1939 and commissioned during 1942.

The next class was conceived in the light of intelligence reports that the Japanese were building ships of 46,000 tons with 16in guns – though in fact the *Yamato* class had 18in guns on 62,000 tons. Nevertheless, the *Iowa* class emerged in 1942–44 as the biggest ever American battleships, and the fastest at 32.5 knots. The four ships were rather wet due to a narrow bow, but were comfortable and manoeuvrable, and perhaps the closest to perfection of any battleships – though they never engaged in the kind of warfare they were designed for.

After Pearl Harbor, some of the remaining slow battleships were kept in reserve to deter any Japanese invasion of the West Coast. Three others remained in the Atlantic to cover vital convoys. As they became ready, the faster ships first went to the Atlantic where they co-operated with the British Home Fleet in containing the German *Tirpitz*, *Scharnhorst* and *Gneisenau*. *Massachusetts* supported the North African landings in late 1942, along with three of the older ships.

By 1943 most of the battleships were in the Pacific, where some of the older ones supported the recapture of the Aleutians, followed by shore bombardment of most of the operations in the Central Pacific Drive. Only twice was there contact between opposing battleships, both one-sided. In November 1942, during the battle for Guadalcanal, *Washington* and *South Dakota* sank the old Japanese battlecruiser *Kirishima*, despite a series of mishaps. In a reversal of pre-war conceptions, the new fast battleships were used mainly used as escorts for aircraft carriers, where their strong anti-aircraft batteries proved useful, along with their command facilities. They provided cover for the main Pacific landings and occasionally fire support, and they shelled Japanese industrial targets late in the war, which ended on the decks of the *Iowa*-class *Missouri*, when the Japanese signed a surrender document in a highly staged occasion.

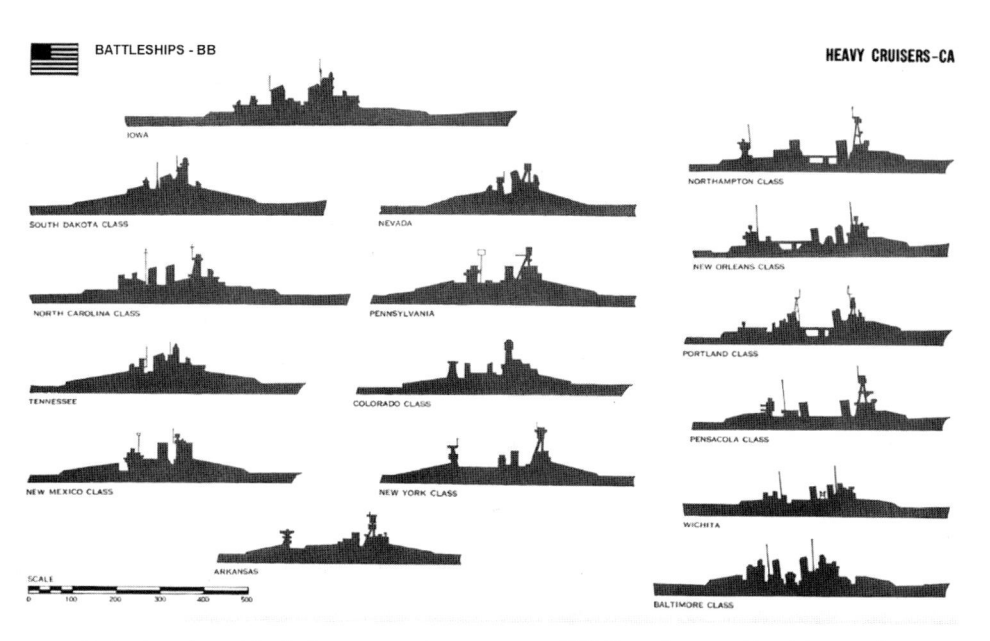

Major American ships in the same series as on page 282. There is a considerable growth in battleships culminating in the *Iowa* class at the top.

The cruiser was second in the traditional naval pecking order, below the battleship but with much smaller guns and thinner armour. They were limited to 10,000 tons by the treaties, and irrespective of size, heavy cruisers were defined as carrying 8in guns and light cruisers as 6in.

The cruiser was versatile, it could scout for the battlefleet (though that was less important in the days of air reconnaissance). It could police the British Empire on five continents, showing the flag and deterring aggression or revolt, or span the wide Pacific for the American navy. In wartime it could patrol the seas against enemy commerce raiders. Cheaper than a battleship, larger numbers could be built, and they could be concentrated with a large fleet or dispersed as necessary. Its 6in or 8in guns were powerful enough to take on enemy ships of the same type, and its armour should keep out their shells. It could run away from an enemy it could not hope to fight.

During the treaty negotiations the British always insisted that they needed a large cruiser force, on the grounds that both their merchant shipping fleet and their empire were bigger than those of other nations. In addition, the homeland had to be protected against invasion.

Before the First World War there were five different types of cruiser, mostly replaced by new 'C'-class light cruisers, which were built in some numbers, armed with a small number of 6in guns on long, narrow hulls. They scouted for the battleships of the Grand Fleet in the North Sea, but were less suitable for worldwide deployment. This led to the larger ships of the *Hawkins* class with 7.5in guns, which could operate throughout the British Empire, fuelled with either coal or oil. Their gun power increased from 500lbs of the 'C' class, to 1400lbs.

In the late 1920 and early 1930s the British built the County classes, three-funnelled, high-sided cruisers with eight 8in guns to meet big enemy cruisers. They introduced twin turrets with a further increase in gun power to 2048lbs. They also built smaller and cheaper ships with six or eight 6in guns, such as the *Leander* and *Arethusa* classes, to provide larger numbers for a worldwide role. In 1931 the Japanese began the *Mogami* class, with fifteen 6.1in guns, and the Americans laid down the *Brooklyn* class with a similar armament. The British disliked the 8in gun – it was overweight and had mechanical problems. More 6in guns could be fitted in a given hull and they could fire much faster. As a further complication, some cruisers were built simply to fill quotas allowed under the treaties

In 1933 the Royal Navy began to design the *Southampton* class, with a hull which was almost as big as a County, though with much less freeboard and armed with twelve 6in guns in triple turrets. Eight were built. *Belfast* and *Edinburgh* had their engines further aft to reduce the chance of damage to the propeller shaft, but that meant that the main anti-aircraft battery was above the engines and was difficult to feed. Ammunition was conveyed by the 'shell conveyor' or 'scenic railway'. Admiral Dunbar-Nasmith was horrified: 'the gear takes up a great deal of space on the upper deck and is extremely vulnerable from hostile aircraft, etc., as it is completely unprotected.' *Belfast* survived a magnetic mine in 1939 and was repaired to take part in the Russian convoys, the sinking of *Scharnhorst* and the Normandy invasion. *Edinburgh* was sunk carrying 'Stalin's gold' from Russia.

The last pre-war design was of the *Fiji* class, named after British colonies. Under what remained of the treaties, they attempted to fit the armament of the *Southampton*s and *Edinburgh*s into a 2000-ton smaller hull. Not surprisingly, they were very cramped, especially when war demanded the fitting of torpedo tubes, radar and more anti-aircraft guns. Eleven ships were completed in 1940–43, the final three with reduced armament, the last 6in ships to see war service except for *Swiftsure* with increased beam. As with capital ships, new building was suspended during the war.

The *Dido* class was conceived in the mid 1930s and were usually seen as light anti-aircraft cruisers, but their 5.25in guns were also suitable for engaging destroyers, rather like the original torpedo boat destroyers in the 1890s, but on a larger scale. In a sense, they were built round the gun, and the first ship was delayed while its new design was got ready. But though they were intended to carry ten of them in five twin turrets, production was delayed, and most had only eight with 4.5in substituted, while two ships, *Scylla* and *Charybdis* were fitted entirely with the 4.5in. Eleven ships were built, followed by four of the *Bellona* class with vertical funnels. Mainly used in the Mediterranean, four of them were sunk by torpedo attack and *Spartan* by a German guided bomb.

British Commonwealth cruisers gained their first glory of the war, when *Exeter*, *Ajax* and *Achilles* forced the scuttling of the German 'pocket battleship' *Graf Spee*. They carried out the traditional role of seeking out enemy capital ships, when *Norfolk* and *Suffolk* were the first to find *Bismarck* in 1941, and for a time *Belfast* was the only ship in contact with *Scharnhorst* before her demise on Boxing Day 1943. They supported the battleships during the Battle of Matapan in 1941 and in the invasion of Crete that spring they destroyed a German troop convoy, but lost two of their number to air attack. With minimal anti-submarine capability they played little part in the anti-U-boat campaign in the Atlantic, but they provided support for the Arctic and Malta convoys, which were attacked by all-comers – two of them were lost in Operation Pedestal in 1942. After that they too found their main role in supporting amphibious landings

In addition to scouting for the battlefleet, patrolling the seas and protecting commerce, the US Navy used cruisers and leaders of destroyer flotillas, a task which was being taken over by specialised 'destroyer leaders' in the Royal Navy. Unlike battleships, the US Navy continued to build cruisers throughout the peace, beginning with two heavy cruisers of the *Pensacola* class started in 1926 and commissioned in 1929/30. They were followed by six *Northampton*s begun in 1928, which established the pattern of nine 8in guns in triple turrets, and *Portland* and *Indianapolis* in 1930–33. The seven ships of the *New Orleans* class used the experience of treaty cruisers already in service, and had thicker armour. The *Brooklyn* class was a response to the Japanese *Mogami,* and it was now believed that the 6in gun, with its much higher rate of fire, might prevail against the 8in – the seven *Brooklyn*s had fifteen of the smaller weapon in its new rapid-firing version, placed in three forward and two after turrets. They introduced longitudinal framing for greater strength, and a new type of aircraft hangar. They were admired by Commander Parry of the Royal Navy in 1941:

> These ships have a smaller tactical diameter than the older light cruisers of the *Omaha* class. They are extremely good sea-boats,

The cruiser *Indianapolis* at speed during her trials in 1932. She was famously sunk by a Japanese submarine at the end of July 1945, after delivering components of the first atom bomb.

the square stern proving no handicap. They have an extremely comfortable action and are an admirable gun platform. … They are very dry, but yaw considerably in a following sea.

The *Brooklyn* class was seminal. Two ships, *Helena* and *St Louis*, had the latest 5in guns and rearranged superstructures, and formed the basis for the *Cleveland* class which was laid down from 1940. Meanwhile, *Wichita* was built as an 8in version and became the basis for the *Baltimore* class. The *Atlanta*-class ships were much smaller, at an intended 6000 tons with 5in guns in response to the 1936 London Treaty. The three ships of the *Alaska* class were an aberration, perhaps hinted at in their naming for territories rather than states or cities. With a tonnage of around 30,000 and 12in guns, they were close to battlecruisers rather than 'super-cruisers', but by the time they were ready in 1944 there was no role for them.

The *Cleveland*s were the best light cruisers available when the war started, and as such they were chosen for mass production, though they were still based on treaty limits. Fifty-two were ordered and twenty-nine completed, making them the largest cruiser class of all time. Main armament was reduced to twelve 6in guns, which allowed space for more 5in guns. By the end of the war, they were top-heavy with extra sensors and armament, and they had steel superstructures instead of the planned aluminium. The *Baltimore*s were heavy cruisers based on the same hull, though it was expanded during the design process. Thirteen of them were commissioned during the war.

With the main threat from Japan, cruisers were mostly concentrated in the Pacific in the 1930s, but the nine 6in ships were sent to the Atlantic in 1938 as the German threat grew. After the Pearl Harbor attack, they returned to the Pacific.

American cruisers had their greatest test in the battles around Guadalcanal in 1942/3, beginning with the disaster at Savo Island in which a poorly organised fleet was taken by surprise in the dark, and four American, as well as one Australian, cruisers were lost. Afterwards they tended to fight in line like battleships, which were in short supply at the time, with destroyers at each end of the line. Performance was still poor, because the Japanese, unlike the Americans, had trained extensively in night fighting. Radar was not always used correctly, there was no flashless powder so the Japanese had a mark for their rangefinders, commanders tended to fight in rigid fashion as they had been trained in peacetime, and there was no real answer to the long range of the Japanese Long Lance torpedo – 8in guns were too slow to tackle the ships which launched them, and 6in guns did not have the range. Nevertheless, the marines and army held Guadalcanal, so the Americans had an important, if costly, victory. And if nothing else, the American cruisers showed their ability to survive serious damage.

After that, the cruisers settled into the same roles as the battleships – escorting carrier groups and amphibious forces, and shore bombardment. In the European theatre they supported the landings in North Africa and Italy, and the Normandy invasion.

Life in the battlefleet

Sick Berth Attendant Sam Wood was impressed when he joined a battleship from boy training: 'The first time I saw the *Prince of Wales* I had come from the Isle of Man, straight from the training ship *St George*. She was the sort of ship you dreamt about as being part of the Royal Navy. It looked awful frightening – I felt like a little ant.' But to boys, their segregated messes on battleships and cruisers were 'just an extension of boys' messes in HMS *Ganges*.'[6] The presence of boys on battleships and cruisers necessitated the use of corporal punishment:

> Punishment for serious crimes by the boys was flogging, or more accurately so many strokes with a thick and heavy cane. This was quite a performance and was enjoyed by nobody ... the boy was brought in wearing a pair of white shorts ... Then the Master at Arms put the boy's head between his knees and the Sergeant administered the first stroke with a sickening thud.[7]

According to Petty Officer John Whelan: 'Big ships are lonely places. There is no camaraderie, no sense of intimacy. Knowing hundreds of people, you don't really know anyone. ... Everything is too big, too impersonal, too lonely.'[8] Large ships operated to a strict routine. In harbour, in the 1939 orders for HMS *Belfast*, the day started at 0505 when men under punishment were called. Hands were called to stow their hammocks at 0530, then the cooks of the messes began work. The crew fell in to clean the ship at six o'clock, with breakfast an hour later. At 0820 'requestmen and defaulters' asking for privileges or facing punishment went before the commander. At 0905 the men were inspected in their 'divisions'. In most ships the seamen were in three divisions, with names dating back to the days of sail – quarterdeck or QD, topmen or 'top', and forecastle or FX. The stokers were in two groups, and there were other divisions for Royal Marines, boys, signallers, artificers and artisans, and the Fleet Air Arm.

Routine work and training resumed until 1200, when the hands were called to dinner, the main meal of the day, which lasted until 1315. There was more work until 1550 when the order 'secure' was given and 'evening quarters' ten minutes later. Then there was 'tea', after which most of the men were off duty. For those who did not go ashore, there was supper at 1900. Boys were expected to turn in at 2045, other ratings at 2200, and chiefs and petty officers half an hour later. Work finished early on Saturday, and on Sunday there was a church service.

At sea, the morning watch was called at 0345 to take up its duties a quarter of an hour later. At 0535 the hands were called to begin scrubbing decks, supervised by the commander. Hammocks were stowed at 0640 and breakfast began at 0700. Both watches fell in for duty just before eight. Some of the seamen had special tasks, such as the quartermaster, who supervised the steering, the duty helmsman, who operated the wheel, and two telegraphmen to transmit orders to the engine room. In peace, there were two lookouts on the bridge at night and one by day, and a boy messenger. Two men stood by to operate warning flags and cones, while the boatswain's mate of the watch was responsible for routine. A seaman gunner of the watch stood by to release a rocket as required, a range-taker might have to measure a distance for navigational purposes, a torpedoman stood by for emergency repair work. There was a sea boat's crew ready to launch in emergency, with five more men to take over the manual steering if the power failed. The marine corporal of the watch reported routines to the commander. Another marine acted as lifebuoy sentry, standing by in case a man fell overboard. The rest of the crew carried out routine duties – physical drill, painting, cleaning and training.

'Divisions' were called at 0905. Dinner lasted from 1200 to 1315 as in harbour. Helmsmen, lookouts and others remained on duty and ate at a different time. At 1600 the first dog watch began and the ship started to wind down for the night. There was supper at 1900, the men set up their hammocks forty-five minutes later and the boys and men turned in, as in harbour. The men of the middle watch took up duty at midnight, and the ship's day began again.

American warships worked the same watch routine as the Royal Navy:

> Watches in the Navy, starting at eight o'clock in the morning, were typically four hours each, though the afternoon watch from four to eight was cut in half so that men would not stand the same watch each day. … That was not too bad, except for the fact that our eight hours off were frequently broken by drills and inspections and the like. … as watchstanders none of us ever had a full night's sleep at sea.[9]

Before the war, battleship sailors were immensely proud of their ships:

> There was pride, understated but ever present, in being a sailor in the battleship navy. I had felt it every time I stepped off that holystoned teak quarterdeck and saluted the flag from the top of the accommodation ladder, every time a civilian asked me what ship I was on and I replied a little smugly the *California*.[10]

Even a cruiser could not match it, to Ted Mason: 'To a battleship sailor, the *Louisville* looked frail and narrow of beam … she … was very weakly protected. I could vividly imagine what one of the murderous torpedoes could do to this eggshell cruiser.'[11] But the battleship's size did not necessarily make it comfortable: 'The old battleship's slow roll is just as apt to make you seasick as the destroyer's quick, pitched roll.'[12]

As a signalman, Floyd Beaver had expected to be put straight onto the signal bridge of *Indianapolis* 'without putting in the traditional first few months in the deck force.' Instead, he was put into a 'slave market' on the fantail, where chiefs selected likely men for their divisions. He would have to learn the technique of cleaning the decks with the holystone. 'To see a line of veteran swabbies swaying rhythmically across a snowy white teak deck striped with black caulking could be a most pleasing sight'. But after transfer to what he regarded as his rightful place, he found life easier:

> Signalmen, along with radiomen and quartermasters, were what was then known as watchstanders. Except for our cleaning stations and drills, we had no routine duties. We were also treated more gently than other sailors. Those having the mid watch were given night rations at sea, thick slabs of meat or cheese on hunks of the Navy's hand-sliced bread.[13]

Ted Mason soon found that *California* was 'like a small city' which resembled a walled, fortified medieval town with a rigid hierarchical structure'. It was divided into twenty-three 'fiefdoms', like 'a collection of fiercely independent Scottish clans, reluctantly gathered together in the face of a mutual enemy.' 'Each fiefdom was run by a chief or first-class petty officer from his command post near the ubiquitous coffee pot. Territory was so jealously guarded that my explorations were sharply proscribed.'[14] Floyd Beaver agreed about the importance of the coffee pot: 'Every duty station had to have its coffeepot and its associated gear. The junior man of every watch was required to stop by the galley on his way to the bridge and pick up coffee, condensed milk, sugar and water.'[15]

The captain of a battleship was usually a remote figure to the crew. During an inspection, E J Jerningham found, 'The captain was the same each time; that is, he didn't notice me as a human being. He was only looking for good posture and the correct dress code, haircut and shave.'[16] But Ted Mason found that a change of captain could make a profound difference:

> Our new CO continued to serve notice on us 'snot-nosed kids' that a battleship skipper's authority was as near absolute as a government of free men could permit. Despite the fact that we had a personnel inspection less than a week before at the change-of-command ceremony, he ordered another one for Saturday 4 January. At captain's mast on Friday, a luckless seaman first was given a general court martial on charges that did not seem to warrant such a grave action.[17]

Surgeon Captain Critchley of the Royal Navy reported on a visit to a new battleship and destroyer in July 1943:

> The most striking feature of these ships is the appearance of great austerity. All comfort has been ruthlessly sacrificed to the demands of damage control and, in particular, to precautions against fire. For this reason all inflammable materials have been discarded. Thus deck coverings. Oil-cloth, corticine, etc, have been torn up exposing everywhere bare steel decks. … all living spaces including state-rooms and especially the wardroom, are bare and comfortless.[18]

Destroyers

Destroyers were another British invention, originally called torpedo boat destroyers and designed to protect the battlefleet against torpedo attack and to launch assaults of their own. They proved to be most versatile ships, capable of convoy escort and independent action among many other functions.

Britain ended the First World War with a large force of fine destroyers, the 'V' and 'W' classes. There was no more building until 1925, when *Arrow* and *Ambuscade* were ordered from the shipbuilders Thornycroft and Yarrow, followed by the 1927 programme of eight ships plus a slightly larger leader. This set the pattern for the next eight years, when successive flotillas delineated by letters were ordered, with slight improvements. They had four 4.7in guns, two sets of quadruple torpedo tubes (quintuple in the 'G', 'H' and 'I' classes) and pom-poms and Lewis guns for anti-aircraft armament. The leaders were named after famous

British destroyer development by 1938. An example of the famous, but expensive, Tribal class is at the top and in the centre of the picture, with its guns in twin turrets. The more economical, single-funnelled 'J', 'K' and 'L' classes are also shown, with heavy torpedo armament. In wartime, even cheaper models were built.

admirals, though it was the 'D' class of the 1930 programme before they caught up with the lettering system, with HMS *Duncan*. But during the subsequent decade, according to one authority, they underwent 'evolution from excellence to obsolescence'.[19]

British destroyers would suffer from the lack of an effective anti-aircraft armament, which might have been provided by a dual-purpose, high angle–low angle gun. This stemmed from discussions with the RAF in 1931, when the navy was assured that dive-bombing was not a real danger, so they remained satisfied with the 40-degree elevation of the standard 4.7in. Another problem was the desire to keep the silhouette low, which was considered important for torpedo attack in the days before radar – dual-purpose guns had a higher profile and would have necessitated the raising of the bridge to see over them. It also caused a redesign of the bridge structure in the 'I' and Tribal classes, so that the helmsman was no longer directly under the bridge, but in a compartment forward with sides and roof sloping aft. They suffered, like nearly all British ships, from short range, which was partly caused by the failure to develop high-pressure steam. And there was always the question of how far they were be gun-armed for defence of the fleet, or torpedo-armed for attack.

The sixteen ships of the famous Tribal class, built from 1935–39, went to one extreme, with eight 4.7in guns in twin turrets, and only four torpedo tubes. They were a response to the 'super-destroyers' being built by Japan and Italy, but they had some of the functions of light cruisers, and 'could not be regarded as part of the normal development of destroyer design', according to an official report.[20] Appointed to *Tartar*, Ludovic Kennedy wrote, 'I could not have asked for a better appointment.'[21] They were glamorous ships and saw heavy service; only four of the British ships survived the war.

The next classes, the 'J's and 'K's, were in a sense a reaction against the Tribals, with ten torpedo tubes and six 4.7s in twin mountings, and they were the first with longitudinal framing. The 'L' and 'M' classes of the 1937 and 1939 programmes were designed for the improved 4.7in Mark XI gun with the heavier 62lb shell and an elevation of 50 degrees, but the last pre-war orders, the 'N' class, reverted to the 'J' and 'K' design and armament. Design of the 'War Emergency' destroyers began in 1939, as a compromise between the 'I' and 'J' classes. They were originally intended to carry four of the 62lb 4.7in, but these fell behind in production, so the 50lb version was substituted. Two flotillas of eight ships each, the 'O' and 'P' classes, were on order or under construction when losses at Norway and Dunkirk showed the need for a more effective AA armament, so eight of the new ships were completed with five 4in guns, one replacing a set of torpedo tubes. Four more were completed as minelayers, also with reduced armament. The 'Q' and 'R' classes had the larger 'J'-class hull for increased endurance, with a transom stern and 4.7in guns. The 'R' class abandoned the ancient practice of accommodating the officers in the stern, where they might be cut off in heavy seas. The 'S', 'T', 'U' and 'V' classes of 1941–44 had Tribal-class bows to make them less wet, and their guns had 55-degree elevation. The 'Z' and 'Ca' classes had the 4.5in gun, a true dual-purpose weapon, and improved fire control. Very few of the 'Ch', 'Co' and 'Cr' classes were ready before the war ended. In all, ninety-six vessels were ordered, and by the end of the war they formed the bulk of the fleet destroyer force.

The Battle class was designed in 1942 with Pacific operation in mind, on a larger hull of 2332 tons standard displacement. They had the new 4.5in gun in two twin mountings with an elevation of 80 degrees. Admiral Cunningham particularly disliked them –'such under-gunned and defensively minded destroyers' were unworthy of the name, and he asked why the Americans could build more powerful ships on a smaller tonnage – though some of his figures were confused. On the other hand, Admiral Edelstein thought them 'grand little ships'.[22] Later destroyers of the Weapons and *Daring* classes were not ready in time

Lieutenant Frank Layard wrote: 'In the piping days of peace between the two world wars, when perhaps there were more opportunities and more time for relaxation, life in destroyers was particularly good.'[23] Some thought that destroyers were relatively free and easy compared with battleships and cruisers, others that it was the worst of both worlds:

> I don't want to serve on a destroyer. You get all the discomfort of a small ship and the pusser routine of a big one thrown in. Pusser? That means 'as per Seamanship Manual.' Rig of the day Number Threes and all that. On a submarine you can wear anything you like.[24]

Nevertheless, destroyers were favoured by many sailors because of the more relaxed discipline, though the captain of HMS *Duncan* complained in 1943, 'The tendency for small ships during this war is to grow steadily more slack in points like dress, appearance of ship, cleanliness and general smartness.'[25] He saw no need for it and ordered his officers 'to help in preserving a high standard.' And there were exceptions. According to Tristan Jones: 'Destroyers on active service were known for their less rigid discipline and friendlier relations between the lower deck and the officers and in some instances – most instances – this was true, but there was usually a bastard in the duff. In *Eclectic* it was the Jimmy.'[26] Even worse, there were captains who had been given a command 'from the hard-pressed Navy List completely running out of Bugginses', who each had to be given a turn. Roderick Macdonald served under one such: 'What drove *Fortune*'s captain, and what tortured him; what fire burned within him; or what it was he sought, was not obvious … But his rough and arrogant treatment of officer and ratings was very much so.'[27]

We know a good deal about life in wartime destroyers, largely because the CW candidates sent to them often left accounts. J P W Mallalieu's group were warned of this while under training, when the Chief told them:

> … they're putting most of you chaps in destroyers, and it's a pretty rough life. I've 'ad good times in destroyers, even in the last war. On quiet days you sit up on your gun and watch or read or smoke in the sun. But you don't get many quiet days. Either the sea's so rough you can't stand, or you're out on some job or other and have to keep your eyes skinned. No, you'll find it hard all right.

Conditions onboard were almost impossibly crowded. Geoffrey Ball asked his leading seaman where he could sling his hammock:

> 'That's the problem. There's twice as many men as hammock places. All the normal places are taken and there's a waiting list for them when anyone leaves. I'll try to find you somewhere but you may have to sleep on the lockers for a time.'
> 'But – won't I fall off?'
> 'Not in harbour you won't, but at sea you'll have to go somewhere else. I'll try to help but it's a real headache.'[28]

Life was particularly hard for destroyers in wartime; they were 'always on the go', according to Joseph Wellings, and impossible to keep clean to peacetime standards. Captain Micklethwaite of *Eskimo* had seen ships during the Spanish Civil War and wondered 'how any captain would allow his ship to get so filthy', but by the end of 1940, 'He now knows and would like to apologize for what he said about the Spanish ships.'[29]

American destroyers were universally known as tin cans, and a conversation with an army officer on the bridge of *Sterett* during an air attack gives some indication why:

> 'How thick is that metal?' he asked, pointing to the pilothouse bulkhead.
> 'About a quarter of an inch.'

'And how thick is the hull?'

'It's about the same.'

He looked at me in disbelief. 'A quarter of an inch? Where the hell do you take cover when they shoot at you?'

'There is no cover.'

He pondered that for a few seconds. Then he said. 'I'll take the army any day. At least we have a foxhole.'

'Well, every man to his own taste,' I replied. 'At least we have three good meals a day, and clean sheets to sleep on every night.'[30]

The United States Navy had neglected destroyers before the First World War, but built a large fleet in response to the U-boat threat. Most were not finished until the war had ended and unfortunately they were the notorious 'flush-deckers', which were already obsolete compared with the British V-Ws. When the fifty ships were transferred to Britain in 1940, President Roosevelt admitted that they were 'on their last legs any way'.[31] But with such a large force throughout the 1920s, Congress did not vote any new destroyers until the *Farragut* class, whose design started in 1933. They had high forecastles in reaction to the flush-deckers and introduced the 5in/38-calibre double-purpose gun, though only in open mountings. The *Porter* class which followed exploited a loophole in the 1930 treaty by which destroyer leaders were allowed to be of 1850 rather than 1500 tons, though there was a tendency to cram too much into them, with eight 5in guns. The seminal *Mahan* class introduced high-pressure steam. The last two of eighteen had the forward 5in guns in enclosed turrets, and that would become universal in later classes.

US destroyers, like all ships, were subject to conflicting requirements. In 1933 the Chief of Naval Operations 'cannot recommend any design which subordinates the gun to the torpedo.' In 1939 the General Board favoured torpedo armament, asking in 1939, 'Since destroyers are primarily torpedo vessels – for use chiefly against the enemy battle line – do not the latest type carry too few torpedoes?'[32] The *Gridley* and *Bagley* classes of 1936–38 had increased torpedo armament at the expense of one gun, while the *Somers* class followed the *Porter*s but had a powerful torpedo broadside. The *Sims* class, on the other hand, placed more emphasis on guns. Since the 1936 treaty limited the total national destroyer tonnage rather than individual ships, they were designed on 1570 tons, though they ended up heavier due to the lack of communication between the Bureaus of Construction and Repair and Engineering. The *Benson* and *Gleaves* classes followed them from 1939, and remained in production in wartime until a newer class was ready; nearly a hundred were built. The *Fletcher* class was the first to be designed after the treaties expired, so it had a tonnage of 2325 standard and 2924 fully loaded. It carried the usual five 5in guns with ten torpedo tubes, and there was room for the anti-aircraft armament that would be added during the war.

A clear distinction was emerging between destroyers for the Atlantic and those for the Pacific. The former needed a forecastle to meet heavy seas, and multiple depth charges for anti-submarine warfare. Pacific destroyers needed speed, long range and a good gun and torpedo armament. The *Fletcher* class had no forecastle, but it was close to perfection for the Pacific War; 175 were built, the largest number ever of any destroyer class. Their successors, the *Allen M Sumner* class, however, were even larger and carried six 5in guns in twin turrets. The final wartime design was the *Gearing* class, slightly longer to accommodate extra fuel tanks and for better hydrodynamics.

American destroyers were effectively at war before the rest of the country. The operated the Neutrality Patrol and from September 1941 they escorted Atlantic convoys. USS *Kearney* was damaged by torpedo that month and *Reuben James* was sunk at the end of October. Destroyers continued to operate in the Atlantic, but had their greatest successes in the Pacific, especially at Leyte Gulf when they attacked the centre force of the Japanese battlefleet in Surigao Strait, sinking a battleship and three destroyers; and off Samar when, against the odds, they and the escort carriers repelled a strong Japanese attack. As in nearly all navies, destroyers took part in practically all operations of any size, including carrier warfare, as plane guards:

> Out of the whole broad spectrum of chores to which *Abercrombie* was assigned … carrier operations were by far the crew's favourites. There was an inherent drama in the burst of bright bunting at the signal halyards, in the sharp, fast turnaway from the crawling convoy and the welcome breeze over bridge and deck as speed built up, and the roar of aircraft engines on the carriers' subby decks that rose to sustained successive snarls and the blue-winged planes made their short runs and took to air, the agile Wildcats leaping skyward, the heavier Avengers lumbering level with the deck or sinking slightly as they picked up speed.[33]

E J Jerningham joined *Saufley* after service in a battleship: 'Comparing the confined feeling of a battleship with its huge size and the freedom found in a destroyer with its smaller structure is impossible. I was born to be a destroyer man.'[34] To Bill Eggenberger of *Dale*: 'One of the good things about serving on tin cans was nobody got excited about how you looked, especially out there in the middle of the Pacific.'[35] But American destroyers had their share of incompetent captains, and Ensign William J Ruhe of *Roe* found that his commanding officer had many of the attributes of the fictional Captain Queeg, including undue fuss over the loss of some ice cream, bullying of the crew and inconsistent reports on his officers.[36]

The characteristic speed had its glory and its drawbacks:

> At thirty knots a destroyer becomes a different entity from a vessel passing through the water at its design hull speed or less. ... At thirty knots, the ship would try to ride over its bow wave; the bow wave rose several feet, and the stern dug deep into the water. To a person standing near the stern at this speed, the surface of the ocean would be higher than eye level. In addition to the unusual fore-and-aft attitude, the ship would acquire a rigidity with respect to its rolling movement ... what remained would be pitch, the rise and fall of the bow ... making it necessary to hold on tightly to avoid being tossed about like a rubber ball.[37]

But Jerningham saw it differently:

> The greatest thing about serving in a destroyer was that we lived so close to nature. Schools of porpoise would come alongside, adjust their speed to us, and seem to play bedside us like kids. ... From the ship's bow, which was maybe 18 or 20 feet above water, you could watch the destroyer cut through the water like a knife through butter.[38]

And it was uncomfortable down below: 'Sleep during the day between watches was virtually impossible. It was too battering an experience to lie in one's bunk with the guardrail raised. The snap and lurch of *Roe*'s motion tossed me thoroughly from guardrail to wall and back again against the heavy metal guardrail.'[39]

British battlefleet tactics were developed during the tactical course at Portsmouth, but unfortunately the records were destroyed so we have only a sketchy idea of what took place. Lieutenant Commander Frank Layard joined a course at the beginning of 1933 consisting of three captains, about fifteen commanders and fifteen lieutenant commanders. He thought that the hours were 'civil', until he discovered that he had to study intensely during Wednesday and Friday afternoons off. When he got a copy of the *Jutland Dispatches* from the port library, he was 'entirely absorbed in them all the evening', to the annoyance of his wife.

And when that battle was discussed it was 'most awfully instructing. It showed what a frightful lack of initiative it was on the part of the cruiser admirals all except Goodenough.' The quality of the lectures varied from very good to 'an awfully bad lecture on destroyers by Clarke'. There were many lectures on the battlefleet and its instructions, on submarines, and three on aircraft. There was nothing specific on amphibious warfare, apart from a lecture on the Zeebrugge raid of 1918. As to anti-submarine warfare: 'Had a lecture on A/S … It's an awfully dull subject', though it was one which would dominate Layard's later career.

There were many exercises, including one on 9 January, when 'We all worked in pairs and kept a strategical plot while enemy reports came in and we had to estimate the position of the enemy battlefleet'. Layard was appointed captain (D) of Japanese destroyers during one exercise, but was frustrated when they never came into action. It was followed by a discussion led by the director which was 'more than usually havering, rambling and long-winded.' A convoy exercise seemed to assume attack by destroyers rather than submarines.

Layard's remarks in March 1933 were prescient:

> In the German elections the Nazis have got in with a big majority. This looks like reviving all the old militarist spirit and may easily lead to trouble. What with this and Japan, the probable failure of the disarmament conference and the financial crisis in America the world is in a pretty explosive state which may easily lead to a big war.

And he was not cheered up two days later when a lecture appeared to show that 'Foreign ships seem in all cases better armed and protected and faster.' It was time to wind up the course, which Layard found 'most interesting and first class value'. However, he 'came in for heavy criticism', after he 'made a bit of a balls of it towards the end.' Perhaps that is why he was not promoted to commander when the time came.

It seems that British battlefleet tactics moved away from the single line of battle to separate squadrons whose commanders could use their initiative. Admiral Cunningham described the Battle of Matapan in March 1941, in which three Italian cruisers and one destroyer were sunk and a battleship damaged:

> … it followed almost exactly the lines of the battles we used to fight out at the table of the Tactical School at Portsmouth, a tribute to the nature and of the studies and the instruction we received there. First we had the contact of long-range reconnaissance aircraft; then the

exact positioning of the enemy relative to our own fleet by the Fleet Air Arm aircraft from the carrier, and the informative and accurate reports of their trained observers. Next the carrier's striking force of torpedo bombers went in to the attack … Meanwhile the cruisers, spread on a line of bearing, pushed in to locate the enemy's battle fleet, and finally the heavy ships themselves came into action.[40]

However, Matapan was the only British action in the war with multiple capital ships and cruisers on both sides.

The American battlefleet reached its peak during the Battle of Leyte Gulf when the Japanese *Yamashiro*, after surviving PT boat and destroyer attack when passing through the Surigao Strait, was pounded by the guns of *West Virginia, Tennessee, California, Maryland* and *Mississippi* and was sunk. It was a classic line of battle action, with the American fleet 'crossing the T' of the Japanese, as Jellicoe had attempted to do to the Germans at Jutland. But it was in exceptional circumstances, in confined waters, and with a Japanese commander who combined faith in the final naval battle with the suicidal bravery of his nation. And it was the last battleship action in history.[41] Other types of ship were already dominating the seas.

12
Naval Aviation

THE WRIGHT brothers produced the first practicable aeroplane in 1903, and they demonstrated it publicly in Europe in 1908. The United States Navy was the first to go into aviation when Eugene Ely flew from *Birmingham* in 1910. The British were not far behind with a flight from the battleship *Africa* in 1912. But a much greater problem was to land an aircraft on a ship, rather than deploy a seaplane, which had a lower performance and was dependent on smooth waters.

The various roles of naval aircraft began to emerge – reconnaissance to find the enemy fleet and fix its position, spotting the fall of shot from the big guns over long ranges, attack by land or sea, using bombs or torpedoes, and fighters to protect one's own fleet and to escort the bombers. There were subsidiary tasks such as rescue from the sea and carrying personnel or messages from ship to ship or to shore.

Sailors and aviators
The Royal Naval Air Service (RNAS) was founded in 1912 and greatly advanced by Winston Churchill as First Lord of the Admiralty. It was a very innovative organisation which pioneered the air defence of cities, strategic bombing and the armoured car. In sea warfare, it instituted anti-submarine air patrols and began to solve the thorny problem of landing on a deck. The Royal Navy commissioned the world's first 'flat top' aircraft carrier, *Argus*, in 1918. It was too late to see service in that war, and meanwhile the RNAS was merged with the army's Royal Flying Corps to form the Royal Air Force (RAF). The RAF was committed to the doctrine, fostered by the Italian Douhet and their own Lord Trenchard, that strategic bombing of cities was the way to deter or win future wars.

All the officers of the RNAS transferred to the RAF. Arthur Longmore, one of the first naval pilots to train in 1912, accepted the change: 'the main reason … was the realization that the air could achieve something more than merely act as an ancillary to the Navy and Army.'[1] As a result, there were no senior naval officers with air experience when the next war began in 1939. According to US Admiral Marc Mitscher: 'by going to the development of its land force, and neglecting its naval air arm, one great nation saved its home islands but lost its empire.[2]

Throughout the 1920s and most of the 1930s, a system of 'dual control' was operated for the Fleet Air Arm, which was technically a branch of the RAF. The navy provided the carriers and 70 per cent of the pilots, the RAF provided the servicing crews, and the aircraft were designed to naval specifications. The navy provided all the observers, who would navigate, send reconnaissance reports, and spot the fall of the shot of heavy guns. It was only in 1937 that it was agreed to return shipboard aircraft (but not shore-based planes operating over the sea) to full naval control, and it was 1939 before it came into operation.

In 1918 Admiral Mayo, the second in command of the US Atlantic fleet, noted 'that the British have undertaken in earnest the very important task of developing the Fleet Air Service. It is of immediate necessity to take up the question of development of airplane carriers and the installation of airplanes on battleships.'[3] The British naval constructor S V Goodall provided advice in 1918, suggesting that both fighter and reconnaissance aircraft would be required, that carriers should be well equipped with air defence, and needed a speed of at least 30 knots. The US still had no carriers in 1922, but war games in the War College indicated some of the practices that might be used.[4]

With no separate air force, American naval aviation developed in a different way from British. The Army Air Corps remained subordinate to its parent service, gaining more independence when it was renamed the Army Air Force in 1941. It supported the idea of strategic bombing and developed heavy bombers, such as the Boeing B-17 Flying Fortress which first flew in 1935, but it had no influence over naval aviation. Instead, the main obstacles were the scepticism of some admirals, and the lack of funds from Congress. The Bureau of Aeronautics (BuAer) was established in 1921, headed by Rear Admiral William A Moffett, not an aviator but in contact with naval air since witnessing a demonstration by Ely in 1910, and using spotting aircraft to good effect during his command of the battleship *Mississippi* in 1920. He would serve three terms in the post. He was a forceful character and extraordinarily skilful in getting his point of view across with Congress and the public. He used publicity, competing in races like the Schneider and Pulitzer trophies, staging flypasts over New York and spectacular, if dangerous, long-distance flights. He went up several blind alleys, including advocacy of the hybrid 'flying-deck cruiser' and the rigid airship – he died in the crash of *Akron* in 1933. More successfully, he oversaw the conversion of the first three carriers and their deployment in Fleet Problems. The

Morrow Board of 1925, set up by President Coolidge, largely backed his policies. In the following year he steered through a five-year plan to build a thousand aircraft, rather than having to negotiate with Congress year by year.

In London to negotiate another treaty in 1930, he was pleased to note: 'our naval aviation is far ahead of theirs, on the whole.' Though the British had more carriers, they had far fewer aircraft operating with the fleet.[5] He campaigned successfully to keep flyers within the navy but not as a separate corps, with small proportions of enlisted pilots, promotion prospects unhindered by lack of sea service, and with 50 per cent flight pay.[6]

He was succeeded by Ernest King, who had learned to fly at the age of forty-eight in order to command a seaplane tender and was known as a 'synthetic' to established flyers. He benefited by the Roosevelt government's allocation of funds voted for public works. The thousand-aircraft plan had 625 more added to it, and the aircraft which would win the coming war were already being planned. In 1934 King proposed the V-5 programme, by which college graduates between eighteen and twenty-eight could begin a year of flying training, followed by three years with the fleet. A great expansion programme began in May 1940 after the president demanded fifty thousand aircraft for the army and navy, though a month later the naval force still only numbered 1741 aircraft and 2965 pilots. Congress authorised 4500 planes, soon rising to 10,000. In December 1941 there were 5260 aircraft, 6750 pilots including those in the Coast Guard and Marines, with 1874 non-flying officers and 21,678 enlisted men. When the Japanese attack came that month, the lack of serviceable battleships meant that they were the main means of defence and eventually attack.[7]

The Bureau of Aeronautics included the Aviation Planning Division, which estimated future needs in aircraft. The Aviation Personnel Division had 'cognizance of matters pertaining to the procurement of naval personnel', though it was often in conflict with BuPers. The training and provision of pilots, technicians and aircrew was supervised by the Aviation Training Division. The Flight Division was concerned with flight rules, air traffic control, and liaison with civil aviation. The Naval Air Transport Service provided flights across the oceans and another division ran Marine Corps aviation. Aviators complained that these divisions were too remote from operations and in August 1943 they were transferred to the control of the Chief of Naval Operations. BuAer was left in charge of design and procurement of aircraft.

Flat-tops

In addition to the pioneering *Argus*, the Royal Navy built *Eagle* (1922), with the first island superstructure on the starboard side of the flight deck. *Hermes* (1924) was the first ship to be built from the keel up as an aircraft carrier, but her tonnage of 10,750 was half that of *Eagle* and she could only operate twenty aircraft. Meanwhile, the eccentric battlecruiser *Furious* was converted to the flat-top format in 1922–25. She had no island until a further conversion in 1939. C A Jenkins, her navigating officer in 1937, commented on 'the oddity of conning the ship from the tiny starboard island navigating position, a little box-like affair which projected only a couple of feet above the level of the huge flight deck'.[8] Two more odd battlecruisers, *Glorious* and *Courageous*, were converted in 1924–30 as allowed by the Washington Treaty. They were similar to *Furious* in dimensions but had substantial islands and funnels. These were the ships on which the pre-war Fleet Air Arm trained and developed its techniques.

The design of the first new large carrier, *Ark Royal*, began in 1932. It was decided to increase aircraft complement to seventy-two by fitting

British aircraft carrier development through the decades. The seaplane carrier *Ark Royal* of 1914 is seen in the left foreground with her contemporaries, two converted cross-channel steamers, in the centre of the picture. The converted liner *Campania* is behind *Ark Royal*, with a flying-off platform forward. To the right is *Argus*, the first 'flat-top', which was still in service in 1939. Behind her is *Hermes*, with an 'island' to starboard. In the background, from right to left, are the converted carrier *Glorious*, *Ark Royal* of 1937 and *Indomitable* of 1940, with the light fleet carrier *Colossus* and an escort carrier behind.

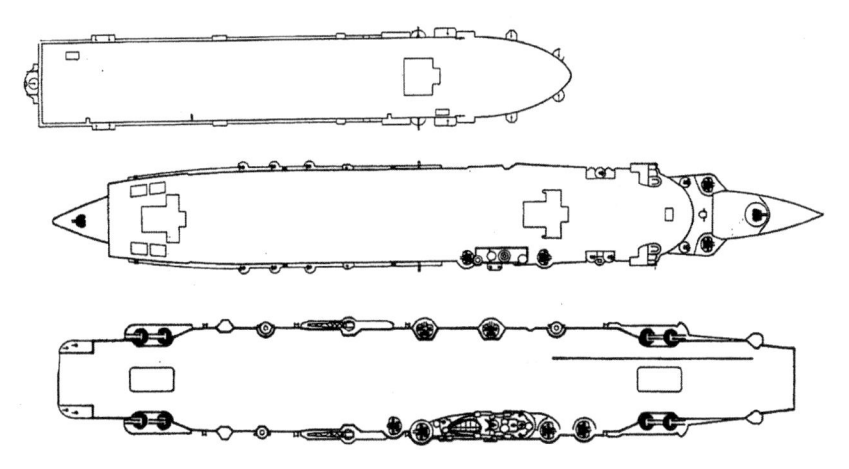

Deck plans of the British carriers *Argus*, *Furious* and *Illustrious*. The origin of *Argus* in a liner and *Furious* in a battlecruiser are apparent; *Illustrious* and her near-sisters were designed as aircraft carriers from the keel up.

two hangar decks. With catapults and arrester wires, a speed of 30 knots was considered adequate. She saw extensive service and gained great fame during the first two years of war, partly because of German claims to have sunk her. In November 1941 she was hit by a single torpedo fired by *U-81* and sank after a failure of damage control.

In 1936 it was decided to build carriers with armoured flight decks, sacrificing the second hangar and reducing the aircraft complement to thirty-six. The three ships of the initial *Illustrious* class entered service during 1940/1 and soon saw active service, but the small air complement caused problems. For the next ship, *Indomitable*, the flight deck was raised by 14ft to fit a small hangar under the first, allowing her to carry forty-five aircraft. The next two, *Implacable* and *Indefatigable*, had a slightly larger lower hangar which allowed sixty aircraft. The armoured deck would prove itself when *Illustrious* survived seven bomb hits in January 1941 and *Indefatigable* was only slightly damaged by a kamikaze in 1945. The repair of *Illustrious* at Norfolk Navy Yard stimulated American interest and the armoured deck was adopted for the *Midway* class, which did not enter service until the war was over.

By the end of 1942, only *Furious* was still in service out of the older carriers. The venerable *Argus* was mostly used for aircraft delivery. *Glorious*, *Courageous*, *Eagle* and *Hermes* had all been sunk, as had the more modern *Ark Royal*, so the brunt of the naval air war fell on the *Illustrious* class and its derivatives.

The flight deck of *Illustrious*, like most British carriers, began aft with a 'round-down', which was intended to improve the airflow for landing, though it was later removed to increase the space available. There were tall wireless telegraphy masts on each side, vertical when transmitting and level when flying was taking place. The original *Illustrious* class had two lifts, 45ft long and 22ft wide, small in order to limit interruption of the armour. *Indomitable, Implacable* and *Indefatigable* had 33ft wide lifts for fighters without folding wings.

The carrier's island included the flight control room at flight-deck level, with the commander (flying)'s control position above. The operations room was on the deck below, 'fitted with plots chart tables, drawers, blackboards, large notice boards for charts, cupboards, telephone and a bunk for the Air Staff Officer.' Carriers had 'waiting rooms' or 'ready rooms' for aircrew 'fitted with notice boards for the rapid distribution of information, … a chart table and desks with a good supply of drawers.' There were settee bunks 'where the crews can rest comfortably while waiting to fly'. The fighter direction room was in the island structure. Below decks was the hangar, running the full length and breadth of the ship, but divided into three by fire curtains. It was fitted with lights and aircraft securing points, and spare parts were hung from the sides or the deck above. Aircraft could be refuelled by pipes, either in the hangar or on the flight deck.[9]

Alongside the relative sophistication of ships like *Illustrious*, much simpler vessels were born out of wartime necessity. The first was the CAM ship, or 'catapult, aircraft, merchantman'. In 1941, in a desperate expedient, aircraft were fitted to be catapulted from the bows of merchant ships in convoy, to shoot down or drive away shadowing Focke-Wulf Kondors. There was no prospect of recovering them and the pilot had to ditch in the sea and hope to be picked up, or try to reach land. Thirty-five ships made 170 round voyages; eight operational launches led to seven kills and the loss of one pilot.[10]

The merchant aircraft carrier, or MAC, ship was a merchantman fitted with a flight deck. They were designed to carry four Swordfish aircraft in addition to a normal cargo, and were manned by the merchant navy with a Royal Navy air group. Six grain ships, which first entered service in April 1943, had hangars, thirteen tankers did not. They had only tiny wheelhouses, and diesel engines whose exhausts issued horizontally rather than through funnels. A typical ship had a crew of 107, half naval. RNVR officers, preferring the freer merchant navy discipline, sometimes painted 'Merchant Navy' rather than 'Royal Navy' on their aircraft.[11] MAC ships made a total of 323 Atlantic voyages and launched aircraft more than four hundred times.

... if to the airborne pilot the flight deck of a fleet carrier appears little larger than a postage stamp, how much more true was that the case in these vessels, and how excellent the pilot's skill in safely landing on this small area [about 420ft], especially with the knowledge that the stops to a plunge overboard were only four arrester wires ...[12]

They made twelve contacts with U-boats, leading to damage to two of them, but their main task was reconnaissance.[13] They were superseded by escort carriers from the United States

The first American aircraft carrier was *Langley*, a collier fitted with a flight deck in 1922, known as the covered wagon, and used for experiments. Under the Washington Treaty, the United States was allowed to complete two large battlecruisers as carriers. Their sharp hulls restricted aircraft storage and the armoured sides prevented the use of open hangars, but after their completion late in 1927, they introduced the navy to the large carrier. *Lexington* and *Saratoga* were of more than 37,000 tons with a speed of 33 knots and a capacity for sixty-three aircraft. Their huge, flat-sided funnels were a major recognition feature. Initially, they were armed with 8in guns as protection against cruisers. In their first appearance in Fleet Problem X of 1929, *Saratoga* launched a strike on the Panama Canal which impressed admirals Hughes and Pratt.[14] During exercises in the 1930s, they established many of the principles for operating aircraft with a fleet. *Lexington* was lost in the Battle of the Coral Sea in May 1942. *Saratoga* survived the war.

Ranger was the first American carrier built from the keel up, to use up treaty tonnage. She was much smaller at under 15,000 tons and slightly slower, but she could carry seventy-six aircraft. She introduced several new features, including the open hangar below the flight deck. There had been some debate about the value of an island, partly based on British experience. A former captain of *Hermes* told an American counterpart that that the pilots liked the island: 'it gave them something in view all the time while coming aboard.' Experience with *Langley* showed that 'When ... the complement was increased to 32 planes, it became difficult and almost impossible for the air officer from his forward position ... to see any plane landing after the 12th or the 15th.' All large American carriers were fitted with islands from then on.[15] But *Ranger's* short length and flared bows caused her to pitch excessively in long Pacific swells and she was mainly confined to second-line duties in the Second World War.

The *Yorktown* class was the first to be designed in the light of operational experience and their building commenced in 1934. They used the open hangar, had a large air group of ninety-six, and retained the high speed

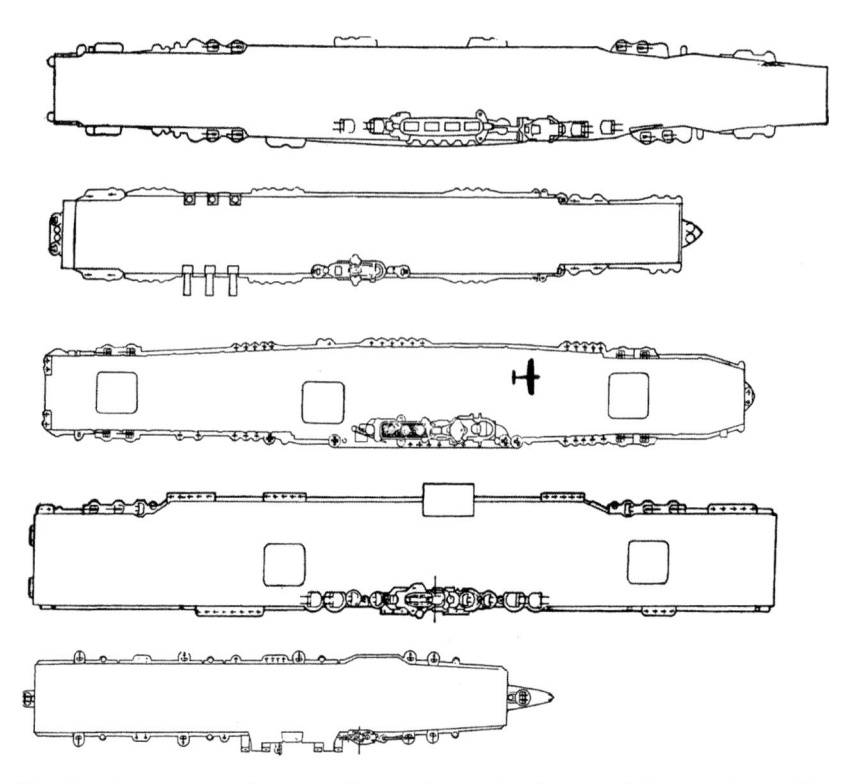

The American carriers *Saratoga, Ranger, Enterprise, Essex* and *Independence*. The huge superstructure of *Saratoga*, a converted battlecruiser, is obvious. *Ranger* was too small to be fully effective, but *Enterprise* and *Essex* represented peak development. The smaller *Independence* class, converted from cruisers, were intended as a stopgap.

of the converted battlecruisers. They abandoned any idea of taking on cruisers, but had the new 5in gun for air defence. James S Russel helped to supervise *Yorktown*'s fitting out after experience in *Ranger*. The 'atrocious' ready rooms of earlier carriers were superseded: 'We put in reclining chairs … all facing in one direction, with a blackboard, and a teletype information system that could be operated from a central point … if you were on a long alert waiting for your flight, you could recline and get some rest.'[16] Thus began a US Navy institution.

Yorktown, commissioned in 1937, was the main American casualty at Midway in June 1942. *Enterprise,* which entered service in 1938, became perhaps the most famous carrier of all time, taking part in nearly all the major battles in the Pacific. Joining her in Pearl Harbor, Alvin Kernan was impressed: 'as the motor whaleboat came up under her counter on her seaward, port, side she towered a hundred feet above us, grayish white, nearly nine hundred feet long, beautifully shaped despite her huge size.'[17] The third ship, *Hornet*, was most famous for launching the aircraft strike against Tokyo in 1942, but was lost later in the year. Between them, they raised American carrier design to a new level.

In the meantime, *Wasp was* ordered in 1936 to use up spare treaty tonnage. She introduced the deck-edge lift, which could be used while flying went on. Otherwise she was unsatisfactory, but the case for smaller carriers continued to be made by Admiral Ghormley, who argued that a large vessel might need an hour to land her whole air group, steaming into the wind and often away from her intended course. In September 1942 *Wasp* was sunk by a submarine in the Pacific.

The *Essex* class were the first post-treaty carriers, of 27,000 tons, 8000 more than the *Yorktown*s. They incorporated all the experience of the

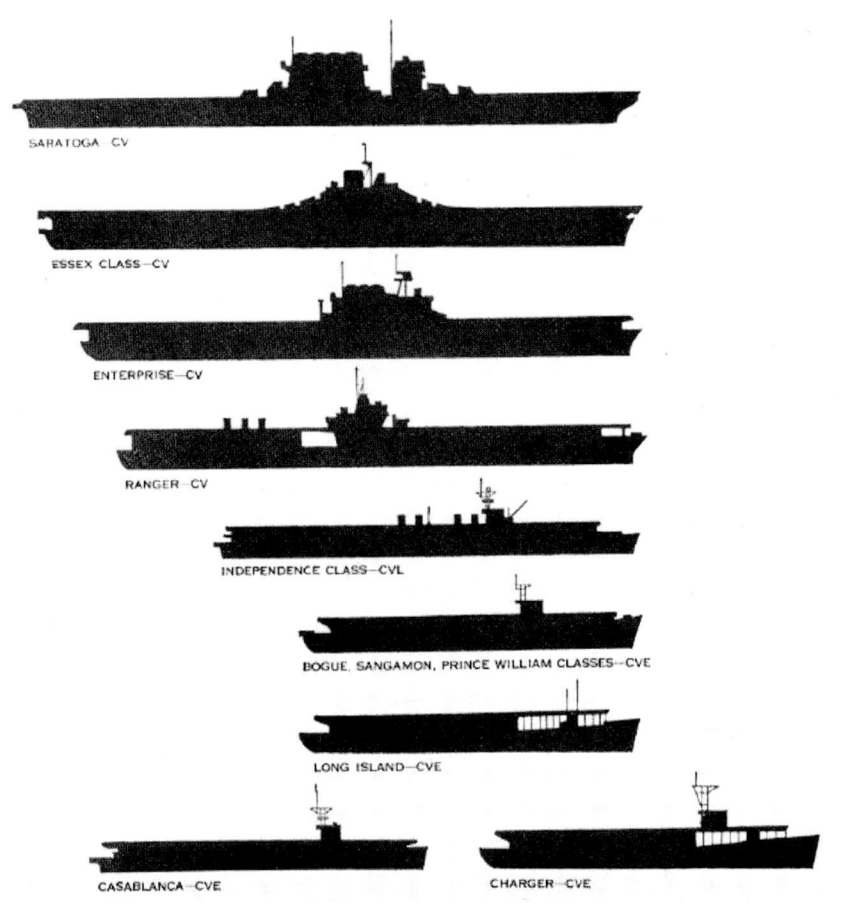

Simplified profiles of the main types of American carrier, showing the contrast in size between *Saratoga* and *Essex*, and several types of escort carrier, or CVE.

last fifteen years, with the deck-edge lift of *Ranger* and the light flight deck with open hangar underneath, which allowed aircraft engines to be warmed up below. The flight deck was square, rather than following the lines of the hull, though BuShips objected that the corners would be difficult to support – in fact, they suffered some damage in typhoons.[18] They were the first to use the new high-pressure steam engines. *Essex* herself was begun at Newport News in April 1941 and commissioned at the end of 1942; a total of fourteen saw war service. More than anything else, they represented the potency of American sea power. *Essex* herself took part in the Battle of the Philippine Sea and the Great Marianas Turkey Shoot, along with *Bunker Hill* and the new *Yorktown*, *Hornet*, *Lexington* and *Wasp*. Unlike other classes, none was lost during the war, though *Franklin* survived very serious damage when hit by bombs off the coast of Japan in March 1945.

Due to unjustified fears that the *Essex*es would not be ready on time, Roosevelt ordered the conversion of nine light cruisers under construction. The *Independence*-class ships were just over a third of the size of the *Essex*es and initially they carried only thirty aircraft but they took part in many campaigns, including *Belleau Wood*, *Bataan*, *Monterey*, *Cabot*, *San Jacinto*, *Princeton*, *Langley* and *Cowpens* at the Philippine Sea. *Princeton* was sunk in October 1944.

Escort aircraft carriers were developed by Anglo-American co-operation, though the two navies had different ideas on their purpose. The British saw them as true to the 'escort' title, to sail with convoys and launch aircraft to deter enemy reconnaissance aircraft, or to force submarines to submerge. The Americans wanted them to support amphibious operations, and indeed the British ships did so in North Africa and Italy, delaying their entry to the Atlantic battle. It began with the captured German merchantman *Hannover*, which was renamed and fitted with a flight deck in June 1941. She was extremely basic, with no island, hangar or lifts and a low speed of 15 knots According to Eric Brown: 'The *Empire Audacity* was certainly a most extraordinary ship … The "bridge" was simply a little metal tray stuck on the ship's side level with the flight deck on the starboard side about a quarter of the way back from the bows.'[19] She was soon lost to a U-boat, but followed by the fast cargo ship *Activity*, and sowed the seeds of an idea.

Meanwhile, Roosevelt wanted carriers which could be built quickly. *Long Island*, formerly the cargo ship *Mormacmail*, was converted using British experience. Her appearance was startling to a conventional seaman. 'My God,' someone said. 'They just chopped off the midships and after houses of a cargo ship and jerry-rigged a flight deck on top. She's a

The escort carrier USS *Block Island*, whose aircraft sank six U-boats before she was sunk in May 1944. It has the short flight deck and small island which was characteristic of these vessels.

seagoing abortion!'[20] She was originally intended as an aircraft transport but soon found a combat role carrying ten observation aircraft and six bombers. She was followed by *Charger*. The British converted four more ships from liners and fast cargo ships during 1943/4, and the Americans provided *Archer*, a sister ship of *Long Island*, *Biter*, *Avenger* which was torpedoed, and *Dasher*, which was destroyed by a petrol explosion in the Firth of Clyde, leading to a dispute between the two navies.

These were overtaken by mass production. The twenty ships of the *Bogue* class, all built at Seattle Tacoma, were an improvement on *Long Island*. Because of their merchant origins, their flight decks had both camber and sheer which made it difficult to handle aircraft in rough weather – the ten ships transferred to Britain as the *Attacker* class were rebuilt to correct this. The four ships of the *Sangamon* class were based on the hulls of tankers, therefore longer than the others. Eleven ships of the *Commencement Bay* class were completed by the end of the war, based on this design and carrying nearly 13,000 tons of oil, which could be used as fuel or delivered at the end of a voyage. They could carry up to thirty-three aircraft and were the only escort carriers able to operate the Hellcat fighter. Henry J Kaiser was already mass-producing Liberty ships in mid 1942, when he was given an order for fifty escort carriers of the *Casablanca* class. They were all built in his Vancouver yard and were smaller and more cramped than the *Commencement Bay* class, but were faster and carried nine each of fighters, bombers and torpedo bombers. They were all completed by the end of 1944.

Unlike the merchant aircraft carriers, the escort carriers were commissioned as warships, which John Godley found intimidating on first ascending to the bridge of HMS *Nairana*: 'Nothing informal here. Three or four officers, all in full uniform. Caps, collars and ties!'[21] He was shown round by a petty officer:

> The hangar deck, to which one by one my Stringbags are being lowered on the lift, then hauled forward by a tractor to their allotted positions, hardly an inch of space between them. … My cabin very far aft … 'You'll not sleep here often when we're at sea, Sir.' More movement … than anywhere else on board.[22]

The escort carriers did indeed help to turn the tide by closing the air gap in the Battle of the Atlantic, as the Royal Navy had intended. They supported numerous amphibious operations and had their finest hour at the Battle off Samar as part of the Leyte Gulf campaign, when their aircraft helped to turn back a much superior Japanese force.

Naval airmen

Ambitious Royal Navy officers were not drawn to flying in the 1920s, partly because it might limit the sea time which was necessary for promotion. The first course of 1924 had fifty members for six months of elementary flying at Netheravon in inland Wiltshire, followed by training in naval aircraft at coastal stations.[23] Caspar John was discouraged from applying, but began his flying training in 1925. He was presented with his wings by Air Marshal Trenchard, the apostle of unified air power, who commented, 'I congratulate you on your wings, but I'm damned if I understand the colour of your uniform.'[24]

With the shortage of officer pilots, the navy wanted to train ratings. It was allowed to do so after transfer of the Fleet Air Arm, but in fact the great majority of its pilots would be officers. In 1938 the navy, which had traditionally offered a career for life for its officers, adopted the principle of short service as pioneered by the RAF, and advertised for unmarried 'British subjects of pure European descent', who were physically fit and between the ages of seventeen and a half and twenty-three for 'Short service commissions in the Air Branch of the Royal Navy.' They would be taken on for seven years, 'including preliminary naval training' and they would be 'instructed in the flying of aircraft both from ships and shore stations'.[25] Early in 1939 three hundred short-service air branch officers were under training, and twenty-seven rating pilots had qualified.[26] Aircrew officers who had not had full naval training wore the letter 'A' in the curl of their stripes. Attempting to order a party of Royal Marines to abandon the sinking *Courageous* in 1939, Charles Lamb found, 'The Corporal just gazed at our left sleeves and went pink with embarrassment. … The badge was designed to warn all beholders that the wearer … could not be expected to answer any question which was not about aviation.'[27]

By the middle of 1939, as the transition from dual control was almost complete, there were still no pilots with the rank of captain, but there were four observers, none currently on Fleet Air Arm duties. Fourteen pilots held the rank of commander. Onboard the carriers the observers were attached to the ship itself, the pilots mostly to the squadrons. There were still many RAF officers; for example *Furious* had a wing commander and squadron leader with junior officers attached, but the senior Fleet Air Arm officer was a commander, RN.

With wartime conscription and volunteering, the navy soon found a supply of well-educated and motivated young men who could be trained as officers and pilots, though it still had a problem, simply because of the existence of the RAF. Unlike its American counterpart, it had a distinctive uniform and it was essential in defending the homeland in the Battle of Britain; pilots were at the centre of the RAF, in the navy the ship came first. Moreover, the naval pilot wore his 'wings' on his sleeve just above his stripes, not prominently on his breast like an RAF pilot. But the prestige of the Royal Navy was high. Raymond Lygo was impressed by the success at Taranto and realised that the airmen were 'more than just pilots, they were in the navy, they were part of our great tradition of the sea.'[28]

Prospective pilots were sent to the shore base HMS *St Vincent* across the harbour from Portsmouth. If they expected to get in the air quickly, they were disappointed:

> At *St Vincent* we learned much. Navigation, meteorology, the Morse code, how to make a reef knot and a bowline and a clove hitch. The only thing we learnt about aircraft was how to recognise some of them in flight. We did our own dhobying [washing], pulled oars in a naval cutter and had lectures on King's Regulations and Admiralty Instructions.[29]

Naval discipline was at the core of the training. 'Chief Petty Officer Wilmot had been the chief gunner's mate in HMS *Nelson*, in charge of the most powerful set of guns in the navy. ... Saved from retirement by the war the fire still burned brightly. He was fierce and had a heart of gold.'[30]

At No 24 Elementary Flying Training School in Cheshire, Dunstan Hadley began in Tiger Moths. Instructors included a flight lieutenant who had joined the RAF in 1922, ex-civil pilots who were too old for operations, and recent trainees who were held back as instructors: 'These young ones usually hated it, and some were inclined to vent their annoyance on the pupils.'[31]

Many other prospective pilots were sent to the USA and Canada for training under a scheme set up by Admiral John H Towers. Among them was Jim Spencer, who found the hosts patriotic: 'While we considered it almost bad form to make a show of patriotism, Yanks in the 1940s were overtly patriotic, everyone wishing to demonstrate a commitment to a great experiment in which people of many races were welded together in one nation.' They were 'the most hospitable people on earth', the accommodation 'magnificent', and the food far superior. He was shocked by the US Navy's tendency to demean its trainees and disliked the demerit system: 'Some rules and restrictions struck us as petty, more akin to peace time guard regiments at home.' But the training at Grosse Ile and Pensacola was very thorough.[32]

Unlike the RAF, the Royal Navy retained the grade of observer after the First World War:

> The Navy insisted on training its own observers, whom it regarded as more important than pilots, believing as it did that the Royal Air Force didn't really know how to navigate anyway and wouldn't know a sixteen-inch gun even if it fell over it, or how to spot the fall of shot from one ...[33]

In wartime, observers were trained either at Arbroath on the east coast of Scotland, or at Piarco Savana in Trinidad. Trainees, still ratings, were flown on exercises by commissioned but disgruntled pilots:

> 'And where would we be going today?' 'If you don't mind, Sir, could we please depart over the Seaforth Hotel swimming pool on a course of 095 degrees.' ... an imaginary aircraft carrier would 'sail' from that point at a speed of 25 knots on a course of 030 degrees, thus bringing it close to the little port of Stonehaven after an hour, by which time we would have completed a dog leg course over the sea and would attempt to arrive over, or 'intercept' the carrier at the appropriate time and place on the coast.[34]

The third crew member in a multi-seat aircraft was a rating known as the telegraphist air gunner, or TAG. He was selected from men who were fit, but not educated enough for pilots or observers. When fully trained, he was given leading rate, though his RAF equivalent would be a sergeant, one rank higher. He was not invited to pre-flight briefings and he had to face backwards and trust the skills of his pilot in taking off and landing. In a Swordfish he only had a single Lewis gun of First World War vintage.

TAGs did not take part in the famous Taranto raid of 1940, but Les Sayer was in a Swordfish for the attack on the *Bismarck* as his pilot went round again:

> So we came right down at sea level. I'm standing up looking forward at the *Bismarck* and she's getting bigger and bigger and still they didn't see us. I thought to myself, well, they've only got us to aim at, they're bound to hit us, this is your lot anyway, so forget it. But we went in, and dropped the fish and turned away and it was only then that they saw us and let us have everything.[35]

Donald Bruce was in the catastrophic attack on *Scharnhorst* and *Gneisenau* in 1942:

> I began swearing away and at the same time fired as much of the feeble .303 tracer in front of the [Focke-Wulf] 190s as I could, stoppages permitting; all drill in this respect went overboard, as indeed went my malfunctioning magazine ... From my backward viewpoint, it was developing into a practice shoot for FW 190s.[36]

Unlike land-based ground crews, maintenance teams in carriers could not call in parts or expertise from a nearby base. They had to deal with aircraft performing several functions which might need conversion, and with the added complication of folding wings. They worked in the confined space of a hangar deck, often moving in the waves. Their aircraft had to be particularly strong to take the stresses of deck landing, while the failure of the single engine over the sea could have catastrophic consequences.

The Fleet Air Arm was initially dependent on the RAF for its servicing crews, though its airmen were reluctant to transfer to the navy. Meanwhile, the navy began to train its own, largely through the auspices of the RAF. At the top level were the artificers, recruited in their teens to serve a very thorough apprenticeship. The first three-year course of three hundred trainees began in 1938, so it was not an instant solution. They were able to 'take charge of workshop and junior maintenance ratings on repair, overhaul, modification and inspection'.

Below the artificers were the 'dilutee' grades, the air fitters, who were divided into airframe, engine, ordnance and electrical, denoted by the letters A, E, O and L. They were selected from the most intelligent 'hostilities only' ratings for a year's training. They wore the fore and aft rig of petty officers and could reach that rating quickly when qualified. More than three thousand airframe and electrical fitters had begun training by August 1943. It was reported: 'Degree of skill varies considerably between individuals; some employed with squadrons on minor inspections, others in workshops on major inspections and overhauls.' But in the defining feature of skill, each was qualified to sign Airworthiness Form 700.

At the next level were the air mechanics, divided into the same four categories and wearing the square rig unform of the seamen. Each was a 'Semi-skilled maintenance rating employed on minor inspection and repair by replacement.' In 1944 a fully-manned fighter squadron with twelve aircraft would have two artificers and nine air fitters of the various branches, four radio mechanics, a chief air mechanic, five petty officers and a total of forty-seven junior air mechanics, plus clerical and catering staff to a total of 106 ratings. In addition, each carrier would have a maintenance crew for more extensive repairs, varying with the type of aircraft carried and having a higher concentration of the more skilled grades.

The United States Navy had already built up a substantial supply of pilots by 1939. There was a certain continuity. The great carrier admiral Marc Mitscher was trained by Kenneth Whiting, who in turn had learned to fly with Orville Wright. Mitscher stressed the importance of the training, and the responsibility of the individual pilot when it came to action:

> You can train a combat pilot for $50,000. ... we spend millions of dollars designing and building a big carrier. We put 3000 men aboard and a big screen of ships around her and then send her 7000 miles from home. Then we launch planes. The whole striking force of this carrier, all we spent in preparation and operation up to this point, is finally spearheaded by a hundred young pilots. Each of these boys is captain of his own ship. What he thinks, his confidence in what he is doing, how hard he presses home the attack is exactly how effective we are.[37]

The US Navy had used large numbers of enlisted pilots before the war, mostly in the rank of chief petty officer. Some became warrant officers, including several in Torpedo Squadron Six onboard the *Enterprise* in

1942, but once the wartime training programme took effect they were greatly outnumbered by newly-commissioned officers.[38]

Early in 1942 Frank Knox announced an ambitious programme to train navy and marine pilots 'at a starting rate of 30,000 a year.' Groundwork for the scheme had already been done by the assistant Secretary of the Navy for Air, Artemus L Gates, who had been a naval pilot in the last war, and by the Chief of BuAer, Admiral John H Towers. Four universities were nominated for pre-flight training, in the east, south, mid-west and west of the country. According to Knox, 'Naval officials attached particular importance to the physical training aspects of the curriculum ... It is intended to condition pilots for any danger they may have to face in, or as a result of, actual naval battle.' Trainees would work a sixteen-hour day with only thirty minutes for rest. It was to include 'dirty fighting', which was 'distasteful to Americans', but was necessary in this war. To Alvin Kernan, 'Learning how to leap over walls, climb ropes, swing on trapezes, and so on came hard and painfully.'[39]

After that the trainees went on to primary flying training, initially in sixteen schools around the country. The navy had to cast its net wide to find instructors:

> Primary flight instructors were of two kinds. One lot had been private pilots before the war – amateurs, mostly, who had flown light planes on weekends ... The other kind ... had been through the same program that we were in ... and been commissioned like any service pilot, and then ... had been sent back to a primary base to instruct us novices ...

Like their British counterparts, they were 'angry and bitter'.[40]

According to Hynes, 'The planes at Memphis were Stearman N2S's, open cockpit biplanes that were painted yellow and were known as "yellow perils". In fact they were anything but perilous; they were probably the safest and strongest air planes ever built.'[41] From the beginning they were trained in naval ways:

> Because of the nature of Naval Aviation, the Naval pilot cannot use the type of approach to a landing which is used by most land-based pilots. So that you won't have to 'unlearn' certain habits, you will begin from the very first to make the carrier type approach to a landing [which is] based on a 'race course' flight pattern ...[42]

They were subject to constant checks on their progress, and the official manual told them: 'The check pilot will merely ride along while you fly the plane through a series of maneuvers. Unlike most examinations, you will know the series of maneuvers which the check pilot will require. You will have practised them many times, both with your instructor and solo.'[43] But it could not help being stressful, as Samuel Hynes recorded:

> When we had learned one set of skills, or at least had flown the prescribed number of hours, there were check-rides, to determine whether we were ready for the next set. These were tests, but not like any test that I had taken at school or university. You couldn't cram for it, and you couldn't fake it. You weren't even being tested on something that you had studied, really, but on what you were. If you were a flier, you passed; if you weren't, you washed …[44]

Later he met his friend from Memphis training days, 'now a seaman pushing a broom.'[45]

The successful candidate went on to intermediate training, which expanded from sixteen to twenty weeks:

> When the aviation cadet finishes primary training he knows how to fly. Entering the intermediate phase, at Pensacola or Corpus Christi, he is taught how to apply his flying in combat … Instrument and night flying, formation flying and air tactics are emphasized at intermediate. He flies heavier planes, graduation from biplanes to SNV, SNJ, PBY, OS2U, SNB.

The first month was devoted to formation flying and divisional tactics, followed by link trainer and instrument flying. The third phase was on individual types of aircraft, and the whole was combined with thorough ground training.

As they neared the end of their intermediate course, trainees were theoretically given the choice of which type they were to fly, but with a strong caveat. Implicitly it was assumed that most would choose fighters:

> Possibly when your turn comes … there'll be a shortage of instructors … Maybe there'll be a need for trained 'big boat' pilots to man the new land-based multi-engined bombers and transports. If such a situation should prevail or be coming up shortly, your choice – for the present, anyway – must become secondary to the Navy's need. As a well-disciplined Navy flier you understand that.[46]

Now wearing his 'wings of gold' on his breast, the pilot went on to the next stage, operational training, for example for fighter pilots:

> … the course of study includes interception of high altitude horizonal bombers with or without enemy VF [carrier fighter]

escorts, dive bomber attacks with or without escort, torpedo attacks under similar circumstances, or any combination of plane types. Pilots learn how to escort bombers, dive bombers or TBFs or any combination of these.

Passing this stage did not guarantee success and the sobering film *This is it* showed six new pilots joining a carrier. Four are killed on their first operation, because of failures in navigation, signalling, discipline and procedures. Another was sent back by the air commander and the last was facing a general court martial for shooting down a friendly plane. But after two years of thorough training, most lived up to Knox's ambition that they would be 'the strongest, most daring and most determined type of airmen in the world.'

For selection at boot camp, an aviation radioman needed a high test score, perfect vision, and a clear speaking voice before entering a twenty-week course. He would learn to transmit encrypted and plain language radio messages, make minor radio repairs and operate a machine gun in flight:

> Whenever the pilot takes off the carrier, … the rear gunner takes off too. He goes bouncing along on the flight deck as if he really liked the work. Some like it. Some don't. …
>
> But usually the little rear gunner, especially when in a torpedo-bomber, is fairly well concealed until the plane already has whirled along the deck for its final spring. Then we can see him curled up and facing us from within the tiny dome … he does not get to see his own take-off from the deck. From all appearances he may be reciting that old roulette phrase: 'Here it goes. Where to, nobody knows.'[47]

Plane captains were enlisted men: 'Each has been assigned to an individual plane, and he is in charge of that one plane as long as it is aboard. He may even sleep in it at times. He is the trustee and guardian of it. The pilot is *his* pilot too.'[48] A prospective aviation machinist's mate needed a high score in tests to begin a twenty-one-week course. He was expected to maintain, adjust and repair aircraft and engines and to understand the principles of their construction and operation. After some experience he might specialise in propellers, fuel systems, brakes, hydraulic systems and other subjects. He could operate machine tools to make small replacements, handle ground gear such as lines and tackle, and make pre-flight inspections. He could also serve as an air gunner.

An aviation ordnanceman needed a similarly high score, though his course was only fourteen weeks long. A candidate was told:

An enlisted plane captain, instructor, and aviation cadet record a flight in an N3N 'Yellow Peril' biplane trainer.

You'll be an expert on all of the guns used by your outfit ... from a cal .22 training pistol up to a 20mm aircraft cannon ... to keep them in tip-top condition – disassemble them, make repairs, put them back together again, install them in airplanes. ... take care of all the bomb releasing gear – the racks, shackles, and other equipment by which bombs are dropped from airplanes.

You'll be handling all of ... the ammunition for the guns, the bombs, torpedoes rockets, mines, pyrotechnics, and their component parts – and loading them into the airplanes.

You'll be working with gunsights, bombsights, torpedo directors ... to correlate sights and guns, and ... install and adjust delicate synchronisers – the mechanisms that fire guns so the bullets pass between the propeller blades.[49]

An aviation electrician's mate might have a slightly lower score in tests and had a sixteen-week course. He would install, maintain and repair equipment such as ignition and light systems, landing gear warnings, generators, armatures, batteries and so on. He was able to carry out simple soldering and brazing, and he could understand electrical diagrams and blueprints.[50]

Aircraft

British naval aircraft fell into four main types. There were obsolescent biplanes which performed surprisingly well in service, in situations where there was little or no threat from enemy fighters. Secondly, there were monoplanes which were designed to misguided specifications or took too long in development, and were largely outdated by the time they were ready. Thirdly, there were adapted landplanes, which had many qualities but did not easily endure the hardships of naval service. Finally, there were American aircraft provided under lend-lease, which avoided most of these problems.

The main British naval aircraft manufacturers were Fairey and Blackburn. In addition, Supermarine, now part of the giant Vickers group, produced the Walrus amphibian and the Seafire, and Hawker the Sea Hurricane. British naval aircraft were made in relatively small numbers, about one in twelve of the total produced in wartime, and they were not subject to mass production except for the Seafire and Sea Hurricane, which were adapted from landplanes. The output of naval aircraft barely increased in the early part of the war and peaked at 279 in May 1944.[51] It was a striking contrast to the massive American effort, which the Fleet Air Arm would come to rely on.

The transition to monoplanes was almost complete when the Second World War began, but the Fleet Air Arm would continue to use biplanes until the end of the war. Visiting the US base at Norfolk, Virginia, Hugh Popham amused the American crews. 'Look at those biplanes, will ya! D'you wonder they're losing the war?'[52] The RAF acquired great aircraft like the Spitfire, Mosquito and Lancaster, along with a few duds. The most successful British naval aircraft, the Swordfish, was obsolete by any normal standards.

With very limited complements on the carriers, each aircraft had to undertake several roles. Thus the Swordfish was originally the TSR 2, for torpedo, spotting and reconnaissance, the Skua was a fighter-dive-bomber (roles which did not combine easily) and the Barracuda was a dive- and torpedo-bomber. Sometimes it worked, but often the aircraft did none of the roles well. The Admiralty, with its usual concern for navigation, insisted on two-seat fighters, such as the Fulmar and Firefly.

In the first category of naval aircraft, the famous Fairey Swordfish which entered service in 1936 was the clear favourite. It got its nickname of 'Stringbag', not because of its old-fashioned profusion of struts and wires bracing the wings, but because it was compared to a string bag in which a housewife would carry a variety of goods. According to John Godley:

She was absolutely stable and even at the lowest speeds the controls were firm and positive. Scream down from an immense height in a dive, the speed would stay well below 200 knots and you could haul back on the stick for all you were worth: a firm, fast pull-out with no fear of that old enemy, the high speed stall.[53]

Its low speed was an advantage: 'Shore-based gunners bluntly refused to believe your speed was eighty-five or ninety whatever their radar might indicate. Shells or tracer would (with any luck) be fifty yards ahead.'[54] The Swordfish gained fame with the attack on Taranto in 1940, in which three major warships were sunk or damaged. One of them launched the torpedo which damaged the steering of *Bismarck*, leading to her destruction. Less happily, six of them were destroyed in an unsuccessful attack on *Scharnhorst* and *Gneisenau* during the Channel Dash of 1942.

The Swordfish's intended successor was the Albacore, described as a 'gentleman's Swordfish', with an enclosed cockpit, a slightly improved speed and a capacity for dive-bombing. It was introduced in 1940 and equipped fifteen squadrons at its peak, but it was unloved. Its controls were heavy and its manoeuvrability did not compare with the Swordfish. It was replaced by the Barracuda from 1943, while the Swordfish found a new lease of life with merchant aircraft carriers in the Atlantic, fitted with radar and armed with depth charges and later rockets.

The Gloster Gladiator was originally an RAF biplane fighter, quite advanced when it was designed in the early 1930s, with an enclosed cockpit and streamlined struts supporting a fixed undercarriage. The Sea Gladiator had a short service life as monoplanes came into service, but it gained fame with the legendary 'Faith, Hope and Charity', which filled a gap in the defence of Malta in 1940.

The Supermarine Walrus, designed from 1932 by R J Mitchell of Spitfire fame, was a flying boat with a square section hull, retractable undercarriage and enclosed cockpit. Its wings were mounted high with a pusher engine between them, keeping it well clear of the water. It became the standard aircraft in ships' flights in battleships and cruisers. Known as the Shagbat, it had a maximum speed of 135mph, robustness and pleasant handling characteristics: 'On a rough day the Walrus behaves more like a cow than a bus – a very friendly cow however.'[55]

The second category was of monoplanes designed for sea service. The Blackburn Skua was advanced when it was designed in 1935, the first all-metal monoplane ordered for the Fleet Air Arm. It had early successes, shooting down the first German aircraft during the war, and sinking the cruiser *Konigsberg* by dive-bombing. But its maximum speed of 225 mph was far behind that of its land-based contemporaries and it was relegated to target-towing. The Blackburn Roc used the same airframe with a four-gun turret aft of the pilot. That concept was soon discredited and the Roc was reduced to second-line service.

The design of the Fairey Barracuda took the term 'observer' literally. It was an ungainly high-wing monoplane to give him a downward view through two curved windows. There was no room for a bomb bay, so torpedoes and bombs were carried externally. Its entry was delayed until 1942 by a change of engine. It had its greatest success as a dive-bomber when carrier-borne aircraft damaged the battleship *Tirpitz* in the steep sided Kaa Fjord.

The Fairey Battle was designed as a light bomber, and the navy ordered a version of it as a two-seat fighter when the Skua fell behind. By the time it entered service in 1940, the Battle had already suffered heavy losses in France. They were powered by Merlin engines like the Hurricanes and early Spitfires, but a Fulmar weighed 40 per cent more, so performance was poor, with a maximum speed of 280 mph. Six hundred Fulmars were delivered and they found a role in the Mediterranean. Their eight forward-firing machine guns shot down ten Italian bombers in three months of 1940 and they supported the Swordfish attack on Taranto.

A Blackburn Skua dive-bombs the cruiser *Konigsberg* in Bergen during the Norwegian invasion of 1940 – a rare success for a type which was obsolescent by the time it entered service.

In contrast, the Hawker Hurricane proved its value in the Battle of Britain. It attracted naval interest in the Norwegian Campaign in May 1940, when RAF aircraft operated from the carrier *Glorious*. A naval version was developed with arrester hook. From October 1941 they were embarked in MAC ships. Sea Hurricanes never had folding wings and early in 1942 many of them were diverted to land-based service in North Africa, while the Spitfire, with its higher performance, was chosen for further development with the name of Seafire. It was one of the classic aircraft of all time, but it had short range and was too delicate for carrier operation: 'the Seafire, if it was not put down in a three-point attitude fairly gently, would bounce back in the air off its pneumatic tyres and deposit you either into the barrier or over the top of the barrier, which was even worse.'[56] In later versions it was fitted with folding wings in a 'Z' pattern due to the large span. It supported the invasion of North Africa and proved useful during the invasion of Salerno in 1943, when the RAF failed to provide adequate cover.

The use of American carrier aircraft began accidentally when a shipment of ninety-one Grumman Wildcats for France was diverted after that country fell. It was renamed the Martlet in British service and Eric Brown found that it was 'a tough, fiery, beautiful little aeroplane.'[57] It served with Arctic and Mediterranean convoys and in the invasion

The upper hangar deck of *Indomitable* with, to the left, a Seafire with its notoriously narrow undercarriage, lashed to the deck. Albacore torpedo bombers, with folded wings, are being serviced behind, with officers inspecting or directing and ratings at work.

of Madagascar. In all, 1182 of its successor, the Hellcat (initially called the Gannet by the Fleet Air Arm), were sent under lend-lease. It served mainly with the carriers of the British Pacific Fleet. Originally, the Americans regarded the high-performance Chance-Vought Corsair as unsuitable for the carriers, but the Royal Navy found ways to land it on ships.

The British only used small numbers of the dive-bombers – Douglas Dauntless and Curtis Helldiver – but took nearly a thousand Grumman Avengers (originally known as Tarpons). Though designed to launch torpedoes, they were mainly used to drop bombs, including raids on Surabaya, Java, and Palembang, Sumatra, in 1944/5. By the end of the war, American aircraft dominated the decks of the British Pacific Fleet.

The Douglas Aircraft Corporation was founded in California in 1928 and became famous for its pioneering transport aircraft including the DC-3 Dakota, known as the R4D to the navy, and the four-engined DC-4 Skymaster, or R5D, which served as a long-range transport in the Pacific. The Grumman Aircraft Engineering Corporation was founded in 1929 when Roy Grumman, a former navy pilot, left the Loening Corporation with two colleagues. Based on Long Island, they began by making floats for seaplanes. In 1930 they designed the XFF-1, the first naval aircraft with a retractable undercarriage, and by 1935 they had become the main supplier of naval fighters with the F2F biplane.

The car-makers played a full part in aircraft production, though mostly in making components rather than the finished product. Ford's gigantic plant at Willow Run near Detroit did produce B-24 Liberators, some of which would play a vital role in the Battle of the Atlantic, but only after enormous teething troubles. Grumman turned most of the Avenger and Hellcat production over to General Motors, and that was more successful due to effective liaison between the companies. American industry produced more than a third of a million aircraft in 1940–45.[58]

The USN used fewer types of carrier aircraft than the RN, mainly because it had fewer failures and it did not need to convert landplanes or take on foreign imports. Naval orders were not subordinate to the needs of the air force, and once the system was in operation the orders were much larger, so American naval aircraft were mostly of very high quality.

In 1935 Douglas produced the TBD Devastator torpedo bomber, which was unfortunate in its timing, with a maximum speed of only 204 mph. Many were lost at Coral Sea and Midway, some going down with their carriers, and it was soon superseded. The Grumman TBF first flew in August 1941 and was soon named the Avenger in response to the attack on Pearl Harbor. Its debut at Midway was catastrophic, with

The Douglas aircraft factory at El Segundo, California, with SBD Dauntless scout bombers under construction on a 1700ft-long production line. British naval aircraft were never manufactured on anything like this scale.

all aircraft being lost without a single hit, but later it took part in all major Pacific operations to great effect. Nearly ten thousand were built. At the Battle of the Philippine Sea, *Hornet* and *Yorktown*'s Avengers had some success with bombs, but would probably have done even better with torpedoes, now that their problems had been solved.[59]

Alvin Kernan compared the Avenger with its predecessor, the TBD:

Heavy bodied, square folding wings, it still carried three men, but the radio gunner was now down in a little compartment at the rear of the plane. Above him and slightly forward was the gunner's power turret containing a single .50-caliber machine gun. The pilot had two fifties in the wings. There was another seat forward of the turret and just behind the pilot designed for an observer. It was, in fact, immediately filled up with new radio gear for which there was no room elsewhere. The engine was much more powerful than the one in the old TBDs, and the plane could turn up 180 knots with a torpedo or full bomb load ...[60]

During an attack the gunner would swap places with the radioman to use the much-vaunted Norden bombsight. 'The radioman who sat down in the tunnel would get up in the turret while the gunner got down in the tunnel seat, opened the bomb bay doors, turned on the sight in front of him and looked down through the bay to line up on the target far below.'[61]

A handbook quoted the experience of the British over Dunkirk with the turrets of the Boulton-Paul Defiant, which had supposedly shot down large numbers of enemy aircraft – but in fact the Defiant was soon reduced to non-operational roles.[62] The turret guns served mainly as a deterrent and the gunner was useful in alerting the pilot to planes on their tail. Kernan attributed the loss of his squadron commander to the

A Grumman Avenger, still with its wings folded, is prepared for a mission on an *Independence*-class carrier, with other aircraft ranged in the background.

fact that he was flying a single-seater and was too absorbed in directing an attack to see what was behind.[63]

The US Navy was the first service to notice the possibility of dive-bombing. Trials were carried out in 1927 using water-filled bombs against a destroyer and hit rates of 38.3 per cent were achieved – though that did not take account of anti-aircraft fire. The technique was incorporated in Fleet Problems, and rules were drawn up in 1932. Dive-bombing allowed the pilot to aim directly at the target, and to adjust his aim as it manoeuvred. Its high speed made it very difficult for anti-aircraft gunners to get the range. A hit on a carrier deck would not necessarily sink it, but would put it out of operation. Dive-bombing had an accuracy of 27.5 per cent at Midway, and 15 per cent overall, while no ships were sunk during the war by high-level horizontal bombing.[64]

The Douglas Dauntless or SBD was known as 'slow but deadly' to its crews, but proved highly effective. According to 'Dusty' Kleiss:

> It had a complex arrangement of controls, and expensive hydraulics required pilots to be trained to fly it blindfolded. We had to read a half-inch thick booklet covering all the new equipment, and then we had to be blindfolded to identify seventy different controls in instruments.

But once in the air:

> I loved flying the Dauntless ... Although exceedingly noisy and drafty, it soared like a dream. It was wonderfully stable, not like a fighter. ... Soon I mastered it so well that I could fly with both hands free. ... The plane's dive control impressed me most of all. I could shift airplane's dive brakes – known as split flaps – to any degree, and regardless of diving speed or g-force, the brakes stayed in place.[65]

Dauntlesses, including one piloted by Kleiss, made the decisive strike against the Japanese fleet at the Battle of Midway, the turning point of the Pacific campaign, and continued to inflict damage for the rest of the war.

The Curtiss SB2C Helldiver was intended as its successor but did not enter service until late 1943. To Hynes it was 'as showy and phoney as the name, like a beach athlete, all muscle and no guts. It was a long, slab-sided, ugly machine, with a big round tailfin. Unlike most service planes it was entirely electrically operated ... and the circuits were very undependable'.[66] Dusty Kleiss, who tested them after the war, 'deemed it an unworthy successor to our beloved Douglas SBD Dauntless.'[67]

In 1938 the Grumman F4F (later the Wildcat) was having technical difficulties, so they lost a contract for the first monoplane fighter to Brewster, who produced the ill-fated Buffalo. The F4F was ready to enter squadron service by November 1940, in time for the beginning of the Pacific War. The Wildcat's folding wing mechanism later won an award for engineering innovation. According to Hynes:

> … the F4F Wildcat was marvellous – very small – so small that it seemed you could reach out from the cockpit and touch both wing tips), simple, maneuvrable, and delicate responsive to the controls. After the TBM, which needed hydraulic boosters to be flown at all, and the humdrum F6F, the Wildcat was like a toy designed especially to please pilots.[68]

Some aircraft, to misquote Shakespeare, are born great, like the Spitfire. Some, like the Lancaster and the P-51D, achieved greatness due to modifications such as engine changes. But the F6F Grumman Hellcat had greatness thrust upon it. It was not exceptionally fast or manoeuvrable or heavily armed, but it was the star of the Marianas Turkey Shoot and overall it achieved the highest kill to loss rate in history – nineteen to one, with 5156 kills. The aircraft was more than adequate, but the most important factors in its success were the failure of the Japanese to update their fighters, the hurried training of many of their pilots, and the thorough training of their American counterparts.

The Hellcat's engine had 800 additional horsepower and was equipped with a supercharger for high-altitude operation; improved and larger auxiliary fuel tanks gave the plane more range; the cockpit was faired smoothly into the top of the fuselage; nearly twice the Wildcat's ammunition supply was available to the Hellcat's six .50 calibres.[69]

The Vought Corsair used the W-shaped 'inverted gull' wing, which created less drag and allowed a short but very robust undercarriage. Like the Hellcat, it was built round the highly advanced Pratt and Whitney R-2800 radial engine of 2500hp.[70] A fuel tank was needed near the centre of gravity, so the cockpit moved aft, which greatly restricted the forward view. The Corsair had a speed of well over 400mph, which equalled almost any land-based aircraft, but difficulty of deck landing meant that initially it was given to the marines, who operated from shore bases, and to the Royal Navy. They soon discovered that it was possible to land on a carrier using a curving approach. Marc Mitscher began to use marine aircraft on his carriers, and part of his motive was to get the use of the Corsair against the kamikazes off Okinawa.[71]

Battleships and cruisers continued to carry observation aircraft and their pilots were integrated with the life of the ship, as prospective pilots were told:

> Your life aboard ship is very different from life aboard a carrier. Your missions against the enemy and in relation to your own squadron or task force call for an exact knowledge of naval tactics and manoeuvres if your radioed reports and advice are to be of any value. Consequently you must know how large or small formations of large craft are operated and directed. You must be prepared to qualify for deck watch, and you must understand ship and formation functions like all deck officers. You must be, in short, a naval officer in the most complete sense of the word.[72]

Scouting aircraft were designed to be fitted as either landplanes or floatplanes (except the Grumman JF Duck which had a striking protruding float as part of the fuselage), but they were invariably fitted with floats for shipboard use. The Curtiss SOC Seagull was one of the last biplanes in service, retained, like the British Swordfish, because of problems with its successors. The most successful was the Vought OS2U Kingfisher, which first flew in 1937. With a large central and two stabilising floats, it was ungainly in appearance but quite effective.

An OS2U Kingfisher observation aircraft attached to the escort carrier USS *Chenango* in the Pacific in 1944/5.

The Consolidated PBY (later known as the Catalina) was a medium-sized flying boat and one of the first monoplanes to enter naval service, in 1936. Three years later, it flew in an amphibian version, the PBY-5, with a retractable tricycle undercarriage. The wing and engines were raised above the water by means of a pylon which contained a claustrophobic station for the flight engineer. In contrast, the gunners had spacious blisters which offered extensive views. A radio operator completed the basic complement of enlisted men, with three officer pilots. Radar was fitted to the 'black cats' in later years.

From a British point of view, Commander Parry wrote in 1941:

> These PBY aircraft should be of very great assistance to us, but I do not think we should be wise to expect too much. They have a very bad take-off and except in almost perfect weather it may not be possible to take off and land in the hours of darkness. Their performance is nothing outstanding, for example with a 2000lb bomb load they would have a range of 1170 miles, or, under over-loaded conditions, which we might be wise to avoid, 1700 miles.

The RAF's Sunderland, in contrast, could carry a 5000lb load for 1700 miles. Throughout the war, from the sighting by a British Catalina that proved fatal to battleship *Bismarck*, the PBY proved its worth, serving with the US Navy and Coast Guard, the RAF, the Soviet Union and other Allied forces. More than three thousand were built. 'Scouting, anti-submarine patrol, rescue missions, bombing and torpedo attacks were all part of the day's work for the lumbering "Cats".'[73]

Like practically all flying boats, the Catalinas had insufficient speed, armament or armour to cope with enemy fighters, or anti-aircraft fire in daylight, and the lower part of the fuselage was designed for water rather than air operation. The navy coveted Consolidated's other great product, the air force's B-24 Liberator, for its strong armament and especially its long range of nearly three thousand miles, essential in both the main oceans. At first the air force resisted acquisition by the navy, but eventually more than a thousand of them, the PB4Y, were delivered. The eleven-man crew was the largest in any naval aircraft, and included three officer pilots and enlisted air bombers, mechanics, radioman and gunners.

Uniquely, the US Navy continued to use airships for military purposes, aided by the fact that it had the world's only supply of non-inflammable helium gas. It had abandoned the use of rigid airships by 1941, but continued to use non-rigid craft, or 'blimps'. Their shape was maintained by the pressure of the gas so their speed was low, a maximum of 75 mph and more typically, 40–50. Eventually they had 167, the largest such fleet ever assembled. Four bases were established on the East Coast, including Lakehurst, where the world saw the dramatic burning of the hydrogen-filled *Hindenburg* in 1937. There were three more in the Caribbean and three on the West Coast. The craft mounted anti-submarine patrols, but there is no evidence that they had any material effect on the war. Some merchant seamen felt reassured by their presence, others feared they might reveal the presence of a convoy. They also participated in rescue work. A typical ship of the 'K' series was 251ft long with 425,000 cubic feet of gas. It had an officer pilot and navigator, with an enlisted naval aviation pilot, two mechanics, a rigger, a radio operator and a radio technician.[74]

Techniques

Aircraft on the forward end of the flight deck were said to be parked, those on the after end were ranged. A large number might be got ready in preparation for an operation:

> Each aircraft had two men on its chocks and armourers and other types were all hanging on in profusion in case anything went wrong at the last minute. At 0520 the signal was given to start up. The Coffman starters had all been carefully lined up and everyone started … The racket made by forty aircraft all running up to test their engines was indescribable. … As the ship steadied on her course and opened up to 30 knots the affirmative came from the island. The DCLO waved the chocks away from the leading Corsair with his wands. The two ratings of the flight deck party, with the chocks grasped firmly by their lanyards slithered across the deck keeping low to miss the propellers, and gained the security of the walkway.[75]

On the return from an operation, according to the 1942 instructions, the aircraft should join a circuit about a mile from the carriers, one on a left-hand and the other on a right-hand turn. They would land in turn on instructions from the carrier.

In the early 1930s the Royal Navy began to adopt arrester wires to bring landing aircraft to a stop, but only adopted the crash barrier around 1937 – pilots disliked it at first because it reduced the chance of 'bolting' after a failed landing. It was assumed that the aircraft complement was equal to the number that could be accommodated in the hangar – there was a shortage of aircraft in any case, while the peacetime navy preferred more carriers to better use of the old ones. In 1936 American pilots were struck by the sloppiness of pilots' approaches to *Hermes*, but around 1937 the deck landing control officer or batsman was introduced to control that.[76] There were further improvements with the *Illustrious* class.

> The most startling innovation in the ship was the new 'safety barrier' across the flight deck. This was a heavy wire net suspended between two hydraulic arms which could be raised or lowered. It was halfway up the flight-deck abreast the bridge … and it divided the deck into a landing and a parking area. In the past we had only been able to land with a clear deck, so that we could open the throttle and go around again if our arrester hook bounced over the wires. The interval between landings had been conditioned by the time it took to taxi the aircraft on to the forward lift, fold its wings, strike it down into the hangar, and bring the lift up to deck level again.

With practice this could be brought down to two minutes, but with the barrier it could be reduced to ten seconds.[77] Dunstan Hadley described the procedure after landing:

> It reached the bottom with a gentle thud and immediately the hangar party swarmed onto it and surrounded the 'Barra' like a tribe of ants. We began to move backwards off the lift. After a few yards the tail was swung to starboard and we were neatly slotted into place between two other 'Barras'.[78]

The US Navy was quick to realise that efficient plane handling on the flight deck and in the hangar was the key to getting the best out of carriers and aircraft, especially with complements of around a hundred planes which might take an hour to launch at the best of times, steaming into wind and usually away from the desired direction of the fleet. Max Miller described the work of the 'Airedales' or 'sheepdogs':

> These crews … push the planes around. They … release the chocks in front of the wheels. They … bound across the flight deck at each landing to release the landing contraptions while another plane is 'in the groove' speeding in. They … jockey the towing jeeps from this end to that of the flight deck, and who on hands and knees slide behind and around the whizzing propellers. And finally they…, on that wind-whipped flight deck, wear just about anything that will cling to them.[79]

Alvin Kernan described the work:

> My days from before dawn until after dark were spent on the flight deck, wearing a dark blue T-shirt and a canvas helmet dyed the

same colour, buckled tightly under the chin, pushing the planes at a dead run back and forth. When planes were landing, all those on board had to be pushed forward to leave room at the rear of the flight deck. Those for which there was no space were pushed into one of the three elevators and taken down to the hangar deck where other crews picked them up and moved them around the hangar deck. ...[80]

'Winkle' Brown of the Royal Navy described the American method of using a catapult:

... a shuttle ran along a slot in the deck for-ard. At the after end of the slot was a hold-back hook. The plane simply taxied over the slot, its belly fixed loosely to the shuttle by a strop, its tail to the hold-back which incorporated a breaking ring in it fixed to break at a certain pressure ... Readying the machine certainly took much less time than with the British catapult.[81]

Take-off could be nerve-racking, according to Kernan: 'Torpedo planes always sank below the deck when fired from the catapult, and looking from the backward-facing turret, I could see the huge black deck rise above us and feel the tug of the waves below. But the engine at full power pulled us up and away.'[82] In fact, his plane did have an accident when a retaining ring snapped and it fell into the water, to be rescued by a destroyer.[83]

The role of the American landing signal officer, or LSO, was described by Max Miller. A trained pilot, he stood on a 'small grilled platform' just off the after part of the flight deck to guide the pilots in, but first he had to know that the deck ahead was clear, though his eyes were concentrated on an incoming plane. An enlisted talker would intone, 'Four-foul-foul', until the space was cleared of planes that had landed already. He also had to take account of up to three squadrons landing at once, and to 'direct the timing between planes, and to see to it that the flight deck doesn't become one beautiful mess of tangled-up propellers.' As the plane approached, the LSO used his coloured paddles to correct for height and speed, and when he was about to complete the operation, he pulled one across this throat to signal 'cut'. Only the 'wave off', used when a landing seemed likely to end in disaster, was compulsory.[84]

There were major differences with British procedure, not just because their operations tended to be less intense with smaller air groups. According to Jim Spencer:

Firstly, the US Navy aimed for a level approach to the deck, not a descending one. Secondly, the US Navy signals for height correction were reversed. The Royal Navy signals were *orders* which the pilot had to obey. Bats up, increase height. Bats down, reduce height. The US navy signals were advice to the pilot. Bats up, you are too high. Bats down, you are too low. This conflict was the reason why throughout our training deck landing instruction had been by our own folk.[85]

Edward Stafford described landing operations as seem from a plane-guard destroyer escort:

> … the returning planes swept in low over the carriers, from stern to bow, to land. They roared overhead in pairs or fours stepped back

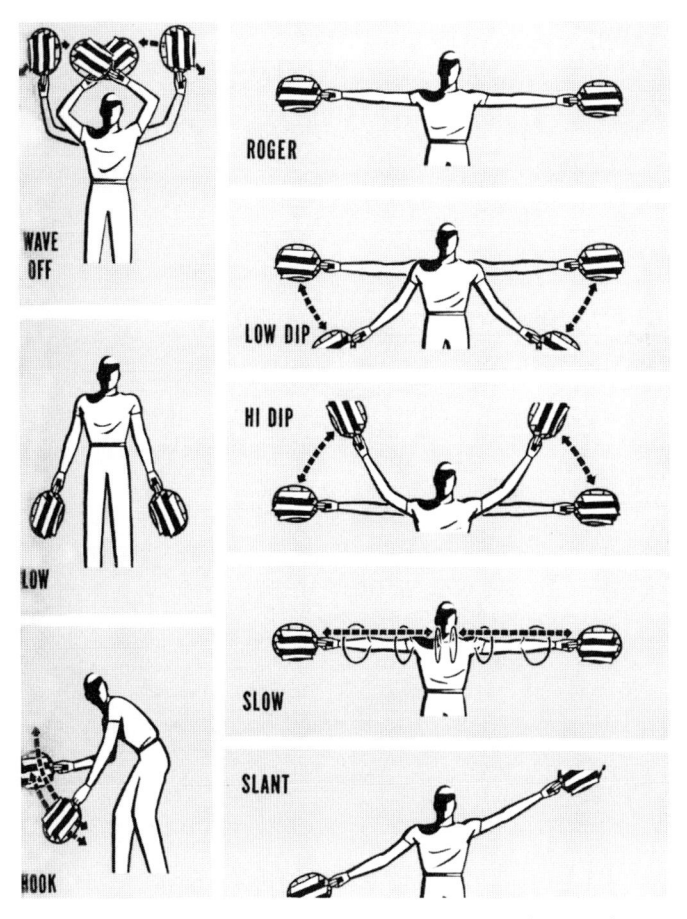

Some of the signals used by American LSOs to guide aircraft onto carrier decks.

in right echelons. At the carrier bow the lead plane flipped into a steep left bank, ... and levelled out downwind, abeam of the ship on an opposite course. Three seconds later the next plane in the echelon duplicated the maneuver, and three seconds later the next and the next until all four were in the landing pattern. Then one at a time they banked and came snarling up the carrier wake, flaps full down, wheels and hooks dangling, seeming to hang on their whirling props, wings dipping slightly, noses high, responding to the precisely moving paddles of the Landing Signal Officer on his little platform on the port quarter of the desk. As the LSO chopped his right paddle down across his body to the left, the pilot cut throttle, the roar of the engine changed to a popping sputter, and the plane bounced slightly then jerked to a stop as the tail hook caught the cross-deck wire of the arresting gear.[86]

Unlike his British equivalent, a US Navy pilot was expected to do his own navigation, using the ingenious but fallible plotting board which was prepared in advance of the flight and was pulled out from under the instrument panel. Jim Spencer was surprised by this:

The board was made of clear transparent plastic and you could write on it with crayons. Beneath the transparent surface, and visible

An SBD pilot uses his plotting board to navigate, while still flying the aircraft. It was carefully prepared before the flight and could slide under the instrument panel when not in use.

through it, was a rotatable disc marked out in a rectangular grid pattern. This one set to a compass bearing and then drew courses, wind directions and ship movements freehand on the transparent top of the board using the grid underneath as a guide. All the while, of course, you were flying the aircraft with your spare hand …[87]

The enlisted men in the back seats were not expected to help with this. A radio system was also used to guide pilots back to their aircraft carrier:

> The second device was what was called ZB. The 360 degree sector around the ship was divided into pie-shaped segments, and a different letter was sent out by radio in Morse code in each segment. For instance, from dead north to 015 degrees might be AA today. Pilots were issued with a little wheel which would show which sectors were for the day, and if a pilot tuned in ZB, got a Morse code FF, he could determine where the ship was. We always tuned in our ZB coming home from flights to make sure we were coming in the right sector.[88]

Tactics

The fighter direction room of a British aircraft carrier tended to follow RAF practice as established in the Battle of Britain, using a filter officer to assess information from radar and lookouts. It was intended 'that constant control of the carrier's own fighters or those of other carriers in company and shore-based fighters can be directed against enemy aircraft, which are usually detected by Radar or, to a lesser degree, by visual methods.' The organisation, it was stated in 1943, 'was developing to include the direction of aircraft other than fighters and against surface as well as airborne targets'. Already the American term 'action information organisation' was beginning to be used.

In 1942 the Admiralty issued instructions for formation attack, though it only catered for a force of one or two carriers. The aircraft would be ranged on the flight deck in sub-flights of three. The leader would take off first, followed by numbers two and three, who would turn to port or starboard to avoid his slipstream. Each group would head slowly towards the target, allowing time for the others to catch up. At night, a flame float should be dropped in the sea about ten miles away and aircraft would circle it to await the rest.

A formation of Barracudas, Tarpons (Avengers) or Helldivers would fly towards the enemy, accompanied by fighters, which would not form a close escort as that would divide it into small units. Instead, the main escort, about two-thirds of the force, would fly 1000 to 3000ft above and up-sun, with the top cover above and held in reserve in the event of an attack. However, the slower Swordfish and Albacore could not be escorted in this way but should be covered by at least sixteen aircraft patrolling 2000 to 6000ft above.

The attacking formation might fly just above the sea or the cloud to protect it from attack from below. Once under attack, a bomber would use its all-round view and its manoeuvrability to protect itself. The leader in the centre would normally fly an undulating course with steep dives and climbs, but still heading in the direction of the target. The outer aircraft would corkscrew, executing violent turns and climbs to about 30 degrees on either side of the course – this had been found effective by RAF heavy bombers and would be even more so in a manoeuvrable Swordfish or Albacore. Crews were warned that they must maintain the objective, shooting down enemy aircraft was secondary, and in any case the gun armament of a naval bomber was feeble. An aircraft which got separated would stay clear and not launch a solitary attack, which might warn the enemy. Slow speed might even be an advantage as a high-performance fighter would quickly pass by, and he had only ammunition for about fifteen seconds.

Fighters generally flew in fours, which might split easily into the basic unit of two. The standard formation had the leader of each pair in the centre with the wingmen on either side and the whole angled downwards on the side of the sun – not unlike the RAF's 'finger four'. When action was imminent, a squadron might deploy in a single line abreast, which had been 'used with great success both over France and in the Western Desert'. Weaving as used by the US Navy was not favoured: 'Mass weaving leads to pilots allowing their attention to be taken up with formation keeping rather than keeping a good look-out.'

Attacking an enemy formation, pilots were advised not to be tempted to go for the leader in the middle, but for the aircraft on the flanks. Head-on attack was likely to be successful, though it was difficult to get a good intercept. Attack Sugar was from astern and the attackers made a curved approach to get on the tail of the enemy. In Attack Queenie they came from the quarter, and from both sides in Double Queenie.

In April 1945 the Admiralty issued 'Air Attack Instructions', presumably intended for the Pacific Fleet and largely based on American experience – attacks by torpedo and dive-bombers should be well co-ordinated, and it was best to hit a carrier first with the dive-bombers to put the flight deck out of action. Torpedo bombers should not attack a well-defended target without the support of dive-bombers. The attack would be led by the senior squadron commander of the flagship, who had been briefed by the admiral. In the case of multiple targets there would be an air co-ordinator, preferably in a two-seater, who would remain independent of the action. Torpedo and bomber aircraft should be escorted by fighters and anti-flak aircraft, which would attack escorting destroyers with rockets and cannon, supplemented by dive-bombers if necessary. Torpedo bombers should attack, one flight of six followed by another. They should start with a shallow approach dive, a steeper attacking dive and then the aiming run. They should only launch between 30 and 90 degrees on a ship on a steady course, 0 to 60 degrees if it was altering course away from the attackers, and 75 to 135 degrees if altering towards – several types of director were available to calculate the aim-off. In a direct dive attack, all twelve aircraft would launch together to produce the greatest concentration. The war would end three months after these instructions were issued, so there was no opportunity to test them, but they show how far the Fleet Air Arm had developed in six years of war.

During the defensive phase of the Pacific War, US Navy fighters used the Thach Weave to deal with the superior manoeuvrability of the Japanese Zero. John S Thach described the procedure:

> Assuming those two sections were cruising in the same direction, they would have to be separated by a standard distance equal to the diameter of the tightest circle the aircraft can make. … the two planes on the right watched over the tails of the two planes on the left and vice versa. We wouldn't use any signals; we would have to wait until an enemy plane was almost within lethal firing range of one section, and then the other section would make a sharp turn toward the one being attacked. That was the signal that somebody was within firing range on his tail. So, if the section being attacked is the one on the left, he turns right, throwing the enemy's lead off. If the enemy tries to follow on around, to get back his aim, it brings him right in the sights of the right-hand section of aircraft, which should have a good shot at him – either head on, if he continues to follow his target, or a good side approach, if he pulls out.[89]

Later in the war, David S McCampbell thought that the weave was no longer necessary with the superior performance of the Hellcat, but US Navy pilots were advised never to get into a dogfight with a Zero.

Offensively, fighters flew in pairs, with the wingman behind and below and on one side of the leader. The pilot on the left searched 180 degrees to the right and vice versa, so that the whole sky was covered, and they did not lose sight of one another. When attacking a single aircraft, they tried to bracket it with one on each side, and one might make a diversionary attack. Four types of attack were recognised.

The side approach needed carefully timed S-turns to get in the right firing position. The high side attack was from an angle of 40 degrees above the target, the flat side within about 10 degrees above or below, and the low side about 20 degrees below. The pilot was expected to pass underneath and get into position for a second attack, if the first one was not successful. The overhead attack began at least 2000ft above the target and 3000ft ahead. The approach was at least 60 degrees, going down to 45 degrees during the attack. It needed practice but would surprise the enemy, whose gunners would be forced to fire upwards. The head-on approach was seldom selected as the range changed rapidly, making aiming difficult, and a second attack impossible, The attack from the stern was the simplest, and was normally used against fighters; it was less successful against bombers because of the dangers from a tail gunner.

The US Navy was well aware that in horizontal bombing, three factors – the speed of the aircraft, gravity and the air resistance of the bomb – had to be taken into account, which made aiming difficult. Moreover, it was impossible to predict the movement of the ship so it was hardly ever successful. In a vertical dive, on the other hand, all three factors were working in the same direction and the aircraft itself could be aimed at the target. The bomb, however, would enter a trajectory after release so it was essential to bring the target under the nose of the aircraft. In a shallow dive it was more difficult to estimate the error in range, in a steep dive, deflection or side to side movement was more difficult to calculate, so as a compromise 65 degrees was recommended. The pilot had to allow for the wind, which would not only affect the aircraft during the dive, but the bomb after its release. He had to estimate the movement of the ship, both forward and in evasive manoeuvres, but dive-bombing proved very effective.

In the crucial Battle of Midway, Dusty Kleiss watched as the first three pilots missed. The next was more successful: 'I watched as Gallagher's bombs smashed onto the aft section of the *Kaga*'s flight deck, just forward of the rear elevator. His 500-pounder landed atop a lone Zero, smashing it to smithereens. ... the aft part of the ship was engulfed in a huge mass of flames.' Then it was Kleiss's turn:

> My plane rolled into a dive and in a few seconds all I could see was the enormous blue ocean coming at me, with the smoking enemy carrier in the middle of it. ... Although I had never targeted a moving ship under combat conditions ... I somehow managed

to deduce *Kaga*'s speed perfectly … I wanted to assure myself of a hit, so I released my bombs when the altimeter read 2000 feet … I pulled sharply on the stick. I felt the awful gut-crushing sensation of 9 Gs squeezing my body. …My 500-pounder slammed into *Kaga*'s forward elevator, …. penetrated *Kaga*'s upper hangar and exploded below the flight deck. My pair of incendiary bombs went in too, igniting fuelled and armed aircraft spotted below.[90]

Skip bombing was another technique, first tried in the Battle of the Bismarck Sea in March 1943: 'the plane to approach at masthead height, drop its bombs and be clear of the target before the five-second delay expired; the bomb, by exploding in the water alongside the ship, to inflict great damage by its mining effect.' Eighteen hits were scored out of thirty-five.

The early model of the Mark 13 wet-heater airborne torpedo had to be dropped at a height of 50ft and speed of 110 knots, which may have contributed to its failure at Midway. It was much improved by 1944 when it was used in attacks on Truk, with a ring tail on stern to reduce pitch and yaw, and a 'pickle barrel' drag ring on nose to decrease impact shock. Its optimum launch was at 260 knots and 800ft, when the aircraft was far less vulnerable to AA fire. It would sink no deeper than 50ft; depth settings could be as little as 5ft: 92 per cent of them ran 'hot straight and normal'. The attacker would dive from cloud from 5000–7000 altitude and glide at 20 to 40 degrees, at 300 knots, levelling off at 260 knots for the release. The best attack was on the beam, aft of that and it might not catch up with the ship. Visual ranging was the most difficult problem: it needed a seaman's eye, but the ideal was about 1400yds. Speed was estimated from the bow wave and the known characteristics of the ship type. Using standard tables, the pilot should allow 1.15 ship lengths for a vessel of 600ft doing 20 knots, and two ship lengths for a similar one at 30 knots. A curved wake indicated a turn, which might decrease speed by about 12 knots in a large ship. Eventually airborne torpedoes had a success rate of nearly 40 per cent.[91]

The US navy went to some trouble to rescue aircrews from the sea. At the first level was the plane-guard destroyer:

> *Dale*'s job was to rush in and pick up survivors. The plane usually floated long enough for the pilot and crew to get out … When we rescued a pilot and crew, we would take them below for a cup of hot coffee and some medicinal brandy. Then, while they were showering, the crew would clean and press their clothes.[92]

Flying boats, or 'Dumbos', were used extensively for rescue work, though it was often difficult to land in rough seas. The PBY Catalina was the most common.

Submarine 'lifeguarding' began with the Gilbert Islands campaign in 1943, when Admiral Pownall suggested that the presence of submarines near the action 'would boost the morale of the aviators.' After that they were in the vicinity of all the Pacific invasions, and they also rescued many army flyers, including Superfortress crews. In all eighty-six submarines rescued 504 flyers, including thirty-one by *Tigrone* in one voyage.[93] Submariners welcomed the 'Zoomies', but it was not always possible to return them immediately to their ships, so they often put them to work. Future president George Bush was rescued by *Finback* in 1944, along with two other officers and two enlisted men. The officers stood night watches, and the boat attacked a convoy and was depth-charged before getting back to Pearl Harbor.[94]

Shore bases

Though the Fleet Air Arm was only intended to operate from ships and aircraft carriers, it needed shore bases for training, maintenance and aircraft storage. Carriers landed their aircraft while in port in order that training could continue, so airfields near the main fleet bases were essential. The RAF handed over five airfields in 1939, none of them completely suitable and the navy had to build its own, its biggest civil engineering project of the war. Each had four runways instead of the RAF's three, because Fleet Air Arm pilots were not used to crosswinds. They were commissioned as ships, nearly all with bird names.

At home, Arbroath (HMS *Condor*) was used for training observers, Crail (*Jackdaw*) for torpedo bombers, and Yeovilton (*Heron*) for fighters. Carriers in the Forth were supported by the base at Donibristle (*Merlin*), off Portsmouth by Lee-on-Solent (*Daedalus*), at Scapa Flow by Hatston (*Sparrowhawk*) and Twatt (*Tern*). In the Clyde, where many ships were based and carrier pilots were trained in deck landing, Machrihanish, 'the uniquely desolate station' on the remote Kintyre peninsula was used.[95] Overseas, the Mediterranean Fleet was supported by North Front at Gibraltar, Hal Far on Malta and Dekheila near Alexandria. Piarco or HMS *Goshawk* on Trinidad was for training observers, and *Saker* in Maine was formally the base for activities in the USA. The Eastern Fleet used Colombo Racecourse in modern Sri Lanka, and Australian bases.

In 1920 the United States Navy had only six fully-fledged air bases in the continental USA, and the army tried unsuccessfully to take control of them – the navy had to use reserve bases for the storage of its aircraft.[96] The oldest was Pensacola, a naval base since 1825 and a naval air station since 1914, known as the 'Annapolis of the Air' (and Jim Spencer remarked that there was no 'Dartmouth of the Air'). Situated on the Gulf of Mexico, the main base was known as Chevalier Field and trained patrol crews. It had six auxiliary stations training in fighters, dive-bombers, formation flying, torpedo bombers and bombers. By 1942, half of naval pilots had their intermediate training there.

In 1938 the Hepburn Board allowed the expansion of eleven existing bases and the setting up of new ones, including Quonsett, Jacksonville and Corpus Christi at home, and Midway, Wake and Guam which would feature in the coming war, but progress was slow and most were barely ready when the country went to war.[97]

Jacksonville, on the Atlantic coast of Florida, was regarded as the postgraduate school of naval aviation, training combat crews in patrol flying boats, as well as technicians and air gunners. Corpus Christi was the world's biggest naval air training centre – situated on a bay of that name in the Gulf of Mexico, it spanned three counties, covered 20,000 acres and had 997 hangars and other buildings. It was built in an area of 'heavy thickets, mesquite brush typical of the southwest, ebony and scrub oak', with sand dunes that had to be levelled. It handled the rest of the intermediate trainees. It too had six auxiliary stations with different tasks. Many more stations were set up – more than forty naval and marine air bases and facilities and seaplane stations in 1942 alone.

Air bases were never more important than in the Pacific War. The Japanese failure to devastate Ford Island during the Pearl Harbor raid allowed its revival. The possession of Henderson Field was the motivation for the Guadalcanal campaign and the numerous naval battles associated with it. Bloody battles in Saipan, Tinian and Iwo Jima were about providing bases to bomb Japan. The taking and construction of air bases was perhaps the most important single task of the Seabees. They built numerous airfields, known as Acorns, defined as:

> ... a self-sustaining unit, packaged and equipped to follow landing forces ashore for the express purpose of establishing an advanced airfield within the shortest possible time. The specific duties of an Acorn are to utilize the trained personnel of which is composed in maintaining the runways, hangars, and all other allied airfield facilities in operating condition. The Acorn operates the control tower, field lighting, aerological unit, transportation pool, communications and medical facilities.

It would operate in conjunction with a Seabee unit in setting the base up, and it would withdraw leaving only a maintenance party.

A CASU, or carrier air service unit, included the personnel for such a base; if it was for flying boats it was a Patsu, or patrol support unit: 'A CASU has many jobs. Its mechanics repair and do minor overhaul on the squadron's planes. Its men rearm the planes, help them taxi around parking strips, and fix their radios. CASUs are responsible for berthing, messing and entertaining pilots and ground personnel of squadrons.' In 1945 they were re-named combat aircraft service units to cover a wider variety of functions.

* * *

Naval aviation followed the usual trajectory – an idea originated by the British was taken up by the Americans and developed much further. The timing was different in this case: the main American development started well before the war, and it was far more extensive than in other cases. It was a pattern which would continue to repeat after the war; the British developed the steam catapult, the mirror landing aid and the angled deck. They never found the resources to deploy the fully angled deck, except on the old wartime *Victorious*, whereas it became standard on numerous American ships.

To the battleship man Ted Mason, 'the bulky carriers were clumsy floating airfields of a surpassing ugliness, not to be remotely compared to the graceful lines of a real fighting ship with a fourteen- or sixteen-inch main battery.' The sailors on these outlandish 'birdfarms' were the 'brown-shoe navy', and were considered little better than landlubbers[98] – otherwise the 'Hooligan navy'.[99] Max Miller suggested that the aircraft carrier was a temporary aberration which would disappear as the range of aircraft increased: 'It may be that carriers have served their purpose with this immediate era … Planes may be so big then, and so fast, and with such great ranges, that these subsidiary landing fields, the carriers, may be inessential.'[100] But aircraft carriers, as well as playing a decisive role in the Battle of the Atlantic, were perhaps the most important single element in winning the Pacific War. They were here to stay and are still regarded as the main element of a sophisticated naval power.

13
Submarines

MANY PEOPLE had dreamed of underwater vessels over the centuries, and a few had attempted to build them, especially Americans. During the War of Independence, David Bushnell designed *Turtle*, manually powered by a screw with a crew of one, which failed to drill holes in the hull of British ships in New York harbour. Early in the next century, Robert Fulton of Pennsylvania offered his design to the French and then the British. Lord St Vincent commented that it was foolish 'to encourage a mode of warfare which those that command the sea did not want, and which if successful, would deprive them of it.' During the Civil War, the Confederate engineer Horace L Hunley built a craft which bore his name and was powered by eight men operating a crank. It sank twice and was raised before its final plunge after ramming and sinking USS *Housatonic* in Charleston Harbour – the first submarine success.

John Holland, an Irish-American schoolteacher, built *Fenian Ram*, which was intended to challenge the supremacy of the Royal Navy. The breakthrough came with the development of the electric motor and torpedo, both used in Holland's later models. In 1900 he sold his patents to the Electric Boat Company of Groton, which remained the main private builder of American submarines during the Second World War, but in a supreme irony they also licensed the British to build them, and the first Royal Navy submarine was known as *Holland No. 1*. And when the Germans began to build submarines in 1906, Holland may have tried to warn the British of the danger.

The Germans adopted the policy of unrestricted submarine warfare, sinking merchant vessels on sight, almost defeating the British and bringing America into the war in 1917. In the Washington Conference of 1921/2 it was proposed that 'the prohibition of the use of submarines as commerce destroyers shall be universally accepted as part of the law of nations.'[1] But that was not agreed and the submarine remained a threat, especially to the stronger navies and the larger merchant fleets.

Until the Germans deployed the snorkel near the end of the war, 'submarines' were really submersibles, which only went underwater when necessary, for their performance there was far poorer. The diesel engines used on the surface consumed vast quantities of air and only electric motors could be used underwater. Speed was much reduced, a maximum of of 15.25 knots on the surface and 9 knots underwater for a British 'T' class, and 20.25 knots and 8.75 knots for an American *Gato* class. But full speed underwater would soon drain the batteries.

Edward Young described the usual structure: 'the pressure hull was roughly the shape of a long cigar, circular in section and tapering slightly towards each end … the lower half was occupied by trimming tanks, fuel tanks, electric batteries and so on.' He also described the technique of diving:

> A submarine dives by allowing her main ballast tanks to fill with water … These tanks are outside the pressure-hull. On the surface they are full of air; when the air is allowed to escape, through vents at the top of the tanks, the sea comes in through holes at the bottom, and the submarine loses buoyancy and dives. Under water the ship is controlled by internal trimming tanks and hydroplanes … external fins which can be tilted from the control-room, one pair for'ard and one pair aft; they are really horizontal rudders.[2]

The boats

The Germans were far less dependent than Britain on seaborne supplies, so the submarine was never likely to be a war-winning weapon for the British. After the First World War they tried very hard to outlaw it, or to ban its use against merchant ships. Having failed in that, they built their own submarines to serve almost every function except what they were best at. They had already tried submersible fleet destroyers with the 'K' class, which suffered heavy accidental losses because of their low profile and the holes which their steam engines made necessary, and the 'R' class, which was designed as an anti-submarine submarine with enormous battery power, but was very wet on the surface, and difficult to steer.[3] They built a submarine cruiser, the enormous *X1*, monitors, and even a submarine aircraft carrier, *M2*. None of this survived by 1939 and the submarine remained a vessel which could fire a torpedo without warning.

Between the wars, six torpedoes was considered the minimum bow salvo, and six tubes were therefore fitted in all submarines built in that period. Stern tubes were out of favour for a time, but revived with the 'T' class of 1939, which was also intended to have as many bow tubes as possible, to fire large salvoes against fast-moving and manoeuvrable warships rather than slow merchantmen. The standard six were supplemented by four external tubes (with no reloads) so that ten could be fired against a 'Very Important Target' – but only three such salvoes were fired during the war, plus ten of eight torpedoes each. The war-built 'U'-class coastal submarines had four internal and two external bow tubes. Torpedoes could be fired straight ahead, or angled at 90 degrees on either side, a facility which was hardly ever used. Aiming was by means of the ISWAS, a simple calculating machine set on the relative bearing ring of the periscope, but enemy course and speed had to be estimated and plotted. British submariners looked with envy at the American torpedo data computer. Until late 1940 a salvo was fired at intervals with the submarine on a steady course. After that it became more common to aim each torpedo individually.[4]

The British submarine's most important service was off the enemy-held coast of Europe, and especially Norway, in special operations and in the Mediterranean, where they tended to mount short-range patrols with little time out of the danger area. Between 15 May and 30 August 1943:

> *Safari* had sailed some 31,312 nautical miles, had spent 259 days at sea with 139 of these dived. We had 158 actions against German and Italian shipping, 30 of these by torpedo attack and 28 by gun action. We had sunk a definite 34 ships and probably 4 more by fire. We had beached a further 3 ships. … We had 129 depth charges dropped against us.[5]

Their greatest success was in disrupting supplies to Rommel's army in North Africa and contributing to Montgomery's victory at Alamein in 1942. From 1943 they were sent increasingly to the Indian Ocean and the Pacific, though by the time they arrived there American submarines had already eliminated most of the targets and they saw little service.

'H'-class boats survived from the First World War and were mainly used for training or as 'clockwork mice' for anti-submarine practice. New building revived in 1924, with several variants of the 'O'-class, long-range 'patrol' submarines for service in the Far East; they were clumsy and noisy with over-complicated electrical systems, and their external fuel tanks leaked. They were succeeded on the building slips by the 'P'-, 'R'- and River-class fleet submarines which were no more successful. Out of twenty-two built, eight were sunk in the first two years of the war, and six more by 1945.

According to Ben Bryant, 'The "S" class was a return to sanity after the flights of fancy which resulted in the clumsy great "O" and "P" class and the long, fast but weak hulled "River" class.'[6] The 'S' class of medium patrol boats began with *Swordfish*, which was designed in 1929. Expectations were reduced and the emphasis was now on reliability rather than high performance. In 1935 the larger 'T' class was ordered, 1090 tons standard rather than 640, and with an exceptionally strong torpedo armament. According to Sir Stanley Goodall:

> In principle the 'T' class followed along lines which many years of experience had shown to be satisfactory. Their displacement was governed by the requirement to provide the desired number of submarines within the overall tonnage allowed by the International Treaties in force at the time. They were of the saddle tank design. Oil fuel was stowed inside the pressure hull in order to minimise the risk of leakage to the surface by depth charge attack, and the pressure hull itself was more robust relatively than that of preceding submarines. In addition to the usual six torpedo tubes inside the hull, four external tubes were fitted. Fuel, stores and water were provided for a 42-day period.[7]

The smaller 'U' class was originally conceived in 1936 to replace the old 'H' class for training in anti-submarine operations, but they soon took on a role in short-range operations in European waters. According to Goodall, 'When the war started it was intended to settle down to a steady programme of "Ts" and "Us", but the reintroduction of the "S" class spoiled this plan'.[8]

British submarines were not spectacular in performance, but in general they carried out the functions allotted to them, according to one commander:

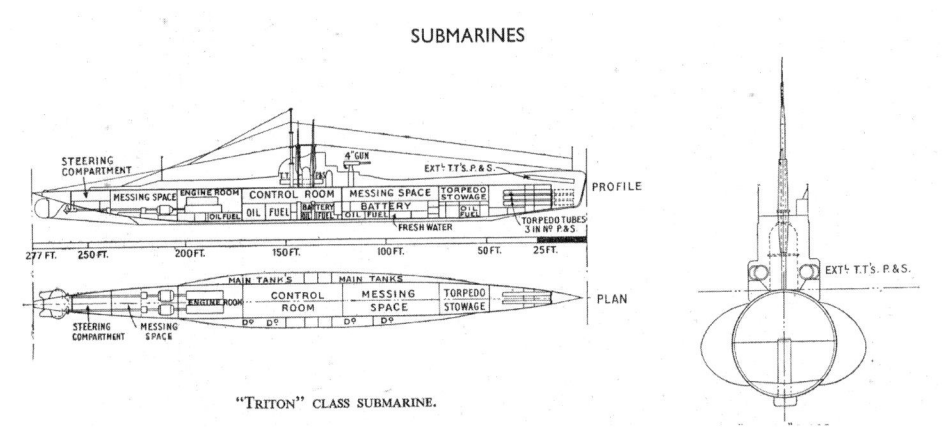

The layout of the British 'T'-class submarine. In contrast to American boats, it is conned from the control room inside the main pressure hull.

Our submarines … were designed for world-wide operations and they did, in fact, operate from the arctic to the equator. Their principal duty was offensive patrol, and for that purpose they had to operate for weeks and months on end completely unsupported and frequently, if not usually, close to the enemy's coast. For that purpose, large battery power and long diving time were absolutely essential.[9]

An entirely new design, the 'A' class, was building at the end of the war for service in the Pacific but none of them saw active service before the Japanese surrender.

British submarines were numbered rather than named after the start of the war, apparently for security reasons, but in December 1942 Churchill was 'grieved to see our submarines described as P212 etc … Not even to give them names if derogatory to their devotion and sacrifice'. The names were to be chosen by the crews, but those of the 'S', 'T' and 'U' classes had to have names with these initials, and the most apt ones had already been taken up by destroyers. Churchill objected to 'Truculent' and 'Trespasser', but supported 'Tutankhamen', while names like *Trenchant* and *Taciturn* were eventually adopted.[10]

In January 1942, after Italian 'human torpedoes' severely damaged the battleships *Queen Elizabeth* and *Valiant*, Churchill decreed, 'Please report what is being done to emulate the exploits of the Italians and Alexandria Harbour and similar methods of this kind.' Midget submarines were already under development, but progress was too slow, so a design was adapted from the standard 21in torpedo with two men sitting astride it, number one operating the controls and number two to cut through enemy nets and operate the detachable warhead. They were encased in rubber suits with a visor in front and equipped with an oxygen breathing apparatus, but it was a highly dangerous occupation, with many men injured in training. Nevertheless, they made an attempt on the battleship *Tirpitz* in the autumn of 1942, with the 'chariots' being lashed to a Norwegian fishing boat captained by the legendary Leif Larsen. The chariots broke loose, the attempt failed and their crews, apart from one man who was wounded and killed by the Germans, escaped to Sweden.

By this time the first midget submarine, or X-craft, was ready. *X-3* (so named because the earlier X numbers had been accounted for) was just over 50ft long, but only half that space was available for the crew, who could not stand up in 5ft of headroom. In the bow was the battery compartment and storeroom, followed by the W and D (wet and dry) compartment which could be flooded to let a diver out; then the main compartment containing the lower end of the periscope, the steering

Views of an X-craft midget submarine. The centre picture looking aft shows the coxswain steering, the captain behind him and the first lieutenant to the rear, in the extremely cramped space.

controls and chart table. It was crewed by two officers, an engine room artificer and a diver. It could make 6 knots and had two charges, known as side cargoes, which could be dropped in shallow water under a target.

In September 1943 six X-craft were towed a thousand miles from the Firth of Clyde to Norway. Only three entered Altenfjord and two dropped their side cargoes under *Tirpitz*, making her unserviceable until she was finally sunk by RAF bombing. Attacks were also made in Bergen harbour, and two X-craft served as markers for the invasion of Normandy. The depot ship *Bonaventure* took a squadron to the Pacific but operations were vetoed by the Americans, who apparently associated them with suicide missions, which they discouraged. Eventually, in July 1945 they were allowed to go into Singapore Harbour to cut the submarine cables and they took the opportunity to attack a cruiser.

The silent service

The submarine was indeed a potential war-winning weapon for the Americans, because Japan was as vulnerable as Britain to attacks on its shipping, though Mahan had discounted such a *guerre de course* as a diversion from the main task of defeating the enemy battlefleet, and the Americans discovered it almost by accident.

At first, the Americans had favoured good underwater performance for their submarines, but during the First World War they came to appreciate the qualities of the German U-boats, with a hull designed for surface operation and submersible when necessary. By the 1920s, they were also looking at boats capable of operating in the vast distances of the Pacific, so they needed to be large. They began to build 'fleet' submarines, defined in 1930 as advanced scouts for the battlefleet while being capable of conducting independent action when required, as well as operating tactically with the battlefleet, rather like the abortive British fleet submarines.

During the 1920s, the US Navy built nine ships of the 'V' classes, ranging from the huge *Argonaut* minelayer of nearly 3000 tons, to the 1120 tons of the *Cachalot* class, limited by the London Treaty. But *Dolphin*, 1688 tons, ordered in 1931 and launched the following year, set the pattern for the future. Rather than high speed she relied on long range of up to twelve thousand miles and endurance for sixty to ninety days, with a good torpedo armament and improved habitability. Boats were ordered in small groups over the next few years, aided by funds from the Industrial Recovery Act, and with incremental improvements. Welding began to be used increasingly, despite the scepticism of some shipbuilders, aiding watertightness, and one observer commented, 'every riveted joint popped, whereas the welded ones just bent like a tin can.' The first version of the torpedo data computer was added in 1934, and air conditioning came in with the *Plunger* class launched in 1936/7. After a conference of submarine officers in 1937, more torpedo tubes were added to make six in the bows and four astern, and a 5in deck gun was added. Admiral Thomas C Hart of the General Board insisted on building two small boats of 825 tons for coastal work and training, but these were the last small submarines to be built for the US Navy. Otherwise, development culminated in the *Gato* class ordered in fiscal year 1941. With the Pearl Harbor attack, design was frozen for mass production, but the type was more than adequate for the tasks in the Pacific.

After a period using letters and numbers, American submarines were again named after 'denizens of the deep', which led to some problems for Lieutenant William Calkins, who was responsible for naming them. With nearly five hundred in service, 'The reasonable names like *Trout*, *Bass*, *Salmon*, and *Shark* were used up long before I appeared. I was reduced to scrabbling around for names like *Sphinx*, *Irex*, *Mero*, and *Sirago*.' He rejected *Big-Eyed Scad* but was forced to use several synonyms, eg *Tiburon* for *Shark* and *Wahoo* for *Ono*.[11]

Seventy-seven boats of the *Gato* class entered the navy, followed by 129 of the *Balao* class and twenty-five of the *Tench* class, with

A *Gato*-class submarine showing the bow designed for surface operation and the prominent conning tower amidships. Her large size is indicated by the crew figures on deck.

incremental improvements, including increased operating depth. They would dominate the American force by the end of the war. As designed, the *Gato* class was 311ft 9in long and 27ft 3in broad, with a standard surface displacement of 1526 tons and 2424 tons submerged. Its surface speed was 20.25 knots, with a maximum of 8.75 knots under water; but to operate underwater for forty-eight hours it could only do 2 knots. It had a range of eleven thousand miles travelling at 10 knots on the surface, and an endurance of seventy-five days.[12]

Externally, the boat had a sharp, raked bow for meeting the sea, and a flat, latticed teakwood deck reaching almost to the stern. The bridge structure was about two-fifths of the way along the length, and was originally streamlined to aid underwater speed. It was cut down in wartime to reduce the silhouette. The ballast tanks were arranged round the cylindrical pressure hull, a double hull type, not blisters as with British saddle tank. The bow planes could be folded up when not needed. The stern planes were much lower down aft of the propellers.

Inside the bows were the torpedo tubes, described officially as having 'a fairly close resemblance to a large naval gun', but the projectile, the torpedo, was self-propelling: 'The tube supplies only the initial impetus or "start" for the torpedo.' This impetus was provided by compressed air. After firing, the tube was filled with water to maintain the trim of the submarine. Aft of that, stretching from frame 16 to 35, was the first of eight watertight compartments, the forward torpedo room which contained the six reloads, plus berths and lockers for up to fifteen men, and an escape trunk. Next, from frame 35 to 47, came the forward battery compartment, named for what was below the platform deck. Above, it contained officers' quarters, the first area on the platform deck which stretched through several compartments for nearly a third of the total length. This included the captain's cabin: 'Aside from his bunk, which was full length and looked comfortable, the room consisted of only of a space about four feet by five feet, with a fold-down desk and a fold-up wash basin. Both could not be used at the same time.'[13] The area also contained the wardroom, with its table and chairs, and two bunks, which were not spacious: 'I'm six feet four in my bare feet – bunks being normally six feet two to six feet four in the navy – I've always been cramped in a bunk onboard a ship.' There were two-bunk staterooms, a pantry, a small office for the ship's yeoman, and a store room. The chief petty officers lived at the after end of the compartment, in a four-berth stateroom.

The next compartment, from frame 47 to 58, was the control room, containing the equipment for steering, diving, controlling the engines and navigating.:

> The control room had two large wheels, one of which operated the stern planes and the other the bow planes. ... Just forward of the bow and stern plane wheels was the hydraulic manifold. This operated the valves for the hull openings and ballast tank vents. It also controlled the flood valve for negative and safety tanks. Hull openings, ballast tank vent valve status and main engine induction valve status were shown in a panel of red and green lights called the 'Christmas tree.' ... The radio shack occupied the after end of the control room behind the housing for the periscopes, which ran from the boat's keel to the top of the periscope sheers above and behind the bridge.[14]

The after battery compartment (frames 58–77) was also used for accommodation above, this time with thirty-six bunks and lockers for the enlisted men. Then came two engine rooms, very similar and stretching from frame 77–88 and 88–99. Each was dominated by two large diesel engines side by side, with electric generators aft of them. Then came the smaller manoeuvring room, frames 99 to 107, with the electric motors which provided the power to the propellers underwater, and various facilities including the crew's heads above. Lucy Williams, an evacuated army nurse, reported: 'There were three heads in the sub and we were assigned to use one. The instructions to flush it was about half a page long and so complicated that they quickly decided to have one of the submariners do it for us after a couple of disasters.'[15] The last

A 1943 watercolour by George Schreiber shows the crowded scene in the conning tower of an American submarine with the captain at the periscope, officers plotting to the right, and a talker on the extreme left, ready to transmit orders.

compartment was the after torpedo room (frames 107–125), similar to the forward one but supporting only four tubes, and containing bunks and lockers for eleven men.

Above the control room was the conning tower, which was a smaller cylindrical pressure compartment from which an attack was controlled: 'The conning tower contains the periscopes and periscope hoist equipment, the radio direction finder, the sonar equipment, the torpedo data computer … the gyro repeater, the conning tower steering stand, and the various pressure gauges and indicators.' It was connected to the control room by a watertight hatch and had communications with all parts of the boat.

The construction of submarines was as specialised a task as any shipbuilder could undertake, in view of the need for all-round watertightness and the demands of water pressure, so it tended to be restricted to a small number of yards. In the 1920s all American boats were built by Portsmouth Navy Yard, apart from one at Mare Island, but in the next decade the Electric Boat Company of Groton, Connecticut, was allowed to bid for alternate boats, creating a healthy rivalry. Electric Boat tended to stress speed and neat internal fittings, Portsmouth worked closely with the operators and fitted the latest equipment. In 1941 Electric Boat was subsidised to double the capacity of their yard to ten building ways and was eventually able to build twenty-one boats at a time. A yard on the Great Lakes at Manitowoc, Wisconsin, built fifteen boats and launched them sideways, to be brought to the sea via the Mississippi to New Orleans. The Cramp Shipbuilding Company of Philadelphia built boats in pairs, one behind another on slipways designed for cruisers, but it found it difficult to recruit enough experienced workmen.

Officers and crews

In peacetime, all Royal Navy submarine ratings were volunteers, but that did not survive war conditions. In July 1941 Arthur Dickison and his colleagues were in a motor boat which took them past a board with the words, '1st Submarine Flotilla': 'It suddenly came to us that we had been drafted into the Submarine Service. We had all thought one had to volunteer.'[16] An Admiralty Fleet Order of 1942 decreed that 'any rating may be drafted to submarines as and when necessary.' Some tried to get out of it by deliberately making themselves liable for detention, but demand was not great and the system could not cope. There were only 9090 ratings in the service in September 1944, a tiny fraction of naval personnel. Trainees were sent to Fort Blockhouse across the entrance to Portsmouth Harbour. According to Arthur Dickinson, they never set foot in an actual submarine during six weeks' theoretical training, but the most impressive part was the famous escape tower. They wore Davis escape apparatus in a mock submarine compartment at the bottom of the tower and it was filled with water:

> The experience of that water slowly rising up my body made the hairs stand up on the back of my neck and when it touched my chin I was not far off panicking. One of my fellow trainees did. When the water was at chin height the pressure was equalised and the instructor opened the hatch at the top of the chamber. In turn we ducked under a canvas tube and floated up to the surface 100 feet above.

About 12 percent of trainees failed the process. After that they went on to practical training in the submarine base at Blyth in northeast England, then to the Firth of Clyde.

Potential submarine commanders were trained and tested by the gruelling 'perisher' course, probably named because of its emphasis on the use of the periscope. First they were trained in the attack teacher in Fort Blockhouse on the western side of the entrance to Portsmouth Harbour.

> The embryo CO was shut in a box containing a periscope. He could train his periscope around and the box, which was like part of a submarine control room, also trained round to simulate the submarine turning, its rate of training varying according to the speed the submarine was supposed to be doing. The periscope looked out at a sort of railway line, along which a small model ship moved; it was all arranged to give a very close simulation of the real thing. The attacks were controlled by other members of the class, who employed much ingenuity in defeating the harassed student down below.[17]

After six weeks at Fort Blockhouse, Edward Young's course was sent to the Firth of Clyde for practical training in an obsolete 'H'-class submarine: 'We took it in turns to act the part of Captain each day, to get used to the routine of taking the submarine to sea, diving and surfacing her in the exercise area, and bringing her back alongside the depot ship in the evening.' But the most testing part was a series of mock attacks on *White Bear*:

> a large, raking motor-yacht with handsome lines that had been taken over by the Navy in wartime as a submarine target … After the first few days, the attacks became more difficult. Target alterations of course were introduced and gradually developed into more complicated zigzags. Finally two old destroyers were added to form an anti-submarine screen for the target, and our attacks were made more exciting because we had to dodge the nearest destroyer or dive under it.[18]

> The submarine captain was in a unique situation during an attack:

> He alone could see what was going on and, further, his vision was limited to one sector at a time – rather like looking round with a telescope; he had to be able to piece the picture together in his head as he swept round the horizon. Some people just never got the knack of judging things through a periscope and however excellent their other qualifications, inevitably failed their perisher.[19]

Lord Ashbourne compared British procedure with American:

> … we have always had the captain in the control room, and in the very closest contact with the first lieutenant and the men under him who are responsible for diving the submarine. On the other hand, most foreign countries prefer to have the captain in the conning tower. For this purpose the conning tower is enlarged so that it

will accommodate the captain and his attack team and the various control instruments. This has the advantage of segregating the captain from the remainder of the boat, and they are unhindered by the other activities that go on inside the submarine.

A submarine commanding officer was usually a lieutenant commander, though Bill Jewell carried out his most notable missions as a lieutenant, and Arthur Hezlett received a very garbled signal announcing his promotion to commander while in charge of *Trenchant*.[20] By the middle of the war, a typical wardroom contained a mixture of regular and reserve officers – *Trenchant* had a regular first lieutenant, who was relieved after a prank involving a smoke candle in the depot ship and returned to 'that convenient receptacle – general service.'[21] *Storm* also had a regular lieutenant under Edward Young, himself of the RNVR. Telegraphist Dickison of *Safari* found that the first lieutenant filled a traditional role: '"Jimmy the One" … got the idea that all our brasswork was a bit dull so it was brightwork cleaning throughout the boat, a lovely pastime that we enjoyed so much!'[22] The navigating officer was RN in *Trenchant* and *Storm*, the torpedo officer was RNVR in both boats, though gunnery duties were allocated differently – combined with navigating in *Storm* and with torpedo in *Safari*. The engineer officers were from contrasting backgrounds. Mike Chambers of *Trenchant*:

> had entered the navy when the war broke out and had a degree in engineering. He was therefore given a temporary commission in the Royal Navy as a Lieutenant (E) and wore the straight stripes of a regular officer. He was … what I would call a theoretical or 'thermo-dynamic' engineer rather than a 'wheel-spanner' engineer with a practical knowledge of submarines.[23]

W H Ray had recently been promoted to warrant rank from chief ERA before being appointed to *Storm*. He was deeply suspicious of his RNVR commanding officer, with 'all the natural antagonism of the professional for the amateur.'[24] A sub lieutenant or fifth officer was attached for training without necessarily taking on any specific role to start with, but as a boarding officer in *Storm*.

As in any small warship, the coxswain was the senior rating. He had medical duties, which Arthur Dickison used occasionally in *Safari*: 'My stomach was really playing up by now, enough to bring tears to my eyes. Cox'n slapped hot bread poultice on it when I did not expect it and did I howl.'[25] *Storm* had an electrical artificer and a torpedo gunner's mate like any submarine. He had a very responsible job servicing the boat's main armament, as observed by Arthur Dickison:

It was quite interesting to watch Figgy do the tests. He had to check the torpedo's gyro and turn its motor, and when he did the latter he had to insert an L-shaped tube into its rear in the centre of the propeller ... During this test it had been known for the torpedo to run out of control so it had to be securely tied down by shackles to ring bolts on the deck.'[26]

He had three torpedomen under him and a fourth who doubled as wardroom steward.

Storm had a yeoman of signals, a petty officer who operated visual signals, plus two leading telegraphists and two telegraphists. Dickison described the duties in *Safari*: 'Wireless watches were split into four, each of four hours duration. During the watch the operator sat with headphones on, reading signals from Admiralty routines, noting the addresses of each signal.'[27] There were two Asdic operators whose duties sometimes overlapped with the telegraphists. The cook in *Safari* sometimes got it wrong: 'Breakfast was a burnt offering because of a slight accident in the galley with Chief Leech. Boy! Did he go through it. Ragged terribly but we never did find out how the eggs and bacon reached the state they were in. Good job that I rather like crunchy bacon.'[28] In addition, *Storm* had two radar operators, two gunlayers and two able seamen. The engineer branch had a chief ERA and three ERAs, a stoker petty officer, three leading stokers and seven stokers. *Trenchant* was similar, with a total complement of five officers and fifty-five men. All had other duties: 'Every man had a special duty at "Diving Stations" and in some cases a different one during a torpedo attack or a gun action. The majority of the Seaman Branch would take their turns as planesmen or helmsmen at "Watch Diving" or as look-outs while on the surface.'[29]

Submarines were cramped and life was basic even by naval standards, but many men preferred the informal discipline, the comradeship and the extra pay. Able Seaman Sydney Hart described joining a boat in 1939:

A narrow gang plank ran down to *Triad*'s slippery deck; we scrambled down it in single file, passed our kits through a small hatch, and so squeezed ourselves into our ship's interior. The atmosphere was warm and stuffy. The lights seemed dull and listless by contrast with the late Autumn sunset outside. So we went through the engine room into the small mess, cramped as it normally was, and now, with our steaming bags all over the place, looking like any London Tube at the rush hour. For us this state of affairs would be normal for three weeks duration or thereabouts.[30]

On patrol, submariners turned night into day:

> By day a submarine proceeds submerged under the power of her electric batteries. Occasionally the periscope is raised and the ocean searched for an enemy ship or aircraft. Always there is the utmost vigilance and a constant listening watch on the asdic ... Men off watch keep as still as possible in order to conserve the air ... Some sleep – sleep comes easily in the close atmosphere of a submarine submerged; others read or play games.
>
> ... Then, when it is dark, the vessel surfaces and the submariner's day begins. The diesel engines that propel the vessel and charge the batteries are started. Instead of the silence there are engine noises and the sound of the sea ... The blowers are started and a draught of fresh air is sucked through the boat. Then comes the welcome order: 'Carry on smoking!' ... 'Midday' dinner is at midnight and supper just before dawn.[31]

Cleanliness was neglected, for:

> Fresh-water showers or baths were a constant luxury compared with the sea-water washed on patrol. Even these could only be taken with the express permission of the TGM ... He would allow a salt-water shower of sorts from a cock at the rear end of one of the torpedo tubes which allowed water to squirt out of a flooded tube. To get any sort of lather it was necessary to use salt-water soap.[32]

> No-one shaved much on patrol; fresh water was limited and in any case hot water gave off steam which added to the damp condensation in the boat. One wore layer upon layer of clothes; it is very cold in a submarine in the Northern winter and submariners get special issues of warm clothing ... As CO, at constant call, I never undressed for weeks on end and, since we all smelled alike, no-one noticed.[33]

Crews still had to take their turn as cook of the mess, as described by Arthur Dickison: 'Dinner was slightly more difficult, since peeling potatoes and getting some stewing meat from Chef, cutting it up in small pieces and taking it along with some onions cut up there in a cramped space was a real challenge.'[34]

American submarine crews were very carefully selected and trained. Enlisted men underwent a six-week course in the Submarine School at New London, with practical work in old 'S'-boats which were 'picked as a type because its construction is relatively simple', but 'the basic principles will not vary between the types of boats'. They would learn 'the basic principles of all submarines, that is the principle of submergence and control of the boat while submerged', including 'the manning of the diving stations and the actual handling of the lines, valves, tanks, controls etc.' Every week everyone was expected to prepare a sketch of a certain aspect of the submarine. Each man was expected to undergo training in the escape tower. The instructor 'fastened the lung to my chest and fixed the clamp over my nose. I fit the mouthpiece over my teeth and bit down. "Can you breathe?" asked the instructor. I nodded. Happy because I had no problems, I made escapes from eighteen and fifty feet.'[35] Even African-American stewards like Hosey Mays were expected to qualify: 'You definitely had to know a lot more than the steward rating. You had to know the ship – electrical systems, air systems, fuel systems and how they worked.' In action he was first loader on the 4in gun.[36]

Eugene Wilkinson volunteered for submarine service from the NROTC after being commissioned in 1940 and joined a course of thirty regular and thirty reserve officers in New London. He found that the results in subjects such as buoyage and Rules of the Road were rigged against reserve officers until he pointed out the anomaly, for 'In the beginning it really made a difference whether someone was a Reservist from the trade school, as we called the naval academy.'[37] John Alden was disappointed with the course in 1944:

> The school was a letdown after serving in a real submarine. Many of the instructors struck us as pedantic, and the courses were cut and dried, based around the antiquated O-class boats that made up most of the training squadron. Instead of learning about the latest torpedo data computer, we were taught to make attacks using old manual devices. I had to make a new notebook, learn the archaic diving routine, and trace out the primitive systems of an O-boat of 1914 vintage.[38]

By the end of the war there were three main training devices. The attack teacher was a mock-up used to practise the attack team. The diving trainer was a replica of the port side of the control room complete with wheels and instruments. The torpedo tube trainer was used to teach men how to reload quickly.

After six months on operations, an officer or man was expected to pass a thorough test, for 'The submarine service expects every man aboard from the captain on down to know his boat from top to keel.'[39] They were supposed to be qualified within a year of service, except that in 1939–41 Lew Parks, captain of *Pompano*, kept three of his officers unqualified, to prevent them being drafted away to new construction and replaced by reservists.[40]

Captains were trained in the potential commanding officers, or PCOs, course. John Alden served in the submarine used for the course: 'The *Cachalot* … was engaged in training prospective commanding officers (PCOs), most of whom were fresh from the Pacific and preparing to command their own boats. In order to give all the PCOs their turns to make approaches and attacks, we were often out quite late'.[41]

A submarine crew, according to Edward L Beach, needed 'indomitable spirit' and 'absolute determination':

> The embodiment and personification of this perspective is the Captain. His men and his ship reflect his will, and a properly organised crew operates with the unity of purpose of an ant colony. Whatever the state of the individual and of internal affairs, his composite exterior is smooth, unruffled; it acts under a single directive force – a single brain – the Captain's.[42]

As in any ship, the executive officer, or XO, was:

> the number two person in charge of the boat. His duties include all the paperwork of the submarine as well as being navigator and operations officer when another officer has not been so designated. He acts as assistant to the captain during battle stations and is in the conning tower next to him giving advice on how to approach a target.[43]

The other officers had their own duties, which might change as they gained in seniority, or others were posted away to new construction. They included an engineer officer and his assistant and others in charge of torpedoes,

The crew was more specialised than on most surface ships, with only about 20 per cent non-rated men, seamen and fireman. Motor machinist's mates, electrician's mates and torpedoman's mates made up about half, with three quartermasters or signalmen, two steward's mates, a pharmacist's mate, a gunner's mate and a yeoman. They were led by the chief of the boat, who was more of a leader and less of a policeman than the master-at-arms of a large ship:

> The natural leader among the crew members seemed to be young Frank Lynes, the gunner's mate. … he had won his promotion to chief petty officer at the age of twenty-five – about the youngest man any of us had seen reach this cherished and respected level. He was young to be a chief but especially young to be a Chief of the Boat. … He was a success from the beginning.[44]

American submariners did not have the excuse for scruffiness and neglect of their British counterparts as their boats were far better equipped. Indeed, according to Jim Calvert:

> ... *Jack* had been ... the USS *Dykers*. His personality, which had moulded the ship far more than those of her other skippers, was of the old school. Paperwork and record keeping were done meticulously, according to Navy regulations. The officers called the men only by their last names. No-one came into the wardroom except in a complete uniform. Meals in the wardroom were always served with linen, silver and china. The boat had a general atmosphere of clean, quiet orderliness.[45]

In *Pompom* the captain's orders stated: 'At sea there is no prescribed uniform. Individuals are expected to be guided by their own common sense, pride in personal cleanliness, and a sense of decency in regard to their shipmates.'[46] But on the other hand, according to one later account: 'Submariners smelled awful. A submarine's smell was a mixture of diesel oil, cork insulation body odor and cooking. Fresh water was limited. The purest water went for the batteries. The crew drank what was left. Showers were limited to a twenty-second dowsing one a week, if that.'[47]

Submarines did not normally carry medical officers, so the responsibility devolved on a pharmacist's mate, who might have to carry out a full range of duties during a six-week patrol. The cooks were also key members of the crew and submarines had a surprisingly high standard of food. Fresh fruit lasted about a week, vegetables two weeks, milk about three and butter about four, eggs lasted about fifty-five to sixty days, and then canned and dehydrated foods were issued.

Techniques and tactics

British attack procedure was described by Ben Bryant:

> At reasonable firing ranges, say under 2000 yards, the target was crossing your sights much faster than you could swing the boat; you had to be lined up in advance. Then you had to attack from ahead. You had not got the speed to catch up.
>
> The ideal firing position was about 600 yards on the beam of the enemy, though anything between 500 and 1500 yards was fair enough ... At its best a torpedo would only run to within a degree of the course set; and at worst it was more likely to torpedo you than the enemy.[48]
>
> If you had got the enemy course and speed right – you had your attack team to help you in computing it from your estimations –

you knew what angle to aim ahead; that angle could be set on the periscope. There was a bearing ring where the periscope passed through the pressure hull and you could read on it the bearing from dead ahead, on which the periscope was pointing.[49]

The main aid for aiming was the torpedo control calculator or 'fruit machine':

> From my settings on the 'fruit machine' I could tell that the moment for firing was drawing near; now all my efforts must be concentrated on producing for the captain what was known as the DA, or Director Angle, or in plainer English the 'aim-off' to allow for the target's speed and the time the torpedoes would take to reach his track. Fortunately this was a simple attack, and when the captain asked, 'What's the DA?' I was able to read off the answer, 'DA five red sir,' with fair confidence.[50]

After an attack on escorted vessels, a counter-attack was highly likely:

> The technique of escape from a hunt was largely a matter of pitting your wits against the enemy. You could glean a certain amount of information on what he was doing by listening to his propellers on the asdic set, and when he was using a echo ranging device you could pick up his transmissions ... But for the most part the Axis relied upon extremely sensitive hydrophones ... To avoid detection the general rule was to go at the slowest speed, to cut down wake which also gave an echo.
>
> Once detected you would have to speed up, make a wake – which you hoped he would mistake for the submarine itself – and alter course and depth ... You wanted him to drop his charges. You waited until he seemed to be committed to steaming over you to drop them; then, and then only, you would speed up and alter course to get out of the light. ... For the CO it was an absorbing business, you had far too much to think about to have time to be frightened.[51]

British submarines fired 5121 torpedoes during the war in 1671 attacks, an average of three per attack. They claimed 20 per cent hits, and a success rate of 46.4 for the attacks, including probables.[52]

Some submarine operations attracted special attention after the war. Lieutenant Bill Jewell was appointed to command *Seraph*, despite his relatively junior rank. In November 1942 he supported the North African landings and transported American General Mark Clark to a conference at Oran. Then he was sent to fetch French General Giraud in hostile waters. In 1943 he was chosen to take part in Operation Mincemeat, a plan to land a body disguised as a Royal Marine officer and carrying secret and deliberately misleading papers off the coast of Spain, where they were certain to be seen by the Germans. He described the dropping of the body off Huelva:

> We closed into the coast and lifted the canister on deck on to the fore casing. We shut everyone else down below and put the hatch down. All the other officers and I went down on to the casing, unscrewed the lid of the canister and took the body out. ... I was supposed to check that he had all his private impedimenta about him. ... Previously I'd had a look through the prayer book and got some idea of how the burial service should be. You never do burials from a submarine, so I'd never done a burial at sea before. So we read this out over him and pushed him quietly over the side.[53]

Lieutenant R P Raikes of *Tuna* played a part in another celebrated operation, to land a party of Royal Marine canoeists off the coast of France to paddle upriver and raid shipping in Bordeaux. It was a challenging feat of seamanship and navigation:

> It was then decided, to the evident delight of the OC military force, to try and disembark close to the coast near the RAF's badly laid mines ... This plot quite evidently required extreme accuracy in navigation, even allowing for rather touching faith of the authorities in the accuracy of the positions given by the RAF – a faith which I dd not share. Further, this plan entailed coming to full buoyancy 4 miles off the coast and 10 miles from the DS/F [radar] station and doing the whole operation in one, cutting out the approach at low buoyancy. But the most important considerations were that in that position the boats had a fair tide for an extra hour, and that our position would be dead accurate.[54]

American submarines were active almost entirely in the Pacific, where their long range and better habitability proved to be great advantages. After the torpedo problems had been solved, their main effort was against Japanese shipping supplying the home islands with vital goods and supporting isolated garrisons. For this they had to abandon the principle, which had brought America into the First World War, that merchant ships should not be attacked without warning. They were very successful in this campaign, sinking 1113 merchant vessels of over 500 tons to a total of more than 5 million tons. The Japanese merchant fleet was reduced from a peak of nearly 6.4 million tons to about 2 million tons by the end of the war, and the navy was desperately short of fuel. Supplies could still come from Asia via the Sea of Japan, until a new sonar system allowed submarines to penetrate it through minefields in the summer of 1945. It is quite possible that Japan would have eventually have been forced to surrender without land invasion or the atom bomb.

Submarines were also used for reconnaissance, especially in advance of amphibious operations. Admiral Barbey noted during the invasion of Hollandia: 'With binoculars I compared the contour of the hills with the photographs taken by the *Dace* just a month before. Yes, we were right "on the beam".'[55] Submarines were increasingly used for lifeguarding duties by 1945, partly because surface targets were becoming rarer, and because the air offensive against Japan was gaining in intensity:

> The concept for lifeguarding was to have the submarine at periscope depth at a precise location known to the carrier aviators before their strike. They had our call sign, and we had theirs – right down to the individual planes. When a strike was scheduled, we would move into position ahead of time to be sure all was in readiness with the rescue party.[56]

American submarine commanders soon found that, with the vast distances in the Pacific, it was best to travel to the operational area on the surface as much as possible, rather than submerge in daytime. The surfaced condition was defined: 'The main ballast, fuel-ballast, negative and safety tanks shall be empty; the variable ballast tanks shall contain such water as will permit the vessel, by flooding the main ballast, fuel-ballast, and safety tanks, to dive with safety and handle at slow speed submerged.'[57] In operational areas the crews had to be ready to dive at any time, especially if an aircraft was sighted: 'Dykers hammered home to us again and again that the ability to spot enemy patrol planes and submerge quickly – in thirty seconds or so – was our main means of survival in the war zone.'[58] Alert lookouts were needed, standing on a small platform round the periscopes and above the bridge and looking to port, starboard and aft. They were relieved regularly to keep them alert.

The dive could be originated by the officer of the deck or the junior officer of the deck, as 'there always exists the possibility of a plane coming on from astern necessitating quick action on the part of the JOOD rather than a report first to the OOD.' Either of them might give the order 'Clear the bridge', when 'all hands topside will repeat it in a loud clear voice and immediately move smartly towards the hatch and avoid jamming.' The klaxon was sounded twice, sounding rather like the horn of an old Model T Ford according to some. Then there was a scramble below. According to a medical report:

Injuries were commonly sustained by personnel of the bridge watch, particularly in the lightning-like maneuvers necessary to clear the bridge in the relatively few seconds that elapse between the time the diving signal is given and the submarine is actually submerged. Smashed fingers, broken ribs, dislocations, bruised shoulders, and lacerations of various degrees were the result of his mass exodus of eight or so men from the bridge through a twenty-four inch hatch and down the slippery and precipitous ladder into the conning tower.[59]

The last man off the bridge was normally the OOD who was responsible for shutting the conning tower upper hatch.[60]

The main engines were quickly shut off and power was switched to the electric motors. Then the planesmen adjusted the surfaces to bring the boat down, especially the stern plane, which was further from the centre of buoyancy and could use the wash of the propeller. The diving officers opened the ballast tanks, except those which were to be used for trimming, and checked their status on the 'Christmas tree'. The boat was then trimmed to the required depth.

Reports on previous patrols were made available to officers, and Jim Calvert noticed:

One thing was clear from reading them – our submarines were using more and more the German U-boat tactic of the night surface attack. Our superior radar and twenty knots of surface speed made a powerful combination for attacking Japanese convoys in the broad Pacific. The night surface attack was a natural for American submarines.[61]

Another tactic adopted from the Germans was the wolf pack, though it was very different in American practice. It was headed by the senior captain present, rather than distant control from a shore base. Instead of twenty or so boats, it typically had three, and as many as seven on a few occasions. *Parche*, *Band* and *Tinosa* divided their patrol area into sixty-mile squares with each assigned to a twenty-mile lane to broaden the front for detecting the targets.[62]

Closely co-ordinated attacks were tried but were too difficult. Instead:

The difference from lonc-wolf operations was primarily the positioning of the submarines. Two submarines would try to get themselves in position ahead on either bow of the target. The third submarine would be the trailer, and she would take station astern in case the target was damaged, and then she could pick up the cripple.

Or, if the target turned or reversed course or eluded either of the two advance submarines, she would be in a position to attack.[63]

In marked contrast to German operations in the broad Atlantic, American attacks were often close to shore.

Sonar was normally used passively, as a ping would alert the enemy to the vessel's presence. When submerged, 'The sonar operators become the main channel of information about the maneuvers of the enemy.' Sonic gear was 'useful for picking up targets at great distances because sonic sound travels further'. Supersonic gear was 'especially superior for catching the bursts of supersonic sound used by enemy escort vessels.'[64] But it was not always successful in the actual attack. According to Jim Calvert, 'many of the first attacks of the war were conducted as sonar approaches, and practically every one was a failure.'[65] This was partly due to torpedo problems, but also to the caution of many peacetime captains.

At the centre of the attacking system was the torpedo data computer, which Ben Bryant of the Royal Navy described as 'a truly wonderful computer'.[66] According to the captain of *Pampanito*:

> The torpedo control system provides means for – (a) determining the course, speed and the position of the enemy with reference to the fining ship at any instant: (b) computing the torpedo angle to cause the torpedo to his, using instantaneous generated values of the target element: (c) continuous setting of the torpedo gyro angles: (d) firing torpedoes with automatic withdrawal of gyro setting spindles: (e) the control officer to issue orders from the tube stations and receive back reports therefrom.

It could be operated using the periscope, or by sonar.

It still needed much skill, which in the case of the USS *Jack* was provided by Jim Calvert, 'a TDC operator with that extraordinary ability, often bragged about but less frequently demonstrated, to make a TDC sing when it came to aiming the weapons.'[67] Calvert described the system:

> Four knobs, or cranks, were located on the machine just under the simulated picture. The operator used three of them to set in the observed bearing, range and target course, as seen by the captain. The fourth knob was used to set the estimated speed of the target. … a skilled operator could soon deduce the correct course and speed.
>
> The TDC made significant use of the feature that enabled the … torpedo … to turn to a predetermined course. This was accomplished by a spinning gyroscope within the torpedo.[68]

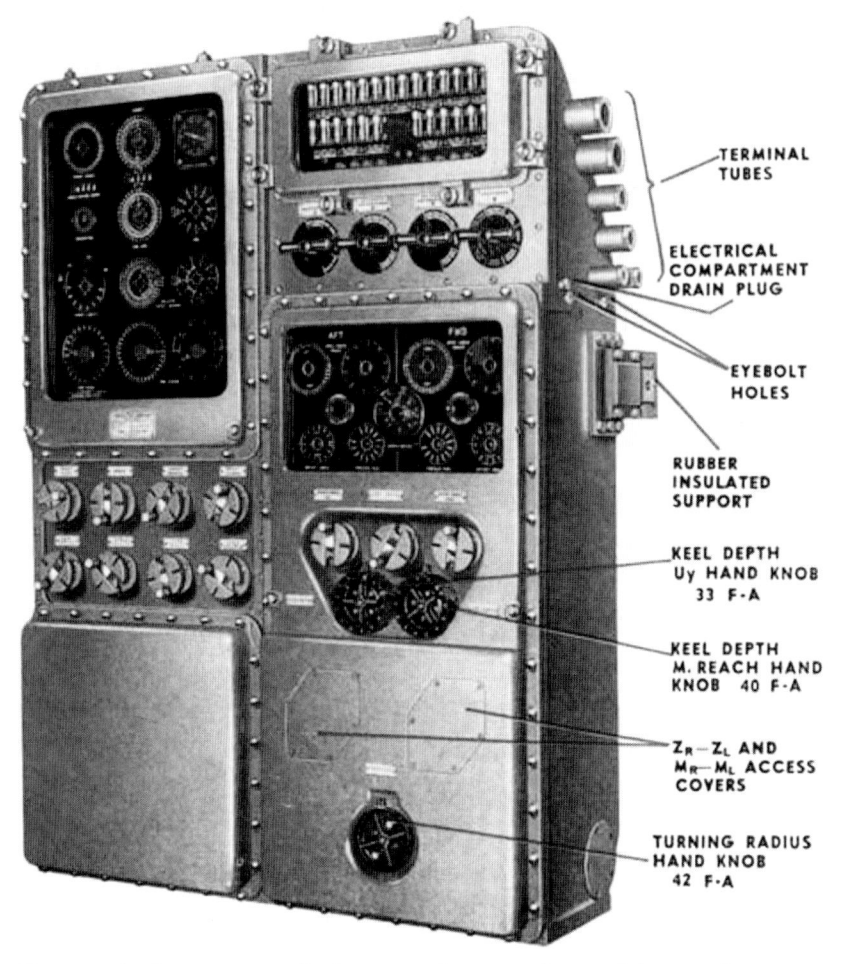

The torpedo data computer, the best torpedo-aiming device of the war, showing its dials and controls.

Dyker [the commanding officer] normally stood about three feet from the TDC where he could see the dials, but when night surface attack was adopted he stood on the bridge and was communicated with by 'talkback.'[69]

There were many improvements during the war years. SJ radar, a development of the SG surface set, was ready by December 1941, was common in submarines by mid 1942 and almost universal by 1943. It used an A-scope, which gave bearing and very accurate range on a surface target of a low-flying aircraft.

Depth-charge attack was the greatest fear of any submariner, and was usually launched by escort vessels after an attack on their convoy:

> It was a nerve racking ordeal. Each time one of the ASW ships would start another run and shift to short-scale pinging, I would be convinced that this would be the time we would get the depth charges. I could see some of my shipmates' faces grow paler as our attacker's screws passed overhead, and I'm sure that mine did also. I can only conclude that our Japanese friend wanted to be sure he had us absolutely to rights before he dropped those charges.[70]

But the Japanese failed to develop effective anti-submarine techniques. Vessels without radar did not know whether the submarine was submerged or surfaced, and often attacked in the wrong way. Or they set the charges for too low a depth, for American submarines, especially of the *Balao* and *Tench* classes, could go deeper than they expected. And often they gave up the hunt because they lacked enough charges, or had to rejoin their convoy, or believed the submarine to be sunk. Despite all that, the United States Navy lost fifty-two submarines during the war.

Jim Calvert noticed the developments over the war years:

> I couldn't help reflecting that earlier in the war – even in early 1943, the time of my first patrol – no American submarine would have dreamed of chasing a convoy on the surface this close to an active base like Manila. But over time we had all learned that if we had really sharp lookouts and could dive in thirty seconds, we usually could get away with it.[71]

Commanders and bases

Admiral Sir Max Horton, a highly successful raider in the First World War, took up command of British submarines in January 1940. He predicted the German invasion of Norway and his boats were in place to sink twenty-one transports and two cruisers and damage a pocket battleship – a rare British success during that campaign. In November 1942 the poacher turned gamekeeper and he was transferred to Western Approaches Command to defend Allied shipping, and his ruthless efficiency proved equally valuable. He was succeeded by Rear Admiral Claud Barry. British submarines were organised in flotillas of around a dozen boats each under a captain (S).

British submarines were mostly based on depot ships, mainly because of the navy's reluctance to construct and use fixed shore bases, rather than the need for tactical mobility, for they were mostly situated in well-established harbours such as the Clyde, and did not have to range across a great ocean like the Americans. Two ships, *Cyclops* and *Lucia*, survived from the First World War. The former became well known as a training ship in the Clyde; *Lucia* served in the East Indies. Several ships were purpose built between the wars. *Medway* of 14,650 tons was built in 1928 and provided support at Alexandria until June 1942 when Rommel's threatened advance caused her to be sent to Haifa; she was sunk by a U-boat on the way, the only loss among depot ships. *Maidstone* (1937), 8900 tons, was the most travelled, serving in the Mediterranean, South Atlantic and Ceylon. Her sister ship *Forth* spent the war in the Clyde. *Adamant* (1940) was in Ceylon from 1943–45, when she moved to Fremantle in Australia. Of converted merchantmen, *Bonaventure* was the depot ship for X-craft and *Wolfe* was in the Clyde until she went to the East Indies in 1944,

The arrival back at a depot ship could be a great relief:

> Once we were secured to moorings there was a dash to the parent ship for baths – a treat we had missed for eighteen mortal days – and a blissful reality when available. Our beards needed clippers instead of razors. But to be back after well-nigh three weeks without the decent comforts of life … Best of all, to breathe fresh, pure air that had not been polluted by the conglomeration of scents bred in a submarine's interior – ah, this was bliss indeed.[72]

Not all the depot ships were comfortable, and one rating complained:

> Submarine depot ships are popularly supposed to be floating palaces where submariners rest after patrols whereas in actual fact, rather than suffer the conditions on this depot ship we prefer to go to sea … There are no baths or showers aboard, and washing facilities are practically non-existent. In my mess, which should accommodate 30 men, there are 97. It is absolutely impossible to find a vacant space in which to sling a hammock and even mess tables are used … Finally the whole ship is over-run with cockroaches …[73]

As always, it was better for officers:

> The ward-room of HMS *Forth* had been nicknamed the Globetrotters' Club, submariners sprawled in the deep chairs and swapped yarns with officers from other boats with whom they had shared depth charges in the Mediterranean. Men back from the Bay of Biscay discussed tactics and experiences with friends down from the Arctic Circle or across from Norway. There was great talk about Norway.[74]

Section of a British submarine depot ship, probably in the Firth of Clyde, with hills in the background. Unlike their American equivalents, they did not range across the oceans.

On the other side of the Atlantic, Charles Lockwood, a member of the Annapolis class of 1912, commanded submarines during the First World War and became chief of staff to the commander of the American submarine force in 1939, before being sent to London to study British submarines. From 1942 he commanded the submarine forces based in Australia and took command of the Commander, Submarines, Pacific Fleet or COMSUBPAC in February 1943, just as they were preparing for their greatest effort. Known affectionately as 'Uncle Charlie', he looked after the welfare of his men, giving them two-week stays in the Royal Hawaiian Hotel between patrols. He also allowed his captain to make decisions on the spot. He was 'A perfect gentleman – smart, meticulous. If he found something wrong, he would confront you with it in a very pleasant manner. He never said anything that was harsh, to my knowledge. That's why everyone in the submarine Force loved him.'[75] He tended to have a light touch over tactics: 'To my knowledge ... no attack doctrine or policy was ever dictated to a skipper before he left on patrol. The submarine tradition of trusting the man on the firing line continued.'[76]

The original base at New London was established just after the Civil War on land given by the state of Connecticut and it was first used for submarine training in 1915, being close to the Electric Boat yard on the same river. According to Fireman 1st Class Stanley Lambkin, 'The base was divided between the instruction buildings on the upper base and the piers on the lower base. There were finger piers that stuck out into the Thames River which gave the officers ulcers because landing a submarine in the swift current was difficult.'[77] The 286 buildings included diesel and sound laboratories, torpedo and periscope shops, attack teachers, compression chamber and the escape tower, with other educational facilities. Nevertheless, it was cramped, with the great number of men passing through, and commandants complained about the obsolete 'O'-class submarines allocated for training. The relatively modern *Cachalot* and *Cuttlefish* were attached from December 1942.[78]

The submarine base at Pearl Harbor, consisting before the war of 32 acres and twenty-eight buildings, was untouched by the Japanese raid. It served as a rear base, giving crews some relief from the isolation of Midway. Submarines also operated from the Australian bases of Fremantle and Darwin: 'Fremantle is the seaport for Perth, in Western Australia, and is separated from it by about ten miles of good road. … There was a certain frontier town atmosphere about both towns … that was, at first, unfamiliar and strange to us Americans.'[79]

Unlike their British equivalents, the depot ships, American submarine tenders gave a great deal of strategic mobility during the advances across the Pacific. According to Jim Calvert:

> A submarine tender is a large ship, usually of ten thousand tons or so, equipped to be a floating submarine base. Torpedo shops, foundries, machine shops, electrical shops, medical and dental facilities, spare parts bins, paint shops, food stores – everything needed to keep a submarine and her crew well and happy – are onboard.[80]

Eight tenders were in service in 1941, increasing to eighteen in 1945, all but one in the Pacific.

Canopus was a merchant ship launched in New York in 1919 and converted to a submarine tender in 1922. She was at Cavite in the Philippines in December 1941 as tender to Submarine Squadron 20. Damaged by bombing, she continued working until scuttled in April 1942. *Fulton* was launched at Mare Island in December 1940 and a year later she was on her shakedown cruise during the Pearl Harbor attack. She went to the Panama Canal Zone to establish seaplane bases in the region, then to Midway, Brisbane and New Guinea. She was at Saipan from April 1945, then Guam.

Signalman 3rd Class Bernie Schwartz (later the actor Tony Curtis) was a member of Submarine Relief Crew 202 on the *Proteus* at Guam in 1945:

> Whenever a sub came in after a war patrol, they would tie up alongside and go on liberty. Our job as relief crew was to go aboard and clean it up, scrape the barnacles from the sides, and assist in whatever repair and other work was needed. It was hard work, sure, but it didn't matter. This was great for us, because the 15 of us were all ready and waiting to be assigned to a submarine – and this was great practice – plus we were making a real contribution to getting those submarines back ready for another war patrol.[81]

The war was over before he was allocated to a submarine; he was still in *Proteus* when she entered Tokyo Bay for the Japanese surrender.

British submarines were given plenty of publicity during the war in an effort to boost morale in hard times. Among the most famous was Ben Bryant's *Safari,* which was known to other crews as a '*Daily Mirror* boat'. The service was also celebrated in film. Arthur Dickison, later of *Safari,* unwittingly played a role:

> … an officer descended from the depot ship and as he left … I saluted him saying. 'Good hunting, Sir.' It was only then that I realised he was the actor John (later Sir John) Mills … When the film *We Dive at Dawn* was released, I was there saluting John Mills![82]

American submarines were manned by only about 1.7 per cent of the navy, but their achievement was enormous. They sank 868,361 tons of Japanese shipping in the autumn of 1944 alone.[83] As such, they were far more successful than the German U-boats, despite the notoriety of the latter. But their achievements were not publicised during the war years. That was partly compensated after the war when the popular TV series *Silent Service,* presented by Rear Admiral Thomas Dykers of *Jack* fame, was shown in 1957/8. It used the submarine *Sawfish* and each episode was based on real events, mostly in the Second World War. It proved highly popular and there are references in the monologues of Bob Newhart and the 1980s sitcom *Cheers.*

The submarine services of both navies would be changed radically after the war. The use of the snorkel allowed hulls to be redesigned for more underwater operation, the use of homing torpedoes allowed them to become anti-submarine vessels in themselves, but by far the most dramatic development was the use of nuclear power, developed by Admiral Rickover in the 1950s and then adopted by the Royal Navy and other forces. It also allowed the fitting of ballistic missiles, creating the most devastating weapons ever devised, and barely recognisable from the wartime craft and their valiant crews.

14

Anti-Submarine Warfare

ANTI-SUBMARINE WARFARE was one area where the Americans learned more from the British than vice versa – the British had more at stake and more years of experience in countering the German U-boat threat to their existence, though they had a false start in the first few months of the war.

Historians and strategists refer to this type of warfare as 'commerce raiding'. The term is appropriate to the age of Nelson, when merchant ships often carried valuable cargoes such as tobacco, sugar and spices. Capturing them would cause the merchants of London, for example, to think twice about the value of the war, or at least use political pressure to force the navy to divert resources to protect shipping. But twentieth-century total warfare was not about commerce, for ordinary economic considerations played a far smaller part. It was about stopping essential supplies – food, fuel, raw materials and munitions – from reaching belligerents such as Britain and Japan, who were completely dependent on imports. In essence, it was about lifeline cutting, and it posed the greatest threat of the war to Britain, which was obliged to expend huge resources to counter it.

Protecting the lifeline

The Battle of the Atlantic was as important as any campaign during the Second World War, especially for Britain – Winston Churchill wrote, 'The only thing that ever really frightened me during the war was the U-boat peril.' The most vital route, from Canada and the USA, kept Britain supplied with essential fuel, food and weapons, and there were times when it was close to being severed. This was also the longest campaign of the war, from the sinking of *Athenia* in September 1939 to the end of the war in Europe in May 1945 – the last two ships were sunk just before VE Day by a U-boat which had not received the orders to surrender. Without a defeat of the U-boats, Britain would have been starved of food and fuel and perhaps have had to surrender. The great build-up of equipment in advance of the invasion of Normandy in 1944 would never have been possible.

The British had defeated a U-boat campaign in the last war and were complacent about this one. They overestimated the value of Asdic in detecting submarines underwater, and had prepared mainly for a war in the North Sea, so they had few long-range escort vessels. Originally, the U-boats were expected to conform to the international rules drawn up in 1930, but the liner *Athenia* was sunk against these rules on the first day of the war and by mid October all British merchant ships could be attacked without warning. By May 1940 all the seas around Britain had been declared unsafe to Allied shipping. In March 1941, after the German bombing campaign had clearly failed to cow the British people and the threat of invasion receded, Churchill declared, 'In view of various German statements, we must assume that the Battle of the Atlantic has begun.'

The Battle of the Atlantic Committee met fortnightly in Downing Street from March 1941, chaired by Churchill himself. Its composition reflected the widespread importance of the campaign, and it included the three service ministers and the ministers of supply, aircraft production, transport, labour and food. It was attended by the chiefs of staff or their deputies, the commander-in-chief of Coastal Command, the controller of merchant shipbuilding and repairs, and Churchill's scientific adviser, Professor Lindemann.

The battle raged over large areas of the ocean, with campaigns at different times off South Africa, the eastern seaboard of the USA, in the Caribbean, and off the North African coast, but the most important campaign was in the jugular vein of the Allied war effort, the route between the USA and Canada to the British Isles. That was the last part of many voyages of ships which had come up the South American coast or passed through the Panama Canal. It was often the most dangerous and uncomfortable. As Captain Walker of HMS *Starling* put it, 'No one in his senses expects anything but foul weather in the North Atlantic in late October and November.'[1]

Britain could not survive without huge volumes of imports. Ships brought in more than a hundred million hundredweight of wheat in 1938, largely from Canada and Australia. Native coal was still used in railway engines, power stations and many merchant ships, but modern war demanded oil to power great numbers of warships, aircraft, fighting vehicles and lorries (trucks). Britain imported 568 million gallons of crude oil in 1938, plus 1478 million gallons of refined motor fuel. By 1944 the latter figure had risen to 2291.

This was a battle which involved everyone in Britain through rationing and shortage, even if they did not work in industries directly connected

An Arctic convoy of 1942, possibly the ill-fated PQ17, showing the arrangement of merchant ships in lines.

with the sea such as shipbuilding and the docks. Food and clothing were strictly rationed. Citizens were urged to 'Dig for Victory' to reduce food shortages and to 'Make do and mend' to minimise the need for new clothes. When a cartoon in the *Daily Mirror* showed a seaman clinging to a raft with the heading 'The price of petrol has been increased by one penny', Churchill threatened to shut the paper down.

The Battle of the Atlantic was divided into several different phases, even as it was in progress. The *Monthly Anti-Submarine Report*, issued to all escort ship officers, was extremely prescient, and in April 1943 it commented: 'Historians of this war are likely to single out the months of April and May 1943 during which the strength began to ebb away from the German U-boat offensive'.

The first phase of the battle lasted until the Fall of France in June 1940; it was a confused period as the British and French prepared escort vessels, and the Germans built U-boats and reduced the restrictions on their operations, while surface raiders like *Graf Spee* seemed a more serious threat. Nevertheless, many merchant ships were destroyed, mainly in the North Sea and the southwestern approaches to the English Channel, and two major warships, the battleship *Royal Oak* and the carrier *Courageous*, were sunk by U-boat. For the second phase, the U-boats quickly developed bases on the west coast of France, which doubled their efficiency, and the British almost gave up on the English Channel and diverted their ocean shipping round the north of Ireland, but for the

U-boats it was the 'happy time' in which 215 merchant ships were sunk. Escort was extended from 17, then 19, then 35 degrees west; air cover from Iceland became available. The British improved their techniques and this phase ended in March 1941 with the death or capture of three 'ace' U-boat commanders – Prien who had sunk *Royal Oak*, Kretschmer and Schepke.

The U-boats moved out into mid-Atlantic to avoid air cover, or attacked stragglers and ships sailing independently. They had a bonanza in May 1941 when a group of six sank thirty-two merchantmen off Freetown in West Africa, and the escort force had to be stretched further to cover that area. Devastating attacks in the western Atlantic meant that end-to-end escort had to be introduced in June, with a force based at St John's in Newfoundland. Catapult aircraft were used to drive off the shadowing Focke-Wulf Kondors which reported the movement of convoys, and the first escort carrier, *Audacity*, was commissioned in the autumn but soon sunk. During this period 325 merchant ships were sunk by German and Italian U-boats for the loss of twenty-eight of their own.

Everything changed in December 1941 when the United States was forced into the war and the U-boat offensive shifted into their waters. That phase ended in July 1942 and the most intensive part of the campaign began as the U-boats returned to mid-Atlantic. Though numbers of escorts were increasing, the 'air gap' in the middle of the ocean was still highly dangerous. Losses fluctuated throughout a long winter, with 117 ships sunk in November and sixty-one in December. Elsewhere, the tide of the war had already turned, with Allied victories at Stalingrad, Alamein and Midway, the invasion of North Africa and the long campaign on Guadalcanal. But in March 1943 two eastbound convoys, HX229 and SC122 (which eventually merged) were attacked by around forty U-boats and lost twenty-one of their number, totalling 141,000 tons, for the loss of one U-boat.

All changed again in the next two months. Escort carriers became available, as did long-range Liberators to close the air gap. There were enough escorts from support groups to go to the aid of convoys under attack, and the escorts themselves were better trained and equipped. In May, Convoy ONS5, led by Commander Peter Gretton until he was forced to leave due to the short range of his destroyer, forced its way through one of the largest packs ever concentrated, with the aid of a support group. It lost twelve ships but sank six U-boats. SC129 was attacked north of the Azores and lost two ships, but several U-boats were sunk by various means. And Gretton had his revenge when escorting SC130, when no ships were lost and five U-boats were sunk. Forty-one

U-boats were lost in May and Admiral Dönitz ordered their withdrawal from the Atlantic to regroup. There were few Allied losses in the ocean after that. In June 1944 the U-boats were in the English Channel in an unsuccessful attempt to disrupt the invasion of Normandy. Them using their new *Schnörchels* (snorkels), they began an inshore campaign in British waters, too late to affect the result of the war.

The other hard-fought convoy routes, in the contrasting climates of the Mediterranean and Arctic, were defended against surface ship and aircraft attack as much as submarines. Nevertheless, the U-boats scored major successes against the old battleship *Barham* in November 1941 and the famous carrier *Ark Royal* in the following month, and the carrier *Eagle* in August 1942. In the Arctic, they sank most of the ships lost after Convoy PQ17 was dispersed due to a threat from the battleship *Tirpitz* in July 1942, and in September PQ18 suffered the loss of ten merchantmen out of forty-one to air attack and three to U-boats – though the sinking of three submarines by destroyer and aircraft showed that tactics were not ineffective.

'We were just plugging along'

The United States Navy had good reason to be aware of submarine warfare by 1941. It was the unrestricted German campaign which brought America into the First World War, and the Neutrality Patrols of 1939–41 led to a battle with USS *Greer*, a U-boat attack on USS *Kearney*, and the sinking of the destroyer *Reuben James* with the loss of more than a hundred lives. These incidents contributed to Roosevelt's anti-German strategy, and affected Hitler's decision to declare war on the USA on 11 December 1941. And arguably the first shot of America's war was fired on 7 December 1941 when USS *Ward* sank a Japanese submarine trying to enter Pearl Harbor just before the air attack. Despite all that, the navy was unprepared for anti-submarine war. In October 1939, while he was still First Lord of the Admiralty, Churchill wrote to Roosevelt, 'We should be quite ready to tell you about our Asdic methods whenever you feel they would be of use to the United States Navy and are sure the secret will go no further.[2] But this upset his colleagues and Admiral Godfrey, the Director of Naval Intelligence.

U-boats had operated off the American coast in the First World War, and in 1941/2 there was plenty of warning by way of the Ultra decrypts sent on by Britain, but the campaign off the East Coast, considered by the British as the fourth phase of the Battle of the Atlantic, came as a surprise. It is not clear how much was due to concentration of minds and resources on the Pacific, where the Japanese advance seemed unstoppable, how much on the lack of preparation due to the primacy of the 'gun club' in the pre-war navy, and how much on the Anglophobia of Admiral King, whose deputy chief of staff observed that 'The Americans wished to learn their own lessons'.[3] Admiral Cunningham, then the British liaison officer in Washington, perceived that the American officials were 'quite determined not to be run by us, in fact rather than benefitting by our experience they prefer to have a disaster of their own to learn by.'[4]

Ultra decoding ended on 1 February 1942, when the Germans introduced a fourth wheel to the Enigma machine, and did not resume until 13 December. Shore lights allowed the U-boats to pick out their targets against them, but commercial interests resisted any attempt to reduce them for three months, and then it was only a largely ineffective 'dim-out', rather than a blackout as was strictly enforced in most of Europe, on shore and inland. According to one visiting British officer, 'The present lighting system in most parts pf Manhattan seems at least equal to, and in other greater than, that of any large British city in peacetime.'[5]

On 12 March Winston Churchill complained that 'I am most deeply concerned at the immense sinking of tankers west of the 40th meridian and in the Caribbean Sea … the situation is so serious that drastic action of some kind is necessary.'[6] But in April King continued to believe that 'Inadequately escorted convoys are worse than none', which was contrary to British experience.[7] He dismissed situation maps as 'little toys and other play things', and ignored the experience of Roger Winn's tracking room at the Admiralty, until Lieutenant Commander Kenneth Knowles was sent to study it and came back with an 'exact clone' in Washington.[8]

On 1 April Admiral Andrews, who commanded the North Atlantic Sea Control Frontier, initiated a partial convoy system known as the 'bucket brigade', by which groups of ships sailed by day and spent the nights in protected anchorages, which had some success. General Marshall, the army chief of staff, was still concerned about losses of his own resources and complained to King on 19 June:

> The losses by submarines off our Atlantic seaboard and in the Caribbean now threaten our entire war effort. … Of the 74 ships allocated to the Army for July … 17 have already been sunk. 22 per cent of our bauxite fleet has already been destroyed. 20 per cent of the Puerto Rican fleet has been lost. Tanker sinkings have been 3.5 per cent per month of tonnage in use.[9]

King finally concluded: 'escort is not just *one* way of handling the submarine menace; it is the *only* way that gives any promise of success.

The so-called patrol and hunting operations have time and again proved futile.'[10] A full convoy system was in force by the autumn.

From the middle of January to the end of July 1941, 360 ships were sunk in American waters. Of course, it is impossible to guess how many would have been sunk in any case if the U-boats had been driven out to mid-Atlantic sooner, but by any standards it was a very severe lesson. Perhaps the naval leadership took on the enthusiasm of the convert, but after July 1942 American anti-submarine tactics and procedures began to improve rapidly. As in many other fields, they took on British experience and improved on it.

Ships

A battleship can earn its keep as a deterrent, swinging round a buoy in harbour, but an escort vessel has to be out at sea to protect a convoy, and large numbers were needed for an ocean war. Many old British destroyers, mainly of the 'S' and 'V'/'W' classes of 1916–18, had survived the peacetime cuts. They were outdated for fleet work and used instead as ocean escorts, though restricted by their short range and instability. Their armament was excessive for convoy escort, as was a speed of up to 36 knots, though it could be useful in moving to an endangered area of a convoy. More modern destroyers could lead escort groups. HMS *Duncan* was a flotilla leader built in the early 1930s. Converted for the Atlantic role, she was:

> well equipped with weapons and detecting instruments and also had the new 'hedgehog', together with a monstrously big depth-charge which was discharged from a torpedo tube. She had kept a couple of guns for use against U-boats and a couple of torpedoes in case a surface warship was encountered. She had all the latest asdic, radio, radar and H/F D/F sets.[11]

Destroyers usually had directors to aim their main guns, and good plotting equipment for directing a hunt. Short range was a serious problem. Commander Donald Macintyre pointed out 'the unsuitability of HMS *Whitehall* [of the 'V'/'W' class] for ocean escort duties owing to her high rate of consumption of fuel', which was 'a cause for constant anxiety to the escort group leader'. She was unlikely to complete a westward passage in winter without refuelling and could not be used on high-speed operations.[12]

Very few of the small First World War escort vessels survived the post-war cuts. Interest in the type revived in 1928 with the *Bridgewater* class with two 4in guns, fifteen depth charges and a speed of 16.5 knots.

Development continued over the next decade, with increases in length, speed and armament, with six 4in guns in the *Black Swan* class, which was laid down in 1939. These vessels proved most useful in areas where enemy aircraft operated, which did not include the central Atlantic.

The conventional destroyer was expensive to build and run, so the Hunt class of 'destroyer escorts' was conceived in the late 1930s as a kind of minimalist destroyer with a speed of 28 knots, six 4in guns and no torpedo tubes. Due to stability problems, two of the guns had to be removed, and the second batch was built with increased beam. They too were more suitable for tasks such as the Gibraltar convoys where anti-aircraft gun power was useful.

The navy had turned to trawlers, the largest and most seaworthy type of fishing boat, during the First World War, and from 1933 it made plans to requisition and convert them for anti-submarine and minesweeping duties. Out of 1700 which were eventually taken over, and besides those built specially to Admiralty specifications, a hundred were used as coastal escorts and 108 as ocean escorts to fill the gap. These were generally about 160ft long with coal-fired engines producing a speed of 11 to 12 knots. They were, of course, fitted with Asdic, and armed with a 4in gun forward, machine guns and Oerlikons. Each carried fifty-five depth charges and was manned by around four officers and forty-six ratings.[13] In April 1943 Sidney Kerslake was onboard one of four trawlers escorting convoy ONS5: 'The *Northern Gem*, though pirouetting about like a cork, was nevertheless weathering the storms well. She took nothing in the way of heavy water onboard, but was continually being swept by spray and spume, which travelling at the speed of bullets, rat-tat-tatted on the bridge window.'[14]

As war approached it became clear that destroyers, and even destroyer escorts, were too expensive to form the extensive screens that were needed round convoys. Sir Stanley Goodall, the Director of Naval Construction, was summoned to the First Sea Lord:

> … he was concerned about ships for anti-submarine duties. We must have great numbers. Of the types then in service, trawlers were too slow, and escorts expensive to build in terms of time and money. He wanted some sort of ship that was faster than the trawler, could be built rapidly, and would not need a big complement such as our escorts required.[15]

Goodall turned to Smith's Dock of Hull, builders of whale-catchers, and based the design of the new class on them. It was assumed that they would be manned mostly by professional seamen. Sixty-one were ordered in 1939, but by the time they came into service France had fallen and they were forced out into the Atlantic. Moreover, they were increasingly manned by hastily trained recruits, some of whom had little or no experience of the sea. One captain complained in the autumn of 1940:

A Flower-class corvette in rough weather, showing the difficulties experienced in ships designed mainly for inshore waters, but forced to fill the gaps in the Atlantic campaign. Depth charges can be seen in racks at the stern and a merchant ship is behind.

> ... the rolling was incredible. In over twenty years in the service in every type of ship, I never encountered anything like it. Officers and men on duty became rapidly exhausted by the mere physical effort of holding on. ... The plight of the numerous seasick members of the crew and some of the older men became pitiable ... Under such conditions, sleep, or indeed any kind of rest, is impossible, as it entails considerable physical strain even to remain in a bunk.[16]

More equipment was fitted, and the standard complement was increased from eighty-five to over a hundred, including seven officers for ocean escort duties. Despite the uncomfortable ride, they were more seaworthy than destroyers in ocean weather:

> In weather in which destroyers with their long sleek lines, designed primarily for speed, would be restricted to courses which would keep them heading into the seas to avoid serious damage or risk of capsizing, the Flowers with their broad beam would ride the huge waves with confidence and steer in any direction with safety.[17]

Improvements included a much longer forecastle, which offered extra accommodation as well as a drier deck, and bilge keels which helped prevent rolling. With a speed of only 16 knots, they were slower than a surfaced U-boat. The Castle class was 50ft longer than the Flowers, with a redesigned hull. Though it had the same engines, it was half a knot faster, but still not fast enough. It was designed to fit onto the slipways of yards which were not able to build larger vessels

The only answer was to build a class of escorts with the Atlantic in mind. Design of what became the River class began in November 1940, soon after the war began to spread into the Atlantic. The new ships were to have a 40 per cent increase in tonnage on the Flower class, on a completely different hull with flared bows to push aside the seas. They were fitted with two of the same engines as the Flower class, giving a speed of 20 knots, which was just enough to overtake a surfaced U-boat (if it could be achieved). They had a much greater range of 3500 miles. The first one, *Rother*, was ready by the spring of 1941.

Captain Humphrey Boys-Smith wrote of *Tay*, 'A very beautiful ship she was too'. They were 301ft long, almost half as long again as the corvettes, and carried two 4in guns, one forward and one aft. The depth-charge armament was eventually increased to 150 and they had the new Hedgehog ahead-throwing weapon, though on an exposed position in the bows because they were fitted as an afterthought.

Captain Gretton commented on the *Tay*: 'These frigates were more comfortable than destroyers although they were slow and could only make eighteen knots'.[18] The substantial quarterdeck aft, originally designed to include minesweeping equipment, allowed room for expansion.

At first the Admiralty objected to the use of the term 'frigate', claiming that 'The introduction of a new class name can only be justified on account of marked change in function or type.' But it was adopted by the Canadians and in 1943 the Admiralty gave way. The Rivers were succeeded by the Lochs, with a slightly redesigned hull to aid mass production – at one stage it was intended to build two hundred of them, but most were cancelled as the Battle of the Atlantic turned in the Allies' favour. They carried the Squid as the main anti-submarine armament instead of the Hedgehog. The Bay class used the same hull with an increased aircraft armament. The Captain class was a version of the American *Evarts* and *Buckley* classes, based on the British destroyer escort design and with diesel-electric propulsion.

Asdic, supposedly named from the Anti-submarine Detection Committee of the First World War, was a means of detecting a submarine by bouncing sound off it. The British placed great faith in it before the war, and Churchill was convinced. After a demonstration in 1938 he wrote to the First Sea Lord, 'I never imagined I should hear one of these creatures asking to be destroyed, both orally and literally.'[19] Across the Atlantic, Raymond Spruance advised his son not to become a submariner, 'Some new-fangled device the British had, called ASDIC, would make the submarine a coffin.'[20] Indeed, plenty of sailors would die in submarines, but only after they had inflicted huge damage. For Asdic's efficiency was greatly exaggerated, and in 1940 it had to move from the North Sea to the broad Atlantic.

Asdic could be used in its normal mode when pings were sent out and bounced off a possible target. It could also be used in passive mode, listening out for movements in the water or 'hydrophone effect', which had the advantage of not alerting the enemy to the escort's presence. The first function of Asdic in an escort vessel was searching. Commander Peter Gretton commented:

> it was hard to keep the asdic operators alert during these long uneventful passages. The noise of the 'ping' of an asdic set is a natural soporific and my sympathies were with the men who had to keep awake. I found that only by continual 'briefing' by the Officer on the Bridge was it possible to keep the operators interested and up to the mark, ...[21]

Once an echo had been found it had to be classified as 'submarine', non-sub' or 'doubtful – operators were warned not to use 'doubtful' every time, but to come to clearer decisions. Factors in classification included any change in the range and bearing of the target; the sharpness of definition, for a U-boat tended to give a clear echo; the presence of hydrophone effect, though that would not be heard from a boat moving at slow speed; change in pitch which might indicate whether the target was moving towards or away from the ship; and the extent of the target.[22]

If a target was clearly identified and it was decided to pursue it, the team closed up in the Asdic hut and a chase began. The Asdic beam was several degrees wide, so with a procedure known as 'cut on', the operator found the edges of the target and pressed a button to mark them on the bearing recorder. By the end of 1943, the experts were recommending a new 'step-across' procedure by which the operator recorded echoes every 2½ degrees across the target to give a more constant reading.

The anti-submarine control officer, or ASCO, was a key man in an escort vessel, the authority on any underwater contact, and able to direct the hunt for a U-boat. But their training was short, and they had difficulty in keeping up with what was expected of them. Often the ASCO had to rely on the experienced leading submarine detector.

Most escort vessels were fitted with radar during 1941. In convoy escort, the main role was to find U-boats attacking on the surface at night. The most common model in the middle of the war was Type 271, with the aerial inside the 'parrot's cage' just aft of the bridge. The data could not be sent over any distance, so the operator had to sit just below the cage. The aerial was turned by hand and could not rotate through more than 360 degrees without reversing. The signal was shown as an A-scan. With the aerial pointed in a particular direction, the distance of any contact could be read off on a line on the tube. A series of contacts had to be plotted by hand to show the relationship of one to another. A U-boat detected outside the convoy was not difficult to track, but if it was inside, good plotting was needed to pinpoint it among the ships. From 1943, ships were fitted with the plan position indicator, or PPI, which gave an overall plan of the radar situation and saved a great deal of plotting. New aerials were introduced, able to rotate constantly and they did not have to be so close to the operator.

U-boats were controlled from their headquarters in France and were encouraged to make regular reports by radio. Bearings taken from Allied shore stations were useful in establishing the number of U-boats in an area, but were too inaccurate to be of any tactical use to the escort. Those taken from ships with the convoy could allow the senior officer to estimate the disposition and tactics of the enemy. Many ships were therefore fitted with high frequency direction finding, HF/DF, or 'huff-duff', which could pick up enemy signals and plot the positions of U-boats. Two separate readings had to be taken to get a cross bearing, but by late 1942 many escort groups were able to do this. This, and intelligence from the shore, meant that convoys were rarely attacked without warning. In 1943 the captain of the training school HMS *Osprey* suggested that it was no longer necessary to keep watch on Asdics unless such warnings had been received.[23]

Commander Donald Macintyre wrote of convoy ONS138:

> The main feature of operations was the astonishing number of enemy signals intercepted, which the use of HF/DF enabled us to plot the movement of U-boats over a period of 24 hours, at the end of which period the U-boats were finally driven off without any attack being delivered on the convoy.

This convoy had two ships fitted with HF/DF, the senior officer's ship *Hesperus* and the rescue ship *Accrington*. It was enough to make an assessment of enemy tactics.

The human eye was still one of the most important sensors, as reported by the captain of *Celandine*: 'as soon as the range was about 500 yards, it was possible, with the aid of binoculars, to make it out as a submarine on the surface, trimmed down, steering at about 12 knots on a course to overtake the convoy'.[24] In July to December 1942, 55 per cent of U-boats were first detected by radar, 11 per cent by sighting, 13 per cent by Asdic transmissions and 9 per cent by hydrophone effect, but figures for HF/DF were not included.

The depth charge had been invented by the Royal Navy during the last war and it remained the primary anti-submarine weapon at the beginning of the next. It was simply a cylinder filled with explosive, set to explode at a certain depth and dropped over the stern or fired on the beam from a thrower. The most common type was the Mark VII, which weighed 290lbs and could be set to a depth of 50ft to 350ft. Originally they were filled with amatol, a mixture of TNT and ammonium nitrate. Later they used minol, with increased explosive power.

A ship needed to make at least 10 knots as it dropped its charges, to avoid its stern being blown off. As it approached the U-boat it would lose the echo, and guesswork was involved as the submarine would take evasive measures. Also, there was no way of determining a submarine's depth until Type 147 Asdic was introduced in 1943. But the charge had to explode within about 25ft to sink a U-boat and about 100ft to do damage. The answer was to saturate the area with a large number of depth charges.

The explosion of a depth charge astern of an American escort. The morale effect on friend and enemy was almost as great as the actual damage by a relatively inaccurate weapon.

Early in the war a fourteen-charge pattern was used, but not too often as each ship had a limited supply. Moreover, with the new minol charges, one interfered with another. The ten-charge pattern was the most common, with charges dropped astern from the rails and others fired from the throwers to land 225ft away on each side. This would produce two exploding diamond patterns, one above the other, 450ft wide and 470ft long. Only about 6 per cent of depth-charge attacks were successful in 1943–45. A U-boat could be 'hunted to exhaustion' and forced to surface as its air ran out after about forty-eight hours, but only if escorts could be spared from the convoy, which was unlikely early in the war. Later, patterns of twenty-six and twenty-eight charges were developed for 'creeping attack', usually by support groups which could afford to spend a long time destroying a contact.

For a repeat attack, the throwers had to be reloaded with great difficulty, as reported by Gretton: 'The depth-charge crew on the quarter deck were having a very difficult time. The ship was pitching and rolling badly; the seas were washing down the quarter deck, soaking the men there, and the heavy and cumbersome depth-charges were difficult to reload.'[25]

The problem of losing contact with the target as it passed under the ship might be solved by firing weapons ahead of the ship. The Hedgehog, put into service in 1941, consisted of twenty-four charges mounted in six rows on a base placed forward in the ship. They would be fired to land in a circle 30yds in diameter and centred 215yds from the ship. They were contact charges so there would only be an explosion if something was hit, so they were much smaller than depth charges, weighing 35lbs instead of 290.

Hedgehog needed more sophisticated aiming techniques, but it was rushed into service ahead of rival systems, without enough training. It also lacked the moral effect of depth-charge explosions. Orders to employ it as often as possible were counter-productive, for it was often fired in unsuitable circumstances. A series of trials off Londonderry early in 1944 allowed it to find its full potential. After that it had a success rate of 28 per cent.

A Hedgehog attack began at a range of about 1200yds; high speed not needed: 8, 9 or 12 knots were recommended. The Asdic team reported the bearings of the target and worked out the deflection needed to counteract the submarine's movements.[26] Gretton described an attack by *Duncan*. After a 'very exciting hunt … using slow speed' and stopping 'every now and then to make quite certain of the course and speed of the submarine', 'I missed with the first "hedgehog" shot, but the second one got three hits and, after some long minutes, gruesome evidence of the destruction of *U-274* began to rise to the surface.'[27]

Hedgehog's main rival was Squid, which was first used in 1944. Instead of contact charges, it fired three depth charges and more care was taken to train the crews properly. It formed the main armament of the new Loch-class frigates and refitted Castle-class corvettes. In the last stages of the war, it had a high success rate of 30 per cent for a single mounting, and 40 per cent if two were fitted.

Details of the Hedgehog anti-submarine mortar in the top left, with other drawings showing its operation. Though developed by the Royal Navy, it was often more successful when used by American escorts; the British tended to favour its rival, the Squid mortar.

Destroyers and sloops had sophisticated gunnery arrangements with more and larger guns than corvettes – modern ones had at least four 4.7in guns, each firing a projectile 1.4 times the weight of a corvette's. Corvettes and frigates only had one or two 4in 'pop-guns' which were barely adequate to penetrate a U-boat's hull, and were aimed by the gunlayers without any mechanical aids. Captains were informed that 'Experience of encounters with U-boats had shown that they can sustain many hits from [semi-armour piercing] or [high explosive] shell without receiving lethal damage.' Escort commanders were advised that gunfire might dazzle their own crews and prevent other means of attack.[28] Gretton became aware of the difficulties of using his guns when they could not be depressed enough: 'I had been horrified by the apparent difficulty of hitting a submarine at night at close range, for only the Oerlikon gun had been any good against the U-boat which nearly scraped the paint off the *Tay*'s bows.'[29]

HMS *Osprey*, the navy's main anti-submarine establishment, was evacuated from Portland on the south coast of England early in 1941 and made its wartime home in Dunoon on the Firth of Clyde, which was usually reached by steamer from Glasgow or Gourock. Besides lectures and exercises, crews were trained on the attack teacher, a simulator 'produced to meet the training requirements for a ship's Asdic team … the sound effects and plotting mechanisms were combined in a single table. The method used was ingenious and realistic.'[30] The American RNVR officer A H Cherry experienced it late in 1941:

> We closed up for exercise. … A quartermaster at the wheel, the A/S operator at his sound gear, Officer-of-the-Watch, who was myself, and the Captain. The operator started sweeping his arc and the drill commenced.
>
> Suddenly: 'Echo … Green three oh,' the sound operator shouted, and the attack was on, 'Range two thousand yards.'
>
> The sweep instantly narrowed down to a small arc governed by a left and right side of the U-boat caught in the sound beam. The warship altered to a collision course and went into attacking speed. Information commenced pouring in to the Officer-of-the-Watch who sifted and passed it on to the Captain: information such as the U-boat's up-to-the-minute course and speed, range and bearings; all essential for the fast approaching moment of 'Fire.'[31]

Crews of newly commissioned ships were trained by HMS *Western Isles* anchored at Tobermory, a sheltered natural harbour on the island of Mull. The unforgettable commander was Commodore Sir Gilbert Stephenson, a former vice admiral known as 'monkey' or 'electric whiskers' because of his apparently uncontrollable facial hair. He was noted for his unpredictable behaviour and great energy. In the most famous anecdote about him:

> Without any preliminaries he flung his gold-braided cap on the deck, and said abruptly to the Quartermaster – 'That's a small unexploded bomb dropped by an enemy plane. What are you going to do about it?' The sailor … promptly … kicked the cap into the sea. Everyone waited for a great roar of protest from the Commodore. But not at all. He warmly congratulated the lad on his presence of mind, and then, pointing to the submerged cap said: 'That's a man overboard! Jump in and save him!'

He outlined his philosophy in 1944: 'The Commanding Officer has to be satisfied that every officer knows not only his own duty but that of every other officer and the whole ship's company has to be moulded into one team'. More privately, he declared:

> My number one priory was *Spirit* … determination to win. Next came *Discipline:* it's no good being the finest men in the world if you are not going to obey orders. Third – *Administration:* making sure the work of the ship was evenly divided … Then, lastly … *Technique* – how to use the equipment. That would have been quite useless unless the spirit was right in the first place.

Crews, such as Cyril Stephens of HMS *Orchid*, found it exhausting: 'Tobermory, oh my God, it was murder … you'd have exercises: "abandon ship", "collision at sea", "fire in the galley", "fire somewhere else"'. It was no easier for officers, the commodore: 'concerned himself with everything and everybody and nothing was too small to escape his notice – he even questioned me thoroughly over a reported shortage of soap.'[32] Most agreed that it could be worse than the actual voyage across the Atlantic.

From late 1942 escort groups were trained in tactics which had been worked out in the tactical school at Liverpool. The school was commanded by A J Baker-Cresswell and based at Londonderry, then Larne, in Northern Ireland. It used the yacht *Philante*, belonging to the legendary aircraft designer Sir Thomas Sopwith, as a mock convoy and several submarines were available to act as U-boats.

By forcing the Allies to adopt convoy, the Germans had already scored a victory of a sort. A convoy cannot sail until all its ships have assembled; at sea, it can only proceed at the speed of the slowest ship; on arrival, even if it is divided into sections for different ports, large numbers of ships will arrive at once, straining the dock facilities. And vast resources were needed to provide adequate escorts. But as well as providing some kind of protection for the ships, convoy bunched them together so that they tended to be harder to find than individual ships; and if the U-boats were to do their job, they would have to confront the convoy's defences, and in that sense the system was far superior to hunting groups searching vast areas of ocean.

At the start of the war, the main convoy routes were on the east coast, across the ocean and to Scandinavia, but the invasion of Norway ended the last. After the Fall of France, a north-about system was introduced to take ships from the east to west coast and vice versa. Gibraltar convoys began in October 1939 to supply forces in the Mediterranean or go south to Sierra Leone. Initially, the ocean convoys only included ships capable of steaming between 9 and 14.9 knots; faster ships sailed independently, slower ones at great risk. In August 1940 a system of slower Atlantic convoys was introduced for ships between 7½ and 9 knots, codenamed SC as they started at Sydney Cove. Westbound convoys assembled at Halifax, Nova Scotia, and were known as HX. They were hopefully met by a naval escort at 12 to 15 degrees west, extended to 17 and then 19 degrees in 1940 and 35 degrees in April 1941 with the use of Iceland as a refuelling base. Westbound convoys were known as ONS and ONF, for outbound north, slow and fast. From 1 June 1941 they were escorted all the way. They were usually routed to the north, especially in the summer when long Arctic days made U-boat attack more difficult.

Transatlantic escorting was shared between the British and Canadian navies, as American ships were devoted to coastal escort after June 1942, and then for the North African and European landings. Transfers took place at Westomp, or West Ocean Meeting Point, south of Newfoundland, and Mid Ocean Meeting Point, or Momp, at 22 degrees west.

The senior officer of an escort group was usually a commander RN, one of the few levels in the escort force where regular officers predominated. Younger than a full captain and better able to withstand the strain and sleepless nights of escort duty, he was an officer of some experience with a mind flexible enough to take in new ideas. After his appointment in

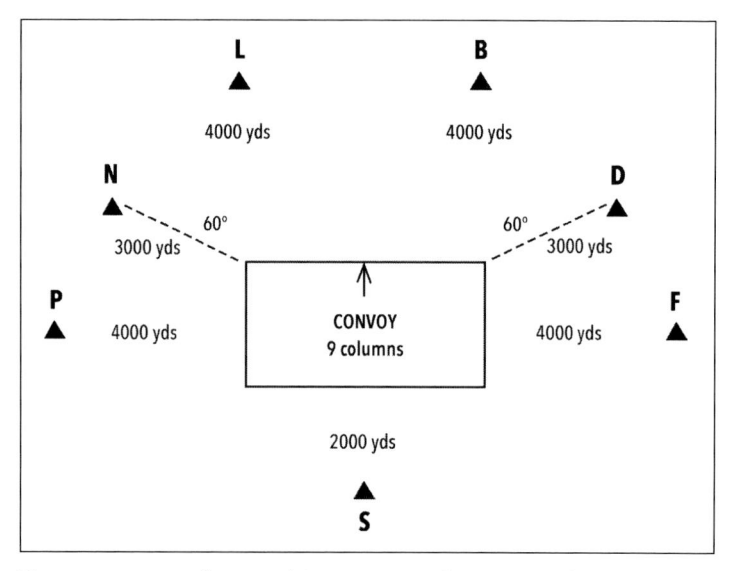

The arrangement of a typical escort group of seven round a nine-column Atlantic convoy, showing the distances from the convoy and the 'whipper-in' 2000yds astern of the convoy. (*Stephen Dent*)

command of B7 group, Peter Gretton realised it was 'the finest job in the navy for a new commander.'[33]

An admiral would have a captain under him to run the flagship. This did not work in the confined space of escort vessels, as D A Rayner found out: 'After years of having my own steward, sea cabin and chart table, I would now lose the captain's pencil, or find that he had carried off my rubber in his pocket.'[34] It was better if the senior officer commanded his own ship as well as the escort group, with a strong first lieutenant to take some of the weight. Most escort group commanders chose to serve in destroyers so that they could move quickly to an area of the convoy under attack. They had more sophisticated equipment, such as gun directors and plotting tables. On the other hand, they were usually old, unstable and needed frequent refuelling.

It was recommended that the senior officer position himself astern of the convoy:

> Had the senior officer of the convoy [SC118] stationed himself astern during the night of the 6th–7th he would have realised at once that ships were being torpedoed and would have had a better idea of the direction of the attack; he would have realised that escorts stationed in the threatened sectors were absenting themselves for long periods and would thus have been able to re-organise the screen so as to fill the gaps or order them back to the convoy.[35]

Some escort groups, on routes to Gibraltar and Freetown where air attack was more likely, were composed mainly of sloops and ex-US cutters. Some consisted entirely of corvettes, such as Unit B5, which operated on the western side of the Atlantic. At the end of 1942 the most typical group in mid-Atlantic had three destroyers and five or six corvettes, perhaps supplemented by one or two frigates in the next few months. B5, for example, had the destroyers *Havelock* and *Warwick* in December 1942, and the corvettes *Buttercup, Columbine, Godetia, Lavender, Pimpernel* and *Saxifrage*.

According to the *Atlantic Convoy Instructions* of September 1943, if only two escorts were available, one should be stationed on each side. With any more escorts, it was normal to have a ship in position 200yds astern of the convoy as 'whipper in'. In addition, in a typical seven-ship escort of the period, there would also be three ships on each side of the convoy, 3000–4000yds out and level with the convoy's centre, 30 degrees from its forward corner and directly ahead of that. There were other dispositions for stronger escorts when a double screen might be attempted, for strong winds and for night-time.

The commodore of a convoy was in charge of the merchant ships; in an ocean convoy he was often a retired flag officer. Even in his current rank, he was two grades superior to a commander, and he might well have been a full admiral when the commander was a junior officer. Gretton worked with Admiral Sir Charles Ramsey, who had been his commander-in-chief at Rosyth earlier in the war.[36] But Donald Macintyre records only one instance of conflict in his own experience. A dispute over the position of the convoy was eventually settled but only after 'A series of more and more acrimonious signals then passed between us and it was a very angry commodore who finally accepted defeat.'[37] The merchant ships were arranged in columns 400yds apart, later increased to 600 and 800yds, and up to five ships in each, so a convoy was far wider than it was long, for research showed that this was the best way to avoid U-boats.

The object of every escort commander was, in the time-honoured phrase, 'the safe and timely arrival of the convoy', and the sinking of U-boats was only a means to that end. If it had been possible to avoid contact with the enemy with nearly every convoy, the campaign would have been just as successful. Yet in the 1950s the authors of the staff history of the conflict, nearly always moderate in their language, called the chapters of the main narrative 'U-Boat Killing, the First Phase', etc. Perhaps this was an attempt to counter the view that anti-submarine warfare was mainly a defensive affair.

But U-boat killing did have its role. If a U-boat was sunk, it was no longer a threat to that convoy, or any future ones. Moreover, making life very dangerous in the vicinity of a convoy was the best way of intimidating U-boat captains and deterring serious attack. And the line between offensive and defensive tactics was not easy to draw. Often the best way counter an immediate threat was to attack the U-boat and force it to dive deep. Even if it was not destroyed it would almost certainly be left behind and was no longer a threat to that convoy.

There were several possible responses to a suspected attack on the convoy. On the code-word 'Raspberry', or the firing of two white rockets, escorts ahead of the convoy would stay in station but fire star shells, the one astern would zigzag, while those towards the rear would sweep in a triangular pattern. It was replaced by 'Pineapple' and 'Banana'. In the former, if a ship was torpedoed all escorts would transit on their Asdics, increase to the maximum speed for Asdic operation, zigzag broadly and fire illuminants. With 'Banana', the escorts carried out more complex manoeuvres including zigzags, triangular searches and U-turns. Others such as 'Artichoke', 'Porcupine' and 'Observant' were added later.

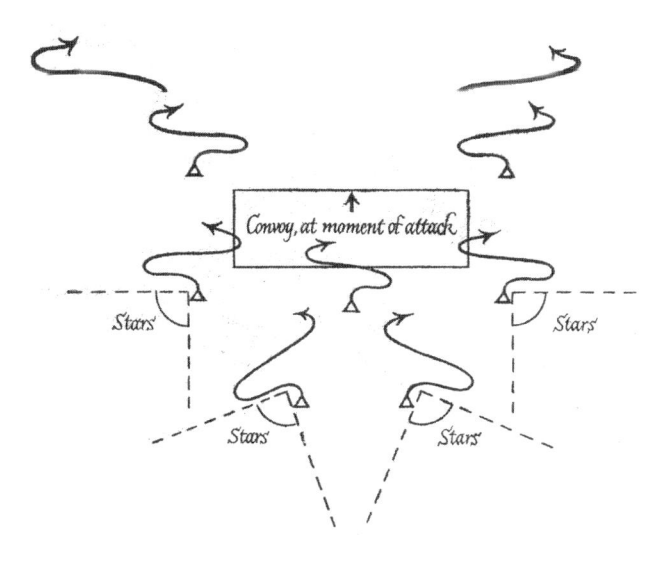

Pineapple was one of the manoeuvres to be carried out by escorts during submarine attack. It was designed to search the largest area possible by Asdic, and at night star shells were fired as shown to illuminate sectors.

Rescue ships were mostly converted merchantmen of around 1500 tons, fitted out with medical facilities for survivors. The lack of them was felt with convoy HX229, when escorts were diverted from their main task, leaving holes in the screen.[38] Thirty rescue ships were commissioned, starting in January 1941, and five were sunk. The most active was *Zamalek* which sailed with sixty-eight convoys and rescued 665 survivors.

Zigzags were designed to ensure that if a torpedo was fired from some distance, the ships would not be on the same course when it arrived at its target. Fifteen different patterns were available for convoys early in the war. Some were very simple: no. 10 only used turns of 22½ degrees, but as the instructions stated, 'The more complex the zig-zag, the greater the protection.'[39] Convoys did not often zigzag in mid-Atlantic, but escorts did:

> The area of the convoy torpedo danger zone is too large for the number of escorts normally available with ocean convoys to provide complete Asdic cover. ... Escorts, by their movement within this area, will seriously embarrass a U-boat closing to a firing position at periscope depth, and zigzags should be so designed and co-ordinated in order to provide the maximum degree of protection ...[40]

There was, of course, the problem of fuel consumption. During the passage of SC130, Commander Gretton decided to keep *Duncan* in the centre of the convoy and travelled a straight course, to conserve fuel.[41]

Counter-attack was stressed in orders: 'When the contact is an immediate danger – A counter-attack must be carried out at once.' This meant that the escort should steer directly for the bearing of the enemy at maximum Asdic operating speed, and then drop the maximum number of depth charges, if the supply permitted.[42]

Ramming was one means of counter-attack. It had been a standard tactic early in the century and the older battleships of the 'R' and *Queen Elizabeth* classes still had bows designed for it, though it was never used that way in practice. It was revived in November 1940 when the destroyer *Hotspur* hit the Italian submarine *Lafole*, which, however, was mainly sunk by depth charges. After that it was used twenty-six times, leading to a sinking in all but three cases – though in only four of these was it achieved by ramming alone. It had a good effect on the morale of a crew: 'it is only natural that ship's company should like to feel the crunch of their bows smashing through a U-boat, and know that one of these pests is definitely destroyed'.[43] It required considerable manoeuvring skill:

> The submarine immediately increased speed and 'snaked the line' commencing to port. *Viscount* followed her swing to port but failed to catch her as she swung back to starboard. The U-boat then 'committed suicide' by swinging back to port right across the bows of *Viscount* who was turning under full starboard rudder.[44]

U-619 was recorded as being sunk.

But by 1943 the Admiralty had serious doubts about the tactic, for escort bows might need several months of repair:

> Whilst it is not desired to prohibit ramming when the opportunity arises, … An analysis of U-boats rammed shows that ramming is in the majority of cases, quite unnecessary to ensure destruction of the U-boat. … full consideration should be given to dealing with the U-boat by all other means …[45]

By the middle of 1942 there were enough escorts to form support groups independent of particular convoys. They differed from the hunting groups which had proved unsuccessful with the British in 1939 and the Americans in 1942. Instead of heading off into the empty ocean, they would usually join convoys which were already under attack, to reinforce the escort and perhaps stay behind to hunt U-boats to destruction. Later in the year, they were mostly withdrawn to support the North African landings, but were back again in 1943. Gretton had his escort group B7 designated as one, just as the U-boats returned to mid-Atlantic. He had some success, participating in the sinking of three U-boats: 'on 5th November the group sailed up the River Foyle feeling very pleased with itself.'[46] It looked very different to the young CW seaman Geoffrey Ball:

> Thus ensued an epic 28 days continuously at sea hunting and attacking U-boats which had come back into force. Action stations more ON than OFF – refuelling 5–6 times in heavy seas: stopping (not recommended) to pick up 2 survivors from a U-boat and attacking with new weapons called 'hedgehogs' … My enduring memory of that time is of feeling so very tired even at age 18. Gretton drove everyone week after week in his relentless pursuit of U-boats. He got the medals (Bar to his DSO) … we, the seamen, did all the hard work.[47]

Captain Frederick J Walker's Second Support Group was the most successful. He developed the 'creeping barrage' technique, by which one escort pinged the submarine from a distance, keeping it unaware of another which was directed over it to drop depth charges. The group sank sixteen submarines before Walker died, probably from overwork, in July 1944, and the crews he had trained went on to sink seven more.

From 1940 the English Channel was virtually closed to merchant shipping and the route south of Ireland was dangerous, so the ports of northwest England, western Scotland and Northern Ireland took on great importance. Liverpool was second only to London among British ports, with a huge complex of enclosed docks protecting ships from the tides of the River Mersey. The headquarters of Western Approaches Command was set up there. It was subject to intensive bombing.

As the hub of Western Approaches command, Liverpool was a target well worth hitting. There were never less than a hundred ships in harbour, loading and unloading; plus their tugs, and oil storage tanks, and eleven miles of docks with their cranes and ammunition barges and ship-repair yards and warehouses and dock-gates and the whole network of rail-linkage to the rest of England. Worth hitting, it was hit with relentless accuracy, for eight nights on end.

The Clyde offered a good anchorage in the Tail of the Bank off Greenock, but Glasgow was a much smaller port than Liverpool. Dock facilities were limited and there were fewer rail links with the rest of the United Kingdom. The Clyde, however, was an excellent escort base. It was close to many of the training bases and there were numerous shipyards to carry out repair work.

With southern Ireland (or the Irish Free State was it was known at the time) maintaining its neutrality, the Northern Irish port of Londonderry was the closest in the United Kingdom to the Atlantic Ocean, which was a key factor when many escorts barely had the range for ocean voyages. Fred Kellett wrote about passage in along the River Foyle:

> Neutral Donegal was indifferent to our steady progress along its coastline until we rounded the headland into Lough Foyle. Our appearance in the Lough awakened the villagers of Moville, who were far from indifferent to the prospect of some trade. The bumboats emerged to move around our ship, and other ships from the same group as we idly awaited the arrival of the boat that would bring our pilot.

On the other side of the Atlantic, the Royal Canadian Navy base *Avalon* was built up in St John's, Newfoundland (known as 'Newfyjohn' to the sailors). The entrance was only 500ft wide between high cliffs and had to be approached at full speed. Inside, the harbour was circular in shape, about a mile in diameter. St John's went very quickly from a defenceless outpost to a major Allied escort base, and the 'key to the western defence system'. By May 1941 Newfoundland also had a huge American naval base along the coast at Argentia. St John's was Canada's major escort base, with up to 545 escort ships based there. The fourth floor of an old warehouse was converted to the 'Seagoing Officers Club', or the Crow's Nest club, which became famous throughout Western Approaches Command.

Halifax was the largest North American base in the early years. Even the dispassionate *Admiralty Pilot Book* was enthusiastic about it:

> It is one of the safest harbours in the world, affording space and depth of water sufficient for a large number of vessels; although the dangers in the approach render great caution necessary during the fogs, … it is easier of ingress and egress than any other large harbour on the coast.

It offered ten square miles of sheltered water and was hardly ever affected by ice.[48] By the late summer of 1942 New York was the main convoy port on that side of the Atlantic, with HX208 sailing from there in September 1942. Ships to and from Canadian ports joined or were detached off Halifax, Sydney and St John's.

East-coast convoys generally sailed from Methil in the Firth of Forth in Scotland, loaded with coal. They sailed towards the Thames Estuary, with some ships detaching for ports along the way, with others heading for the south coast with escorts from Dover Command. Minesweepers went on ahead. They sailed close to the land and Coastal Command provided aircraft cover in the daytime against enemy aircraft and E-boats, but the danger came after dark as the latter preferred to attack at night. They were protected by the East Coast Mine Barrage twenty or thirty miles offshore, which kept submarines out, but not shallow-draught E-boats. On being appointed to a corvette on the east coast, Monsarrat was told, 'you know what that means: Hitler's front doorstep. A bomb every five seconds. E-boats for tea, mines in your soup.'[49] Derek Rayner recorded:

> Long lines of ships wound their way up the east coast. Destroyers of the east coast escort force fussed round them. One or two anti-submarine trawlers would be there, and we cast envious glances at them. At least they went from one port to another, whereas we flogged the same bit of sea, day in and day out.[50]

Air power

Even after the Fleet Air Arm transferred to naval control in 1939, shore-based aircraft, including flying boats, remained part of the RAF. To operate them, Coastal Command was formed in 1936, nominally an equal with Fighter and Bomber Commands, but actually far behind in prestige. At the beginning of the war it had five flying boat squadrons, eleven squadrons for general reconnaissance and two of torpedo bombers, a total force of 296 aircraft. None of them were fitted or trained for anti-submarine warfare: they were mainly intended to find enemy surface raiders. By November 1939 they were preparing to attack submarines, though their bombs were ineffective and they were fitted with naval depth charges. In March to December 1941, in the third phase of the Battle of the Atlantic, they began to drive the U-boats out of the Western Approaches to the north of Ireland, but the aircraft, even the mighty Short Sunderland, lacked the range to pursue them in mid-Atlantic, even with Icelandic and Canadian bases. Thus the 'air gap' emerged in mid ocean, by far the most dangerous area for merchant ships.

The RAF put its main effort into strategic bombing and suggested that the best way to beat the U-boats was to bomb their shipyards and bases, which, even if effective, would do nothing about those already at sea, and did not take account of the bomb-proof pens erected in the French Atlantic ports. Coastal Command was brought under the operational control of the Admiralty in December 1940, though still manned and trained by the RAF.

A hundred and twenty Consolidated B-24 Liberator bombers were to be supplied to France but were diverted to the RAF in 1940. Initially, they were used for transport duties, as they lacked defensive fire power, but it became evident that their range of 2400 miles made them the only aircraft capable of closing the air gap. There were problems in the early stages as aircraft failed to find the convoys they were supposed to protect, or were unable to communicate with them. Lieutenant Commander Chavasse of convoy ON179 reported in April 1943:

> An RCAF Liberator arrived over the convoy and identified itself. I flashed 'Viper' at him, but he did not appear to understand and must have thought I was being rude. When I translated into plain language, he flew off happily on his task. Then another aircraft appeared, identified itself and then disappeared. He called me on R/T and asked for our position and number of ships in convoy. A minute later it appeared again quite close and I tried to reply. … The aircraft flew right over the convoy and circled at a distance of one mile before disappearing again, and I received the astonishing signal by R/T: 'Am unable to locate you. Am returning to base.'[51]

Soon they were operating much more efficiently with Torpex depth charges. Coastal Command only destroyed fourteen U-boats in the first three years of war, but between August 1942 and January 1943 they sank eleven while on patrol, and sixteen on convoy escort. In 1943 the command sank eighty-seven boats and shared in the destruction of others. Many of these were sunk in the 'Bay Offensive' against boats leaving and returning to their French bases. Convoys were generally safe while Liberators were on hand.

On the American side, the lines of demarcation were drawn differently, but not necessarily with better results. The navy was responsible for shore-based flying boats, but not wheeled bombers, which remained with the air force. This caused difficulty during the U-boats' 'second happy time', when the navy's Catalinas were too few and Mariners were too slow to catch the U-boats unawares. The army crews had little or no training in oversea navigation and ship identification, and used a different signal and command system. They believed in offensive hunting of U-boats, while the navy preferred to give close support in the vicinity of convoys. In March 1941 there were eighty-four army planes, eighty-three naval and four navy airships based at 128 different fields to patrol the whole East Coast.

The Army Air Force set up its Anti-Submarine Command, modelled on RAF Coastal Command, in May 1942, but it was not operational until October, just as the U-boat campaign off the East Coast had ended. Command difficulties and tactical differences with the navy continued and in June 1943 the AAF accepted that 'The Army is prepared to withdraw Army Air Forces from anti-submarine operations at such time as the Navy is ready to take over those duties completely.' Seventy-seven much desired Liberators were transferred to the navy. It was already being used effectively by the RAF, and in July 1942, despite the demands for a future strategic bombing offensive, the navy was allocated a share in its production and it became the PB4Y to the US Navy.

Two-ocean escorts

From 1940 there was an interaction between the two navies in the design and building of ocean escorts, which paralleled that in amphibious warfare vessels. It also reflected the difference between the two navies. The Americans started with the two established British designs for ocean escorts, the River-class frigates and the Hunt-class destroyer escorts. Back in 1940 the General Board ordered design studies for escorts, while Captain E L Cochrane was an attaché in Britain; he had a close relationship with Sir Stanley Goodall. American interest developed in the Hunt-class destroyer escorts, but in the meantime the US Navy preferred to concentrate on conventional destroyers, perhaps because Congress did not distinguish their sizes, and more capable ships could be obtained from a particular vote.

In June 1941 the British delegation in Washington requested a hundred destroyer escorts and Roosevelt approved the building of the first fifty in August. Cochrane, now with the Bureau of Ships, had produced a design based on the Hunt class. After Pearl Harbor they became part of the US Navy's programme. Eventually it was planned to build more than a thousand of them, though only 498 were completed, 306 by the end of 1943 by a massive effort. The earlier ships had British-style open bridges, but the planned 5in guns were not available and they had to make do with 3in, which were barely adequate against U-boats. They were originally designed for geared turbines, but these were precious, so submarine diesels were substituted, adding 3½ft to the length; again there were supply problems and turbo-electric was substituted, with a further increase in length. In that format they could make 24 knots. In addition to the main guns, they had Bofors and Oerlikons, depth charges, Hedgehog and three torpedo tubes. As the anti-submarine war wound down, some of them became fast transports or APDs, others were radar pickets. Edward Stafford was excited as he joined *Abercrombie*, under construction at Consolidated Steel Corporation, Orange, Texas:

> It was obvious that when the tangle and mess of the yard was cleared away, the DE would be beautiful in a clean-cut, deadly, efficient way.

> ... The clean, straight sweep of the deck from the anchors in her high, sharp bow to the depth-charge rails low on her fantail and the ordered symmetry of her armament made her as graceful as a yacht.

In British service they became the Captain class, without the torpedo tubes. Thirty-two were diesel powered, with a speed of 20 knots, and forty-six had turbines. The officers complained about rolling:

> The violent 'lurching' is the principal control factor in efficiency. As gun platforms these ships are satisfactory only under the most favourable conditions. ... Under average conditions it must be an even bet whether the throwers lob their charges vertically upwards and on to the quarter deck or immediately alongside the propellers.[52]

The Americans made no such complaints; one theory is that the ships had a natural period of roll which coincided with a typical north Atlantic wave, which did not apply in the Pacific; another is that the Americans were more used to such rolling.[53]

The Americans also took over the River-class design, calling them gunboats in the early stages, and later, patrol frigates. The structure was redesigned by Gibbs and Cox to allow them to be built quickly in merchant yards, but the result was not entirely satisfactory. The hull was perceived as being weak with too many discontinuities, and the messdecks were too stuffy and warm, which had not bothered the British sailors in the North Atlantic. More fundamentally, the turning circle was much larger than a DE because, as in the original Rivers, there was only a single rudder, whereas the Hunts and DEs had one aft of each propeller. Two prototypes were ordered from Canada and a hundred more were built. They were all manned by the Coast Guard, often as weather ships. Many were transferred to other navies, including twenty-eight to the Soviets in 1945.

To the British they became the Colony class, and Monsarrat transferred to one after service in a River:

> She had the same overall measurements as *River* (they had used the British hull design), but the fact that she was welded throughout instead of riveted, gave her lines a clean flowing look which I liked a lot. The absence of portholes (forbidden in American ships since Pearl Harbor), a lot of extra radio equipment, and some really beautiful AA guns, power operated from individual directors, were the only differences which caught the eye.

But inside it was very different:

> The refinements came thick and fast ... a steam laundry, ice-water plants in each mess-deck, dishwashing machines, potato peelers, ice-cream makers, typewriters, two sets of cinema equipment ... Meals were to be served on the cafeteria system, each man receiving an aluminium tray with two depressions stamped in it, one for meat and the other for pudding. ... The stringent anti-fire regulations which were the outcome of the Pearl Harbor disaster ... meant all-metal furniture ...[54]

The class was dogged by 'an engine defect, common to all of them, which nothing seemed able to cure', as Monsarrat recorded. 'We ran fourteen sea-trials altogether, before those engines came right: fourteen separate repetitions of the same disheartening, and largely futile process – out to sea, breakdown, creep home, fortnight in dock, and out to sea again.' After eight months, 'She did come right in the end', but like others of the class her armament was largely obsolete and the anti-submarine battle was already won.[55]

In 1937 Roosevelt urged a competition for the design of small wooden anti-submarine craft, which was won jointly by Luders Marine and Elco, while the Bureau of Ships produced its own version, which turned out to be the most successful. These three were the only ones available when the German onslaught began in 1942. They were known as '110s' from their length and were intended for patrol off harbours and estuaries. With a standard crew of twenty-six, they were powered by 'pancake' diesels originally intended for railway use. Thirteen were available in the middle of 1941, fifty-four a year later, and 306 in June 1943. They were far from comfortable as H G Jones found in *SC-525*: 'the enlisted men ... bunked in the aft crew quarters, which, when the bunks were folded against the wall, doubled as the mess hall. The galley was little more than a cubbyhole, and abaft the compartment was tiny lazarette.' The three officers lived in 'the cramped ward room just forward of the engine room and beneath the bridge. ... additionally the deck was so cluttered that walking from stem to stern was hazardous even when in port'. They were notoriously unstable in heavy seas. 'Every small ship sailor can tell stories of hanging on to the railings during violent seas in blizzard conditions, and every helmsman can recall valiant efforts to hold the correct compass heading as huge waves tossed the little "Donald Duck" as if it was a cork.'[56] They were not ready for the U-boat offensive of the East Coast and were diverted to other duties – only one ever sank a U-boat.[57]

There was also a competition for a longer boat, but again the Bureau of Ships produced the best alternative, which became known as the

PC or 'Peter Charles'. Only that prototype and the 165ft winner of the competition were ready by the beginning of 1942, but mass production began and 154 were in service in mid 1943. They and the SC boats were used for convoy escort between New York and Brazil and in the Mediterranean. Only the young could serve in the 'Donald Duck Navy'; older men could not stand the strain.[58]

Anti-submarine training began in 1939 at New London, where submarines were available for practice, and four old flush-deckers, the first in the Atlantic to be fitted with sonar, were used. The area was foggy and had poor sound conditions. The school moved south in December 1940. H G Jones was an early trainee:

> The first weeks at Key West were spent largely on an Attack Teacher, a British invention that had been installed in the year before to train sailors in antisubmarine tactics. The shorebased contraption mimicked shipboard echo-sounding and offered experience in operating the equipment and in honing the operator's interpretation of echoes. Lessons on the Attack Teacher resembled a twenty-first century computer game in which an elusive target (a makebelieve submarine) seeks to outwit the sonar operator on an imaginary surface vessel ...[59]

No badge had yet been allocated for the new rating of 'soundman' or 'sonarman', so Jones and his colleagues were obliged to wear quartermaster insignia on the left sleeve with the eagle pointing in the wrong direction; they were called 'queer quartermasters' until the badge of a set of headphones and an arrow was authorised. The Key West School continued to expand and in the first quarter of 1943 it trained 250 officers in an eight-week course, with 1033 enlisted men entering and 969 graduating.[60]

USS *Abercrombie* worked up in the 'Shake-Down Group' at Bermuda, which was shared with HMS *Malabar,* intended to work up US-built destroyer escorts in British service:

> Those days and weeks went by in a whirl of work and a fog of fatigue while the raw material of the new ship and green crew was forged and hammered into a usable weapon for warfare at sea. On all but a few of those days, *Abercrombie* was underway at first light ... Once clear of the outlying reefs, the drills began and continued till later afternoon when it was time to run the ninety-minute channel back to Great Sound. Evenings were spent reviewing the results of the day's drills, correcting the discrepancies and preparing for the next day's exercises.[61]

The Americans were happy to adopt the British Hedgehog mortar and it was used to great effect by the destroyer escort *England* in May 1944:

> Again, the *George* attacked, and again she missed. Between 0730 and 0810, she made three more firing runs and each time came up empty. Like the *Raby*, she found herself baffled by an opponent who was tricky, elusive, disconcertingly sharp – and lucky. After two frustrating hours, Commander Hains yielded to what was beginning to appear as the inevitable. With a touch of exasperation, he ordered the *George* to sheer off and give way to the *England*.
>
> We missed on our first firing run, then went back for another attack. At 0834, the hedgehogs plunged resolutely into the sea, and in a few seconds, we were rewarded with a V-R-R-R-OOM! of unprecedented and magnificent proportions. We estimated 10–12 hits, at 300 feet. The first ripple of hits was followed, in the next half minute, by several more minor explosions. Then, three minutes later, came the now-to-be-expected WHAM! Once again, a crashing underwater explosion sent the *England* reeling.
>
> At 1045, the first debris began to bob to the surface, along with a steady flow of oil. We lowered a boat to collect the grisly evidence. After half an hour, we had sufficient wreckage, plus oil samples, and I decided to go below for a cup of coffee.
>
> Our third success had produced a muted response: some grim satisfaction but little jubilation. We were, it would seem, beginning to take time for second thoughts.

England sank six submarines in an exceptional series of attacks, but it is significant that none of the other ships with her made any hits at all despite being offered chances. Overall, Hedgehog attacks launched by American ships in May 1944 to May 1945 had a success rate of 9.9 per cent, compared with 4.5 per cent for depth charges.[62]

For smaller vessels like PCs and SCs, a smaller version known as Mousetrap, with only four or eight rails, was adopted. To Edward Stafford on *SC 692*, 'all the way forward, aft of only the ground tackle, was another improvement over the days of World War I, a double rack of launchers, known as "mousetraps", which could hurl eight fast-sinking, contact-firing projectiles two hundred yards ahead to rupture the pressure hulls of her enemies.'[63]

Depth charges, or 'ashcans', remained in use throughout the war. From the destroyer *Dale* off Okinawa, summer of 1945, Sonarman Dan Ahlberg reported:

> We were screening the fleet and I was standing mid-watch on the sonar. After about every fourth sweep, I would search ninety degrees to starboard and ninety degrees to port. Suddenly, I came up with the biggest darn sonar contact I had ever heard about fifteen degrees off the bow. The skipper's cabin was right next to the sonar shack, so I punched his intercom and said, 'Sir, I've got a big one.'
>
> The captain came into the sonar shack, gave a listen, and then ordered, 'Sonar bearing fifteen degrees off the starboard bow, come right fifteen degrees. Steady. … On my mark a shallow pattern. Mark!' We launched a pattern of depth charges, but when the water settled down the sub was still down there. We … chased it around for a while before finally losing it.

After the war it was established that a submarine had indeed been sunk at that time and place.[64]

The Japanese, with their interpretations of Mahan's doctrine, tended to attack warships rather than merchantmen, and they did indeed have some successes in 1942, before the American anti-submarine system was developed. After a distinguished role in the Battle of Midway, the carrier *Yorktown*, already damaged by aircraft, was attacked by the submarine *I-158*. None of the six escorting destroyers had picked up her echo and *Hammann* was hit and blew up as her depth charges exploded. Two torpedoes hit the carrier and attempts to salvage her were abandoned. *I-158* escaped, despite searches by the remaining destroyers.[65] And in the Guadalcanal campaign the carrier *Wasp* was sunk by *I-19*.

Transports carrying vital supplies were allowed to proceed unmolested, and SS *John A Johnson* was the first merchant ship sunk by the Japanese in the Pacific in 1944, on 29 October. The fast carrier groups seemed immune until the night of 3/4 November when the cruiser *Reno* was hit by two torpedoes, but saved due to good damage control. While operating off the Philippines, the groups' manoeuvres were becoming predictable and escorts were concentrated on the more immediate threat from the air. Admiral McCain recommended the setting up of specialised hunting groups of destroyers, as DEs were too slow, more training in anti-submarine technique, and the deployment of more pilots trained in anti-submarine warfare.[66]

The Merchant Navy

The British Merchant Navy was given the title just after the First World War, in recognition of its vital services during the conflict, and it was combined with a standard uniform for officers. But it was a far more diverse organisation than its royal counterpart, with many different companies, ranging from British India Steam Navigation with more than a hundred ships to firms such as the Chine Shipping Company and Ampleforth Steamship with one each. It included men (and a few women) of many nationalities, most notably the Lascars or Indian seamen who numbered more than fifty thousand in 1938, alongside 132,000 British and nearly ten thousand of other nationalities.[67] About a quarter of them were deck officers, engineers and pursers. Britain and the Dominions still had the largest merchant fleet in the world, but it had remained at around 20 million tons for many years, whereas other fleets, such as the American, Norwegian and Japanese, had expanded greatly. By 1937 Britain had 28 per cent of world tonnage.[68]

It was divided into liners and tramps. Liners were not necessarily passenger vessels, but ships which followed a regular route, for which they were often designed specially. In 1935 there were 940 oceangoing cargo liners on the British registry, along with 556 cargo-passenger liners, a total of eight million tons. Conversely, tramps were not necessarily as run-down as the name might suggest, for it was perhaps derived from the Victorian labourer's habit of 'going on the tramp'. They were simply vessels which picked up cargoes wherever they could. There were more than a thousand of them in 1936, of nearly 4.5 million tons. The officers of liners were generally better qualified and paid and had more secure employment.[69] Merchant ships were often more sea-kindly than their escorts, and the *Atlantic Convoy Instructions* decreed that 'In bad weather the escort of a fast convoy may be unable to maintain the convoy speed without risking serious damage.' In that case, the senior officer had to decide whether to slow the convoy down or let it proceed unescorted.[70]

Oil tankers became increasingly important during the war. There were 287 of them in ocean-going trades in 1935, totalling nearly 2 million tons. Passenger ships were not often found in the convoy system. Short-sea ferries were redundant after the enemy conquest of Europe and were often converted to amphibious warfare vessels. The great ocean liners were fast enough to evade U-boats and were converted to armed merchant cruisers in the early stages of the war, and troop transports later on. *Queen Mary* could carry up to sixteen thousand men.

Everything changed for the merchant seaman in wartime. Ships no longer sailed independently, with the captain choosing the most economic route. Instead, they travelled in convoy, with liners and tramps in apparent equality. Owners no longer had to find cargoes: goods were allocated to them by the naval authorities. The crews had to control

An average ship type as below has a:	Length of	When loaded floats in	Speed Loaded of	Tonnage of	Loading capacity of
Passenger Liner	657·6 ft.	34 ft. 1½ in.	19 knots	17,350 gross	658,960 cub. ft. 517 pass.
Cargo Liner ...	516·3 ft.	29 ft. 7 in.	17 knots	12,320 gross	750,839 cub. ft. 12 pass.
Oil Tanker ...	462·8 ft.	27 ft. 0 in.	11 knots	8,012 gross	12,000 tons oil
Tramp ...	414 ft.	25 ft. 3½ in.	11 knots	4,719 gross	585,420 cub. ft.
Ore Carrier ...	387·1 ft.	24 ft. 4 in.	10 knots	5,787 gross	161,380 cub. ft.
Cross-Channel Ship ...	353 ft	15 ft 1 in.	17½ knots	4,320 gross	725,755 cub. ft. 1,000 pass.
Tug (Salvage)...	198·3 ft.	17 ft. 11 in.	17 knots (without tow)	793 gross	No loading capacity: carries fire and salvage pumps
Coaster...	197 ft.	8 ft. 6 in.	9 knots	200 gross	62,480 cub. ft.
Trawler	134·6 ft.	11ft. 9in.	11 knots	130 gross	400,000 lb. fish

Merchant ship types in their peacetime categories. In war, the fast liners sailed independently, but liners and tramps, tankers and cargo ships, sailed together in convoy. Cross-channel ships were mostly converted to Landing Ships, Infantry.

course and speed very accurately to stay in station, which some found very difficult. One officer said, 'convoy work … we HATED it. The soul destroying frustration; The physical strain of watch-keeping and station-keeping.'[71] It had always been a dangerous occupation, with a high accident rate, but now it was the most hazardous part of the whole war effort, with higher casualty rates than any of the armed services with more than twenty-five thousand deaths in action. In compensation, in 1943 an able seaman was paid £24 per month, compared with a maximum basic rate of £5.10 for his naval equivalent. There was never any shortage of volunteers for the Merchant Navy during the war.

Merchant seamen had a very different culture. According to one convoy commodore:

> One of their pet jibes at the Royal Navy was the fact that a large number of men in smart uniforms were always turned out … whenever a ship came to a buoy or went alongside or dropped anchor. … The Merchant Service considered it far more chic to do the same with one officer and a couple of usually grubby and picturesque characters fore and aft.[72]

Merchant seamen might serve under Royal Navy command on T124 agreements, perhaps in armed merchant cruisers or merchant escort carriers. Naval gunners were carried on 'defensively equipped merchant ships', as well as army artillerymen. Though the Merchant Navy did not expand to anything like the extent of the Royal Navy or the American Merchant Marine, HMS *Gordon* was used to train men who did not quite come up to naval standards.

The Merchant Navy was supplemented by ships from the European maritime nations, whose vessels were overseas when their homelands were conquered. At the end of 1941 there were 156 Greek ships on time charter to the British government, 147 Dutch and 180 Norwegian, out of a total of 840 foreign dry cargo ships, totalling 5,109,000 tons. There were heavy losses and few replacements, so by 1945 the fleet was depleted to 590 ships of 3,746,000 tons.[73]

The Merchant Marine

The American Merchant Marine had been a significant force in in the mid nineteenth century, almost rivalling the British until the Civil War when Confederate raiders captured many ships and caused others to change their flags. It had a short-lived revival after the First World War, but only two dry cargo ships plus a few tankers were built from then until 1936, when Roosevelt's Merchant Marine Act attempted to remedy this by means of subsidies and create a shipping industry both to service national needs, and to be mobilised in the event of war. The Maritime Commission was set up under the act with an aim to build five hundred ships in ten years. Four standard designs were evolved. C-1, C-2 and C-3 were freighters ranging from 9137 to 12,438 tons, the T-3 was a tanker of 18,300 tons. Most of them were taken over by the army and navy at the start of the war. The War Shipping Administration was set up in February 1942 to control the ever-expanding fleet.

The most common merchant ship ever built was the famous Liberty. Initially regarded as a stopgap, it was based on a design by J L Thompson of Sunderland, England, but adopted by the US Maritime Commission for mass production largely in Henry J Kaiser's yards.

Initially there were doubts about their strength due to unfamiliarity with welding, but with improvements many of them lasted for decades after the war. Reciprocating engines were fitted due to the shortage of turbines, and therefore they only had a speed of 11 knots. There was a large, square deckhouse amidships with three large hatches forward and two aft, equipped with derricks for cargo handling where there were no regular port facilities. Victory ships were slightly larger, with turbines and a speed of up to 17 knots. C-4 troopships could carry 2500 men, P-2 troopships 5200. Altogether, over seven million troops were shipped overseas. Eventually, the Maritime Commission would build 2708 Libertys, 414 Victory ships and 523 T-2 tankers. By June 1945 the WSA controlled 4125 vessels of more than 44 million tons.[74]

Whereas the British Merchant Navy was largely concentrated in the Atlantic, North Sea and Mediterranean, the American Merchant Marine ranged over the oceans. During 1944 it shipped 15 million tons of goods to the UK and Europe, 13 million to the Pacific, 8 million to the Mediterranean, 6 million to South America and the Caribbean, 5 million to the USSR, and 3 million to India and Ceylon.[75]

A section of a Liberty ship showing its five holds and the crew accommodation amidships, and space for the armed guard right aft.

John Stagg, a tanker-type Liberty ship built in New Orleans in 1943. The rectangular life rafts can be seen ready to launch above the decks.

Extensive programmes were set up to man the new ships. The US Merchant Marine Cadet Corps had been set up in 1938 and a major training school was established at King's Point, New York, in 1942. The course started with ten or twelve weeks of basic training. The *Preliminary Manual* of 1943 was rather frightening, in that it had a great deal on lifeboats and first aid. Deck trainees were issued with another manual which placed emphasis on steering: 'Remember the lubber's line is the line you must move. Do not attempt to move the compass around to the lubber's line.' In addition, there were chapters on 'marlinspike seamanship', or rope work, cargo handling, ground tackle, lookout work, and an introduction to submarine warfare. Engineering trainees were told:

> The first sight of the ship's power plant in operation is apt to be a fascinating spectacle of large whirling cranks; gleaming piston rods, sliding in and out of huge lofty cylinders, and of roaring fires in the furnaces. The maze of pipelines and smaller machinery gives the impression of a complicated assembly requiring much time to understand. Nothing could be further from the truth.[76]

After King's Point they were supposed to go to sea for a minimum of six months, but according to James H Ackerman, 'Because the war was on they couldn't govern the time you were at sea; ... I had an extraordinarily long time. I left Los Angeles and a liberty ship ... and ended up in New York and a one way round-the-world-voyage sixteen months later.'[77] One new seaman recalled:

> My first time relieving the man on the bridge, I approached Mr Heyme the Chief Mate. I saluted him snappily and said, 'Relieving the watch, Sir.' The Chief Mate stood there a moment, dumbfounded, and them he replied, 'Oh my, how lovely!' … I soon learned there were no formalities on merchant ships.[78]

The final stage was more training at King's Point, followed by an examination, on passing which a cadet could become a third mate or third engineer.

Seamen's unions played a part in allocating men to crews. Bill Bailey was the port agent of the New York branch of the Pacific Firemen, Oilers, Watertenders and Wipers Association:

> I decided I just couldn't take it any longer, you know watching his kids come in. I said to myself, 'How the fuck can I go through this war – when people ask me "What did you do during the war?"' All I'll be able to say will be I helped win it by pushing kids out, by manning ships.[79]

A merchant crew might include a great variety of ages:

> One of the ABs on my watch had sailed around the world in Teddy Roosevelt's Great White Fleet. He didn't have to go. And my [watch] partner and I were both 4-F. We'd both been rejected by the draft … that's what kept a Merchant Marine going: old-timers who couldn't quit and young guys who didn't have to worry about the draft.[80]

Merchant seamen were paid much more than their naval counterparts, and relations with the US Navy reached a low point in October 1944 when a merchant ship came alongside a destroyer and taunted its crew: 'Suckers! Suckers! I get twenty bucks a day, whadda you guys get?' while the master 'sat up on his bridge in his undershirt and cursed and yelled at our officers and men.'[81] Most ships had a naval armed guard, who would be helped by the merchant seamen in action: 'We had guns fore and aft, guns on the bridge, and a gun crew and gunnery officer. He was a real character from some freshwater College in Minnesota or Wisconsin. And I believe this was his first the first time he'd seen the ocean.'[82] The Liberty ship *Jacksonville* had forty-nine crewmen and twenty-nine armed guards.

Merchant seamen suffered heavy losses during the war, equalling or exceeding those of the armed forces. Britain lost 22,490, India 6093, China 2023, the United States 5638, Norway 4795, Greece 2000. But there is no doubt that the war could not have been won, or even fought, without them.

15

Coastal Navies

Coastguards

HIS MAJESTY'S Coastguard had had many roles in the past, including prevention of smuggling and as a kind of naval reserve, and it had served several masters, including the Admiralty and HM Customs. In 1921 it was put under the Board of Trade and concentrated on safety at sea. Its members lived in rows of white cottages strategically sited on cliffs and headlands round the coast, and worked in stations from which they could radio to ships standing into danger, or call out the lifeboats – which were themselves run by an enthusiastic and efficient charity, the Royal National Lifeboat Institution. In 1939 it reverted to Admiralty control for the duration of the war. The coastguard had about nine hundred members at the beginning of the war and these were boosted by five thousand auxiliaries. With the invasion scare of 1940 they began to mount beach patrols armed with Sten guns and wearing battledress, though they continued with the rescue duties. Lighthouses and buoyage were serviced by Trinity House in England and Wales, the Commissioners of Northern Lights in Scotland, and the Commissioners of Irish Lights.

The United States Coast Guard was formed in 1915 by the merger of the Life-Saving Service and the Revenue Cutter Service. It was a very different animal from its British counterpart, though it too could serve different masters – the Treasury in peacetime when it was part of the revenue-raising establishment, and the Navy Department in war, when it took its place alongside the Marines and the Navy proper. In the first of these roles it was expanded in the 1920s, with the addition of more than thirty cutters, as large as small warships, in a doomed attempt to enforce the prohibition laws and stop the illegal import of alcoholic drinks. In 1938 it had 550 commissioned and 542 warrant officers (a far higher proportion than the other services), 145 cadets and 9000 enlisted men, wearing uniforms identical to the navy except for a shield which replaced the star on the officers' sleeves, and was worn on the shoulder of the enlisted uniform. Arriving in Glasgow, Marvin Perrett found that

A Landing Ship, Tank, or LST, manned by the US Coast Guard has opened its bow doors and is landing amphibious tanks off Iwo Jima.

the regular navy men had told the local girls that the shield meant they had had 'a social disease ... after a few bar room fights we straightened that mess out.'[1] It had numerous small craft and an aviation wing with sixty-three aircraft operating from ten stations. In 1939 the duties of the Bureau of Lighthouses were transferred to it from the Department of Commerce along with five thousand personnel, and in 1942 it took over responsibility for inspection of merchant ships. The Coast Guard Reserve was formed in February 1941, modelled on the Navy Reserve.

Prospective regular officers were trained in the Coast Guard Academy at New London, Connecticut, which had been completed in 1932 in redbrick colonial Georgian style. They were selected by competitive examination, with none of the political influence associated with Annapolis and West Point. The four-year course placed emphasis on 'the fundamentals of science and engineering', including seamanship, of course, but it also included 'History of Western Civilisation' and 'Contemporary Problems' to give a broader picture. Annual practice cruises were held at the end of the first and third years, and were 'planned to include carefully selected ports in European and South American waters', with the cadets taking on many shipboard duties during a voyage of about ten thousand miles over ten weeks. The cruise at the end of the second year was coastwise, in sail or patrol boats of the service. On graduation, 'A young ensign leaves the realm of school boys and walks into a world of men. He would probably join a large cutter for his first service.'[2]

As soon as the war in Europe started, the Coast Guard began neutrality patrols and weather services. Clyde Allen enlisted after Pearl Harbor because of a memory of a Coast Guard recruiting poster he had seen as a boy.[3] Marvin Perrett, wanting to avoid the army and the marines, went to the naval recruiting office in New Orleans just before he became eligible for the draft and was told they had taken up their quota, but he should try the Coast Guard, which took him on right away.[4]

After Pearl Harbor, it used more than twenty-five thousand men for beach patrols in the United States and they were partly responsible for catching a German sabotage team. To Clyde Allen, 'it was a good life. You met a lot of people … in patrolling up and down the beach … and there was nothing really drastic that ever happened, but the weather … in Oregon, was wet'. It was equally quiet in observation stations set up in peninsulas: 'you reported airplanes even though they were American airplanes, which that was the only thing.'[5]

In May 1942, as the U-boats continued their ravages off the East Coast, they were organised in the 'Hooligan Navy', or 'Corsair Fleet', using private yachts and amateur sailors: 50–100ft sailing yachts were favoured; it was hoped that their seakeeping qualities, long range and silent movement would be helpful. An act of June 1942 authorised the Coast Guard to recruit 'such officers and members of the crew of any motorboat or yacht placed at the disposal of the Coast Guard, and such men who by reason of their special training and experience are deemed by the Commandant to be qualified for such duty'. George B Keyes was a crewman on the schooner *Mohawk*, owned by Albert Sterns who offered her to the Coast Guard. She was given the designation CGR-2543 and, despite his lack of naval experience, Keyes was rated chief boatswain's mate; the others given appropriate ratings and green hands were recruited and trained. They were eventually armed with a Springfield rifle, a Browning machine gun, a BAR and a Thompson sub-machine gun. They patrolled off Nantucket Island, but by this time the U-boats had moved back to mid-Atlantic.[6]

Despite the name, Coast Guard services were not confined to the American coast. It manned numerous escort vessels in the Battle of the Atlantic, sinking eleven U-boats in various theatres, starting with *U-352* off North Carolina in May 1942. They operated landing craft which took part in all major amphibious operations, with Signalman First Class Douglas A Munro winning the Medal of Honor at Guadalcanal. Marvin Perrett was selected as coxswain of an LCVP and eventually rated as boatswain's mate second class. He took part in the landing on Utah Beach, then at Napes and the south of France, which he found much easier. Back in the States, he hoped he had done enough, but was told by an officer, 'You're experienced. That's what we need', and found himself at Iwo Jima.

They continued regular duties in the Aids to Navigation branch, operating lighthouses and buoys. Lieutenant (JG) Harriet Writer, then a quartermaster, enjoyed her service in Boston: 'I worked with nautical charts that showed the location of buoys and other navigation aids in the harbor. I had to keep watch of the nearby lighthouses. If a lighthouse went out, we'd find out why they were out. Was it a monetary thing, or was it 24 hours?'[7] True to their original role, they rescued survivors in the Atlantic, 1600 off the American coast and two hundred in the Mediterranean.[8]

Mine warfare

Sea mines were an often ignored but potentially very deadly weapon. They came in many forms. Contact mines were set off when target ships touched them, influence mines by sound, pressure or magnetic field. The former were usually moored mines attached to weights on the bottom of the sea; the latter were ground mines lying on the bottom in relatively shallow water. Mines could be laid defensively to protect one's ports or shipping routes, or offensively to threaten those of the enemy. Minelaying was not a popular naval activity: the results were rarely immediately apparent. It might be weeks or months before a mine was hit by its target, but more often it never was. But it was a deterrent, perhaps denying an area of sea to the enemy or causing him to expend large-scale resources to clear it. Minefields were supposed to be 'declared' to allow neutral shipping to keep clear, but that too had its paradox – it might be used to keep ships out of an area for security reasons, though it was only lightly mined, if at all. Minesweeping was an essential task in any navy, but it too was unpopular. To Charles McAra of the Royal Navy, 'minesweeping was a fairly menial task. Minesweepers were the housemaids and skivvies of the Fleet'.[9]

Britain was vulnerable to mining and had already fought an intense campaign against it from the first day of the First World War. There was a certain amount of defensive planning, but no offensive mining strategy at the beginning of the second war. British mine warfare was the responsibility of the Torpedo Branch, which had its main depot in HMS *Vernon*, a shore base at the entrance to Portsmouth Harbour. It was evacuated to Roedean girls' school near Brighton. Naval trainees were amused by the notices in the dormitories: 'If you require a mistress in the night, ring the bell.'

The classic mine was a metal sphere with protruding spikes, or 'horns', contact with which would set it off. It had a heavy 'sinker', which would rest on the bottom when the mine was in place, with a wire set at the right depth for the mine to float just under the surface – though that had to take account of the rise and fall of the tide in British waters, and it was often safer to sweep at high tide when the mine was further under the surface. Despite newer types it remained in service throughout the war: 'in spite of the advent of new and complicated mines, the plain moored contact mine retains its effectiveness.'[10]

In 1919 the Royal Navy developed the Oropesa sweep, tested on a trawler of that name. It was a streamlined float which would be attached to a long wire from the sweeper, and held at the correct depth along most of its length by a 'kite', looking rather like a set of large, shaped shelves, at its inner end and a similar 'otter' near the float. The wire was serrated and it was intended to cut the mine's wire so that it would float to the surface to be destroyed by gunfire. A vessel called a danlayer, perhaps a fishing drifter or a converted yacht, followed, dropping buoys to mark the cleared channel. It was the most efficient known method for sweeping contact mines in any navy.

The paravane was a another development of the last war and was described just after it. It 'had as its basis the suspension of a submerged wire around the bow of the ship, which caught and deflected the mine-mooring wire before the horns of the mine itself could reach the sides of the ship.' For:

> It seldom happens that a vessel strikes a mine dead on the bow or stem-post. The cushion and dislocation of water formed by a big and fast ship is usually sufficient to cause the mine to swing a few inches away from the bow and to return several feet back … The paravanes themselves are submerged torpedo-shaped bodies which hold the wires under the surface and away from the ship's side.[11]

At the beginning of the Second World War, all merchant ships were fitted with 'A' or 'M' frames in the bows to support paravanes, and they were able to operate at speeds up to 31 knots.[12]

There were several unexplained sinkings of British ships in the first weeks of the war, and the cruiser *Belfast* was badly damaged by an explosion under her hull in the Firth of Forth. The idea of the magnetic mine had been anticipated. The 'M-sweep' went into service in December 1939. It consisted of seventy 27in magnets spaced 10ft apart on a cable towed between two ships. Known as the 'bosun's nightmare', it had very limited success, but a much better method was already on the way.

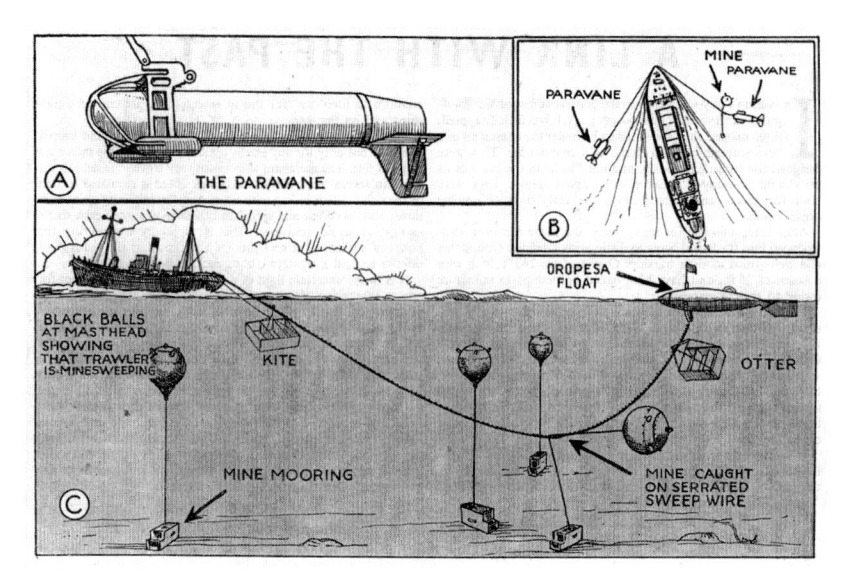

Details of the paravane towed by a trawler, in this case used to cut the cables of moored mines.

Initially, the Germans had laid the mines by submarine, but began to drop them from aircraft, which raised the possibility of them falling in shallow water. On the night of 22 November 1939 a bomber was observed dropping objects 'like sailors' kitbags suspended from parachutes' in the Thames Estuary. Lieutenant Commander J G D Ouvry was wakened at three next morning and ordered to the Admiralty and then to the coast where a mine had been found at low water: 'It was cylindrical in shape, made of some aluminium alloy, had tubular horns on the nose and a hollow tail containing a massive phosphor bronze spring. There were two unpleasant looking fittings near the fore end and these looked like being Public Enemies Nos 1 and 2.' Using non-magnetic tools, he defused it with the aid of a chief petty officer and its secrets were discovered.[13] 'Examination showed that it operated on the dip-needle principle, that it required a change of vertical magnetic field of the order of 50 milligauss, and that it was actuated by a ship with its red pole down (ie one built in the northern hemisphere).'[14]

There were several ways to counter it. Towed skids were tried, but they would be destroyed by any explosion. A bomber fitted with a large electrified coil could fly low over the area, but it was impossible to mark the cleared channel accurately. The answer was to be found in the 'LL sweep'.

It was a buoyant cable with a short leg of 125yds and a long leg of 525yds, each leg terminating in a 50yd electrode. The legs were married together throughout the length of the short leg to cancel out magnetic fields near the sweeper. Car batteries and two 35kW petrol generators were employed and the set could pulse in one direction only at 3000 amps. Two ships so fitted could sweep an 80 milligauss path 200yds wide at 8 knots.[15]

It entered service in March 1940 and was far better than anything previously produced. Simple improvements followed – 'pulsing' was used to provide high power for a short period, better batteries were designed, and pulses could be sent in two directions. Two standard formations were adopted. In the 'P' formation, two ships sailed abreast followed by as many more pairs as available; and in the 'Q' formation, three to seven ships operated abreast. The Germans introduced improvements over the years, but the British minesweeping effort was able to keep up with them. The Germans had made the classic mistake of introducing a new weapon before they had enough of it to make a difference.

Ernest Goodall described the procedure in a motor minesweeper:

Once under way and the skipper had given the order 'Out Sweep', four seamen would lower the cable into the sea over the rollers at the stern while I got the 54kW generator running and set charging the batteries at 200 amps. When the cable was fully streamed, all 547 yards of it, this left me to connect the very large brass cable lugs to terminals in a steel connection aft. ... you had to get synchronised with your partner ship so that both ships were sending out the magnetic field of the same polarity.[16]

Individual ships were protected by a process known as degaussing – winding a coil round a ship and energising it with direct current, which was done to all ships as soon as possible. Degaussing ranges were used to test the magnetic fields of ships, including one off Helensburgh in the Firth of Clyde, as described by a Wren who served there:

There was deep water close offshore to our offices, deep enough for the biggest aircraft carriers and warships to make several runs through a selected passage, marked by buoys, while taking the degaussing tests.

Special underground cables ran from that area up into one of the buildings, where the information was processed in a temperature controlled room furnished with camera equipment.[17]

Acoustic mines were set off by sound and countered by an acoustic hammer, or Kango. In *MMS41* Ernest Goodall reported, 'the large bucket-like steel container housing the "Kango" was lowered over the bow on an "A" frame and made fast with steel cables. This was carried out prior to launching the magnetic minesweeping cable.'[18] Pressure mines, set off by the wash of the ship, were more difficult They were encountered for the first time in large numbers off Normandy, in the form of 'oysters'. The British believed that ships passing at 4 knots or less would be safe. For the Americans the most effective means was to sail expendable 'guinea pig' ships over them, but that was mainly to check cleared passages.[19] Fortunately, they were not extensively deployed by the Japanese before the war ended.

It became apparent that 'means could be produced to counter any single mine and that the most effective offensive minefield was one which contained a wide mixture of different types of mine. Then a vessel sweeping for one variety was a likely victim for another type.'[20] The British used this 'mixed bag' policy when laying their own offensive fields, and were fully aware that the Germans might do the same. Another trick was to set the fuse for a time lapse of up to two hundred days, or to activate the mine only after the area had been swept up to a dozen times.

To start with, British minesweeping was the province of fishermen, especially the warrant officers of the Royal Naval Reserve known as 'skippers', with commissioned skipper lieutenants to lead groups of them. At the beginning of the war, Derek Rayner found one of the best of them in Skipper Lang, 'a perfect example of a Devon trawler skipper'. He had a fisherman's eye for weather: 'See those gulls, Sir, throwing water over their backs – sure sign of a southerly wind that Sir', and could navigate without the usual aids.[21] But such men had their limitations: 'Most of them were splendid seamen, but they did not take easily to filling in forms or writing official reports; they were often puzzled by the Confidential Books issued to them ... They had but a hazy idea of naval discipline.'[22]

Modern minesweeping needed a more disciplined approach to station-keeping, and a certain amount of scientific knowledge, which might be found among well-educated temporary RNVR officers. Although he frankly regarded it 'menial', Charles McAra volunteered for it because he wanted to serve in small ships, and his officers approved: 'Here was a lad with no fancy notions above his station like wanting to be in a Tribal class destroyer.'[23] By the end of the war, skippers RNR only made up about 6 per cent of minesweeper officers, with the RNR as a whole providing 34 per cent. Only 3 per cent were regular navy and the remaining 63 per cent were RNVR.[24] In summary:

> There was a tendency throughout the war to regard minesweeping forces as a private Navy, and the degree of ignorance of mines and minesweeping matters among officers of the Fleet was

deplorable. Among the minesweeping personnel there was a high degree of enthusiasm balanced by an almost complete disregard of handbooks.[25]

The Royal Naval Patrol Service provided most of the ratings for minesweeping duties. It was originally intended for fishermen, but the supply was limited, and in October 1940 Vivian Cox, who confessed to being 'the world's worst sailor', began his training, inspired by his yachtsman brother-in-law. He was not impressed by the Sparrow's Nest, a park in Lowestoft taken over for the duration: 'It may have been a pleasant pleasure garden in times of peace … but the Navy had moved swiftly and inexorably. … Temporary buildings covered the once open spaces. The trampling of countless Navy-issue boots had obliterated every trace of what had been grass lawns'. Like any new entrant, he went through 'the process known as being "kitted up"', medical examinations 'too hideous to detail', and learned 'the rudiments of how to march in step'.[26]

The patrol service mainly used naval ranks and ratings, but with specialised categories like 'engineman'. The second in command of a trawler was often a petty officer known as a mate who, unlike the skipper, did not have a Board of Trade certificate. According to Derek Rayner, 'This rank was never a success, and as soon as the Patrol Service got properly under way it was dropped and the mates were replaced by young Sub-Lieutenants.'[27] On the other hand, Vivian Cox found that the most important person onboard the trawler *Euclase* was the mate Tom, 'a weather-beaten old fisherman', who 'had swept mines in trawlers all through the last war … a man of deeds and not words.' Under them were second hands (small craft only).

Ernest Goodall passed the trade test to become a wireman electrical rating and was allocated to the Patrol Service. He asked his chief if that was good and was told, 'You won't effing last long!' After a two-week course he was sent to *MMS41* at Lowestoft and had two hours' tuition from an electrical officer on 'how to operate and control the magnetic sweeping gear and the acoustic hammer.' Then he went to sea and blew up his first mine off Harwich, when the crew gave him a big cheer.[28]

There were different opinions about the quality of Patrol Service seamen. Finding that many of them failed officer training, the captain of a training base claimed that they did not 'compare favourably with candidates from other sources.' At the same time, an anti-submarine trainer noted, 'Almost certainly the P/S gets a better quality of rating'. It seems that they were good seamen who did not have what the Admiralty felt was needed in an officer.[29]

Minesweeper officers and Patrol Service members were sent to HMS *Lochinvar* in the Firth of Forth to learn the trade. It used the artificial harbour of Port Edgar in the shadow of the Forth Bridge:

> First, we had a week or two of instruction in which we were introduced to the various types of British and German mines and initiated into the methods and technique for dealing with them. After that off we went to the minesweeping trawlers to gain some practical experience, taking turns to work on the sweep-deck or on the bridge as officers of the watch. It was a strenuous, cheerful time but very dirty as the trawlers were coal-burning and the washing-facilities were minimal.[30]

Lochinvar produced 4050 officers and thirteen thousand ratings during the war, but that was not nearly enough for a service which peaked at forty-three thousand officers and men in September 1944, with a further fourteen thousand in Dominion navies, so the great majority came to minesweepers untrained in their operation.[31]

Minesweepers came in a variety of shapes and sizes – large in the form of fleet sweepers, small for inshore work, wooden to counter the magnetic mine, and improvised in the case of trawlers and paddle steamers. Commercial trawlers were already fitted with equipment to trail wires or nets, but they were steel hulled, and had a comparatively deep draught. They had a great variety of names from their original owners, including *Lady Philomena*, *Sweet Promise*, *Sir Gareth* and *Preston North End*. Four at least were approved of by Skipper Lang: 'That *Loch Tulla* Sir – that's a fine ship for us sir. ... and the *Regal*, *Brontes* and *Istria*, Sir – there's three good sound ships – not as you might say extra modern Sir, but real good seaboats that any man would go fishing in.'[32] Four classes of trawler were purpose-built for the navy during the war, all based on *Basset* of 1935. They were coal-fired, with vertical triple-expansion engines, and copied most of the features of commercial trawlers, except for their shallower draught of 11ft.

In peacetime, paddle steamers were common on coastal and estuary passenger routes and had the advantage of shallow draught, but only thirty-two could be found out of fifty needed at the beginning. They had poor endurance, of two to three days, and could only work in fine weather. Fairmile motor launches with their shallow draught could also be fitted: '*ML137* was equipped for minesweeping and was of shallow enough draft (1.75 metres) to permit close approach to the beach. ... The ship's company was composed of three officers and seventeen ratings ...

Types of British minesweeper. In the left foreground is the stern of a sweeper showing the cable drum and the sweeping gear, including Oropesa floats, kites and cranes. Behind is a column of *Algerine*-class fleet minesweepers with numerous conversions and older, smaller types behind that.

Relations between officers and men in *ML137* were much less formal than in the *Jason*.[33]

Motor minesweepers, or MMS, were built in wood to nullify the effect of magnetic mines (though, of course, they needed metal engines). They came in two classes, 105ft long, of which 294 were built, and 126ft, of which 102 were built. They concentrated on the LL sweep, for they did not have enough power to tow an Oropesa sweep. After service in larger vessels Sub Lieutenant James Clark was appointed to *MMS56*, which:

> carried a captain, a Lieutenant, and a chief Petty Officer but had a smaller crew of fifteen men, mainly fishermen and hostilities only ratings. I was Number One (Lieutenant) on board and we were a happy bunch, more like a family, as it was more relaxed than a fleet minesweeper.[34]

Fleet minesweepers were manned by the navy proper, rather than the Patrol Service. They were intended to travel with the main fleet and to sweep ahead of it, so they needed higher speed – the *Algerini*s could travel at 16 knots when not sweeping, 12 knots with an LL sweep, and 11 with an Oropesa sweep; with two sweeps that was reduced to about 8 knots.[35] At the beginning of the war the main group consisted of twenty-two ships of the *Aberdare* class, coal-fired and known as the 'Smokey Joes'. The seventeen ships of the *Halcyon* class were built in 1933–39 and would suffer heavy losses in the war, ten being destroyed by U-boat, mine, gunfire, accident and friendly fire. Brendon Maher served in *Jason* in 1944: 'a happy ship, although (or perhaps because) discipline was strict. The facilities were good – sick-bay, medical officer, ship's canteen for the crew, good food, and a good atmosphere in the wardroom'.[36]

The first ships of the *Bangor* class had diesel engines and were found to be too cramped for modern gear. The second batch were enlarged from 162 to 180ft and had vertical triple-expansion engines, giving a free speed of 16.5 knots. Charles McAra was delighted at his first sight of *Bude*: 'For a start she wasn't a rather grubby, cramped converted fishing-trawler'.[37] The final development was the *Algerine* class, the name ship being launched in December 1941. They were turbine or VTE powered with a length of 225ft, enough to accommodate all the necessary gear for sweeping contact, magnetic and acoustic mines; so large that they were sometimes diverted as escort vessels. The *Catherine* class, or BAMS vessels of the *Auk* class supplied under lend-lease, were American-built. The British minesweeping fleet rose from seventy-five vessels in 1939 to over seven hundred in 1940, manned by about fifteen thousand officers and men. By the end of the war it had risen to 1500 vessels, with 237 being lost; 497 merchant ships were sunk by German mines, and 14,300 of them were swept.

In home waters, the smaller minesweepers cleared the east-coast shipping channel of aircraft-launched mines, and swept the various ports and estuaries. After completing the course at *Lochinvar*, Brendan Maher was appointed to a sweeper in the same area, 'part of a flotilla responsible for sweeping for real mines in the Firth of Forth. Because the mines laid in the Forth were generally dropped by night by German aircraft, they were nearly always of the magnetic type and we swept them with electrical sweeps.'[38] Ernest Goodall reported:

> We worked out of Queenborough for 18 months, generally doing four days out and two days in, which consisted of up to Harwich and back, and round to Dover and back. … During that spell … we destroyed a large number of mines [over a hundred] but even so a number of merchant ships was sunk, especially in the Thames Estuary. You couldn't get them all.[39]

It was tiring for Vivian Cox in the trawler *Euclase* off Lowestoft:

> at sea the four hours off watch were purely nominal. If at any time during your spell below, day or night, the Skipper sounded 'Out

Sweeps' or 'In Sweeps' then the watch below had to be turned out on deck, for those were evolutions that demanded the presence of all seven seamen and the Mate.[40]

And there was constant danger of air attack, despite the RAF's fighter cover.

Overseas, minesweepers cleared channels in the Mediterranean and led the way on invasions. At Salerno, there were too few of them to clear the anchorage and the channels leading to the beaches, but no craft were lost, due to the skilled use of radar. At Anzio they suffered from shortage of intelligence.[41] For the Normandy invasion, the Royal Navy provided forty-seven out of fifty-six fleet minesweepers for the American beaches and forty-six out of sixty-two smaller sweepers, in addition to forty-two fleet sweepers and eighty-seven others for the British sector.[42] The minesweeping organisation was 'perhaps, the most intricate of all the many measures taken to ensure the safety of the invasion convoys', with swept channels along the coast and in the vital areas in the English Channel.[43] And on the final approach, Brendan Maher was in *MMS84*:

> Our task was to sweep mines to leave a safe depth for the larger fleet sweepers of the 1st Flotilla, led by the *Harrier*. They, in turn, swept at an even greater depth and width to clear the water necessary for the larger invasion vessels coming in behind them … The plan also called for us to remove ourselves into the unswept water outside Channel 9 when the time came for the assault craft to make their run to the beach.[44]

After that the sweepers continued to be employed, clearing ports such as Cherbourg and Antwerp to ensure the Allied supply routes.

HMS *Abdiel*, a ship of light cruiser size, was designed:

> … to produce a vessel able to lay as many mines as possible by day and by night in waters which might be under the control of the enemy. It was required to lay mines without escort and therefore had to rely on speed to avoid action with hostile surface vessels. A maximum speed of 40 kts in the standard condition was required, giving an expected 37–38 kts in the deep condition. …
>
> All the mines were to be under cover and capable of being laid in one operation, under all conditions that the ship could keep at sea.[45]

A hundred were to be carried, plus fifty more if the speed was reduced. Six of the class were built but they were mainly used for carrying supplies and special operations. They saw hard service and three were sunk. Mines could also be laid by submarines and two of the Mark II magnetic mine could be fitted in each torpedo tube, but production only lasted until 1942. Most offensive minelaying was done by aircraft. Bomber Command crews might see it as a diversion from their campaign against Germany, but they often welcomed operations which did not involve deep penetration of enemy territory. By the end of the war they had dropped 47,303 mines, 87 per cent of all those laid by the Navy and RAF, and the Germans attributed 842 vessels were lost due to their efforts.[46]

Defensive minelaying took the form of fields restricting entry to ports, and mine barrages. The Dover Barrage was laid at the start of the war and soon sank three U-boats, causing the Germans to revert to the longer northern route, a policy which continued even after they had occupied France,. The East Coast Mine Barrage, declared in December 1939, was a few miles offshore and was intended to protect convoys supplying London and the south with coal. It used up thirty-five thousand mines, but did not stop shallow-draught E-boats, which continued to sink ships, mainly off the coast of Norfolk. The Northern Barrage, between Scotland and the Denmark Strait, used eighty-one mines, nearly a third of the total British minelaying effort, and only sank one U-boat, with no appreciable effect on the conduct of the campaign.[47]

'Damn the torpedoes'

American sailors had often encountered sea mines in the past. David Glasgow Farragut's famous exclamation, 'Damn the torpedoes', actually referred to what would later be called mines – the 'locomotive torpedo' came a few decades later. In 1918 American ships helped lay a great barrage across the North Sea to prevent the exit of U-boats, and they stayed behind after the war to remove it. Nevertheless, the US Navy neglected mine warfare over the next two decades. Only two old Bird-class sweepers were still in use as such in 1928. Mining played a part in all the Fleet Problems between the wars, though rarely extensively or realistically, and mine warfare vessels were sometimes assigned roles outside their primary function, for example in Fleet Problem VIII of 1938, when they formed a patrol line eight hundred miles west of Hawaii. Mine warfare remained 'a perennial orphan on the service.'[48]

In 1939 the then Chief of Naval Operations assigned Captain Alexander Sharp to build up a minesweeping force, initially for base defence. He collected commercial and fishing boats and obtained permission to man them with reservists. Meanwhile, Lieutenant Commander Edward C Craig, at the minesweeping desk of the Bureau of Construction and Repair, surveyed available gear for sweeping influence mines, and found that the British system was the best. Mine depots were set up at Yorktown,

Virginia, and New London, Connecticut, followed by a research and testing station on Solomons Island, Maryland.[49]

Mining was less of a danger to the United States, as the ports tended to be deeper and were much further from German and Japanese bases. However, during the U-boats' 'second happy time' in June 1942, the Germans did lay mines which closed some East Coast ports for days, until they could be swept. A field of fifteen laid off the Chesapeake by *U-701* was by far the most successful, sinking a cargo ship, a trawler and a coal barge, and damaging two other vessels, including USS *Bainbridge*. Those off Delaware, Jacksonville, Chesapeake, Charleston and New York were discovered and swept. Four more, off Newfoundland, Boston, Mississippi Passes and Charleston, were so badly laid and irrelevant that their existence was not known until after the war.[50] This kind of war was not easy for the Germans to sustain: a U-boat could only carry fifteen mines for a voyage across the Atlantic by sacrificing most of its torpedo armament.

The threat did not end there as James Leland Jackson recorded:

> I was called in the fall of … nineteen forty-two to go to Miami to be minesweeping officer for the Seventh Naval District . … It was my responsibility to oversee all the exploratory minesweeping in the particular harbors. All the big harbors had a couple of YMSs. Supposed to … be checking to be sure the German submarines hadn't laid any mines.

In fact none were found: 'The only mines that were laid were laid by us at Key West. And they were supposed to be … defensive mines.'[51]

As war approached, old First World War Bird-class minesweepers were reconverted or recommissioned, degaussed and fitted for magnetic sweeping. Fishing boats, yachts and coastal craft were taken up and converted. Most new American minesweepers were intended to double as subchasers and, indeed, the 220ft fleet sweepers were designed for minelaying as well, which is why they were made so large. Often they played a part in escorting a convoy for an assault, then swept the landing area in advance.

Raven, a large 220ft steel sweeper, was designed to replace the ageing Birds and was followed by *Osprey*. It soon became clear that more electric power was needed for magnetic sweeping so a diesel-electric drive was adopted in place of pure diesel, with enough capacity left over to operate LL sweeps, so the hull was redesigned and the first of them, *Auk*, was launched in August 1941. Sonarman Houston Jones wrote, 'The steel-hulled AMs were large ships in the eyes of YMS and SC sailors. The Two Twenties, like *Speed*, carried a complement four times that of a subchaser, and its armament put to shame my previous ship's peashooters.'[52] Though they were expensive and complex, large numbers were built during the war.

In 1940 the Bureau of Ships began work on a design with 'excellent sea-keeping qualities permitting the minesweepers to sweep and keep station in all kinds of weather; second, simplicity of design to permit production in large numbers with minimum cost in time and money.'[53] The resulting *Admirable* class was simpler and smaller at 184ft. It reverted to pure diesel propulsion with engines powerful enough to generate electricity for magnetic sweeping and had a speed of 14 knots. The Royal Navy rejected it as too small for its needs and opted for *Raven*s instead. The *Admirable*s were found to be too slow for subchasers, but 174 were built.

The YMS, or yard minesweeper, was wooden-hulled and small at 136ft, but capable of crossing oceans. It was closely related to the PCS and SC submarine chasers as Houston Jones observed:

> ... in the Mediterranean I had become more familiar with YMSs than AMs because, like SCs, the yard minesweepers were made of wood, were only 26 feet longer than out SC ... Besides, their small complement lived in cramped quarters without desalination equipment and thus shared the discomforts of subchaser sailors.[54]

This is different from the experience of Yeoman John Desrosiers, who thought *YMS-380* was 'the most beautiful ship constructed for the navy', and 'even had a desalination plant aboard for drinking water.'[55]

The principal Naval Mine Depot was at Yorktown, Virginia, three miles from the historic town. It suffered several explosions, including one in November 1943 when a warehouse blew up, causing seven deaths and twenty-five injuries. By the end of the war, it had 148 officers, 1314 enlisted men and 1592 civilians. Training was among its responsibilities. In December 1941 James Leland Jackson:

> ... went to Naval Mine Warfare School for three months in Yorktown, Virginia. ... That was a training school for officers for mine warfare. ...we enjoyed it thoroughly. It was very simple. They had an MIT professor, who was the smartest guy I ever saw, teaching us electricity and magnetism and stuff like that. 'Course, we knew everything he was talking about cause most fellas, all this was new to them. But you know, going to Georgia Tech you'd studied all that stuff. ... It lasted three months... They demonstrated on the York River how to do it and all that sort of stuff. It didn't seem to be too intense to us.[56]

Over ten thousand reserve officers were trained in mine warfare during the war.[57] From the enlisted point of view, Houston Jones was involved in training at Little Creek in the same state: 'Our job was to take personnel assigned to mine sweepers, instruct them on deploying the different types of gear.'[58]

For contact mines, the British system was adopted:

> This type of sweeping used Oropesa gear (named after the British ship that perfected the gear); the procedure was spoken of as 'Making an O-sweep'. The Oropesa (or pig-float) was a streamlined steel float shaped like a fish … This was the most commonly used sweeping procedure in Far Eastern Waters.[59]

One American authority concluded: 'Few Navy leaders realized how much of their success in countering mines during World War II was due to the adaptation of British MCM technology, tactics and applications.'[60]

Raven and *Osprey* did exploratory minesweeping before the invasion of North Africa, and then served as landing craft control vessels. At Salerno, not enough time was allotted for clearance, leading to the loss of one ship. At Anzio, a large group of twenty-three minesweepers caused congestion off the beaches.[61] Houston Jones saw the effects of mines:

> Only a few hundred feet from us a submerged mine struck the stern of USS *Portent* (AM-106) sending up billows of black smoke and a 150-foot-tall column of white water. The ship quickly began to settle as several nearby small craft, including our sister ship *SC692,* risked their own safety by speeding into the minefield to rescue the captain … and more than seventy-five officers and enlisted men … I stood on our flying bridge and watched helplessly as the smoking 221-foot minesweeper gently sank stern-first and, at the same time rolled onto her starboard side until the ship was literally upside-down.[62]

John Desrosiers was onboard *YMS-380* for the invasion of Normandy:

> Having been fortunate enough to survive the Germans' first counter attack on Normandy, the Y squadron took up places on the starboard side of the swept channel in intervals between ships to extend over one mile back in the channel. The radar on, the sound gear on and both manned by experienced personnel and the flying bridge manned by two officers and two enlisted men with binoculars scanning the horizon for German fighter planes, as well as German E-boats, trying to disrupt the invasion.[63]

After that they went on to help clear liberated harbours:

> The four minesweepers of the YMS class entered the outer harbor of Cherbourg we formed up in echelon position, all deployed gear on the starboard side ... to sweep for acoustic mines and on the starboard [sic] side the O-type gear was also streamed to cut the cable holding the moored mine ... Some acoustic mines were activated, also some moored mines brought to the surface to be destroyed, we then deployed the magnetic sweep and gear and began to sweep for magnetic mines ... We continued to sweep for 30 days maybe even more, declared the harbor clear and safe. Days later mines began to sink ships. ... the mines had counters and only exploded after a certain amount of ships had passed over.[64]

In the Pacific war, the minesweepers also found their main role in supporting landings. Off Okinawa:

> The sweepers formed a row twelve miles long and moved across the sea in echelon formation, cutting a swath six miles wide ... Within three hours *Speed* struck our first blow against the Japanese when our starboard leg cut a mine. The next morning we cut another with the port leg. We were on a roll. Sweeping was usually limited to daylight hours when floaters could be spotted by eye; furthermore, the ships were strictly blacked out at night.[65]

TF-39 destroyed 404 mines in all, but only two were credited to *Speed*.[66]

> For eleven days, our tasks were repetitive. Each morning, dozens of ships would position themselves to form, collectively, an inverted fan, following the lead ship, and covering a miles wide triangle of the East China Sea ... Daily, each ship streamed intricate gear, recorded mines exploded by the gear or by gunshot on the surface, retrieved the gear ...[67]

Japan was just as vulnerable to mining as Britain potentially had been. American offensive minelaying in the Pacific began in October and November 1942, partly because a torpedo shortage made it necessary to find other employment for submarines. Two of them laid mines in the Gulf of Siam, two more in the Gulf of Tonkin, one off Indochina and one at the eastern entrance to Japan's Inland Sea. The last operation was carried out by *Whale*, whose officers used their initiative to lay close inshore where mines would not be expected. As usual they were unable to confirm any sinkings, but it was later found that two ships were damaged. The mines included the Mark 10, a moored contact mine which was cylindrical to fit into a torpedo tube and could be laid in 50–300ft of water. It was held in place by an anchor, and a hydrostatic mechanism took it to the right depth. The Mark 12 was a magnetic mine which could be laid in 16–25ft and contained 1095lbs of TNT or 1225lbs of Torpex.[68]

A second mission was mounted by three submarines in December, this time in Japanese waters. *Trigger* stayed in the area and had the unusual experience of seeing some of results of her actions:

> At this instant the leading ship which had reached the exact bearing of our mine plants, commenced smoking at least five times as great as before and the three other ships scattered to the northward. The smoke of our mine plants lasted only a few minutes while the other three columns of smoke disappeared to the northward. Consider that as freighter of at least 5000 tons was damaged, if not sunk by this mine.
>
> As a result of this experience it was decided to concentrate on harbor approaches rather than sea lanes, and CinCPac set up an analytical section which concluded that it was best to lay mines close inshore so that shipping would be forced into deeper water to become prey to torpedoes.[69]

Operation Starvation involved laying mines in Japanese inshore waters by the mighty B-29 bombers. General Curtis LeMay, despite his commitment to ruthless bombing campaigns against cities, was enthusiastic about the project as an alternative to land invasion. Most mines were laid in the Shimonosek Straits at the entrance to the Inland Sea, through which 80 per cent of Japanese merchant shipping passed. Naval officers assisted with the planning and material and new radar navigation ensured accuracy, though most bombing was by night. The first mission was flown on 27 March 1945 to lay the Mike and Love fields in the Straits.

A B-29 carried 20,000lbs of mines, including the Mark 25, which weighed 2000lbs and was cylindrical with a parachute in its tail. According to a later account, it possessed 'great damaging potential', but was 'quite sensitive'.[70] It could be laid in depths of 40–100ft against surface craft and 400ft against submarines. The Mark 26 and 36 weighed 1000lbs each, with 465lbs of TNT, or 525 of Torpex. Raids of fifty to a hundred planes in a total of 1529 sorties were mounted and 12,135 mines were laid. Eventually the Japanese were obliged to employ 349 vessels and twenty thousand men to clear mines. Despite that, 2 million tons of shipping were sunk or damaged, besides the disruption to ship movements.[71]

Coastal forces

It was a longstanding dream of naval inventors to attack mighty battleships and cruisers with small, fast craft carrying deadly weapons. The Royal Navy had used torpedo-carrying coastal motor boats during the First World War, and fast power boats were highly publicised in the 1920s and 1930s, with dramatic races and constant attempts on the world speed record. The RAF developed fast air–sea rescue launches, using the work of 'Aircraftman Shaw', alias Lawrence of Arabia.

The fast, light coastal forces of both navies in the Second World War owed much to Hubert Scott-Paine, who headed the Supermarine company making seaplanes, which had much in common with speedboats. He founded airlines which used flying boats. In 1927 he started the British Power Boat Company at Hythe, near Southampton, and built *Miss Britain III*, the first successful metal-hulled motor boat powered with an aeroplane engine. In 1935 he persuaded the Admiralty, mainly in the person of the enthusiastic Admiral Sir Reginald Henderson, to order six 60ft boats and a dozen more orders ensued. Like most of the craft which followed, they used the 'hard chine' form, in which the boat was partly raised out of the water at high speed:

> A hard chine design has very little V-shape on its bottom whereas a soft chine boat has a considerable V which gives a sharper entrance into the seas. The hard chine design gives greater speed due to the fact that it causes the boat to plane but it also causes the boats to be extremely wet in choppy or very rough weather, particularly at slow speeds.[72]

Scott-Paine's commercial methods did not please one of his rivals, Sir Jack Thornycroft, who claimed that:

> Between 1934 and 1938, owing to great showmanship and intensive publicity on the part of a firm, newcomers to the small boatbuilding industry, officials and responsible naval officers were … persuaded that a 'V' bottom or hard chine type of hull was something new … which made obsolescent all former designs of round bilge hulls.

In fact, as Thornycroft pointed out, it was only viable for craft of up to 110ft.[73] After losing to Scott-Paine in 1935, Thornycroft built fast craft for the Philippines, China and Finland, among others, until getting more Admiralty work in 1938.

Another rival was Commander Peter Du Cane, who had left the Royal Navy in 1929 and became head of the Vosper Company, which built Sir

Malcolm Campbell's record-breaking speedboat *Bluebird*. He too had an interest in aviation, as a pilot in the Royal Auxiliary Air Force, and later the Fleet Air Arm. He built the 70ft *MTB 102* as a private venture and it attained a speed of 47–48 knots and was taken on by the Royal Navy. His company would build more than three hundred MTBs during the war and the 70ft boat became standard.

Another contender was Camper and Nicholson, famous for their yachts, including challengers for the America's Cup. The designer Uffa Fox described the hull of their boat:

> Here we see a very easily-driven set of lines. At the waterline the angle of entry is 20 degrees but then the flaring bow extends this to 76 degrees at the deck-line; thus we see the waterlines fanning out from a very fine angle down at the water to a coarse angle of 76 degrees at the deck-line; all a good compromise between an easy motion through head seas combined with dryness on deck and not too much rake forward on the stern.[74]

As a result of competition, wartime developments, imports from America and the weakness of central control, more than forty different types of MTBs served during the war. They were made in wood to avoid using precious steel and built by dozens of large and small companies.

The greatest problem with fast British craft was finding suitable engines. There was no high-speed diesel engine like the one which made the German S-boat or E-boat so formidable, so they had to use highly inflammable petrol. Scott-Paine used the famous Rolls-Royce Merlin for his private venture of 1939, but in wartime it was reserved for aircraft. Before the war, some boats were equipped with the Italian Isotta Fraschini giving 1100hp per unit but, of course, that supply dried up. The Hall-Scott Defender, designed for the American Coast Guard in the Prohibition era, was procured but only offered 620hp, so speed was reduced. The Packard was more powerful and even his rival Thornycroft credited Scott-Paine with helping to procure it with his American connections.[75]

The boats were often compared with aircraft. They were like bombers in that they contained 'almost a maze of complicated and fragile fittings which need constant attention.' They were crewed by young men with 'the sense of duty and courage associated in the public mind with the "Battle of Britain" pilot.'[76] But, as L C Reynolds pointed out, bomber crews rested after an operation and did not see the aircraft again till the next one; coastal forces crews lived onboard and were responsible for maintenance.[77]

The 21in torpedo was standard, as the warhead of the 18in was considered inadequate, but submariners took priority, and coastal forces had to make do with older models until late 1942. Scott-Paine's original MTB followed the practice of the coastal motor boats in dropping its torpedo over the stern and getting out of the way, but that had obvious disadvantages. The 70ft Vosper boat had a single torpedo tube in the bow, but they were soon replaced by a tight-fitting torpedo tube which was designed in 1938/9 and may have been influenced by Thornycroft's design for the Philippine government. Early MTBs had one on each side. They worked well, except at high speed when the torpedo would dive deep – but MTBs rarely fired at such speed. They were angled 7½ degrees outward, but gyros were set to angle them 6½ degrees inward, so that there was a spread of 2 degrees. By 1943, 18in torpedoes with more powerful warheads were available, and subsequent MTBs were armed with four of them. Peter Dickens describes the preparations for attack in an MTB: 'Action Stations! Torpedoes ready with stop valves open, impulse cartridges inserted and firing mechanisms checked, safety pins out of the whiskered pistols; intense look-out; muted voices'.[78]

In all, MTBs and steam gunboats fired 1328 torpedoes in action in 689 separate attacks, making an average of just under two per attack. They claimed 318 certain hits and thirty-seven probables, with an average of 39.7 per cent success, which compares favourably with attacks by other vessels.[79]

Early MTBs concentrated on the torpedo armament and only carried .303 machine guns in addition. Some of the first Oerlikon guns were fitted on British ships. It became clear that while torpedo targets were comparatively rare, the main enemy was the German E or S-boat, with a 37mm and a 20mm gun as standard. Once the Germans were in possession of the opposite shores of the North Sea and English Channel, they used their E-boats to raid British coastal convoys. With their shallow draught and high speed, they were immune to torpedoes, so equally fast and numerous gunboats were needed to counter them. At first, various craft were converted or refitted. Motor anti-submarine boats built by BPB or provided under lend-lease from Higgins of New Orleans, and submarine chasers building for the French, had no real role as the U-boats tended to avoid inshore operations, so they were fitted with machine guns, and 75 and 20mm guns, in the case of the French vessels. They soon proved inadequate, and even with light armaments they could not cope in a seaway, while their engines were placed under undue stress. It was decided to adapt the BPB designs for MTBs, mostly around 70ft long, but they were given a 'hogged sheer', that is, the deck was curved downwards in the bow to improve the field of fire of forward guns when at speed. Some carried a 2pdr gun forward, others had Oerlikons and machine guns, but improvised armament was often fitted unofficially. As well as BPB, such boats were produced by Higgins, White of Cowes and Elco.

Meanwhile, the Fairmile Company was developing in its own way. It was founded in 1939 by Noel Macklin, whose personality and breadth of experience matched Scott-Paine and Du Cane. Of Australian origin, he was a big-game hunter and film-maker. During the First World War, he was both an army and an RNVR officer. Afterwards, he designed and built racing and sports cars and took up flying. In 1939 he read an article by Vice Admiral Usborne on the need for naval small craft and set up the Fairmile Marine Company, named after his home village. He designed the Fairmile A motor launch, based on a fishery protection boat, and eventually persuaded the Admiralty to order a dozen, entering into a unique hybrid commercial relationship with them. The A was not well liked, and was used for minelaying; the Fairmile B was sketched out by the Admiralty with a round bilge rather than a hard-chine hull and Fairmile developed it into a 112ft boat. Only two Hall-Scott engines were available instead of three, so speed was reduced to 30 knots, but it proved a remarkably versatile craft, quickly convertible to torpedo boat, anti-submarine boat, air-sea rescue craft or gunboat.

Meanwhile, Fairmile was developing a remarkable system of mass production for the wooden boats. Timber yards cut the frames, a bell foundry cast propellers, wire net manufacturers made rudders and a linoleum company turned the shafting – in all, 145 slipways in forty-five shipyards, most of them very small, would be involved in Fairmile production.

The Fairmile C was fitted with the three Hall-Scott engines and twenty-four were built, used for convoy escort. In 1939 W J Holt of the Admiralty produced a hard-chine design:

> The form was developed by, in imagination, splicing a destroyer type bow onto a fast motor-boat type of stern, in an attempt to obtain less pounding of the hull when driven at high speed into ahead sea. The form also produced a dry boat forward by ploughing over the bow wave.[80]

It was turned over to Fairmile, who began work on it in March 1941, and the first example began trials eleven months later. It proved to be the classic design:

For a small boat, 658 had an impressive array of guns. She carried a 40mm pom-pom in a power-operated turret on the fo'c'sle; twin Vickers 0.5 turrets on each side of the charthouse; twin Vickers .303s on the wings of the bridge; a power-mounted twin Oerlikon (20 mm) over the engine-room, and a 6pdr (nearly 3in calibre) aft.[81]

The relative lack of speed was not a problem: 'low speeds were far more effective during close attacks than high speeds, and the lack of bow-wave and wake gave the enemy less chance of sighting accurately, and our own gunners were conversely able to hold the target more easily'.[82]

The steam gunboat was conceived in 1940 as an answer to the E-boat, in view of the lack of a lightweight, high-power, diesel engine. Unlike the motor boats, it used traditional methods, designed by the Admiralty in co-operation with the established shipbuilders Yarrow's and Denny's, and nine of them were built in steel by these yards and Hawthorn Leslie's and Whites. They were allowed names rather than numbers because they were more than 130ft long.[83] Peter Scott was aware of their essential flaw: 'although they did not carry high-octane petrol, and risk thereby was much reduced, they only had one boiler, one feed pump, only one extractor pump. If any of these were put out of action by a machine-gun bullet the boat was bound to stop'.[84] Fuel consumption was very high, but they were strong and heavily armed, with two 6pdr guns and two 21in torpedo tubes. They were quite successful against E-boats, but no more were ordered.[85]

It was generally true that coastal forces were manned almost entirely by temporary RNVR officers and HO ratings, though *MGB 658* had four 'active service' regulars out of 30.[86] Eric Denton had his own reason for applying: 'If I was in Coastal Forces I would get into all sorts of smaller harbours and places where I would get a varied interest and would get a chance to see some life away from the strict rigours of the Navy'.[87] But more common among officers was the prospect of an early command. That was enough to win over Peter Dickens, despite his initial prejudices as a regular officer: 'Command! The word rang in my ears; but then I thought of those scruffy boats of which I had heard little except that they usually broke down when in the presence of the enemy'.[88] An MGB or MTB usually had a lieutenant or sub lieutenant in command, and a sub lieutenant or midshipman as first lieutenant – later a third officer was often added.

Coastal forces produced a whole litany of heroes, of which Robert Hichens ('Hitch') was the most prominent. He was a solicitor, motor racer, oarsman and yachtsman who joined the Supplementary Reserve in 1936.

He was in one of the first courses at *King Alfred*, which he completed in six weeks. After service in minesweepers, he transferred to motor anti-submarine boats in 1940, then found his metier as commander of an MGB in 1941. He was a superb leader and Peter Dickens, a regular RN officer, was not upset to defer to 'a hostilities only amateur. ... his burning passion was rigidly controlled by the self-discipline of a gentleman; ... he was interested personally in every one of his sailors. Add to that a personal magnetism which flowed from his steady eyes and carried strength, courage and inspiration.'[89] After numerous actions in the North Sea and Channel and several decorations, he turned down a nomination for the Victoria Cross on the grounds that his actions had led to several losses. He was killed shortly afterwards, and the award of a posthumous VC was vetoed for the same reason. As it turned out, the only coastal forces VC was awarded to Able Seaman William Savage, a gunlayer in the St-Nazaire operation.

An MGB usually had a petty officer or leading seaman as coxswain, a petty officer motor mechanic, leading stoker and stoker, able seamen torpedoman and gunner, a telegraphist and an ordinary seaman, though crews tended to expand as more guns were added, and the Fairmile D had thirty or more.[90] As in most small craft of the Royal Navy, the coxswain was a significant figure, though often in an awkward place between the officers and crew. In Peter Dickens's boat: 'Some coxswains went ashore with their crews but that was slap-happy. When we went ashore the Coxswains used the Saloon Bar and the crews the Public Bar.'[91] The coxswain's views on his cabin-mate, the PO motor mechanic, reflected the typical 'oil and water' antipathy in the navy: 'Proper grease-monkey, covered in it and used to bring it into the cabin, and I used to sling his gear out in the alleyway ... Good fellow, though, knew his job first class.'[92]

But all ranks and trades shared the hardships:

> The crashing rise and fall of the boats in heavy weather was often the cause of serious stomach disorders, not to mention the occasional broken bone, and in general a severe strain was imposed upon the physical and nervous systems. This was particularly true for engine-room personnel, who had to wear ear-plugs to deaden the noise of the supercharger, and whose health was constantly endangered by gas fumes.[93]

And cooking was far from easy:

> Even a first class cook with good sea legs would have found it difficult in light weather to prepare a meal in the galley of a small

MTB, and in moderate weather, with the contents jumping out of the pan and the pan jumping off the stove, cooking was out of the question.[94]

Habitability was a serious problem in port, for in general the crews lived onboard: 'The worst conditions occurred ... when the boat was ... made fast at a deep quay, with three or four boats abreast. In such a place on a cold night with the crews sleeping below the amount of "sweating" had to be seen to be believed.'[95]

Individual training for coastal forces was done in HMS *St Christopher* at Fort William in Scotland, which occupied five hotels and numerous Nissen huts, with a staff of thirty officers and nineteen MLs, eight MTBs and nine MGBs at its peak.[96] HMS *Bee* at Weymouth was:

> a working-up base to polish newly commissioned crews or refitted boats into operation order, and the routine was indeed tough. A very complicated timetable was arranged so that lectures ... occupied the days, and frequent tactical exercises occupied the nights. The programme for each boat gradually worked up to a crescendo ...[97]

It was commanded by a 'retired old swashbuckler called Roland Swinley... No young RNVR officer could accuse him of hidebound RN pomposity',[98] Peter Dickens recalled: 'We "sank" the old Bob-a-nob-round-the-Fleet paddle steamer time and time again, after which our performance was critically examined by Lieutenant Commander Younghusband whose judgement at the beginning was likely to be "You might as well try to manure a 40 acre field with a fart".'[99] In October 1943 *Bee* moved to Holyhead, where Peter Scott became a slightly reluctant member of staff: 'There were lectures to give and long days, and sometimes nights, to be spent at sea in other people's boats on various exercises.'[100]

In operational bases, maintenance was a key problem, for breakdowns were frequent, according to Peter Dickens: 'MTBs broke down because they were too hastily designed and thrown together; that was much less the fault of those who built them than the Navy's own.'[101] There was a constant shortage of spares, as the boats had relatively low priority in production. Structural damage often had to be dealt with: 'If a boat is given big engine power and will travel fast, it is human nature – and especially young human nature – to open up the throttle and make it travel fast despite weather conditions.'[102]

Nore Command, the principal operator, had forty-five MGBs, twenty-four MTBs and thirty-five MLs in November 1942. Its commander-in-chief, Admiral Sir George D'Oyly Lyon, was 'the vicar on earth of Simple

Goodness', according to Peter Dickens.[103] By September 1943 it had an offensive force of sixteen MTBs at Felixstowe with seven MGBs and nine launches. HMS *Mantis* at Lowestoft 'provided everything spiritual and material that our aggressive purpose needed',[104] but was more defensive, as it had to protect some of the most dangerous areas for convoys, and it had only eight MTBs alongside twenty MGBs and sixteen MLs. Yarmouth just to the north had fifteen MTBs, twenty MGBs and twelve MLs.

Dover Command operated within range of the guns of Dover Cliffs and Cap Gris-Nez on the other side, and was known as 'Hell-fire Corner'. It had twenty MGBs, seven MTBs and seventeen MLs in November 1942, rising to twenty-four MGBs and twenty-one MTBs ten months later, but with a reduced force of nine MLs. A few miles away at Ramsgate, the officers' mess, formerly the Royal Ramsgate Yacht Club, 'stood out in all its dignity. Its interior was filled with yellowed pictures of bygone yachting days.'[105]

Portsmouth Command was the main base for the steam gunboats, as well as fifteen MGBs, sixteen MTBs and twenty-eight MLs in November 1942. Its other bases included Newhaven, which accommodated the SGBs from July 1943, as well as eleven MTBs, six MGBs and twenty-four MLs in September: '*Aggressive* was housed in the London and Paris Hotel. We lived on board our boats, but I had an office in the building … After a night patrol we normally had a bath and breakfast in *Aggressive*. Often the night's activities were discussed over the partitions in the bathroom'.[106]

The sheltered harbour at Portland, and nearby Weymouth, catered for a total of eight MGBs, nine MTBs and a dozen MLs. Plymouth was further from the action but had eight MTBs and twenty-eight MLs in November 1942. The command also included bases at Dartmouth with a total of forty-two boats in September 1943, and Falmouth with a dozen MLs. Western Approaches Command had twenty-five MLs in November 1942, for convoy escort in the Irish Sea. At Milford Haven, the antiquated ironclad frigate *Warrior* was used as a depot ship: 'to get on shore we had to go up on deck on the *Warrior*, over to the other side where she was moored and down through a long tunnel which carried an oil pipeline ashore to storage tanks.'[107] At the opposite end of the country, Orkney and Shetland Command had eight MTBs and twenty-five MLs in November 1942. At Lerwick, it supported a famous Norwegian flotilla which raided their homeland across the North Sea.

In the Mediterranean, the main base was HMS *Gregale* on Malta, which was 'housed in a row of hotels and villas on the other side of Marxamaxett Harbour'.[108] In that sea:

Slipping and docking of small MTBs presented a very difficult problem. They cannot be docked on their keels, a cradle being required. All docking facilities were limited [which] tended to force the coastal force craft to the small, ill-equipped ports where there were small slips with operators not mindful of the relatively delicate nature of an MTB.[109]

Much of the work of coastal forces was in the North Sea, where they protected coastal convoys from E-boats, which were shallow enough to cross the mine barrage, and fast enough to hit and escape. By 1941, the main policy was to employ the Fairmile motor launches to defend the convoys through the most vulnerable points, especially at night. The motor gunboats were fast enough to chase the E-boats, but at first there was no role for the MTBs, according to Peter Dickens, who believed that 'You can knock things out with guns, but if you give it half a chance the torpedo will do the job for you, suddenly and completely.'[110] The Commander-in-Chief, Nore thought that 'we of the MTBs had little or no part to play in his master plan. His all-absorbing concern was the safety of his coastal shipping against constant attrition by mines, aircraft and E-boats, and … offensive operations off the enemy's coast seemed to have small relevance'. It was pointed out that coastal iron ore traffic from Sweden towards Rotterdam was essential to German war production, and raids on these convoys began. MGBs played their part, and in March 1942 they frustrated a squadron of E-boats leaving Ijmuiden. Offensively, it became common for one MTB and one MGB flotilla to co-operate on raids.

MTBs took part in the unsuccessful operation to stop the 'Channel Dash' of *Scharnhorst* and *Gneisenau* in February 1942:

> It was an impossible situation. The 24 E-Boats kept close station, preventing any attempt to break through the screen. We were forced to fire our torpedoes from about 4000 yards or more, a far from ideal range for Torpedo Boats. But there was nothing for it but to try, so we fired away gamely, loosing the torpedoes from all five boats.[111]

They were also involved in the even less successful Dieppe raid of 1942, where Peter Scott recorded the confusion:

> All this time it was very hard to know what was going on either ashore or afloat. From time to time signals came through calling for closer support. But how to do that, was the question. How to know where one's troops were. The blanket of smoke between us and the shore was almost complete.[112]

Radar played an increasing part, both from shore stations and from sets fitted to coastal craft from that autumn. MLs carried out minelaying operations in the North Sea, with eighty-one laid in July 1943, but that was only a tenth of the number laid by aircraft in the same period. Warfare in the English Channel intensified after the Normandy invasion; in July there were ten clashes between MTBs, supported by radar-equipped frigates, and German light craft off Le Havre, with losses balanced on each side. And in the North Sea, there were nine actions in July and August 1944, with seven small enemy war vessels sunk for the loss of one MTB.

In the Mediterranean, coastal forces operated from bases in Corsica against shipping supplying the German forces in northwest Italy. In April 1944 a well-trained force under Commander Robert Allan RNVR, consisting of landing craft gun, motor gunboats and British and American MTBs destroyed several barges, a tug and a patrol vessel off Livorno. By July, coastal forces were in action almost every night between the south coast of France and Genoa. In the Adriatic, the boats co-operated with Yugoslav guerrillas:

> Our boats … had hidden, camouflaged in creeks by day and patrolled by night. Now they were joined by Commandos, units of the Royal Artillery, and a squadron of Hurricanes. … the situation at Vis, where we would be operating, was unique; it was an island fortress containing about 4000 allied servicemen and 8000 Partisans, but surrounded on all but the seaward side by islands held by the Germans.[113]

They raided German lighters and barges coming out of Venice and Trieste to disrupt communications.

Were they expendable?

By mid 1938 the US Navy was taking an interest in fast boats, largely to defend the Philippines. A design competition attracted twenty-four entries for a 53ft boat and thirteen for a 70ft. A winner was chosen in both categories and four of each were ordered, to become *PT-1–8*.

In 1939 Scott-Paine was disappointed when the British Admiralty adopted the Vosper design instead of his 70ft boat. He shipped it to New Jersey, where he linked up with the Electric Boat Company, or Elco, of Bayonne. Registered as *PT-9*, it was tested against US designs and found to be superior, 'but no miracle', according to the assessor. However, it was ready, unlike the other designs, and Elco was given a contract for twenty-three more boats, enlarged to 77ft to allow for four torpedoes instead of two.

In the meantime, Higgins of New Orleans produced an 81ft boat and Huckins of Florida built another. In the summer of 1941 they were tested off New London along with a BuShips design in the 'plywood derbies' – though three of the boats were actually built of mahogany and the Bureau one of aluminium. That was its undoing; it was clearly uninhabitable. Contracts were awarded for the three others, but experience showed that the Huckins boat was too weak. Only eighteen were ordered, and they were used for training. The Higgins boat was inferior to the Elco in speed and seakeeping, though it was cheaper and had a better turning circle. The training school at Melville wanted to abandon the Higgins craft, but it was decided not to end production, which had already been tooled up. The length of the Elco boat was increased again to 80ft.[114]

These two became the standard motor torpedo boats, for, in accordance with normal American policy, design was largely frozen at the start of the war. Eventually 296 Elco 80ft boats were built for the US Navy, out of a total of 535 MTBs, compared with 146 Higgins boats. In addition, seventy-three were built for the Royal Navy, mostly of the Vosper 70ft type.

The official *Motor Torpedo Boat Manual* of February 1943 gave a detailed account of the boat's characteristics in various sea conditions:

> Up to about a 4-foot sea, the PT boat can make her maximum speed on any course.
>
> When the seas increase to about 8 feet, she can still make her maximum speed down wind or across it, in fact on every course except dead into the seas. If the normal course is directly into the wind and sea, in heavy weather, the boat may be injured by trying to make maximum speed. In addition, the crew will be unable to man their stations properly and may even be injured … Perhaps most serious of all is the fact that, forcing the vessel at high speed into the seas causes so much spray to come-over the bow that visibility is reduced to a very great degree. This is particularly undesirable, because the very success of a mission, … usually depend, upon spotting the enemy before being spotted, … All these considerations point to the necessity for tacking the boat. This means to steer a zigzag course, taking the wind and seas quartering over the bows instead of from dead ahead. Then the boat can resume much of its speed, and visibility will improve notably.[115]

According to the same manual:

> The torpedo boat is designed to carry four torpedoes in tubes and to discharge them by expansion of ignited gun powder. There are two

tubes on each side. Tubes train inboard for cruising and loading, and train outboard for expected action and firing. The forward tubes train outward to an angle of 8° 30′ with the ship's centerline, the after tubes to an angle of 12° 30′. All torpedoes are fired forward and at the stated angles with the centerline.[116]

As well as their weight, the tubes caused problems in night operations, according to Donald B Frost:

> … it was gunpowder that went off. As the torpedo cleared the torpedo tube, a lot of times the powder from the shell would also light off the grease … There'd be a flash of light. Now it didn't last too long. Most of the time somebody would douse it… to keep it from flaming anymore. But it was a kind of giveaway device …[117]

There was a shortage of 21in torpedoes in the early stages, and Higgins designed a tube to accommodate the airborne 22.5in Mark 18, but by the time it was ready, another answer had been found. Reportedly, Lieutenants Sprugel and Costigan of *PT-188* first conceived the idea of a torpedo to be carried in a rack and rolled into the water, and it was ready by August 1943. Before firing, a lanyard was pulled to start the torpedo gyro and motor, and it could be launched as soon as the latter reached full speed. Each rack weighed 540lbs compared with 1450 for a tube, and lighter torpedoes were now used, so boats could carry increased gun armament without sacrificing their torpedoes.[118]

An Elco 80ft motor torpedo boat launching torpedoes at speed during an exercise; they were rarely used effectively in this way in action.

Early PT boats had a basic anti-aircraft armament of machine guns, mostly 0.50s and 0.30s. Boats in the Southwest Pacific began to acquire 40mm Bofors from various sources, including the Royal Australian Navy, but in the South Pacific they were considered to be too heavy and the 37mm gun was favoured for 'barge busting', mostly using redundant models from Bell Airacobra aircraft. As torpedoes were used less than guns, the question of removing them arose, but that was only done on a few vessels to make gunboats in the British style. It was decided to retain the flexibility which a torpedo armament allowed, helped by the lighter torpedo and gear. In November 1944 the standard armament was to be four torpedo racks, but only two torpedoes were carried in normal circumstances. There was a 37mm gun forward with a Bofors aft, with a total of four 0.50s. Rockets were fitted to many craft to illuminate the night sky, while others carried depth charges in place of some of their guns.[119]

PT boats were not commissioned warships in the fullest sense of the term:

> The organization of the motor torpedo boat squadron is similar to that of an aircraft squadron in that the squadron, rather than the individual boat, is the commissioned unit. However, each motor torpedo boat functions as a commissioned vessel when acting singly.
>
> For operations and tactics, the squadron is organized into several divisions of two or three vessels each which usually are the basis for task assignments. For administration and maintenance, the squadron is organized into departments.[120]

It was decreed that: 'Each boat boat shall be under the command of an officer of suitable rank and ability, assigned as boat captain. The executive officer on each boat shall assist the boat captain in every way and he should strive to qualify in all respects for the position of boat captain.'[121] PT boat officers were an elite in more senses than one. According to Donald M Frost, 'we did end up with a lot of officers then who came from very wealthy families or were ... above the average kid that comes out of college.'[122] To Ted Mason, who had endured a 'friendly fire' attack by them in *Pawnee*, they were 'skippered by glory-hunting ensigns and jay-gees from the Ivy League colleges whose basic qualifications were wealthy parents and summer experience handling sailboats off Cape Cod.'[123] The most famous, of course, was the young John F Kennedy, whose wealthy and influential father Joseph pulled strings to get him appointed, though he was medically unfit for the role.

Originally, it was expected that each boat would have nine enlisted men: a torpedoman, gunner's mate, quartermaster, radioman, three engineers, one seaman and a ship's cook. Extra guns naturally needed more men, and by the end of the war the typical boat had around fourteen enlisted men, making their quarters very crowded.

Donald Frost was training as an aviation machinist's mate in Jacksonville but was reluctant to go to a rear base:

> Gee, I don't want to spend the whole war sitting in a PBY or a PBM. I want to go out where the action is. … on the bulletin board there was a poster that said if you were interested in volunteering for PT boats, you know, put your name down. Well, about 20 out of my particular company … said they'd love to go to the PT boats … and we were accepted. … aviation engines were quite similar to the engines that were in PT boats, which were Packard V-12 engines and that were water-cooled rather than air-cooled, and a different type of engine. But basically if you were an engine man, as we were then, then you wouldn't have as much problem in working on a PT boat engine.[124]

As with the British, the crews did much of their own maintenance:

> Then we'd have to come back and do, you know, check the engines and strip the guns down, clean them, get them ready. Because even if they're not fired, they do get salty, and you can't leave them too long. … Then for the engine, then, of course, we're down there changing plugs or changing oil and all the other things that are needed to keep the engines in good shape. Even the radioman would have to do something with his radio and make sure that was okay. And, you know, we had to do some map work, navigation; that was the quartermaster's job. And so everybody was busy during the day. And the problem was, though, when do you sleep?[125]

PT boat crews were considered to be irregular by regular navy men, but even the official orders allowed some slack:

> The cleanliness and appearance of a boat should never be sought at the expense of the care and upkeep of its equipment; however, unless particularly heavy operating schedules have been maintained, boat personnel should be able to keep top side and below compartment spaces clean and shipshape. … A clean and smart looking boat reflects on the efficiency and ability of the officers and men on board.[126]

Edgar D Hoagland trained in the Motor Torpedo Boat Squadrons Training Center at Melville in the Rhode Island, like around two thousand fellow officers and 12,500 enlisted men: 'The training at the school was good. ... Our gunnery and torpedo classes were comprehensive. Most of the instructing officers were fresh from combat in the Pacific and gave us good tips on how to fight and survive.'[127] From the enlisted point of view, Donald Frost commented:

> There was a lot more to it than just training for the engine work. Because if you were in a small crew of say 12 people on a PT boat, you couldn't just say, Well, I only work on engines, nothing else. You had to learn how to work on guns because you were going to be firing the guns, and you had to be able to clean guns and so forth. You also had to know something about navigation and something about torpedoes and the whole bit.[128]

After that boats were formed into flotillas and transited the Caribbean and the Panama Canal to Taboga, a few miles offshore, for a five-week course, which also satisfied Hoagland:

> There were comfortable sleeping facilities far up a mountainside. The food was good, with lots of fresh local fish. The weather was warm, and for recreation, we enjoyed swimming, volleyball, and liberty in Panama City. ...
>
> Our training was superb. There was a huge rock that we shot at by day and by night as our gunners became professional. ... There was practice with torpedoes against patrol ships by night and day, and we fired at sleeves towed by aircraft. We made long navigational cruises and simulated practice runs against aircraft carriers and other capital ships.[129]

The Pacific campaigns needed a great deal of mobility, which was reflected in PT boat bases. Boats usually operated near a base in the Solomons, while those in the Southwest Pacific often operated several hundred miles from a base.[130] As a result of the movement, bases often changed role: 'We docked in a beautiful little harbor at Kana Hope that had been an active combat patrol torpedo base before the war had moved north.'[131]

By the beginning of 1944, standard Seabee equipment included PT boat moorings, a pontoon dry dock suitable for PT boats, a mooring catwalk and a frame for lifting engines. The most memorable was the 'Marine Railway for PT Boats', which was:

a ramp of pierced steel plank which extends into the water, a cradle on wheels which is equipped to accommodate the hulls of PT boats or other craft …, and a winch for pulling the load cradle up into the hull repair shop at the inshore end of the ramp.[132]

Mios Woendi is an island off the northwestern coast of New Guinea, triangular except that the eastern side was a shallow bay. The PT boat base was at the southern end of that bay, with piers and a torpedo loading dock, and the armoury torpedo shop and warehouses on land. West of that, on the west side of the island, were the officers' quarters and administration office, all in Quonset huts. Further up that side were the enlisted quarters, mess hall and a movie area. The rest of the east shore was undeveloped, but the northern shore was dominated by tents for the Seabees. Near the centre of the island was a chapel, library and yet more warehouses. The central part of the east shore included the Bob Hope theatre, a seaplane base and a dock for bigger ships.[133]

Three private yachts were taken over as gunboats and converted to PT boat tenders in 1941. *Niagara* was sunk in 1943, *Jamestown* and *Hilo* proved inadequate. LSTs were far more suitable: the tank decks could be used for support facilities and they already had troop accommodation – ten of them were converted. They were supplemented by four seaplane tenders which also had good accommodation, and plenty of fuel stowage. To Donald Frost:

> … a tender is like a mother ship, and they were made to raise boats out of the water. They mostly had some sort of a davit, a derrick, or whatever, that would hook onto a boat and be able to pick it up out of the water if need be. They also supplied us with food supposedly. But it being so rough, it wasn't easy to get the food from the tender to the boat.[134]

Douglas MacArthur, then a field marshal in charge of the defence of the Philippines, was enthusiastic about motor torpedo boats in 1940:

> A relatively small fleet of such vessels, manned by crews thoroughly familiar with every foot of the coast line and surrounding waters, and carrying, in the torpedo, a definite threat against large ships, will have a distinct effect in compelling any hostile force to approach cautiously and by small detachments.

It was decided to adopt the British Thornycroft model, but the builders were soon distracted and only three were available when the Japanese invaded, besides Lieutenant John Bulkeley's six USN boats.[135] They fought a celebrated campaign against Japanese advances and evacuated MacArthur himself, and the president of the Philippines, after all was lost. W L White's book supposedly describing their exploits, *They were Expendable*, publicised the boats but was highly optimistic; they did not sink the two cruisers and two merchant ships as claimed. The John Wayne film, released at the end of the war, exaggerated the claims even further.

MacArthur retained his enthusiasm throughout the campaign. If he appeared unenthusiastic about the support he received from most of the navy, it was different when he spoke of the PT boats.[136] Roosevelt himself began to take an interest in February 1942: 'The action by those little Italian boats in the Eastern Mediterranean on December 22 was pretty good. I would say it was damned good. If they can do it, why can't we do it?'[137]

In fact, they would take a key role in the battle for Guadalcanal later that year, though not by attacking capital ships, as intended. They operated in 'The Slot' or 'Ironbottom Sound' to disrupt the 'Tokyo Express' bringing supplies to the hotly contested island. On the first anniversary of Pearl Harbor, eight boats out of Tulagi attacked a destroyer already damaged by air attack. They scored no hits with their torpedoes, but the Express failed to deliver any supplies on that occasion. Their inshore attacks against barges were more devastating. It was there in August 1943 that John F Kennedy's *PT-109* was cut in half by a Japanese destroyer.

General Douglas MacArthur in his trademark cap crosses Leyte Gulf in a PT boat in October 1944. Before the war, he had planned to use such craft for the defence of the Philippines, and he was evacuated in one in 1942. He used them effectively during the Southwest Pacific campaign, though not in their planned role.

The PT boats were most effective during MacArthur's advance along the north coast of New Guinea in 1943/4. Operations were conducted by Commander Selman Bowling, who was awarded the Distinguished Service Medal for:

> … exceptionally meritorious service to the Government of the United States in a duty of great responsibility as Commander Motor Torpedo Boat Squadrons, Seventh Fleet, during action against enemy Japanese forces from Wakde through and including the Philippine Islands and Borneo Areas, from February 1944 to 25 August 1945. An inspiring and dynamic leader, highly skilled in the comprehensive planning and coordination of supporting operations launched by his units against a fanatic, determined enemy, Captain Bowling consistently operated in uncharted waters and under extremely difficult conditions, expertly deploying and directing his command in advance strikes to disrupt vital hostile communications, intercept enemy supplies and reinforcements, carry out liaison missions with friendly guerrilla scouts and parties and perform extensive escort and reconnaissance duties.

Barge busting became increasingly dangerous as the victims acquired armament. The captain of *PT-342* wrote after one attack:

> These 110 foot heavily armed and sometimes armored barges are at least an even match for a PT and if numbers are in enemy's favor the odds are decidedly with them, not taking the speed factor into consideration. It is remarkable in this instance that [our] PT boats came through unscathed, as there was an enormous concentration of fire power emanating from the barges, to say nothing of shore battery fire.[138]

In October 1944, during the Leyte Gulf campaign, thirty-nine PT boats were available to face a Japanese fleet proceeding through the Surigao Strait, but they lacked recent torpedo training. Lieutenant Howard Terry captained *PT-326* in the attack:

> As we got within a few thousand yards the secondary batteries on the big Japanese ships opened up and it looked like a solid wall of fire ahead of you. You just knew that nothing could survive in there. And here we were going at them in a plywood boat.

Anther captain recalled, 'From then on, brother, we weren't scared. We were terror stricken.'[139] They fired thirty-four torpedoes between them, nearly all of which ran 'straight and normal', but scored only one hit, which did no serious damage to the light cruiser *Abukuma*. Soon afterwards the destroyers launched a devastating torpedo attack.[140]

* * *

The real value of fast motor boats, especially MTBs, weas always controversial. Their crews tended to believe that they could have done much better had old-fashioned admirals been prepared to let them off the leash. Peter Dickens was approached by his coxswain, who told him the crew 'want to go to sea more often.'[141] Edgar Hoagland conceded that 'Some observers have stated that PT boats did not sink many ships with torpedoes in World War II, despite being called patrol torpedo boats. Actually, in terms of confirmed kills they are right.' He explained that kills against the Japanese were very difficult to confirm, and often they did not acknowledge their losses even amongst themselves, but that does not explain why US submarines had a much higher kill rate.[142]

The motor torpedo boat, in particular, did not live up to original expectations. It rarely used its torpedoes with success, and hardly ever against major warships, and its high speed was often useless since it could not launch torpedoes when going fast, so its two main features were not as useful as they might have been. The official naval historians tended to be sceptical or patronising about their exploits. To Captain Stephen Roskill of the Royal Navy, in British coastal waters: 'Our Coastal Forces accounted for comparatively few German merchantman (40 ships totalling 59,650 tons); but they sank no less than 70 enemy warships (mostly of a small size).'[143] Rear Admiral Samuel Eliot Morison of the US Navy wrote of the PT boats:

> One of the interesting and baffling things about naval history is the way in which a type of ship or weapon designed for one purpose turns out to be useless for that purpose, but very useful for another. … their torpedo tube rapidly becoming a sort of vermiform appendix for lack of employment.[144]

And despite his title *Engage the Enemy More Closely*, Correlli Barnett's highly critical history of the wartime navy only mentions coastal forces once, in connection with the failed attack on *Scharnhorst* and *Gneisenau*.

But that is not to deny that, as small craft, they were mostly built without eating into the resources needed for larger ships, and were manned by daring and dedicated officers and adventurous crews. In that sense, they provided good value for money and, more important in a wartime context, for their use of manpower and material resources.

16

Amphibious Warfare

NO CONFLICT in history depended more on amphibious warfare – on bringing land and air forces across water – than the Second World War. In the European and Mediterranean theatres it allowed the invasions of North Africa, Italy and France. In the Pacific it was the principal feature of the Central Pacific Drive, and a vital part of General MacArthur's parallel campaign to the south. It was an excellent example of co-operation between nations in the development of suitable vessels.

By 1940, modern firepower and mass armies meant that an invader was far less likely to find a quiet spot to land. Moreover, for a sustained campaign he would need artillery, armoured vehicles, transport, and fuel and supplies. Air support was essential, but it had to be directed at precise targets on the battlefield. Amphibious warfare was now at the centre of strategy. To win the war, Britain and her allies would eventually have to re-enter Continental Europe against fierce resistance. In the meantime, there would be raids to harass the enemy and perhaps build up some experience.

The main burden of amphibious warfare falls on navies. The air force would conduct photo-reconnaissance and provide fighter protection and bombing, but that was a variation on what they did anyway. The army or marines would provide the bulk of the personnel, who might face a long and very uncomfortable voyage. They would have to acquire skills in getting themselves and their vehicles ashore, but after that they would move on and fight as they had always done. The navy, on the other hand, had to provide thousands of specially designed ships and boats, and tens of thousands of officers and men to operate them.

Origins

British wars usually involved some amphibious operations, though less so in 1914–18. Troops had invaded enemy colonies dozens of times in the last few centuries, usually rowed ashore in ships' boats and unopposed on the beaches. There was very little interest in the subject before the 1939 war – the alliance with France would remove any need for it, while the Gallipoli operation of 1915/16 was an unhappy memory, not least for Churchill. In 1940 the British intervention against the German invasion of Norway was poorly planned and amateurish, establishing the principle that major amphibious operations cannot be improvised. After that, the Fall of France changed the picture completely.

Within days of the Dunkirk evacuation, Churchill foresaw a return to Europe, and he set up the Combined Operations Organisation to plan and co-ordinate it. It signalled that amphibious warfare was the responsibility of all the services and, unlike in the USA, the marines played a relatively small part. Its first head was Admiral of the Fleet Sir Roger Keyes, who had led a raid on Zeebrugge in 1918 and had as much experience of amphibious operations as anyone. He bombarded Churchill with unwelcome suggestions, which led to his replacement in October 1941. Captain Lord Louis Mountbatten was related to the royal family, confident and full of ideas. He took over an organisation mainly designed for raiding and expanded it into one to conduct a full-scale invasion. Quickly promoted to acting vice admiral, he joined the chiefs of staffs meetings. By May 1943, Combined Operations comprised nearly 5500 officers, 38,000 men, eighty-nine landing ships, 2600 landing craft and more than a thousand barges.[1] In September 1943 Mountbatten left to become commander-in-chief in Burma. His successor was the much more modest but highly efficient Major General Robert Laycock, who had led commandos in the Middle East (and was fictionalised in a very favourable light by Evelyn Waugh in *Officers and Gentlemen*), then played a key role in the landings on Sicily and at Salerno.

Aware of the possibilities of a war in the Pacific, the United States Marines began to study amphibious warfare in the 1920s. An exercise of 1924 proved unsuccessful: 'In short, almost all the mistakes conceivable in a landing operation were made.'[2] After that, the force was committed to operations in Nicaragua and interest did not revive until 1933 when the Fleet Marine Force was founded. The *Tentative Manual for Landing Operations* was devised in the following year and established six main principles – the need for a clear command structure, for naval gunfire and aerial support, for efficient ship-to-shore movement, for securing the beachhead, and for logistics, including the unloading and distribution of supplies and equipment.

These were tested in exercises beginning in 1934, when it was found that large naval shells were useless in this kind of warfare, and that ships' boats were unsuitable – though it would take some years to have them superseded. In 1935 daylight landings were tried, with and without smoke cover, and also night landings, which proved farcical even in unrealistic conditions. The 1936 exercises saw improvements in naval gunnery technique and the full use of marine air power (such as it was). The third exercise, off San Clemente near San Diego, incorporated army units and further illustrated the faults of naval boats:

> Navy standard boats are totally unsuited for landing troops of the leading waves, even under moderate surf conditions. They were in no sense tactical vehicles, for they are lacking in speed and manoeuvrability and are extremely difficult to handle in the surf. They do not permit the rapid debarkation of troops at the water's edge.[3]

In addition, their naval coxswains were almost obsessively anxious to avoid damage to them.

The year 1938 saw the first tests of the famous Higgins boat (though without its bow ramp) and moves towards the fast destroyer transport, later known as the APD. Exercises continued until the summer of 1941 under General Holland M Smith. They involved sixteen thousand officers and men of the army and marines, three hundred vehicles, 2200 tons of supplies, forty-two naval vessels and four aircraft carriers, along with 266 landing craft of different types. Smith concluded: 'Such a high degree of realism was attained following the seizure of a beachhead, an advance of nine miles inland was ordered', but 'the maneuver was again hampered by lack of equipment and personnel.'[4] The exercises and the *Tentative Manual* had not provided all the answers, but they had raised most of the questions, and the US Marines were better prepared for amphibious warfare than any other force in the world, except perhaps the Japanese navy, and they had the best integrated air support.

But the experience was not wholly transferred to the army, which would do most of the land fighting in the North African, Mediterranean and European theatres where the US marines barely had a presence.

Ships and craft

More than any other field, amphibious warfare craft saw unprecedented co-operation between the two navies, especially in the medium-sized vessels. Amphibious warfare vessels can be divided into three main categories – for landing personnel, for landing vehicles, or to carry out various subsidiary functions such as gunfire support. In addition, they fell into another three groups – those which could carry out the whole operation from loading in port to beach landing by themselves, such as tank landing ships and tank landing craft; or those which would carry a number of smaller vessels to the area, such as Landing Ships Infantry of various sizes; and the craft which would be launched from them for the final attack such as the British Assault Landing Craft and the American Landing Craft, Vehicle, Personnel. And finally there were amphibious vehicles including the Landing Vehicle Tracked and the famous DUKW, nearly all originating in America. All this, plus the practice of converting existing craft and the innovative spirit of many officers, led to a great variety of craft. By April 1944 there were seventy different types of landing craft in service or projected in the two navies, with twenty-six types of landing ship.

Most amphibious warfare vessels, particularly those used in the opening waves of an assault, used opening bow doors to allow the quick egress of men and vehicles under fire. This went against the grain of traditional naval architecture, and K C Barnaby of Thornycroft reminisced, 'Having been brought up to fear all leaks from such trivial matters as side scuttles and so forth, the ... barn doors right in the eyes of the ship were somewhat alarming as I visualized them punching into head seas.' He later admitted his fears were groundless.[5]

At the end of June 1940, even before the Battle of France was over, Churchill asked for tank landing craft to be designed and on 9 August

Mainly British landing craft and ships depicted in 1944. In the foreground an ALC, followed by an American DUKW battling through the waves. To the left, a Landing Craft, Infantry (large) with a Landing Craft, Flak, behind. In the background, Landing Ships, Infantry are lowering their LCAs and LCMs, which set off towards the left. On the right side of the picture is a classic Landing Craft, Tank, with support craft behind.

1940 he wrote to his aide Ismay: 'Get me a further report about the designs and types of vessels to transport armoured vehicles by sea and land on beaches.'[6] The first vessel, the LCT(1), delivered in November, was able to carry three tanks of 40 tons, the largest then planned, and land them in 2ft 6in water. It was designed for operations as far as the west coast of France.[7] It was the first heavy vehicle landing craft in the world and it set the pattern, with a flat bottom for beach landing, a shallow draught which was greater aft than forward, an opening ramp in the bows and the engines and crew's quarters aft, leaving an open deck for tanks and other vehicles.

The next version, the TLC(2), was 2ft wider but was difficult to handle:

The Mark 2 must have been designed by a madman. It had three Scott-Paine Sealion engines, using high-octane petrol, with a home-made reverse gear which required a man on each gear lever, each pulling back with all his strength to operate a friction band which had a life of 50 hours. ... Although we had three engines there were only the usual double telegraphs, so we had to use our ingenuity to rig up a telegraph for the centre engine. This was the vital one, for the craft would only steer with the slipstream from this engine on to the single rudder in the centre.[8]

The LCT(3) was longer, with a 32ft section added amidships. It drew 3ft 10in of water forward and 7ft 10in aft and could make a speed of 10 knots, but its sailing qualities were not much better.

... there was no feeling of cutting through the waves; instead, these craft 'butted' their way ahead. In rough weather, they suffered a fairly high degree of juddering, while in smooth weather progress was made by a sort of straight slide. ... In addition these craft were powered by engines originally designed for tanks, and had both screws turning in the same direction, which caused a bias in their movement at slow speeds. ... More than once I have seen a Royal Navy officer gallantly attempting to demonstrate to a newcomer the art of coming alongside, and making a considerable pot-mess of his endeavours.[9]

The LCT(4) was mainly built by non-maritime structural engineers, which raised some eyebrows among naval architects. With its structural weakness, it was initially considered expendable after one landing only, but it proved far tougher than expected. After that, the baton passed to the United States. In November 1941 the Admiralty asked the Americans for a 100ft lighter capable of carrying three 50-ton tanks. The design, designated Mark 5, was ready in a month; it was followed by the 119ft LCT(6) which had an open stern so that it could be used as a floating bridge for unloading tank landing ships; 500 of the former were built, 965 of the latter.

They were not considered suitable for ocean voyages, but might be transported whole on the deck of a tank landing ship, or in three sections in a freighter.

Churchill wanted to raid overseas colonies in enemy possession and was not satisfied with the short range of the LCT. According to one of the designers:

> The first LCT had hardly completed its trials [when] the Prime Minister demanded ships that could land tanks … on beaches anywhere in the world. The problem was difficult physically because of the obvious fact that we should have to have an ocean-going ship of limited draught; it was difficult psychologically because it seemed certain that any ships so used would need to be written off after the first assault.[10]

The only ships suitable for conversion were shallow-draught oil tankers used on Lake Maracaibo in Venezuela and three of them were fitted with bow ramps. Their draught of 4ft 2in forward was still too much and their speed of 10 knots was too low, so three ships of the *Boxer* class were built with a speed of 17 knots, and disembarkation via a long bow ramp – both classes were known as the LST(1).

By 1941 it was recognised that a return to the European Continent would take hundreds of LCTs to transport the numbers of tanks needed. A British mission in Washington explained the need and the details of a 300ft-long ship were worked out jointly. More than a thousand of these LST(2) were built in American yards. It was 'a lesson to the world of the essential ingenuity of British naval architecture, and a tribute to US mass production possibilities.'[11]

The Landing Ship Tank (2) was 327ft long and displaced 1468 tons, equivalent to a medium-sized warship. It could carry eighteen Churchill tanks on its lower deck, which could be toxic when too many were running up: 'Their engines were already running and in spite of huge fans, there were an awful lot of fumes. … People started getting sick.'[12] More than thirty vehicles could be carried on the upper deck. It could beach in 3ft of water. The tanks would discharge through the bow doors and the vehicles on the upper deck would be lowered by lift then through the bow. In British service it was manned by thirteen officers and seventy-three men and could carry around 180 soldiers. The British tried to build their own LSTs despite a shortage of diesel engines and a lack of welders and their equipment. The LST(3) was largely riveted, and its steam engines restricted space on the tank deck. It had a deeper forward draught of 4ft 7in.

The lack of LSTs was felt in the North Africa landings, which took place before any of them were ready. The Western Task Force had to take the small port of Safi in order to disembark 28-ton Sherman tanks from a converted ferry.[13] The shortage of LSTs for all the fronts led to dissension at the highest levels. General Marshall asserted that the only bitter fight he had seen in the joint chiefs of staff was over twenty-seven LSTs, and in 1944 Churchill complained that 'The destinies of two great empires seem to be tied up in some God-damned things called LSTs.'[14] In June 1944 there were 168 serviceable American-operated ships in UK waters alongside sixty-one British; twenty-three American and two British in the Mediterranean; ninety-five more on the US East Coast and 102 in the Pacific.

The LST was a vessel of great flexibility. It was rarely used to land tanks in the Pacific theatre, where these vehicles were less important. Instead, it launched amtracs carrying marines, as at Tarawa; and it brought Seabees and their equipment ashore soon after the first landing. Their long range was not relevant to the Normandy invasion, but 237 of them took part, including three of the old LST(1)s. They brought in hundreds of tanks to meet an expected Panzer counter-attack, and their upper decks were filled with supply trucks and other vehicles. After the war it was the ancestor of the roll-on, roll-off ferries used today.

As a passenger, Eugene Sledge reported:

> Each rifle company assigned to the assault waves against Peleliu made the trip in an LST carrying the Amtracs that would take the men ashore. Our LST lacked sufficient troop compartment space to accommodate all of the men of the company, so the platoon leaders drew straws for the available space. The mortar section got lucky. We were assigned to a troop compartment in the forecastle with an entrance on the main deck. Some of the other platoons had to make themselves as comfortable as possible on the main deck under and around landing boats and gear secured there.[15]

Not all beaches were suitable for the LST, which ideally needed a gradient of about 1 in 50. More than that and the stern would be afloat while the bows were grounded, less and the ship would ground some way offshore, leaving the men and vehicles with a long and hazardous drive or walk. The answer was to bridge the gap with a causeway formed of Seabee pontoons.

Despite the hopes of the planners, the LST did not exceed the speed of 10 knots which justified its nickname of 'large slow target'. At the beginning of the Central Pacific Drive in October 1943, Kelly Turner believed that this gave the Japanese twenty-four hours' warning of the attack on Makin.[16] One crewman of the sleek destroyer *Dale* noted:

> At Canton Island we picked up some bug box-shaped LSTs to screen. They were real slow, and our cruising speed went from twenty-four knots down to six, which made us extremely vulnerable. … *Dale* was ordered to lead them to Makin Island several days before the rest of the fleet so that all the ships would arrive at the same time.[17]

The Landing Ship Medium, or LSM, originally known as the LCT(7), was designed as a compromise between the LST and the LCT, able to operate alongside the LCI(L)s. It was relatively fast at 13 knots.

The smallest vehicle able to land a tank was the Landing Craft, Mechanised, or LCM. British development began as early as 1926 and led to the MLC10, a slow, clumsy, round-bottomed monstrosity able to land a 12-ton tank. It resumed on a better path with the orders for the LCM(1) in 1938, but it was essentially a powered lighter, with the 16-ton tank carried above the waterline, thus raising the centre of gravity. The US Marines had a version by the spring of 1941, but soon saw its flaws. They approached Higgins, who was building four shallow-draught tugs for the Peruvian government, which could be modified for the task. A visiting British mission saw them at the end of the year and realised that, with a lower centre of gravity and some modifications, they could land a 30-ton tank, such as the Grants and Shermans which would soon enter service. According to the manual of 1945:

> The general lines of the tank lighter are similar to those of the 'VP'. The draft is shallow, the freeboard high, and the screws and rudder mechanisms are protected by skegs. These characteristics cause the LCM to handle like the LCVP. However, because the tank lighter is larger and has twin screws there are distinct differences too.[18]

The concept was of limited application, tanks were becoming larger and would be too heavy to be lifted by ship's davits. Other ways would have to found to land tanks from ships.

The smallest and most common types of landing craft, the British Assault Landing Craft and the American Landing Craft Vehicle, Personnel, looked similar and had identical functions – to be lowered from the davits of a landing ship and to put a platoon ashore – but they evolved in totally different ways.

Though amphibious warfare was unfashionable in the British services in 1938, the Inter-Service Training and Development Centre was set up in Portsmouth, with an officer from each of the services and a Royal Marine as adjutant. An exercise at Slapton Sands in Devon turned to farce, but the Centre began work on a landing craft. Designed by K C Barnaby of Thornycroft, it was intended to be lowered from the standard lifeboat davits of a passenger ship, and to carry an infantry platoon. Its engines were aft and the steering position was well forward, and protected by an armoured box. Following standard ship practice at the time, the coxswain did not control the engine directly but telegraphed messages to a stoker (so-called) in the engine room. The troops sat on three fore-and-aft benches and they disembarked through a pair of conventional doors, then over a lowered ramp. The craft was built in wood, often by non-nautical contractors such as furniture makers, but was soon fitted with light armour, including some on each side half covering the port and starboard troop benches. Opposite the coxswain's station was an armoured position for a Bren gun.

The Assault Landing Craft, or LCA as it was later called following American practice, had its debut landing the French Foreign Legion in the abortive Norway expedition. It took part in the withdrawals from Dunkirk, Greece and Crete, as well as early commando raids, and in the

A Landing Craft, Assault, or LCA, the unsung hero of all British withdrawals and landings. In this case, it is ferrying American troops, which often happened. The coxswain is in the lightly armoured steering position directly above the letters LCA painted on the side.

invasion of Madagascar in 1942. After that it played a vital role in all the landings in North Africa, Italy and Normandy. Nearly two thousand were built.

The two most important American craft were developed, almost accidentally, from vessels used on southern rivers. Andrew Higgins designed his Eureka craft in 1926 'for use in the shallow waters of the Mississippi River and along the Gulf Coast, where it could run its bow up on river and bayou banks and back off easily.' It was adopted by the Marines under H M Smith and the two worked closely together against the scepticism of the navy: 'Andrew Higgins was willing to go to bat with anybody and when we got lost in the morass of crippling detail and Washington procrastination, he came to our assistance. His heart and soul were pledged to building the vessels we so desperately needed for amphibious warfare.'[19]

The Higgins boat was fitted with a bow ramp to become the Landing Craft, Vehicle, or LCV, which was soon superseded by the famous Landing Craft, Vehicle, Personnel, or LCVP. The steering controls and gunners' cockpits were fitted aft, and unlike the British LCA the coxswain operated the engine controls directly: 'The "V"s now in general use are equipped with simple controls; a steering wheel and the single lever which controls forward and reverse gears and the throttle.'[20] Its decks were more open than the LCA, which allowed the transport of a vehicle of up to 6000lbs, though it was more commonly used to land thirty-six men, the equivalent of a platoon. Eventually more than twenty thousand were built.

Eugene Sledge experienced it as a passenger:

> A Higgins boat, like any powerful motor-driven boat under full throttle, normally settled down at the stern end with bow elevated and moved easily over the water. But our boat was so loaded with men and equipment that, even though we crowded as far back in the stern as possible, the squared-off bow ramp wasn't elevated sufficiently to skip over the waves. It drove straight against some large waves.[21]

Majors Grant and Ascoli of the Royal Marines compared the British and American craft in 1944. The LCVP, they thought, was noisier, it had a higher silhouette, the coxswain was exposed, a large amount of space was taken up by the engine, it would not stand rough usage, and it was not so well armoured. On the other hand, it handled as well as the LCA, had better astern power and got off beaches more easily in surf. Though they believed the LCA to be superior, they recognised that it had better engines and gearing and a redesigned bottom 'to get rid of its tendency to stick when beached.' But in the end, according to a British assessment:

> ... in spite of the success of the LCA, American type boats were generally more satisfactory for operations under the conditions they had to meet, and at the end of the war, when large-scale British operations were planned in the Western Pacific, the demand was beginning to arise for British production to be changed over; this never actually arose.[22]

The Landing Vehicle, Tracked was designed by Donald Roebling Jr and was another discovery of the Marine Corps and General Smith:

> Like our landing boat, his tractor was a product of the shallow waters and creeks of the south. Roebling, an engineer who had retired to Florida for his health, had built his tractor for rescue work in the Everglades. He called it the Alligator and his model, which he manufactured that year [1938], included all the essential features of the military vehicle used since.[23]

The first version, the LVT(1) arrived just in time in August 1941 and was first used at Guadalcanal, but the Tarawa landings showed that such a vehicle was essential for surmounting the coral reefs which surrounded most Pacific islands, and it had the added advantage of taking men or goods some way inshore. The improved LVT(2) had a crew of three and could carry twenty-four troops, though only at a speed of 5.4 knots in water, as it was propelled by its caterpillar tracks. The LVT(3) was fitted with a rear ramp for disembarking men ashore and was succeeded by the improved LVT(4). Meanwhile, the LVT(A)s were developed, fitted with armour plate and mounting a 37mm gun. Amtracs were mostly used in the Pacific but also in the North African landings.

Infantry land ships were intended to carry troops and assault craft to the beaches and launch them. The Royal Navy filled this role by converting passenger ships. The first were *Glenearn*, *Glenroy* and *Glengyle*, new ships of nearly 10,000 tons built for the Glen Line for their Far Eastern services. Between them, they were in all the major British operations of the war from 1940 onwards. They had 1200hp diesel engines, giving a speed of 18 knots. A large deckhouse above contained army officers' accommodation aft and naval officers' forward, as well as the galley, bakery and refrigerated stores. The crew lived forward and the army other ranks aft. A typical messdeck had tables for seventy-four men on each side, with kitbag lockers and rifle racks. The troops slept in hammocks provided by the ship, but they brought their own

Amphibious tractors, or amtracs, in this case fitted as assault vehicles, head for the beach at Okinawa in 1945.

bedding, plates and cutlery.[24] Originally, each carried twelve LCAs, on standard merchant ship davits which were only just adequate for the job. In 1942 these were replaced with luffing davits, which allowed the LCA complement to be doubled. They also carried a few LCMs, which were mainly intended to launch motor transport or Bren gun carriers, rather than tanks. They were launched by derricks of standard cargo type, but cranes might have been preferable.[25] The landing craft were under a lieutenant commander RNR, with a junior officer in charge of each of four divisions of LCAs and another for the MLCs, plus a boatswain for the support landing craft.

Other landing ships were ferries which had been made redundant by the severing of communication with Europe. Vessels named after members of the Belgian royal family, such as *Princes Astrid* and *Prince Leopold*, became Landing Ships, Infantry, small while the Dutch *Queen Emma* and *Princes Beatrix* became LSIs medium. Landing ships (hand-hoisting) were three former Irish sea ferries whose landing craft had to be hoisted by manpower. These ships always found it difficult to disembark landing craft carrying tanks and heavy vehicles. The landing ship (gantry) was intended to solve this problem with fifteen LCMs.

The Americans converted merchantmen into landing ships, which they called attack transports and code-named APAs (Auxiliary Personnel Attack) from 1942. They also built ships specially for the purpose, including 117 of the *Haskell* class, which entered service late in 1944, in time to take part in the final drive across the Pacific. Based on the Liberty ship hull, they were of 14,800 tons and carried 1475 troops under fifty-seven officers at a speed of 16.5 knots. They could be landed by means of twenty-two LCVPs, two LCM(3)s and three LCP(R). Robert Leckie travelled in one but did not enjoy the experience: 'Squat, dark, uncomfortable, plodding ship it served only to take us from place to place, like a ferry, without character, without interest, without adventure'. And the facilities were not good: 'A galley shed had been constructed above decks and there were also topside heads. In a strong wind, we fought to keep our food down on those unimaginable instruments of exasperation we called our mess kits – or to keep it down in the stomach, once the wind blew from the heads.'[26] In all 388 APAs and AKAs (cargo transports) entered service.

The concept of the APD, or High Speed Transport, began in 1938 when the old flush-decker destroyer *Manley* had two of her funnels and engines removed to make more room for troops. Her speed of 24 knots was still faster than most AW vessels. She was followed by others, and then from mid 1944, by converted destroyer escorts. They often launched the first wave of personnel landing craft in the Southwest Pacific landings, largely because infantry landing ships were not available.

The Landing Ship, Stern Chute, was a British attempt to launch LCMs with tanks or goods. Two train ferries were converted to launch vessels over the stern. *Princess Iris* took part in the Normandy invasion. The Landing Ship, Gantry was another British attempt to solve the problem, three ships fitted with prominent lifting gear which could be extended over the sides. Designed to British specifications but built in America, the Landing Ship, Dock was the ultimate answer to the problem of landing heavy tanks from ships. It had a large rear compartment which could be flooded to allow the landing craft to float out. It was 'a shotgun marriage between an LST and a floating dry dock'.[27] Eight ships of the *Ashland* class were built, along with fifteen of the *Casa Grande* class. It was used for the first time in the South Pacific in the Arawe landing in late 1943. Four were supplied to the Royal Navy, where they formed the basis of the post-war landing ships *Fearless* and *Intrepid*.

The British were particularly keen on support craft and developed them for several different purposes. The most common was for gunfire support, using craft which could come much closer to the landing than conventional warships and concentrate on the beach battle. Landing Craft, Support, came in various sizes – motor boats or LCAs armed with machine guns, and slightly larger craft that might deploy turrets from armoured cars. The Landing Craft Gun (Large) carried two naval 4.7in guns which were operated by an officer, two NCOs and twenty men of the Royal Marines. The medium version used 17pdr or 25pdr army field guns:

> The first military requirement in the LCG(M) was that she should be able to meet a tank or pill box on equal terms; the second was that she should be able to give artillery cover to troops ashore up to ordinary artillery ranges. The first naval requirement was that the craft should be capable of making ocean passages.[28]

Landing Craft Tank (Rocket) fired a battery of up to a thousand rockets with 29lb heads from an LCT hull, at a fixed range of 3500yds; the LCA (Hedgerow) was much smaller, but used the standard Hedgehog anti-submarine mortar to similar effect. Single-shot weapons, their effect was probably more moral than material, but LSIs equipped with 288 rockets each proved very successful in the South Pacific – for example, at Hollandia.[29] Admiral Keyes, the former head of Combined Operations, was impressed at Leyte:

> This time a surprise awaited them. The LCIs darted out ahead of the first wave and ran in close to the shore and turning parallel to it, blasted the foreshore some 100 yards inland with a tremendous concentration of rocket fire, which wiped out the Japanese, and the troops following close after this new barrage landed apparently without opposition ...[30]

The battle for Crete in 1941 led to the view that any major landing had to be closely protected from air attack. This led to the design of the Landing Craft, Flak, which after much discussion between the services was armed with a combination of 4in guns, pom-poms and Oerlikons. The Landing Craft, Flak, Large was an LCT(3) fitted with a larger number of pom-poms and Oerlikons. The Landing Barge, Flak was designed to carry army artillery including Bofors guns to defend a zone 3000–5000yds from the beach, until such time as the guns could be landed. Aside from gunnery, the Landing Craft, Control was developed from the Fairmile motor launch as navigation leader for a group of craft, and other vessels were converted for similar purposes. The Landing Barge, Kitchen was designed 'to serve as a floating kitchen to groups of landing craft.' To a Canadian officer, it 'closely resembled an overgrown caboose on a barge, and its many smoking stove-pipes made this unseaworthy Noah's Ark look most out of place battling it out in the mean sea towards Normandy.'[31] Other barges served as emergency repair ships, water carriers and oilers.

The Americans developed their own Landing Craft, Control, 'As lead-in navigational craft for landing boats, to mark line of departure, for traffic control, for preliminary hydrographic surveys.' In the middle stages of the war, they tended to improvise shallow-draught gunboats: for example, in the attack on the Treasury Islands in October 1943, when two LCIs were converted but gave up their troop capacity. The Motor Gunboat PGM used the same hull fitted with Bofors, bazookas and mortars. But their most important support craft were the LCI(L)s which were fitted with 120 5in rockets and Bofors and Oerlikon guns and titled the Landing Craft Support (Large). They were first used at Iwo Jima in 1945, and at Okinawa in April a dozen of them went in ahead of the landing and formed a line, with the landing craft proper weaving through them when their time came.[32]

By early 1944, as the amphibious war approached a climax on both oceans, the US was planning to expand its force of landing craft from twenty thousand to eighty thousand. That included twenty thousand ranging in size from a landing ship to an amphibious tractor, with twenty-five thousand to follow, and fifteen thousand small craft, including rubber boats and rafts. Craft were already being built by sixty-seven shipyards, and twenty to thirty thousand subcontractors would be needed.[33]

The British were ingenious in devising inventions in support of amphibious landings. Churchill claimed to have been the inspiration for artificial harbours with a minute of May 1942: 'They must float up and down with the tide. The anchor problem must be answered. ... Let me have the best solution worked out. Don't argue the matter. The difficulties will argue for themselves.'[34] After the failure of the Dieppe raid it was clear that a port could not be captured intact so the Mulberry harbours were devised.

The main breakwaters known as Phoenixes were huge concrete structures which were built in various sites to be towed to the invasion beaches. Once there they formed a line enclosing an area as large as Dover Harbour. They were interspersed with sunken merchant and warships, or 'corncobs', including the battleship *Centurion*, which had fought at Jutland, and outboard of that were floating 'bombardons', intended to help break the waves. Within the sheltered enclosure were floating piers or 'whales' up to half a mile long, with heads or 'spuds' against which ships could unload. It was a massive effort, costing about £20 million and deploying 105,000 tons of steel and 1¼ million tons of ballast.

On 19/20 June a storm damaged Mulberry B, the British artificial harbour at Arromanches, and wrecked the American Mulberry A at Omaha Beach, which was never completely repaired, for it was found that 'Gooseberries', created by blockships, were adequate for the purpose. As with many of the D-Day inventions, the simplest solution was the best.

Pluto, or Pipe Line Under the Ocean, was intended to supply the armies in France with fuel, but by the time it was ready the war had moved on. Rockets were launched from landing craft, but were very inaccurate and could not penetrate enemy bunkers. Many of the swimming tanks, used by both the British and the Americans on the Normandy beaches, were either not launched due to bad weather, or foundered with loss of life. Only on the British Sword to the east were they completely successful; on Omaha Beach they all foundered, leaving the infantry to face devastating fire. 'Hobart's funnies', converted tanks intended to clear obstacles and bridge gaps, and named after the eccentric general who designed them, were landed on the British and Canadian beaches in advance of the troops in the LCAs. Whatever their success in their intended role, they did have the effect of supporting the troops during the crucial stage, and they might have helped the Americans on Omaha Beach.

Personnel

A major invasion would require many hundreds of officers who would largely operate outside the traditional naval ethos. Mountbatten declined to take on regular naval officers and instead relied on a few retired officers as squadron commanders, and a huge number of temporary RNVR. Late in 1941 the commodore of HMS *Quebec II* complained that very few of his officers had any naval background. They were 'of an age when youthful enthusiasm and *esprit de corps* infuse them with the necessary energy to acquire experience'.

For a new officer, Combined Operations was less exciting than destroyers or coastal forces, but it offered quick promotion and an early command. Mountbatten made a point of visiting *King Alfred* to meet the cadets. Most had destroyers as their first choice, but Mountbatten urged them to consider Combined Operations as well: 'The result was that almost everybody put down their first choice as destroyers and their second choice as Combined Ops. There were few vacancies for destroyers, and we scooped the rest of the cream of the officer entry.'[35]

By August 1942 it was recognised that *King Alfred* could not keep up with the demand for landing craft officers, and the full training was not always needed. A new course was established in the remote Scottish village of Lochailort. Readers of the Combined Operations magazine *Bulldozer* were invited to:

> … use a little introspection and see if you find in yourself some of the qualities that are wanted, remembering that the Nation wants leaders and wants them now, and that it is your duty if you think you can achieve it, to give all that you have got towards the Service to which you belong and not to be content with the fact that you have done enough already.

They were warned, however, that the course was a hard one:

> … when you leave the train after, perhaps, a 20-hour journey, you will march into the camp and the candidates on course will tell you that you swim the Loch each morning, you climb the highest mountain before breakfast and, having dodged a couple of land mines, you work in an open lecture room for eight hours. This has a fair semblance of truth in it.

The course included:

> seamanship (mostly as applied to C.O. craft) handling of craft, divisional work and elementary knowledge of paper work required in a flotilla; navigation and pilotage from a coastal point of view; elementary tides, compasses, etc; signals (morse 8 w.p.m., semaphore 12 w.p.m. and theoretical signals as used in C.O.); gunnery (parade work for power of command. Sub-machine guns, only an elementary knowledge).[36]

Paul Lund who did the course believed that:

> As seagoing officers in major and minor landing craft they would find that all their intensive physical training had been to little purpose. Most of their time at sea would be spent standing on the bridge of an LCT or LCI or in some minor landing craft; and the strain would not be so much physical as mental – keeping awake and alert for long periods of duty and being able to go for long periods without rest or sleep.[37]

An LCT was as large as a corvette, though with a much smaller crew, who had to be adaptable:

> Character is, perhaps, far more important in L.C.T.s than in any other craft. That is because with so small a crew in so small a space

no one can adequately hide his real character as is the case in bigger ships. And the key to success and happiness in these craft is for each officer and man to aim a step higher than his rank or rating. The C.O. and First Lieut must realise they have got to be real leaders. ...

Similarly coxswains are in effect doing the work of C.P.O.s: they are the 'Buffers' of L.C.T.s. If they realise that, they will make good coxswains. The way to make them feel that is to delegate more responsibility to them.

Almost everybody aboard an L.C.T has to be better than he would be aboard a bigger ship.[38]

The spartan accommodation came as something of a shock to Peter Bull when he joined *TLC 168*:

Where I now found myself was in theory the galley, and certainly a large stove took up most of the space; but in a small alcove I espied two bunks one above another in a cubby-hole the size of a small wardrobe. Apart from two drawers under the bunks and a minute table affixed to the deckhead, this was all there was in the way of wardroom and cabins for the two officers. Separated from the galley by a blue curtain, it was still possible ... to take a more than active interest in what was cooking.[39]

After basic training, amphibious warfare trainees were sent to HMS *Northney*, a series of holiday camps near Portsmouth. Their wooden huts were 'in great need of repair', according to the medical officer.[40] The site was restricted and subject to bombing, but trainees learned the rudiments of the new craft before being sent north. HMS *Quebec* at Inveraray was the oldest of the Combined Operations bases, set up in 1940 almost as soon as the Dunkirk evacuation had finished, and named after the combined operation under General James Wolfe which captured that city in 1759. It was on the shores of Loch Fyne, a three-hour bus ride from Glasgow – there was no railway, but regiments might arrive by steamer. The Duke of Argyll's eighteenth-century, mock-medieval castle was half a mile from the town, and its park was covered with huts for the army. Rear Admiral L E H Maund wrote that it was 'as far distant as possible from attack but yet within the umbrella of some fighter organisation. ... Here the rains might fall almost continuously, but it gave sheltered water and was, as it were, behind the defences of the Clyde.'[41] Inveraray trained the army to operate with the navy, and new landing craft crews worked up under their officers. It was also the pool for men awaiting draughting. It was took about a dozen officers and 150 men from Northney each fortnight. There was a pier in the town and several slipways near the naval encampment. The loch had sixty-four sites where men or vehicles could land, though it was rarely more than two miles wide and did not allow large-scale exercises.

The term commando originated with the Boer Cavalry units of the South African War, which Churchill had admired. He wanted a raiding force and Lieutenant Colonel D W Clarke 'produced the outline of a scheme ... The men for this type of irregular warfare should, he suggested, be formed into units to be known as Commandos.' In August 1940 Churchill, always keen on the offensive, told Eden the War Secretary that any campaign of 1941 would depend on 'surprise landings of lightly equipped, nimble forces accustomed to work like packs of hounds instead of being moved about in the ponderous manner which is appropriate to the regular formations.'[42]

Initially, the commandos did not flourish. Three of them were sent to the Middle East early in 1941 and lost six hundred men out of two thousand in the defence of Crete.[43] But Churchill proclaimed in August 1942: 'the policy of [His Majesty's government] is to maintain and develop the Commando organization with the utmost energy and to make sure that the wastage and losses are replaced by good quality men.'[44] Their raids at Vaasgo and the Lofoten Islands cause Hitler to divert more troops to Norway for fear of an invasion. At Bruneval they captured a vital part of a German radar, and in the Mediterranean they raided behind Rommel's lines. They led in the raid on St-Nazaire when the ex-American 'four-piper' *Campbeltown* was expended to immobilise a huge dry dock, but they were far less successful in the assault on Dieppe in 1942, which fell unhappily between a raid and a full-scale invasion. And they seized key sites during the major invasions.

The US Army formed the Ranger battalions based on British experience and they were mainly used to support major landings rather than isolated raids – most famously scaling the cliff at the Pointe d'Hoc during the Normandy invasion. The US Navy was far less keen on this type of warfare. A premature raid on Makin in August 1942 only caused the Japanese to fortify the Gilbert Islands, raise the garrison and round up the coast watchers, making it much more difficult when the real invasion came.

In contrast with the situation with Combined Operations in Britain, amphibious warfare was still an orphan in the United States in 1941, with responsibility 'badly scattered' in the Navy Department. Or more aptly, it was the subject of a custody battle between army, marines, coastguard and the navy's two main fleets. Early in 1942 it was suggested that it should be conducted by the navy in the Pacific theatre and the army in the

Atlantic, on the grounds that: 'In the one case, landings would be repeated many times, and continuous Naval support is essential; whereas, in the second case, after the initial landing, the navy's chief interest would be the protection of the line of sea communication.'[45] But the navy formed commands for amphibious warfare in both oceans in March and April 1942 with all amphibious units assigned to them. The army continued to train its own crews until February 1943, when it agreed to 'discontinue all amphibious training activities', except for certain engineer units being established. The navy would 'continue amphibious training of boat operating and maintenance personnel to meet Army requirement of this nature, and will also train at a later date Army replacements for existing amphibian units if this should become necessary.'[46]

Landing craft officers were mostly the products of midshipman schools, and the V-7 and V-12 programmes. Early in 1944 it was found that the assignment was popular among young officers who looked forward to action and an early command. According to Admiral Barbey in the Southwest Pacific:

> If there was any one group of Reserve officers for whom I had the greatest admiration and sympathy, it was the young LCT officers. Usually, they were the only officer aboard and as such were responsible for the safety of the craft, and also for the harder job of maintaining discipline among the small crew, many of whom were often older than themselves.[47]

The captain of one LST, a former chief quartermaster's mate, found that three of his officers were teachers and three lawyers. He appointed the first three as communications and navigation officer, first lieutenant and engineering officer. One of the lawyers became the executive officer, and another gunnery officer on the grounds that he had once gone duck hunting.[48]

After the North African landings of late 1942 one American officer complained:

> ... we had only a figurative crew. They were unskilled in handling their boats, they were unlearned in even the simplest elements of seamanship such as the rules of the road ... Some attention had been paid to the art of landing through surf and retracting again [but] the supreme test of their training was made under conditions where only experts could hope to succeed part of the time ...[49]

But a suggestion that the boats should be manned by army crews was quickly rejected: 'The solution is that, whatever uniform the crews wear, they must be *trained seamen* with special practice in the technique of landing operations, and in close touch with the requirements of the troops they have to land and maintain.'[50] The conclusion was that 'It is therefore recommended that LVTs which are being used for landing assault waves be considered as boats rather than vehicles, that they be manned by Navy personnel who have been trained in seamanship and boat handling … and that they be assigned to vessels in which embarked'.[51]

Initially, the training bases for amphibious warfare were on the East Coast, because most of the craft were built there or on the Great Lakes, and because the North African landings had priority. Andrew Higgins himself came to New River to teach the crews how to handle his boat, but it remained a specialised skill. Coxswains were told:

> Because of its design the 'VP' has several characteristics that distinguish its handling from that of less specialised boats. … The shallow draft and high freeboard tend to make the boat swing very easily in wind and current. The spoon bow has a more helpful influence. It helps trap aerated water (that is, water filed with air bubbles) under the boat. As this body of water bubbles moves under the hull it has a roller-bearing effect and enables the 'VP' to pivot easily and quickly.[52]

By 1945 they had the use of the booklet *Skill in the Surf* which consolidated the experience of the last three years:

> If you are the coxswain, some of the responsibilities that fall to your lot include the daily boat check, a knowledge of rules of the road, buoyage systems, care of gear, and your part in ship-to-shore movements. Your boat and how she handles should become as well-known to you as the taste of bacon and eggs. Docking, or lowering from a transport, coming alongside, beaching, and retracting will be all in the day's work.
>
> As an engineer, the daily engine check becomes your job, but only one small part of it. You will need to know how to make repairs, and how to spot motor trouble before it has a chance to cause damage. As a signalman, you will find yourself using the blinker light and semaphore flags in the somewhat technical field of amphibious communications. In ship-to-shore movements, the maneuvering signals are to be learned accurately and completely, and you will need to recognize the various signals for control of landing craft at the transport.

Familiarity with marlinspike seamanship, buoyage systems, rules of the road, and ship-to-shore movements, plus a thorough knowledge of what your boat will do are demanded of the deckhand who is 'on the ball.'

Officers for LSTs, LCTs and LCIs were trained at Tucson, Arizona. Crews came together at Norfolk, Virginia, though facilities were limited in 1942/3: 'At Norfolk there had been seven crews training aboard the LST at the same time, all trying to squeeze into quarters meant for one, and trying to learn about the ship without stumbling over each other.'[53] By early 1944, more bases had been set up at Morro Bay, Camp Pendleton, Coronado and San Diego in California.[54] The base at Morro was described in a newspaper article of June 1944. It was under Amphibious Training Command Pacific and had expanded from a former patrol craft base and included sixty-two Quonset huts for the sailors, while the soldiers under training were driven in every day, so it was 'dotted with hundreds of uniforms of nearly every branch of the armed forces'. A former hotel was used as a fort which was 'captured' every day:

> … the Navy's Amphibious trainees – Landing Craft Units – demonstrate boat handling which they have been taught. Through the narrow channel of Morro Bay stream hundreds of landing craft towards the open sea for a rendezvous. At a given time and place they go into action, racing through the swells and surf of the Pacific to the nearby beaches of Estero Bay where 'enemy' troops offer simulated resistance by blowing up the beach with land mines, sending a stream of machine gun fire over the heads of the troops and throwing up barriers whenever possible to make the 'invasion' approximate the real thing.[55]

Training for amphibious warfare never ended, especially in the Atlantic where a man's whole career might be concentrated on a few days of intense action, in contrast to other fields of naval activity where much might be learned on the job. The build up to the Normandy invasion culminated in a series of exercises known as Fabius in May 1944, for each of the five major assault forces, deploying all arms including armies and air forces. Notoriously, Force U for Utah Beach was exercising off Slapton Sands in Devon when German torpedo boats got among the landing craft and caused six hundred casualties, raising fears about what could happen during a real invasion.

Techniques and tactics

In the past, British amphibious operations had been dogged by bad relations between the naval and army commanders, and that applied at the Dardanelles and Norway as much as anywhere else. In Britain Combined Operations was expected to resolve some of this by encouraging co-operation, though initially Churchill did not go so far as to appoint a supreme commander.

It was relatively simple in the Central Pacific Drive, where the bulk of the forces were under the same service – marines carried out the initial landings and air cover was largely provided by naval and marine aircraft. And the islands were so small that the land forces never moved far beyond naval influence, though Saipan was big enough to cause major friction between army and marines. Even so, it could become complicated as Admiral Kelly Turner wrote:

> Although I had command of the entire Joint Expeditionary Force, I also exercised command of the Northern Attack Force, for the capture of Saipan. But I divided these duties, assigning to Admiral Hill all *naval* duties concerned with the landing of troops, and retaining in my own hands the gunfire and air control, all protective measures at the objective, and SOPA duties at Saipan. But for the Tinian attack, we formed a new attack force under Admiral Hill, but he exercised all naval duties at Tinian.[56]

He concluded: 'We found the most important technique of amphibious warfare was to be the willingness and ability to co-operate in spite of difference of opinion or viewpoint between the different Services themselves, including allied Services.'[57]

With the South Pacific campaign, there was never any doubt that General MacArthur was in overall charge and he selected the targets. He often landed on the beach amid publicity, but to the concern of the local commanders: 'He stalks a battlefront like a man hardly human, not only arrogantly but lazily.'[58] But he was a good delegator, leaving the decisions to the men on the spot. Admiral Barbey concluded, 'General MacArthur proved to be the finest commander I ever worked for. He delegated authority far more than most commanders. He gave his subordinates a job and left to them the details of how it was to be done.'[59] Despite MacArthur's claim that his headquarters were 'without service bias', relations were often strained, amounting at best to 'mutual cooperation', rather than 'unity of command', according to Admiral Kincaid.[60] As often happened, the air force was the most difficult. The Allied Air Force, which included the American Fifth Air Force, was under the command of Lieutenant General George Kenney. He was 'thoroughly competent in his own field and highly regarded by his men, but not interested in any phase of warfare that was not centered around an airplane, particularly a bomber.'[61] The transfer of power during a landing was another difficulty, until Admiral Kincaid came up with the suggestion that the navy should be in charge until the army had set up its headquarters on shore, after which the services would operate separately unless naval support was needed.

The Mediterranean landings involved co-operation between nations, as well as services, and were conducted under a British 'committee' system under the American General Eisenhower:

> The Combined Chiefs named Ike commander in chief for the Sicily operation. But he had no direct command responsibility for planning and execution the operation. The Combined Chiefs delegated this responsibility to Ike's deputies for ground, air and sea … Ike had become in his own description 'chairman of the board', presiding over a committee of three to run the war.[62]

And there were differences in approach. Bradley again:

> Unlike the US Army where an order calls for instant compliance, the British viewed an order as a basis for discussion between commanders. If a difference of opinion developed, it would be ironed out and the order might be amended. In contrast, we in the American army sought to work out our differences before issuing an order. Once an order was published it could not be changed except by the issuing authority.[63]

Admiral John Lesslie Hall, who commanded in both oceans, wrote: 'never in my experience in the Mediterranean and in the United Kingdom did we ever approach the efficiency of joint command that existed in the Central Pacific. The US Army Air Force was never willing to be under our command.'[64] And there were other problems. During the invasion of Sicily, General Patton ordered the landing of his reserves without consulting the naval authorities, leading to delay and confusion.

This became more complicated with the Normandy invasion, partly because it was launched from British home waters. Royal Naval vessels were exempted from the usual control by Plymouth and Portsmouth commands over ships in their areas, but the strategic bombing forces – Bomber Command and the Eighth Air Force – remained independent. The supreme commander was General Eisenhower, with a British air marshal as his deputy. At the next level, the naval, army and air force commanders were also British, including Admiral Bertram Ramsay for the navy. They carried out the planning and made the key decision to launch the invasion on 6 June despite the weather, but the subsequent decisions were made by the admirals and generals on the spot with the invasion forces – to send later waves into Utah Beach where the troops had landed, and to continue with Omaha Beach despite the near disaster.

One question that had to be settled was whether the operational commander was to be in a regular warship such as a cruiser or destroyer, or in a specialised vessel. After the abortive British attempt on Dakar in 1940, General Irwin wrote: 'Seldom have I felt so impotent, as during this expedition, when I was separated from my forces and tied to any naval operations that might become necessary. The Commander of any such enterprise must retain his independence from the fleet.' Mountbatten claims to have provided the solution, persuading the Ministry of War Transport to hand over *Bulolo,* an Australian passenger ship, which was converted by the summer of 1942. According to a later American account:

> A communication plan called for each service to have its own network and inter-service channels for combining the individual networks. This plan required radio equipment far in excess of any existing in *Bulolo* and each channel required both a transmitter and receiver. To prevent interference between the transmitting and receiving antennas, separation was required. Transmitters were located aft and the receivers forward. Numerous operations rooms were provided for the individual services and a joint room for command decisions was strategically located.[65]

She first saw service in the North African landings of 1942, with high-ranking Americans, including General Mark Clark. Churchill had her stationed off Casablanca for the conference of 1943, and he used maps and documents onboard to help persuade the Americans to follow his Mediterranean strategy. HMS *Largs* was converted at almost the same time, to be followed by many others, including specialised fighter direction ships. The Normandy invasion of June 1944 deployed seventeen British headquarters ships, some converted from destroyers and frigates, and three American.

The American cruiser *Augusta* was fitted with extra radio and radar equipment for the North African landings but was not a success:

> Enroute to the area, living, planning and operational spaces were so crowded that the personnel were barely capable of performing their

duties. Communication facilities were inadequate, both as to the total number of circuits available and the equipment for handling internal traffic. The most serious problem was the difficulty experienced in positioning the ship to provide gun fire support and still be able to perform command and communication functions.[66]

It was clear that specialised ships were needed, and *Bulolo* was 'The prototype of our AGCs', according to Samuel Eliot Morison.[67] The first American one was USS *Ancon*, a luxury liner of 1938 used as a troopship by the army and then the navy. She was fully converted for the new role at Norfolk and completed by April 1943, in time to take part in the invasion of Sicily. In the same campaign, *Monrovia* carried an admiral and staff, an Army Air Force fighter control group, and General Patton and his staff. She had 126 officers and 670 men besides her normal complement of forty-eight officers and 466 men.[68] More ships were built using the Merchant C-6 type hull with a speed of 16 knots and seventeen were in service by 1945. Turner used *Rocky Mount* for the Marshalls, but found:

> The initial reaction was that the ship was wonderful. But by the time the staff had shaken down the Commander, Fifth Amphibious Corps and his staff had come on board, it was apparent that there were problems in the communication equipment – primarily interference between the many, many radio sets and radar needed and used simultaneously.[69]

But the headquarters ship was now standard for all major landings.

Techniques and tactics

One vital task during an operation was to transfer the troops from the ship to the landing craft. The British LCA had the advantage that the troops could embark direct from the ship without using landing nets. At 'military boat stations' on *Glengyle* in 1942, on the order 'First flight embarkation stations':

> First flight of soldiers proceed from the mess-decks to their boat stations. Cox'ns will give senior officer of his boat orders to man. When the boat is manned it is reported by the cox'n to the telephone operator and thence to the bridge. Tackles are then unrigged and boat made ready for lowering.[70]

Then:

> Boats remain alongside ship until Divisional leaders haul out (no signal is made). They then follow in line ahead, a boat's length

apart, the two divisions converge ahead of the ship and the flotilla then proceeds in two columns in line ahead keeping station on the senior officer's boat. On approaching the beach, divisional leaders show red and green steady lights, reduce speed to 750 revs on one engine, columns then deploy to port and starboard respectively. ...[71]

In American practice, most davits were considered too weak to cope with loaded boats and cargo nets had been used to disembark men into landing craft since the exercises of 1935. New men:

> ... had to be taught to grasp only the vertical cords while descending or climbing the cargo nets. ... A dislodged entrenching tool or rifle falling 20 or 30 feet onto the men already in the landing boat would injure or even kill. And, a slow learner who grasped the horizontal cords of the cargo net received a painful lesson when the man above him stepped on his hand in descending the net.[72]

'Before going over the side, troops are cautioned to unfasten the straps of their packs and helmets ... so that heavy gear may be shed if a soldier falls into the water.'[73] But even so it was a frightening experience even for hardened marines:

> Three feet above the rolling Higgins Boats the cargo nets came to an end. One had to jump, weighted with fifty or more pounds of equipment. No time for indecision, for others on the nets above were all but treading your fingers. So there it was – jump – hoping the Higgins Boat would not roll away and leave only the blue sea to land in.[74]

Marvin J Perrett described the procedure from an LCVP coxswain's point of view:

> ... the ship dropped anchor 12 miles offshore at Normandy and at 2.30 in the morning darkness and in three foot seas they put us over the side and we would then move out off the bow, amidships and astern, down both sides in configuration of about 12 boats to the circle ... as a wave of boats. ... they would go out there and immediately start a slow moving circle and it was clockwise, and one by one we'd be hailed alongside the ship at certain debarkation stations and there these 36 troops would come down the debarkation net ... Once getting those troops then you'd go back to your circle ... and it took time to fill that circle of 12 boats ... As it developed I didn't bring my troops ashore until maybe seven o'clock in the morning.[75]

African-American marines practise disembarking with cargo nets in a training camp in North Carolina in 1945. It was even more difficult carrying full equipment in a pitching sea.

During the attack on Bougainville in November 1943, the ships used the British system, which they called 'rail-loading' and found it more efficient:

> Initial troop waves were rail-loaded in LCVP instead of crawling down into them by cargo nets, and the boats shoved off right away. There was no confusion among boat waves, no landing craft milling about for hours making the troops seasick. *Clymer* had all her boats in the water in 19 minutes, and her assault waves were loaded 37 minutes after the order was given.

Though 'the speed and smoothness of this unloading was astonishing', it was not adopted generally.[76]

Another hazard was broaching to, when the stern of a craft was afloat and the bows beached, and the stern was swept round by the tide:

> One of the most common problems in making a landing is to avoid broaching or letting your boat swing parallel to the beach. The unwary coxswain's boat can broach in a few seconds. When this happens the LCVP takes a pounding from the waves, and if the surf is high, may fill with water or even capsize.[77]

This could be avoided with skill: 'On reaching the beach, the bowman controlled the ramp and door while the sternsheetman let out the kedge anchor. The platoon commander unbolted the armoured door and troops disembarked, with the centre section leaving first.'[78]

Plenty of mistakes were made during the North African landings of 1942, and it is fortunate they were carried out against light or non-existent opposition by the French Vichy regime. One general asserted: 'The combination of inexperienced landing craft crews, poor navigation, and desperate hurry resulting from lateness of hour, finally turned the debarkation into a hit-or-miss affair that would have spelled disaster against a well-armed enemy intent upon resistance', while an admiral claimed that success 'could only have been possible through the intervention of Divine Providence'.[79] Tactics for amphibious warfare evolved quickly after that, alongside the vast improvement in equipment.

Normally a landing would be scheduled for at or around dawn, so that the boats could approach in darkness and the troops could move inshore in daylight, but the North African landings were planned for four in the morning. A night landing was planned for Anzio in view of the light opposition to be expected, and it succeeded. At Finschafen in New Guinea, it took place an hour before dawn, but that caused difficulties.[80]

There were many factors in the choice of beach, including tide, gradient, likely opposition, distance from base and possibilities of moving inland. Europe was heavily populated and its beaches were likely to be well defended, though they were well charted and relatively free of offshore obstacles, apart from rummels or false beaches. Central Pacific islands, on the other hand, were often very heavily defenced, poorly mapped, and often had coral reefs offshore which demanded special techniques. And according to Admiral Barbey:

> In the Southwest Pacific, the many excellent beaches scattered throughout the area were vulnerable to assault and difficult to

defend. The Japanese could not be strong everywhere, nor could they readily shift troops from one point to another. They had to spread themselves too thin throughout the islands of the Pacific, China, the Philippines, and Southeast Asia.[81]

An expedition might be over a broad front – in the case of Sicily, the American landings alone were over a 37-mile front in the Gulf of Gela. And in Tinian surprise was achieved by landing on two beaches 60 and 160yds wide, where no more than four or eight LVTs could approach abreast. Individual beaches were usually wide enough for several waves of boats to land at once.

Intelligence was key and was often obtained at some trouble. Charts might be out of date, inaccurate, or lacking in detail, so aerial reconnaissance was essential. It did not provide the answers on heights of structures or hills, or depth of water, but some of these could be

Follow-up landings on Iwo Jima photographed from an aircraft flying over Mount Suribachi, with LSTs, LSMs and LCTs unloading and other vessels anchored offshore.

answered by sending in a submarine. The British deployed combined operations pilotage parties, or COPPs, who landed at night from canoes. Another problem was the firmness of the ground to be traversed – in the invasion of Sicily, some beaches had to be covered in matting before vehicles could move over them.

Shore bombardment might be used as an end in itself to attack enemy assets, but it was more often used in direct support of a landing. During the First World War, the British developed the monitor, with the largest possible guns on the minimum hull, and a few still served as late as the Normandy invasion. But it was more commonly done by battleships, cruisers and destroyers, whose traditional role was gradually replaced as enemy surface fleets declined.

The landings in Sicily were not preceded by a bombardment, in order to keep the enemy unaware, but some though that a mistake. Conversely, shore bombardment was a turning point at Salerno, as the German Panzers counter-attacked. But in the next landing at Anzio there was no bombardment, which caused many of the problems on that assault.

Shore bombardment had difficulties, for often the target was not visible from the ship. That could be corrected by air spotting or by army officers on the spot, known to the British as forward observers, bombardment, or FOBs. Moreover, naval guns did not have the precise accuracy of land weapons, and their shells were designed to penetrate naval armour, so they were far less effective against concrete bunkers. Their trajectory was lower than army howitzers, which could lob shells over friendly forces. British trainee officers were told:

> Naval guns are normally High Velocity/Low Trajectory Guns. Problem of 'crest clearance' therefore arises. Special reduced charges, known as 'bombardment charges', are used to produce a howitzer effect. Accuracy is slightly affected and maximum range of guns, is, of course, decreased.

It was easy to overestimate the effect of a bombardment. General Holland M Smith noted a signal by one of the admirals before the Tarawa invasion: 'It is not our intention to wreck the island. We do not intend to destroy it. Gentlemen, we will obliterate it.' But the reality was very different, as Smith commented afterwards: 'Obliterate it? I entered every pillbox and blockhouse on the western end of the island and found only one had even been hit by naval gunfire. Not one had been destroyed. All of them had to be destroyed by Marines with explosive charges and hand grenades.'[82]

However, the morale effect was powerful. Leckie was on the receiving end on Guadalcanal:

> We could see the flashes of the guns far out to sea. We heard the soft pah-boom, pah-boom of the salvoes. Then rushing through the night, straining like an airy boxcar, came the huge projectiles. The earth rocks and shakes upon the terrifying crash of the detonation, though it be hundreds of yards away. Your stomach is squeezed, as though a monster hand were kneading it into dough; you gasp for breath like a football player who falls heavily and has the wind knocked out of him.[83]

Men in the landing craft were comforted by the support of big ships. Lieutenant R B Davies, in command of LCT 647, commented:

> Well, we are going in now, the guns of HMS *Belfast* firing over us. Landmarks were clear – we were coming in line abreast, six craft covering a mile of beach, my craft on the left flank. … Tanks were manned and revving up, the ramp door eased, … all of us dressed and armed and provisioned against an enforced stay ashore, feeling and looking like pirates. …

Communication with the troops ashore was essential, as at Iwo Jima:

> I was up in *Dale*'s gun director, talking directly with the marines fighting on Mount Suribachi. We spent about two days helping them out with our 5-inchers. The Japs were encased in deep caves and fortifications. Whenever the marines would come up against one of the strong points they would call for help. We would lay a few rounds in the distance, and the marines would call back, 'Down a hundred! Now, right fifty!'

Tides had two effects on a landing: the rise or fall of the water might affect the ability of craft to reach the beach in a suitable place or pass over a reef, which had serious effects at Tarawa; and the movement of the tides along a coast could displace the landing force. In general, the British were more aware of this with strong tides on their own coast, and everyone who had ever had a seaside holiday knew to go to the beach when the tide was in. But they too could make mistakes. Landing in the supposedly tideless Mediterranean, 'Evidently a westward sweep of current along the Algerian coast was not considered and a number of Beer landing craft wound up on the Apples beaches.'[84]

It was conventional to land just before high tide, so that the troops would have the shortest possible distance to reach the shore, and the craft would be able to retract before the level fell, but in Normandy, where the tidal effect was greatest of all the landings, it was decided to land at low tides so that the beach obstacles were uncovered. Other considerations had an effect in Normandy. The Utah landing force was swept 2000yds southwards, but it turned out to be a safer site than the intended one, and the subsequent waves were ordered to follow. It was far less happy on Omaha Beach. The British-manned LCAs launched from *Empire Anvil* landed Company A of the First Battalion 116th Infantry on Dog Green Beach on the western flank, but they found themselves alone. Company G in LCVPs was intended for neighbouring Dog White, but was swept two beaches eastwards to Easy Green, while Company F landed on the wrong side of Company G, and Company E was strung out a mile further east.[85] But it is doubtful if these errors caused the slaughter on Omaha Beach.

In effect, the landing craft operated in three different theatres – the central Pacific, South Pacific and European and North African. In the central Pacific, fierce resistance could be expected on tiny but well-defended islands, and the LVT was the most important, after Tarawa emphasised the need to get over coral reefs where LCVPs might ground. They were taken to the area by LST and launched. Different types were used to provide slightly heavier armament, and then the LSTs came in with heavy equipment and Seabees. This was well honed at Okinawa, when the first wave of four LSTs launched fourteen LVTs, each followed by five waves of LSTs, launching about six LCVPs each, then a seventh wave including LSMs, followed by more LSTs.[86]

Following his policy of 'Hit him where he ain't', MacArthur's attacks in the south were planned to use less well defended beaches as the enemy was more spread out – the classic example was Hollandia, when he leapfrogged many miles of enemy territory to take him by surprise. But his command was hampered by the lack of priority in the allocation of equipment. As Admiral Barbey put it:

> As it became apparent that the Southwest Pacific was not likely to get any more of the big amphibious transports, that is the APAs, and only a few of the smaller fast transports, the APDs … it became necessary to change our thinking regarding the conduct of future amphibious operations. It was obvious the seventh Amphibious Force would have to rely mainly on beaching type ships, that is, the LSTs, LCIs and the LCTs, not only for the reinforcement echelons but for the assault landings as well.[87]

In this theatre the LCI(L)s came in early, perhaps behind a wave of LCVPs launched by APDs, landing a large number of troops, even though they might be vulnerable as they came down the bow ramps in single file. Then the ubiquitous LSTs arrived with vehicles and heavy equipment.

European landings were normally led by LCAs and LCVPs, relying on the infantry to attack the immediate beach defences to clear the way for the following forces. Tanks and artillery were essential in this kind of warfare, so the LCTs usually came in next with the LSIs for infantry reinforcements, then the LSTs with many more tanks as well as heavy equipment. The Normandy invasion varied this procedure. It was intended that DDs, or swimming tanks, would land first, but few of them made it to the beach in the weather conditions. Instead, the first American forces landed on Utah and Omaha beaches in LCVPs, and the occasional British-manned LCA. On the British and Canadian beaches – Gold, Juno and Sword – LCTs came first, carrying Hobart's 'funnies', which were intended to clear obstacles, but found themselves fighting against German bunkers.

For the Normandy landings, the British spread small groups of specialists – signallers, beach parties, engineers, police and so on – in different craft and interspersed them among the infantry boats, so that the loss of a single craft would not destroy one element of the plan.

This panorama of a Normandy beachhead shows an LSI(L) landing men via bow ramps, after which they are led ashore by ropes. There is a sunken landing craft just behind, with LCAs arriving. The picture emphasises the crowded and potentially chaotic situation on the beach itself, demanding careful control by the beachmaster and his staff.

American landing craft usually circled until the whole force was ready and the time arrived, then formed a up on a prescribed line of departure. The *Tentative Manual for Landing Operations* suggested a V-formation within each group, as did the army's *Landing Operations on Hostile Shores* of November 1944, which was clearly based on practice in the European theatre. The V-formation had the advantage of identifying the leading craft, but a line abreast was clearly far more common, if not universal, as it was with the British.

During a landing, a beach was likely to become an improvised but exceptionally busy port under constant threat of enemy shelling and counter-attack, and with the possibility of huge traffic jams building up as more and more vehicles headed for limited numbers of exits. On Gela Beach in Sicily:

> Tiny infantry landing craft were coming in all up and down the sea front, and other larger boats were edging towards the shore to swell the monstrous and ever-growing heap of beached material. There was an endless, confused mass of men, of tiny jeeps, huge highsided DUKWs and more jeeps and heavily loaded trucks, stuck and straining in the thick sand or moving clumsily on the wire netting that the engineers had already laid down in some places as a road.[88]

During the long voyage out to the Madagascar landings in 1942, the officers onboard the transports worked out the need to have parties to control the movements on the beaches. In 1942 *Glengyle* had a party of twenty-four. Two were put in each of the LCAs, where they could help with the unhooking as the craft entered the water.[89]

Major European landings such as Salerno were guided by a beach battalion of 450 men divided into companies and platoons of about forty-six men, each of which had four sections – signals, medical, hydrographic and boat repair:

> … the beachmaster and some of his men trained in hydrographic duties are locating the beach, surveying the approaches, charting underwater obstacles and determining the best passages for the armada of landing craft yet to come. …
>
> Focal point of all Battalion operations is the Beachmaster's command post, located near the high-tide mark and within easy reach of beach exits and a cooperating army CP.[90]

The landings on the smaller Pacific islands were guided by beach platoons, each under an officer and attached to an individual APA. They only used the equipment they could carry ashore, though they had small boats for hydrographic work. They departed with the APA when it left after the landing. The major landings, such as Leyte and Okinawa, were closer to the European model.[91]

In the Southwest Pacific, after several failures, Admiral Barbey found the ideal formula:

> Their duties would be hazardous. They were to go ashore with the first assault boats and commence their job of buoying channels, erecting markers on the beach for incoming craft, handling assault casualties, taking offshore soundings, blowing up beach obstacles, and maintain voice communication between the troops ashore and incoming boats and nearby ships. They would work closely with the Army shore party which would unload the ships at the shoreline, but it was up to the beach party to see that the ships arrived in the right slot for quick unloading.[92]

* * *

MacArthur's forces alone conducted eighty-seven landings, though many of these were on Philippine islands after the enemy was practically defeated. Though they had plenty of experience of withdrawing troops by 1942, the only real failure of a British landing was at Dieppe, where the whole operation was misconceived. The Americans never had an unsuccessful landing, despite the great hazards involved. The least successful was at Anzio, where the landing itself succeeded, but the failure to press inland made the operation a waste of resources. But the war could not have been won in either the Atlantic or Pacific theatre without the rapid development of amphibious equipment and techniques.

Wars are not often won by navies alone and in this case it was armies landed by amphibious forces which defeated Italy and Germany, though in the latter case it has to be conceded that the land forces of the Soviet Union did the great bulk of the fighting. In the Pacific, the invasion of Japan proved unnecessary, but the capture of various islands by amphibious forces created the situation in which the nation could be bombed into surrender. Amphibious warfare, though seemingly marginal before 1940/1, had been at the centre of naval strategy ever since.

17
Enemies

ALL THREE of the main enemy powers were relatively new regimes. Germany had been unified in 1871 after a triumphant war against France and largely under the domination of Prussia. The unified Italian state was founded in 1866. Japan claimed to be a very ancient state dating back centuries, but it took its modern form with the Meiji Restoration of 1868.

The Third Reich

Germany had never been clearly defeated by land or sea during the First World War, which fostered the myth of a 'stab in the back', creating an atmosphere in which the extreme-right Nazi Party flourished. The Weimar Republic, founded by the malevolent Treaty of Versailles, was probably doomed from the start, but it was further hit by rampant inflation, mass unemployment and the fear of Communism. 'It was at this time', according to U-boat crewman Hans Goebeler, 'a politician appeared who promised to solve our nation's problems; give food and work to the unemployed, regain our lost territory, re-establish safety in the streets, and restore dignity and honour to our people.'[1] Adolf Hitler's Nazi Party took power in 1933. He became chancellor, an Enabling Bill gave him absolute power, and he took over the post of president, so there was no formal authority to challenge him. His grand vision for world domination was set out in his *Mein Kampf* of 1923, but it was an idea rather than a plan. Policies tended to emerge by accident: for example, the sinking against orders of *Athenia* on the first day of the war led eventually to an unrestricted U-boat campaign. 'Working towards the Führer' was the standard practice for officials and military leaders.

The army had always been the primary service in Germany. The Prussian force created by Frederick the Great had enormous respect and prestige, and the situation of the country, between France and Russia, made land defence essential. The new air force, the Luftwaffe, was near the centre of power, with Hitler's close associate Hermann Göring at its head. It subscribed to the airman's belief that bombing alone could win wars, but never developed aircraft heavy enough to execute it. Like many navies of the period, the Kriegsmarine had poor relations with the Luftwaffe, and it made a minimal contribution to naval operations by mounting patrols over the Atlantic. It was reported to Hitler in July 1941, 'the Air Force considers reconnaissance an inferior task, since it does not show immediate results.'[2]

The German navy was created by Admiral von Tirpitz at the end of the nineteenth century and was immensely proud of its tactical victory against the mighty Royal Navy at the Battle of Skagerrak, or Jutland, in 1916. Its U-boats came close to winning the war against Britain. In 1918 naval mutinies at Kiel and Wilhelmshaven led to the downfall of the empire, but honour was restored when the interned High Seas Fleet scuttled itself at Scapa Flow. This ambivalent history was referred to by Hitler, formerly a soldier on the Western Front, after a failure to attack British shipping. In a ninety-minute diatribe he complained that the old navy had 'lacked men of action who were determined to fight … a large amount of fighting-power lay idle, while the army was constantly heavily engaged.'[3]

The navy was cut down in size by the savage terms of the Versailles Treaty, but its three 'pocket battleships' built in 1929–34 would give the Royal Navy much trouble. The British unwisely accepted the resurgence of the Kriegsmarine in 1935, allowing it to reach 35 per cent of British warship tonnage and even a revival of the much-feared U-boats. But the navy was a weak link in Germany's plans for world domination, because it was still too small when war broke out. Under Plan Z of March 1939, it was to have eight battleships and four aircraft carriers, but not until 1943. It actually had no modern battleships until the great *Bismarck* and *Tirpitz* were ready.

The German navy had a vast expansion, from the 15,000, including 1500 officers, allowed by Versailles to a peak of 810,000 in 1944, though that included shore services such as coastal artillery. A million and half men passed through its ranks, because of casualties and transfers between services. In the late 1930s officers were selected over a two-week course, using typical Nazi methods:

> We had to grasp the two hands of a bar, and once the apparatus was switched on and the current began to flow we couldn't let go of them. Many of us just screamed – quite the wrong thing – but others bit their cheeks and by drawing them to give impression of stern endurance. All this was filmed …[4]

Those selected would spend five months on the naval island of Danholm, oppressed by petty officers who were themselves failed officer candidates. The main object was 'to take note of our behaviour and character'. Then there were four months on one of three sail training ships, which continued despite the war situation in 1940. On arrival they were told: 'You have the honour to learn your seamanship on this fine ship. ... you have everything to learn'. That included 'knots and splices, boat-pulling, reading a compass and taking bearings. Above all, we learnt mast-work, to go and come down from aloft.' Heinz Schaeffer served in the forward turret of the old battleship *Schleisen* in the Baltic, then on patrol boats off the newly conquered French coast. Then he went to the Naval Academy at Flensburg with a course in which celestial navigation featured largely, as 'it seemed unnecessary to learn everything in detail' due to the great variety of ships – though it did also include tactics, weapons and naval history. After graduation, receiving their sword belts and being promoted to *Oberfanrich zur See*, or senior midshipmen, he and some of his colleagues were sent to serve on a U-boat where they were told, 'You are nobodies and know nothing. The most junior hand knows more than you do.' Finally, after three years he was commissioned as *Leutnant zur See*.

Though Nazi Germany, as a warlike state, tended to offer a full career to a higher proportion of its wartime officers, reserves had to be called on. The great U-boat commander Günther Prien joined from the merchant service. Hans Groebeler found a variety of officers during three years in *U-505*. The first was Axel Olaf Lowe: 'his quiet, casual demeanour was based on a firm foundation of first-rate professionalism and ability. ... the very best officers don't need to throw their rank around, but rather lead by example.' He had to be relieved after a nervous breakdown and his successor Peter Zschech was the opposite: 'intelligent, self-confident, but a little aloof ... like an aristocrat. ...his aloofness hid an explosive temper.' He killed himself while on operations. At forty-three, Harald Lange was very old for a U-boat commander. He had been a merchant seaman and had 'a good understanding of what life was like for us crewmen ... His main concern was the good of the boat. Everything else was small fish'. As to the junior officers, Zschech's executive officer was in the same mould and was even suspected of having an intimate relationship with him. However, 'in the following months, Thilo Bode gradually transformed from a martinet into an officer men could have confidence in.' Watch officer Paul Meyer 'had been promoted to officer rank for his bravery in action. His experience as an enlisted man made him relate to us more as a comrade than as a superior.'[5]

Training of ratings also began in army style: 'To my infinite disappointment, we were issued green uniforms ... just like army soldiers. ... The only skill I learned was how to crawl like a snake on my belly through the mud.'[6] Potential petty officers were identified early, by previous experience as mechanics, or good hearing and basic electronic knowledge for radio operators, or excellent vision and good handwriting for signallers. Wolfgang Hirschfeld recalled, 'Following the basic three-month infantry induction period at Stralsund in early 1936, I was posted to Flensburg for the first of numerous courses in telegraphy at the Naval Signal School.' After service in a minesweeper, he was promoted to leading telegraphist in October 1938 and six months later he passed the examination for *Funkmaat*, or telegraphist petty officer.[7] And in July 1943 he was sent on a four-week platoon commander's course at Emden followed by a four-month warrant telegraphist course at Flensburg.[8]

The navy was far less political than the army, partly because most were at sea – though early in 1945 the High Command included 8000 officers and men, reduced to 2800 in the extreme war situation.[9] Admiral Dönitz, though non-political in theory, expressed his enormous loyalty to Hitler.

> The enormous strength which the Führer radiates, his unwavering confidence, and his far-sighted appraisal of the Italian situation have made it very clear in these days that we are all very insignificant in comparison with the Führer, and that our knowledge, and the picture we get from our limited vantage are fragmentary. Anyone who believes that he can do better than the Führer is foolish.[10]

Among the enlisted men, Hans Goebeler commented, 'It never entered our minds for a moment whether this one was a Nazi or that one was not. We considered ourselves patriots, pure and simple.'[11] It is reasonable to believe that very few navy men knew much about the terrible events in central Europe, though most of them must have noticed the use of slave labour in shipyards and factories. On the other side of the coin, the navy did nothing to resist Nazi rule. After the July 1944 plot against Hitler, nearly five thousand alleged conspirators were executed, but only three were naval officers, including the brother of the plot leader.[12]

The strength of the German surface fleet was not likely to increase, for Hitler expected a short war in 1939 and no more large ships were built. The only aircraft carrier, *Graf Zeppelin*, was never completed, largely due to the lack of suitable aircraft and equipment. In April 1942:

> The total time necessary to complete the carrier does not depend on completing the hull and engines, but on changing the flight

installations for the use of aircraft adapted from the JU87D [Stuka] and [Messerschmitt] BF109F. About two years are required to develop construct and test the catapults necessary for these planes.[13]

Nevertheless, the surface ships were effective, especially in the early stages. As the smaller naval power, Germany used the classic strategy of building each ship to be superior to its opponents. The 'pocket battleships' *Graf Spee* and *Deutschland* were already at sea when the war started and the former sank nine merchant ships before being cornered in Montevideo by British cruisers and scuttled. The battlecruisers *Scharnhorst* and *Gneisenau* were completed with relatively light 280mm (11in) guns and sailed on a cruise at the start of the war. They took part in the invasion of Norway, sinking the carrier *Glorious,* and on a second cruise they sank twenty-two ships. Early in 1942 they embarrassed the British by leaving Brest and escaping up the English Channel, but that was in effect a retreat. *Gneisenau* was immobilised by bombing, *Scharnhorst* was sunk in an attack on the Russian convoy route on Boxing Day 1943.

The great battleships *Bismarck* and *Tirpitz* had 15in guns and a speed of 30 knots. *Bismarck* escaped into the Atlantic in May 1941, sank the revered battlecruiser *Hood* and threatened the whole Atlantic convoy system until she was damaged by air attack and sunk by a powerful British force. One surviving crewman reported:

Before our own guns fired, enemy shells dropped close to the ship. After about one hour the first hits scored on our ship. I myself was

The mighty German battleship *Bismarck* at sea, photographed from her consort, *Prinz Eugen*, during her fatal raid of May 1941.

wearing the telephone. The connection broke off. I took off the telephone. From this time onwards no orders were given by the anti-aircraft control to my gun. As the hits increased the anti-aircraft crews went undercover. We had the impression that we were being fired from all sides.[14]

Tirpitz remained moored in a Norwegian fjord, but by January 1943 Hitler was exasperated by the lack of action: 'Due to the present crucial situation, where all fighting power, all personnel, and all material must be brought into action, we cannot permit the large ships to ride idly at anchor for months. They require constant protection by the air force as well as by numerous smaller surface craft.'[15] He ordered their scrapping, which led to the resignation of Admiral Raeder. His successor, Dönitz, though a U-boat man, pointed out that their very existence tied up disproportionate British resources, until *Tirpitz* was damaged by midget submarines then sunk by RAF bombers in 1944.

Apart from three cruisers lost in the Norway invasion, *Prinz Eugen* sailed with *Bismarck* and with *Scharnhorst* and *Gneisenau* in the 'Channel Dash'. *Admiral Hipper* was deployed as a commerce raider in 1940/1, then was one of the few heavy units in the Baltic.

Amphibious warfare had never been the German strength, though it had conducted a landing against Russian forces on Osel off Estonia in 1917, and a few exercises in the Baltic during the peace. Despite all this, in April 1940 an invasion of Norway was launched in the face of a superior fleet and against all the rules of naval warfare. Admiral Raeder warned on 1 April 1940:

> The execution and protection of the landing operations by the Navy will take place mainly in an area in which not Germany, but England with her superior naval forces is able to exercise control of the sea. In spite of this we must succeed, and we will, if every leader is conscious of the greatness of his task and makes a supreme effort to reach the objective assigned to him.[16]

The Norwegian armed forces were very weak and the cabinet failed to alert them in time. Two German cruisers were sunk as they entered Oslo Fjord, but at Narvik, Trondheim, Bergen, Stavanger, Egersund, Kristiansand and Arendal resistance was slight. Troops landed in sheltered fjords from destroyers, sometimes with paratroops in the rear and with strong support from the Luftwaffe. The British fleet was successfully evaded and counter-attacks at Narvik and Trondheim failed, though the German navy lost ten destroyers. The affair had many lessons, though not in amphibious warfare as it would later develop.

After the Fall of France, the navy would have played an essential role in any invasion of Britain, but it was not ready for it, with many ships out of action. Raeder probably never believed that a landing was practicable:

> an invasion should be used only as a last resort to force Britain to sue for peace. He is convinced that Britain can be made to ask for peace simply by cutting off her import trade by means of submarine warfare, air attacks on convoys, and heavy attacks on her main centres.[17]

And at one point Raeder remarked that 'Our attacks on England, particularly on London, must continue without interruption. ... The attacks may have a decisive outcome'[18] – highly unusual support for strategic bombing by an admiral.

The army proposed a broad front, but Raeder commented, 'The task allotted to the Navy in operation "Sea Lion" is out of all proportion to the Navy's strength'. He was 'therefore of the opinion that the crossing should be concentrated at first entirely on the Straits of Dover as far as Eastbourne, and that this route should be protected as strongly as possible by guns, mines, and the available naval forces.'[19] A compromise was reached by 27 August. Landings would be made in four areas between Folkestone and Selsey Bill. Since previous landings had been in the tideless Baltic or in sheltered fjords, there was some debate about the time of landing, but it was decided that about two hours after high tide was best. And the coast was highly exposed to wind, weather and enemy attack.

The navy improvised a fleet, for there was no time to design and build anew. Heinz Schaeffer noticed:

> Everywhere we find preparations for the invasion of England. All available shipping was being adapted for it. Auxiliary motors were being put into riverboats and, to increase speed in emergency, one or even two aeroplane engines installed, while the bows were cut away and a collapsible ramp fitted to land tanks in a flat beach.[20]

In July the operation was estimated to require 1722 barges, mostly requisitioned from German and Dutch waterways, 471 tugs, 1161 motorboats and 155 transports.[21] This fleet would consist of 'Large numbers of slow, unwieldy transport units concentrated in a small space, mixed with motor boats of the most varied types, and escorted by light units of the Navy and auxiliary vessels'. Perhaps the greatest weakness of all was in landing craft for tanks, vehicles which were essential to German success on land. One solution was to lower watertight

Panzerkampfwagens into the water from a barge and have them drive ashore, but any obstacle would be fatal.[22]

Manning was also improvised:

> Because I had been in the Naval Hitler Youth I was put into a blue uniform ... and ordered aboard a Rhine barge as a deckhand. This barge had been rebuilt ... for landing operations and fitted with two airscrews ...These boats were manned by three men from the Navy, some of whom have previously been in the army; five engineers operated on the equipment ... and there were two aircraft engine mechanics.[23]

After several delays and the Luftwaffe's failure to gain air superiority, the operation was stood down and the barges and other vessels returned to their duties where they were desperately needed. It has always been a matter of speculation how far Hitler really intended to invade, but perhaps it is not necessary to reach a conclusion. He was an opportunist and so far every time he had kicked at a door the whole structure had collapsed, but the British refusal to compromise did not fit that scenario and he looked elsewhere.

Since invasion was impracticable and the air attack on Britain was faltering, it was natural to turn to the U-boat as the only means of defeating the British. This was aided by the capture of bases in Norway

A Type VIIC U-boat returning to its base in Norway in November 1943, with many of the crew on deck and on the conning tower.

and France, solving Germany's problem of being cut off by British sea power and allowing the boats to reach the Atlantic without running the gauntlet of patrols. But Hitler's eyes were already turned towards the east with his invasion of Russia in June, so the U-boats did not have priority.

The U-boat force was headed by Admiral Karl Dönitz, a submarine commander in the last war, and a determined and forceful character: 'The visit of the tall, distinguished Admiral to our sub made an everlasting impression on me. We U-boat men had unbounded confidence and respect for both his abilities and devotion to duty.'[24] He issued praise and rebuke in equal measure.

'Men of the *U-109*! You were off the coast of Africa, and you achieved nothing.' He paused. 'But you cannot be faulted for that.'

Fritz-Julius Lemp, on the left, sank the liner *Athenia* at the beginning of the war in *U-30*. Here he is congratulated by Admiral Dönitz after a successful mission. In May 1941 he was killed when *U-110* was captured by the British, along with an Enigma machine.

He spoke slowly and quietly, yet his voice was sharpening as he went on. 'Off the coast of Spain, you found a convoy and sank nothing.' He paused again, and then resumed with a deeper harsher tone. 'I have the impression that you didn't even try.'[25]

In mid 1940 the navy was still not strong in U-boats with only forty-six in service, reduced to twenty-eight after some losses. The most common model (567 out of 1131 commissioned) was the Type VIIC, which was an excellent craft in many ways but was not designed for Atlantic warfare. It could travel for 9700 miles on the surface at 10 knots, but only 3450 miles at 17 knots. Submerged it could travel 130 miles at 2 knots, 80 miles at 4 knots, but only one hour at its maximum speed of 7.6 knots. It was armed with four bow and one stern torpedo tubes, with a maximum of eleven torpedoes. It had a standard crew of forty-four. The next type, IXC, was exemplified by Goebeler's *U-505*: 'one of the larger Type IX boats designed to operate independently on long-range patrols on the periphery of the Atlantic.'[26]

The Type XXI was truly revolutionary. It abandoned the ship-like bows of earlier submarines in favour of a streamlined shape designed for underwater operation, and with much increased battery power, so it could hopefully attack undetected. According to Dönitz:

> ... it could possibly be detected by listening devices, but the range is not anywhere near so great as that of the high frequency location-finding equipment used in aircraft against submarines operated on the surface. It is still true that the ship is sunk if the submarine is able to get close in. The difficulty lies in getting close enough to the target, because it still has to be done on the surface. With the new submarine it is possible under water.[27]

Under armaments minister Albert Speer it became the object of a huge mass-production effort, but German industry was not ready for it. Boats were to be made in sections at inland sites and then assembled in yards such as Blohm und Voss in Hamburg, but the prototype, put together for Hitler's birthday in 1944, leaked badly and with others the sections were inaccurately made and did not fit together without modification.[28] Even more revolutionary was the boat designed by Helmut Walter to use highly unstable hydrogen peroxide to reach high underwater speeds and stay down for a long time. Fortunately for Allied shipping, none were operational by the end of the war.

More generally, air raids disrupted production, as did shortages of steel and labour. Dönitz was sanguine in August 1943: 'I believe that air raids can hardly endanger our essential industries in a material way. I saw machines standing right next to a bomb crater in the machine shops of the Hamburg shipyards. Even though the bombs scored a direct hit on the shop, the machines were absolutely undamaged'.[29] But conversely, mass production could be vulnerable to bombing:

> Since thirty or forty parts of one kind are built simultaneously in one shipyard, a loss of thirty or forty submarines may be caused by a single air raid. The same condition exists in the assembly plants. In Hamburg for instance, thirteen submarines are assembled each month. Since it takes more than two months to complete assembly, more than thirty boats are always under construction on the building slips.[30]

The greatest failure was to appreciate the Allied use of centimetric radar and radio intelligence. Instead, the problems were attributed to the radar-detecting device Metox fitted to U-boats, as Dönitz told the Führer in August 1943:

> … the Metox radiations which may have been responsible for grievous losses. These radiations may explain all the uncanny and unsolved mysteries of the past, such as the enemy avoiding traps set for him, and losses on the open sea while comparatively few boats were destroyed during convoy attacks because the Metox was always turned off then.[31]

U-boat crews were not necessarily volunteers, though Radioman Werner Hess apparently was:

> I went to the U-boat arm of my own free will. The first reason for this was that one could earn a lot of money. The second reason was that in this way I could help my father. He was a well-known Social Democrat and had enormous difficulties under Hitler. … after I became a U-boat man my father was left in peace.[32]

Hans Goebeler was pleased to be selected: 'I suppose they were impressed by my enthusiasm, not to mention the fact that in the cramped conditions inside a sub was one place where my small size would be an advantage.'[33] U-boat men had to get used to lack of space and washing facilities. The torpedo room 'doubled as the forward crew quarters. There were not enough bunks for everyone in the crew, so someone slept in your bed while you were on duty. The bunks folded up out of the way whenever we needed to fire or reload the torpedoes.'[34]

There was a regular pattern to operations in the middle years of the war. There was a riotous send-off the night before sailing on an operation: 'In the evening we attended the traditional farewell banquet. As usual there was much drinking and toasting as we consumed the last of our private stocks of beer and liqueur. With our money gone and our goodbyes said, we were finally ready to leave.'[35] The first hazard, which got worse as Allied air patrols intensified, was to exit across the Bay of Biscay:

> The Brits maintained constant surface and air patrols designed to catch departing or returning submarines moving through the area. We would soon come to call the place 'the U-boat Graveyard' because of all the unfortunate subs sunk there. By the end of the war, most U-boats never got a chance to engage the enemy before they were snared by their allies' cordon of death around our submarine sally ports.[36]

The next job of the U-boat command was to find the convoys, no easy task in a vast ocean. Kondor aircraft might help in some waters, but there was no effective air reconnaissance in mid-Atlantic. It might be aided by signal intelligence, but the most common solution was to form lines of U-boats across the likely path. According to Wolfgang Hirschfeld: 'Late in the following day the BdU finally managed to assemble around Newfoundland a reconnaissance approximately 200 miles in length and consisting of eight boats including *U-109*. This wolf pack was collectively known as "*Westboote*."'[37] Once a convoy was found, the nearest boat would be ordered to follow it. 'Every two hours we transmitted fuller details. We were the first U-boat to contact the convoy and our job was to call in all other U-boats in the area, this being the whole point of a Wolfpack tactics.'[38] When enough boats were gathered round the convoy the attack began. The usual technique was to attack on the surface to avoid Asdic, though that became less and less effective as radar improved. But apart from that, the wolf pack was not under central control; once the order had been given each boat attacked on its own, so much depended on its commander:

> ... I do not mean to imply that we were all acting under unified command. Action in the Battle of the Atlantic merely meant calling up all available forces, for once in touch with the convoy every ship acted on its own, yet in this way we could annihilate convoys of 50 ships and more in actions that went on for days.[39]

A large proportion of successful attacks were carried out by a limited number of commanders – the 'aces': 2 per cent of U-boat commanders were responsible for sinking 30 per cent of Allied tonnage lost, while around 850 U-boats never sank or damaged any ships. This was not the case with one captain:

> We wanted to torpedo four ships, so we picked out the big ones, preparing to attack the furthest first and the rest afterwards … If possible all four must hit simultaneously, so to leave no time for alterations of course. We were quite close to the nearest ship already – 650 metres perhaps.
> 'Fire!'
> The ship throbbed four times – we were now using our after tube along with the rest. In fifteen seconds we should hit. We grew impatient; they seemed such very long seconds. …
> A spurt of flame and then two thuds. Sound travels through water faster than through the air. One more explosion aboard the same ship. She was breaking apart now, and in a moment she had gone down.[40]

In this case they evaded the pursuers by staying surfaced among the ships of the convoy, but all submariners had to get used to the horrors of depth charge attack:

> The skipper immediately ordered a crash dive to 200 meters. We had barely passed the 40 meter depth point when four gigantic explosions rocked the boat. Now we really understood what a depth charge sounded like at close range! After 10 minutes of manoeuvring the pings began to gradually fade into the distance.[41]

Germany declared war on the United States four days after Pearl Harbor. It has always been a matter of speculation as to what would have happened if it had failed to do so. Would American resources have been diverted to the Pacific, leaving Britain in the lurch? But the Nazis saw America as a mongrel nation run by Jews, and conflict with it was inevitable – there would never be a better chance. The U-boat crews enjoyed their 'second happy time' off the largely unprepared American coast. According to Hirschfeld:

> … Witte whispered, 'Palm Beach over there.'
> The coast was very near: we could see the lights in the houses. There seem to be a coastal road. We could see the headlights of a lot of motor traffic. The boat was edging ever closer to the foreshore. The purpose of this was to prevent the tanker we were following from attempting to beach herself after our torpedoes had hit.[42]

After American defences improved in mid 1942, the boats returned to mid ocean for the climax of the campaign in 1943. They were refitted to cope with increasing air attack:

> The entire conning tower had been removed and was being replaced with a completely new and improved style unit. The 105mm deck gun had also been removed ... In lieu of the single cannon, we would now be armed with a four-barrelled 20mm anti-aircraft weapon. Two twin barrelled 20 mm guns were also installed.[43]

Some U-boats were used as oceangoing tankers:

> East of the Antilles we rendezvoused with *U-463* ... one of the 'Milk Cow' submarines specially designed to replenish U-boats on the high seas fuel, torpedoes and other supplies. Luckily for us, the sea was smooth as a mirror and there was no difficulty in making the Diesel hose connection.[44]

The new T-5 *Zaunkönig* (Wren) acoustic homing torpedo could be used against targets with speeds of between 10 and 18 knots – that is, escort vessels; it had its first success against HMS *Lagan* in September 1943. But it could be countered by noise-making machines, and it made life even more difficult for the crews:

> These complex, electrically-propelled eels were nicknamed 'Destroyer Killers' because, it was hoped, we could fire them in the general direction of the enemy escorts and they would automatically chase down our tormentors. Unfortunately they contained delicate instrumentation that required constant attention ... since the fore and aft torpedo rooms doubled as our crew's sleeping quarters, the mechanics had to fold up our bunks ... in order to perform their daily maintenance ...[45]

In the bases at Lorient, La Rochelle, St-Nazaire and Brest, impenetrable U-boat pens or shelters were constructed by the Todt organisation, partly using slave labour. Heinz Schaeffer noted:

> ... in the cliffs, the first U-boat pens were being constructed: formidable armoured underground wharves and docks. Air attacks were becoming more frequent and we didn't want to let up on our U-boat attacks at any rate through delays from ship refits. The work went ahead at unimaginable rate, unending streams of lorries with sand and cement pouring through the streets. ... it was altogether a masterpiece of organisation.[46]

Between operations, crews had luxurious recreation, unlike their opponents in the escorts, who had yet more training. Goebeler and his shipmates were sent to Chateau Neuf near Lorient: 'The resort was absolute heaven! It had big double-sized rooms, a huge swimming pool, a fully stocked bar, there was no standing in line for food, and best of all, the delicious meals were served to us individually by a staff of beautiful young mademoiselles.'[47]

But all was not well in the bases. Though the U-boat pens were immune from bombing, the surrounding towns could be flattened, and the people were not to be trusted:

> We immediately suspected sabotage from the dock workers. In an effort to reduce the chances of sabotage, virtually all of the men working on U-boats were *Volksdeutsch,* ethnically-German residents of Poland and other Eastern European countries. It was discouraging to imagine that if it was sabotage, out ethnic brethren were the ones plotting our demise.[48]

The development of the *Schnörchel*, or snorkel, copied from the Dutch, allowed a revival of the U-boat campaign in British inshore waters in the last year of the war. They caused much diversion of Allied resources, including the laying of protective minefields, but the inexperienced crews suffered high casualties themselves. Only about six thousand out of thirty-seven thousand U-boat men survived the war, a higher casualty rate than any other service.

Germany took up the idea of a fast torpedo boat sooner than Britain and the USA, partly to evade the restrictions of the Treaty of Versailles. The process began with the motor yacht *Otaka II* built in 1928 by Lürssen, ironically for an American client. Powered by three 550hp Maybach engines, she had a speed of over 30 knots and claimed to be the fastest in the world. The Kriegsmarine obtained the plans and ordered the first *Schnellboot*, with a projected speed of 37 knots on a 39-ton hull incorporating two torpedo tubes. Unlike British boats, it had a displacement hull, so it needed great engine power. Completed in 1930, it did not attain that speed, but development of the S-boat, to be known as the E-boat to the British, continued. A tendency to dip its bows in the water was corrected by a 'knuckle' which allowed the lower bows to be flared outwards, size was increased to nearly 100 tons and three Daimler-Benz 2000hp engines were fitted, diesel so that they did not need highly inflammable petroleum (gasoline). It was superior to anything the British had and two flotillas, a total of eighteen boats, were in service by August

1938. Another was added at the start of the war.[49] Altogether, 249 were commissioned, each with a normal crew of twenty-one.

The S-boats supported the invasion of Norway by landing troops from larger ships, and with the invasion of the Low Countries and the Fall of France they had the whole coastlines of the North Sea and the English Channel to operate from. They attracted much less attention from on high than the surface raiders and the U-boats, except in April 1943 when Dönitz explained their use to Hitler: 'He emphasises the construction of E-boats, the mission of which is obvious, ie to force the British to maintain escorts along the English coast, in order to keep them from attacking our convoys and to supplement submarine warfare by sinking the many ships moving in English coastal waters.'[50] Their most dramatic success was when they intruded on an American D-Day rehearsal off Slapton Sands in Devon, when they sank two LSTs with considerable loss of life, and caused some tension between the Allies.

Empire of the Sun

At a time when almost all the world was subjected to Western rule, Japan was unique as a truly independent and very powerful Asian state. Closed to foreigners for centuries, Japan was forcibly opened by the expedition led by Commodore Perry of the US Navy in 1853 and the state was modernised with the Meiji Restoration in 1868. The power of the feudal clans was reduced, the samurai ceased to be the ruling class, and the country looked to Western technology, founding a modern navy in 1872. Internal dissent was largely silenced by a decisive naval victory over China in 1895, giving Japan territory and power in the region. In 1901 Britain, finding that 'splendid isolation' was not enough, sought its first alliance with the new Asian power. In 1904/5 Japan fought a decisive war against Russia to make her a great power on an international scale. The Anglo-Japanese alliance, strengthened in 1905, brought the country into the First World War, and she captured German colonies and Chinese concessions without any great risk, while expanding her industry to fill the gaps left by the warring powers. She had a place at the Versailles conference of 1919, and for the next ten years or so the state was run on relatively liberal lines under the emperor. The Diet was elected by universal suffrage, but its power was limited, and no cabinet could be formed without the support of the high commands of both the army and the navy. There was growing resentment when the Washington Treaty restricted the fleet to three-fifths of the American and British, and in 1923 when the US introduced racist immigration legislation. From 1930

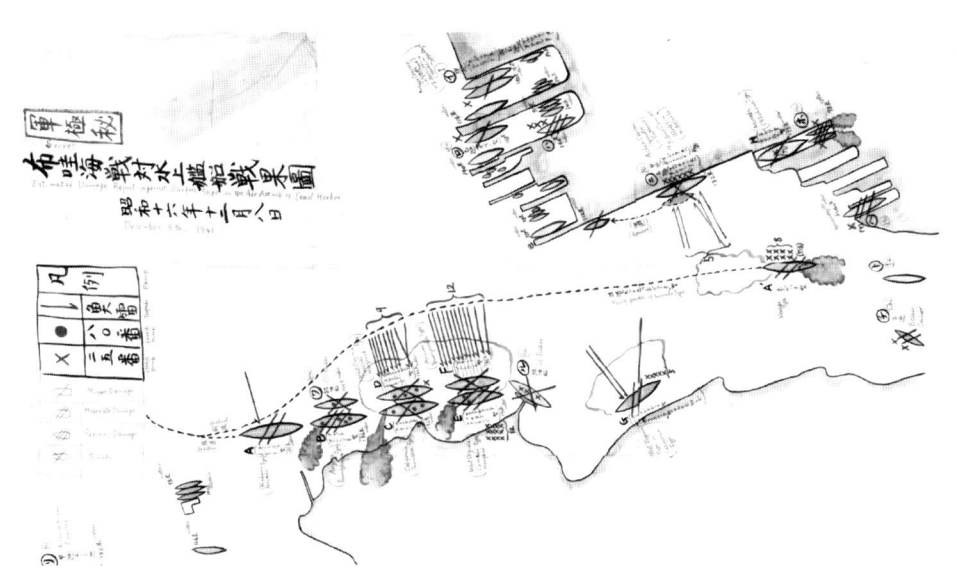

A map showing the damage to American ships in Pearl Harbor, as assessed by Mitsuo Fuchida immediately after the attack. Arrows show torpedo hits, and crosses, bomb impacts. Lines indicate the damage to particular ships.

the army, always a powerful force, began to take control of politics and lead the country into aggression and war in China.

Japan combined traditional values with Western technology. The Shinto faith was only formally separated from Buddhism in 1875 and it became the state religion. It promoted worship of the emperor and loyalty to the family, both of which inspired fanatical devotion to the national cause. There was no separate heaven or paradise, but the dead might be absorbed into life. One kamikaze wrote in his last letter: 'Though my body departs, I will return home in spirit and remain with you forever.'[51] The code of the samurai forbade surrender and led to suicidal bravery – not just from the elite kamikaze pilots, but from defeated marines and infantry who were expected to finish off the battle and their own lives with a banzai charge; or later, when they hid in tunnels to await burial or death by flame thrower. Conversely, they had no respect for those who did surrender, At best, they might harsh face imprisonment and slave labour, at worst death by torture. They never appreciated how much this infused enemies with the resolve to fight harder.

Like Britain, Japan was highly dependent on imports and had easy access to the sea, so that no one and nothing was far from the shore. In a sense, she was even stronger, since there was no great power close to her capable of invasion or bombing, until the Americans fought their way there at great effort and cost in 1944. The Japanese learned much from the British, both in surface warfare and naval aviation. On the other hand, they had taken the lead and catapulted navies into the new age with their victory over the Russians at Tsushima. The tactics were studied in the West and inspired the building of *Dreadnought*, beginning the new battleship age. More recently, the attack at Pearl Harbor followed the British success at Taranto and began a new age of naval air warfare.

Other warring powers had a single leader during nearly all of their period of hostilities – Hitler, Churchill, Roosevelt, Stalin and Mussolini. Japan, of course, had Emperor Hirohito: though he was more than a figurehead, he was not involved in day-to-day decision-making. Instead, there was a succession of three prime ministers, none powerful enough to overcome army–navy rivalry. All nations suffered from this to some extent, but none so much as Japan. One officer wrote much later, 'During the war and today I abhorred the Japanese Army.'[52] The navy tended to see itself as men who had travelled the world, and army officers as boors.

Entry to the naval academy at Etajima, near Nagasaki, was more meritocratic than its British or American counterparts, by competitive examination rather than parental wealth and status or political influence. It was modelled on Royal Navy practices, and red bricks were imported from Britain to build the cadet quarters: 'The layout of the college is very attractive, its most prominent feature being an avenue of cherry trees, … leading from the main College gates to the "daikido" or Great Hall, an imposing building of white stone which is the centre of the spiritual life of the college.' But the cadets, who entered between the ages of sixteen and nineteen, had little time to appreciate the beauty, working hard for most of their waking hours. Violence was common: 'After a few months of such treatment the newcomers became sheeplike in their obedience. Every man's face bore evidence of the brutality we endured.'[53] They learned Kendo or Judo, languages, the usual naval subjects, and sailed round the coasts of Japan. The most gruelling feature was the long-distance swim over eight to ten miles, during which many withdrew due to cramp. After graduation they spent eight months on foreign cruises.

The wartime reserve officers were a different breed: 'My students were all in their early twenties. They were serious and enthusiastic but, being reservists, complete amateurs, and totally unlike the Academy men to whom I had taught … some years before. I quickly discovered a great need for patience.'[54] Yoshida Mitsuru highlighted the difference as *Yamato* sailed on her suicidal last mission:

Those ensigns and lieutenant who had graduated from the naval academy speak as if with one voice: 'We die for the nation, for the emperor. Isn't that enough? Do we need anything more than that? ...'

An OCS man colours and asks in return: '... But isn't there more to it than that? My death, my life, the defeat of Japan as a whole: I'd like to link those with something more general, more universal, something to do with values. What is the purpose of all this?'[55]

Warships were spartan inside, and it was noted, 'most Japanese officers regard foreign warships as luxury ships'. Traditionally they spent less time on spit and polish than Western ships in peacetime.[56] They had no regular sleeping quarters for enlisted men or cadets: 'At night we spread hammocks in any available space to sleep. Meals consisted of rice and barley with some canned fish or meat.'[57] Again, violence was common. Yoshida Mitsuru was reprimanded for not striking a sailor who failed to salute him, with at least five blows of the fist: 'On the battlefield, no matter how nice and understanding an officer you are, it won't work. You must be strong.'[58] But others, including destroyer captain Hara, saw it differently: 'To beat men like cattle merely deprives them of the initiatives thought necessary in the destroyer which must be manned by a closely knit team.'[59]

Senior Japanese naval officers had even more faith in the battleship than their opposite numbers in Britain and the USA, perhaps because of an exaggerated belief in Mahan and the concept of the great battle. Restriction of battleship numbers by the Washington Treaty was one of the primary causes of the dispute with Britain and the USA. The six ships of the *Fuso*, *Ise* and *Nagato* classes were all built in 1913–21 and were extensively modernised just before the war. They were similar to British ships and had poor armour protection. They were supplemented by the four battlecruisers of the *Kongo* class, also reconstructed. All were armed with 14in guns, except the *Nagato* class with 16in.

Yamato and *Musashi* were laid down in 1937/8 and largely built in secret. At nearly 70,000 tons full load and with nine 18in guns, they were by far the largest battleships ever built and were treated with great reverence in Japan, perhaps as a vindication after the humiliations of Washington and London. To Seaman Tsukada of *Musashi*:

> Unsinkable, was really what you would describe them. The upper decks were curved upwards as it headed forward from the main mast towards the bow and slightly angled funnel was surrounded by anti-aircraft guns, and it was like a fortified castle, and from the sides the sleek figure was more like an enlarged cruiser.[60]

Yamato, the pride of the Japanese surface fleet and, along with her sister *Musashi*, the largest battleship ever built, fitting out in the Kure naval base in September 1941.

The nearest approach to the great battle was at Leyte Gulf in 1944, when Admiral Nishumura's force was ambushed in the Surigao Strait and *Musashi* was sunk. Then in April 1945 *Yamato* was sent on a suicide mission to relieve Japanese forces at Okinawa. After his own cruiser was sunk, Captain Hara witnessed the attack on her from the water:

> I was heartened to see that *Yamato* was still fighting. Scores of American planes swarmed gnatlike over and around her, launching their deadly missiles, but the giant ship still fought on. ... But the sight was short lived. At 1420 a frightening pillar of fire and white smoke came belching from the battleship hiding everything. The smoke towered 20,000 feet into the sky.[61]

Japan was the first nation to resume building of cruisers after the Washington Treaty, with the *Sendai* class. The first heavy (8in) cruisers were the *Furutaka* class of 1922–26 and the design was improved through several other classes. The *Mogami* class caused a sensation in the early 1930s with its fifteen 6.1in guns, but it was built to a very ambitious specification and the four ships had to be altered to heavy cruisers, with ten 8in guns and bulges to increase displacement. In 1941 Japan had eighteen heavy cruisers, all fast, heavily armed and well armoured – though only by exceeding treaty limits. Light cruisers were neglected in comparison, consisting mainly of the ageing and under-gunned *Sendai* class. The three ships of the *Agano* class of 1940–42 were designed for officer training, with a large bridge and a combination of turbine and diesel power plants for the engineers. When the war started they were converted to flagships. Only *Oyodo* with 6.1in guns was new-built during the war; *Ibuki* was completed as a carrier.

As in most navies, destroyers did much of the real fighting:

> … it was the destroyer flotillas, totalling never more than 130 or at any one time, which shouldered the heaviest burden of the war. They were the workhorses of the Imperial Navy. These destroyers were assigned not merely as fighting ships, but also as escorts to transport and even *as* transports for many months of the war.[62]

The *Fubuki* class of 1923–30 was another game-changer, introducing the 5in gun in twin turrets, making them the best armed destroyers in any navy. Out of twenty ships built, one was sunk by collision in 1934 and all but one of the rest were sunk in wartime. The six ships of the *Hatsharu* class of 1932–34 were designed for maximum performance on a displacement limited by the London Treaty, but had to be rebuilt due to instability. The *Shiratsuyu* class followed them in their rebuilt format, with only five 5in guns. The *Asashio* class was post-treaty and larger. The similar *Kagero* and *Yugumo* classes followed and building of them continued during the war. The wartime *Atisuku* class were intended as anti-submarine escorts with 3.9in guns.

The torpedo was the main weapon of destroyers and the 'long lance' was a great success:

> The Japanese torpedo, in addition to being much faster and longer ranging than the best American or British torpedoes had another great advantage. Ordinary torpedoes, driven by compressed air, leave a long, white, tell-tale track which is usually detected and divided by a fast ship. But an oxygen-fuelled torpedo runs without leaving a trace on the surface.[63]

Most wartime attacks were a range of 4000–5000yds, which outranged American torpedoes.[64] Hara describes action during the naval Battle of Guadalcanal, in November 1942:

> Eight big fish jumped in rapid succession and sped on their way. I watched prayerfully … The second ship, *Barton*, stopped short to

avoid collision with *Aaron Ward*. And that moment, two minutes after the launching of my torpedoes, two pillars of fire shot high in the air from *Barton*. ... The ship, broken in two, sank instantly.[65]

The Japanese rated American torpedo boats highly, perhaps more than the Americans did themselves: 'In its preoccupation with big ships the Navy high command had not developed torpedo boats and their tactics. Japanese naval officers were appalled the brisk activity of American torpedo boats in the Solomons, and a rapid attrition of Japanese destroyers.'[66] But the boats produced were far from satisfactory:

> The first new boat arrived at the school in February and I was totally disgusted with its performance. After a test run of the 20-ton craft I returned it to the pier and ranted, 'This is not a torpedo boat. It is nothing but a barge. This scow would be of no value in a real fight.'[67]

Japanese submarines also benefited from the torpedo, though not as much as they might have done. After 1919 larger British and American designs were copied, producing long boats with poor manoeuvrability. Many more were built to different designs at the expiry of the treaties, including A-type headquarters boats, B-type for scouting and C-type for attack. According to Mochitsura Hashimoto:

> The Japanese policy was to use submarines primarily for attacking enemy naval forces. Attacks on merchant shipping had only second priority. Thus enemy aircraft carriers were the chief target, then battleships and other naval craft. Merchant ships were legitimate targets only when there are no warships to be considered.[68]

They did, however, have a successful campaign against shipping in the Indian Ocean in 1942/3, claiming an estimated eighty ships sunk for the loss of two of their own.[69] Against warships, they did sink the carriers *Yorktown* and *Wasp*, and the cruiser *Indianapolis* near the end of the war.

Japanese submarines were even less habitable than their counterparts in other navies, as Mochitsura Hashimoto reported:

> ... I went to lie down on my bunk in the wardroom. ... Two-thirds of the crew were turned in. They slept completely naked on top of torpedoes, on top of the rice sacks, or between shelves. ... The remaining third of the crew were on watch, ... One must not forget the rats, which there were plenty![70]

The Japanese continued to use submarine-launched aircraft longer than other navies, despite the difficulties – low performance, and the need to stay surfaced and vulnerable for an hour or so during recovery. Midget submarines were used, but had no success in the Pearl Harbor attack. The Kaitens were another kind of suicide weapon: 'small submarines – or large torpedoes, depending on how one looked at them – fitted with a tiny compartment in which the pilot rode on his one-way mission.'[71] They were carried into action by a conventional submarine.

Paradoxically, the Japanese army, with its operations on Chinese coasts and estuaries in the 1930s, was ahead of the navy in the development of landing craft. *Shinsu Maru*, the world's first purpose-built landing ship, was built for the army in 1935 and could launch twenty landing craft through stern doors, but it was not repeated. More typically, infantry landing ships were usually converted merchantmen with landing craft nested three deep on the decks and hoisted out by crane. For the navy, the Daihatsu, known to the Americans as the Type A, used a fishing boat hull with a bow ramp and had capacity for up to ninety troops or a Type 98 tank. When adopted by the navy, it had a wheelhouse and part of the deck was covered. The larger version, the Toku Daihatsu, could land twice as many troops or two tanks. The Type E, as the Americans called it, driven by an aeroplane propeller, narrow and with a very shallow draught, was used to capture upriver Palembang from the Dutch.

Amphibious forces played a key role in the Japanese advances of 1941/2 through British-held Malaya and the Dutch East Indies. Typically, the troops landed on an isolated beach on an island or peninsula where road communications hardly existed, so control of the sea was vital, and they overwhelmed small Dutch or British garrisons. They were initially repulsed at Wake, which was defended by US marines, but returned with two fleet carriers and three heavy cruisers. Troops landed where the American guns could not be brought to bear and the marines were forced to surrender.

The Japanese had studied British progress in naval aviation during the First World War and in 1919, while the Anglo-Japanese Alliance was still in force, the Sempill mission arrived to train them. Several members became enamoured with Japan and spied for it in later years – Lord Sempill himself escaped prosecution because of his high connections. In the meantime, the Japanese navy was building *Hosho*, the first carrier to be built as such from the keel up, and some British ideas were incorporated in her design. Like her British near-contemporary, *Hermes*, she was used for training and experiments, though the Japanese made rapid progress while the British stagnated. The second carriers, *Akagi* and *Amagi*, were built on the hulls of battlecruisers banned at Washington, as in Britain and America. The Japanese were reluctant to adopt the island superstructure. It was only fitted to *Akagi* during a modernisation, was set to port and was very small. Smoke was discharged through funnels at flight deck level, which could be angled downwards during flying. *Hiryu* (1939) had a larger island, still to port, but that set up dangerous currents. *Shokaku* and *Zuikaku* had it to starboard but others dispensed with the island, until *Hiyo* and *Junyo* of 1942 had a funnel running through it, angled outwards. *Taiho* (1944) had a more conventional layout to Western eyes, not unlike the British *Illustrious* class, but it was sunk within three months of completion. Many of the Japanese carriers were conversions from merchant ships and submarine tenders, giving an improvised 'covered wagon' appearance in some cases.[72] Out of thirty-one completed, twenty were sunk.

The Japanese aircraft industry was largely independent of foreign designs by the mid 1930s, though the firms, including the big three, Mitsubishi, Nakajima and Kawasaki, were tightly controlled by the government. They produced nearly fifty-nine thousand aircraft during the war, a great achievement, but less than a quarter of the American total. Like most industries outside America, it was too dependent on skilled craftmanship, and Japan had no system of reserved occupations so key workers might volunteer for the fighting services, or be conscripted. The industry began a rapid downturn after the raids by B-29s started at the end of 1944. Jiro Horikoshi, the designer of the Zero fighter, was shocked to see the effects as he returned from sickness in May 1945: 'My former factory is a ghostly, steel-ribbed wreck, shattered by bombs and torn apart by the dispersal crews.' Plans to disperse the industry into underground tunnels merely caused more disruption.

The Mitsubishi Zero fighter was so called because it entered service in the year 2600 (1940) in the Japanese calendar – its Allied code name Zeke was rarely used. It pioneered the use of light alloys and had a competitive speed with superb manoeuvrability and range. It was beloved by pilots such as Kamane Harada: 'I thought the Zero was simply the best fighter in the world, and I trusted it. The fighter also looked very sleek, and the manoeuvrability was superb.'[73] But like most Japanese aircraft it lacked armour and self-sealing tanks, and it was poor in a dive. Eventually it was outclassed by new American types like the Hellcat, Corsair and Lightning, and replacements such as the Mitsubishi A7M Reppo and J2M Raiden did not materialise in time.

The Nakajima B5N, codenamed Kate by the Allies, was the best carrier-based torpedo bomber in the world in 1941, superior to the American Devastator and the British Swordfish; it did most of the damage at Pearl Harbor and struck the carriers *Lexington*, *Hornet* and *Yorktown* in later

The second wave of Aichi D3A1 (codenamed Val) dive-bombers about to take off from the carrier *Akagi* during the Pearl Harbor attack.

actions. The other attacker at Pearl Harbor, the Aichi D3A Val dive-bomber, was old-fashioned in having a spatted undercarriage like its contemporary, the Stuka. It was replaced by the Yokosuka D4Y Suisei, or Judy, in 1942/3. The twin-engined Mitsubishi G4M Betty was a land-based bomber with a crew of seven, noted for its long range. The Aichi E13A was a floatplane which could be catapulted from cruisers. The most common type of flying boat was the Kawasaki H6K, with four engines on a wing mounted on a pylon above the fuselage. The Kawasaki H8K had a much deeper fuselage and a superior performance to the British Sunderland and the American Sikorski XPBS-1.

Potential officer pilots were selected at the academy, like Yoshio Shiga, who 'became interested in being a pilot during my senior year ... after seeing a demonstration by a group of three fighter planes called "Genda's Circus."'[74] But the Imperial Japanese Navy relied far more on petty officer pilots than the British or Americans.

Takeshi Maeda, then PO 2nd class, recounted: 'Regarding the aviators I flew with during the Pearl Harbor attack, PO3c Yoshiro Yoshikawa, the pilot, was skilled in doing torpedo attacks, and PO2c Koji Ohjino, the navigator, was the plane captain. ... the three of us had been trained as a team and always worked together.'[75] As one flier commented: 'What's important in the world of naval aviators are your flying abilities, not your rank or number of lines on your good conduct badge. If you don't have good skills as an aviator, people would laugh behind your back.'[76]

Lieutenant Sadao Takai of the Genzan Air Corps described the torpedo attack against *Prince of Wales* and *Repulse*:

> We dropped below cloud level. We were on the side of the enemy battleship, which was just swinging in a wide turn. Our luck was good – no better chance would come!
>
> I pushed the throttles forward to reach maximum speed and flew just above the water. This time I yanked hard on the torpedo release. Over the thudding impact of bullets and shrapnel smashing into the airplane, I felt the strong shock through the bomber as the torpedo dropped free and plummeted into the water.

He would never know where his torpedo had hit and contributed to one of Britain's greatest naval defeats.[77]

The kamikaze was the most startling Japanese innovation during the war, to Western eyes at least – Admiral Nimitz later said that it was the only thing they did not predict. It arose largely by chance. In October 1944, as the Americans triumphed at Leyte Gulf, and Japanese resources in pilots and aircraft were depleted, Admiral Ohnishi told his officers: 'there is only one way of assuring that her meager strength will be effective to a maximum degree. That is to organise suicide attack units composed of Zero fighters armed with 250kg bombs, with each plane crash dive into an enemy carrier.'[78] Thus began the kamikaze force, named after the 'Divine Winds' that had dispersed Kublai Khan's invasion fleets in 1274 and 1281. It was also known as 'Special Attack', but according to one commander that was 'just a name. The tactic, while unusual in form, is just another way of performing our military obligation.'[79] After some delays the first attack was mounted:

> It was simple justice that Lieutenant Seki, who had been the first volunteer, should be the first to succeed. On four consecutive days he had sortied, only to return each time in miserable disappointment. But it was different the fifth time – on 25 October … The five bomb-laden planes, escorted by four Zero fighters, had located an enemy carrier task force. Each pilot had selected his target, and at a banking signal from Seki, who was in the lead, the planes plunged. Seki's plane hit first, at 10.45, striking squarely into a carrier.[80]

In the early days, pilots were more than willing to volunteer and those who were rejected were deeply disappointed: 'The requests of our best flyers … to become kamikaze pilots had to be denied. Such men were so urgently needed to guard the suicide planes that they could not be spared to pilot them'.[81] On the other hand, Petty Officer First Class Isao Matsuo wrote to his parents:

> Please congratulate me. I have been given a splendid opportunity to die. ... The destiny of our homeland hinges on the decisive battle in the sea to the south where I shall fall like a blossom from a radiant cherry tree. I shall be a shield for His Majesty and die cleanly along with my squadron leader and other friends. I wish that I could be born seven times, each time to smite the enemy.[82]

By the spring of 1945 pressure had to be applied, but those chosen, while reluctant at first, accepted the kamikaze ethos after a time. Ensign Teruo Kamaguchi wrote to his parents:

> I was selected quite unexpectedly to be a special attack pilot ... Once the order was given for my one-way mission it became my sincere wish to achieve success in fulfilling this last duty. Even so, I cannot help feeling strong attachment to this beautiful land of Japan. Is that a weakness on my part?[83]

According to Captain Rikhei Inoguchi:

> The indoctrination for the new Kamikaze Corps pilots lasted seven days. The first two days were spent exclusively in take-off practice. This covered the time from the moment the order to sortie was given until the planes of a unit were airborne and assembled. During the next two days, lessons were devoted to formation flying ... The last three days were given primarily to the study and practice of approaching and attacking at the target.[84]

The standard of pilot skill deteriorated over the months and eventually men were sent on raids with practically no training.

In the initial stage of special attack operations, a standard sortie consisted of three kamikaze and two escort planes, on a theory that each formation must be kept small for maximum mobility.[85] According to Rikhei Inoguchi, 'For such light and speedy planes as the Zero fighter ('Zeke') and the Suisei carrier bomber ('Judy'), two methods of approaching for a special attack were found to be most effective. The approach should be made either at extremely high or extremely low altitude.' In the latter case, the plane would approach at 10–15m height to avoid detection then rise to 400–500m to dive on the target.[86]

In the Leyte campaign the kamikazes were credited sinking thirty-seven ships, though American records suggested only sixteen, with a further eighty-seven damaged. But the shock effect was profound, as James A Fahey witnessed from his station at a gun in the cruiser *Montpelier*:

A photograph taken on board USS *Missouri*, off Okinawa in April 1945. A kamikaze, just visible in the top left-centre of the picture, is about to strike.

> Right off the bat a Jap plane made a suicide dive at the cruiser *St Louis*, there was a big explosion and flames were seen shortly from the stern. Another one tried to do the same thing but he was shot down. A Jap plane came in on a battleship with its guns blazing away. Other Jap planes came in strafing one ship, dropping their bombs and another and crashing into another ship. The Jap planes were falling all around us, the air was full of Jap machine gun bullets.[87]

At first, aircraft carriers were the main targets and it was considered best to aim at the central elevator as one of the weakest points. Later, transports were attacked, and then the radar picket destroyers which protected the rest of the fleet. Pilots were ordered to release their bomb safety catch only when the enemy was sighted, to avoid having to jettison the bomb if no target was found. But in the excitement, some forgot.

Kamikaze attack reached its peak during the Okinawa campaign of 1945, as Task Force 58 had to remain on station while the land battle dragged on. The Japanese navy and army co-operated for the first time and mounted ten different raids The first one on 6/7 April involved 230 navy planes and 125 army. American records show no carriers were sunk, but seven were damaged. The Japanese claimed a dozen battleships sunk and eighteen damaged, but the Americans only admitted ten damaged. In all sixteen ships were sunk and 185 damaged.

The Okha (Cherry Blossom), known to the Allies as the Baka, was a rocket-propelled single-seat suicide aircraft, made mainly in wood for mass production and intended as a last-ditch defence against invasion. It was carried in the bomb bay of a G4M2e Betty bomber, but that was too slow and the first raid of sixteen aircraft in March 1945 was intercepted and the Okhas had to be released too soon. It had its first success in the following month against an American destroyer. An improved version was designed to be fitted under the faster P1Y1 Ginga bomber and a further version used a turbojet, while the Model 43B was intended to be launched from a catapult at the mouth of a cave, but none of these entered service.[88]

Failure in anti-submarine technique was perhaps the weakest single point of Japanese naval power. According to Atushi Oi, who served in the Grand Escort Command Headquarters from 1943, it was partly a matter of 'racial temperament': 'Compared with the Europeans the Japanese are generally said to be more impetuous and less tenacious. They preferred colorful and intensive fighting to monotonous and defensive warfare. It was only natural that convoy escort and A/S warfare were not jobs welcomed by the Japanese naval men.'[89] Trade protection had played very little part in the wars with China, Russia and Germany, and it was only during the last conflict that Japan, once fanatically self-sufficient, had developed a export trade and become dependent on imported oil. That was an essential cause of the war but senior officers, obsessed with battleships, gave little thought on how to protect imports. And in the early stages of the war, the failure of American torpedoes meant that there was no immediate cause for concern. According to Atushi Oi:

> In peace time no A/S craft were built, in the expectation that they could be easily and quickly built after a war was actually declared. In 1941 when the construction of four frigates was first approved, these craft were intended to be used not as escort vessels but for coastal defence or fishery protection. ... Though frigates were later used, almost exclusively, as ocean escorts in the face of acute A/S problems, it was not until June 1943, that the building of 40 ships of the type was approved. And this belated approval does not seem to have been a willing one, judging by the fact that the A/S branch requested to have 360 of them built.[90]

This began to change, according to Atushi Oi, in August 1943, when 'we first realized that some innovation had come to the American submarine torpedoes', and sinkings rose alarmingly. Convoys were begun, but were very small to aid the flow of shipping – typically two to five ships with a single escort, which might have to decide whether to pursue a contact or stay with the convoy. In the spring of 1945 'large' convoys were instituted, ten to twenty ships with perhaps three escorts, but still tiny by Atlantic standards. Radar was still rare in escorts and American submarine commanders were often pleased to hear depth charges while they were actually on the surface. The Japanese did nothing to develop ahead-throwing weapons like the Hedgehog, and depth-charge attack was still the only means, as described by Tameichi Hara:

> My head was filled with calculations of bearings, angles, and distance. The answer came almost reflexively; 'The submarine is 180 degrees, or dead ahead, moving at 9 knots, now 1000 meters away, at a depth of 30 meters.' I ordered speed boosted to 21 knots, and looked at the second hand on my watch. I rapidly diagrammed the two ships' navigation curves. At 2158 we released eight depth charges when I believed the enemy sub was directly below. I put their *Amatsukaze* about and turned back, poised for another series of depth-charge attack. The surface of the sea gave a strong odour of diesel oil in the dark night. We could see nothing. The smell of oil grew stronger.[91]

He wrote the submarine off as sunk, though he was 'well aware of skunk tactics used by submarines under attack', by releasing oil to make the attackers believe they have been sunk. But Japanese commanders had a tendency to break off an attack too soon, on flimsy evidence. Furthermore, they failed to appreciate how deep American submarines could go, and set the charges wrongly. And liaison with aircraft was poor due to radio problems.

Japan had four main naval bases in the home islands. Yokosuka in the Tokyo Bay had been set up by the French engineer Bertin in the last century, and resembled his native port of Toulon. During the Second World War it employed forty thousand workers and occupied 280 acres. Maizuru was on the opposite side of the island of Honshu. Its location made it the main base during the Russo-Japanese War, but it was mothballed after 1923 and not reopened until 1936, when it was mainly used to service destroyers and smaller craft. Kure Naval Arsenal near Hiroshima in the Inland Sea was another project of Bertin's, and became the largest yard, building ships such as *Yamato*. It was heavily bombed with the loss of 1900 lives and the destruction of 70 per cent of buildings and equipment. Sasebo, near Nagasaki, on the southern tip of Honshu, was dominated by a 250-ton crane and took over the building of destroyers when Maizuru was closed. It employed fifty thousand workers during the Second World War.

Overseas, the Japanese built a huge base at Rabaul round the beautiful natural refuges of Simpson Harbour and Blanche Bay, with three airstrips added to the existing two, with underground hangars, workshops and barracks, defended by the great majority of nearly ten thousand troops stationed on New Britain. But the building of bases was far less efficient than with the Americans. The Americans and Japanese had very different approaches to building their bases in combat zones. The Japanese relied on manpower to clear jungles and build airstrips, while the Americans used large amounts of mechanical equipment to prepare the bases as quickly as possible. Moreover, the Japanese paid little attention to sanitation and suffered many casualties due to malaria and dysentery.

So, overall, the performance of the Japanese forces was uneven. The literally suicidal bravery was unique among all the combatants. Innovations in cruiser and destroyer design, torpedoes, naval aviation and amphibious warfare were accompanied with very significant gaps, especially in anti-submarine warfare. The Japanese war machine, typified by the highly flammable Zero fighter, was designed only for attack and quick victory, and ill-adapted for a long and defensive war in which the huge industrial resources of the United States came into play. And perhaps most of all, they grossly underestimated the resolve of the American people, especially after the Pearl Harbor attack.

The new Roman empire

Italy was the birthplace of Christopher Columbus, Amerigo Vespucci and Guglielmo Marconi. It had been the base of the Venetian navy, a dominant force in the early modern age, but the embryonic Italian fleet was decisively defeated at the battle of Lissa in 1866, arguably the first modern naval battle. It was on the winning side in the First World War, despite an ineffective performance against Austro-Hungary, but it resented the lack of gains with the Treaty of Versailles. That contributed to the rise of Mussolini, and the first Fascist state – they invented the term, based on the bundle of sticks and an axe carried as a symbol of the authority of a Roman emperor. A new empire dominating the Mediterranean, the *Mare Nostrum*, was Mussolini's aim – though as with most dictators, it is often difficult to separate rhetoric from actual plans.

Italy might have been a major sea power with its commanding position in the Mediterranean, long coastlines and numerous harbours, but it had a relatively small seafaring population, slender industrial resources, despite a world-class motor industry, and depended on imported iron and oil, with no obvious source of supply in wartime. And the position in the Mediterranean was a weakness as well as a strength. There was a fear that the navy might be 'imprisoned' within it, with British control of the Straits of Gibraltar and the Suez Canal.

Mussolini was never all-powerful like Hitler and Stalin. The king still retained influence, and the army was inclined to support him, while the state council had some power. Nevertheless, he usually took the initiative, as with the invasion of Abyssinia in 1936, which almost caused a war with Britain, intervention in the Spanish Civil War, and when he made an opportunist declaration of war on Britain and France, just as the latter was about to fall to the German onslaught. But the Italians were not motivated. In May 1943 Mussolini told Dönitz:

> ... the results of British air raids on Italy will be that the people will learn to hate the British ... If there is one Italian who hates the British he says it is he himself. He is happy that his people are now learning the meaning of the word hate as well.[92]

Sailors' morale was always poor, in a war which they had not wanted, and Edward Stafford noted among the prisoners of war in Oran, 'the Germans sullen and taciturn, the Italians smiling and loquacious.'[93] The 'Pact of Steel' signed by Hitler and Mussolini had formalised a ten-year alliance in 1939, but as often happens in such cases, the weaker partner took it more seriously than the stronger. The Germans were drawn into the campaign in Greece, though it was 'definitely a regrettable blunder on the part of the Italians.'[94] As Hitler stated in May 1943, 'The Axis must face the fact that it is saddled with Italy.'[95]

Italy did comparatively well in the Washington Treaty, with tonnage equal to that of France, but limited budgets meant that they did not attempt to build up to it until 1934. Naval policy in the immediate pre-war period was dominated by Admiral Cavagnari, a battleship man who was obsessed with Jutland, like many of his kind, and expected to win any war against Britain by a decisive fleet battle in the central Mediterranean. He did not encourage the building of aircraft carriers, which matched Mussolini's view that Italy was a giant carrier, and he took no interest in the light craft which would prove to be Italy's only success. Four battleships of the *Littorio* class were laid down. They were innovative ships in many ways, and exceeded the tonnage limitations set

A magazine cover celebrating Hitler's visit to Italy in May 1938, with Mussolini and King Victor Emmanuel to the left, onboard the battleship *Cavour*, and a view of a *Zara*-class cruiser passing as part of an elaborate naval manoeuvre.

by the treaties, but only two were ready when Italy entered the war and one was never completed.

The ships of the Italian navy were designed for a war against France, with whom there were disputes over imperialist expansion in Libya and Morocco. The navy lacked radar, aircraft carriers, anti-submarine and anti-aircraft ships, amphibious capability, night-fighting technique and suitable mines – all the trappings of modern naval warfare. Its ships were designed for speed and the cruisers were capable of 36–37 knots, but had only 70mm armour belts. The exception was the *Zara* class of 1929–32, which were well-balanced ships with 150mm belts, but with speed reduced to a more conventional 32 knots. To save weight, guns were mounted in pairs on single cradles, which tended to slow the rate of fire, and they were so close together that when both were fired, as was intended, one shell would interfere with the other. In destroyers, the *Navigatori* class 1922–30 had a speed of 38 knots, but tended to instability, wetness and poor habitability – less serious in the Mediterranean than in the ocean. The *Maestrale* and *Oriani* classes of 1934–36 were sounder, but less spectacular, and set the pattern for later ships. Other navies started off with ships designed on wrong premises, but were able to correct them during the war – Italy was short of shipbuilding resources so very few new ships were built. None of the thirteen cruisers lost was replaced, only five out of forty-five destroyers, sixteen out of forty-four torpedo boats, and forty-six out of 106 submarines. Only in minor vessels was there any increase, with 239 replacing 119 lost.[96]

The navy remained cautious. It did not invade Malta in 1940, when the island's defences were extremely weak – the island would remain a thorn in the Italian side for the rest of the war, despite being largely neutralised by bombing and shortage of supplies. The neglect of naval air power had its reward in November 1940 when carrier aircraft from HMS *Illustrious* damaged the battleships *Littorio*, *Caio Duilio* and *Conte di Cavour* in the confines of Taranto harbour. And the nearest approach to a general fleet action came in March 1941 off Cape Matapan when with the aid of aircraft, the Royal Navy sank three cruisers and two destroyers. The navy had inadequate support from its own air force, the *Reggio Aeronautica*, which was favoured by the government as a creation of the Fascist state and was firmly committed to the strategic bombing principles of its own Douhet – though it soon abandoned them after war started, without developing any ideas to replace them.

The main function of the navy was to protect the supply routes to the campaign in North Africa, which started from Italy's established colony of Libya and led to a see-saw campaign towards Egypt and the Suez Canal – 'this miserable business of transportation', as one admiral called it.'[97] It had to do this without the help of the Germans, for their surface ships could not penetrate the Straits of Gibraltar. It was quite successful: out of 896 convoys, 151 ships or 8.35 per cent were sunk.[98]

The Italian Naval Academy was situated in the Hospital of St James, originally built in 1640, in Livorno in northwest Italy, where 'speak the revered traditions of the sea: from the names of the Etruscan cities and from the ruined towers of the ancient Pisan port from which sailed the conquerors of the Saracens', according to its founding commandant in 1881. Cadets were trained in a three-year course to become line officers, engineers, ordnance supply and medical officers, as well as shore-based port captains. They spent their summers sailing in the full-rigged ships *Cristoforo Colombo* and *Amerigo Vespucci*, built in 1928 and 1931. Compared with Annapolis, according to an Italian officer, 'The cadets enjoy much less freedom, they are much more supervised and are treated less like grown men.'[99] Members of the *Corpo Reale Equipaggi Marittimi* were commissioned from enlisted rank and were only eligible for promotion to lieutenant. The line officers used traditional continental naval ranks such as *capitano di vascello*, *capitano di corvetta* and *tenente di vascello*; the corps officers had army titles such as *colonnella* and *maggiore*.

Some of the Italian submarines were in poor condition, such as *Vettor Pisani* of 1927:

> She was an old ship back on, with many wheezy whims, and leaking all over the place; to take her on war missions was quite a feat … In order to deal with the infiltration of water through the hull, a reserve stock of rubber hose was kept in every compartment of the submarine and used for conveying the water as it entered direct to one of the trimming tanks …[100]

Others were poorly designed, according to Aldo Cocchio: 'Unfortunately, Italian submarines are equipped with conning towers of truly prodigious size, which provided space for galleys, lavatories and what have you. … the bridge was in fact dominated by two massive periscope housings to which were attached the radio aerials and a short mast.'[101]

However, the submarines constituted the only attempt to break out of the 'prison' of the Mediterranean. Twenty-seven of them avoided British patrols in the dangerous passage through the Straits of Gibraltar. Under German command, they mostly operated off the Azores, where the weather was suitable for the inexperienced crews. Though they boosted numbers when the U-boat force was at a low ebb, Dönitz was dismissive: 'The overall effect of the Italian boats remained slight.'[102]

The navy was far more successful with its 'human torpedoes'. The 'pig' was described by its inventor:

> The new weapon is in size and shape very similar to a torpedo but is in reality a miniature submarine with entirely novel features, electrical propulsion and a steering wheel similar to that of an

aeroplane. … the crew, instead of remaining enclosed and more or less helpless in the interior, keep outside the structure. … at night, under cover of the most complete darkness and steering by luminous controlled instruments, they will be able to … attack their objective while remaining quite invisible to the enemy. The operators …. are free to move and act at will, to reach the bottom of the sea and travel along it …, and able to cut nets and remove obstacles with special compressed-air tools and therefore reach any target.[103]

The navy took over Villa Carmela, nominally inhabited by Antonio Ramognino and his retiring wife, in neutral Algeciras opposite the British base of Gibraltar, but in fact a base for human torpedo operations, while the weapons themselves were hidden in a wrecked merchant ship in the bay. Several raids were mounted, attaching limpet mines to the hulls of Allied merchant ships.

The raid on Alexandria in December 1941, mounted by three 'pigs' carried by the submarine *Scire*, was the most spectacular naval success of Italy's war. The veteran battleships *Valiant* and *Queen Elizabeth* were both sunk (though not fatally), along with a large tanker. Luigi de la Penne was taken prisoner after fixing the charges and held onboard *Valiant*. He told the captain that they were about to explode and described his reaction when they did: 'The vessel reared, with extreme violence. All

An Italian human torpedo of a type which had some success in Alexandria Harbour, and was the model for the British 'Chariots'.

the lights went out in a hold became filled with smoke. I was surrounded by shackles which had been hanging from the ceiling and had now fallen. ... The vessel was listing to port.'[104] President Roosevelt was impressed. In Parliament, Winston Churchill described the operation as being conducted with 'extraordinary courage and ingenuity', and the Royal Navy began the development of similar weapons.

The Italian navy did very little to obstruct the invasion of Sicily in 1943, and the Fascist regime collapsed soon afterwards. The fleet surrendered, and Admiral Cunningham signalled his superiors in London: 'Be pleased to inform their Lordships that the Italian battlefleet now lies at anchor under the guns of the fortress of Malta' – the culmination of a record of failure.[105]

18
Allies

THE BRITISH like to believe that they 'stood alone' against German aggression in 1941/2, though that was never literally true. Even when they lost their Allies, they had support from the Commonwealth and were able to support 'free' forces by land sea and air, which sometimes had a substantial effect on the war, but their contribution was often complex, and efficiency was highly variable.

Lost Allies

Various countries fell to German attacks in 1939–41. Most formed governments in exile, based in London. Usually part of the fleet escaped and formed the nucleus of a free navy, which was supplemented by ships built in Britain and manned by officers and crews who still sailed under their national flag, wore their national uniform and were subject to the naval laws and discipline of their home country. They tended to have high morale because of the often unprovoked attacks on their homelands, and some made substantial contributions to operations. Perhaps even more importantly, they promoted the idea of a united world effort against the Axis powers and helped maintain the pride of their native countries in extremely hard times.

Poland had been partitioned by her powerful neighbours in the eighteenth century and was only restored as a state in 1919. Her access to the Baltic Sea, the Polish Corridor, was the cause of the war in 1939. She was quickly overrun by Germany and the Soviet Union, but Poles had a long tradition of fighting from exile. The Polish-designed, British-built destroyers *Błyskawica* and *Grom* were already in British waters and the submarine *Orzeł* made an epic voyage, escaping internment in Estonia and using charts drawn from memory to get out of the Baltic. Churchill broadcast in March 1940: 'when these Polish sailors have finished their work with the British Navy we will take particular care that they once more have a home to go to.'[1] Eight Polish merchant vessels helped with the Dunkirk evacuation. New warships were added, including one French and three British-built destroyers, three Hunt-class escorts,

The celebrated Polish submarine *Orzeł* flying the national flag from her bow, with part of the crew on deck.

and two British and one American submarine. The largest ship was the cruiser *Dragon* of 1918, lost during the Normandy invasion and replaced by *Conrad*, ex-*Danae*. After losing four destroyers, two submarines and several other craft, it remained a small force, with 3840 men at the end of the European war, compared with more than 170,000 Polish soldiers. It never achieved the fame of Polish aircrews, but it set the pattern for navies of defeated nations operating under a government in exile.

The Poles fought in a wide range of actions as described by the First Lord of the Admiralty: 'In view of its small size, and the number of operations in which the Polish Navy has taken part is almost incredible ... Narvik, Dunkirk, Lofoten Islands, Tobruk, Dieppe, attacks on enemy shipping in the Channel, Sicily, Italy, Oran, patrols notably in the Mediterranean, and convoy escorting.'[2] They were especially motivated and much respected by the Royal Navy.

The advancing Soviet army occupied the whole of Poland by 1945, so it was perhaps inevitable, despite Churchill's promise of March 1940, that there would be some concession at the Yalta Conference – but more than that, the Soviets were eventually allowed to take over the country as a satellite state. The London government in exile was disavowed and the armed force were left in limbo, in what many regard as one of the greatest betrayals of the war.

Norway was neutral before the war and had a very small navy, including four old coast defence vessels, all launched by 1900. Four of the seven destroyers were relatively new, but small at less than 600 tons. The twenty-six torpedo boats were also old, dating from 1917 or earlier and ranged from 220 to 45 tons. There were eleven minelayers, the largest and newest of nearly 1600 tons and launched in 1933. The nine submarines were also old. Based mainly at Horten in Oslo Fjord, the navy included 1600 men at the start of the war, augmented by the crews of requisitioned fishing boats.

Norway was quickly overrun by German forces in 1940, though the common belief that the fifth column of Vidkun Quisling undermined the defence does not bear examination. Several German ships were damaged, mainly by coastal defence guns. King Haakon and the royal family escaped in the cruiser *Devonshire* to provide a focus for resistance. He was not the only one:

> Many thousands of Norwegians had found themselves in exile with the king, and thousands more had followed him, escaping from Norway in fishing boats, yachts, small steamers and even through rowing boats across the North Sea. ... But in Norway there still remained a large army, disorganised and disbanded and only partly trained, but still ready to risk a lot to drive the Germans out of the country.[3]

Thirteen warships escaped, including the destroyers *Sleipner* and *Draug*, the submarine *B-1*, two gunboats and eight trawlers. Motor torpedo boats already under order were added, along with minesweepers and four of the 'four-piper' American destroyers, followed by corvettes. Men could be found from the extensive Norwegian merchant fleet, which was distributed around the world when the attack came.

More famous in retrospect was the Norwegian Naval Independent Unit, or the 'Shetland Bus', which in fact had no connection with the regular navy and was manned by fishermen. None of them were considered suitable to be commissioned, but skippers were put into uniform as petty officers and the rest as seamen; however, they knew little of naval discipline. Under the British Special Operations Executive they maintained links between Norway and their base at Lunna, Shetland. The best known of them was Leif Larsen, who escaped by fishing boat in February 1941 and made fifty-two trips across the North Sea. He skippered the fishing boat *Arthur* during the attempt to sink *Tirpitz* by human torpedo in 1942, was awarded an exceptional array of decorations, and was described as 'one of the most remarkable personalities of the entire Second World War.'

The unit was allocated three subchasers by the American navy to supplement the fishing boats. They were manned by twenty-two men each, and Larsen and another fishing skipper were commissioned to take charge of them, along with a regular officer. Though the fishermen 'hardly knew enough drill to march in step ... and had the most rudimentary ideas of naval etiquette', they learned to use them after a week's training.[4] In all, the unit landed nearly 400 tons of armaments and picked up 350 refugees, as well as keeping the Germans on edge and feeding Hitler's paranoid fear of an invasion in that area.

The history of the French navy stands alongside that of the British. It was briefly superior in the 1690s, but soon overtaken, and had little success in fleet battles, up to the disaster at Trafalgar. As a result it turned to commerce raiding, though that was condemned by Mahan the naval evangelist, 'even for its special ends such a mode of war is inconclusive, worrying but not deadly'.[5] But major warships such as *Jean Bart*, *Duguay-Trouin* and *Surcouf* were named after privateer captains. The French built the first iron battleship, *Gloire* of 1860, though that was soon overtaken. In the First World War it took part in the unsuccessful Dardanelles Campaign, but otherwise it was confined to Mediterranean patrols and escorting troop convoys from North Africa, while the French army suffered catastrophic casualties before victory on the Western Front. In the Washington Treaty, it was allocated three-tenths of British and American tonnage, half that of Japan and equal to Italy – though France had a vast empire with colonies in the Caribbean, north and West Africa and. The navy began to revive under Minister of Marine Georges Leygue, succeeded on his death in 1933 by François Darlan, a powerful figure for whom the rank of admiral of the fleet was specially created.

The French navy operated on the Atlantic and Mediterranean coasts. It had its great and historic bases at Brest and Toulon, a nineteenth-century one at Cherbourg, and the main overseas one at Mers-el-Kébir, near Oran in North Africa. In 1936 the navy had 2340 *officiers de marine*, almost half the officer corps. They were mostly trained in the Ecole Navale at Brest, 'an imposing building on a hilltop visible for miles around'.[6] According to American observers, the education was general, with comparatively little on technicalities. They were the *Grand Corps*, eligible to command ships. Father tended to follow son and they were generally conservative, even by military standards, and often anti-British. In the *Petit Corps*, the 516 *ingénieurs méchaniciens* were shipboard engineers, while the 225 officers of the *Génie Maritime* were naval architects, who would have been civilians in most other navies. There were 464 medical officers, 231 in the commissariat, 155 ordnance officers, thirty-one surveyors and 392 for *musique et train*, or music and supply. There were very few reserves, so the navy would not expand much on the onset of war. For its lower deck, the *Marine Nationale* relied less on conscription in its usual form than the other French services: under the *Inscrits Maritime*, professional seamen were expected to serve four years with the merchant or fishing fleet and one in the navy on a rotating basis. Others were volunteers, some came from the *écoles professionales* and others changed service. Matelots might rise through the grades for *quartier-maître* to *maître principal*.

The rise of Hitler caused an uneasy alliance with Britain. In September 1939 the French navy was the fourth largest in the world, with five old battleships, two fast battleships and two new light battleships with 13in guns. The only aircraft carrier, *Béarn*, completed in 1927 on a battleship hull, was too slow for fleet work and saw no active service. There were nineteen heavy and eight light cruisers, twenty-four destroyers, thirty-nine torpedo boats and eighty submarines including the massive *Surcouf*, with an 8in gun and an aircraft. The navy escorted convoys and took part in the disastrous Norway campaign of 1940. Unlike the army and the air force, it took no blame for the national defeat that year and it played its part in evacuating 338,000 troops, a third of them French, from the beaches of Dunkirk. The Vichy regime, including much of central France and the Mediterranean coast, was set up under German patronage, with Darlan as prime minister and Marshal Pétain as head of state.

The regime had an impossible dilemma – to maintain relations with the conquerors while preventing the fleet falling into the hands of the Germans. Darlan's word was not good enough for Churchill: in July 1940 he ordered the powerful Force H to Mers-el-Kébir, near Oran, where the bulk of the fleet was concentrated. The terms of capitulation proved impossible for the French Admiral Gensoul to accept. Force H was ordered to open fire, which horrified the navy from top to bottom. To Admiral Somerville in charge of the operation, 'the idea of slaughtering our former allies (or being slaughtered by them) was most repugnant.'[7] Stoker Vernon Coles commented: 'It was a sad irony,' but went on, 'What a bombardment! I had never seen anything like it.'[8] But Somerville thought the lower deck attitude was 'they never 'ad no use for them French bastards.'[9] The battleship *Bretagne* blew up, *Dunkerque* and *Provence* were severely damaged, along with smaller ships, but *Strasbourg* and five destroyers escaped to Toulon so the object was not fully achieved. Nearly two thousand French sailors were killed and great resentment was created. Three cruisers and three destroyers escaped from Toulon in September and passed through the Straits of Gibraltar due to a failure in the British command structure. They were instrumental in preventing a

The French battleship *Strasbourg* under attack by the Royal Navy at Mers-el-Kébir on 3 July 1940 – an event which soured relations between the two navies.

takeover of the West African colony of Dakar. But in the end, the Vichy regime did keep its word – when Germany invaded the remaining part of France at the end of 1942, it did indeed scuttle the ships left at Toulon.

The operation of July 1940 went better in Alexandria, where Admiral Cunningham was able to reach agreement with the French admiral. In Operation Catapult, French ships in British ports were brutally boarded and their crews were initially treated almost like prisoners of war.

Meanwhile, Brigadier General Charles de Gaulle, junior war minister in the collapsing French government, reached Britain and broadcast on the BBC on 14 July: 'France, although divided and pillaged, has not lost.' Churchill recognised him as leader of Free French forces which would continue the fight. Admiral Émile Muselier, a classmate of Darlan, escaped from Marseilles to Gibraltar in a British collier to take command of the *Forces Navales Française Libres*, or FNFL. He was as difficult to deal with as de Gaulle and much senior to him in military rank. He was replaced in April 1942.

Of thirty-five thousand French military personnel in Britain when the armistice was signed, the great majority chose to be repatriated via Morocco. There were a few French ships, including the battleship *Courbet* which served as a floating barracks and anti-aircraft ship at Portsmouth, three destroyers and torpedo boats seized during Operation Catapult, five submarines, including the mighty *Surcouf* and *Narval* which joined the force at Malta, plus five corvettes and sixteen auxiliaries.

Recruitment to the force was slow to start with: only about a thousand men had joined in August 1940, rising to 3300 by the end of the year, half of them navy veterans, the others merchant seamen or civilians. It had increased to 5700 officers and men by the end of 1942. They were allowed to retain their uniforms and flags, including the Cross of Lorraine which Muselier had designed, but they would serve under British command. Eventually, nine British-built Flower-class corvettes were added to the force, along with a dozen Fairmile motor launches and eight Vosper MTBs. Though they never achieved fame as the Free French Army did at Bir-Hakeim and the liberation of Paris, they saw a good deal of active service. The destroyer *Leopard* and the corvettes escorted Atlantic convoys. *Surcouf* was sunk by collision in the Caribbean, but the other submarines laid minefields and landed commandos off the coast of Norway. Three ships arrived separately in the Pacific to patrol Micronesia and escort convoys. Four Fairmiles were lost in the raid on St-Nazaire in 1942, and an expedition led by Muselier secured the support of the island of St Pierre et Miquelon off the Canadian coast in 1941, to the annoyance of Roosevelt. In all, 567 sailors were reported lost or missing before the FNFL was merged with Vichy forces in August 1943.[10] It was a tiny force, about 3.5 per cent of the French navy at the start of the war and minuscule compared with the British navy, not to mention the American, but it did achieve its object of salvaging French pride on the high seas.

During the Anglo-American invasion of North Africa, General Eisenhower reached a rather controversial deal with Admiral Darlan, who was soon assassinated by an unforgiving opponent of the Vichy regime. But the new French navy would take part in the liberation of the country, supplying two light cruisers for shore bombardment, a Hunt-class destroyer, which carried de Gaulle to his homeland on the French national day, three frigates and three trawlers.

The Netherlands (then known as the United Provinces and later popularly as Holland) was a major sea power in the seventeenth century, vying with England with some success. It declined due to the threat of invasion by France, and because ever larger ships could not navigate the Dutch ports until the country's great civil engineering industry improved them in the nineteenth century. The country had a large and efficient shipbuilding industry and a major merchant fleet. It remained determinedly neutral, hosting conferences at The Hague in 1899 and

1907 which regulated the rules of warfare. It managed to stay out of the First World War and offered refuge to the Kaiser at its end.

The Dutch had a vast empire in the East Indies comprising the islands of Java, Sumatra and Celebes and large parts of Borneo and New Guinea, as well as thousands of smaller islands. Unlike most empires of the period, it was highly profitable, supplying the world with oil, rubber, tin and other strategic goods, and giving the homeland the highest standard of living in Europe. This was badly hit by the Great Depression, which affected naval budgets even more than in other countries. The main function of the *Koninklijke Marine* was to defend the East Indies against the rising power of Japan, leaving only light forces in home waters. It would be impossible to defend the three-thousand-mile range of the archipelago, so the strategy, advocated by Admiral Furstner, was to form task forces to raid Japanese lines of communication in co-operation with the British and Americans, and thus deter an attack. A planned battlecruiser similar to *Scharnhorst* was halted by the German invasion; if completed, it would probably have shared the fate of *Prince of Wales* and *Repulse*. Light cruisers included the *Java* class of 1926 and *De Ruyter* (1942), which was considered inferior to the British *Leander* class. The destroyers of the Admiralen class of 1930 were unique, in that originally they carried floatplanes to be lowered into the water, but that proved impracticable. They were succeeded by the *Gerard Callenburgh* class, including *Isaac Sweers*. Submarines, including the seven ships of the *O21* class of 1939–41, were another part of the plan.

Despite its difficulties, the Dutch navy produced two game-changing innovations. The Hazemeyer triaxial mount was the best system available at the start of the war for stabilising an anti-aircraft gun. It was fitted to the minelayer *Willem van der Zaan* and adopted by the British after she fled in 1940. The Dutch had tested the *snuiver*, or snorkel, as early as 1916, and it was fitted in the *O19* and *O21* classes of submarine which were built in 1936–40. The Germans later took up the idea, and if they had done so sooner it might have affected the outcome of the war.

When the Germans invaded without warning on 10 May 1940, only the destroyer *Van Galen* offered resistance by sailing up the Nieuwe Waterweg canal towards Rotterdam and shelling German positions. The cruisers *Sumatra* and *Jacob van Heemskerck* sailed to British ports, and the uncompleted destroyer *Isaac Sweers* was towed across and joined by several submarines. Other ships were scuttled. Queen Wilhelmina fled to Britain and set up a government in exile. Some of the cadets of the naval college at Den Helder were evacuated in the cargo ship *Westland* and the minesweeper *Medusa*. On arrival at Portsmouth they were treated to 'an extensive English tea, a meal which was taken in a very large hall on the walls of which were pictures of the great battles Nelson fought.'[11] Studies continued, modelled on Dartmouth, despite the lack of Dutch textbooks and all the evacuated cadets were serving afloat by 1942.[12]

The East Indies colonies recognised the exiled government, as did the navy, but the resources of the area were tempting to the Japanese, and indeed the oil was their main motivation for beginning the Pacific war. When Pearl Harbor was attacked, the Dutch government declared war right away. The East Indies Fleet contained the cruisers *De Ruyter, Java, Sumatra* and *Tromp*, seven destroyers and fifteen submarines. They formed part of the ABDA (American, British, Dutch, Australian) command, but a force under Admiral Doorman was heavily defeated in the Battles of the Java Sea in February 1942 with the loss of the cruisers *De Ruyter* and *Java* and several destroyers, along with the British *Exeter*. The East Indies were taken over by the Japanese. Dutch submarines had some successes, but most were scuttled or fled to Australia. *Tromp* was the only major survivor of the ill-conceived campaign.

A new Dutch navy was formed in European waters and gunboats took part in the invasion of Sicily in 1943 with corvettes and frigates in the Battle of the Atlantic and in the invasion of Normandy. As the European war came to an end, there were plans for a revived Dutch fleet in the East Indies.

Belgium had only a small coast defence force when the country was overrun in 1940, and the government refused to allow even these ships to be transferred to Britain, so they were taken over by the Germans or sought refuge in Spain. The *Section Belge* continued to fight on, recruiting men serving on merchant ships and fishermen. Three trawlers took part in the Dunkirk evacuation and the corvettes *Buttercup* and *Godetia* were manned by Belgians, along with the 118th Minesweeping Flotilla.

The Greek navy was old-fashioned by any standards in 1940, having been acquired mainly to fight the Turks before the First World War. It included two ex-American pre-dreadnought battleships, an armoured cruiser of 1910 and several old destroyers – though four relatively new ones had been in Italy in 1931 and two more in Britain in 1939. Mussolini's opportunistic invasion was successfully resisted with the navy, especially the six French-built submarines, disrupting transport across the Straits of Otranto. But when Hitler reluctantly came to the aid of his embarrassing ally in April 1941, the Greek army was defeated, despite British aid, and the navy was largely sunk, including the two battleships by Stukas in Piraeus Harbour. However, the old cruiser *Giorgio Averof* escaped to Egypt with three destroyers and five submarines to form the core of the

Free Greek Navy. They were supplemented by British-built destroyers, escorts and smaller craft. *Averof* escorted convoys through the Red Sea to India. After the Mediterranean was largely cleared in 1943, two destroyers supported the Normandy invasion.

The Soviet Union

The Russian navy was founded by Peter the Great after a visit to Amsterdam and London in 1698 and the city of St Petersburg (later Leningrad) was built to give access to the sea. The navy was heavily defeated by the Japanese at the Battle of Tsushima in 1905, followed by the *Potemkin* mutiny and a failed revolution. Mutiny by the sailors at Kronstadt helped to trigger the initial revolution of 1917. The cruiser *Aurora* shelled the Winter Palace during the Bolshevik Revolution later in the year. The Soviet Union, product of that revolution, took over most of the extensive territory of the old Tsarist empire, but remained a pariah state devastated by civil war. Joseph Stalin, now established as dictator, initiated the first Five Year Plan in 1928 with aims to build industry and improve education, both of which were essential to a strong navy. The navy suffered heavily from Stalin's purges of 1938, with about three thousand officers killed, imprisoned or dismissed, resulting in fast promotion for many, including Nikolai Kuznetsov to People's Commissar of the Navy. The officers who survived tended to support Stalin's idea of a large blue-water navy, but that was never to be realised until much later. Commands were given to very young men, with the youngest fleet commander aged only thirty-five, and most of them were insecure in the role. Allied officers tended to discount the Russian navy as ill-trained, ill-equipped, bureaucratic and over-cautious – not without reason. It had practically no role in the oceanic warfare. Soviet fleets operated in five main areas, which were almost self-contained, despite efforts to build ship canals and open up the Arctic route.

The Northern Fleet, based at Polyarnoe and Murmansk, was neglected before the war as the region was isolated and undeveloped. It supported the British and American supply convoys, but only in the last stage of the voyage when close to Russian ports. It operated against German attempts to disrupt in the Arctic region and staged largely ineffective raids against German forces in Norwegian waters. The Baltic fleet was the strongest and had some combat experience in the war against Finland in 1939/40. After the invasion of 1941 it outnumbered the Germans, who did not deploy their major sea power in the region, but was used cautiously and retreated into the Gulf of Finland. After that it fought for the possession of islands and supplied the naval base of Kronstadt, helped to maintain the outpost at Oranienbaum, and played a major role in defending the besieged city of Leningrad where the battleship *Marat* was sunk but continued to use its guns.

The Black Sea Fleet also suffered from the loss of its bases to the German advance, but the attackers had great difficulty in getting naval forces into the sea. Like other navies early in the war, the Soviets became experts at evacuation. They got eighty-six thousand soldiers and fifteen thousand civilians out of Odessa. They were less successful at Sevastopol, which fell after a 250-day siege. In their largest amphibious operation, they landed forty-two thousand men on the Kerch peninsula using fourteen major warships but no specialised landing craft. Inland, the Soviet Fleet operated on Lake Lagoda and the Dnieper and Don Volga rivers, in which they maintained a bridgehead during the siege of Stalingrad.

The Pacific Fleet was based at Vladivostok, which was reached by a week-long journey on the Trans-Siberian railway. It was based on the shores of a curved inlet, Golden Horn Bay. It claimed to have deterred Japanese aggression in the region in the 1930s with its submarine fleet, but since the Soviet Union remained neutral against Japan, it played no part in it until the declaration of war at the very end.

Officers were selected from those with a 'ten-year school' education, as distinct from those who had only had seven years. Kuznetsov describes an early course in Leningrad:

> I spent four years in the naval school. In winter we attended classes and in summer we sailed in ships. We learnt seamanship from the start. We were taught to clean the deck, polish the copper, and keep watch as beginners. But with every passing year our duties became more and more complicated.[13]

The navy continued to rely on Tsarist officers for many years and the system of political commissars was set up to supervise them. To American eyes, the training was highly technical, with nothing on the broader issues. At the beginning of the war the school was moved to an isolated site near Baku, away from the German advance, but with the Caspian Sea for training. According to American observers, there was much emphasis on navigation and some of the equipment was good:

> ... students are seated at long tables. Between each two students are mounted a gyro repeater, engine room counter and clock. The instructor changes the course of speed from a control station, simulating tracking or dead reckoning exercises at high speed in close waters. Each student plots a track on his chart taking into account the currents and winds.[14]

Enlisted men were mostly recruited by conscription, and in peacetime they had to serve three or five years in the navy, compared with two years in the army. According to the American observers:

> In the Red Navy, as in the British, greater dependence is placed in 'enlisted' men in the supervision and maintenance of special equipment. Red Navy petty officers are sent to shore schools for considerable periods to master below-decks specialities – in the case of radio as long as two years. The officers, in general, apparently function more exclusively in the capacity of administrators than in the US Navy and bend most of the efforts to keeping the ship off the rocks, while the petty officers keep the engines and radio functioning.[15]

Despite Stalin's grand plans, the Soviet fleet only had three old battleships in 1941 and they hardly left port during the war. In 1944 they were lent the old British battleship *Royal Sovereign*, renamed *Arkhangelsk*, which sortied on convoy duty, but was narrowly missed by a torpedo and remained at anchor after that. The Soviet navy had seven cruisers at the start of the war, at least two of them very outdated, and three more entered service during the conflict. Distributed between the Baltic, Black Sea and Pacific, they played a role in defending the besieged cities of Leningrad, Odessa and Sevastopol and supported the Soviet advance by shore bombardment.

At the time of the German invasion the Soviet Navy had seven destroyer leaders and forty-seven destroyers, with the largest number in the Baltic Fleet. They were all relatively new and the majority were of the *Gnevnyi* class, based on Italian designs, with all the faults including structural weakness and poor seakeeping, compounded by the fitting of a heavier armament of 130mm guns. They were followed by the *Storozhevoi* class, with stronger hulls and more powerful engines. They suffered heavily from mining and bombing in the Black Sea. The extensive Soviet submarine fleet of more than two hundred boats was its greatest failure. For the loss of ninety of its own number it only sank ninety-one Axis merchant vessels, including three at the very end of the war in the Baltic, killing thousands of retreating Germans. A large fleet of around 388 motor torpedo boats was built up, more than half of them in the Pacific, where they had no effect on the war. There were eighty minesweepers at the beginning of the war and many more were built or supplied under lend-lease, but the Soviets were slow to learn how to deal with influence mines, to their cost.

The resistance of the Soviet people made the USSR highly popular in Britain and the United States. The Humphrey Bogart film *Action in the North Atlantic* did not mention Britain at all, apart from a brief glimpse of a red ensign. Instead, it highlighted the role of American merchant seamen in supporting the Soviet Union. But internally, the Communist revolution was played down. It was known as the Great Patriotic War and Tsarist uniforms, ranks and decorations were revived. The Soviet Union played an essential, and often ignored, role at enormous cost in in winning the land war against Germany, but it was often a liability in oceanic affairs, with the need to run highly dangerous convoys in its support. But though it could have been far more efficient, the Soviet navy played a part in the Allied victory.

Commonwealth and Empire

Britain was unique among the colonial powers in exporting a large volume of population thereby creating countries – Canada, Australia and New Zealand – which were dominated by educated, English-speaking, white people, with largely powerless indigenous minorities. All were fully independent by this time, but remained loyal to the British Crown and had no hesitation in supporting Britain's wars. With the implicit racism of the times, this meant that they were considered capable of producing effective navies, while other colonies produced ground troops.

The empire's contribution to British naval power had been controversial for most of the century. Churchill was deeply disappointed in 1912 when the Canadian parliament refused finance for three battleships. After the First World War, Admiral Jellicoe was sent round to get opinions. The idea of a unified naval force was only supported by New Zealand and Newfoundland and was dropped. Dominions were urged to develop fuelling facilities, but the main agreement was that they should build and train their navies to British standards. The uniforms were identical to the British ones, except for the buttons worn by officers and petty officers, incorporating the name of the country in the case of Canada and Australia, and a complex star design for India, and sometimes with shoulder flashes, or 'mudguards', with the name of the country.

But financially the standard was uneven. In 1922 the British government spent the equivalent of £1.50 per head on the navy, Australia 49 pence, New Zealand 20 pence, Canada 9 pence and South Africa 3½p.[16] The situation became more complex as the Second World War approached. Unlike the last one, it would not be dominated by a single theatre of naval action, and Australia and New Zealand were directly under threat in the middle years of the war.

Australia was colonised by the British from 1786, firstly as a penal colony. The Gold Rush of 1851 increased the population, and a strong export market in wool was developed, encouraging migration from Britain. In 1900 the five colonies of Queensland, New South Wales, Victoria, South Australia and Western Australia came together to form the Commonwealth of Australia, with a government modelled on British practice. Though usually classed as a continent, Australia is also an island with more than twelve thousand miles of coastline, all usable by shipping, except that the Great Barrier Reef restricted access to the east coast. Its area was almost equal to that of the United States, though most of the interior or 'outback' was desert, and it had a population of less than seven million in 1936/7. It already had a strong beach culture; John Collins of the RAN helped to rescue two girls off Cornwall in 1933 and commented modestly that it was 'a standard affair such as happens at Bondi any afternoon.'[17] Immigration, mostly from Britain, had declined sharply during the 1930s, so the newly arrived 'pommie' (supposedly shortened from pomegranate, rhyming slang for immigrant) was much rarer. Most Australians were fanatical about sport, and the 'bodyline' tactics used by the English cricketers during their tour of 1931/2 led to near riots, and a real risk of a trade war; some of the bitterness still lingered in 1939. Nevertheless, they accepted the aristocratic Lord Gower as governor general and King's representative.

In 1926 the Australian government stated:

> The guiding principle on which all our defence preparations are based, … is uniformity in every respect – organisation, methods of training, equipment &c – with the fighting services of Great Britain, in order that in time of emergency we may dovetail into any formation with which our forces may be needed to co-operate.[18]

The Royal Australian Navy was ruled by a naval board modelled on the British Admiralty and under the Minister of State for Defence. At the outbreak of war, the First Naval Member was Admiral Sir Ragnar Colvin, until he was succeeded by Sir Guy Royle, another Briton, in 1940. The Second Naval Member was responsible for personnel and stores, the Third for ship construction. In addition there was a rear admiral commanding the Australian Squadron. From 1942 to 1944 the post was held by Rear Admiral Sir Victor Crutchley, son of a royal courtier, who had won the Victoria Cross in the last war and commanded *Warspite* with great success at the Battle of Narvik.

The RAN had served well in the First World War, sinking the German raider *Emden* in 1914 and providing the battlecruiser *Australia* to augment the Grand Fleet. Australia was hard hit by the economic crisis of 1929, but its navy began to revive in 1933, building up 'from bedrock' according to the Minister of Defence. In 1937 the prime minster, Joseph Lyons, stated that the navy was the 'first line of defence, with the Army and Air Force supplementing and cooperating.' This was not unchallenged; the Labour Party favoured a policy of isolation, but with a strong air force. But expansion went ahead, the naval budget increased to over £20 million, two new Tribal-class destroyers and some motor boats were to be built, and anti-submarine defences were set up round the major ports. The question of acquiring a capital ship was even considered. But it had to be admitted: 'we cannot, single-handed, defeat a powerful aggression.'[19] British support was considered essential and the base at Singapore was a key part of that.

Cruisers were at the centre of the Australian navy, for they could cope with the long distances in the Pacific. HMAS *Australia* was built on the Clyde and served for twenty-eight years. She was 'a good ship', though her 8in turrets had 'more than their fair share of teething troubles.'[20] *Canberra,* another heavy cruiser, was lost after the Battle of Savo Island in 1942.

Shropshire was given to the RAN as a replacement, and King George decided to keep her original name, in accordance with Australian wishes. At first she was something of a lame duck, until it was discovered that one of her thrust-blocks had been wrongly fitted. After that, 'she "ran like a sewing machine for the rest of her life"; and she "handled like a picket boat"'.[21] In addition, there were four light cruisers at the start of the war. In 1933 the flotilla leader *Stuart* and four old destroyers sailed from Britain to join the fleet.

The *Bathurst* class of minesweepers was designed because, unlike Britain, Australia had no large fleet of trawlers to requisition. They proved very successful, not only in local areas but ocean-wide, and more than fifty of them were built: 'Simplicity was the watchword, reciprocating engines, one gun, elementary control, but good anti-submarine and minesweeping capability.'[22] The first venture in naval aviation was the seaplane carrier *Albatross*, built locally but paid off in 1933. However, aircraft were needed for launching from cruisers, initiating the development of the famous Supermarine Walrus.

The Royal Australian Navy had a total strength of 5440 men at the start of the war. The Australian Naval College was founded at Osborne House, Geelong, with entry at thirteen. John Collins was one of the first twenty-eight cadets to join in 1913.[23] Discipline was as brutal as in the English namesake: one cadet 'was awarded the most serious punishment other

A Walrus aircraft being lifted onto a *Leander*-class cruiser of the Royal Australian Navy. The aircraft was originally designed for the Australians, as the Supermarine Seagull V of 1933.

than dismissal, namely a caning strapped over a box horse before the assembled cadets and ships company.'[24] It moved to Jervis Bay in 1915, then to Flinders Bay in 1930 as an economy measure. There were no fees for entry. Yachtsmen were commissioned at the start of the war, as with the Royal Navy. Other candidates for commissions were selected at the end of recruit training and went on a sixteen-week course based on the working of a frigate. They were given two months' further instruction before beginning seagoing duty.

Trained by the Royal Navy, Australian ratings were perhaps less individualistic than their colleagues in the army with their famous slouch hats. Nevertheless, Admiral Sir William Fisher, 'the Great Agrippa', was pleased with the men of HMAS *Sydney*: 'You've got a good ship's company ... I like the way they speak up.'[25] In wartime, all male citizens had to enrol for military service at the age of eighteen, but only 10 per cent of those who applied for the navy were accepted. They were trained in the New Entry School at the Flinders Naval Depot with methods familiar in boot camps all round the world, according to Nial Roberts: 'training ... seemed to be mainly involved in marching, and getting straight lines, and learning how to shoulder a rifle, and running around'.[26] They would be selected for the same specialisations as their British cousins, with an anti-submarine school being set up in Balmoral, Port Jackson, in 1939.

The RAN had the use of the great port of Sydney, which contrasted with the British ports where Australian sailors often had to spend time:

> Instead of the slush of the dockyard, or the desolation of Scapa Flow or the mud flats of Half-Acre-Creek, there was Man-of-War steps in a garden setting and almost in the heart of the city. I would nominate No 1 Buoy Farm Cove, Sydney harbour, as the best berth in the world.[27]

Cockatoo Island was eight miles from Sydney Heads and was fully equipped with dry docks, workshops and a great 'Titan' crane. As well as Australian ships, it serviced American ones, such as the cruiser *New Orleans* after damage at Savo Island. Another facility was built from 1940 on Garden Island outside the iconic Harbour Bridge, with a thousand-foot dry dock and more giant cranes, but it was not officially opened until 1945. Further south, Melbourne was developed because it was further away from enemy activity. To the west, Fremantle on the Swan River served mainly as a base for American submarines, though it was also used to train radar operators like Nial Roberts, who was 'camped there in fairly primitive circumstances', and then served in escort vessels, helping to train the Americans by dropping depth charges on them.[28] According to Jim Calvert, 'we would be based in Fremantle, the seaport for Perth. Our rest periods would not be spent on some gooney-bird infested island but in a large city with all that can mean … our response was overwhelmingly favorable.'[29] And the base did not disappoint. Darwin in the north was very different, for it had been damaged by Japanese air raids from February 1942:

> A ghost town expecting invasion was hardly the place to revitalise exhausted submarine crews, and the harbor was scarcely suitable for the overhaul of submarines. But Captain Fife and his staff pitched in. The Salvation Army turned up with a hut on the town's outskirts, and there was plenty of desert available for a baseball diamond.[30]

Australian warships rarely operated independently in any numbers – they were usually under British command in the Mediterranean and American in the Pacific. In peacetime, a cruiser might be the only Australian ship on station, but during the Mediterranean Crisis of 1936 the crew of HMAS *Sydney* was pleased when they found *Australia* at Alexandria: 'It was good to have a chummy ship from our own country in the squadron.'[31]

Apart from home waters, the Mediterranean was the obvious station for Australian ships, for they could be sent home through the Suez Canal in an emergency. By 1940 the cruiser *Sydney* and five destroyers bombarded Italian positions and in June *Sydney* put the cruiser *Bartolomeo Colleoni* out of action, 'the result obtainable by an efficient gunnery team backed by good material', according to Admiral Cunningham.[32] *Australia* left the inland sea to join the unsuccessful operation against Dakar in July 1940, while other ships patrolled the Red Sea and Indian Ocean, where HMAS *Sydney* was lost in November 1941 in action with a German raider. Australian ships helped with the evacuations of Greece and Crete.

Everything changed with the attack on Pearl Harbor, and Australia declared war on Japan on 9 December. Darwin was raided and Port Jackson attacked by midget submarines. HMAS *Perth* was sunk in February 1942. The offensive began after the Battle of Midway in June, with *Australia* and *Canberra* supporting the landing on Guadalcanal in August, but *Canberra* was sunk at Savo Island. Australian ships supported General MacArthur's advance though the Solomons and along the coast of New Guinea, and *Shropshire* played a part in the great victory of Surigao Strait after the landing in the Philippines: '*Shropshire's* broadsides were really something at night. Unlike most US ships we didn't have "flashless" charges … at the first DING … DING I shut my eyes, but many didn't and were blinded for many minutes. Broadsides went on the regular beat but every 30 seconds'. There were still ships in the Mediterranean and seven of them supported the invasion of Sicily in 1943.

By 1945 the RAN had four cruisers, eleven destroyers, six frigates, two sloops, fifty-three minesweeping corvettes and three landing ships, infantry, two old and nine modern destroyers, fifty-three minesweepers, and numerous smaller craft. It had 36,976 officers and men, and 2600 members of the Women's Royal Australian Naval Service, or WRANS.[33]

Canada had by far the longest coastline in the world, even before Newfoundland and Labrador were incorporated in 1949, but much of it was north of the Arctic Circle and practically unusable. Halifax, the largest port on the east coast, had a population of less than sixty thousand in 1931, Vancouver on the west had nearly a quarter of a million people, but Canada would play little part in the Pacific War. Nearly two-thirds of the population lived inland in Ontario and French-speaking Quebec, but the country depended on the St Lawrence River and the Great Lakes for most of its trade. Though the English speakers were usually enthusiastically pro-British, they were influenced by American culture, as a Canadian officer attached to *King Alfred* reported in 1940: 'We must ask to be "put down" from a bus or train, not "let out"; the Subway is the Underground; "Long Distance" is "Trunks" – but the less said about the telephones the better ... nothing can reconcile Canadians to the telephone system or the coffee.'[34]

Canada declared war on Germany on 10 September 1939 after it had been approved by Parliament, and the Francophone minority did not object to a war in support of France, though Canada was never under direct threat and had tiny armed forces at the time. Prime Minister Mackenzie King proclaimed, 'Canada, as a free nation of the British Commonwealth, is bringing her co-operation voluntarily.' Herb Roberts commented, 'We were part of the British Empire. This was still a big thing at that time. So because Britain was at war we were of the view that it was our duty to support them in their defense.'[35]

The very existence of the Royal Canadian Navy had been threatened in 1933 when the chief of staff had suggested that one service should be sacrificed to preserve the others. It remained a traditional navy with faith in the gun. Since battleships and cruisers were out of the question, the ideal navy, in the eyes of most Canadian officers, was a force of glamorous Tribal-class destroyers. In the meantime, it had to make do with six destroyers of the River class, based on the British 'B', 'C' and 'D' classes of the early 1930s. The complex Tribals were beyond the capabilities of Canadian shipbuilders, so it was planned to build fifty-four corvettes and exchange some of them for British-built Tribals – which fell through when an exchange rate could not be agreed. As a result, the RCN was left with a large escort force and no definite plan to use it.

When the war began, the RCN had a total force of 3684, all ranks including reserves, but with ambitious plans to increase that to fifteen thousand. The Rivers were sent across the Atlantic in 1940 to guard against invasion, and when that threat seemed less serious they went to the Clyde to join escort groups. The first ten corvettes were delivered there by 1941 and, due to misunderstanding, their crews were retained to join the escort force, and six ex-American Towns were added; thus Canada was drawn into a kind of war it had not planned for. Its role increased in April 1941 when escort was extended across the Atlantic and the Newfoundland Escort Force was set up to cover the western end. Alan Easton was awarded the Distinguished Service Cross for an action of August 1942: 'when a U-boat was sighted on the surface [and] he immediately shaped course to ram and through skilful handling of his ship and devotion to duty contributed to the almost certain destruction of one enemy U-boat and the probable destruction of another.'[36]

Canadian officers and ratings on the bridge of the corvette *Trillium*, with the compass binnacle in the centre. The scene would not look any different on a Royal Navy corvette.

The RCN had always been keener than other Dominion navies to show its independence of the Royal Navy and used few British instructors. In 1939 all the staff of the depot and training ships *Stadcoma* at Halifax and *Nader* at Esquimalt were Canadian and there was only one lieutenant (E) RN in the rest of the navy. Whereas the Australian and New Zealand navies had British officers at their heads, the RCN was led by Percy Nelles of Ontario, who was appointed as chief of naval staff in 1933 and retired from the post as vice admiral in 1944.

Before the war, regular officers had usually been trained as part of the RN Special Entry scheme. Admiral Nelles was largely responsible for setting up a naval college at Hatley Park in British Columbia in 1942. There was some debate about whether to adopt the Dartmouth or the Annapolis system, and it came down on the side of the former because it had to be adapted to Royal Navy practices, and because of the need for greater specialisation. Cadets lived in dormitories, rather than cabins as at Annapolis.[37]

Most of the early corvette captains were merchant seaman from the Royal Canadian Naval Reserve with a wide variety of experience.

Lieutenant Harman of *Matapedia* had been a schooner skipper; his navigator had worked on merchant ships on the Great Lakes. Alan Easton served with Canadian Pacific from 1919 to 1929 but left the sea, only to be recalled ten years later. George Skinner had been in the Reserve since 1929, but it was reported of him:

> He unfortunately knows very little about the Navy and never seems to train and is intolerant of Naval etiquette and custom ... but he is very jealous of the reputation of his ship and he understands Canadians, and so by his unorthodox methods he achieves efficiency and instils into officers and men a good team spirit and pride of ship.[38]

Commander Layard of the Royal Navy concluded: 'so many RNCR officers were given commands in the early expansion days that they have given all the VR officers much more a merchant service than a naval outlook.'[39] Later he noticed the difference between Reserve officers who then commanded frigates, and Volunteer Reservists: 'I'm damn sorry to lose the corvettes, especially the COs who are a really fine keen bunch of VRs. The NR types I'm likely to get in the frigates probably will be better seamen and more experienced but not half as keen and alive.'[40]

The RCN was wary of the British system of selecting and training volunteer reserve officers. They came directly from shore until February 1943, when the equivalent of the CW scheme was introduced. It was found that British officers on selection boards did not understand Canadian methods, so they were excluded. Officer training took place in HM Canadian Ships *Royal Roads* in Victoria, *King's* in Halifax and the frankly-named *Stone Frigate* at Kingston.

At *King's*, converted from a university: 'The academic environment familiar to civilian students gave way to the regimented military schedule complete with drills on the parade square and the chimes of the bell.' As to staff: 'If a teacher wasn't available they would call on the King's College President, Rev Dr Stanley Walker ... At an hour's notice he could teach marine law, naval history and other subjects the young officers should know something about.'[41]

The initial training of ratings was spread among reserve divisions throughout the country:

> Murray and I presented ourselves to the Naval Reserve division HMCS ... *Unicorn* on Third Avenue north in Saskatoon. It was just a building but the fiction of being a ship was vigorously maintained. Soon we were looking like sailors in 'bell bottom' trousers and

middy with the huge collar and learning to salute, ranks, badges and such.[42]

After that they came together for more specialist training as seamen, stokers, gunners, and so on, at *Nader*, and especially HMCS *Cornwallis* in Halifax, which claimed to be the largest naval training base in the world. When that port became overcrowded, it was moved to Deep Brook, Nova Scotia, though the extremely high tidal range restricted boat work. Don Bowman wrote: 'I had several experiences that very clearly demonstrated the need to be knowledgeable about the rapid rise and fall of the tide.'[43] Anti-submarine training only began in a hut in Halifax in September 1939, but it was replaced by a new school which, it was claimed, was the best in the British Empire. Radar training began at Halifax in August 1941, but was inefficient to start with due to the lack of experienced instructors.

One problem peculiar to Canada was that the nation was in theory bilingual. But it had to be accepted that English was the language onboard ship, and Quebecois who did not speak the language would have to learn it. Training schools were set up, but there was no satisfactory solution when the war ended.

Nearly a hundred thousand men – 6621 officers and 93,067 ratings, passed through the navy during the war and it expanded fifty-fold. It was too fast, especially in the early stages, and that, combined with the unexpected role in convoy escort, led to a number of disasters. Canadian escort groups were allocated to the slower convoys, which increased time in the danger area and provided a softer target for the U-boats. Of convoys escorted largely by Canadian ships, SC42 lost fifteen ships in August and September 1941, SC44 lost four plus an escort in September, and SC48 lost ten plus three escorts torpedoed, including USS *Kearny* in October. The results may have confirmed Admiral King in his belief that 'Inadequately escorted convoys are worse than none', with disastrous results.

They lagged about eighteen months behind British ships in key fittings such as the latest Asdic and radar. The captain of the destroyer *Ottawa* wrote of her as she left with convoy ON 127:

> … what really mattered was our ability, or want of it, to cope effectively with the U-boats. Our Type 286M radar with its antenna at the foretruck was of marginal utility. … against a submarine, trimmed down on the surface at night, its performance was lamentable. *Celandine* was the only ship in the group with the latest and most effective radar for such work … (but then she was RN.

They – the RN – always got to the head of the queue ...) Also, none of our group had HF/DF ...[44]

Most of the early corvettes were completed with the short forecastle which made them very wet and crowded. Ted Cunningham, who served in HMCS *Arrowhead* in 1940/1 commented: 'it wasn't unusual to be sitting at the mess table ... and have two smelly feet suddenly set next to your coffee or breakfast, but you got used to it.' To Ivan Chamberlain, 1943 plus: 'Arriving in Londonderry was the most beautiful sight anyone could ever see.'[45]

Royal Navy officers were not slow to blame the Canadians for their deficiencies, especially Captain Donald Macintyre. In 1942 the Canadian ships were 'travesties of warships ... dirty and seamanlike.' He was particularly outraged to discover that the captain of one corvette allowed the men's hammocks to be slung permanently on the messdecks, 'In case they got tired during the day'[46] – which might seem reasonable for a crew which had spent long and hard hours at sea, but not to a highly traditional officer like Macintyre. That might just have been a collision of worlds, but there was no doubt that the hastily expanded navy lacked training.

Commander Frank Layard RN had no specific complaints about the individual Canadian officers under him, but he sometimes despaired about the crews of his escort group: 'I went on mess deck rounds. Disappointed to find that there is hardly a corner I can walk into without finding dirt.' On leaving Scapa Flow: 'I've never been so ashamed of a ship's company. There were men in khaki trousers, in filthy duffel coats, sea boots, jerseys, mostly smoking and not one man in No. 3s'.

It was no better on shore. At Gibraltar, 'Capt D's staff came down on board to say that the ship's companies of the 9th DF had been breaking up the town last night ... Oh these Canadians!' He made little impression with his RN discipline: 'I've been awfully weak and done nothing to buck things up in this group.' Yet he could defend them against a senior officer: 'I told him I thought the RN treated the RCN unfairly – all criticism and no help and we'd never seen a senior RN officer on board.' And when he left, 'At about 1600 I was asked to come aft to the quarter deck, where all the sailors were assembled, and they presented me with one of the beautiful scale models of the ship which have been made in the ship. Very touching how kind and friendly these Canadians are.'[47] Interviewing former Stoker Davy Jones many years later, 'One got the impression that there was a strong streak of Canadian democracy at play between the decks.'

The Canadian ships were diverted to the less active areas such as the Caribbean and West Africa, and so missed most of the crucial battles of the spring of 1943. They returned to the Atlantic and dominated the escort groups in the later stages of the war. They took part in Arctic convoys as reported by the first lieutenant of the destroyer *Huron*:

> It seemed that gales were forever sweeping over the dark, clouded sky. The dim red ball of the sun barely reaching the horizon as the ship pitched and tossed, the musty smell of damp clothes in which we lived, the bitter cold, the long frequent watches that seemed to last forever.[48]

For the Normandy invasion, HMCS *Rimouski* was tasked with escorting some of the blockships that would form part of the Mulberry harbours, and therefore was one of the first to sail for the Normandy invasion, from the Scottish port of Oban:

> … as we were steaming sedately down the Irish Sea we were passed at some speed by the bombardment force of battleships and cruisers. … We felt awfully insignificant, but a minute later felt like kings again when one of those giants took the trouble to send 'Good luck' by light.[49]

A large part of the naval budget was devoted to preparing bases on the east coast, mainly to serve the Battle of the Atlantic. The great natural harbour at Halifax was the only base on the east coast before the war, but in 1938 it was 'in a peculiarly bad state'. In the early stages, it was the base for the Third Battle Squadron of old British 'R'-class ships, intended to deal with surface raiders. It was also used by French ships, including the battleship *Lorraine*, the carrier *Béarn* and cruisers, and submarines. But its main function was as an assembly point for ocean convoys, and as the depot for the RCN. There was much investment, a 35,000-ton floating dock was built, and 3 million dollars was spent on armament facilities alone from 1942.[50]

Though Newfoundland was not part of Canada at the time, the RCN shared with the Royal Navy the building up of a base at St John's. Some of it was taken over by the United States as part of the 'destroyers for bases' deal, while it was agreed that the British Admiralty would bear the capital cost. It was designed to support a force of sixty destroyers and escorts, and a hospital, workshops, administrative centre, armament depots and fuel depots were established along with naval barracks and a tactical training centre. Sydney Cove in Nova Scotia became the assembly point for slower convoys, with some repair facilities being set up. On the other coast, Esquimalt, near Vancouver, was the principal base, heavily defended by guns but comparatively little used in this war.

Many Canadian officers would serve with the Royal Navy. Some yachtsmen were sent to *King Alfred* early in the war, for they were little regarded by the RCN at the time – one officer thought that yachting bore as little relationship to naval command as kite flying to the air force.[51] Cornelius Burke was captain of *MGB 658* and:

> … was typical of a Canadian who had been educated at a very 'English' school on Vancouver Island. Although his ideas and energy were characteristic of the New World, he had a tremendous respect for British institutions, even though he was not above making cracks at them to provoke an argument.[52]

The RCN turned out to be the most specialised of the oceangoing navies during the war, though two cruisers were added towards the end. There was a plan to send a task force to the Pacific after the defeat of Germany, though it is doubtful how serious that was and, of course, it was ended by the atom bomb. Though the achievements of the RCN were often ignored by British and American historians, Canada did use the experience to achieve a more balanced naval force after the war, with a carrier, cruisers and a full range of supporting ships.

New Zealand had a very small population of about 1.6 million when the war started, not enough to support a fully-fledged navy, so the local force was known as the New Zealand Division of the Royal Navy until it was renamed the Royal New Zealand Navy in October 1941. It was ruled by a naval board like the Australian one, though smaller, and at the start of the war the posts of First Naval Member and Commodore Commanding the New Zealand Squadron were combined in the person of J W Rivett-Crane, succeeded by H E Horan.[53]

Initially, the main effort was to support the light cruisers *Achilles* and *Leander*. At the outbreak of war twelve officers and 801 ratings were available, supplemented by officers and ratings lent by the Royal Navy.[54] *Achilles* achieved early fame in the Battle of the River Plate in 1939. *Leander* had a very active career in New Zealand waters, the Mediterranean and Red Sea. She sank an Italian raider in the Indian Ocean and in July 1943, with US forces, she engaged Japanese forces in the Solomons, where she was damaged by a torpedo. She was repaired in Boston and reverted to the Royal Navy. The force acquired other light vessels over the years, including minesweepers and a dozen Fairmile motor launches built in the country.

Several schemes were set up for recruiting and training officers. Scheme A for qualified yachtsmen operated between January and December 1940. Scheme B was for those who would enter as ordinary seamen, with the expectation of a temporary commission in the RNZNVR, and Scheme R was for potential airmen, which would prove to be one of New Zealand's main contributions to the war effort – all were sent to Britain for training.[55] HMS *Tamaki*, the initial training base, was set up in January 1941 in Haurake Gulf. According to Brian Breen: 'A favourite punishment doled out to trainees was taking "Jimmy for a walk." HMNZS *Tamaki* was set up on a hill on Mutuihe Island, so we had to roll "Jimmy" the 112-pound, 6-inch shell down the hill and then carry it back up!'[56]

Floyd Beaver of the US Navy was seconded to HMNZS *Moa* in 1942 and was amazed at customs, which were largely identical to those of the Royal Navy:

> No cool drinking water for one thing, and one rudimentary washroom about the size of those found Pullman cars in the states. There was a bathtub I discovered, but it was officer gear and not for the likes of me. … One interesting thing for me, was to see officers on board a naval vessel with drinks in their hands and bottles standing ready on a cloth-covered table. An American did not expect to see anything like that on a Navy ship.[57]

Moa took part in the Guadalcanal campaign and sank a Japanese submarine in co-operation with *Kiwi*.

South Africa, though also dominated by a white population, was different from the other Dominions. Fewer than two million whites lived among a non-European population of African and Asian stock of around 6.4 million. The whites themselves were split between the English-speakers and the Afrikaners, with their own language, descended from Dutch, who were less likely to offer unconditional support to Britain. Though they had been treated generously after their defeat in the Second Anglo-Boer war of 1899–1902, much resentment still lingered. The country entered the war reluctantly with a vote of eighty to sixty-seven in the whites-only parliament.

The British had long valued the Cape of Good Hope for its strategic position, and maintained a naval base at Simonstown, but the South Africans showed little interest in naval affairs. The first naval force was only formed in 1922 as the South African Naval Service, with a surveying vessel and two minesweepers. Even these were disposed of during the Great Depression, and at the start of war in 1939 the force had three officers, three ratings and no ships. A hundred and thirty-three ships were sunk off the coast during the war and minesweepers and anti-submarine vessels were acquired to counter that. Other vessels were sent to the Mediterranean. It was renamed the Seaward Defence Force in January 1940 and in August 1942 it was merged with local volunteer reserve forces to form the South African Naval Force. 'Non-whites' were only recruited as cooks and deckhands. By the end of the war the force included 1436 officers and 8896 ratings, while 2937 South Africans joined the Royal Navy. The SANF had eighty-seven vessels during the war, mostly small but with three Loch-class frigates arriving at the end.[58]

Britain's other African colonies maintained small volunteer reserve units before the war. Kenya had a skeleton force with a commanding officer, a warrant officer instructor and two probationary officers. The Gambia Naval Volunteer Force had six officers, the Gold Coast (Ghana) had thirteen, including instructors.[59]

India (which included Pakistan until 1947) had been dominated by the London-based Honourable East India Company since General Clive's victory over the French in 1757. After the mutiny of 1857, the British government took over the government, through a viceroy. Queen Victoria became Empress of India, her great-grandson George VI was still the King-Emperor, and India was known as the 'Jewel in the Crown' of the British Empire. It was a huge subcontinent with a land area of 1,766,000 square miles (about the same as non-European Russia) and a population of nearly 389 million in 1941, 250 million of them Hindus and 92½ million Muslims. British rule was being increasingly challenged, with the rise of nationalist movements. Mahatma Gandhi and his National Congress advocated pacifism, Chandra Bose attempted to form the Indian National Army against British rule with German and Japanese support, and Muhammad Ali Jinnah campaigned for a separate Muslim state.

The East India Company had always maintained some kind of naval force, with Indian ratings under white officers, and it became the Bombay Marine and then the Royal Indian Marine in 1892. In 1919 the Fourth Sea Lord poured cold water on any suggestion of a fully-fledged Indian navy: 'it would be hopeless to expect the natives of India themselves to provide the officers. The intelligence and brain power would be quite unequal to this.' As to ratings, the divisions in society would 'present well nigh insuperable difficulties in the manning of ship. It would lead to such a thing as the foretopmen being Pathans and the quarter deck men being Sikhs'.[60]

Until 1934 the Royal Indian Marine was mainly involved in surveying, transport and harbour inspection until an act passed by the Council of State in Simla, forming the Royal Indian Navy with real military status under a Naval Discipline Act modelled on that of the Royal Navy and the other Dominions. 'Indianisation' was favoured by the government of India, and one Indian executive officer and two engineers had been appointed by 1934, with four and seven under training. Engineers were sent to Plymouth for training, but in in 1938 engineer cadets were 'relegated to the position of apprentices. They live on their own in lodging in the town and usually go home for their meals in solitude. The have hardly a chance of getting to know anybody outside their small circle'.[61] The British Admiralty continued to resist allowing Indian officers to sit on courts martial on white officers and ratings, and to have command over them. They claimed that they would mainly serve in ships with Indian ratings, and would only join Royal Navy ships for training, when they would have no executive authority, but Indian officers continued to be aggrieved.

In 1939 the Royal Indian Navy included a rear admiral, six captains, thirteen commanders and fourteen lieutenant commanders, all British. There were four Indian lieutenants, four sub lieutenants, one midshipman and five cadets, with eight engineer officers and four cadets. The warrant officers included four Indian boatswains and the education of the lower deck was in the hands of six warrant schoolmasters, one with a PhD.[62] Vice Admiral John Henry Godfrey took command in 1943, after disagreeing with Churchill about the role of naval intelligence.

D C Dutt had only grudging respect for the typical white officer:

> Tough, sun-tanned, stern disciplinarians of Kipling's India, they … loved the land, the uneducated sepoys and ratings of the regular services in their own fashion. Living in India, some for generations, they spoke of England as home. To home they went for higher education and for finding their brides, if one of their own kind was not available in India.[63]

He had no more regard for Indian officers, who with rare exceptions, were 'no better in our eyes than their white counterparts. … Like most British officers, they preferred to keep the ratings in their place.'[64] He much preferred a Royal Navy officer sent out to India: 'We developed a great respect for his human qualities. He was tough, generous, kind-hearted and without a trace of colour prejudice.' But his colleague 'treated us with the usual hauteur of a British officer.'[65]

The RIN expanded to twenty thousand men in 1943 and around thirty thousand by the end of the war. Sloops and minesweepers were added, along with gunboats and motor launches, but a corvette and two frigates arrived too late to be of service. The ships served mainly in convoy escort in the Atlantic, Mediterranean and Indian Ocean, but *Sutlej* and *Jumna*

Sir Bruce Fraser, commander-in-chief of the Eastern Fleet, inspects Indian sailors, including a Sikh wearing a turban, in October 1944. The caps of the others are worn at a variety of angles.

supported the invasion of Sicily in 1943. The minesweeper *Bengal* was mainly used as an escort like many others, and in 1942 she was escorting a Dutch tanker when attacked by two Japanese commerce raiders, and sank one. *Godavark* sank a German submarine near the Seychelles in 1944.

D C Dutt, from a remote village which had never seen a white man, enlisted in February 1941 after his mentor advised him to 'get recruited to some specialised branch of the armed forces.' He was well educated, although thin and underage, but Chief Petty Officer Suleiman advised him on how to be accepted for training as a wireless telegraphist. He was bewildered on joining the training ship *Dalhousie* in Mumbai, where the course had much in common with that undergone by British boys. The uniform was 'probably the strangest outfit created for a human being.' The petty officers shouted and swore in English and Hindustani. The schedule was intense, starting at 5.30 and lasting until 9pm. The food, which would later play a major part in his and India's story, was strange. The 'E' ration had beef curry and bread, the 'I' ration had mutton and chapatti instead. The curry was 'a unique invention of the fraternity of chefs' with 'a flavour and taste that the ratings from no part of India had tasted before. ... I never came across upon any rating who would eat that witch's brew ... willingly.'[66]

Dutt served well onboard the minesweeper *Baluchistan* and gained promotion. He did not encounter blatant race prejudice, in that all the ratings were Indian, but it was very different when he came ashore for combined operations training alongside British and Australian soldiers and sailors, to find that, 'they lived in better quarters, ate better food, wore uniforms made of finer quality material, enjoyed amenities we could not even dream of.' A horrific train journey in a grossly overcrowded carriage confirmed his resentment. Five months after the end of the war, he was one of the leaders of a mutiny, initially against bad food but also against prejudice. Heavy-handed repression caused it to spread to other cities and military units, and it accelerated the British government's decision to give independence to India.

The Royal Indian Navy saw little action and had only a small impact on operations, but in a sense it bridged two eras. It began when the white race was supreme and prejudice was undisguised. The mutiny of 1946 catapulted the countries of India and Pakistan, and their navies, into a new age. But the sailors of the RIN bore no responsibility for the Hindu-Muslim violence that killed thousands. As Dutt put it: 'We came from widely different regions and religious backgrounds. ... They belonged to Hindu, Muslim, Christian and Sikh families. The years spent in the Navy had made them – the ratings of the Royal Indian Navy – Indians.'[67] Again an element of sea power led the way, though not as anyone had intended.

19
Conclusions

AS FAR as possible I have tried to see the numerous aspects of naval warfare from the point of view of those concerned – British and American politicians, admirals, officers and enlisted men, marines, women and so on. I have also tried to see it through the eyes of U-boat crews, kamikazes, human torpedoes as well as the ordinary officers and men of the German, Japanese and Italian navies, and of the numerous allies, 'free' forces and Commonwealth navies. It is now time to stand aside and make a judgement on the details and the overall performance of the two great forces that endured early defeat but went on to victory.

The Royal Navy was often assumed to be ultra conservative up to the early twentieth century, but actually it was ahead in technology, if not in social development. It was the first to use radio, but later fell behind in its development. Likewise with turbine engines, it peaked around 1910 and then failed to use high-pressure steam (though their lack of progress in naval aviation can be ascribed to external factors). Was it some kind of malaise which affected the navy? Certainly it was short of funds and run by officers with an overriding fear of failure, but that was equally true in the US Navy. And this backwardness is not to be found in other aspects of British society: Britons played leading parts in the development of radar, nuclear research, television and the jet engine which would change the post-war world.

The British and American navies were the only ones which attempted to maintain a full range of seaborne activities. The Germans had no aircraft carriers in service and did not develop amphibious warfare. The Soviet navy was always a secondary force and had no aircraft carriers or large amphibious vessels. France's participation was short and they lacked effective carriers and amphibious capability. The Commonwealth and 'free' navies were dependent on British and American supplies. Italy produced some fine cruisers and was expert at attack by torpedo boats and underwater craft but had no success in any other area. Japan came closest to all-round capability, with very effective carriers and aircraft, amphibious craft, the largest battleships ever built and many other attributes, but its failure to develop anti-submarine warfare would prove to be a major weakness. The Soviet Union had relatively small forces operating in the Baltic, Black Sea, Arctic and Pacific, and Japan made incursions to the Indian Ocean, but the Royal and United States navies were the only ones which operated in strength in more than one ocean.

No navy was fully prepared at the start of the war, except perhaps the Japanese. The Germans had started from a very low base. The Royal and American navies were starved of funds until the mid 1930s. The British were surprised by the fall of France, which negated all their planning, the Americans by the losses at Pearl Harbor, and later by the kamikaze attacks. The British had not anticipated the need for amphibious warfare or an oceanic anti-submarine campaign.

It was only the British Commonwealth and the Americans who expected a long war and continued to build surface ships in large numbers after the start of it, which was a major factor in victory. The British commissioned large numbers of escort vessels and landing craft, and smaller numbers of carriers, cruisers and destroyers. That, of course, was dwarfed by the huge American effort. Meanwhile, in Germany, building of surface ships largely ceased and production concentrated on U-boats in the expectation of a short war mainly fought on land. Japan did not have the productive capacity to renew war losses in ships and aircraft, and Italy had even less. Therefore victory was almost inevitable, as long as the Allies did not lose their determination.

To some extent, the operations in the Atlantic and Mediterranean, except amphibious landings, were conducted separately by different elements; the battlefleet was only occasionally involved in the Battle of the Atlantic, and submarines mainly fought their own campaigns. Escort vessels rarely saw other branches of the fleet. and the different 'navies within the navy' had their very different personnel, practices and tactics. But US naval operations in the Pacific largely consisted of amphibious landings, and these involved all the elements. The assault on an island would begin with reconnaissance by air, by submarines looking at the beaches or by clandestine landing parties. The island would be bombarded first by aircraft from the fast carrier groups, then by battleships and cruisers. Landing ships and craft, particularly the LSTs and LVTs, would put men ashore, mostly marines in the early stages. With the army and with the support of naval gunfire, and bombing by carrier or land-based aircraft, they would fight a fierce battle against determined Japanese resistance. Carriers and battleships would be ready to deal with any Japanese naval counter-attack. As soon as this was completed, the Seabees would construct harbour facilities, roads and especially runways, so that they were ready to begin the next stage of the advance across the ocean.

The system of quasi-independent bureaus was a major weakness of the American naval administration. In a sense it reflected the 'separation of powers' in the national system of government, and it only worked in 1941–45 because there was a strong leader. Naval strength and success also depended on the support of Congress, which was forthcoming in wartime and also after the war, with the Soviet Union clearly in view as the potential enemy. But the US Navy's Bureau of Personnel was generally more efficient than the then office of the Second Sea Lord in Britain, largely because it had real control, whereas in the Admiralty the selection, training and appointment of officers and men was largely left to the individual branches, creating a rather incoherent system. It is not clear that the British system of specialised officers was in any way superior to American generalism. Indeed, in the highly specialised field of naval engineering, it was the Americans who produced the great innovations of high-pressure steam and later nuclear propulsion, though in the post-war period the British would lead the way in gas-turbine propulsion.

Generally, the senior American naval officers had a broader outlook and world than their British contemporaries because of their training system. Leahy was a powerful force as the president's chief of staff, King directed strategy, especially in the central Pacific, and Nimitz directed the largest fleet in history over thousands of miles of sea, with all the logistical problems that entailed. In Britain, Churchill formulated strategy and the admirals were confined to their own commands. One exception was Lord Louis Mountbatten, who was as political as any American admiral or general, but that can perhaps be ascribed to his family background rather than his naval training. In America, presidents Kennedy, Johnson, Nixon, Ford, Carter and George H W Bush had all served as naval officers, though only Carter was a permanent one who had trained at Annapolis. In Britain, most male members of the royal family served in the navy, but the only naval prime minster was James Callaghan, formerly a lieutenant RNVR.

It is a striking paradox that, in the case of both navies, the war began with professional sailors conducting themselves in a rather amateurish way against enemy advances, but proceeding later in the war with largely amateur forces that fought with great professional skill. This is not to denigrate the professional officers – at the start of the war they found themselves in circumstances not of their own choosing and against enemies with many surprises up their sleeves, while the amateur forces which completed the war were still commanded by captains

Men crowd every available space onboard *Missouri*, to watch the formal Japanese surrender on 2 September 1945, almost exactly six years after the war in Europe started, with film crews and photographers in the foreground. A panel on the right centre records the ship's achievements, including landings supported and aircraft shot down.

and admirals from the regular navies who had learned to cope with the changing circumstances. And the amateurs had the advantage of knowing exactly what kind of war they were fighting, and mostly with ships and equipment designed for it.

The navies could learn from one another, but mostly the Royal Navy from the USN. Americans were best in aircraft carriers, submarines and in building a modern battlefleet (not that it was much needed, as such). The British mastered anti-submarine warfare out of sheer necessity. Both had strengths and weaknesses in amphibious warfare, but they came together in the Normandy invasion of June 1944. Part of the legacy was preparation for the Cold War which followed and navies co-operated far more than ever before, through NATO and its regular exercises.

It is not the intention of this work to assess the post-war performance of the two navies, but a brief glimpse does give some indication of what worked best. Mostly, the British ended up adopting American practice while trying to maintain some independence. At first the Royal Navy tried to go back to its pre-war status. The thirteen-year-old entry to Dartmouth had already been proved less efficient at producing motivated officers than the Special Entry at eighteen, and the standard age of entry was raised to sixteen in 1949, and eighteen in 1955, matching nearly every other navy. Promotion from the lower deck became far more common by the late 1950s, with up to 40 per cent of officers starting as ratings. Onboard ship, the Royal Navy remained reluctant to adopt the American system of bunks and canteens for about ten years, maintaining that mess life was a key factor in morale, but it did so in the end. It was a slow process: sailors mobilised for the 'Cod Wars' with Iceland in the 1970s found themselves sleeping in hammocks in ships dug out from the reserve fleet. The steam engine was greatly improved and range was increased for oceanic war, before it was superseded by diesel, gas turbine and nuclear power. Amphibious warfare was unfashionable among the traditional officers who took power in the late 1940s, but became one of the main functions of the Royal Navy after the Suez operation of 1956. In contrast, the US Navy did not have to address any of these issues after 1945.

Many things are needed for a strong navy. There has to be the political will to maintain it and taxpayers have to be reasonably willing to support it, which was always the case in Britain and in the United States from the mid 1930s onwards. It needs tradition which, of course, was stronger and longer in Britain, but was developing fast in America. Both nations were as unified as at any time in their history, with a deep sense of purpose. In contrast, the British are deeply divided today about whether it was wise to leave the European Union, and there is a real prospect of Scotland voting for independence, while among other issues, Americans are divided about the legitimacy of the most recent presidential election.

National motivation is a strong factor in naval or military success. In Germany that was provided by the Treaty of Versailles and the fear of Communism; in America by the attack on Pearl Harbor; in the Soviet Union by the aggressive German attack; in Japan by the perceived racism and restrictive policies of America and the European colonial powers. Italy had no such motivation, which might explain her poor performance.

The British situation is more complex. Ostensibly, she went to war in 1939 to maintain the balance of power in Europe, which was not something that touched the hearts of the people. The bombing of cities in 1940/1 did provide the right kind of motivation, but interestingly the British were already galvanised before that, during the summer of 1940 when they flocked to join the Local Defence Volunteers, later the Home Guard and served, mostly willingly, with the army, navy and air force. Some of them were motivated by a desire to protect the empire, others by fear of Fascism and especially its Nazi variant, which had already demonstrated its untrustworthiness and cruelty even before it embarked on mass exterminations. There was a residual fear of Germany dating from the First World War, but most of all it was a compulsion to defend the 'island fortress' at all costs. But there was a sense of fair play, and mutinies were not unusual when the sailors felt cheated, and when the men who had joined to defend the foresaid 'island fortress' in 1940 found themselves in danger of being sent to restore the British Empire in the East.

It was, of course, a unique war, with tanks, aircraft and aircraft carriers fully developed for the first time, with submarine and anti-submarine warfare practised in both the main theatres on an unprecedented scale, and huge resources devoted to amphibious operations. New technologies – jet engines, atomic weapons and power, guided missiles and ballistic missiles – were already emerging by 1945 and would make it impossible to fight anything like the Second World War again.

The ultimate question is, 'Was the American Navy better than the British during the Second World War?' In absolute terms the answer is yes, the US Navy had far greater numbers in the end, and better techniques especially in aviation and engineering. But taken in context the answer is far less clear and a more revealing question might be, 'How well did the navies adapt to the circumstances that were forced upon them?'

America had many overall advantages in the war, size being fundamental. She is forty times as large as Great Britain, with three times the population. Remoteness was another factor, and the USA was never under serious threat of bombing or invasion. Britain had already been fighting for two years before America entered the war and, even then, America did not have to begin its major offensives for another two years after that. It already had a tradition of mass production, which contrasted with the European reliance on craftsmen's skills. It had money, and a highly motivated population, which tended to override endemic political differences. That does not diminish the great achievement of the navy in fighting a war across two oceans, especially the massive effort required in the Pacific. And if it is clear that that the Royal Navy had far more to learn from the Americans than vice versa, that does not negate its effort in defending the country and its lifelines though difficult early years. Both navies, despite some flaws and some mistakes, adapted well to unforeseen circumstances and can be immensely proud of their superb heritage.

The United States Navy went from strength to strength after the war. It developed the nuclear submarine and the submarine-launched ballistic missile, while maintaining a huge and powerful fleet of aircraft carriers, supported by abundant finance and popular support. It played a relatively minor role in the Vietnam War compared with the army, air force and marines, which is perhaps fortunate for its reputation. The Royal Navy has struggled to maintain a full range of activities. The decline of empire, though not a catastrophe for the nation at large, tended to reduce the belief in naval power. The Royal Navy was innovative in its aviation, mainly through necessity. It pioneered the jet engine, mirror landing aid, steam catapult and the angled deck, though it could only afford to fit it to the old *Victorious* in its fullest form. Most of the post-colonial wars were fought on land, but it did gain some glory and prestige in the Falklands Conflict of 1982. It has now regained a force of aircraft carriers, but smaller than the American ones and using American aircraft. It is generally agreed that the two navies work well together as part of the NATO alliance, but there is no doubt about which is supreme.

Notes

1 The Structure of Naval Power

1. A Short Account of the Several General Duties of Officers, of Ships of War.
2. Bureau of Naval Personnel, *Naval Orientation*, June 1945, p39.
3. *The Roosevelt Letters*, London, 1952, vol 3, p267.
4. Margaret Halsey, *With Malice Towards Some*, London, 1938, p239.
5. Albert H Jones and Michael H Jones, *No Easy Choices*, Worcester, 1994, p151.
6. Alex H Cherry, *Yankee RN*, London, 1951, p149.
7. Navy Records Society, *Anglo-American Naval Relations*, ed Michael Simpson, vol 1, p347.
8. Ibid, pp601–2.
9. S W Roskill, *Naval Policy Between the Wars*, London, 1978, vol 2, pp65–7.
10. Navy Records Society, *Anglo-American Naval Relations*, ed Michael Simpson, vol 2, p229.
11. Harold Gardner Bowen, *Ships, Machinery and Mossbacks*, Princeton, 1954, p5.
12. R G Albion, *Makers of Naval Policy*, 1980, pp449–50.
13. E J Whitehill, *Fleet Admiral King*, London, 1953, p461.
14. Albion, *Makers of Naval Policy*, p394.
15. W S Churchill, *The Second World War*, vol III, *The Grand Alliance*, London, 1966, p608.
16. *Alanbrooke War Diaries*, 1939–1945, ed Alex Danchev, London, 2001, Diary, pp440–3.
17. Navy Records Society, *The Cunningham Papers*, ed Michael Simpson, vol 2, 2006, p203.
18. J P W Mallalieu, *On Larkhill*, London, 1983, p198.
19. Navy Records Society, *Cunningham Papers*, vol 2, pp158, 166.
20. R G Albion, *Makers of Naval Policy*, 1980, p248.
21. Ibid, p379.
22. *Alanbrooke War Diaries*, p272.
23. William Emmerson, *Franklin Roosevelt as Commander-in-Chief in World War II*, Military Affairs, 1958–59, pp181–207.
24. Whitehill, *Fleet Admiral King*, p630.
25. Albion, *Makers of Naval Policy*, p448.
26. Orvill Raines, *Good Night Officially*, Boulder, 1994, P182.
27. *With Malice Towards Some*, p239.
28. Henry Eccles, *To the Java Sea*, ed Hattendorf, Newport, 2021, p169.
29. C L Mowat, *Britain Between the Wars*, Cambridge, 1987, pp259–83.
30. *A People at War*, New York, 1943, passim.
31. War Production Board, *Industrial Mobilization for War*, Washington, 1947, p53.
32. Churchill, *Grand Alliance*, pp596–7.
33. Arthur Herman, *Freedom's Forge*, New York, 2012, pp338–9.
34. Brian Lavery, *Hostilities Only*, Greenwich, 2004, pp24–5.
35. Whitehill, *Fleet Admiral King*, p647.
36. Theodore C Mason, *Battleship Sailor*, Annapolis, 2013, p44.
37. R G Albion, *Brief History of Civilian Personnel*, Washington, 1943.
38. Norman Friedman, *US Battleships*, London, c1985, p311.
39. Roosevelt, *Letters*, vol 3, p257.
40. S W Roskill, *The War at Sea*, vol 1, London, 1954, p27.
41. Ibid, p583.
42. Robert Finch, *The World's Airways*, London, 1938, p69.

2 Naval Society and Culture

1. Robert Burgess and Roland Blackburn, *We Joined the Navy*, London, 1943, p1.
2. E J Jerningham, *Tin Can Man*, Annapolis, 1993, p21.
3. Paul Fussell, *Wartime*, Oxford, 1989, p84.
4. Ben Warlow, *Shore Establishments of the Royal Navy*, Liskeard, 1992, pp60, 68.
5. Edward P Stafford, *Little Ship, Big War*, London 1986, p32.
6. Leonard Charles Williams, *Gone a Long Journey*, Havant, 2002, p185.
7. Frank Muir, *A Kentish Lad*, London, 1997, p62.
8. Theodore C Mason, *We Will Stand By You*, Columbia, pp190–2.
9. John Fernald, *Destroyer from America*, London, 1942, p25.
10. James F Calvert, *Silent Running*, New York, 1995, p20.
11. Mason, *Battleship Sailor*, p61.
12. US Naval Institute, *The Bluejacket's Manual*, Annapolis, 1940, p423.
13. Admiralty, *Manual of Seamanship*, BR 68, vol 2, 1932, p24.
14. *Bluejacket's Manual*, p209.
15. Mason, *Battleship Sailor*, p58.
16. Admiralty, *The Gunnery Pocket Book*, BR 224/45, 1945, pp179–80.
17. National Archives, ADM 116/3060.
18. Len Wincott, *Invergordon Mutineer*, London, 1974, p68.
19. National Maritime Museum, KEL/109.
20. William W Rogal, *Guadalcanal, Tarawa and Beyond*, Jefferson, c2010, p18.
21. Alvin Kernan, *Crossing the Line*, Annapolis, c1994, p152.
22. Admiralty, *Manual of Seamanship*, vol 1, 1908, p4.
23. Ralph Ransome-Wallis, *Two Red Stripes*, London, 1973, p25.
24. *Naval Orientation*, pp3, 7, 9.
25. Samuel Eliot Morison, *Operations in North African Waters*, Oxford, 1947, p194.
26. Raymond Calhoun, *Tin Can Sailor*, Annapolis, 1993, p35.
27. Ibid, p35.
28. Walter R Borneman, *The Admirals*, New York, 2012, p154.
29. Joseph H Wellings, *On His Majesty's Service*, ed Hattendorf, Newport, 1983, p234.
30. H G Jones, *The Sonarman's War*, Jefferson, 2010, pp1, 55, 67.
31. John Kilbracken, *Bring Back my Stringbag*, London, 1979, p18.
32. Hannen Swaffer, *What would Nelson Do?*, London, 1946, pp92–3.
33. S Gorley Putt, *Men Dressed as Seamen*, London, 1943, pp34–5.
34. Mason, *Battleship Sailor*, p31.
35. Jerningham, op cit, p18.
36. Mason, *Battleship Sailor*, p41.
37. Ibid, pp14–15.
38. James J Fahey, *Pacific War Diary*, New York, 1963, p14.
39. Jones, *The Sonarman's War*, p171.
40. Mason, *Battleship Sailor*, p137.
41. Martin Middlebrook, *Convoy*, Harmondsworth, 1978, p70.
42. *The Royal Navy Officer's Pocket Book*, ed Lavery, London, p104.
43. National Archives, ADM 239/335.
44. *Lost Voices of the Royal Navy*, p298.
45. *Naval Orientation*, pp371–86.
46. Mason, *Battleship Sailor*, p59.
47. George Melly, *Rum, Bum and Concertina*, London, 1977, p183.
48. Jean O'Hara, *Honolulu Harlot*, 1944, p4.
49. Mason, *Battleship Sailor*, pp23–4.
50. Christopher McKee, *Sober Men and True*, London, 2002, pp177–80.
51. *Rum, Bum and Concertina*, pp121, 59, 57, 29.
52. Mason, *Battleship Sailor*, pp135.
53. Lawrence R Murphy, *Perverts by Official Order*, London, 1988, p293.
54. Alan Berube, 'Marching to a Different Drummer', p90, in *My Desire for History*, North Carolina, 2011.
55. Ibid, p100.
56. Ibid, p312.
57. *The Royal Navy Officer's Pocket Book*, pp27–34.
58. *Destroyer from America*, pp61–4.

59. John Whelan, *Home is the Sailor*, London, 1959, pp185–6.
60. Peter Bull, *To Sea in a Sieve*, London, 1958, p222.
61. *Naval Orientation*, pp276–93.
62. Mason, *Battleship Sailor*, p105.
63. Stafford, *Little Ship, Big War*, pp229–30.
64. Mason, *Battleship Sailor*, p65–6.
65. *Naval Orientation*, pp62–8.
66. Ibid, pp445–51.
67. Mason, *Battleship Sailor*, pp78.
68. Ibid, p31.
69. Theodore C Mason, *Rendezvous with Destiny*, Annapolis 1997, p80.
70. Calhoun, *Tin Can Sailor*, pp81–2.
71. *Rum, Bum and Concertina*, p3.
72. Herman Wouk, *The Caine Mutiny*, 1978 edition, p411.
73. *Naval Courts and Boards*, section 46, p14.
74. Michael Keith Olson, *Tales from a Tin Can*, St Paul, 2007, pp237, 277–8.
75. Jerningham, op cit, p170.

3 Officers
1. Olson, *Tales from a Tin Can*, p14.
2. Stafford, *Little Ship, Big War*, p296.
3. William James, *The Sky was Always Blue*, London, 1951, pp24–5.
4. Brian Lavery, *In Which They Served*, London, 2008, p167.
5. Bob Whinney, *The U-Boat Peril*, Poole, 1986, p21.
6. Stephen King-Hall, *My Naval Life*, London, 1952, p39.
7. Michael Partridge, *The Royal Naval College Osborne*, Stroud, 1999, p96.
8. Ibid, p162.
9. Rebecca John, *Caspar John*, London, 1987, p45.
10. Partridge, *The Royal Naval College Osborne*, p60.
11. King-Hall, *My Naval Life*, p46.
12. Partridge, *The Royal Naval College Osborne*, p63.
13. King-Hall, *My Naval Life*, p42.
14. B B Schofield, *With the Royal Navy in War and Peace*, Barnsely, 2018, p8.
15. Ibid, p5.
16. Gieves Ltd, *How to Become a Naval Officer*, London, 1934, p16.
17. Bob Whinney, *The U-Boat Peril*, pp19–20.
18. Louis Le Bailly, *The Man Around the Engine*, Emsworth, 1990, p15.
19. *Navy List*, 1937, p573.
20. C A Jenkins, *Days of a Dogsbody*, London, 1946, pp9–10.
21. *How to Become a Naval Officer*, p13.
22. John H Beattie, *The Churchill Scheme*, 2010, p65.
23. Roderick Macdonald, *The Figurehead*, Edinburgh, 1993, p199.
24. *Naval Review*, 1913, pp181, 281.
25. Bailly, *The Man Around the Engine*, p28.
26. National Archives, ADM 116/3058.
27. *Hansard*, vol 378, cols 1088–89.
28. National Archives, ADM 116/3926.
29. Peter Dickens, *Night Action*, London, 1978, p20.
30. Edward Stafford, *Subchaser*, Annapolis, 2003, p93.
31. Lavery, *Hostilities Only*, pp59–60.
32. John M Iago, *And Home There's No Returning*, Fleet Hargate, 2004, p76.
33. Jenkins, *Days of a Dogsbody*, p73.
34. Lord Chatfield, *It Might Happen Again*, London, 1947, p133.
35. Chatfield, *The Navy and Defence*, London, 1942, p201.
36. National Archives, ADM 116/3060.
37. Angus Cunningham Graham, *Random Naval Recollections*, Ardoch, 1979, p126.
38. *The Royal Navy Officer's Pocket Book*, pp94–5.
39. B Lavery, *All Hands*, London, 2012, p31.
40. United States Naval Academy, *General Information Pamphlet*, Annapolis, 1941, p21.
41. Calvert, *Silent Running*, p9.
42. Theodore Taylor, *The Magnificent Mitscher*, Annapolis, 1991, p19.
43. Thomas B Buell, *The Quiet Warrior*, Annapolis, 1987, pp8–9.

44. Borneman, *The Admirals*, pp14, 56.
45. Whitehill, *Fleet Admiral King*, p24.
46. *Lucky Bag*, 1931, pp, 1, 287.
47. Ibid, pp302–8.
48. Ibid, pp326–43.
49. Whitehill, *Fleet Admiral King*, p30.
50. *Lucky Bag*, 1931, pp346–7.
51. Bowen, *Ships, Machinery and Mossbacks*, p4.
52. Brian Schofield, *With the Royal Navy in War and Peace*, Barnsley, 2018, p3.
53. Borneman, *The Admirals*, p474.
54. Ibid, p469.
55. Donald Chisholm, *Waiting for Dead Men's Shoes*, Stanford, 2000, p756.
56. George Carrol Dyer, *The Amphibians Came to Conquer*, vol 2, Washington, 1972, p158.
57. Chisholm, *Waiting for Dead Men's Shoes*, p763.
58. Calhoun, *Tin Can Sailor*, passim.
59. Ibid, pp83, 96.
60. National Archives, ADM 18/223.
61. Bowen, *Ships, Machinery and Mossbacks*, p14.
62. Daniel E Barbey, *MacArthur's Amphibious Navy*, Annapolis, 1969, xx.
63. D A McElduff, 'The Wardroom of the USS *Tuscaloosa*', in *US Naval Institute Proceedings*, July 1935.
64. 'Dusty' Kleiss, *Never Call me a Hero*, London, 2017, p79.
65. Mason, *Battleship Sailor*, p118.
66. Ibid, p117.
67. Bowen, *Ships, Machinery and Mossbacks*, pp17–18.
68. Samuel Eliot Morison, *The Struggle for Guadalcanal*, Oxford, 1949, p132.
69. Mason, *Battleship Sailor*, pp151.
70. Mason, *Rendezvous with Destiny*, p225.
71. National Archives, ADM 1/18698, 1/18959.
72. John Davies, *Stone Frigate*, London, 1947, p6.
73. Ibid, p5.
74. D A Rayner, *Escort*, London, 1955, p23.
75. *King Alfred Magazine*, vol 1, no 5, p2.
76. Lennox Kerr and Wilfred Granville, *The RNVR*, London, 1957, p151.
77. Nicholas Monsarrat, *Life is a Four Letter Word*, vol II, *Breaking Out*, London, 1970, p6.
78. Ludovic Kennedy, *On My Way to the Club*, London, 1990, p93.
79. *King Alfred* Syllabus, Hove Library.
80. *King Alfred Magazine*, vol 6, p29.
81. F S Holt, *A Banker All at Sea*, Newton, Victoria, 1983, pp108–9.
82. Norman Hampson, *Not Really What You'd Call a War*, Caithness, 2001, p29.
83. Brendan A Maher, *A Passage to Sword Beach,* Shrewsbury, 1996, p29.
84. *King Alfred, General Information*, leaflet, 1941, p17.
85. *Royal Navy Officer's Pocket Book*, p15.
86. *A Passage to Sword Beach*, pp28–9.
87. *To Sea in a Sieve*, pp35–6.
88. *King Alfred* website, p2.
89. Ibid.
90. *HMS King Alfred, 1939–1945*, p21.
91. *The Diaries of Evelyn Waugh*, ed Michael Davie, London, 1976, p490.
92. *In Which they Served*, p187.
93. C Snelling Robinson, *200,000 Miles Aboard the Destroyer Cotton*, Kent Ohio, 2000, pp1–3.
94. *Information for Applicants* ... May 1942, p2.
95. Herman Wouk, *Sailor and Fiddler*, New York, 2016, p38.
96. Douglas Edward Leach, *Now Hear This*, pp8, 14, 15.
97. Ibid, pp16–17.
98. *The Caine Mutiny*, p39.
99. *Recollections of Ensign Leonard W Tate*, US Naval Heritage and History Command, p2.
100. Jones, *The Sonarman's War*, p44.
101. Turner Publishing Company, *Navy V-12*, 1996, p92.
102. Jones, *The Sonarman's War*, p30.
103. Eugene Sledge, *With the Old Breed*, London, 2011, p6.
104. Ibid, p24.
105. Gerald Ford Presidential Library, Ann Arbor.

106. Bureau of Naval Personnel, *All Hands*, June 1945, p33.
107. Jones, *The Sonarman's War*, p27.
108. Naval History and Heritage Command, *The Logistics of Advanced Bases*, OP-30, pp123–30.
109. *All Hands*, June 1945, p34.
110. Dyer, *The Amphibians Came to Conquer*, vol 1, p158.
111. Mason, *Battleship Sailor*, p14.
112. Olson, *Tales from a Tin Can*, pp236, 270.

4 Ratings and Enlisted Men

1. Hannen Swaffer, *What Would Nelson Do?*, London, 1946, p89.
2. Tristan Jones, *Heart of Oak*, 1984, reprinted Shrewsbury, 1997, pp29, 44–5.
3. Rick Jolly, *Jackspeak*, Liskeard, 2000, pp429–30.
4. Mass Observation, Reports 886–7, Sussex University.
5. National Archives, ADM 1/21955.
6. George Melly, *Rum, Bum and Concertina*, London, 1977, pp5–6.
7. Alec Guinness, *Blessings in Disguise*, London, 1985, p154.
8. Admiralty, *Royal Naval Handbook of Field Training*, London, 1920, p19.
9. J Lennox Kerr and David James, *Wavy Navy, by Some Who Served*, London, 1950, p194.
10. Kernan, *Crossing the Line*, p7.
11. Mason, *Battleship Sailor*, p135.
12. Ibid, p33.
13. Floyd Beaver, *Sailor from Oklahoma*, Annapolis, 2009, p24.
14. Ibid, p28.
15. Fahey, *Pacific War Diary*, pp4–5.
16. Beaver, *Sailor from Oklahoma*, p31.
17. Bureau of Naval Personnel, *Yearbook of Personnel Statistics*, 1944, pp59–60, 84–5.
18. US Navy, *Interviewer's Classification Guide*, December 1943, pp2–3.
19. John W Davies, *Jack, the Sailor with the Navy Blue Eyes*, Edinburgh, 1995, p21.
20. Admiralty, *Gunnery Pocket Book*, p1.
21. Ibid, p1.
22. Ibid, p2.
23. Lavery, *All Hands*, pp46–7.
24. *Home is the Sailor*, p55.
25. National Archives, ADM 1/8371/212.
26. John L Brown, *Dairy of a Matelot, 1942–45*, Lowesmoor, Worcester, 1991, p8.
27. Fahey, *Pacific War Diary*, p100.
28. *Interviewer's Classification Guide*, op cit.
29. Monmouth University, DSEA Oral History Project.
30. Mason, *Battleship Sailor*, p56.
31. *Bureau of Naval Personnel Manual*, 1942, p345.
32. Beaver, *Sailor from Oklahoma*, 35.
33. Kernan, *Crossing the Line*, p17.
34. Ibid, p23.
35. Mason, *Battleship Sailor*, p35.
36. Stafford, *Subchaser*, p19.
37. Mason, *Rendezvous with Destiny*, p58.
38. US Naval Institute Oral History, Roger L Bond, pp121, 127.
39. Jones, *The Sonarman's War*, p9.
40. Interview, New York State Military Museum.
41. Mason, *Battleship Sailor*, p102.
42. Jerningham, op cit, p108.
43. Nicholas Monsarrat, *Three Corvettes*, reprinted London, 2000, p188.
44. National Archives, ADM 116/3060.
45. George Melly, *Rum, Bum and Concertina*, London, 1976, p7.
46. H Oram, *The Rogue's Yarn*, London, 1993, p229.
47. *Naval Orientation*, p40.
48. Mason, *Battleship Sailor*, p49.
49. *Naval Orientation*, pp40–1.
50. Kernan, *Crossing the Line*, p62.
51. Beaver, *Sailor from Oklahoma*, p209.
52. Mason, *We Will Stand By You*, p27.
53. Mason, *Battleship Sailor*, p130.
54. Ibid, p61.
55. Stafford, *Little Ship, Big War*, p29.
56. Kernan, *Crossing the Line*, p155.
57. Beaver, *Sailor from Oklahoma*, p209.
58. Ibid, p220.
59. Ibid, p231.
60. Mason, *We Will Stand By You*, p20.
61. Mason, *Battleship Sailor*, p107.

62. *Very Ordinary Seaman*, p88.
63. National Archives, ADM 298/341.
64. *Home is the Sailor*, p147.
65. Noel Wright and AC G Sweet, *How to Prepare Food; Tips and Wrinkles for Cooks of Messes in Standard Ration Ships*, Ipswich, 1941.
66. G G Connell, *Jack's War*, London, 1985, p79.
67. National Archives, ADM 101/623.
68. Fred Kellet, *A Flower for the Sea, a Fish for the Sky*, Carlisle, 1995, p11.
69. National Archives, ADM 239/335.
70. *Anglo-American Naval Relations*, vol 2, pp358, 361, 362.
71. Jerningham, pp41–2.
72. Kernan, *Crossing the Line*, p40.
73. Beaver, *Sailor from Oklahoma*, p138.
74. Jerningham, op cit, pp84–6.
75. Mason, *We Will Stand By You*, p119.
76. Fahey, *Pacific War Diary*, p49.
77. Raines, *Good Night Officially*, p14.
78. Rogal, *Guadalcanal, Tarawa and Beyond*, p41.
79. Edward Monroe-Jones and Michael Green, *The Silent Service in World War II*, London 2012, p20.
80. Beaver, *Sailor from Oklahoma*, p75.
81. Ibid, p129.
82. Raines, *Good Night Officially*, pp14, 26.
83. Mason, *We Will Stand By You*, p119.
84. Kernan, *Crossing the Line*, pp91, 93.
85. Fahey, *Pacific War Diary*, p54.
86. Beaver, *Sailor from Oklahoma*, p155.
87. Mason, *Battleship Sailor*, p25.
88. W S Churchill, *The Gathering Storm*, London, 1965, p689.
89. Frederick S Harrod, *Manning the New Navy*, Westport, 1978, p60.
90. Mason, *Battleship Sailor*, p153.
91. Richard E Miller, *The Messman Chronicles*, London, 2003, p163.
92. Mason, *We Will Stand By You*, p133.
93. Miller, *The Messman Chronicles*, op cit.
94. Studs Terkel, *'The Good War'*, London, 1985, pp392–9.
95. Naval History and Heritage Command, *The Negro in the Navy*, 1947, passim.
96. Bureau of Personnel, *Guide to the Command of Negro Personnel*, p10.
97. Lavery, *All Hands*, p152.
98. *What would Nelson Do?*, pp7.

5 Non-combatants
1. Admiralty, *Handbook of the Royal Naval Sick Berth Staff*, BR 888, 1944, p487.
2. *Biographical Memoirs of Fellows of the Royal Society*, 1956.
3. National Archives, ADM 116/4550.
4. Ransome-Wallis, *Two Red Stripes*, p10.
5. *The Royal Navy Officer's Pocket Book*, pp56.
6. National Archives, ADM 101/620.
7. National Archives, ADM 116/4550.
8. *Nursing in the Senior Service*, ed C M Taylor, Gosport, 2002, pp19–20.
9. *Healers in World War II*, ed Patricia W Sewell, Jefferson, 2001, p240.
10. George Clark, 'Doc', *100 Year History of the Sick Berth Branch*, London, 1984, p153.
11. *The Royal Navy Officer's Pocket Book*, pp49.
12. *'Doc'*, p151.
13. *'Doc'*, p140.
14. *Handbook of the Royal Naval Sick Berth Staff*, p482.
15. Kathleen Harland, *A History of Queen's Alexandria's Royal Naval Nursing Service*, 1990, p28.
16. Ibid, pp26, 28.
17. National Archives, ADM 101/653.
18. Nicholas Monsarrat, *Life is a Four letter Word*, vol II, London, 1970, pp24–5.
19. *The Royal Navy Officer's Pocket Book*, p8.
20. Ibid, p60.
21. Macdonald Critchley, *Shipwreck Survivors, a Medical study*, London, 1943, passim.
22. *Navy V-12*, pp24–5.
23. Jan K Herman, *Battle Station Sick Bay*, Annapolis, 1997, p15.
24. Calhoun, *Tin Can Sailor*, p41.

25. Ibid, p71.
26. Bureau of Medicine and Surgery, *The History of the Medical Department of the United States Navy in World War II*, p115.
27. Naval History and Heritage Command, Ann A Bernatitus, Oral hist.
28. Ibid.
29. Diane Burke Fessier, *No Time for Fear*, East Lansing, 1996, p257.
30. Ibid, p54.
31. Ibid, p54.
32. Ibid, p52.
33. Ibid, p75.
34. *Naval Orientation*, p431.
35. Ibid, p434.
36. *Healers in World War II*, p219.
37. Ibid, p230.
38. Naval History and Heritage Command, Oral History, *The Battle of Guadalcanal*, Louis Ortega.
39. *Healers in World War II*, p139.
40. Mason, *Battleship Sailor*, 141.
41. *Battle Station Sick Bay*, p15.
42. C W Shilling, *A History of Submarine Medicine in World War II*, New London, 1947, p12.
43. Theodore Roscoe, *United States Submarine Operations in World War II*, Annapolis, 1949, p167.
44. Shilling, *A History of Submarine Medicine*, p68.
45. Ibid, p10.
46. Louis Ortega oral history, op cit.
47. National Archives, ADM 298/454.
48. Mason, *Battleship Sailor*, pp140–1.
49. *Battle Station Sick Bay*, p16.
50. Mason, *Battleship Sailor*, 141.
51. Paulo E Coletta, *United States Navy and Marine Corps Bases, Domestic*, Westport, 1985, pp105, 350, 400, 564, 595.
52. *Battle Station Sick Bay*, p205.
53. Ibid, p206.
54. *No Time for Fear*, p148.
55. Ibid, p54.
56. *The History of the Medical Department of the United States Navy in World War II*, vol 1, p172.
57. Ibid, p171.
58. Ibid, p172.
59. *Battle Station Sick Bay*, p171.
60. *Healers in World War II*, p221.
61. *The History of the Medical Department*, vol 1, p175.
62. Ibid, p176.
63. Ibid, p178.
64. Ibid, pp184–5.
65. *Battle Station Sick Bay*, p204.
66. *The History of the Medical Department*, introduction, iii.
67. Roland Gittelsohn, *Pacifist to Padre*, Quantico, 2021, p75.
68. Gordon Taylor, *The Sea Chaplains*, Oxford, 1978, p406.
69. *Navy List*, 1937, pp168–9.
70. Taylor, *The Sea Chaplains*, p451.
71. Ewen Montagu, *Beyond Top Secret U*, London, 1977, p18.
72. Ibid, p173.
73. Taylor, *The Sea Chaplains*, pp443–4.
74. Mason, *Battleship Sailor*, p91.
75. Kernan, *Crossing the Line*, p87.
76. Mason, *Battleship Sailor*, p112.
77. Gittelsohn, *Pacifist to Padre*, pp37–8.
78. Mason, *Battleship Sailor*, p158.
79. Fahey, *Pacific War Diary*, p240.
80. Mason, *Battleship Sailor*, p96.
81. Fahey, *Pacific War Diary*, p186.
82. Joy Bright Hancock, *Lady in the Navy*, Annapolis, 1972, p246.
83. *All Hands*, February 1945, p17.
84. US Coastguard Oral History Program, interview, 7 June 2012.

6 Marines
1. Waugh, *Diaries*, p453.
2. Holland M Smith, *Coral and Brass*, London, 1958, p50.
3. John St John, *To the War with Waugh*, London, 1973, pp1–3.
4. National Archives, ADM 1/20545.
5. Waugh, *Diaries*, p461.
6. St John, *To the War with Waugh*, pp11–12.
7. John Day, *A Plain Russet-coated Captain*, 1993, pp10–15.
8. Waugh, *Men at Arms*, London, 1952, p123.

9. *Sheet Anchor*, vol XVII no 1, Summer 1992.
10. Ted Ford, *The Nearly Man*, Wolverhampton, 1997, p16.
11. J E Pollitt, *Marine to Mayor*, Exeter, c1989, pp28, 30, 33.
12. Ibid, p23.
13. Ibid, p26.
14. Ibid, p25.
15. James D Ladd, *By Sea and by Land*, London, 1998, pp523, 527, 528.
16. War Office, *Infantry Section Leading*, 1938, pp18, 19, 37, 38.
17. Leckie, *Helmet for my Pillow*, p163.
18. Ladd, *By Sea and by Land*, pp501-4.
19. Ibid, pp473-5.
20. Smith, *Coral and Brass*, p32.
21. Rogal, *Guadalcanal, Tarawa and Beyond*, p5.
22. Samuel Hynes, *Flights of Passage*, London, 2005, p112.
23. Mason, *Battleship Sailor*, p16.
24. Sledge, *With the Old Breed*, p8.
25. Robert Leckie, *Helmet for my Pillow*, New York, 2010, p7.
26. Ibid, p7.
27. Ibid, p18.
28. Sledge, *With the Old Breed*, p13.
29. Smith, *Coral and Brass*, pp32-3.
30. *Administration of the Navy Department in World War II*, Chapter IX, 'The United States Marine Corps', pp568-71.
31. Leckie, *Helmet for my Pillow*, p120.
32. Joseph Grasso, *Manila John*, 2010, p45.
33. Rogal, *Guadalcanal, Tarawa and Beyond*, pp47-8.
34. *Marine Corps Manual*, 1940, p183.
35. Julia D Dye, *Backbone*, London, 2011, p76.
36. Leckie, *Helmet for my Pillow*, pp18, 28, 29.
37. *Manila John*, pp174-5.
38. *Marine Corps Manual*, 1940, p183.
39. Leckie, *Helmet for my Pillow*, p172.
40. Ibid, p164.
41. Ibid, p178.
42. Ibid, p23.
43. *Manila John*, p153.
44. Condit, Diamond and Turnbladh, *Marine Corps Ground Training in WWII*, Washington, 1956.
45. Leckie, *Helmet for my Pillow*, p108.
46. Dye, *Backbone*, p25.
47. War Department, *Basic Field Manual*, 1941, p1.
48. Rogal, *Guadalcanal, Tarawa and Beyond*, p40.
49. *Basic Field Manual*, pp1-3.
50. Sledge, *With the Old Breed*, p17.
51. Ibid, p118.
52. Rogal, *Guadalcanal, Tarawa and Beyond*, pp51.
53. Smith, *Coral and Brass*, p2.
54. Leckie, *Helmet for my Pillow*, p163.
55. Ibid, p50.
56. Sledge, *With the Old Breed*, p34.
57. Ibid, p98.
58. Leckie, *Helmet for my Pillow*, p165.
59. Sledge, *With the Old Breed*, p27.
60. Leckie, *Helmet for my Pillow*, p92.
61. Ibid, p78.
62. Ibid, p88.
63. Terkel, 'The Good War', p60.
64. Leckie, *Helmet for my Pillow*, p144.
65. Robert Sherrod, *A History of Marine Corps Aviation in World War II*, Washington, 1952, pp37-8.
66. Hynes, *Flights of Passage*, p77.

7 Bases and Logistics
1. Mason, *Battleship Sailor*, p81.
2. Monsarrat, *Life is a Four Letter Word*, p103.
3. Calvert, *Silent Running*, p102.
4. Mason, *Battleship Sailor*, p81.
5. Raines, *Good Night Officially*, p66.
6. Mason, *Battleship Sailor*, 51.
7. Ibid, p110.
8. Yates Stirling, *Sea Duty*, 1939, Chapter XVII, 'My Last Command'.
9. Holden Evans, *One Man's Fight for a Better Navy*, New York, 1940, pp264-5.
10. Portsmouth Naval Shipyard Cultural Resources Fact Sheet.
11. Bettina A Norton, *The Boston Naval Shipyard 1800-1974*, Boston, 1975.

12. Mason, *Battleship Sailor*, p79.
13. Olson, *Tales from a Tin Can*, p211.
14. Calvert, *Silent Running*, pp101.
15. National Archives, ADM 178/223.
16. Calvert, *Silent Running*, p39.
17. Buell, *The Quiet Warrior*, p168.
18. William Bradford Huie, *Can Do, The story of the Seabees*, Annapolis, 1997, p137.
19. Catalog, p635.
20. Huie, *Can Do*, p139.
21. Jack Cornwell, *A Seabee on Iwo Jima*, in Historynet.
22. Bureau of Yards and Docks, *Building the Navy's Bases in World War II*, pp160–2.
23. Kernan, *Crossing the Line*, p151.
24. Huie, *Can Do*, p46.
25. Richard K Smith, 'Marston Mat', in *Air Force Magazine*, Apil 1969, pp84–8.
26. Morison, *The Struggle for Guadalcanal*, p77.
27. Bureau of Yards and Docks, *US Navy Advanced Base Equipment Catalog*, 1944, p305.
28. Huie, *Can Do*, p135.
29. Taylor, *The Magnificent Mitscher*, p287.
30. Macintyre, *U-Boat Killer*, p62.
31. Fahey, op cit, pp102–3.
32. Morison, *Leyte*, pp47–54.
33. Stafford, *Little Ship, Big War*, p231.
34. Kernan, *Crossing the Line*, p143.
35. Donald Macintyre, *U-Boat Killer*, London, 1999, p106.
36. Peter Gretton, *Convoy Escort Commander*, London, 1964, p138.
37. Macintyre, *U-Boat Killer*, p107.
38. Ibid, pp106–8.
39. Samuel Eliot Morison, *New Guinea and the Marianas*, Annapolis, 1953, p30.
40. Thomas Wildenberg, 'Chester Nimitz and the Development of Fueling at Sea', *Naval War College Review*, 46, no 4, Autumn 1993, pp50–62.
41. Stafford, *Little Ship, Big War*, pp105–6.
42. Roskill, *The War at Sea*, Volume III, Part II, 1961, p374.
43. Ibid, Appendix P, pp426–30.
44. Samuel Eliot Morison, *Leyte*, pp75–7.

8 The Ships
1. Alfred Thayer Mahan, *Naval Strategy*, Boston, 1911, p44.
2. William Hovgaard, *General Design of Warships*, London, 1920, p4.
3. D K Brown, ed, *The Design and Construction of British Warships, 1939–1945, Major Surface Vessels*, London, vol 1, 1995, p17, *Atlantic Escorts*, Barnsley, 2007, pp128–9, 163.
4. *Oxford Dictionary of National Biography*.
5. D K Brown, *A Century of Naval Construction*, London, 1983, p163.
6. *Naval Estimates*, 1937, p256.
7. D K Brown, ed, *The Design and Construction of British Warships, 1939–1945*, vol 3, *Landing Craft and Auxiliary Vessels*, London, 1995, pp8–9.
8. Dyer, *The Amphibians Came to Conquer*, vol 1, p29.
9. Wooldridge, *Carrier Warfare in the Pacific*, p95.
10. Norman Friedman, *US Cruisers*, London, 1985, p9.
11. Ibid, p260.
12. Norman Friedman, *US Destroyers*, Annapolis, 1992, p88.
13. Paul Stillwell, *Submarine Stories*, Annapolis, 2007, p95.
14. Louis Le Bailly, *From Fisher to the Falklands*, London, 1991, pp55–6.
15. Bowen, *Ships, Machinery and Mossbacks*, pp51–2.
16. Ibid, p61.
17. Ibid, p62.
18. Ibid, p74.
19. E T Wooldridge, ed, *Carrier Warfare in the Pacific*, Washington, 1993, pp94–5.
20. Bowen, *Ships, Machinery and Mossbacks*, p95.
21. Ibid, pp98–9.
22. Ibid, p113.
23. Ibid, pp127–33.
24. Calvert, *Silent Running*, pp16–17, 50, 54, 101.

25. Alistair Borthwick, *Yarrow and Company*, Glasgow, 1965.
26. D D Strohmeier, 'A History of Bethlehem Steel Company's Shipbuilding and Ship Repairing', in *Naval Engineer's Journal*, 1963, pp269–72.
27. Nicholas Monsarrat, *HM Frigate*, London, 1946, pp57–8.
28. Augusta H Clawson, *Shipyard Diary of a Woman Welder*, Ann Arbor, 1992, ix.
29. Herman, *Freedom's Forge*, p338.

9 Weapons

1. 'The Evolution of the Modern Gun Mounting', part 1, in *Papers on Engineering Subjects*, 1945, p82.
2. Max Arthur, *Lost Voices of the Royal Navy*, London, 2005, p442.
3. Mason, *Battleship Sailor*, p15.
4. Buford Rowland and William B Boyd, *US Navy Bureau of Ordnance in World War II*, Washington, c1947, p262.
5. Ibid, p263.
6. John Brooks, *Dreadnought Gunnery and the Battle of Jutland*, Cambridge, 2016, p272.
7. *The Gunnery Pocket Book*, p104.
8. Wellings, *On His Majesty's Service*, p234.
9. Ordnance Pamphlet 1140, *Basic Fire Control Mechanisms*, 1944, p8.
10. Calhoun, *Tin Can Sailor*, p91.
11. Olson, *Tales from a Tin Can*, p160.
12. Calhoun, *Tin Can Sailor*, p44.
13. Captain (E) G C Jerry, 'The Development of Destroyer Main Armament, 1941 to 1945', *Journal of Naval Engineering*, 1953, pp393–9.
14. Rowland and Boyd, *US Navy Bureau of Ordnance in World War II*, p258.
15. Ibid, pp258–60.
16. Jerningham, op cit, p122.
17. Calhoun, *Tin Can Sailor*, p49.
18. Olson, *Tales from a Tin Can*, p129.
19. Ibid, p132.
20. Bureau of Ordnance, *5-Inch Twin Mounts ... Description and Instructions*, 1944, pp29–46, 75.
21. Ordnance Pamphlet 1140, *Basic Fire Control Mechanisms*, Washington, 1944, p8.
22. Macdonald, *The Figurehead*, p6.
23. NavWeaps, Tony DiGulian, *The British High Angle Control System*; Peter Marland, *HACS: a Debacle or Just in Time?*
24. NavWeaps, Tony DiGulian, *The British High Angle Control System*; Rowland and Boyd, *US Navy Bureau of Ordnance in World War II*, pp377–8.
25. Morison, *The Struggle for Guadalcanal*, p215.
26. Navy Records Society, *Cunningham Papers*, vol 2, pp365, 359.
27. US Navy, *Motor Torpedo Boat Manual*, February 1943, p70.
28. Rowland and Boyd, *US Navy Bureau of Ordnance in World War II*, pp2343.
29. *Gunnery Pocket Book*, 1945, p170.
30. Jerningham, op cit, p143.
31. *Motor Torpedo Boat Manual*, p70.
32. Navy Records Society, *Cunningham Papers*, vol 2, pp365, 359.
33. L C Reynolds, *Motor Gunboat 658*, London, 2002, p70.
34. Headquarters, US Navy Department, *Antiaircraft Action Summary*, Washington, 1945, pp5–7.
35. Tristan Jones, *Heart of Oak*, London, 1984, p251.
36. Edward Young, *One of our Submarines*, London, 1982, pp225–6.
37. National Archives, ADM 239/239, Staff Monograph, Torpedoes, p69.
38. Calhoun, *Tin Can Sailor*, pp20.
39. Calvert, *Silent Running*, pp62–4.

10 Intelligence and Electronics

1. F H Hinsley, *British Intelligence in the Second World War*, 1979, pp115–25.
2. National Archives, ADM 239/241, Staff Monograph, Naval W/T Organisation, p10.
3. Ibid, passim.
4. Macintyre, *U-Boat Killer*, p25.
5. National Archives, ADM 239/241, Staff Monograph, Naval W/T Organisation, pp12–13.
6. CIC Manual, *Radar Bulletin No 6*, Radsix, 1945, p15.

7. Mason, *Battleship Sailor*, op cit, p32.
8. Navy Records Society, *The Battle of the Atlantic and Signals Intelligence*, ed David Syrett, 2002, p7.
9. Ibid, p29.
10. Ronald Lewin, *The American Magic*, Harmondsworth, 1983, p46.
11. Ibid, p126.
12. Ibid, p134.
13. Stephen Phelps, *The Tizard Mission*, Westholme, 2010, p101.
14. Bowen, *Ships, Machinery and Mossbacks*, p155.
15. Derek Howse, *Radar at Sea, The Royal Navy in World War II*, Basingstoke, 1993, pp83–6, 100, 109–15, 149ff.
16. Ibid, pp141–2, 173–4; Raymond C Watson, *Surviving the Naval Radar Crisis*, Trafford Publishing, 2007, pp270–3.
17. National Archives, ADM 239/307.
18. Mason, *Battleship Sailor*, p187.
19. Ibid, p79.
20. Morison, *The Struggle for Guadalcanal*, p154.
21. Phillip Ziegler, *Mountbatten*, London, 1985, pp77–86.
22. National Archives, ADM 239/241, Staff Monograph, Naval W/T Organisation, p99.
23. Watson, *Naval Radar Crisis*, op cit.
24. Olson, *Tales from a Tin Can*, p193.
25. Navy Records Society, *The Battle of the Atlantic and Signals Intelligence*, ed David Syrett, 2002, p390.
26. *Combat Information Center Magazine*, May 1945, pp17–19.
27. Samuel Eliot Morison, *Breaking the Bismarcks Barrier*, p108.
28. *Combat Information Center Magazine*, May 1945, p27.
29. Radsix, op cit, part I.
30. Samuel Eliot Morison, *Leyte*, p218.
31. Edward P Stafford, *The Big E*, Annapolis, 1988, 307.
32. *Combat Information Center Magazine*, September 1945, p3.
33. Ibid, October 1945, p23.
34. Ibid, November 1945, p5.
35. Olson, *Tales from a Tin Can*, p173.
36. Morison, *Breaking the Bismarcks Barrier*, p188.
37. Taylor, *The Magnificent Mitscher*, pp170–1.
38. Eric Feldt, *The Coast Watchers*, Oxford, 1967, p15.

11 The Battle Fleet

1. Chatfield, *It Might Happen Again*, p99.
2. Navy Records Society, *Anglo-American Naval Relations*, pp199–200.
3. National Archives, PREM 3/324/16.
4. B Lavery, *Churchill Goes to War*, London, 2012, pp31, 45, 63–4, 83, 96.
5. Navy Records Society, *Cunningham Papers*, vol 2, p382.
6. Ian Hawkins, ed, *Destroyer*, London, 2003, p21.
7. Ransome-Wallis, *Two Red Stripes*, p29.
8. *Home is the Sailor*, p38.
9. Beaver, *Sailor from Oklahoma*, pp65–6.
10. Mason, *Battleship Sailor*, p193.
11. Ibid, p190.
12. Jerningham, op cit, p48.
13. Beaver, *Sailor from Oklahoma*, pp52–3, 65.
14. Mason, *Battleship Sailor*, pp55, 58.
15. Beaver, *Sailor from Oklahoma*, p72–3.
16. Jerningham, op cit, p38.
17. Mason, *Battleship Sailor*, p101.
18. National Archives, ADM 298/454.
19. D K Brown, *Major Surface Vessels*, vol 1, p125.
20. Ibid, p128.
21. Kennedy, *On My Way to the Club*, p105.
22. Navy Records Society, *Cunningham Papers*, vol 2, pp376, 389, 364.
23. Arthur, *Lost Voices of the Royal Navy*, p207.
24. *In Which They Served*, p130.
25. *The Royal Navy Officer's Pocket Book*, p86.
26. Jones, *Heart of Oak*, p165.
27. Macdonald, *The Figurehead*, pp32, 183.
28. Communication to author.
29. Wellings, *On His Majesty's Service*, pp75, 76.

30. Calhoun, *Tin Can Sailor*, p86.
31. *The Roosevelt Letters*, vol 3, p329.
32. Friedman, *US Destroyers*, pp87, 112.
33. Stafford, *Little Ship, Big War*, pp120–1.
34. Jerningham, op cit, p80.
35. Michael Keith Olson, *Tales from a Tin Can*, St Paul, 2007, p198.
36. William J Ruhe, *Slow Dance to Pearl Harbor*, Washington, 1995, passim.
37. Robinson, *200,000 Miles Aboard the Destroyer Cotton*, p133.
38. Jerningham, p78.
39. Ruhe, *Slow Dance to Pearl Harbor*, p51.
40. Cunningham, *A Sailor's Odyssey*, London, 1951, p260.
41. Samuel Eliot Morison, *Leyte*, pp224–6.

12 Naval Aviation

1. Arthur Longmore, *From Sea to Sky*, London, 1946, p75.
2. Taylor, *The Magnificent Mitscher*, p320.
3. *Anglo-American Naval Relations*, vol 2, p355.
4. Friedman, *US Aircraft Carriers*, Annapolis, 1993, pp33–4.
5. William F Trimble, *Admiral William A Moffat*, Washington, 1994, p245.
6. Ibid.
7. Archibald Douglas Turnbull and Clifford Lee Lord, *History of United States Naval Aviation*, New Haven, 1949.
8. Jenkins, *Days of a Dogsbody*, pp191, 193.
9. National Archives, ADM 239/361.
10. Arnold Hague, *The Allied Convoy System*, Chatham, 2000, pp77–82.
11. Kilbracken, *Bring Back my Stringbag*, p15.
12. Royal Institution of Naval Architects, *British Warship Design*, 1983, p49.
13. Hague, *The Allied Convoy System*, p85.
14. Albert A Nofi, *To Train the Fleet for War*, Newport, 2010, pp148, 150.
15. Friedmann, *US Aircraft Carriers*, pp63, 67, 72, 75.
16. Wooldridge, *Carrier Warfare in the Pacific*, pp93–4.
17. Kernan, *Crossing the Line*, p22.
18. Wooldridge, *Carrier Warfare in the Pacific*, pp96–7.
19. Eric 'Winkle' Brown, *Wings on My Sleeve*, London, 2007, pp17–18.
20. Mason, *Rendezvous with Destiny*, p84.
21. *Bring Back my Stringbag*, p168.
22. Ibid, pp168–9.
23. John Winton, *Carrier Glorious*, London, 1999, p11.
24. Rebecca John, *Caspar John*, p74.
25. National Archives, ADM 116/4036.
26. Roskill, *War at Sea*, vol 2, pp409–10.
27. Charles Lamb, *To War in a Stringbag*, London, 1978, p43.
28. Raymond Lygo, *Collision Course*, Lewes, 2001, p62.
29. D L Hadley, *Barracuda Pilot*, Shrewsbury, 1992, p26.
30. Ibid, p22.
31. Ibid, p32.
32. H J C Spencer, *Ordinary Naval Airmen*, Tunbridge Wells, 1992, passim.
33. Hadley, *Barracuda Pilot*, p29.
34. Gordon Wallace, *Carrier Observer*, Shrewsbury, 1993, p23.
35. Arthur, *Lost Voices of the Royal Navy*, p308.
36. Ibid, pp530–1.
37. Taylor, *The Magnificent Mitscher*, p242.
38. Kernan, *Crossing the Line*, p53.
39. Ibid, p125.
40. Hynes, *Flights of Passage*, pp47–8.
41. Ibid, p45.
42. *US Navy Flight Training Manuals*, 1 Elementary, 2 Primary, p59.
43. Ibid, 1, p9.
44. Hynes, *Flights of Passage*, p25.
45. Ibid, p145.
46. Bureau of Aeronautics, *Using Your Navy Wings*, Washington, 1943, p1.
47. Max Miller, *Daybreak for our Carriers*, New York, 1944, pp31–2.
48. Ibid, p7.
49. Bureau of Naval Personnel, *Aircraft Armament*, 1945, p3.

50. *Interviewer's Classification Guide*, op cit.
51. William Hornby, *Factories and Plant*, London, 1958, pp401–3.
52. Hugh Popham, *Sea Flight*, London, 1954, p76.
53. Kilbracken, *Bring Back my Stringbag*, p31.
54. Ibid, p32.
55. Quoted in Owen Thetford, *British Naval Aircraft*, London, 1991, pp324–5.
56. Lygo, *Collision Course*, p84.
57. Brown, *Wings on My Sleeve*, p11.
58. Herman, *Freedom's Forge*, p338.
59. Morison, *New Guinea and the Marianas*, p299.
60. Kernan, *Crossing the Line*, p61.
61. Ibid, pp98–9.
62. Bureau of Naval Personnel, *Aircraft Turrets*, 1946.
63. Kernan, *Crossing the Line*, p122.
64. Nofi, *To Train the Fleet for War*, pp34, 188–90.
65. Kleiss, *Never Call me a Hero*, pp85–6.
66. Hynes, *Flights of Passage*, p142.
67. Kleiss, *Never Call me a Hero,* p228.
68. Hynes, *Flights of Passage*, p192.
69. Stafford, *The Big E*, p280.
70. Herschel Smith, *A History of Aircraft Piston Engines*, Manhattan, Kansas, 1986, p241.
71. Taylor, *The Magnificent Mitscher*, p169.
72. *Using Your Navy Wings*, p9.
73. *The Struggle for Guadalcanal*, p330.
74. Swanborough, pp565–80; Morison, *Atlantic*, pp250–1.
75. Hadley, *Barracuda Pilot*, p159.
76. Norman Friedman, *British Carrier Aviation*, London, 1988, pp110–11.
77. Lamb, *To War in a Stringbag*, pp91–2.
78. Hadley, *Barracuda Pilot*, p151.
79. *Daybreak for our Carriers*, p9.
80. Kernan, *Crossing the Line*, p25.
81. Brown, *Wings on My Sleeve*, p45.
82. Kernan, *Crossing the Line*, pp110–11.
83. Ibid, pp139–40.
84. *Daybreak for our Carriers*, pp46–9.

85. Spencer, *Ordinary Naval Airmen*, p104.
86. Stafford, *Little Ship, Big War*, p121.
87. Spencer, *Ordinary Naval Airmen*, p44.
88. Wooldridge, *Carrier Warfare in the Pacific*, p228.
89. Ibid, p11.
90. Kleiss, *Never Call me a Hero*, pp176–8.
91. John Campbell, *Naval Weapons of World War Two*, London, 1985, p159.
92. Olson, *Tales from a Tin Can*, p191.
93. Roscoe, *United States Submarine Operations*, op cit, pp465–74.
94. Robert B Stinnett, *George Bush, His World War II Years*, Washington, 1992, pp147–65.
95. Popham, *Sea Flight*, op cit.
96. Turnbull and Lord, *History of United States Naval Aviation*, p301.
97. Trimble, *Admiral William A Moffat*, p83.
98. Mason, *Battleship Sailor*, p18.
99. Ibid, p126.
100. *Daybreak for our Carriers*, p4.

13 Submarines
1. Navy Records Society, *Anglo-American Naval Relations*, vol 2, p51.
2. Edward Young, *One of our Submarines*, London, 1982, pp18, 21.
3. Ben Bryant, *Submarine Command*, London, 1975, p25.
4. National Archives, ADM 239/239, Staff Monograph, Torpedoes, pp24–9.
5. Arthur Dickison, *Crash Dive*, Stroud, 1999, p187.
6. Bryant, *Submarine Command*, p36.
7. Goodall, *TRINA*, 1946, p6.
8. *British Warship Design,* p72.
9. Ibid, p74.
10. National Archives, PREM 3/324/20.
11. Stillwell, *Submarine Stories*, p243.
12. John D Alden, *The Fleet Submarine in the US Navy*, London, 1979, p101.
13. Calvert, *Silent Running*, p203.
14. Monroe-Jones and Green, *The Silent Service in World War II*, p17.
15. Ibid, p67.

16. Dickison, *Crash Dive*, ix.
17. Bryant, *Submarine Command*, p35.
18. Young, *One of our Submarines*, pp124–35.
19. Bryant, *Submarine Command*, p35.
20. Arthur Hezlet, *HMS Trenchant at War*, London, 2000, p108.
21. Ibid, pp110–11.
22. Dickison, *Crash Dive*, p35.
23. Hezlet, *HMS Trenchant at War*, pp2–3.
24. Young, *One of our Submarines*, pp150–1.
25. Dickison, *Crash Dive*, p67.
26. Ibid, p115.
27. Ibid, p10.
28. Ibid, p83.
29. Young, *One of our Submarines*, p336.
30. Sydney Hart, *Discharged Dead*, London, 1958, p34.
31. Admiralty, *His Majesty's Submarines*, 1945, p7.
32. Dickison, *Crash Dive*, p5.
33. Bryant, *Submarine Command*, p73.
34. Dickison, *Crash Dive*, p175.
35. Monroe-Jones and Green, *The Silent Service in World War II*, p26.
36. Stillwell, *Submarine Stories*, pp204.
37. Ibid, p138.
38. Ibid, p227.
39. Submarine Division Forty-One, *Submarine Information and Instruction Manual*, 1942, pp1, 4, 64.
40. Stillwell, *Submarine Stories*, pp16–17.
41. Ibid, p228.
42. Edward L Beach, *Salt and Steel*, Annapolis, 1999, pp21–2.
43. Monroe-Jones and Green, *The Silent Service in World War II*, p12.
44. Calvert, *Silent Running*, p109.
45. Ibid, p248.
46. USS *Pompom*, *Ship's Orders*, 1944, p15.
47. Monroe-Jones and Green, *The Silent Service in World War II*, p20.
48. Bryant, *Submarine Command*, p58.
49. Ibid, p60.
50. Young, *One of our Submarines*, pp43–4.
51. Bryant, *Submarine Command*, p50.
52. National Archives, ADM 239/239.
53. Arthur, *Lost Voices of the Royal Navy*, pp405–8.
54. C E Lucas-Phillips, *Cockleshell Heroes*, London, 1977, p255.
55. Barbey, *MacArthur's Amphibious Navy*, p170.
56. Calvert, *Silent Running*, p222.
57. USS *Pampanito*, *General Information Book*, 1943, p22.
58. Calvert, *Silent Running*, p6.
59. Ivan V Duff, *Medical Study of the Experiences of Submariners*, Washington, 1947, p22.
60. USS *Pompom*, *Ship's Orders*, p123.
61. Calvert, *Silent Running*, p109.
62. Stillwell, *Submarine Stories*, p208.
63. Ibid.
64. Comsublant, *Submarine Sonar Operator's Manual*, 1944, p1.
65. Calvert, *Silent Running*, p52.
66. Bryant, *Submarine Command*, p57.
67. Calvert, *Silent Running*, x.
68. Ibid, p13.
69. Ibid, p117.
70. Ibid, p63.
71. Ibid, p178.
72. Hart, *Discharged Dead*, p38.
73. *What Would Nelson Do?*, p36.
74. J D Drummond, *HM U-boat*, London, 1958, p149.
75. Stillwell, *Submarine Stories*, p247.
76. Calvert, *Silent Running*, p55.
77. Monroe-Jones and Green, *The Silent Service in World War II*, pp73–4.
78. Roscoe, *United States Submarine Operations*, p88.
79. Calvert, *Silent Running*, p136.
80. Ibid, p40.
81. Tender Tale website.
82. Dickison, *Crash Dive*, xii.
83. Samuel Eliot Morison, *Leyte*, p413.

14 Anti-submarine Warfare

1. National Maritime Museum, Ships covers, 573A.
2. *Churchill War Papers*, ed Martin Gilbert, vol 1, London, 1993, p247.

3. Michael Gannon, *Operation Drumbeat*, New York, 1990, p340.
4. Navy Records Society, *Cunningham Papers*, vol 2, p14.
5. *King Alfred Magazine*, January 1944, p13.
6. Gannon, *Operation Drumbeat*, p339.
7. Roskill, *War at Sea*, vol 2, p97.
8. Gannon, *Operation Drumbeat*, p342.
9. Ibid, p390.
10. Barley and Waters, *The Defeat of the Enemy Attack on Shipping*, p86.
11. Gretton, *Convoy Escort Commander*, p131.
12. National Archives, ADM 237/126.
13. Brown, *The Design and Construction of British Warships, 1939–1945*, vol 3, p93.
14. S A Kerslake, *Coxswain in the Northern Convoys*, London, 1984.
15. B Lavery, *River Class Frigates and the Battle of the Atlantic*, London, 2006, p18.
16. Ibid, p20.
17. Macintyre, *U-Boat Killer*, p59.
18. Gretton, *Convoy Escort Commander*, p107.
19. Quoted in B Lavery, *Churchill, Warrior*, Oxford, 2017, p372.
20. Buell, *The Quiet Warrior*, p79.
21. Gretton, *Convoy Escort Commander*, p109.
22. National Archives, ADM 239/298.
23. National Archives, ADM 1/13680.
24. National Archives, ADM 237/90.
25. Gretton, *Convoy Escort Commander*, p137.
26. National Archives, ADM 239/298.
27. Gretton, *Convoy Escort Commander*, p175.
28. National Archives, ADM 239/298.
29. Gretton, *Convoy Escort Commander*, p133.
30. National Archives ADM 239/248, p4.
31. *Yankee RN*, p150.
32. B Lavery, *In Which They Served*, London, 2008, pp283–7.
33. Gretton, *Convoy Escort Commander*, p106.
34. Rayner, *Escort*, p230.
35. Admiralty, *Monthly Anti-Submarine Report*, vol 3, p23.
36. Gretton, *Convoy Escort Commander*, p116.
37. Macintyre, *U-Boat Killer*, p22.
38. Martin Middlebrook, *Convoy*, Harmondsworth, 1978, pp225–7 and passim.
39. National Archives, ADM 1/13415.
40. Atlantic Convoy Instructions, Article 129.
41. Gretton, *Convoy Escort Commander*, p118.
42. National Archives, ADM 239/298.
43. *Monthly Anti-Submarine Report*, August 1942, p11.
44. National Archives, ADM 199/714.
45. CAFO P603/43.
46. Gretton, *Convoy Escort Commander*, p176.
47. Lavery, *In Which They Served*, p145.
48. *Admiralty Pilot Book*, 1921 ed, p120.
49. Monsarrat, *Three Corvette*, London, 1945, p73.
50. Rayner, *Escort*, p41.
51. David Boler, *Hostilities Only*, 2013, p294.
52. Brown, *Atlantic Escorts*, p135.
53. Norman Freidman, *British Destroyers and Frigates*, London, 2006, p81.
54. Monsarrat, *HM Frigate*, pp60–1.
55. Ibid, pp62–4.
56. Jones, *The Sonarman's War*, pp23–5.
57. Samuel Eliot Morison, *The Battle of the Atlantic*, p229.
58. Ibid, pp230–1.
59. Jones, *The Sonarman's War*, p11.
60. Morison, *The Battle of the Atlantic*, pp213–15.
61. Stafford, *Little Ship, Big War*, pp57–8.
62. Alan M Sternhell and Alan B Turnbull, *Anti Submarine Warfare in World War II*, Washington, 1946, p143.
63. Stafford, *Little Ship, Big War*, p10.
64. Olson, *Tales from a Tin Can*, p276.
65. *Dictionary of American Fighting Ships*, vol VIII, Washington, 1981, p538.
66. Ministry of Defence, *War With Japan*, vol VI, 1995, pp101–4.
67. C B A Behrens, *Merchant Shipping and the Demands of War*, London, 1956, p157.

68. Ibid, p17.
69. R H Thornton, *British Shipping*, Cambridge, 1939, p127.
70. *Atlantic Convoy Instructions*.
71. Martin Middlebrook, *Convoy*, pp24–5.
72. Quoted in Woodman, p49.
73. Behrens, *Merchant Shipping*, pp114–18.
74. George J Billy and Christine M Billy, *Merchant Mariners at War*, University Press of Florida, 2008, p28.
75. Ibid, p9.
76. United States Maritime Service, *Training Manual, Preliminary Training*, 1943, p3.
77. Billy, *Merchant Mariners at War*, p36.
78. Middlebrook, *Convoy*, p109.
79. Michael Gillen, *Merchant Marine Survivors of World War II*, Jefferson, 2015, pp20–1.
80. Ibid, pp30–1.
81. Samuel Eliot Morison, *Leyte*, pp78–9.
82. Gillen, *Merchant Marine Survivor*, p28.

15 Coastal Navies
1. *US Coast Guard Oral History and Memoir Program*, p12.
2. The United States Coast Guard Academy, Washington, 1939, passim.
3. *US Coast Guard Oral History and Memoir Program*, 2 8 2004.
4. Ibid, 18 June 2003.
5. Ibid.
6. Ibid, Captain Bob Desh.
7. Ibid, 7 June 2012.
8. William H Thiesen, 'The Coast Guard's World War II Crucible', *Naval History*, October 2016.
9. Charles McAra, *Mainly in Minesweepers*, London, 1991, pp55–6.
10. *British Minesweeping*, p71.
11. Charles W Domville-Fife, *Submarine Warfare of Today*, London, 1919, pp175–6.
12. National Archives, ADM 239/245, *British Minesweeping*, 1950, p18.
13. Winston G Ramsey, ed, *The Blitz Then and Now*, London, 1987, vol 1, pp52–5.
14. *British Minesweeping*, p20.
15. Ibid, p21.
16. Ernest Goodhall, *Wartime Minesweeping Memories*, in mcdoa.org.uk website, passim.
17. Patricia B Farley, *Birds of a Feather: A Wren's Memoirs, 1942–1945*.
18. Goodhall, *Wartime Minesweeping Memories*, op cit.
19. Tamara Moser Melia, '*Damn the Torpedoes*', Washington, 1991, p59.
20. *British Minesweeping*, p45.
21. Rayner, *Escort*, pp30–1.
22. Admiralty, *His Majesty's Minesweepers*, London, 1943, pp38–9.
23. McAra, *Mainly in Minesweepers*, pp55–6.
24. *British Minesweeping*, p12.
25. Ibid, p71.
26. Vivian A Cox, *Seven Christmases*, Sevenoaks, 2010, pp26–8.
27. Rayner, *Escort*, p33.
28. *Wartime Minesweeping Memories*, op cit.
29. B Lavery, *All Hands*, London, 2012, p92.
30. McAra, *Mainly in Minesweepers*, p57.
31. *British Minesweeping*, p11.
32. Rayner, *Escort*, p32.
33. Brendan A Maher, *A Passage to Sword Beach*, Shrewsbury, 1996, pp101–2.
34. *WW2 People's War*, James Clark.
35. *British Minesweeping*, p77.
36. Maher, *A Passage to Sword Beach*, p59.
37. McAra, *Mainly in Minesweepers*, pp57, 64.
38. Maher, *A Passage to Sword Beach*, p48.
39. *Wartime Minesweeping Memories*, op cit.
40. Cox, *Seven Christmases*, p50.
41. Roskill, *War at Sea*, vol 3, part 2, pp174, 303.
42. Ibid, p18.
43. Ibid, p29.
44. Maher, *A Passage to Sword Beach*, pp118–19.
45. Brown, *Major Surface Warships*, pp39–45, 120.

46. Norman Longmate, *The Bombers*, London, 1983, pp118–19.
47. Barley and Waters, *The Defeat of the Enemy Attack on Shipping*, Navy Records Society, 1997, pp150–4.
48. Nofi, *To Train the Fleet for War*, pp64n, 292.
49. Melia, '*Damn the Torpedoes*', pp48, 49.
50. Morison, *Battle of the Atlantic*, Appendix IV.
51. Digital Library of Georgia, Oral history interview of James Leland Jackson.
52. Jones, *The Sonarman's War*, p180.
53. Rob Gardiner, ed, *Conway's All the World's Fighting Ships*, London, 1980, p151.
54. Jones, *The Sonarman's War*, p180.
55. Naval Historical Foundation, Oral History Program, 2004, p7.
56. Digital Library of Georgia, Oral history interview of James Leland Jackson.
57. Melia, '*Damn the Torpedoes*', p50.
58. Jones, *The Sonarman's War*, p10.
59. Ibid, p182.
60. Melia, '*Damn the Torpedoes*', p64.
61. Ibid, p55.
62. Jones, *The Sonarman's War*, p65.
63. John B Desrosiers, *Minesweeping During World War II*, Naval Historical Foundation Oral History Program, 2004, p14.
64. Ibid, p19.
65. Jones, *The Sonarman's War*, p183.
66. Ibid, p183.
67. Ibid, p187.
68. US Navy Bomb Disposal School, *Mine Disposal Handbook*, 1945, pp9–10, 11.
69. Roscoe, *United States Submarine Operations*, pp180–2.
70. Bureau of Ordnance, *Operational Characteristics of US Naval Mines*, 1959.
71. Gerald A Mason, *Operation Starvation*, Air War College, Maxwell Air force Base, Alabama, 2002.
72. *Motor Torpedo Boat Manual*, p357.
73. *British Warship Design*, p156.
74. Uffa Fox, *Seamanlike Sense in Power Craft*, London, 1968, p101.
75. *British Warship Design*, p160.
76. Ibid, pp143, 147.
77. Reynolds, *Motor Gunboat 658*, p118.
78. Peter Dickens, *Night Action*, op cit, p67.
79. National Archives, ADM 239/239, Staff Monograph, Torpedoes, pp9–10, 29, 39–40, 49, 69.
80. *British Warship Design*, p141.
81. Reynolds, *Motor Gunboat 658*, p25.
82. Ibid, p116.
83. Peter Scott, *The Eye of the Wind*, London, 1961, p447.
84. Ibid, p428.
85. *British Warship Design*, pp140–1.
86. Reynolds, *Motor Gunboat 658*, pp21–2.
87. Eric Denton, *My Six Wartime Years in the Royal Navy*, London, 1999, p61.
88. Peter Dickens, *Night Action*, p33.
89. Ibid, pp58–9.
90. Ibid, p231.
91. Ibid, p45.
92. Ibid, p45.
93. C Anthony Law, *White Plumes Astern*, Halifax, 1989, p16.
94. *British Warship Design*, p165.
95. Ibid, p153.
96. B Lavery, *Shield of Empire*, Edinburgh, 2007, p384.
97. Reynolds, *Motor Gunboat 658*, p19.
98. Peter Dickens, *Night Action*, p39.
99. Ibid, p39.
100. Scott, *The Eye of the Wind*, p484.
101. Peter Dickens, *Night Action*, p34.
102. *British Warship Design*, p138.
103. Peter Dickens, *Night Action*, p55.
104. Ibid, p65.
105. Law, *White Plumes Astern*, p46.
106. Scott, *The Eye of the Wind*, p474.
107. Denton, *My Six Wartime Years in the Royal Navy*, p73.
108. Reynolds, *Motor Gunboat 658*, p48.
109. *British Warship Design*, p162.
110. Scott, *The Eye of the Wind*, p474.
111. Law, *White Plumes Astern*, intro.
112. Scott, *The Eye of the Wind*, p416.
113. Reynolds, *Motor Gunboat 658*, p164.
114. Norman Friedman, *US Small Combatants*, Annapolis, 1987, p141.

115. *Motor Torpedo Boat Manual*, pp274–5.
116. Ibid, p193.
117. Donald B Frost, oral history interview, John Fitzgerald Kennedy Library, 2005, p21.
118. Friedman, *US Small Combatants*, pp156–7.
119. Ibid, pp157–66.
120. *Motor Torpedo Boat Manual*, p1.
121. Ibid, p3.
122. Donald B Frost, op cit, p4.
123. Mason, *We Will Stand By You*, p69.
124. Donald B Frost, op cit, pp1–2.
125. Ibid, p26.
126. *Motor Torpedo Boat Manual*, p4.
127. Edgar Hoagland, *The Sea Hawks*, Presidio Press, 1999, p56.
128. Donald B Frost, op cit, pp2–3.
129. Hoagland, *The Sea Hawks*, pp75–6.
130. Friedman, *US Small Combatants*, 149.
131. Hoagland, *The Sea Hawks*, p80.
132. *US Navy Advanced Base Equipment Catalog*, 1944, pp451, 499, 513, 519, 521, 527–8.
133. Howard L Terry, *A PT Boat Captain in the Pacific*, terryfoundation.org, p6.
134. Donald B Frost, op cit, p60.
135. William Manchester, *American Caesar*, London, 1979, p167.
136. Barbey, *MacArthur's Amphibious Navy*, p24.
137. Roosevelt, *Letters*, vol 3, p416.
138. Terry, *A PT Boat Captain in the Pacific*, p3.
139. Ibid, p11.
140. Samuel Eliot Morison, *Leyte*, pp205–11.
141. Dickens, *Night Action*, p54.
142. Hoagland, *The Sea Hawks*, p212.
143. Roskill, *War at Sea*, vol III, part II, p283.
144. Samuel Eliot Morison, *New Guinea and the Marianas*, pp56–7.

16 Amphibious Warfare
1. National Archives, DEFE 2/697, p59.
2. Peter A Isely and Phillip A Crowl, *US Marines and Amphibious Warfare*, 1951, p31.
3. Ibid, p53.
4. Smith, *Coral and Brass*, p81.
5. *British Warship Design*, p199.
6. *Churchill War Papers*, vol 2, p638.
7. R Baker et al, *British Warship Design in World War II*, London, 1983, p181.
8. Paul Lund and Harry Ludlam, *The War of the Landing Craft*, Slough, 1976, p40.
9. *Mariner's Mirror*, 2002, p213.
10. *British Warship Design*, p19.
11. Ibid, pp19–30.
12. *Battle Station Sick Bay*, p97.
13. Samuel Eliot Morison, *Operations in North African Waters*, p137.
14. Morison, *The Invasion of France and Germany*, p28.
15. Sledge, *With the Old Breed*, p43.
16. Dyer, *The Amphibians Came to Conquer*, vol 2, p655.
17. Olson, *Tales from a Tin Can*, p170.
18. Landing Craft School, Coronado, *Skill in the Surf*, 1945, p38.
19. Smith, *Coral and Brass*, pp72, 96.
20. *Skill in the Surf*, p29.
21. Sledge, *With the Old Breed*, p177.
22. *British Warship Design*, p171.
23. Smith, *Coral and Brass*, p97.
24. National Archives, DEFE 2/838.
25. Ibid.
26. Leckie, *Helmet for my Pillow*, pp206–7.
27. Mason, *We Will Stand By You*, p196.
28. *British Warship Design*, p190.
29. Barbey, *MacArthur's Amphibious Navy*, p170.
30. British Library, Add Ms 82532.
31. Maher, *A Passage to Sword Beach*, pp124–5.
32. Morison, *Victory in the Pacific*, pp37–8, 149–51.
33. Bureau of Naval Personnel, *Information Bulletin*, February 1944.
34. National Archives, PREM 3/216/1.
35. Phillip Ziegler, *Mountbatten*, London, 1985, p162.
36. National Archives, DEFE 2/703.
37. *The War of the Landing Craft*, p91.
38. National Archives, DEFE 2/703.
39. *To Sea in A Sieve*, p46.

40. National Archives, ADM 101/641.
41. L E H Maund, *Assault from the Sea*, London, 1949, p75.
42. National Archives, PREM 3/103/1.
43. Kings College, Alanbrooke Papers, 6/2/11.
44. National Archives, PREM 3/256.
45. Dyer, *The Amphibians Came to Conquer*, vol 2, p216.
46. Ibid, p217.
47. Barbey, *MacArthur's Amphibious Navy*, p51.
48. Bureau of Naval Personnel, *Information Bulletin*, May 1945.
49. Morison, *Operations in North African Waters*, p81.
50. Ibid, p202.
51. Dyer, *The Amphibians Came to Conquer*, vol 2, p822.
52. *Skill in the Surf*, p27.
53. Bureau of Naval Personnel, *Information Bulletin*, May 1945.
54. Ibid, February 1944.
55. *San Luis Obispo County Telegram Tribune*, 10 June 1944.
56. Dyer, *The Amphibians Came to Conquer*, vol 2, p876.
57. Ibid, p930.
58. Manchester, *American Caesar*, p341.
59. Barbey, *MacArthur's Amphibious Navy*, p24.
60. Gerald E Wheeler, *Kincaid of the Seventh Fleet*, Washington 1994, p347.
61. Barbey, *MacArthur's Amphibious Navy*, p27.
62. Adrian R Lewis, *Omaha Beach*, Stroud, 2021, p153.
63. Ibid, p124.
64. Ibid, p82.
65. David A Rogers, 'Development of Amphibious Force Flagship', *Bureau of Ships Journal*, February 1962, p11.
66. Ibid, p12.
67. Morison, *Operations in North African Waters*, p190n.
68. Morison, *Sicily, Salerno, Anzio*, pp63–4.
69. Dyer, *The Amphibians Came to Conquer*, vol 2, p781.
70. National Archives, DEFE 2/838.
71. Ibid.
72. Rogal, *Guadalcanal, Tarawa and Beyond*, p43.
73. *Skill in the Surf*, p32.
74. Leckie, *Helmet for my Pillow*, p56.
75. US Coast Guard Oral History Program, 18 June 2003.
76. Morison, *Breaking the Bismarcks Barrier*, p300.
77. *Skill in the Surf*, p35.
78. National Archives, DEFE 2/838.
79. Morison, *Operations in North African Waters*, pp123, 177.
80. Barbey, *MacArthur's Amphibious Navy*, p101.
81. Ibid, p182.
82. Smith, *Coral and Brass*, pp130–1.
83. Leckie, *Helmet for my Pillow*, p91.
84. Morison, *Operations in North African Waters*, p204.
85. Morison, *The Invasion of France and Germany*, pp100, 136–7.
86. Morison, *Victory in the Pacific*, p150.
87. Barbey, *MacArthur's Amphibious Navy*, p43.
88. Morison, *Sicily, Salerno, Anzio*, pp106–7.
89. National Archives, DEFE 2/838.
90. Morison, vol IX, *Sicily, Salerno, Anzio*, p83.
91. *All Hands*, August 1945.
92. Barbey, *MacArthur's Amphibious Navy*, p103.

17 Enemies
1. Hans Goebeler, *Steel Boats, Iron Hearts*, London 2005, pp26–7.
2. *Fuehrer Conferences on Naval Affairs*, p223.
3. Ibid, p306.
4. Heinz Schaeffer, *U-Boat 977*, London, 1973, p31.
5. Goebeler, *Steel Boats, Iron Hearts*, pp37, 84, 85–6, 134, 156, 209.
6. Ibid, p29.
7. Wolfgang Hirschfeld, *The Secret Diary of a U-boat*, London, 2000, pp16.
8. Ibid, p299.

9. *Fuehrer Conferences on Naval Affairs*, p438.
10. Ibid, p360.
11. Goebeler, *Steel Boats, Iron Hearts*, p240.
12. *Fuehrer Conferences on Naval Affairs*, p391.
13. Ibid, p274.
14. Ibid, p216.
15. Ibid, p307.
16. Ibid, p90.
17. Ibid, p114.
18. Ibid, p137.
19. Ibid, p124.
20. Schaeffer, *U-Boat 977*, p48.
21. *Fuehrer Conferences on Naval Affairs*, p120.
22. Peter Schenk, *The Invasion of England 1940*, London, 1990, pp107–10.
23. Ibid, p182.
24. Goebeler, *Steel Boats, Iron Hearts*, p65.
25. Hirschfeld, *The Secret Diary of a U-boat*, p126.
26. Goebeler, *Steel Boats, Iron Hearts*, p32.
27. *Fuehrer Conferences on Naval Affairs*, p384.
28. Adam Tooze, *The Wages of Destruction*, London, 2007, pp615–18.
29. *Fuehrer Conferences on Naval Affairs*, p361.
30. Ibid, p391.
31. Ibid, p362.
32. Martin Middlebrook, *Convoy*, p59.
33. Goebeler, *Steel Boats, Iron Hearts*, p29.
34. Ibid, p33.
35. Ibid, p160.
36. Ibid, p41.
37. Hirschfeld, *The Secret Dairy of a U-boat*, p54.
38. Schaeffer, *U-Boat 977*, p80.
39. Ibid, p81.
40. Ibid, pp81–2.
41. Goebeler, *Steel Boats, Iron Hearts*, p51.
42. Hirschfeld, *The Secret Dairy of a U-boat*, p257.
43. Goebeler, *Steel Boats, Iron Hearts*, p152.
44. Ibid, p79.
45. Goebeler, *Steel Boats, Iron Hearts*, p238.
46. Schaeffer, *U-Boat 977*, p88.
47. Goebeler, *Steel Boats, Iron Hearts*, p211.
48. Ibid, p162.
49. Bryan Cooper, *The E-Boat Threat*, London, 1978, pp21–3, 39–48.
50. *Fuehrer Conferences on Naval Affairs*, p317.
51. Rikhei Inoguchi, *The Divine Wind*, Annapolis, 1994, p198.
52. Ron Werneth, ed, *Beyond Pearl Harbor*, Aglen, Pennsylvania, 2008, p252.
53. Tameichi Hara, *Japanese Destroyer Captain*, New York, 2006, p17.
54. Ibid, p178.
55. Yoshido Mitsuru, *Requiem for the Battleship Yamato*, London, 1999, p52.
56. Cecil Bullock, *Etajima, The Dartmouth of Japan*, London, 1942, pp78, 81.
57. Tameichi Hara, *Japanese Destroyer Captain*, p18.
58. Yoshido Mitsuru, *Requiem for the Battleship Yamato*, p44.
59. Tameichi Hara, *Japanese Destroyer Captain*, pp76.
60. World of Warships website.
61. Tameichi Hara, *Japanese Destroyer Captain*, p11.
62. Tameichi Hara, *Japanese Destroyer Captain*, p10.
63. Ibid, p30.
64. Ibid, p31.
65. Ibid, p104
66. Ibid, p177.
67. Ibid, p178
68. Mochitsura Hashimoto, *Sunk*, London, 1954, p54.
69. Ibid, Appendix B.
70. Ibid, p203.
71. Ibid, p9.
72. A J Watts and B G Gordon, *The Imperial Japanese Navy*, London, 1971, pp169–96.
73. Werneth, *Beyond Pearl Harbor*, p219.

74. Ibid, p245.
75. Ibid, p109.
76. Ibid, p104
77. Ibid, p178.
78. Rikhei Inoguchi, *The Divine Wind*, p7.
79. Ibid, p83.
80. Ibid, p57.
81. Ibid, p62.
82. Ibid, p200.
83. Ibid, p198.
84. Ibid, p90.
85. Ibid, p61.
86. Ibid, pp91–2.
87. James J Fahey, *Pacific War Diary*, p229.
88. R J Francillon, *Japanese Aircraft of the Pacific War*, London, 1979, pp476–82.
89. Atushi Oi, 'Why Japan's Anti-Submarine Warfare Failed', *US Naval Institute Proceedings*, June 1952.
90. Ibid.
91. Tameichi Hara, *Japanese Destroyer Captain*, p47.
92. *Fuehrer Conferences on Naval Affairs*, p324.
93. Stafford, *Little Ship, Big War*, p74.
94. *Fuehrer Conferences on Naval Affairs*, p147.
95. Ibid, p330.
96. James K Sadkovich, *The Italian Navy in World War II*, Westport, 1994, passim.
97. Ibid, p132.
98. Aldo Cocchi, *The Hunters and the Hunted*, 1958, p105.
99. Richard Stockton Field, 'The Royal Italian Naval Family', *US Naval Institute Proceedings*, June 1937.
100. J Valerio Borghese, *Sea Devils*, 1952, p39.
101. Cocchi, *The Hunters and the Hunted*, p24.
102. Barley and Waters, *The Defeat of the Enemy Attack on Shipping*, p59.
103. Borghese, *Sea Devils*, pp14–15.
104. Ibid, p150.
105. Cunningham, *A Seaman's Odyssey*, p565.

18 Allies
1. Peter Jordan and Alexander Janta, *Seafaring Poland*, London, *c*1944, passim.
2. Michael Alfred Peske, 'The Polish Armed Forces in Exile', *The Polish Review*, 1987, nos 1 and 2, p170.
3. David Howarth, *The Shetland Bus*, Edinburgh, 1957, p4.
4. Ibid, p211.
5. Mahan, *Influence of Sea Power upon History*, p136.
6. Schaeffer, *U-Boat 977*, p88.
7. Navy Records Society, *The Somerville Papers*, ed Michael Simpson, 1996, p108.
8. Arthur, *Lost Voices of the Royal Navy*, p256.
9. *The Somerville Papers*, p110.
10. Hugues Canuel, 'An Ambiguous Partnership', *Northern Mariner*, October 2015.
11. H George Franks, *Holland Afloat*, London, 1942, p160.
12. Ibid, p161.
13. Kuznetsov, *Memoirs of Wartime Minster of the Navy*, Moscow.
14. *All World Wars, USSR Navy* by Division of US Naval Intelligence, 1943, Part 1, np.
15. Ibid.
16. Nicolas Tracy, ed, *The Collective Naval Defence of Empire*, Navy Records Society, 1997, xxx.
17. John A Collins, *As Luck Would Have it*, Sydney, 1965, p55.
18. Tracy, ed, *The Collective Naval Defence of Empire*, p415.
19. *Brassey's Naval Annual*, 1938, p21.
20. Collins, *As Luck Would Have it*, p44.
21. Ibid, pp43, 128–9, 143.
22. Ibid, p70.
23. Ibid, p18.
24. Ibid, p17.
25. Ibid, p65.
26. Australian War Memorial, Roberts, p5.
27. Collins, *As Luck Would Have it*, p21.
28. Australian War Memorial, Roberts, p5.
29. Calvert, *Silent Running*, p105.
30. Roscoe, *United States Submarine Operations*, pp63–4.

31. Collins, *As Luck Would Have it*, p64.
32. Navy Records Society, *Cunningham Papers*, vol 1, p118.
33. George Hermon Gill, *Royal Australian Navy, 1939–1945*, Canberra, 1968, Appendix 3, p710.
34. *King Alfred Magazine*, October 1940, p5.
35. Herb Roberts, 'Recollections from the Battle of the Atlantic', *Action Stations*, Winter 2015, pp22–4.
36. Carl Anderson, 'Profile of Lt-Cdr Alan Easton', *Action Stations*, Winter 2020, p29.
37. Gilbert Norman Tucker, *The Naval Service of Canada*, vol 2, Ottawa, 1952, pp257–61.
38. A F C Layard, *Commanding Canadians*, Vancouver, 2005, p75.
39. Ibid, p93.
40. Ibid, p109.
41. *Action Stations*, Spring 2016, p21.
42. Ibid, p20.
43. Ibid, p22.
44. T C Pullen, 'Convoy ON127 and the Loss of HMS *Ottawa*', *Northern Mariner*, April 1992, p5.
45. Ivan E Chamberlain, 'World War 2 Memoirs', *Action Stations*, Fall 2020, p25.
46. Macintyre, *U-Boat Killer*, p79.
47. Layard, *Commanding Canadians*, pp155, 171, 206, 226, 264, 286.
48. *Action Stations*, Winter 2018, p17.
49. Ibid, Spring 2019, p29.
50. Tucker, *The Naval Service of Canada*, vol 2, pp107–135 passim.
51. Marc Milner, *North Atlantic Run*, Toronto, 1985, pp16–17.
52. Reynolds, *Motor Gunboat 658*, p45.
53. Beaver, *Sailor from Oklahoma*, p193.
54. T D Taylor, *New Zealand's Naval Story*, Wellington, 1948, p79.
55. Ibid, pp89–90.
56. New Zealand Navy Museum.
57. Beaver, *Sailor from Oklahoma*, p193.
58. Andre Wessels, 'The South African Navy and its Predecessors', King-Hall Conference, Canberra, 2009.
59. *Navy List*, June 1939, pp614–15.
60. Tracy, *The Collective Naval Defence of Empire*, pp248–9.
61. Ibid, p620.
62. *Navy List*, 1939, pp620–3.
63. R C Dutt, *Mutiny of the Innocents*, Bombay, c1970, p100.
64. Ibid, p112.
65. Ibid, pp65–6.
66. Ibid, pp35–53.
67. Ibid, p62.

Bibliography

General history
British
Anon, *A People at War*, New York, 1943
Calder, Angus, *The People's War, Britain 1939–1945*, London, 1982
Churchill, W S, *The Second World War*, esp vol III: *The Grand Alliance*, London, 1966
Danchev, Alex (ed), *Alanbrooke War Diaries, 1939–1945*, London, 2001
Gilbert, Martin (ed), *Churchill War Papers*, vol 1, London, 1993
Hornby, William, *Factories and Plant*, London, 1958
Lavery, B, *Churchill Goes to War*, London, 2012
Mowat, C L, *Britain Between the Wars*, Cambridge, 1987
Plummer, Alfred, *New British Industries in the Twentieth Century*, London, 1937
Ramsey, Winston G (ed), *The Blitz Then and Now*, London, 1987

United States
Bernstein, Irving, *Turbulent Years, 1933–1941*, Boston, 1969
Berube, Alan, 'Marching to a Different Drummer', in *My Desire for History*, North Carolina, 2011
Herman, Arthur, *Freedom's Forge*, New York, 2012
Lowitt, M, and L Beasley, *One Third of a Nation*, Chicago, 1981
Murphy, Lawrence R, *Perverts by Official Order*, London, 1988
The Roosevelt Letters, London, 1952
Terkel, Studs, *'The Good War'*, London, 1985
Vatter, Harold G, *The US Economy in World War II*, New York, 1985

World
Finch, Robert, *The World's Airways*, London, 1938
Fussell, Paul, *Wartime*, Oxford, 1989
Kennedy, Paul, *The Rise and Fall of the Great Powers*, London, 1989
Millett, Allan, and Williamson Murray, *Military Effectiveness*, vol 3: *The Second World War*, London, 1988

Interactions
Brogan, D W, *The American Character*, New York, 1956
Halsey, Margaret, *With Malice Towards Some*, London, 1938

Naval policy and social history
Naval interchange
Cherry, Alex H, *Yankee RN*, London, 1951
Simpson, Michael (ed), *Anglo-American Naval Relations*, vol 1, Navy Records Society
Wellings, Joseph H, *On His Majesty's Service*, ed Hattendorf, Newport, 1983

British

Beattie, John H, *The Churchill Scheme, 1913–1955*, np, 2010
Burgess, Robert, and Roland Blackburn, *We Joined the Navy*, London, 1943
Clark, George, *'Doc', 100 Year History of the Sick Berth Branch*, London, 1984
Critchley, Macdonald, *Shipwreck Survivors, a Medical study*, London, 1943
Domville-Fife, Charles W, *Submarine Warfare of Today*, London, 1919
Feldt, Eric, *The Coast Watchers*, Oxford, 1967
Gieves Ltd, *How to Become a Naval Officer*, London, 1934
Glenton, Bill, *Mutiny in Force X*, London, 1986
Harland, Kathleen, *A History of Queen Alexandra's Royal Naval Nursing Service*, 1990
Jolly, Rick, *Jackspeak*, Liskeard, 2000,
Kennedy, Paul, *The Rise and Fall of British Naval Mastery*, London, 2017
Kerr, J Lennox, and Wilfred Granville, *The RNVR*, London, 1957
——, and David James, *Wavy Navy, by Some Who Served*, London, 1950
Ladd, James D, *By Sea and by Land*, London, 1998
Lavery, Brian, *In Which They Served*, London, 2008
——, *Shield of Empire*, Edinburgh, 2007
——, *Hostilities Only*, Greenwich, 2004
McKee, Christopher, *Sober Men and True*, London, 2002
Partridge, Michael, *The Royal Naval College Osborne*, Stroud, 1999
Phelps, Stephen, *The Tizard Mission*, Westholme, 2010
Roskill, S W, *Naval Policy Between the Wars*, vol 2, London, 1978
Swaffer, Hannen, *What Would Nelson Do?*, London, 1946
Syrett, David (ed), *The Battle of the Atlantic and Signals Intelligence*, Navy Records Society, 2002
Taylor, C M (ed), *Nursing in the Senior Service*, Gosport, 2002
Taylor, Gordon, *The Sea Chaplains*, Oxford, 1978
Thornton, R H, *British Shipping*, Cambridge, 1939
Warlow, Ben, *Shore Establishments of the Royal Navy*, Liskeard, 1992

American policy

Albion, R G, *Makers of Naval Policy*, 1980
Chisholm, Donald, *Waiting for Dead Men's Shoes*, Stanford, 2000
Coletta, Paulo E, *United States Navy and Marine Corps Bases, Domestic*, Westport, 1985
——, *United States Navy and Marine Corps Bases, Overseas*, Westport, 1985
Duff, Ivan V, *Medical Study of the Experiences of Submariners*, Washington, 1947
Fessler, Diane Burke, *No Time for Fear*, East Lansing. 1996
Harrod, Frederick S, *Manning the New Navy*, Westport, 1978
Herman, Jan K, *Battle Station Sick Bay*, Annapolis, 1997
Huie, William Bradford, *Can Do, The story of the Seabees*, Annapolis, 1997
Isely, Peter A, and Phillip A Crowl, *US Marines and Amphibious Warfare*, 1951
Lewin, Ronald, *The American Magic*, Harmondsworth, 1983
Mahan, Alfred Thayer, *Naval Strategy*, Boston, 1911
Melia, Tamara Moser, *'Damn the Torpedoes'*, Washington, 1991
Miller, Richard E, *The Messman Chronicles*, London, 2003
Naval History and Heritage Command, *The Negro in the Navy*, 1947
Nofi, Albert A, *To Train the Fleet for War*, Newport, 2010
Norton, Bettina A, *The Boston Naval Shipyard 1800–1974*, Boston 1975
Sewell, Patricia W (ed), *Healers in World War II*, Jefferson, 2001

Shilling, C W, *A History of Submarine Medicine in World War II*, New London, 1947
Sherrod, Robert, *A History of Marine Corps Aviation in World War II*, Washington, 1952
Truxton, Thomas, *A Short Account of the Several General Duties of Officers, of Ships of War*
Turnbull, Archibald Douglas, and Clifford Lee Lord, *History of United States Naval Aviation*, New Haven, 1949
Turner Publishing Company, *Navy V-12*, 1996
US Coast Guard Academy, *Entrance Requirements*, Washington, 1939

Naval warfare
General
Pemsel, Helmut, *Atlas of Naval Warfare*, London, 1977
Potter, E B, and Chester W Nimitz, *The Great Sea War*, London, 1960
Sadovitch, James J (ed), *Reevaluating Major Naval Combatants of World War II*, New York, 1990

Royal Navy operations
Cooper, Bryan, *The War of the Gunboats*, Barnsley, 2022
Hague, Arnold, *The Allied Convoy System*, Chatham, 2000
Lucas-Phillips, C E, *Cockleshell Heroes*, London, 1977
Lund, Paul, and Harry Ludlam, *The War of the Landing Craft*, Slough, 1976
——, *Trawlers Go to War*, London, 1972
Maund, L E H, *Assault from the Sea*, London, 1949
Middlebrook, Martin, *Convoy*, Harmondsworth, 1978
Reynolds, L C, *Dog Boats at War*, Stroud, 1998
Roskill, S W, *The War at Sea*, vol I: *The Defensive*, London, 1954; vol II: *The Period of Balance*, 1956; vol III: Part I, *The Offensive*, 1960; Part II, 1961
Syrett, David (ed), *The Battle of the Atlantic and Signals Intelligence*, Navy Records Society, 2002
Warren, C E T, and James Benson, *Above us the Waves*, London, 1953
John Winton, *Carrier Glorious*, London, 1999

US Navy operations
Barbey, Daniel E, *MacArthur's Amphibious Navy*, Annapolis, 1969
Hoagland, Edgar, *The Sea Hawks*, Presidio Press, 1999
Howarth, Stephen, *To Shining Sea*, London, 1991
Lewis, Adrian R, *Omaha Beach*, Stroud, 2021
Mason, Gerald A, *Operation Starvation*, Air War College, Maxwell Air Force Base, Alabama, 2002
Miller, Edward S, *War Plan Orange*, Annapolis, c1991
Miller, Max, *Daybreak for our Carriers*, New York, 1944
Monroe-Jones, Edward, and Michael Green, *The Silent Service in World War II*, London 2012
Morison, Samuel Eliot, *History of United States Naval Operations in World War II: 1 The Battle of the Atlantic; 2 Operations in North African Waters; 3 The Rising Sun in the Pacific; 4 Coral Sea, Midway and Submarine Actions; 5 The Struggle for Guadalcanal; 6 Breaking the Bismarcks Barrier; 7 Aleutians, Gilberts and Marshalls; 8 New Guinea and the Marianas; 9 Sicily – Salerno – Anzio; 10 The Atlantic Battle Won; 11 The Invasion*

of France and Germany; *12 Leyte*; *13 The Liberation of the Philippines*; *14 Victory in the Pacific*; *15 Supplement and General Index*
Polmar, Norman, and Samuel Loring Morison, *PT Boats at War*, Osceola, 1999
Roscoe, Theodore, *United States Submarine Operations in World War II*, Annapolis, 1949
Stafford, Edward P, *The Big E*, Annapolis, 1988
Stillwell, Paul, *Submarine Stories*, Annapolis, 2007
Toll, Ian W, *The Conquering Tide*, New York, 2015
Wooldridge, E T (ed), *Carrier Warfare in the Pacific*, Washington, 1993

Ships, shipbuilding and equipment
General
Campbell, John, *Naval Weapons of World War Two*, London, 1985
Gardiner, Rob (ed), *Conway's All the World's Fighting Ships*, London, 1980
Hovgaard, William, *General Design of Warships*, London, 1920
Lindberg, Michael, and Daniel Todd, *Anglo-American Shipbuilding in World War II*, Westport, 2004
Manning, George C, *The Basic Design of Ships*, New York, 1945
Winser, John D, *The D-Day Ships*, Kendal, 1994

British
Bassett, G A, 'The Repair and Upkeep of HM Ships and Vessels in War', *Transactions of the Institutions of Naval Architects*, vol 88, 1946
Borthwick, Alistair, *Yarrow and Company*, Glasgow, 1965
Brown, D K, *Atlantic Escorts*, Barnsley 2007
D K Brown, *A Century of Naval Construction*, London, 1983
—— (ed), *The Design and Construction of British Warships, 1939–1945*, vol 1: *Major Surface Vessels*; vol 3: *Landing Craft and Auxiliary Vessels*, London, 1995
Fox, Uffa, *Seamanlike Sense in Power Craft*, London, 1968
Friedman, Norman, *British Battleships, 1906–1946*, Barnsley, 2015
——, *British Cruisers, The Two World Wars and After*, Barnsley, 2012
——, *British Destroyers and Frigates*, London, 2006
——, *British Carrier Aviation*, London, 1988
Goodall, Stanley V, 'The Royal Navy at the Outbreak of War', *Transactions of the Institutions of Naval Architects*, vol 88, 1946
Hobbs, David, *Royal Navy Escort Carriers*, Liskeard, 2003
Lavery, B, *River Class Frigates and the Battle of the Atlantic*, London, 2006
Macdermott, Brian, *Ships Without Names*, London, 1992
Newton, R N, *Practical Construction of Warships*, London, 1941
Royal Institution of Naval Architects, *British Warship Design*, 1983
Wingate, John, *HMS Belfast*, Windsor, 1972

American
Alden, John H, *The Fleet Submarine in the US Navy*, London, 1979
Clawson, Augusta H, *Shipyard Diary of a Woman Welder*, Ann Arbor, 1992
Dictionary of American Naval Fighting Ships, Washington, 1959–1991
Friedman, Norman, *US Aircraft Carriers*, Annapolis, 1993
——, *US Destroyers*, Annapolis, 1992
——, *US Small Combatants,* Annapolis, 1987
——, *US Battleships*, London, *c*1985

——, *US Cruisers*, London, 1985
——, *US Naval Weapons*, London, 1983
Sawyer, L A, and W H Mitchell, *The Liberty Ships*, Newton Abbot, 1970

Aircraft
British
Harrison, W A, *Fairey Swordfish and Albacore*, Marlborough, 2002
Jackson, A J, *Blackburn Aircraft Since 1909*, London, 1968
Taylor, H A, *Fairey Aircraft Since 1915*, London, 1974
Thetford, Owen, *British Naval Aircraft Since 1912*, London, 1991

American
Francillon, Rene J, *Grumman Aircraft since 1929*, London, 1989
——, *McDonnell Douglas Aircraft since 1920*, vol I, London, 1988
Smith, Herschel, *A History of Aircraft Piston Engines*, Manhattan, Kansas, 1986
Swanborough, Gordon F, and Peter M Bowers, *United States Naval Aircraft Since 1911*, London, 1976

Technical subjects
DiGiulian, Tony, 'The British High Angle Control System', *NavWeaps*, http://www.navweaps.com/index_tech/tech-066.php
Gardner, W J R, *Decoding History*, Basingstoke, 1999
Hackman, Willem, *Seek and Strike*, London, 1984
Howse, Derek, *Radar at Sea, The Royal Navy in World War II*, Basingstoke, 1993
Le Bailly, Louis, *From Fisher to the Falklands*, London, 1991
Marland, Peter, 'HACS: a Debacle or Just in Time?', *NavWeaps*, http://www.navweaps.com/index_tech/tech-111.php
Rippon, P M, *Evolution of Engineering in the Royal Navy*, vol 1: 1827–1936, Tunbridge Wells, 1988; vol 2: 1939–1992, London, 1994
Watson, Raymond C, *Surviving the Naval Radar Crisis*, Trafford Publishing, 2007

Official and staff histories
British
Barley and Waters, *The Defeat of the Enemy Attack on Shipping*, Navy Records Society, 1997
Behrens, C B A, *Merchant Shipping and the Demands of War*, London, 1956
Hinsley, F H, *British Intelligence in the Second World War*, 1979
Ministry of Defence, *War With Japan*, vol VI, 1995
National Archives, ADM 239/245, *British Minesweeping*, 1950
National Archives, ADM 239/241, Staff Monograph, Naval W/T Organisation
National Archives, ADM 239/239, Staff Monograph, Torpedoes

American
Administration of the Navy Department in World War II, Chapter IX, *The United States Marine Corps*
Albion, R G, *Brief History of Civilian Personnel*, Washington, 1943
Bureau of Medicine and Surgery, *The History of the Medical Department of the United States Navy in World War*
Bureau of Yards and Docks, *Building the Navy's Bases in World War II*

Condit, K W, G Diamond, and E T Turnbladh, *Marine Corps Ground Training in WWII*, Washington, 1956
Naval History and Heritage Command, *The Logistics of Advanced Bases*, OP-30
Naval History and Heritage Command, Oral History, *The Battle of Guadalcanal*, Louis Ortega
Rowland, Buford, and William B Boyd, *US Navy Bureau of Ordnance in World War II*, Washington, c1947
Sternhell, Alan M, and Alan B Turnbull, *Anti Submarine Warfare in World War II*, Washington, 1946
US Navy Department Headquarters, *Antiaircraft Action Summary*, Washington, 1945
War Production Board, *Industrial Mobilization for War*, Washington, 1947

Service manuals, etc
British
Admiralty, *The Gunnery Pocket Book*, BR 224/45, 1945
Admiralty, *Handbook of the Royal Naval Sick Berth Staff*, BR 888, 1944
Admiralty, *Manual of Seamanship*, vol 1, 1908
Admiralty, *Manual of Seamanship*, BR 68, 1932
Admiralty, *Monthly Anti-Submarine Report*
Admiralty, *Royal Naval Handbook of Field Training*, London, 1920
Lavery, B (ed), *The Royal Navy Officer's Pocket Book*, London, 2007
National Archives, Atlantic Convoy Instructions
War Office, *Infantry Section Leading*, 1938
Wright, Noel, and A C G Sweet, *How to Prepare Food; Tips and Wrinkles for Cooks of Messes in Standard Ration Ships*, Ipswich, 1941

American
Bureau of Aeronautics, *Using Your Navy Wings*, Washington, 1943
Bureau of Naval Personnel Manual, 1942
Bureau of Naval Personnel, *Aircraft Armament*, 1945
Bureau of Naval Personnel, *Aircraft Turrets*, 1946
Bureau of Naval Personnel, *Guide to the Command of Negro Personnel*
Bureau of Naval Personnel, *Information Bulletin*, February 1944
Bureau of Naval Personnel, *Naval Orientation*, June 1945
Bureau of Naval Personnel, *Yearbook of Personnel Statistics*, 1944
Bureau of Ordnance, *5-Inch Twin Mounts … Description and Instructions*, 1944
Bureau of Ordnance, *Operational Characteristics of US Naval Mines*, 1959
Ordnance Pamphlet 1140, *Basic Fire Control Mechanisms*, 1944
Bureau of Yards and Docks, *US Navy Advanced Base Equipment Catalog*, 1944
Comsublant, *Submarine Sonar Operator's Manual*, 1944
Landing Craft School, Coronado, *Skill in the Surf*, 1945
Marine Corps Manual, 1940
Naval Courts and Boards
Submarine Division Forty-One, *Submarine Information and Instruction Manual*, 1942
US Naval Institute, *The Bluejackets' Manual*, Annapolis, 1940
US Navy, *Interviewer's Classification Guide*, December 1943
US Navy, *Motor Torpedo Boat Manual*, February 1943
US Navy Bomb Disposal School, *Mine Disposal Handbook*, 1945
US Navy Flight Training Manuals, 1 Elementary, 2 Primary

USS *Pampanito*, *General Information Book*, 1943
USS *Pompom*, *Ship's Orders*, 1944
United States Maritime Service, *Training Manual, Preliminary Training*, 1943

Biography and autobiography, senior (flag) officers
British
Chatfield, Lord, *It Might Happen Again*, London, 1947
——, *The Navy and Defence*, London, 1942
Cunningham, Andrew, *A Sailor's Odyssey*, London, 1951
Graham, Angus Cunninghame, *Random Naval Recollections*, Ardoch, 1979
James, William, *The Sky was Always Blue*, London, 1951
Longmore, Arthur, *From Sea to Sky*, London, 1946
Oram, H P K, *The Rogue's Yarn*, London, 1993
Simpson, Michael (ed), *The Cunningham Papers*, vol 2, Navy Records Society, 2006
——, *The Somerville Papers*, Navy Records Society, 1996
Ziegler, Philip, *Mountbatten*, London, 1985

American
Borneman, Walter R, *The Admirals*, New York 2012
Bowen, Harold Gardiner, *Ships, Machinery and Mossbacks*, Princeton, 1954
Buell, Thomas B, *The Quiet Warrior*, Annapolis, 1987
Dyer, George Carroll, *The Amphibians Came to Conquer*, vol 2, Washington, 1972
Evans, Holden, *One Man's Fight for a Better Navy*, New York, 1940
Manchester, William, *American Caesar*, London, 1979
Smith, Holland M, *Coral and Brass*, London, 1958
Stirling, Yates, *Sea Duty*, 1939
Taylor, Theodore, *The Magnificent Mitscher*, Annapolis, 1991
Trimble, William F, *Admiral William A Moffat*, Washington, 1994
Wheeler, Gerald E, *Kincaid of the Seventh Fleet*, Annapolis, 1996
Whitehill, E J, *Fleet Admiral King*, London, 1953

Other officers
British
Boler, David, *Hostilities Only*, Privately published, 2023
Bryant, Ben, *Submarine Command*, London, 1975
Bull, Peter, *To Sea in a Sieve*, London, 1958
Cox, Vivian A, *Seven Christmases*, Sevenoaks, 2010
Davie, Michael (ed), *The Diaries of Evelyn Waugh*, London, 1976
Day, John, *A Plain Russet-coated Captain*, 1993
Denton, Eric, *My Six Wartime Years in the Royal Navy*, London, 1999
Fernald, John, *Destroyer from America*, London, 1942
Gretton, Peter, *Convoy Escort Commander*, London, 1964
Guinness, Alec, *Blessings in Disguise*, London, 1985
Hampson, Norman, *Not Really What You'd Call a War*, Caithness, 2001
Hezlet, Arthur, *HMS Trenchant at War*, London, 2000
Holt, F S, *A Banker All at Sea*, Newton, Victoria, 1983
Jenkins, C A, *Days of a Dogsbody*, London, 1946
John, Rebecca, *Caspar John*, London, 1987
Kennedy, Ludovic, *On My Way to the Club*, London, 1990

Kilbracken, John, *Bring Back my Stringbag*, London, 1979
King-Hall, Stephen, *My Naval Life*, London, 1952
Lamb, Christian, *I Only Joined for the Hat*, London, 2007
Law, C Anthony, *White Plumes Astern*, Halifax, 1989
Le Bailly, Louis, *The Man Around the Engine*, Emsworth, 1990
McAra, Charles, *Mainly in Minesweepers*, London, 1991
Macintyre, Donald, *U-Boat Killer*, London, 1999
Maher, Brendan A, *A Passage to Sword Beach*, Shrewsbury, 1996
Mallalieu, J P W, *On Larkhill*, London, 1983
Monsarrat, Nicholas, *Three Corvettes*, reprinted London, 2000
——, *Life is a Four Letter Word*, vol II: *Breaking Out*, London, 1970
——, *HM Frigate*, London, 1946
Ransome-Wallis, Ralph, *Two Red Stripes*, London, 1973
Rayner, D A, *Escort*, London, 1955
Reynolds, L C, *Motor Gunboat 658*, London, 2002
St John, John, *To the War with Waugh*, London, 1973
Schofield, B B, *With the Royal Navy in War and Peace*, Barnsley, 2018
Scott, Peter, *The Eye of the Wind,* London, 1961
Whinney, Bob, *The U-Boat Peril*, Poole, 1986
Young, Edward, *One of our Submarines*, London, 1982

American
Beach, Edward L, *Salt and Steel*, Annapolis, 1999
Calhoun, Raymond, *Tin Can Sailor*, Annapolis, 1993
Calvert, James F, *Silent Running*, New York, 1995
Cooper, Page, *Navy Nurse*, New York, 1946
Dickens, Peter, *Night Action*, London, 1978
Eccles, Henry, *To the Java Sea*, ed Hattendorf, Newport, 2021
Gerald Ford Presidential Library, Ann Arbor
Gittelsohn, Roland, *Pacifist to Padre*, Quantico, 2021
Hancock, Joy Bright, *Lady in the Navy*, Annapolis, 1972
Jerningham, E J, *Tin Can Man*, Annapolis, 1993
Leach, Douglas Edward, *Now Hear This*, 1987
Robinson, C Snelling, *200,000 Miles Aboard the Destroyer Cotton*, Kent Ohio, 2000
Ruhe, William J, *Slow Dance to Pearl Harbor*, Washington, 1995
Stafford, Edward P, *Little Ship, Big War*, London 1986
——, *Subchaser*, Annapolis, 2003
Tate, L W, *Recollections of Ensign Leonard W Tate*, US Naval Heritage and History Command
Terry, Howard L, *A PT Boat Captain in the Pacific*, terryfoundation.org
Wouk, Herman, *Sailor and Fiddler*, New York, 2016

Aviators
Brown, Eric 'Winkle', *Wings on My Sleeve*, London, 2007
Hadley, D L*, Barracuda Pilot*, Shrewsbury, 1992
Hynes, Samuel, *Flights of Passage*, London, 2005
John, Rebecca, *Caspar John*, London, 1987
Kellet, Fred, *A Flower for the Sea, a Fish for the Sky*, Carlisle, 1995
Kleiss, 'Dusty', *Never Call me a Hero*, London, 2017
Lamb, Charles, *To War in a Stringbag*, London, 1978

Lygo, Raymond, *Collision Course*, Lewes, 2001
Popham, Hugh, *Sea Flight,* London, 1954
Spencer, H J C, *Ordinary Naval Airmen*, Tunbridge Wells, 1992
Stinnett, Robert B, *George Bush, His World War II Years*, Washington, 1992
Wallace, Gordon, *Carrier Observer*, Shrewsbury, 1993

Anthologies
Arthur, Max, *Lost Voices of the Royal Navy*, London, 2005
Billy, George J, and Christine M Billy, *Merchant Mariners at War*, University Press of Florida, 2008
Block, Leo (ed), *Aboard the Farragut Destroyers in World War II*, Jefferson, NC, c2009
Connell, G G, *Jack's War*, London, 1985
Eadon, Stuart (ed), *Kamikaze, The British Pacific Fleet*, np, 1995
Gillen, Michael, *Merchant Marine Survivors of World War II*, Jefferson, 2015
Hawkins, Ian (ed), *Destroyer*, London, 2003

Ratings and enlisted men
British
Brown, John L, *Dairy of a Matelot, 1942–45*, Lowesmoor, Worcester, 1991
Davies, John, *Stone Frigate*, London, 1947
Davies, John W, *Jack, the Sailor with the Navy Blue Eyes*, Edinburgh, 1995
Dickison, Arthur P, *Crash Dive*, Stroud, 1999
Farley, Patricia B, *Birds of a Feather: A Wren's Memoirs, 1942–1945*
Ford, Ted, *The Nearly Man*, Wolverhampton, 1997
Gritten, John, *Full Circle*, Dunfermline, 2003
Hart, Sydney, *Discharged Dead*, London, 1958
Iago, John M, *And Home There's No Returning*, Fleet Hargate, 2004
Jones, Albert H, and Michael H Jones, *No Easy Choices*, Worcester, 1994
Jones, Tristan, *Heart of Oak*, 1984, reprinted Shrewsbury, 1997
Kerslake, S A, *Coxswain in the Northern Convoys*, London 1984
Melly, George, *Rum, Bum and Concertina*, London, 1977
Pollitt, J E, *Marine to Mayor*, Exeter, c1989
Putt, S Gorley, *Men Dressed as Seamen*, London, 1943
Whelan, John, *Home is the Sailor*, London, 1959
Williams, Leonard Charles, *Gone a Long Journey*, Havant, 2002
Wincott, Len, *Invergordon Mutineer*, London, 1974

American
Beaver, Floyd, *Sailor from Oklahoma*, Annapolis, 2009
Fahey, James J, *Pacific War Diary*, New York, 1963
Kernan, Alvin, *Crossing the Line*, Annapolis, c1994
Leckie, Robert, *Helmet for my Pillow*, New York, 2010
Mason, Theodore C, *Battleship Sailor*, Annapolis, 2013
——, *Rendezvous with Destiny*, Annapolis 1997
——, *We Will Stand By You*, Columbia, 1990
Olson, Michael Keith, *Tales from a Tin Can*, St Paul, 2007
Raines, James Orvill, *Good Night Officially*, Boulder, 1994
Rogal, William W, *Guadalcanal, Tarawa and Beyond*, Jefferson, c2010
Sledge, Eugene, *With the Old Breed*, London, 2011

Other navies
Germany
Cooper, Bryan, *The E-Boat Threat*, London, 1978
Fuehrer Conferences on Naval Affairs
Goebeler, Hans, *Steel Boats, Iron Hearts*, London, 2005
Hirschfeld, Wolfgang, *The Secret Dairy of a U-Boat*, London, 2000
Schaeffer, Heinz, *U-boat 977*, London, 1973
Schenk, Peter, *The Invasion of England 1940*, London, 1990
Stern, Robert C, *Type VII U-Boats*, London, 2002
Tooze, Adam, *The Wages of Destruction*, London, 2007

Japan
Bullock, Cecil, *Etajima, The Dartmouth of Japan*, London, 1942
Francillon, R J, *Japanese Aircraft of the Pacific War*, London, 1979
Hara, Tameichi, *Japanese Destroyer Captain*, New York, 2006
Hashimoto, Mochitsura, *Sunk*, London, 1954
Inoguchi, Rikhei, *The Divine Wind*, Annapolis, 1994
Jansen, Marius B, *The Making of Modern Japan*, Harvard, 2002
Johns, Leslie W, *Japan; Reminiscences and Realities*, 1943
Mitsuru, Yoshido, *Requiem for the Battleship Yamato*, London, 1999
Oi, Atushi, 'Why Japan's Anti-Submarine Warfare Failed', *US Naval Institute Proceedings*, June 1952
Werneth, Ron (ed), *Beyond Pearl Harbor*, Aglen, Pennsylvania, 2008
Watts, A J, and B G Gordon, *The Imperial Japanese Navy*, London, 1971

Italy
Borghese, J Valerio, *Sea Devils*, 1952
Cocchi, Aldo, *The Hunters and the Hunted*, 1958
Field, Richard Stockton, 'The Royal Italian Naval Family', *US Naval Institute Proceedings*, June 1937
Mallett, Robert, *The Italian Navy and Fascist Expansionism, 1936–1940*, London, 1998
Sadkovich, James K, *The Italian Navy in World War II*, Westport, 1994

Allies
Andenaes, Johs, Olav Riste, and Magne Skodvin, *Norway in the Second World War*, Lillehammer, 1983
Carr, John C, *RHNS Averof*, Barnsley, 2014
Division of US Naval Intelligence, *All World Wars, USSR Navy*, 1943
Franks, H George, *Holland Afloat*, London, 1942
Howarth, David, *The Shetland Bus*, Edinburgh, 1957
Jenkins, E H, *History of the French Navy*, London, 1973
Jordan, K Peter, and Alexander Janta, *Seafaring Poland*, London, *c*1944
Kuznetsov, N G, *Memoirs of Wartime Minster of the Navy*, Moscow
Marine National, *Manuel des Recrues des Equipages de la Flotte*, Paris, 1935
Mitchell, Donald W, *A History of Russian and Soviet Sea Power*, London, 1974
Muselier, Émile, *Marine et Résistance*, Paris, 1945
Peske, Michael Alfred, 'The Polish Armed Forces in Exile', *The Polish Review*, 1987, nos 1 and 2

Commonwealth
Anderson, Carl, 'Profile of Lt-Cdr Alan Easton', *Action Stations*, Winter 2020
Britts, Angus, *A Ceaseless Watch*, Annapolis, 2021
Chamberlain, Ivan E, 'World War 2 Memoirs', *Action Stations*, Fall 2020
Collins, John A, *As Luck Would Have It*, Sydney, 1965
Duffell-Canham, John, *Seaman Gunner do not Weep*, Simonstown, 2014
Dutt, R C, *Mutiny of the Innocents*, Bombay, c1970
Gill, George Hermon, *Royal Australian Navy, 1939–1945*, Canberra, 1968
Layard, A F C, *Commanding Canadians*, Vancouver, 2005
Milner, Marc, *North Atlantic Run*, Toronto, 1985
Pullen, T C, 'Convoy ON127 and the Loss of HMS *Ottawa*', *Northern Mariner*, April 1992
Roberts, Herb, 'Recollections from the Battle of the Atlantic', *Action Stations*, Winter 2015
Tracy, Nicholas (ed), *The Collective Naval Defence of Empire*, Navy Records Society, 1997
Tucker, Gilbert Norman, *The Naval Service of Canada*, vol 2, Ottawa, 1952
Waters, S D, *The Royal New Zealand Navy*, Wellington, 1956
Wessels, André, 'The South African Navy and its Predecessors', King-Hall Conference, Canberra, 2009

Periodicals
All Hands, June 1945
Brassey's Naval and Shipping Annual, 1935–40
CIC Manual, 'Radar Bulletin No 6' (Radsix), 1945
Combat Information Center Magazine, September 1945
Emerson, William, 'Franklin Roosevelt as Commander-in-Chief in World War II', *Military Affairs*, 1958–59, pp181–207
Jerry, Captain (E) G C, 'The Development of Destroyer Main Armament, 1941 to 1945', *Journal of Naval Engineering*, 1953
King Alfred Magazine, vol 1, no 5; vol 6, p29
McElduff, D A, 'The Wardroom of the USS *Tuscaloosa*', *US Naval Institute Proceedings*, July 1935
Rogers, David A, 'Development of Amphibious Force Flagship', *Bureau of Ships Journal*, February 1962
Strohmeier, D D, 'A History of Bethlehem Steel Company's Shipbuilding and Ship Repairing', *Naval Engineer's Journal*, 1963, pp269–72
Thiesen, William H, 'The Coast Guard's World War II Crucible', *Naval History*, October 2016
Wildenberg, Thomas, 'Chester Nimitz and the Development of Fueling at Sea', *Naval War College Review*, 46, no 4, Autumn 1993

Oral history
Digital Library of Georgia, Oral history interview of James Leland Jackson
John Fitzgerald Kennedy Library, Donald B Frost, oral history interview, 2005
Naval Historical Foundation Oral History Program, John B Desrosiers, Minesweeping During World War II, 2004
Naval History and Heritage Command, Ann A Bernatitus, Oral history
US Coast Guard Oral History Program, interview, 7 June 2012
US Naval Institute Oral History, Roger L Bond

Picture Credits

AKG-Images/Ullstein bild 497
Alamy 154
All Hands magazine, 1944 337
*Britain's Merchant Navy, c*1943 410
Bluejacket's Manual, 1940 46
Bofors Quadruple Mount Manual 244
Computer Mk 1 Manual 236
Destroyer from America, 1942 53
Division of Naval Intelligence, JANI no 1 72, 103
Douglas SBD-3, Pilot's Handbook, 1942 338
German Federal Archive 258
Gunnery Pocket Book, 1945 229, 246
historyofwar.org 274
How to Serve Your Country in the Waves, 1942 156
Illustrated London News (Mary Evans Picture Library) 11, 74, 114, 134, 148, 184, 218, 261, 280, 294, 306, 325, 326, 352, 373, 384, 391, 420, 425, 456, 486
Imperial War Museum 21, 40, 554
King Alfred Magazine, 1941 86, 87
Library of Congress 19, 215, 505
Lucky Bag, 1931 77
Lucky Bag, 1940 79
Mary Evans Picture Library 521
Men Dressed as Seamen, 1943 43
Museo della Scienza e Technologia 524
National Geographic magazine 63, 105
National Maritime Museum, Greenwich, London 186, 213
Navy Uniforms, Insignia and Warships of WWII 282, 285, 307, 310, 321
Naval Heritage and History Command 3, 8, 12, 92, 116, 138, 144, 192,197, 231, 322, 328, 356, 378, 389, 416, 422,482, 496, 508, 516, 527
The Negro in the Navy, 1947 123
Principles of Naval Engineering, 1970 220
Radar Manual, 1945 264
Radar Operator's Manual, 1945 266
Royal Naval Museum, Portsmouth 97
Shipshub.com 354
The Royal Navy at the Outbreak of War, 1946 350
Torpedo Data Computer, Manual 370
Torpedoes Mk 14 and 23 Types, Manual 262
US Coast Guard 423
US National Archives 559
United States Naval Institute 26, 35, 179, 203, 313, 329, 332, 464
To the War with Waugh, 1973 161
Wikipedia Commons 205, 258, 513
World War II Database 24, 67, 178, 172, 199, 216, 226, 284, 288, 445, 450, 461, 480, 493, 531, 541, 545

General Index

APD, 403, 455, 485, 486
Abyssinia, 69, 520
Ackerman, James H, 413
Acorns, 93, 345
acoustic mines, 421, 423, 426, 432, 502
Action Information Organisation (AIO), 272, 339
admirals, 72
Admirals of the Fleet, 45, 64
Admiralty, 20*ff*
Admiralty Fleet Orders (AFOs), 52
African-Americans, 121–3
Ahlberg, Dan, 407–8
Aichi D3A (Val), 513
air artificers, 317
air fitters, 318
air mechanics, 318
Airedales, 335
airships, 241, 304, 333, 402
alcohol, 41
Alden, John, 362, 363, 575, 588
Alexandria, 130, 165, 184, 186, 257, 344, 351, 372, 524, 531, 542
Alexander, A V, 21
Allen, Thomas, 121
America, British, Dutch, Australian (ABDA), 534
amtrac (LVT), 20, 198, 459, 463, 473, 482, 485, 557
'Anchors Away', 78
Anglo-Japanese Alliance, 504, 511
Annapolis, 6, 48, 75–81, 89
anti-aircraft gunnery, 79, 152, 165, 279: against dive bombing, 330; aiming, 236, 240–1, 533; British weakness, 237–8; fitting of guns, 167, 208, 209, 210, 287, 446, 502, 507; fuses, 248; gunners, 102, 78; types of gun, 238, 239, 283; use of radar, 263; *see also* Bofors, Oerlikon etc
anti-Semitism, 66, 150
anti-submarine branch, 95
anti-submarine control officer (ASCO), 387
appendicitis, 139, 140
Arbroath, 316, 344
Argentia, 201, 400
armoured flight deck, 307
Army Air Corps, US, 181, 304
Army Air Force, US, 13, 194, 304, 402–3, 476, 478

arrester wires, 307, 309, 334, 335
Arromanches, 468
Articles of War, 52
artificers, 22, 102, 193, 104, 110, 204, 218, 269, 352, 359
Asdic (sonar), vii, 260, 377, 380, 547: development, 386; evading, 262, 365, 500; installation, 271, 382–3; operators and training, 103, 360–1, 392; use of, 210, 387–8, 390, 392, 396–8
Ashbourne, Lord, 358
Atlee, Clement, 11
attack teacher, 357, 362, 374, 392, 406
attack transports (APA), 112, 465, 485
atom bomb, 23, 59, 250, 288, 367, 550, 561
Australia, 30, 32, 49, 119, 130, 142, 178, 189, 206–7, 277, 372–4, 377, 538–40
Auxiliary Repair Docks, 201
aviation cadets, 320, 322
aviation electrician's mate, 322
aviation machinist's mate, 321, 441
aviation ordnanceman, 106, 321
aviation radioman, 321, 329

badges, ratings, 102–3; enlisted men, 104–5
Bailey, Bill, 414
Baker-Cresswell, A J, 393
Ball, Geoffrey, 98, 297, 399
Banana, 396
Bancroft Hall, 76
Barbey, Daniel E, 367, 472, 475, 481, 485, 488
barge busting, 446, 451
Barnaby, K C, 456, 461
Barnard, Elizabeth,155, 371
Barret, David, 51
Barry, Claud, 371
Basilone, John, 171, 172, 173, 175
Bath, 213
Bath Iron Works, 225
Battle of the Atlantic Committee, 377
Battle of Britain, 31
Battle Force, 28
'Battleship Holiday', 281
Beaver, Floyd, 100, 101, 104, 106, 111, 112, 118, 119, 292, 551
Befehlshaber der Unterseebote (BdU), 500
Belgium, 10, 534
bell bottoms, 42, 120, 546

597

Bermuda, 27, 130, 141, 257, 406
Bernatitus, Ann, 136
Bethlehem Shipbuilding, 224
Biscay, Bay of, 372, 500
Blackburn Skua, 323, 324, 325
Blaw Knox, 224
Bletchley Park, 257, 258, 259
Blohm und Voss, 498
Bluejackets Manual, 37, 46, 117
boatswain's mates, 58, 104, 291, 417
Boeing B-17, 304
Bofors gun, 243–5, 247, 248, 403, 446, 466–7
boilers, 217, 218
Bolshevik Revolution, 10, 536
bombing, effects on land, 18, 27, 130, 184–5, 189, 213, 223; at sea, 342, 352; strategic, 181, 241, 303–4, 377, 399, 401, 403, 433, 470, 495, 503; *see also* dive bombing, skip bombing, torpedo bombing
Bond, Roger, 107–8, 343
boot camps, 99, 100, 101, 541
Bordeaux, 377
Borneo, 451, 533
Bose, Chandra, 552
Bougainville, 181, 480
Bowen, Harold G, 6, 26, 77, 81, 83, 214, 219, 220, 225
Bowling, Selman, 451
Boys-Smith, Humphrey, 385
Bradley, John, 140
Bremerton, 192, 193
Bren gun, 165, 461
Brest, 207, 493, 502, 529
brig, 57, 58
British Pacific Fleet, 22, 28, 29, 65, 130, 148, 221, 327, 340
British Power Boat Company, 434, 435
Brooke, Sir Alan, Lord Alanbrooke, 8, 13
brothels, 49–50
Brown, Eric 'Winkle', 336
Browning automatic rifle, 175, 176, 177, 417
Bruce, Donald, 327
Bruneval, 471
Bryant, Ben, 349, 364, 375
bulldozers, 196, 197, 200
bunks, 34, 36, 98, 113, 116, 117, 138, 198
bureau system, 25, 26, 558
Bureau of Aeronautics (BuAer), 155, 214, 304, 305, 403
Bureau of Construction and Repair, 25, 214, 221, 298, 428
Bureau of Engineering, 214, 219, 221, 298
Bureau of Medicine and Surgery (BuMed), 141
Bureau of Navigation (BuNav), 25, 80, 155
Bureau of Ordnance (BuOrd), 25, 230, 232–3, 239, 252–3, 265, 266
Bureau of Personnel (BuPers), 25, 124

Bureau of Ships (BuShips), 82, 215, 216, 265, 405, 430, 440
Bureau of Yards and Docks, 195
burial, 151, 366
Burke, Cornelius, 550
Burns, 136, 146
Bush, George H W, 344
Bushnell, David, 347

CW scheme, 70, 88, 114, 115, 118, 297, 399, 546
Cadogan, Sir Alexander, 16
cafeteria, 118, 119, 124, 405
Calhoun, Raymond, 41, 59, 81, 236
California, 18, 99, 192, 226, 327, 474
Calkins, William, 353
Calvert, Jim, 49, 75, 183, 193, 194, 364, 369, 371, 374
Cammell Laird, 222, 223
Camp Lejeune, 157, 170
Camper and Nicholson, 435
Canada, 5, 30, 206, 316, 376, 377, 538, 543*ff*
canteens, 115, 120, 187, 188, 426, 550
capital ships, 5, 278: armament, 228, 233–4, 251; in battle, 302; classes, 279, 281, 282; fitting out, 184–5; in fleets, 27; marines in, 164; radar, 265
captain, ship's, role and status: character, 84, 94, 267, 293, 300, 369; duties, 271, 273, 275, 356, 358, 368, 373, 408, 446, 451; promotion to, 73; ranks of, 93; relations with officers and crew, 74, 107; training, 363
Caribbean, 7, 10, 30, 191–2, 217, 243, 334, 377, 381, 412, 448, 529
Carrier Air Service Unit (CASU), 346
Case, Richard, 85
cash and carry, 6, 19
catapults, 307, 336, 346, 379, 493
catapult, aircraft, merchantman (CAM), 308
cathode ray tube, 263, 268
Cavagnari, Admiral, 520
Cavite, 194, 374
cavity magnetron, 260, 261, 262
Celebes, 553
Central Pacific Drive, 32, 285, 453, 460, 475
Chambers, Mike, 359
Chance-Vought Corsair, 327, 331, 334, 512
chapels, 148
chaplains, 67, 92, 125, 144, 146-50, 174, 200
Charleston, 191, 347, 429
Chatfield, Lord, 72, 242, 278, 282
Chatham, 27, 96, 102, 127, 129, 130, 159, 160, 212
Cherry, A H, 4
chief of the boat, 363
Chief of Naval Operations, 25, 28, 215, 298, 305, 428

chief petty officers, 42, 51, 98, 100, 103, 109–11, 291, 292, 355
chiefs of staff, 12, 13
China, 414, 434, 482, 504, 505, 517
Christianity, 146, 150
Chrysler, 244
Churchill, Winston S: and allies, 526, 527, 530, 532, 538; American connections, 3, 7, 8, 13, 19, 206; career, 30, 454, 471; on combined operations, 454, 458, 459, 467, 471, 475; First Lord of the Admiralty, 20–1, 61, 68, 121, 166, 217, 279, 283, 380; in Parliament, 11, 23, 525; prime minister, 9, 506; as strategist, 31, 282, 376–7, 381, 558; regard for, 10; relations with senior officers, 12, 21, 271
CinCPac, 29, 433
Civil Engineering Corps, 196
Civil Service, 22, 124, 168, 211
Civil War, 23, 48, 411
Clark, Mark, 365, 477
Clarke, D W, 471
Class A schools, 101, 106, 122
class and caste in Britain, 14–17
classification of recruits, 101
Clemens, Martin, 277
Clyde, 196, 188, 201, 222–4, 249, 258, 268, 313, 344, 352, 357, 358, 372–3, 392, 421, 470, 540, 544
Coast Guard, US, 26, 156, 305, 332–3, 404, 416–17, 435, 471
coast-watchers, 277
Coastal Command, 401, 402
Coastguard, British, 415
Cochrane, E L, 214, 403
Cockatoo Island, 542
coffee, 38, 41, 107, 117, 119, 282
Collins, John, 539, 540
Columbia University, 81
Columbus, Christopher, 519
Combat Information Center (CIC), 256, 272–6
Combined Chiefs of Staff, 7, 8, 476
Combined Operations Organisation, 167, 454, 471, 475
Combined Operations Pilotage Parties (COPPs), 483
commander, 73, 80
commandoes, 31, 159, 162, 165–7, 181, 443, 641
commerce raiding, 2, 376, 529
commissioning of ship, 36
Commons, House of, 10, 11
Commonwealth, 30, 188, 287, 526
Communism, 20, 489, 538, 561
conning tower, 281, 356, 359, 363, 368, 496
convoys, 394–7: commodores, 396, 411; HX229, 379, 397; ON 127, 547; ONS138, 388; PQ17, 21, 378, 380; PQ18, 389; SC42, 547; SC44, 547; SC118, 395; SC122, 379; SC129, 379; SC130, 379, 398
Congress, 5–7, 9, 13, 25, 56, 64, 79, 80, 95, 154, 195, 214, 231
Conservative Party, 9, 10
Consolidated: Catalina (PBY), 320, 333, 344, 402; Liberator (PB4Y), 181, 333, 403
Construction Corps, 213
cooking, 107, 114, 118, 119, 361, 439, 440
Coolidge, President, 305
Copeland, Captain, 135
Coral Sea, 32, 204, 260, 309, 327
Corbett, Sir Julian, 2
cordite, 229, 230, 243
Corpus Christi, 181, 320, 345
corvettes: Canadian, 544–8; command of, 84, 401; design and build, 212, 223, 383–4; guns, 392; in service, 395, 528, 532, 534; engines, 218; medical facilities, 129, 132; radar, 262–3, 265, 268; range, 203; seakeeping, 36, 384
courts martial, 52, 54, 56–8, 80, 122, 163, 293, 321, 563
Cox, Vivian, 423, 426
coxswain, 53, 132, 362, 359, 417, 439, 452, 455, 461, 470, 473, 479, 481
Craig, Edward C, 428
Crail, 344
Cramp Shipbuilding, 357
Crete, 165, 207, 287, 461, 466, 471, 543
Critchley, Macdonald, 133, 140, 293
cruisers, heavy, 227, 228, 282, 286, 288, 508–9, 511, 530, 540
cruisers, light, 227, 286–8, 295, 312, 509, 530, 532–3, 540, 550
cruising stations, 38
Crutchley, Sir Victor, 539
Cunningham, Sir Andrew, 7–9, 12, 21, 27, 65, 71, 94–5, 282, 296, 301, 381, 525, 543
Cunninghame Graham, Sir Angus, 73, 563
Curtiss: Helldiver (SB2C) 327, 330, 339; Seagull (SOC), 332
Cuthbertson, Lt Cdr, 84

DUKW, 456, 487
Daihatsu, 511
Daily Mirror, 375, 378
Dakar, 28, 166, 477, 531, 543
Dalrymple-Hamilton, Frederick, 67
Danholm, 491
Daniels, Josephus, 154
Dardanelles, 10, 475, 529
Darlan, 529, 530, 531, 532
Dartmouth, 46, 65, 67–70, 72, 76, 94–5, 441, 560
Darwin, 374, 542, 543
David W Taylor, 216

David W Taylor tank, 211
dead reckoning tracker (DRT), 274, 275
defaulters, 53, 290
demerits, 77, 90, 316
Denny shipyard, 222, 438
dentistry, 135
depth charge, 209, 271, 299, 372: on aircraft, 324, 401–2; attack by, 344, 349–50, 365, 371, 501, 508, 542; creeping attack, 399; history of, 388; loading, 36; patterns, 389, 408; in ships, 382–4, 390, 398, 403–4, 407, 446; throwers, 389–90, 404
Desrosiers, John, 430, 431
destroyer escorts, 190–1, 212, 383, 403, 406, 465
Dewey, George, 23, 48
Diamond, Lou, 173
Dickens, Peter, 70, 436, 438–42, 452
Dickison, Arthur, 357, 359–60, 361, 375
Dieppe Raid, 129, 442, 467, 471, 488, 527
diesel engines, 386, 438
directors, 230, 233–6, 240, 242, 264, 266–7
distributing stations, 132
dive bombing, 181, 241–2, 295, 321, 323–7, 330, 341–3, 345
docks, 182, 184–5, 190, 192–4, 201
dockyard workers, 182–3
Donibristle, 344
Dönitz, 399, 492, 494, 497–9, 502, 504, 520, 523, 542
Douglas: Dauntless, 327–8, 330; Devastator (TBD), 327, 512; DC-3 (R4D), 181, 327; DC-4 (R5D), 327
Douhet, Guilio, 303, 522
D'Oyly Lyon, Sir George, 440
draughtsmen, 196, 212–13, 215
dreadnought battleships, 68, 208, 217, 226–8, 231, 508
drill, foot, 85, 89, 92, 97–100, 102, 158–62, 164, 170–1, 173, 304, 315, 546
Du Cane, Peter, 434, 437
dual control, 304, 315
Dudley, Sir Sheldon, 125, 126
Dunkirk, 10, 27, 31, 65, 166, 238, 295, 329, 454, 461, 526–7, 539, 534
Dutch East Indies, 533, 534
Dutt, D C, 553–5
Dykers, Thomas W, 252, 364, 367, 375

Easton, Alan, 544, 546
Eccles, Henry, 15, 563
echoes, classification of, 387
Edison, Charles, 24, 221
Edward VIII, Duke of Windsor, etc, 9, 68
Eggenberger, Bill, 299
Eisenhower, Dwight D, vi, 9, 476, 532
El Segundo, 328
Electric Boat Company (Elco), 225

electric drive, 219
electricity, 71, 76, 95, 101–2, 107, 117, 219, 232
Elizabeth, Princess, 152
emigration, 3
Empire, British, 29ff, 59, 120, 188, 278, 304
engineer officers, 65, 69–70, 72, 81, 83, 91, 218, 359
Engineering Duty Only, 81, 214
Enigma code, 58, 257, 381, 497
enlisted men, 39, 42, 45, 57, 80, 96ff, 135, 150, 194, 198, 265
enlisted pilots, 305
Ennor, Patrick, 161
ensign, 62, 78, 80, 91, 93, 416, 446
escape tower, 357, 362, 374
escort carriers, 206–8, 226, 299, 309, 311, 313–14, 379
escort groups, 394–5, 547: senior officers, 394–5
Espirito Sancto, 199, 207
Esquimalt, 545, 549
evaluator, 275

Fahey, James, 45, 104, 129, 201, 515
Fairey: Albacore, 324, 326, 340; Barracuda, 323–5, 339; Battle, 325; Fulmar, 323, 325; Swordfish, 308, 317, 323–5, 332, 340, 350
Fairfield shipyard, 222–4
Fairmile, 424, 437, 439, 442, 466, 532, 550
Farragut, David Glasgow, 48, 428
Fascism, 10, 561
Federal Shipbuilding and Drydock, 225
Felixstowe, 441
Filipinos, 83, 104, 121, 129
finger four, 340
fire control, 230, 232–6, 239, 240, 242–3, 265–7, 293
fire controlmen, 235–6
First Sea Lord, 21–2
First World War (Great War), 1, 3, 23, 47, 48, 51, 52, 66
fishermen, 55, 422, 425, 528–9, 534
flag plot, 276
flags, etc, 45
fleet admirals, 64
Fleet Air Arm, 35, 55, 62, 159, 304ff, 314–15, 317, 323, 327, 341, 344, 401
Fleet Problems, 309, 330, 428
fleet train, 206, 207
Flensburg, 491, 492
flight control room, 308
flight nurses, 137
Flinders Bay, 541
flogging, 52, 290
flush deckers, 239, 298, 406, 465
Focke-Wulf: FW 190, 317; Kondor, 308, 379, 500
Force H, 27–8

Forces Navales Française Libre (FNFL), 531, 532
Ford, Gerald, 92
Ford, Henry, 17, 18, 20, 225
Ford Island, 345
Forester, C S, 46, 47
Forgy, Howard L, 147
Forrestal, James, 25, 26, 157, 180
Fort Blockhouse, 185, 186, 357–8
Fox, Uffa, 435
France, 10, 42, 156, 168, 325, 401, 428, 443, 468, 489, 524, 544: fall of, 6, 27, 31, 166, 245, 378, 384, 393, 454, 456, 495, 556–7; First World War, 3; inter-war, 29; rivalry with Britain, 30, 184, 208; U-boat and S-boat bases, 387, 497, 504; Vichy regime, 13, 530, 531; war with Italy, 520; Washington and London treaties, 5, 529
Fraser, Sir Bruce, 28, 41, 64, 65, 554
Freetown, 27, 131, 237, 257, 379, 395
Fremantle, 372, 374, 542
French Navy, 529*ff*
Friedman, Norman, vii
frigates: armament, 247, 390–1; Castle class, 223; command, 271; design and building, 212, 224, 385–6; engines, 218; Loch class, 224; officers and crews, 75, 115, 127; radar, 263, 265; River class, 403–4; service, 395, 443, 447, 517; sick bay, 132
Frost, Donald B, 445
fuel, 17, 33, 36, 206, 209, 218–19, 221, 279, 286, 376, 377, 382, 398, 438, 453, 468
fuel tanks, 182, 194, 200
Fulton, Robert, 347
Fursland, Stoker, 148, 149, 219
Furstner, Admiral, 533
Fussell, Paul, 34

Galbreath, John H, 144
Gallipoli, 454
gambling, 113, 120
Gandhi, Mahatma, 552
Gates, Artemus L, 319
gedunk sailors, 48, 124
Geelong, 540
General Board, 122, 214–15, 221, 278, 283, 298, 353, 403
General Electric, 219
General Motors, 20, 221, 244, 327
general quarters, 38, 107
Geneva Convention, 125, 140, 143
George V, King, 9
George VI, King, 9, 12, 30
Germany: blockade of, 31; bombing of, 18, 428; British rivalry with, 208, 278; campaign against, 7, 488; effects of Versailles, 29; First World War, 489; Great Depression, 17; industry, 243; Navy, 282, 490*ff*; unification, 489
Gerrits, Burt, 84, 186, 208, 222
Gibbs and Cox, 216, 221, 404
Gibraltar, 27–8, 54, 130, 154, 185, 257, 344, 383, 395, 520, 522–4, 530–1, 548
Gilbert Islands, 207, 344
Giraud, General, 365
Gittlelsohn, Roland, 147, 150
Glasgow, 223–4, 392, 399, 415, 470
Glenwood Springs, 141
Gloster Gladiator, 324
Godfrey, John, 271, 380, 553
Godley, John, 42, 314, 323
Gold Coast (Ghana), 552
Goldberg, Rube, 252
Golden Gate Bridge, 193, 196
Goodall, Ernest, 421, 423, 426
Goodall, Sir Stanley, 211, 304, 350, 383, 403
Goolsbee, Daniel, 139
Government Code and Cypher School, 254, 257
Gower, Lord, 53
Grand Corps, 529
Grantham, Guy, 69
Great Depression, 3, 6, 16–18, 99, 189, 196, 222, 533, 551
Great Lakes, 99, 122, 357, 473, 543, 546
Great White Fleet, 207, 225
Greece, 414, 461, 520, 543
Greenock, 201, 399
Gretton, Peter, 203, 279, 386, 390–1, 395, 396, 398–9
Groebeler, Hans, 491
Grosse Ile, 316
Groton, 225, 347, 356
Grumman: Avenger (TBF), 299, 327–9, 339; Duck (JF), 332; Hellcat, 313, 327, 331, 341, 512; Wildcat (Martlet, F4F), 299, 326, 331
Guadalcanal: battles, 83, 273, 289, 408, 509, 543; campaign, 259, 267, 551; importance, 32, 277, 345; landing vessels, 463; marines, 140, 170, 173, 176–8, 290, 484; PT boats, 450; Seabees, 196, 200
Guam, 23, 29, 189, 194, 345, 374
Guantanamo Bay, 141, 192
Guinness, Alec, 98
gun club, 13, 227
gun design and construction, 228, 230
gun turrets, 25, 38, 102, 109, 158, 162, 208, 228–34, 238–40, 281, 283, 286–8, 294–5, 298–9, 491, 509, 540
gunnery branch, 71, 102, 124, 269
guns (calibres): 18in, 281, 284, 507; 16in, 25, 35, 228, 231–2, 281, 283–4, 507; 15in, 184, 228, 279, 493; 14in, 23, 228, 230, 232, 281, 283, 507; 13.5in, 231, 279; 8in,

227–8, 232, 286, 288–9, 309, 508, 530; 6in, 214, 227, 229, 248, 286–90; 5.25in, 238; 5in, 232, 239, 248, 253, 267, 289, 296, 299, 310, 353, 403, 509; 4.7in, 237, 293, 296, 391; 4.5in, 238, 296; 4in, 236, 238, 296, 362, 382, 391, 393, 466; 40mm, 104, 243–4, 267, 438, 446; 20mm, 245–6, 249, 322, 502

HF/DF, 387, 388, 548
HOR MAN engines, 221–2
Haakon, King, 528, 316, 335
Hadley, Dunstan, 316, 335
Halifax, 131, 189, 394, 400, 543, 545–7, 549
Hall, John Lesslie, 476
Hall-Scott Defender, 435, 437
Halsey, 'Bull', 2, 14, 29, 64, 78
Halsey, Margaret, 3
Hamburg, 259, 498, 499
hammocks, 100, 113–14, 117, 132, 149, 164, 291, 463, 507, 548, 580
Hampton Roads, 99, 191
Hancock, Joy Bright, 155
happy time, 379, 402, 429, 501
Hara, Tameichi, 507–9, 518
hard chine, 434, 437
Harland and Wolff, 222
Harman, Lieutenant, 546
Hart, Sydney, 360
Hart, Thomas C, 214, 353, 375
Haslar, 129, 130, 211
Hatley Park, 545
Hawaii, 28, 49, 157, 193, 424
Hawker Sea Hurricane, 323, 326
Hazemeyer mount, 533
Hedgehog, 382, 385–6, 390, 391, 399, 403, 407, 466, 518
Helensburgh, 1, 421
Henderson Field, 345
Henderson, Sir Reginald, 434
Hess, Rudolf, 15
Hess, Werner, 499
Hezlett, Sir Arthur, 359
Hichens, Robert, 438
hidden economy, 115, 120
high angle control system (HACS), 242, 243
Hirohito, Emperor, 506
Hirschfeld, Wolfgang, 492, 500
Hitler, Adolf, 7, 15, 259, 380, 471, 489–90, 492, 494, 497–8, 504, 506, 520, 529–30, 534
Hoagland, Edgar D, 448, 452
Hobart's funnies, 468, 486
Holland, John, 208, 347
Holland, Thomas, 148
Home Fleet, 27, 242, 285
homosexuality, 50, 51, 66
Honolulu, 48, 136, 193, 552

Honourable East India Company, 552
Hoover Dam, 226
Hoover, President, 6, 12, 18
Horan, H E, 550
Horikoshi, Jiro, 512
horizontal bombing, 330, 342
Hornblower novels, 46, 47
Horton, Sir Max, 61, 65, 94, 371
hospital apprentices, 137, 138
Hospital Corps, 137, 138, 139
hospital ships, 128–31, 137
hospitals, 51, 126, 129–30, 138–9, 141–2, 144, 202
Hostilities Only (HO), 318, 425, 439
housing, 16
Hove, 85, 87
Hovgaard William, 209, 214
hull lines, 211, 215, 216
human torpedoes, 185–6, 351, 353, 524, 528, 556
Hunley, Horace L, 347
Hunter College, 157
Hynes, Samuel, 169, 181, 319–20, 331

ISWAS, 349
Iago, John, 171
ice cream, 41, 60, 92, 120, 204, 300, 405
Identification Friend or Foe (IFF), 262, 269
immersion foot, 133, 134
imports, British, 376, 377
imprisonment, 52, 55, 58
India, 10, 17, 23, 30, 121, 550*ff*
Industrial Recovery Act, 353
industry: American, 7, 18, 20, 327; British, 17, 222
Inoguchi, Rikhei, 515
instructor officers, 67, 75
Inter-Service Training and Development Centre, 461
intermediate flying training, 320, 345
Inveraray, 470
Invergordon Mutiny, 39, 59
Irish-Americans, 2
Ironbottom Sound, 450
island superstructure, 306, 512
isolationism, 6, 208, 211, 260
Italy, 5, 7, 31, 290, 295, 312, 443, 453, 462, 488, 519*ff*, 556, 561
Iwo Jima, 32, 137, 140, 144, 171, 173, 180–1, 198–9, 345, 416, 418, 467, 482, 484

JGs, 62, 93, 136, 155
Jackson, John Leland, 429
James, William, 27, 64
Japan: advances, 28, 184, 186, 254, 277, 305, 345, 374, 380, 450; aircraft, 331, 341, 512*ff*; alliance with Britain, 504; American attitudes to, 179, 194, 289; attack on Pearl

Harbor, 7; codes, 259–60; history, 32, 168, 489, 504–5; First World War, 504; Geneva Convention, 140, 143; merchant shipping, 409; navy, 2, 267, 284, 286, 288, 295, 299, 302, 508*ff*; need for imports, 367, 376; prisoners, 144; religion, 507; shipping, 253; submarine warfare, 351, 366, 368, 371, 433; surrender of, 132, 232, 375; strategy and tactics, 180, 408; torpedoes, 509; treaties of Washington and London, 5, 189, 281; underestimation of, 29
Jarrow, 222
Jellicoe, Admiral Sir John, 249, 302, 538
Jenkins, C A, 68, 71, 72, 306
Jerningham, E J, 293, 299, 300
Jewell, Bill, 359, 365
Jinna, Mohamed Ali, 155
John Brown's, 222, 223
John, Caspar, 66, 314
Johnson, Augustus P, 106
Johnson, Lyndon, 92
Joint Chiefs of Staff, 13, 459
Jones, Houston, 42, 45, 91, 93, 108, 429, 430–1
Jones, John Paul, 48
Jones, Tristan, 96, 250, 296
Judaism, 151
Judge Advocate General, 56
Juno Beach, 69, 486
Jutland, Battle of, 47, 235, 249, 255, 278–9, 281, 300, 487, 490, 520

Kaiser, Henry J, 225–6, 313, 412
Kaiten, 511
kamikaze, 146, 247–8, 253, 265, 307, 331, 505, 514–16, 557
Kawasaki H8K, 513
Kelly Turner, Admiral, 80, 93, 213, 460, 475
Kennedy, John F, 446, 450, 558
Kennedy, Ludovic, 85, 186, 295
Kenney, George, 476
Kenya, 30, 257, 552
Kernan, Alvin, 39, 106, 111–12, 117, 120, 150, 202, 310, 319, 328–9, 335–6
Kessing, Oliver, 202
Key West, 406, 429
Keyes, Sir Roger, 454, 466
Kincaid, 474, 476
King, Ernest J, 7, 8, 13–14, 25–6, 76, 155, 214, 305
King-Hall, Stephen, 65, 66
King's Regulations, 52
Kleiss, 'Dusty', 82, 330, 342
Knox, Frank, 13, 24–6, 319, 321
Knudsen, William, 20
Kolombanga, Battle of, 276
Koninlijke Marine, 553*ff*
Kronstadt, 536

Kuznetsov, Nikolai, 535, 536
La Rochelle, 502
Labour Party, 9, 10–11, 21, 540
Lake Maracaibo, 458
Lamb, Charles, 315
Lambkin, Charles, 373
Lancing College, 85, 86
Landing Barge: Flak (LBF), 167; Kitchen (LBK), 466
Landing Craft: Assault (LCA), 167, 456–7, 460; Flak (LCF), 167, 456, 466; Gun (LCG), 167, 443, 466, 468; Mechanised (LCM), 460–1; Support, 466; Tank (LCT), 130, 456, 482; Tank (Rocket) (LCTR), 466; Vehicle (LCV), 20, 462; Vehicle and Personnel (LCVP), 20, 456, 464–5
Landing Ship: Gantry, 464–5; Infantry (LSI), 410, 455, 458, 464; Medium (LSM), 460, 482; Stern Chute, 465; Tank (LST), 416–17, 465, 485
landing signal officer (LSO), 336, 338
Landing Vehicle Tracked (LVT), 20, 351, 463, 473, 482, 485, 528, 557
Larsen, Leif, 352, 528
Laughton Matthews, Vera, 152, 154
Lawrence, T E, 'of Arabia', 434
Layard, Frank, 296, 300–1, 546, 548
Laycock, John N, 198
Laycock, Sir Robert, 454
Le Bailly, Louis, 70
Leach, Douglas, 90
Leach, Sir Henry, 230
leading seamen, etc, 101–2, 109–10, 360, 439
leading stoker, 360, 439
leading telegraphist, 360, 492
Leahy, 7, 8, 13, 26, 64, 75, 78–9, 95, 204
Leckie, Robert, 172–4, 176, 178–80, 465, 484
Lemp, Fritz-Julius, 497
lend-lease, 19, 245, 255, 323, 327, 426, 436, 537
Leningrad, 535, 536, 537
Lewin, Terence, 242
Leyte Gulf, 2, 32, 94, 143, 206, 232, 253, 273, 299, 324, 451, 466, 488, 508, 514–15
Liberal Party, 9, 10, 66
Liberty ships, 200, 225, 313, 412–13, 465
Libya, 168, 521, 522
lieutenant, 55, 68, 69–70, 75, 80, 267, 365, 422, 438
lieutenant commander, 61–2, 72, 93, 359
lifeboats, 133–4, 413, 415
lifeguarding, 344, 367
Lillicrap, Sir Charles, 212
Lindemann, Frederick, 377
liners, 30, 190, 217, 222, 225, 313
Lines, Wheeler B, 139
Liverpool, 27, 130, 182, 185, 188–9, 201, 271, 393, 399

Livorno, 443, 622
Lochailort, 469
Lockwood, Charles, 373
Lofoten Islands, 258, 471, 527
London Treaty, 6, 211, 231, 281, 283, 289, 353, 509
Londonderry, 130, 185, 189, 201, 390, 393, 400
Long Lance torpedo, 509
Longmore, Sir Arthur, 303
Lords, House of, 10, 14
Lorient, 502, 503
Lowe, Axel Olaf, 491
lower deck, 49, 70, 74, 85–6, 96, 109, 115, 124, 296
lower deck attitudes, 88
Lowestoft, 423, 426, 441
Lucky Bag, 78
Lyness, 187
Lyons, Joseph, 540

McAfee, Mildred H, 155
McAra, Charles, 418, 422, 426
MacArthur, Douglas, vi, 9, 29, 32, 271, 449, 450, 451, 453, 475, 485, 488, 543
McCampbell, David S, 341
Macdonald, Roderick, 69, 297
McElduff, D A, 82
McHale, Clemen, 200
Macintyre, Donald, 201, 203–4, 255, 382, 356, 396, 548
Machrihanish, 344
Mack, Angela, 153
magnetic mines, 420–2, 424–5, 428, 430, 432–3
Maher, Brendan, 426, 427
Maizuru, 518, 519
Malaya, 511
Mallallieu, J P W, 10, 149, 287
Malta, 129, 130, 166, 184–5, 257, 287, 324, 344, 441, 522, 525, 532
Manila, 23, 32, 371
Manitowoc, 357
Marconi, Guglielmo, 254, 519
Mare Island,193, 224, 356, 374
Mare Nostrum, 519
Marines, Royal, 158*ff*: bands, 164; NCOs, 162–3; officers, 159–61; shipboard, 164; training, 162–3; uniform, 158, 161–2
Marines, United States, 167*ff*: aviation, 181*ff*; fire team, 173, 175–6; landing operations, 170–1; NCOs, 170; officers, 171–2; roles, 169–70; shipboard, 169; specialists, 174–5; training, 170–1; uniform, 168, 178; weapons, 177–8
marriage, 70
Martinez, Richard, 240

Mason, Ted, 25, 38, 44–5, 50–1, 56, 58, 73, 82, 93, 108, 112, 119, 140, 151, 169, 183, 192, 292–3, 346, 446
Mass Observation, 97
mass production, 4, 17, 18, 20, 145, 226, 243–5, 289, 313, 353, 386, 406, 412, 437, 458, 498–9, 517, 562
master at arms, 52, 57, 113, 290
masturbation, 49
Matapan, Battle of, 283, 287, 301, 522
Mathis, Sam, 199
Maugham, Somerset 82
Maund, L E H, 470
Mayo, Admiral, 5, 304
Medical Director General, 125, 126
Mediterranean Fleet, 22, 27, 267, 287
Melly, George, 49, 50, 59, 75, 98, 109
Memphis, 319, 320
merchant aircraft carrier (MAC) ship, 308
Merchant Marine, 411*ff*: Cadet Corps, 413
Merchant Navy, 408*ff*
Mers-el-Kébir, 529, 531
messdecks, 109, 113–15, 133, 149, 164, 404, 463, 548
messmen, 121, 123
Metox, 499
Mid Ocean Meeting Point (Momp), 394
midshipman, 48, 75–8, 89, 91, 428, 472, 553
Midway, 32, 260, 294, 310, 327, 330, 342, 345, 374, 379, 408
Miller, CPO, USN, 41
Miller, Max, 335, 336, 346
Mills, Sir John, 375
Mincemeat, Operation, 365
mine barrages, 23, 401, 428, 442
minelaying, 418, 432–3
mines, 418*ff*, 428–30
minesweepers, 424*ff*, 430–2
minesweeping, 419*ff*, 431–2
Mios Woendi, 449
Mitscher, Marc, 29, 75, 77, 94, 200, 278, 303, 328, 331
Mitsubishi: A7M Reppo, 512; G4M (Betty), 513, 517; J2M Raiden, 512; Zero, 341–2, 514–15, 519, 612
Mobile Naval Base Defence Organisation, 165
Mobile Service Squadron, 207
Moffet, William A, 216, 304
Mogmog , 202
Monsarrat, Nicholas, 84–5, 89, 109, 132, 225, 401, 404–5
Montagu, Ewen, 149
Morocco, 521, 531
Morrow Board, 305
Morton, H V, 73
motor gunboats (MGBs), 428, 439–42, 550

motor launches (MLs), 143, 437, 440–1
motor torpedo boats (MTBs), 251, 435–6, 438, 440–4, 452, 532
Mountbatten, Lord Louis, 9, 67, 154, 167, 245, 267–8, 454, 468, 477, 558
Mountfield, Reginald, 234
Mousetrap, 407
Mulberry Harbour, 467, 468, 549
Munich Crisis, 69
Murray, Stuart, 216
Muselier, Emile, 531, 532
Mussolini, Benito, 506, 529, 520–1, 534
Mustang officers, 82
mutiny, 39, 50, 57, 60, 535, 555
mutiny on the *Bounty*, 59

NROTC, 89, 362
Nagasaki, 506, 519
Nakajima B5N (Kate), 512
naming of ships and bases, 6, 34, 48, 287, 293–4, 351, 353
Narvik, 279, 494, 527, 539
naval architects, 25, 209, 219, 457, 529
Naval Discipline Act, 52
Naval Estimates, 22
Naval Independent Unit, 528
Naval Mine Warfare School, 430
Naval Ordnance Laboratory, 76, 230, 265
Naval Research Laboratory, 230
naval staff, 22
Naval War College, 32, 278
navigation: American practice, 81, 107, 276, 447–8; aviation, 315, 321, 323, 338, 366, 433; British officers, 39, 65; lack of training, 402; landing craft, 466–7, 469, 472, 481; radar, 265, 267, 271; specialisation in, 71–2 ; training, 76, 87–8, 91, 315
Navy Department, 24
Navy Nurse Corps, 136
Navy Regulations, 56, 59–60, 94, 364
Nazism, 301, 489, 491–2, 501, 561
Nelles, Admiral Percy, 545
Nelson, Horatio, 46, 132, 376, 534
Netherlands, 532
Netley, 142
Neutrality Act, 6
Neutrality Patrol, 28, 299, 380, 417
New Deal, 19, 20
New Guinea, 32, 277, 374, 449, 451, 481, 533, 543
New Hebrides, 201, 277
New London, 225, 361–2, 373, 406, 416, 429, 444
New York, 35, 90, 156–7, 190, 221, 225, 304, 347, 374, 406, 413–14, 439
New York Navy Yard, 221, 243
New York Shipbuilding, 216

New Zealand, 30, 49, 119, 142, 189, 538, 545, 550–1
Newport News, 225, 312
Newport, Rhode Island, 225
Nicholls, Sir Percival, 126
Nightingale, Florence, 127, 142
Nimitz, Chester W, vi, 9, 24, 26, 29, 41, 64, 75–6, 80, 89, 94, 150, 155, 177, 204, 253, 514, 558
'ninety-day wonders', 89*ff*, 508
Nishumara, Admiral, 508
Nixon, Richard, 92, 558
Norden bombsight, 260, 329
Nore Command, 27, 440, 442
Norfolk, Virginia, 122, 139, 191, 224–5, 307, 323, 474, 478
Normandy, 22, 71; build-up, 376; casualties, 130, 142, 145; chaplain, 148; coastal forces, 443; command, 9, 65, 67, 69, 477; commandoes, 167, 471; landing craft, 459, 462, 465, 467–8, 479, 496; mines, 422, 427, 431; naval gunfire, 228, 287, 290, 483; navigation, 352, 485; preparation, 474, 476; U-boats, 380
North Africa: Churchill and, 10, 31; command, 22, 477; hospital ship, 131; landing craft, 459, 462, 463, 472, 485; mines, 431; Roosevelt, 13; submarines, 349, 365; support, 191, 285, 290, 312; tactics, 481
North Atlantic Sea Control Frontier, 381
North, Sir Dudley, 28
Norway, 31, 76, 243, 254, 259, 295, 349, 352, 371, 372, 393, 414, 454, 461, 471, 475, 494, 496, 504, 528, 530, 532
nurses, 127–30, 135–7, 142–3, 146, 355
Nyce, Harry, 136

Oban, 549
Observant, 396
observers, 159, 302, 304, 315–17, 325, 329, 344
Odessa, 536, 537
Oerlikon gun, 241, 245–7, 249, 271, 284, 383, 391, 403, 436–8, 466, 467
officer-like qualities, 88
O'Hara, Jean, 49
Oi, Atushi, 517, 518
oil tankers, 203–7, 313, 409
Okha (Baku), 517
Okinawa, 32, 82, 143, 179, 200, 205, 274, 331, 432, 464, 467, 485, 488, 508, 516
Oléron, Laws of, 52
Oliver, Geoffrey, 59
Olson, Michael Keith, 94, 193
Omaha Beach, 468, 477, 485, 486
Oram, H, 110
Orange, War Plan, 32

ordinary seamen, 97
Oropesa sweep, 419, 425, 431
Orkney, 27, 186, 441
Ortega, Louis, 138, 140
Orwell, George, 16, 17
Osborne House, 65, 67, 68, 540
Ouvry, J G D, 420
Owen, Charles, 67

PAMETRADA, 217
Pact of Steel, 520
paddle steamers, 424, 440
Palm Beach, 510
Panama Canal, 23, 92, 191, 192, 309, 374, 377, 448
parking, 335, 346
Parry, 48, 81, 117, 169, 194, 256, 273, 288
Parsons, Charles, 217, 219
parts of ship, 38, 290, 552
patrol torpedo (PT) boat, 65, 107, 199, 225, 265, 302, 444–52
Pearl Harbor, 90, 157, 327, 353, 403–5, 417, 450, 501, 506, 512–13, 519, 534, 543, 557, 561: airfields, 345; attack on, 7, 24, 42, 89, 107, 147, 170–1, 189, 193, 195, 221, 239, 270, 283, 285, 289, 380, 505; as base, 29, 32, 194, 201, 310; hospital, 141; intelligence, 254, 259–60; submarines, 253, 344, 374, 511; Waves at, 157
Pelly, John, 86–7
Penne, Luigi de la, 524
Pensacola, 181, 316, 320, 345
Perishers, 357, 358
Perret, Marvin J, 415, 417, 419
Perry, Commodore, 168, 504
Pétain, Marshal, 530
Peterson, Frederick, 122
petty officers, American, 45, 59, 91, 101, 104–7, 110–13, 122
petty officers, British, 22, 51, 54, 86, 102, 109–10
pharmacist's mates, 136
Philippines, 23, 28, 32, 131, 181, 189, 194, 259, 374, 408, 434, 443, 449, 450, 482, 543, 588
Phoenixes, 467
Phoney War, 31, 254
Piarco Savana, 316
pin-on badges, 63, 64
Pineapple, 396–7
Pipe Line Under the Ocean (Pluto), 468
plane captains, 321, 322
plane guard destroyer, 343
planing hulls, 211
plebes, 76, 78
plotting board, 338
Plunkett, Reginald, 69

Plymouth, 27, 49, 96, 98, 102, 127, 129, 130, 159–60, 182, 184–5, 212, 441, 476, 553
Poland, 503, 526, 527
Pollen system, 233, 235
pontoons, 198, 448, 459
Port Chicago, 57, 122
Port Edgar, 130, 424
Port Jackson, 542, 543
Portland (UK), 103, 392
Portland (USA), 225
Portsmouth (UK) 49, 66: airfields, 344; amphibious warfare, 461, 470, 476; as base, 182, 184; command, 27, 64, 441; employees, 22, 212; French at, 531, 533; harbour, 185–6; hospital, 127–9; marines, 159–60, 165–6; tactical courses, 300–1; training, 70–1, 96–7, 102, 254, 268, 316, 357; wardroom, 46
Portsmouth, New Hampshire, 190, 224, 356
Potter, E B, vi
Pound, Sir Dudley, 21
Pratt, William V, 8, 214, 309
Preble, Edward, 4
primary flying training, 319, 320
promotion, officers, 66, 72–3, 80, 89, 93
prostitution, 49, 50
Protestantism, 150, 151
Puget Sound, 192, 224

Quakers, 150
quartermasters, 41, 65, 81, 104–5, 107, 291–2, 406, 418, 447, 472
Quebecois, 547
Queen Alexandra's Royal Naval Nursing Service (QARNNS), 127, 128
Queen Bee target, 242
Queenborough, 426
Quincy, 224
Quisling, Vidkun, 528
Quonset huts, 198, 345, 449, 474
Quonsett, 34

Rabaul, 519
race, 4, 120*ff*
radar aerials, 210, 262, 263, 264, 265, 387
radar, British types: GA, 263; GS, 263; WA, 263; WS, 263; Type 79, 263; Type 271, 262–3, 265, 269, 271, 387; Type 273, 262; Type 276, 262, 269; Type 277, 262; Type 279, 263; Type 281, 263; Type 284, 264; Type 285, 242, 263; Type 286, 262, 547; Type 293, 269
radar displays: A-scope, 263, 265, 269, 370; PPI, 263, 265, 269, 272, 275
radar, microwave, 261, 262, 265–6
radar plotter branch, 269
radar, US types: CXAM1, 265, 267; FJ, 267; Mark 3, 267; Mark 4, 267; Mark 8, 267;

SC, 265; SC2, 265; SG, 265, 267, 370; SJ, 370; SK, 265; XAF, 265
radarman, 108, 270
radio technician, 104, 108, 270, 334
Raeder, Admiral, 494, 495
Raikes, R P, 366
rail loading, 480
Raines, Orvill, 14, 108, 117, 119
ramming, 347, 398
Ramsey, Sir Bertram, 27
Ramsey, Sir Charles, 396
Ramsey, Nurse Helen, 142
rangefinders, 102, 233, 235, 236, 269, 289
Rangers, 471
rank structure, officers, 61
Ransome Wallis, Dr R, 126
Raspberry, 396
ratings, 70, 96*ff*
rationing, 145, 377
Rayner, D A, 85, 188, 395, 401, 422, 423
Red Cross Society, 128
reduction gears, 217, 220
refuelling at sea, 203–4, 206–7, 217
rescue ships, 134
Revenue Cutter Service, 416
Reynolds, L C, 435
Rickover, Hyman, 81, 375
rifles, 34, 107, 161–2, 164, 169–72, 175–9, 417, 479, 541
riveting, 211, 222, 224
Rivett-Crane, J W, 550
Robbs of Leith, 223
Robinson, C Snelling, 89
Roebling, Donald, 20, 463
Rogal, William, 39, 118, 168, 172, 178
Roman Catholicism, 49, 147–51
Roosevelt, Eleanor, 12, 155
Roosevelt, Franklin D, 6, 7, 12–15, 18, 20, 26, 31, 76, 121–2, 190, 298, 305, 312, 380, 403, 405, 411, 450, 506, 526, 532
Roosevelt, Theodore, 2, 23–4, 207, 226
Roskill, Stephen, 61, 452
Rosyth, 27, 96, 130, 184–5, 396
Royal Air Force, 47, 66, 96, 152, 255, 316, 434, 435
Royal Australian Navy (RAN), 540, 541, 545
Royal Canadian Naval Reserve (RCNR), 545, 546
Royal Canadian Navy (RCN), 400, 544–6, 548, 550
Royal Corps of Naval Constructors, 211–13
Royal Fleet Reserve, 84, 96
Royal Hawaiian Hotel, 373
Royal Indian Marine, 552
Royal Indian Navy (RIN), 552*ff*
Royal National Lifeboat Institution, 415
Royal Naval Air Service (RNAS), 52, 303
Royal Naval Patrol Service, 423

Royal Naval Reserve (RNR), 62, 85, 422
Royal Naval Volunteer Reserve (RNVR), 4, 36, 62, 85, 89, 127, 147, 272, 308, 359, 422, 438, 440, 468
Royal New Zealand Navy (RNZN), 441, 550, 551
Royal Ramsgate Yacht Club, 441
Ruffing, Bob, 51
Ruhe, William J, 300
Rum, 114
Ryder, 'RED', 69

SPARS, 156, 157
safety barrier, 335
sailorettes, 165
St Clair Morford, 160
St John, John, 160, 165
St Johns, Newfoundland, 379, 400
St Nazaire, 69, 129, 471, 502, 532
St Vincent, Lord, 347
Salerno, 66, 131, 263, 326, 427, 431, 454, 483, 487
saluting, 47, 83, 85, 88, 170, 292, 375, 414, 507, 547
Samar, 94, 299, 314
San Diego, 99, 113, 141, 168, 170, 174, 183, 193–4, 455, 474
Santa Cruz, Battle of, 244
Savo Island, 267, 289, 540, 543
Scapa Flow, 3, 27, 130–1, 185–6, 188, 202, 279, 283, 344, 490, 542, 548
Schaeffer, Heinz, 491, 495, 502
Schneider Trophy, 304
Schofield, Brian, 66, 67, 78
schoolmasters, 74, 553
schools, public, 15, 50, 69
Schwartz, Bernie (Tony Curtis), 374
Scott, Peter, 434, 436, 438, 440, 442
Scott Paine, Hubert, 434–7, 443, 457
Scouting Force, 28
Sea Lion, Operation, 495
Sea Lords, 21–2
Seabees, 142, 195*ff*, 557: equipment, 93, 199, 448, 459, 485
seasickness, 36, 135, 292, 385, 480
Seattle, 192, 193, 313
Secretary of the Navy, 6, 13, 24, 26, 93, 154, 180
Sedberry, Robert, 107
selection of officers, 64, 68, 94–5, 546, 558
Selective Service Act, 6, 121, 196
Sempill Mission, 511
Sharp, Alexander, 428
shells: design, 228; fusing, 243, 247–8; in service, 229–30, 287, 493; shore bombardment, 454, 483, 487; star, 396–7; types, 237–40, 295, 391
Shetland Bus, 528
Shinto, 505

ship-handling, 39, 64
shipwreck survivors, 133, 146
shore bombardment, 206, 274–5, 283, 285, 290, 483, 532, 537
shore patrol, 59, 108
Short Sunderland, 333, 401
Sicily, 9, 31, 69, 166, 198, 454, 476, 478, 482–3, 487, 525, 527, 534, 543, 554
sick berth attendants, 128–9, 132, 166
sick quarters, 126, 130
Sierra Leone, 27, 237, 257, 393
Silent Service (TV series), 375
Simonstown, 130, 184, 551
Singapore, 28, 184, 186, 189, 259, 352, 540
Skinner, George, 546
skip bombing, 343
Slapton Sands, 461, 474, 504
Sledge, Eugene, 91, 170–1, 177, 180, 459, 462
sloops, 102, 391, 395, 543, 553
Small, Joseph, 122
Smith, Holland M, 159, 175, 171–2, 176–8, 455, 483
Smith, Ralph M, 176
Smith's Dock, 223, 383
snorkel, 347, 375, 380, 503, 533
sonar, vii, 104, 108, 139, 209, 210, 356, 367, 369, 406–8, 429
Somerville, Admiral, 28, 61, 530
Sopwith, Sir Thomas, 393
South Africa, 10, 30, 184, 377, 538, 551
South African Naval Force (SANF), 552
Southport, 130
Soviet Union, 20, 29–31, 333, 488, 526, 535*ff*, 557–8, 561
Spanish-American War, 23, 48
Spanish Civil War, 242, 243, 297, 520
Special Entry Scheme, 68, 69, 545, 560
speed of warships, 209, 210, 211
Speer, Albert, 498
Spithead, 182, 188
Spruance, Raymond, 14, 29, 74, 94, 177, 386
square rig, 42, 88, 104, 153–4
Squid, 386, 390, 391
stability, 209–11, 243, 383, 509, 522
staff, naval, 22
Stalin, Joseph, 20, 506, 520, 535, 527
Stanford, Edward, 202
Stark, Admiral, 89
stars, rank, 64
Starvation, Operation, 433
steam gunboats, 136, 441
steam, high pressure, 24, 26, 81, 214, 216, 219–21, 295, 298, 312, 556
steam turbines, 208, 218–20, 222, 403–4, 412, 426, 509, 556, 558, 580
Stearman N2S, 319, 393
Stephens, Cyril, 393

Stephenson, Gilbert, 392
stevedores, 122, 200
Stimson, Henry L, 13
stokers, 103, 110, 217, 290, 360, 439, 547
stone frigates, 35
Stonehouse, 129, 130
Stralsund, 492
strikers, 105, 107, 196
stripes, rank, 62–4
sub lieutenant, 62, 71, 88
subchasers 110
submarine depot ships, 352, 371–4
submarine tracking room, 271, 272, 381
substantive and non-substantive rates, 102–3, 110, 158
Suda Bay, 165, 207
Suez Canal, 520, 522, 543
suffragettes, 152
Sumatra, 327, 533, 534
Supermarine: Seafire, 323, 326; Spitfire, 323–4, 326, 331; Walrus, 323–4, 540, 541
surf, 169, 455, 462, 472–4
surgeons, 115, 118, 125–7, 135
Surigao Strait, 267, 299, 302, 451, 508, 543
Sydney, 130, 542
Sydney Cove, 394, 400, 549
synthetic fliers, 305
swearing, 115, 118, 148, 252

tachymetric system, 242–3
tactical course, 300–1
Takai, Sadao, 514
Talk Between Ships (TBS), 255
Tarawa, 143, 180, 459, 463, 483, 484–5
task force, 29, 254, 275–6, 332, 459
telegraphist air gunner (TAG), 317
telephones, 174, 255, 273, 308, 478, 544
teleradio, 277
test tanks, 211
Thach Weave, 341
Thompson, 'Big Bill', 2
Thornycroft, Sir Jack, 434
three-badge AB, 106, 109
'tiddly' sailors, 42, 43
tides, 167, 399, 469, 484–5
Tinian, 321, 345, 476, 482
Tizard mission, 260, 262
Tobermory, 392, 393
toilet facilities, 177, 198
Tokyo, 204, 311, 375, 518
torpedo bombing, 283, 302–3, 314, 321, 323–9, 341, 343–4, 401, 505, 512–14
torpedo data computer, 349, 353, 356, 362, 369, 370
torpedoes, 209, 227, 249*ff*: British, 250–1; US, 252*ff*; faults of, 252
Torpex, 249, 251, 402, 433

Toulon, 518, 529, 530, 531
Towers Scheme, 316
Trafalgar, 132, 529
tramp steamers, 409, 410
trawlers, 36, 218, 237, 383, 401, 423–4, 528, 532, 534, 540
Treasure Island, 51, 139, 193
Treasury: British, 23; US, 415
Trenchard, Hugh, 303, 314
Trinity House, 415
Tsukada, Seaman, 507
Tsushima, Battle of, 32, 506, 535
Tucson, 474
turrets, aircraft, 379

U-boats, 396, 496, 498, 502, 503
Ulithi, 49, 143, 182, 201–3
Ultra, 257–9, 271, 380–1
Union flag (jack), 36, 45, 46
Usborne, Vice Admiral, 437
Utah Beach, 417, 477, 485, 486

V-5, 305
V-7, 90–1, 472
V-12, 91–2, 135, 172, 472
VHF radio, 255, 256
VT fuses, 248, 249
Vaasgo, 471
Versailles Treaty, 489–90, 503–4, 519, 561
Vespucci, Amerigo, 519
Vian, Philip, 66, 94
Vichy regime, 13, 28, 481, 530, 532
Vickers-Armstrong, 222, 228, 238
Victoria, Queen, 40, 65, 552
Villa Carmela, 524
Vinson, Carl, 14
Vinson-Trammell Act, 1, 5, 211
Vladivostok, 536
Voluntary Aid Detachments (VADs), 128
Vosper, 434, 436, 443–4, 532

Walker, F J, 61, 377, 399
Walker, Forrest, 137, 138, 144
Wall Street Crash, 18
War Cabinet, 11, 26
War of 1812, 3, 48, 76, 168
War of Independence (American Revolution), 48
War Shipping Administration, 412
wardrooms, 57, 70, 73, 74, 82–3, 121, 132, 136, 151, 164, 293, 355, 359, 364, 426, 476, 510
wargaming, 32, 214, 304

warrant officers, 51, 74–5, 80*ff*, 95, 129, 318, 359, 416, 422, 553
Washington Treaty, 1, 5, 6, 189, 208, 228, 231, 278, 281, 306, 309, 504, 507–8, 520, 529
watches, 37–8, 98, 108, 117, 188, 269–70, 291–2, 344, 360–1, 368, 388, 408, 411, 414, 426, 519
watertender, 104, 108
Waugh, Evelyn, 88, 158, 160, 454
Waves, 155–7
Wavy Navy, 62, 83
Webb, Aston, 67
welding, 182, 222–4, 226, 253, 412
Wellings, Joseph, 297
Western Approaches Command, 27, 61, 65, 86, 271–2, 371, 399–401
Western Ocean Meeting Point (Westomp), 394
Westinghouse, 219
Whale Island, 70, 185
Whelan, John, 54, 75, 103, 114, 290
Whinney, Bob, 65, 67
White Ensign, 46, 47, 538
Whiting, Kenneth, 318
Wilhelmina, Queen, 533
Wilkinson, Eugene, 362
Willans, Geoffrey, 47
Williams, Leonard Charles, 36
Williamsburg, 150, 151
Willow Run, 20, 327
Wilmot, CPO, 315
Wincott, Len, 39
Winn, Roger, 381
wolf packs, 368, 500
Wood, Sam, 290
Woodgate, Miss J, 128
Wouk, Herman, 91
Wrens, 98, 152*ff*, 188, 421
Wright brothers, 303, 318

Y stations, 257
yachtsmen, 36, 84, 85, 541, 550
Yalta, 8, 527
Yamamoto, 260
Yarrow, 223, 224, 293, 438
yeomen, 104, 108
Yeovilton, 35, 344
Young, Edward, 348, 358, 359

Zaunkönig, 502
Zeebrugge, 301, 454
zigzagging, 275, 358, 397, 444
Zscech, Peter, 491

Ship Index

Australian warships
Albatross, 540
Australia, 543
Bathurst class, 540, 543
Canberra, 540
Shropshire, 540, 543
Sydney, 541, 543

British warships
SB = Shore base

'A'-class submarines, 351
Abdiel class, 211, 427
Adamant, 372
Africa, 303
Aggressive (SB), 441
Aire, 127
Ajax, 287
Algerine class, 426
Ambuscade, 293
Arethusa class, 212, 286
Argus, 303, 306, 307
Ark Royal, 27, 55, 243
Arrow, 293
Attacker class, 313
Battle class, 296
Belfast, 148–9, 212, 217, 219, 282, 287, 290, 419, 484
Bonaventure, 352
Bridgewater, 382
Britannia (SB), 84
Bulolo, 477, 478
'C'-class cruisers, 71
'C'-class destroyers, 296
Campanula, 132, 182
Campbelltown, 471
Captain, 208
Captain class, 386, 404
Castle class, 223, 385
Celandine, 388, 547
Centurion, 467
Charybdis, 238, 287
Colony class, 404
County class, 286
Courageous, 280, 282, 306, 307, 315, 378
Cyclops, 372
Delhi, 243
Devastation, 208
Devonshire, 528
Dido class, 238, 287
Dreadnought, 208, 217
Dryad (SB), 71
Duke of York, 41, 230, 281–2, 283
Duncan, 295–6, 382, 390, 398
Eagle, 54, 243, 306, 307, 380
Edinburgh, 287
Effingham, 280
Eskimo, 297
Euclase, 423, 426
Excellent (SB), 70, 102, 227
Exeter, 287, 534
Fiji class, 287
Flower class, 384, 532
Forth, 372
Frobisher, 69
Furious, 306, 307, 315
'G'-, 'H'- and 'I'-class destroyers, 293
Ganges (SB), 35, 96, 98, 114, 290
Glenearn, 463
Glengyle, 463, 478, 487
Glenroy, 89, 463
Glorious, 280–1, 306–7, 326, 493
Glowworm, 213
Gordon (SB), 411
Gregale (SB), 441
'H'-class submarines, 349
Hermes, 131, 306, 307, 309, 335, 511
Hesperus, 133, 388
Hood, 27, 109, 281, 283, 493
Hotspur, 398
Howe, 222, 223
Hunt class, 383, 403, 526
Illustrious class, 191, 238, 307, 308, 335, 512, 522
Impregnable (SB), 96
Indomitable, 69, 74, 148, 306, 307, 308, 326
Isle of Jersey, 131
'J'- and 'K'-class destroyers, 294, 295
'K'-class submarines, 348
King Alfred (SB), 65, 85–9, 149, 439, 468, 543, 550
King George V class, 206, 209, 212, 226, 281
Lady Philomena, 424
Lagan, 502
Largs, 477
Leander class, 286, 533, 541

SHIP INDEX   611

Lion, 282
Loch class, 224, 386, 390
Lochinvar (SB), 424, 426
Lucia, 372
ML137, 424–5
MMS41, 421, 423
MMS56, 425
Maidstone, 372
Maine, 131
Malabar, 406
Mantis (SB), 441
Mauritius, 218
Medway, 372
Nairana, 314
Nelson, 22, 228, 233, 281, 283, 315
Norfolk, 132, 287
Northney (SB), 470
'O'- and 'P'-class destroyers, 295, 349
Orchid, 393
Orchis, 262
Osprey (SB), 103, 388, 392
Oxfordshire, 131, 150
Penelope, 147
Philante, 393
Preston North End, 424
Prince Leopold, 464
Prince of Wales, 73, 230, 283, 290, 514, 533
Princes Astrid, 464
Princes Beatrix, 464
Princess Iris, 465
'Q' and 'R' classes, 296
Quebec II (SB)
Queen Elizabeth class, 227–8, 279–80, 351, 398
Renown, 150, 279, 282
Repulse, 279, 280, 283, 511, 533
River class, 127, 132, 271, 385, 403, 404
Rodney, 150, 225, 233, 234, 263, 281, 283
Royal Arthur (SB), 98
Royal Oak, 185, 186, 187, 279, 283, 378
Royal Sovereign ('R')-class battleships, 54, 227–8, 279, 398
'S'-class submarines, 349–50
'S'-, 'T'-, 'U'- and 'V'-class destroyers, 296
Safari, 349, 359–60, 375
St Christopher (SB), 440
St George (SB), 97
St Vincent (SB), 97
Scylla, 238, 287
Southampton class, 287
Starling, 377
Storm, 359, 360
Suffolk, 287
'T'-class submarines, 348, 350
Taciturn, 351
Tay, 392
Temeraire, 282
Trenchant, 351, 359–60
Triad, 360

Tribal class, 237, 250, 290, 295–6, 422, 540
Tyne, 41
'U'-class submarines, 350
'VW' classes, 292
Valiant, 164, 242, 351, 524
Valkyrie (SB), 268
Vanguard, 222, 228, 243, 282
Vasna, 131
Verbena, 85
Vernon (SB), 71, 185, 254, 418
Victorious, 148, 346, 562
Vindictive, 69
Viscount, 398
Warrior, 208, 441
Warspite, 73, 279, 280, 359
Western Isles, 292
White Bear, 358
Whitehall, 382
Wolfe, 372
X craft, 351–2
X1, 348
Zinnia, 4

British merchant ships
Anglo-Saxon, 133
Athenia, 376, 377, 489, 497
Empire Audacity, 312
Lancastria, 129
Queen Mary, 222, 409

Canadian warships
Arrowhead, 548
Cornwallis (SB), 547
Huron, 549
Matapedi, 546
Nader (SB), 545, 547
Rimouski, 549
Royal Roads (SB), 546
Stadcoma (SB), 545
Unicorn (SB), 546

Dutch warships
Admiralen class, 533
De Ruyter, 533, 534
General Callenburgh, 533
Isaac Sweers, 533
Java class, 533
O21 class, 533
Sumatra, 534
Van Galen, 533
Willem Van der Zaam, 243

French warships
Béarn, 530, 549
Bretagne, 530
Dunkerque, 530
Provence, 530
Strasbourg, 530, 531

German warships
Admiral Hipper, 494
Bismarck, 26, 230, 234, 251, 258, 281, 283, 287, 317, 324, 490, 493–4
Deutschland, 493
Gneisenau, 285, 317, 324, 442, 452, 493–4
Graf Spee, 27, 287, 378, 493
Graf Zeppelin, 492
Königsberg, 324, 325
Krebs, 258
Lauenberg, 258
München, 258
Prinz Eugen, 493–4
Scharnhorst, 219, 230, 234, 250, 283, 285, 287, 317, 324, 442, 452, 493–4, 533
Schleisen, 491
Tirpitz, 283, 285, 325, 351–2, 380, 494, 528
U-47, 185–6
U-109, 500
U-110, 497
U-463, 502
U-505, 491, 498
U-559, 258
U-619, 398
U-701, 429

Greek warship
Giorgio Averof, 534–5

Indian warships
Baluchistan, 555
Bengal, 554
Dalhousie (SB), 554
Godavark, 554

Italian warships
Amerigo Vespucci, 523
Caio Duilio, 522
Conte di Cavour, 521, 522
Cristoforo Colombo, 523
Lafole, 398
Littorio class, 520, 522
Maestrale class, 522
Navigatori class, 522
Oriani class, 522
Vettor, 523
Zara class, 521, 522

Japanese warships
Agano, 509
Akagi, 511–13
Amagi, 511
Fubuki, 509
Furutaka class, 508
Fuso, 507
Hatsharu, 509
Hiryu, 512
Hiyo, 512
Hosho, 511
Ise, 507
Junyo, 512
Kaga, 342–3
Kagero, 509
Kongo, 507
Mogami class, 286, 288, 508
Musashi, 507–8
Nagato, 507
Oyodo, 509
Sendai, 508, 509
Shinsu Maru, 511
Shiratsuyu, 509
Shokaku, 512
Taiho, 512
Yamato, 284, 506–8, 518
Yugumo, 509
Zuikaka, 512

New Zealand warships
Achilles, 287, 550
Moa, 551
Tamaki (SB), 551

Norwegian warships
B-1, 528
Draug, 528
Sleipner, 528

Polish warships
Błyskawica, 526
Grom, 526
Orzeł, 526, 527

United States warships
Abercrombie, 35, 299, 403, 406
Admirable class, 430
Alaska class, 214, 289
Ancon, 478
Argonaut, 353
Arizona, 107, 283
Atlanta class, 214, 289
Augusta, 477
Bagley class, 298
Balao class, 371
Bataan, 312
Belleau Wood, 312
Benson class, 298
Birmingham, 303
Bogue class, 313
Brooklyn class, 120, 215, 288
Buckley class, 386
Bunker Hill, 265, 312
Cabot, 312
Cachalot class, 216, 353, 374
California, 37, 74, 82, 113, 151, 169, 183, 192, 230, 232, 265, 267, 283, 292, 302

Ship Index

Canopus, 374
Casablanca class, 314
Cimarron class, 206
Cleveland class, 216, 289
Comfort class, 143
Commencement Bay class, 313
Cowpens, 312
Dace, 367
Dale, 60, 94, 118, 240, 276, 299, 343, 407, 460, 484
England, 407
Enterprise, 82, 117, 151, 204, 225, 244, 266, 273, 310, 318
Escambia class, 206
Essex class, 214, 310–12
Evarts class, 386
Fletcher class, 299
Fulton, 374
Gato class, 348, 353
Gearing class, 299
Gleaves class, 298
Greer, 380
Gridley class, 298
Hornet, 204, 311, 312, 328, 513
Indianapolis, 118, 288, 292, 510
Independence class, 312
Iowa class, 24, 25, 192, 214, 215, 231–2, 284, 285
Jack, 37, 183, 222, 252, 364, 369, 375
Kearney, 299, 380
Langley, 309, 312
Lexington, 6, 120, 204, 216, 265, 309, 312, 512
Louisville, 292
Mahan class, 216, 219, 225, 298
Maine, 23
Manley, 465
Marlin class, 214
Maryland class, 230–2, 283, 392
Mason, 123
Missouri, 35, 191, 232, 284–5, 516, 559
Monitor, 208
Monterey, 93, 312
Montpelier, 104, 151, 515
Nevada class, 230, 231, 283
New Mexico class, 230, 283
New Orleans class, 288
North Carolina class, 215, 232, 283
Omaha class, 288

Osprey, 429, 431
PC-1264, 123
PT-1 to 9, 443
PT-109, 450
PT-188, 445
Pampanito, 369
Parche, 368
Pawnee, 111–12, 122, 446
Pecos, 136
Pensacola class, 288
Plunger class, 353
Pompano, 362
Potomac, 12
Princeton, 312
Proteus, 374, 375
Ranger, 225, 309–10, 312
Raven, 429–31
Refuge, 143
Reuben James, 7, 299, 380
Roe, 300
SC-525, 405
St Louis, 83, 169
Samuel B Roberts, 135
San Jacinto, 312
Saratoga, 6, 100, 107, 192, 309–11
Saufley, 60, 299
Sawfish, 375
Seadragon, 139
Sims class, 298
Somers class, 220
South Dakota class, 225, 232, 244, 283, 285
Sterett, 41, 59, 81, 135, 236, 239, 251, 297
Suamico class, 206
TF-39, 442
Tench class, 353, 371
Texas class, 230, 283
Tinosa, 253, 368
Trigger, 453
Turtle, 347
'V'-class submarines, 353
Washington, 215, 221, 267, 284
Wasp, 83, 168, 224, 275, 311–12, 408, 510
West Virginia, 231–2, 267, 283, 302
Wyoming class, 283
YMS class, 429–32
YMS-380, 431
Yorktown, 6, 121, 138, 204, 220, 225, 265, 309–12, 328, 408, 510, 512